MW01626316

Collector's Value Guid

Japanese Woodblock Prints

Sandra Andacht

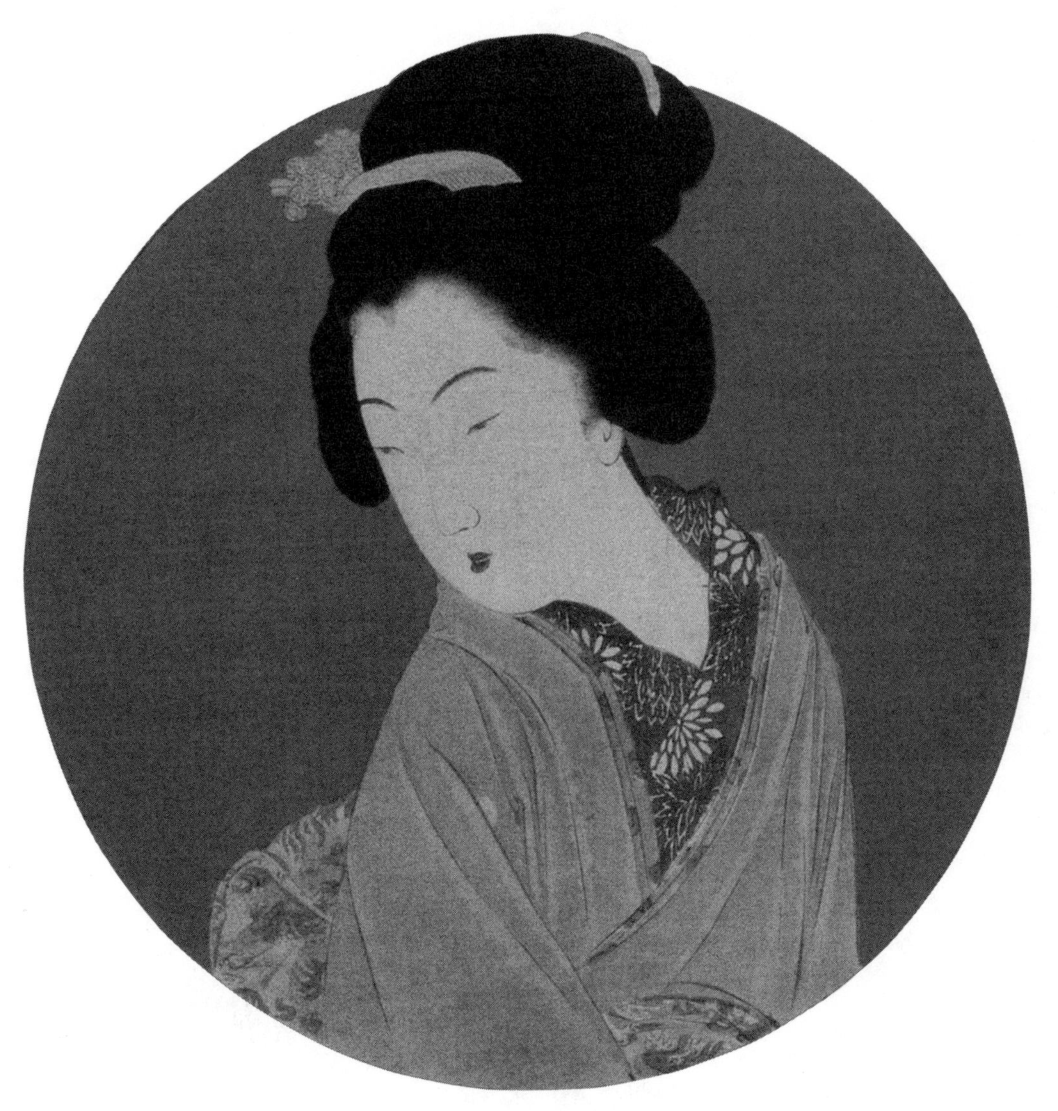

© Copyright 2000
by
Sandra Andacht

All rights reserved.
No part of this publication may be reproduced or transmitted in any form or by any means, electronic or mechanical, including photocopy, recording or any information storage and retrieval system, without permission in writing from the author, except by a reviewer who may quote brief passages in a critical article or review to be printed in a magazine or newspaper or electronically transmitted on radio or television. The author and publisher assume no liability or responsibility for any loss incurred by users of this book because of errors, typographical, clerical, or otherwise.

Published by

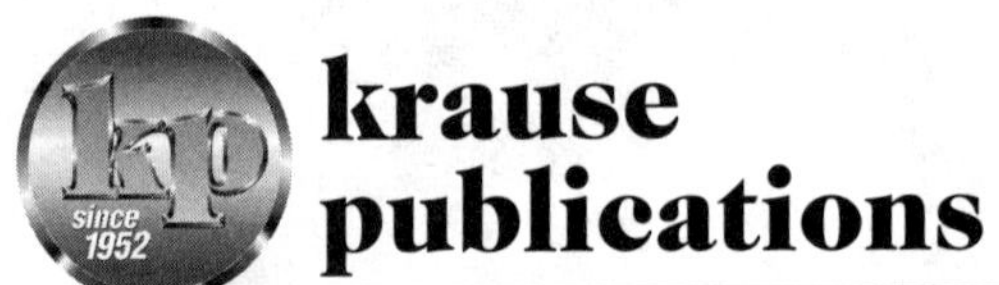

700 E. State Street • Iola, WI 54990-0001
Telephone: 715/445-2214

Please, call or write us for our free catalog of publications. To place an order or receive our free catalog, call 800-258-0929. For editorial comment and further information, use our regular business telephone at (715) 445-2214 or www.krause.com

Library of Congress Catalog Number: 00-104097
ISBN: 1-58221-005-5

Printed in the United States of America

Contents

Acknowledgements 4
An Introduction to Japanese Woodblock Prints 5
Format and Size of Prints 11
Identifying a Print 11
Care of Prints 11
Woodblock Artists and Print Listings 12
Color Plates 97
Appendix A Japanese Numerals 209
Appendix B Japanese Year Dates and Chronology 212
Appendix C Common Character Index 217
Appendix D Characters Commonly Found in Artists Names 218
Appendix E Signatures of Ukiyo-e Artists of the 18th and 19th Centuries 221
Appendix F Signatures and Seals of 20th Century Woodblock Artists and Publishers 237
Appendix G Ukiyo-e Artists by School 247
Appendix H Trademarks of Edo Publishers 255
Appendix I Date and Censor Seals 260
Appendix J Actor's Mon (Crests) 262
Appendix K Famous Courtesans Depicted in Woodblock Prints 265
Appendix L Genji Mon 269
Appendix M Kabuki Plays 270
Glossary 272
Bibliography and Sources 277
Index 279
Index to Illustrations 282
About the Author 284
Woodblock Artist's Signature Pull-out Section 286

Acknowledgments

The author extends her sincere appreciation to the following for their contributions and support: Jeffrey Andacht, Stuart Andacht, Debbie Andin, Connie Bennett, Richard Berger, The Browning Collection, Philip Cadeaux, David Camisa, Joseph Camisa II, Enes Carnesseca, Dennis Carroll, Arlene and Jim Constantine, Dorothy Egan, John Emerson/The Emerson Collection, The Salomon Epstein Collection, Lisa Field, Mark Fogel, The Garcia Collection, The Gernhart Collection, Kyle Husfloen, The Iannou Collection, Emmanuel Jenkins, The Johnson Collection, Mike Kaye/ The Mike Kaye Collection, Shelly Kaye, Spyros Konitsiotis, Virginia and Frederick Korz/The Korz Collection/Wing Antiques, Liza McCrory, Bernard McManus, Robert Miller/A Step Behind, Miracle Ventures Inc. Oriental Art, Lita Payerle, Michael Pearce, Louie Pharr and David Greenbaum/The Pharr-Greenbaum Collection, Peter Piacentini/The Piacentini Collection, Jennifer Ramirez, Linda and Jaime Ramirez, Calvin Rasweiler/The Rasweiler Collection, Peter Sherry, Florence Simon, Roni Simon, The Orientalia Journal, Harvey Weinreb, Mike Zadrow, Charles Zicari.

Photography:
Arthur Field, Field Studio, Little Neck, New York

An Introduction To Japanese Woodblock Prints

Until the second half of the seventeenth century Japanese art was nurtured almost exclusively by the aristocracy, which consisted of the nobility and warrior class. At that time, the wealthy merchant class and the wealthier citizens of Edo, modern-day Tokyo, began to cultivate and support a new art form. This art form was termed ukiyo-e, which literally means "pictures of the floating world." Ukiyo, first a Buddhist term referring to the transitory nature of life and suffering, evolved to refer to the transitory pleasures and luxuries of the present world. Pictures, either done in brushwork or as woodcut prints, depicted subject matter from, or associated with, the everyday life of commoners. Ukiyo-e prints depict the lives of people who, although well aware of the snares and tricks in store for them, still do their best to take as much pleasure and enjoyment out of life as possible. From its start, ukiyo-e developed as a kind of souvenir art of Edo, the seat of the central feudal government.

Artists, who emerged from the ranks of the commoners, created ukiyo-e art for the common people during the Edo period (1615-1868). Having little connection with other styles of Japanese painting, ukiyo-e drew its support from the patronage of the townspeople of Edo and other cities. This becomes clearer when ukiyo-e is compared with painting(s) produced prior to the Edo period.

Historical Background

Until the twelfth century, Japan had a centralized government based on the Chinese model of an all-powerful monarchy. The emperor was viewed as a Supreme Being, and the seat of government was in Kyoto. Beginning in the ninth century, this centralized form of government began to break down and by the end of the twelfth century Japan had a feudal system of government. Decentralized in nature, a warrior class of samurai served feudal lords known as daimyo. Over the next three centuries, a series of civil wars were fought among the competing daimyo. Hideyoshi Toyotomi's rise to power in the late sixteenth century put an end to a long period of civil wars. The period of Hideyoshi's overlordship is known as the Momoyama period (1582-1603). He was the son of a peasant and following his rise to power he took considerable interest in art and architecture which were the tools of self-glorification.

Grandeur in scale and dazzling in splendor were the chief characteristics he sought in art. Castles, which during the civil wars had primarily served as strongholds, were now built on level ground with greater emphasis on palatial magnificence rather than military strength. The wall painting of the Kano School answered the demand for a luxuriant art. The artists of this school painted beautiful birds, flowers, and landscapes on immense expanses of gold or silver covered walls, on sliding doors, and on folding screens. The social function of Kano School painters was that of samurai who served their master with the painter's brush rather than the sword. The Kano School created art for the ruling class and the artists themselves were samurai, Buddhist priests, or their social equals. Other groups of painters carried on earlier traditions of Chinese ink painting (*syuigokuga*) based on the philosophy of Zen Buddhism, and the Tosa School, a style patronized by the Imperial Court in Kyoto.

The Edo period started when Tokugawa Ieyasu, a minor daimyo, overthrew the military dictatorship of Hideyoshi Toyotomi after Hideyoshi's death. Taking the title of shogun, Tokugawa became military ruler of Japan. Tokugawa had been a vassal lord under Hideyoshi, controlling the fiefdom of Edo. He continued to reside there after assuming power as shogun, and Edo became the new center of government. A powerless emperor continued to reign, but not rule, from the seclusion of his palace in Kyoto.

By a series of governmental measures, it became impossible for jealous daimyo to combine against and overthrow the Tokugawa rule. The result was a period of peace that lasted for nearly three hundred years. Although their services as soldiers were no longer required, samurai maintained their positions as a privileged class bound to their feudal code. Below the samurai in the social hierarchy were the farmers, then the artisans and, finally, the lowest of all—the merchants.

Before long, however, the merchant class reaped the gains of this era. With peace came increasing luxury of life, fostered in part by the government, increased consumption, and internal tranquillity. These factors brought about a greater degree of economic interdependence and exchange of goods throughout Japan. The beneficiaries of this prosperity were the merchants who grew in wealth and numbers, and the artisans and shopkeepers catering to urban demands. The sufferers were the peasants who paid taxes in the form of goods and services on which the whole feudal structure rested.

The chonin, or townsmen, considered the lowest class in the feudal hierarchy, had the most reason to enjoy the peace. The chonin largely created the glittering urban environment. The two main urban centers were Osaka and Edo (now Tokyo). Ukiyo-e was almost entirely the product of Edo. The spirit and attitude of the chonin toward life is the content and spirit of ukiyo-e.

The masters of ukiyo-e came from a much lower level of society. They were usually the sons of artisans, merchants, actors, or lower officials of the Tokugawa government. The Tokugawa rule lasted 270 years. During this period, because of the ban on Christianity, there was no contact with foreign nations except for restricted trade at Nagasaki. No Japanese were allowed to leave the country either. Stability was of utmost importance to the government. They were afraid that this stability would be undermined if foreign ideas were permitted to enter Japan. Other policies of the Tokugawa government were directed at freezing the country's political and social status quo created by Ieyasu and his immediate successors.

The typical townsman of Edo was dashing, happy-go-lucky, and high-spirited, living each day to the fullest and not worrying about where tomorrow's rice would come from. A proverb of the time evoked this spirit: "An Edokko despises money which has been kept overnight."

The places where he sought his pleasure and spent his money were the red-light district and the kabuki theater. The red-light district was more than a place for gratifying physical pleasure. In the rigid feudal society there were barriers to social equality, not only between people of varied professions, but of varied social status. The red-light districts, such as the Yoshiwara, were the one place that such barriers did not exist. Here a commoner and samurai could meet and have discussions on equal terms. Women who inhabited the red-light districts were free of the restraints imposed upon women in ordinary life. They could converse with men and have romance, which was largely lacking outside these districts.

Courtesans and Kabuki

Subjects of ukiyo-e were all but completely devoted to bijin-ga (portraits of beautiful women) and of yakusha-e (kabuki actors). Landscapes and kacho-e (flowers and birds) made their appearance towards the end of the Edo period. Ukiyo-e was born with the world of commoners' entertainment as its background. As the main enjoyments for commoners of the time were within the pleasure quarters and the kabuki theater, ukiyo-e first dealt with subjects from these areas. Ukiyo-e pictures had their *raison d'être* simply as pin-up pictures of courtesans, the heroines of the red-light quarters, and kabuki stars, the heroes of the theatrical world.

While the warrior class was a votary of Chinese taste and the nobility adhered to classicism, the commoners conducted their lives in the here and now. The Kano school of painters, working for the warrior class, used Chinese stories, figures, and landscapes in their art. The Tosa School, patronized by the nobility, derived their subjects from literary works. Both schools tended to ignore contemporary Japan. In contrast, ukiyo-e, an art for and by the commoners, stood face to face with the actual world. Free from the oppression of the upper classes, ukiyo-e provided an art form that found joy in daily life.

Representative of the pleasure quarters during the Edo period (1615-1868) was Yoshiwara in Edo and Shimabara in Kyoto. Prostitution in Japan has a long history. By the end of the Heian period (794-1184) groups of brothels appeared in various parts of the country. Women calling themselves miyagi and eguichi, with groups of courtesans under them respectively, were engaged in businesses in various localities. By the middle of the seventeenth century women of this type began to live in large groups in Edo and Kyoto, where they formed red-light districts. The government sanctioned these districts, and prostitution was considered legal within these licensed areas.

During this period, commoners, overborne by the nobility and the warrior class, were next to nothing in social position. Due to the development of a currency system, they grew wealthy, and spent their money in the pleasure quarters. The quarters supplied them with a place to vent their resentment against the social system; they were the only places where commoners could be free. The women working there were from peasant families, but they gradually learned arts and tricks that were used to entertain their guests of the commoners' class.

Kabuki, the other primary subject of ukiyo-e prints, also originated in the seventeenth century. In 1603, O-Kuni, a maiden in service of the Izumo Shrine in Izumo Province (now Shimane Prefecture), went to Kyoto, the capital at that time, and performed a kind of religious dance in the neighborhood of the Kitano Shrine in order to collect donations for the Izumo Shrine. She appeared in unusual attire: she wore a hat, concealed half of her face with a piece of cloth, hung a gong at her chest, and danced while ringing the gong. Her strange dance became so popular among the citizens of Kyoto that she later built a stage at the riverside resort of Shijo. Other women began imitating her. Gradually the Shijo resort, already crowded with show-houses and street entertainers, had kabuki houses built. Performances by these women were collectively called onna kabuki, onna meaning woman or women; and kabuki, song and dance performance. Some of the women appeared in men's attire and played short simple dramas, but all staff members always danced the finales. The music was played on a samisen, a three stringed musical instrument that, at the time, was a novelty.

The onna kabuki spread from Kyoto to Edo as well as to local districts, and became a national vogue. Its height of popularity was circa 1610. Many of the onna kabuki dancers had previously been courtesans, and frequently continued in both occupations. The feudal government, thus, banned the onna kabuki, around 1614. In its place appeared the wakasashu kabuki (young men's kabuki), played by teenage boys who wore female costumes. The wakasashu attracted interest through their unusual appeal, but their kabuki was also soon prohibited, as the young men became objects of sodomy. After the ban on wakasashu kabuki, actors had to cut off their forelocks in order to mar their feminine loveliness. The actors, thereafter called yaro (male), played with their bare foreheads concealed with pieces of ornamental cloth. Kabuki was now called yaro kabuki.

This Japanese stage drama, connected in its origin with sexual overtones, depended for its popularity upon the beauty of actresses, and, later, actors. As a matter of necessity the kabuki evolved into a performance with due dramatic representation. Such a history accounts for the style of present-day kabuki which is rich in elements of both drama and dance, and the unusual organization of kabuki in which there are no actresses. Actors play all roles, female and male.

Development of Ukiyo-e

The first artist to deal with these subjects, the pleasure quarters and the kabuki, was Hashikawa Moronobu who was active in the late seventeenth century. He designed images of women from the Yoshiwara, Edo's most popular red-light district. At that time these woodblock prints were used to illustrate fictional books. Brush paintings could not keep up with demand for the extremely popular ukiyo-e. Woodblock printing allowed for mass production of these prints. Moronobu made ukiyo-e pictures easily available to the populace both in quantity and price by utilizing the woodblock printing method. The woodblock print was, at this time, a sumi-e—done only in black ink. Color could only be added by hand brushwork and was only done for special orders, as it was so time consuming.

The Torii School of artists, specializing in theater program illustrations and billboards, began producing woodblock prints shortly after Moronobu began working. Torii Kiyonobu (1664-1729), founder of the Torii School, produced pin-up pictures of kabuki actors, and sometimes courtesans. Kaigetsudo Ando, working in the early 18th century, had his atelier at Suwacho, Asakusa near Yoshiwara, where, with many assistants, he mass-produced brush paintings of women. His works were all paintings, but two of his students, Kaigetsudo Doshin and Kaigetsudo Dohan, produced sumizuri-e, black and white prints portraying women in standing poses. Ukiyo-e prints from the Genroku to Hoei eras, 1688-1710, were sumizuri-e, although some had vermilion added in brushwork. These prints were called tan-e (vermilion pictures) and were generally large in size, so that they could be mounted as kakemono-e (hanging scrolls).

During the Kyoho era (1716-1735), Okumura Masanobu, an artist and ukiyo-e publisher, devised a method of elaborate color brushwork by using pink in lieu of vermilion, with the addition of yellow, green, and a few other hues. Often the black portions of the images, such as hair and obi (sash) were rendered in black ink blended with glue for the purpose of producing a glossy black that simulated urushi (lacquer). The pictures were called beni-e (pink pictures), and those with glossy black were termed urushi-e or lacquer pictures. The size of these prints became smaller, with the hosoban or 'long narrow' print, approximately 6 inches by 12 inches, becoming very popular.

Adding color to prints by means of brushwork was a painstaking process. The cost of brush colored prints was too high. By the end of the Kyoho era artists employed a method, inspired by Chinese prints, of printing in two colors, pink and green, in addition to black. Known as benizuri-e (pink pictures), these were the first color prints. Prints became a bit larger in size and a distinctive color effect, different from brush painting, came into being. Benizuri-e should not be confused with beni-e, which were hand colored. Beni-e and benizuri-e existed side by side for approximately ten years after the true color printed print was introduced. Color printing, involving one or more blocks in addition to the one for black, first appeared in 1741—the first year of the Kampo era. These early color prints are termed benizuri-e because they had only two colors, pink and green. The development of blocks and colors, and then overprinting, was a series of short steps after benizuri-e appeared.

Torii Kiyomitsu (1735-1785), head of the third generation of the Torii family, and Ishikawa Toyonobu (1711-1785) specialized in benizuri-e. In this form everything was done in two colors, pink and green. As this was not the natural color of real things, ukiyo-e artists sought a new printing method for adding color to their works. In 1765 the discovery of nishiki-e, or polychrome printing, overcame the unnatural benizuri-e.

In 1765 it became popular amongst poets to exchange picture calendars as New Year's gifts. New ideas for producing innovative concepts and designs were worked out and given to Suzuki Harunobu (1725-1770). The innovations were engraving and printing methods that enabled the printing of more than ten colors. The polychrome prints or nishiki-e (brocade pictures) were so named because they were as colorful and beautiful as fancy brocade. The first nishiki-e woodblock prints were single-sheet prints which depicted the fast floating world of the pleasure quarters, the theater, and the life of the townspeople. In early prints the kabuki actors and courtesans were depicted with rigidity in form. The bold full-length portraits of heavily dressed beauties lacked expression and appear sluggish in style, but are expensive in today's market.

The paper used for nishiki-e is termed hosho. The new paper size, chuban, measuring approximately 10 inches by 7 inches, became popular. Engraving (kimekomi) and printing (karazuri) techniques evolved. The beauty of woodblock prints was created with the marriage of design, engraving, color and printing, making these prints different from the early prints produced prior to 1765.

By the mid-eighteenth century designs became more fluid, conveying a sense of shaping or plasticity. It is in this transitional period that the semi-nudes enjoyed popularity. With the development of the polychrome print ukiyo-e achieved maturity. This is known as the period of the "great masters." Artists were in great competition and flourished and declined rapidly according to the quickly changing vogues of the times.

From 1765 on, when an artist became popular, his style was copied. When Harunobu became famous such contemporaries as Isoa Koryusai and Suzuki Harushige copied his style. When Harunobu died, ukiyo-e took on a new style. Torii Kiyonaga (1752-1815) brought a new style to woodblock prints. Kitao Shigemasa (1739-1820), Chobunsai Eishi (1756-1815), Katsukawa Shunsho (late 18th c.) et al, followed the style of Torii Kiyonaga. The Torii School artists portrayed different actors with similar faces. One would have to read the name of the actor and the role, which was part of the print design, in order to recognize the portrait.

Early period prints were replaced by the nishiki-e print. Artists' specialties were established; there were specialists in bijin-ga, which included Harunobu and Utamaro, and artists specializing in yakusha-e such as Toshosai Sharaku. Some artists produced portraits of actors or beautiful women as well as other subjects.

The nigao-e (likeness print) brought a new style to portraits of actors with regard to their features. Frequently the styles of varied artists within a school continued to be almost identical one to another, but the artists of these groups that were highly distinctive had their own styles. Amongst these were Utamaro, Harunobu and Kiyonaga, all specializing in prints of beautiful women. Utamaro captured the intimate qualities of the women he portrayed. Harunobu's style answered the patrons who desired elegance and refinement. Kiyonaga achieved classicism in his compositions. Sharaku was considered an iconoclast because of his powerfully realistic and exaggerated depictions of kabuki actors at the moment of dramatic climax. Other artists experimented with the use of Western perspective. The polychrome print brought attention to background and detail, making the subject depicted more realistic.

Following the development of bijin-ga and yakusha-e, the art of ukiyo-e was given new styles with the landscape prints of Katsushika Hokusai (1760-1849) and Ando Hiroshige (1787-1858). Their landscape prints were images that represented traditional Japanese painting; they were aspects of nature with which the Japanese were familiar.

In the nineteenth century there was a gradual decline, as the Tokugawa shogunate became unsteady. Censorship and restrictions were imposed. However, by this time, a very large audience bought prints.

Following the publication of *Perry's Japan Expedition*, reproduction in full color of Japanese prints came to the attention of Westerners. Using the new process of chromolithography, each volume included fold out copies of the Hiroshige print "Boat On the Yedo River." In 1856 a copy of Hokusai's manga found its way to Paris and soon followed with many other prints. The impact abroad was monumental. However, the woodblock print, in Japan, was in decline.

The Opening of Japan and the Meiji Restoration

When the determined American Commodore Matthew C. Perry (1794-1858) arrived with his tall black ships in the Japanese port of Uraga on July 3, 1853, he intended to force the Japanese to end their 250-year policy of national seclusion. His aim was to promote American domination of the lucrative China trade.

Perry wanted the Japanese to enter into a trading agreement with the United States and open at least two ports to American ships. Western countries, including the United States, were seeking additional outlets for their industrial and agricultural goods in East Asia, and Japan lay strategically on the most direct shipping route between San Francisco and Shanghai.

At the time of Perry's arrival Japan was undergoing dramatic societal changes that had already brought pressure against isolationism. While the emperor resided in Kyoto, the imperial capital since 794 C.E., the Tokugawa shogun controlled the administration of the country from Edo. By 1853 the feudal system that had supported the powerful Tokugawa shogunate was in decline.

The early 1800s saw the Japanese economy in a state of transition. As cities grew, increased demands for goods and services expanded commerce and increased the importance of currency, banking, and capital. The peasant class, long oppressed by members of the ruling order, was increasingly exploited as the privileged class accumulated ever-expanding levels of debt. These difficulties were compounded in 1833-1836 by a series of famines that led to the breakdown of the agricultural economy, a decline in the status of the military classes, and the rise of a new elite—the merchant class.

In 1639 the Tokugawa shogunate had instituted an exclusionist policy as a reaction to the influx of European Christian missionaries, whose presence was seen as a political menace. No Japanese were allowed to leave or, having left, return. The size of sailing vessels allowed to be built in Japan was restricted. Foreign trade was severely limited, with only a small, closely watched Dutch settlement permitted at Nagasaki.

By 1853, when Perry arrived in Japan, the shogun's power had already eroded too much to risk a military confrontation with the United States. Furthermore, progressive forces in Japan held that the end of isolationism and the development of foreign trade would solve some of Japan's economic problems. The Japanese therefore agreed to receive Perry's delegation. When Commodore Perry dropped anchor in Japan's Edo Bay on July 8, 1853, he and his crew of "barbarians" and their mysterious steam-powered ships caused a great commotion. The morning after the Americans arrived, several small Japanese boats filled with artists making sketches approached the black ships. Within a week the first pictures of the foreigners and their ships were carved, printed and available for sale in print shops throughout nearby Edo.

Communication between Perry and the Japanese was cumbersome. None of the Americans knew Japanese and Dutch translators had to intercede in all transactions. Written and spoken communications were translated from English to Dutch and from Dutch to Japanese and vice versa.

In spite of such difficulties, Perry made his demands and vowed to return for an answer the following spring. He docked at Edo Bay in February 1854 and in March signed the Treaty of Kanagawa, which provided limited landing rights for American ships and a diplomatic residence at Shomoda. Townsend Harris (1804-1878), the United States' first diplomat to Japan, arrived in 1856 with his Dutch interpreter to negotiate a commerce treaty, commonly known as the Harris treaty. Concluded in 1858, the treaty provided for the opening one year later of the ports of Nagasaki and Kanagawa. Japanese officials later substituted nearby Yokohama for Kanagawa. In the summer of 1858, Lord Elgin arrived to negotiate a similar treaty for the British. The French, Russians, and Dutch quickly sent their own delegations.

Yokohama was a fishing village located on the western shore of Edo Bay, just three miles opposite the site first proposed for the foreign settlement at Kanagawa. Tokugawa officials moved the site because Kanagawa was situated on the Tokaido, the great highway linking the seat of the Tokugawa shogunate at Edo with Kyoto, the imperial capital and home to the Emperor. They feared disruption of traffic caused by conflict between the foreign residents and the samurai and daimyo who frequently traveled the road.

By the time the port opened at Yokohama in July 1859, two piers, a customhouse and the "godowns" (warehouses) of foreign trading firms had been constructed along the waterfront. The pleasure district, located inland across a small canal, boasted the *Gankoro*, an establishment that catered to foreigners. Residential areas for Europeans and Americans were initially limited to the eastern part of the city but later spread to the bluffs overlooking the port. Japanese residences and businesses were in the western section, and the Chinese, who acted as intermediaries between the Japanese and foreign traders, lived in separate quarters.

After initial problems in reaching an equitable currency valuation, business in Yokohama prospered. By the 1860s the port had become a "boom town" filled with opportunists of all nationalities and classes.

The Japanese were fascinated with Yokohama, its ships, its strange foreigners and their clothing, customs, and technology. Artists recorded Yokohama's exotic life in countless editions of multicolored woodblock prints. From 1860-1862, 40 or more publishers issued more than 400 "Yokohama prints" by 25 artists.

In 1868 the Japanese monarch was restored and the emperor whose reign name was Meiji (Enlightened Government) ushered in a period of institutional and social change. Less than 10 years had passed since the opening of the new foreign settlement in Yokohama, and Japan was well on its way to modernization through the selective adaptation of Western models.

Among the first types of Yokohama prints to be published were panoramic landscapes of the newly built city as seen across Edo Bay from the nearby hills. Artist Sadahide's "Complete Picture of the Newly Opened Port of Yokohama," completed during the winter of 1859-1860, is one of the largest woodblock prints published in Japan during the Edo period. Assembled from eight oversized sheets of paper, this detailed landscape map of Yokohama and its topography includes features such as mountains, rivers, temples, bridges, buildings, and roads, all of which are individually labeled. Prints of foreign ships arriving in Yokohama's harbor were also extremely popular. The Tokugawa shogunate had forbidden the building of large ships, but the arrival of foreign vessels powered by steam and sail revived interest in Western-style ship building.

In making prints, a few Japanese artists relied on their immediate observations and impressions of the foreign settlers and their lives. Most, however, borrowed from secondary sources such as Western newspaper and magazine illustrations. Scenes of foreign lands were inspired by many sources, including illustrations from newspapers and magazine. Since artists could not read the foreign language captions, they frequently incorporated images of buildings, for example, from localities unrelated to the title of the print or its text.

Because the Japanese had a well established artistic tradition of portraying beautiful women, Western women were represented in great disproportion to their actual numbers in Yokohama. Artists were fascinated with Western clothing, furnishings of Western residences, and everyday utensils and habits. Common were series of five prints, one representing each of the five nations, with the occasional addition of a sixth print for China. Prints accurately depicted the furnishings and activities of Western mercantile offices. Print artists were struck with behaviors of the foreigners at such leisure pursuits as dinner and drinking parties, as well as riding excursions in the nearby countryside.

With the end of the Edo period, the social and cultural roles of ukiyo-e changed. Meiji-period (1868-1912) ukiyo-e was a continuation of the art form, but with differences. Censor seals were replaced with date seals (see section on seals) that contained year, month, day, publisher's address, etc. The Japanese realized that in order to defend themselves from and compete with the West, they would have to learn to adopt Western technologies and systems, adapting them for their own use. During the Meiji Restoration Japan embarked on a course to modernize its economy, government, and military.

Woodblock prints of the Meiji period recorded the modernization of the times and of Japan. Brick buildings, gas lamps, Western dress, the circus, etc., were depicted in vivid aniline dyes in hues of red, blue, violet, and yellow. New developments in engraving and photography are partially responsible, historically, for this period of decline. In today's market, prints of the Meiji period are highly collectible and sought after. Print artists such as Kunichika, Chikanobu, Yoshitoshi, and Gekko, are extraordinarily popular. Prints depicting the horrors of the wars, the Satsuma rebellion at Kagoshima, the Sino-Japanese war, and the Russo-Japanese war, are highly collectible. Yokohama prints tended to depict the lifestyles of Westerners in that city. Sadahide's series, "Things Seen and Heard at the Open Port of Yokohama," made him a leader in such prints. He was the first Meiji artist to be exhibited in the West—in Paris in 1867. He also incorporated Western elements in his work, including perspective and shading to indicate figures.

Following the Meiji period the development of the Japanese print fell behind the other arts. The public became apathetic toward ukiyo-e. It was not considered mainstream art and ukiyo-e artists were considered inferior to the artists of classical paintings. An important reason for the decline was the commercial venture of ukiyo-e. The artist who designed the print was not responsible for cutting the blocks or for printing and publishing. During the second decade of the twentieth century, when young print artists turned away from ukiyo-e tradition and techniques, the print medium progressed.

Twentieth Century Prints

The sosaku hanga ("creative print") movement advanced the new concept of the artist/printmaker. Young artists involved themselves in all stages of the printmaking process thereby producing original art. The early sosaku hanga artist sought a natural realism; this displaced by a striving for individualistic expression with a more abstract and simple statement and an emphasis on composition.

In 1904 Yamamoto Kanae (1882-1946) made a sketch of a fisherman and created a print. Woodblock printing, up to this point in time, was a commercial means of reproduction and was not considered art. In 1904 Shozaburo Watanabe had not yet begun to produce shin hanga for export. The majority of Japanese artists during the Meiji period studied Western style painting. They were influenced by Impressionist artists such as Van Gogh and Cezanne (and vice versa). Utagawa Kuniyoshi reportedly owned Western style pictures. Though Japanese, many of his prints show the assimilation of Western influence. Kanae trained as an artist, not in the ukiyo-e tradition and not in the methods employed for reproducing Japanese style paintings, but in wood engraving. White line wood engraving is a technique for reproducing a detailed drawing and achieving subtle tonal effect. Used in Europe in the nineteenth century, this relief process differed from the traditional Japanese technique. In wood engraving, fine lines were scratched into the end grain of a cross cut block of hardwood. When printed it created gradations in value and chiaroscuro (the use of light and dark in pictorial representation). Kanae made two printing surfaces by carving two sides of a single plank of wood. He printed on one side in ochre covering the whole surface and the second block in black to provide details. His carving technique allowed him to scoop out unwanted wood rather than cut it away from the line in the traditional manner. At that time other new methods being used included the use of gauges and chisels. Print artists were becoming self-carvers as well as printers, lithographers, stencilers, and etchers.

Shozaburo Watanabe began publishing new prints when he commissioned Takahashi Shotei (1871-1945) to make hanashita-e, a drawing on thin paper that is reversed and glued to the block for cutting. Watanabe intended to produce prints directly from hanashita even though it was common by this time to work from a finished painting. From 1907 Shotei made designs for Watanabe, often in long and narrow format, either vertical or horizontal. The 1923 Tokyo earthquake virtually destroyed all the blocks in Watanabe's establishment. Under the name of Hiroaki, Shotei made an additional 150 or so more prints for Watanabe. Before the earthquake, Shotei had produced approximately 500 designs.

In 1915, Watanabe hired Fritz Capelari, an Austrian artist, to produce print designs. A total of 12 were completed. This was a short-lived relationship. Hashiguchi Goyo (1880-1921) had a brief collaboration with Watanabe as well. The 1915 print "Bathing," by Goyo, published by Watanabe, was the start of the shin hanga ("new prints"). Watanabe revitalized woodblock printmaking. His clientele was Western and his prints sold for high prices. Some prints were limited editions. Watanabe discovered brilliant young artists including Kawase Hasui, Yoshida Hiroshi, Kasamatsu Shiro, Tsuchiya Koitsu, Ishiwata Koitsu, Oda Kazuma, Natori Shunsen, and Ohara Koson.

Following shin hanga was moku hanga, circa 1926. These were popular prints that showed Westernized Japan. Influenced by what was happening in Paris and New York, Japanese women were shown in Western dress, with short bobs, and as modern nudes.

Woodblock Printing

During the Edo period production of a woodblock print required the collaboration of four people: the artist, the woodcutter, the printer, and the publisher. The artist designed the print and determined the coloration of the print. The woodcutter carved the blocks from which the prints were made, and the printer printed from these blocks. The publisher coordinated the efforts of these different craftsmen and distributed the prints. After the artist completed the design, a master woodcarver cut a key block. Several proofs were made from this block and the artist would indicate coloration of the print on these proofs. The master woodcarver would assign his assistants to cut the blocks for the print—a separate block was needed for each color in the print. A kento, a right angle cut into the lower right hand corner and a straight edge at the upper left of the block, allowed the printer to align the blocks when making the print. Dampened paper was laid on each block in turn, aligned with the kento, and the paper was hand rubbed with a pad called a baren. After each impression the blocks were recharged, again, allowing for tones and colors. Removing wood at a right angle allowing a gradation would also create bokashi or gradation in color.

Woodblock printing consisted of the creation of lines and planes by carving along the grain of the woodblock with a knife. Ukiyo-e artists, when drawing the original picture for a print, had to take into consideration the fact that they were limited to compositions of lines and flat color planes. Woodblock printing, therefore, differs from other forms of graphic arts that are also used for mass production (e. g. a lithograph allows a greater degree of gradation through juxtaposition of light and dark and of expression of volume through bokashi or shading.) In woodblock printing the line does not stop at its simplest function of tracing the outlines of the motif but is much more complex. It is the same in the case of the plane: objective, visual images have to be expressed, not by the use of bokashi to express the three dimensions, but by breaking up the image(s) into patterns of flat color planes, and then recomposing them.

Regardless of what style, period, format, or artist, it appears, at the time of this writing, that ALL Japanese prints are highly collected throughout the world. In the realm of prints we must also include serigraphy, intaglio, etchings, mezzotints, and stencils. Many modern artists worked in more than one medium.

Japanese Woodblock Prints

Format and Size of Prints

The sizes of woodblock prints were and are dependent upon the stock sizes of the papers used for printing. In addition, sheets of paper were folded and cut in different ways thus allowing the production of different size prints from the same sheet of paper. Knowing the approximate size a print should be helps determine if it has been trimmed.

Sizes are approximate and can vary up to 1 inch.

Aiban 34.5 x 22.6 cm (13 x 10 inches)

Chuban 25.5 x 19 cm (10 x 7 inches)

Dai-oban 45.7 x 34.5 cm (18 1/4 x 13 3/4inches)

Ebankiri 19 x 51.5 cm

Hashira-e 73 x 13 cm (28 x 4 1/2inches) A pillar print produced by pasting two sheets together.

Hosoban 33 x 14.3 cm (13 x 5 inches)

Kakemono-e (prints wider than *hashira-e*) 30 x 9 inches

Kaku-surimono 21.3 x 18 cm (used for square shape *surimono*-syn. *shikishiban*)

Kamban posters

Koban 22.8 x 17.2 cm

Ko-tanzaku 34.5 x 7.6 cm

Naga-ban 51.5 x 23 cm

Oban 38.2 x 23 cm (15 x 10 inches)

Ogata-chuban 29.3 x 21.7 cm

O-hosoban 38 x 17 cm

Shikishiban 9 x 8 inches

Sho-tanzaku 25.5 x 9.5 cm

Tate-e vertical format

Yoko-e horizontal format

Identifying a Print

The first step in identifying your print is locating the signatures. This is not always an easy task. Signatures can appear anywhere on a print, usually accompanied by a publisher's seal and a date seal. In the 1820s artists started to enclose their names in boxes, referred to as cartouches. The signature is almost always followed by one of two characters: the ga (drawn by) or fude (painted by), the ga being more common. On older prints zu (picture) is found. No two artists wrote these in the same way. The following examples are by a wide selection of artists.

Examples:

Ga (Gwa)

Fude

Zu

Once you have located the ga or fude, the two or three characters above is the artist's name or his go. The go is the art name used by the artist to sign his work. The go is usually used in conjunction with the artist's given name, school name, or another go. In this book only the name most commonly used is given, for the artists used many different go at different periods. For example, Kunisada used 13 go, the most common being Gototei Kunisada, Ichiyusai Kunisada, Kochoro Junisada, Utagawa Kunisada, Utagawa Toyokuni, and Toyokuni. In this book the names Kunisada and Toyokuni are given.

Once you have located the ga or fude try to locate the characters above in the Common Character Index. The character you are looking for may not look exactly the same as the writing style of the artist varies from print to print, and from artist to artist. If you cannot locate the signature in the index, the next step is to compare it to the other signatures in the book.

Collecting, Buying, and Caring of Prints

If you have decided to collect Japanese prints, the most important thing to do is become familiar with them. This can be done by visiting local museums and galleries, and by reading the many books on the subject.

If you are planning to buy an expensive print for investment purposes, contact a reputable dealer or appraiser for it takes an expert to tell an original from a 100 year old fake. Famous artists such as Hiroshige, Hokusai, and Utamaro were widely reproduced and copied, even while they were living. If you are at a garage sale or flea market and find a print you like at a low price, buy it. Keep in mind that it is safer buying a print by a lesser-known artist of the Meiji era like Kunichika or Yoshiiku, for the chances of it being a reproduction are slim.

Print Condition

A collector will come across the following terms and grades referring to the condition of a print.

Impression Fine, very good, good, moderate, poor

Condition Fine, very good, good, moderate, poor

Fading Slightly faded, faded, heavily faded, minor oxidation, oxidation

Toning Margins and edges slightly toned, paper slightly toned, paper toned, paper heavily toned

Foxing Minor foxing (here and there), foxing

Soiling Margins and edges slightly soiled, slightly soiled (here and there), soiled

Stains Lightly stained, stained from gluing, water stains, tape stains on the front and/or verso

Creasing Lightly creased, creased, light centerfold, centerfold, folds

Rubbing Lightly rubbed, moderately rubbed, rubbed

Holes Minute holes, minor holes, minor worm holes, worm holes, binding holes

Trimming Slightly trimmed, trimmed, trimmed outside or to the margin, trimmed within the margin(into the image)

Wear Corners worn, edges worn, minor tear(s), thin areas, part(s) missing

Backing Partially backed, backed, glued down corners and/or edges, taped down, laid down on board, board laid on (attached to top of image around the edges or into the image)

Restoration Restored wormholes and/or holes, restored tear(s), restored margins, partially remargined, remargined, minor restorations in general

Retouching Outlines retouched, black areas retouched, color areas in painted

Care and Keeping of Prints

Prints should be mounted on 100% acid free rag mat, front and back. Regular paper has a high acid content that will harm your print. If not mounted, store the print in an acid free folder.

Never frame a print directly against the glass, as this cuts off airflow and can allow mold to grow.

Use only acid free archival quality tape for mounting a print. Never have your print trimmed or cut. Ask your framer what materials will be used, and make sure she/he is well versed in conservation techniques.

Exposing a print to sunlight will cause fading. Keep your print away from direct sunlight. Many galleries and museums use uf-3 plexiglass which blocks ultraviolet rays and is lightweight. Conservation quality glass, which blocks approximately 98% of ultraviolet rays, is also available. Discuss these points carefully with your framer. It is a small price to pay to insure the preservation of your print.

Woodblock Artists and Print Listings

Following are known woodblock print artists working from the eighteenth through twentieth centuries. Dates for the artists are given and their specialties listed when known. Signatures for many of these artists can be found in Appendix E and Appendix F, and can aid in identifying the print and artist.

All print listings are woodblock prints unless otherwise specified.

A

Abe Jiro (b. 1910) (aka Muro Juni, Saito Jiro) specialized in moku hanga.

Abe Koji (b. 1839)

Abe Koun (b. 1908) studied with Munakata Shiko.

Abe Sadao (1910-1969) specialized in moku hanga.

Abo Hiroshi (b. 1919) studied with Munakata Shiko.

Aigasa Masayoshi (b. 1939) etching, other, usually produced editions of 30.

Akagi Yasunobu (1889-1955) moku hanga artist, also produced lithographs and etchings.

Akagawa Isao (b. 1940) known for woodblock prints, generally in editions of 30.

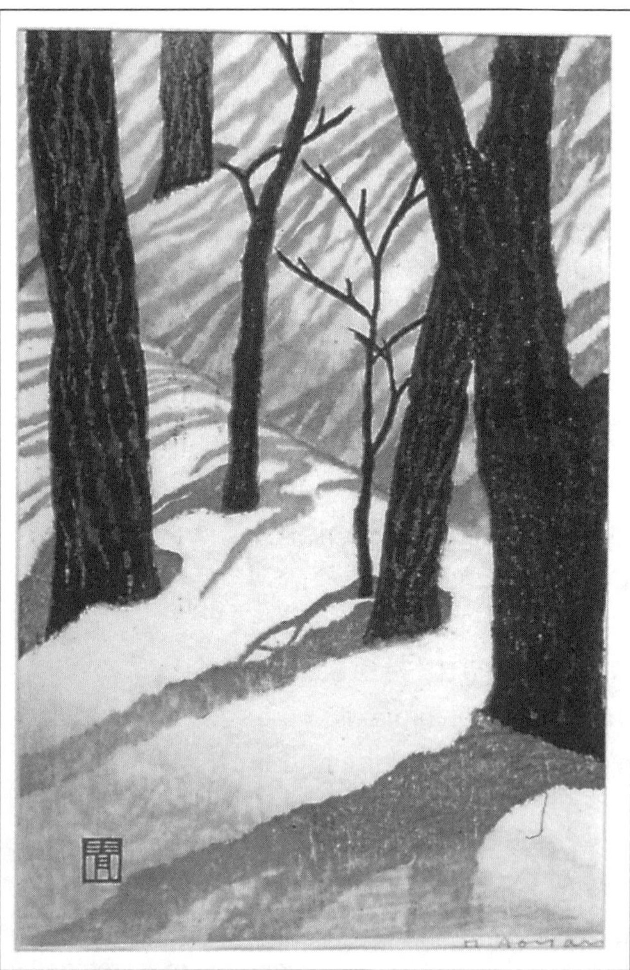

Aoyama M., oban tate-e, "Trees in Winter," c. 1960, very good impression, slightly toned, margins with mat burn, $100-150.

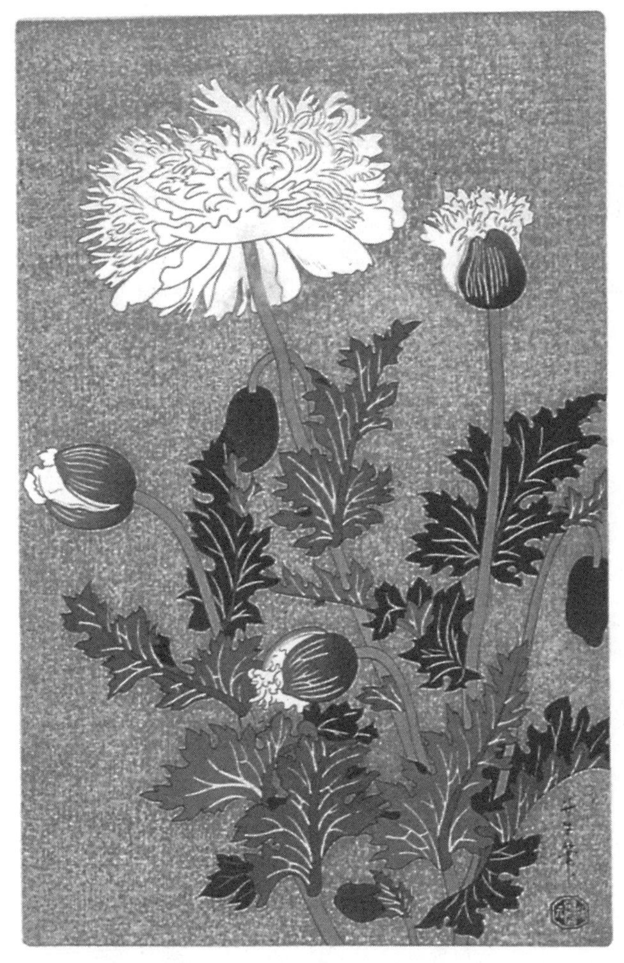

Asada Benji, oban, 17 3/4" x 12", "Poppy," published by Uchida, c. 1960 with original folio, fine impression, condition, and color, $175-275.

Akimoto Yukishige ( ) known for woodblock prints and serigraphy, usually in editions of 40.

Akiyama Iwao (b. 1921) studied with Munakata Shiko, known for woodblock prints, etchings and moku hanga, usually limited editions of 100.

Akiyama Shizuka (b. 1932) prints with oil base pigments, metal plate prints, and moku hanga.

Amano Kamumi (b. 1927) influenced by Munakata Shiko.

"Adaption-A," woodcut and embossing, signed in pencil "Kazumi Amano," dated '73, from an edition of 30, framed and glazed, frame size 36" x 36", $900-1200.

Amano Kunihiro (b. 1929) known for bold abstracts.

23" x 29" (58.9 x 74.3 cm), "Fuyu," (Winter), woodcut, 1957, signed in pencil "K. Amano" in the image and in the margin, dated in pencil 1957, 10, backed with paper, margins stained, $600-900.

Ando Futaba (b. 1946) worked in woodblock, lithographs (editions limited to 20).

Aoki Shigeru (1882-1911)

Aoki So (b. 1921) sometimes sealed Ao and signed Seiji on prints.

Aoyama Kosuke produced woodblock prints, lithographs, serigraphs, usually in editions of 30.

Araki Tetsuo (b. 1937) known for etchings (editions of 50).

Arai Toru sometimes signed TO carved in the blocks, known for shin hanga.

Arishima Ikuma (1882-1974) known for moku hanga and metal plate prints.

Asada Benji (1899-1984) father of Asada Takaji and Asada Horishi; founding member of Kyoto Sosaku Kanga Kyokai.

Asano Takeji (1900) Many of his prints have the title, in English, in the lower margin.

Oban tate-e 15 1/4" x 10 1/2", "Bamboo Shrine," fine condition, impression, and color, $375-500.

Oban tate-e 15 1/2" x 10 3/4", "Wakanoura," early edition, fine condition, impression, and color.

Ashiaki (fl. c. 1820s) Osaka School artist.

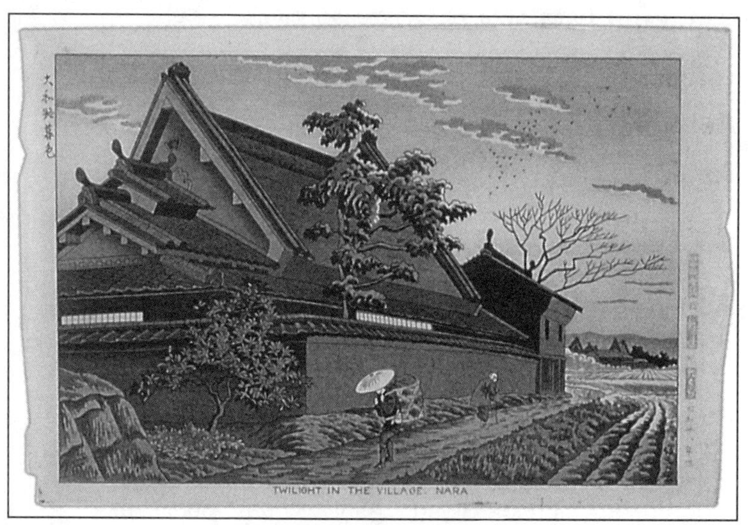

Asano Takeji, oban yoko-e, "Twilight In The Village, Nara," early edition, published by Unsodo, fine color, impression, condition, $450-650.

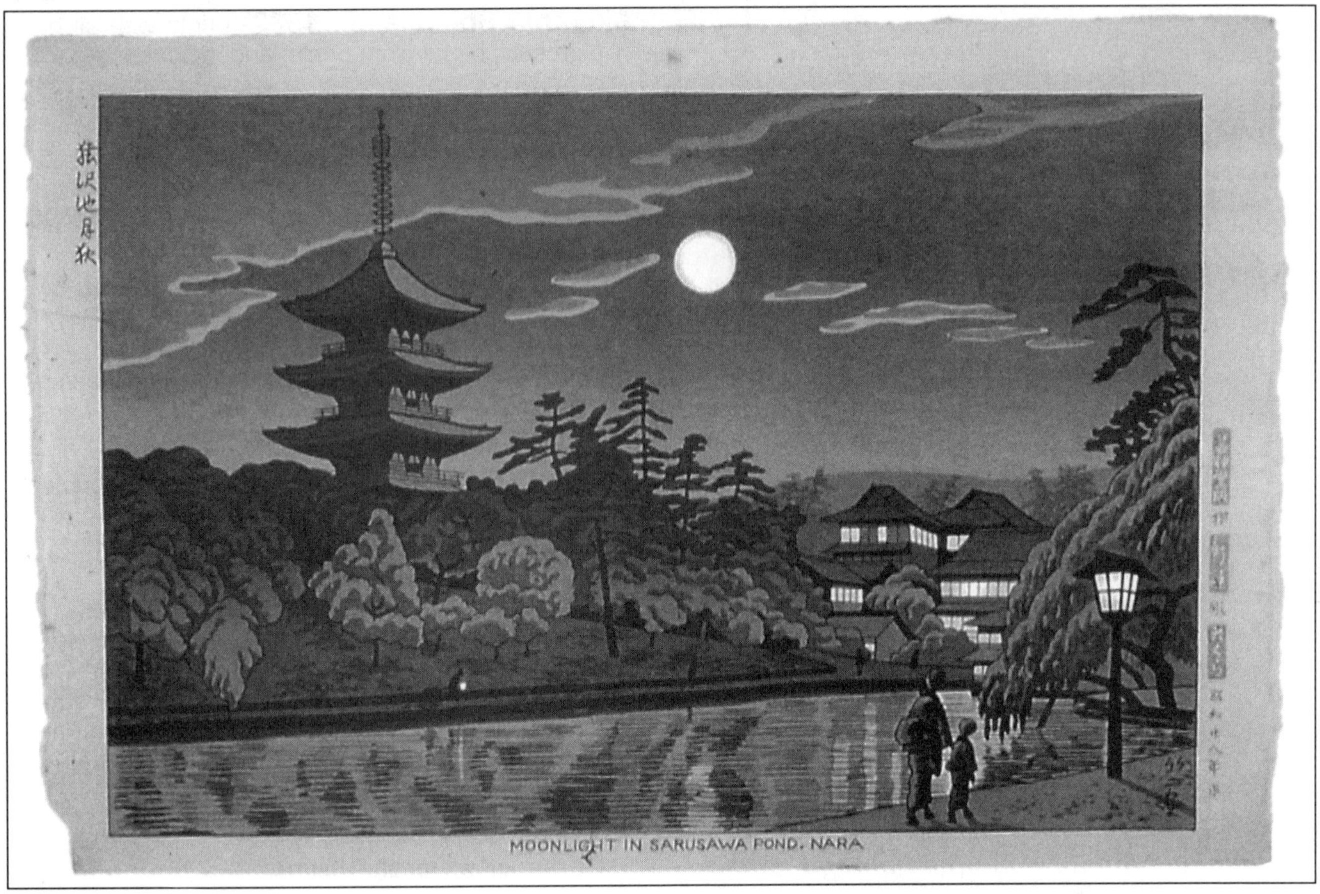

Asano Takeji, oban yoko-e, 10 3/4" x 16", "Moonlight In Nara," early edition, published by Unsodo, fine color, impression, and condition, $400-600.

Ashifuni (fl. c. 1814-1825) Osaka School artist.

Ashihiro (fl. c. 1816-1836) Osaka School artist, pupil of Ashikuni.

Ashihisa (fl. c. 1817) Osaka School artist.

Ashikaga Shizuo specialized in kacho-e prints, published by Uchida.

Ashikiyo (fl. c. 1816-1817) Osaka School artist.

Ashikizu (fl. c. 1820) Osaka School artist.

Ashikuni (c. 1775-1818) Osaka School artist.

Ashimaru (fl. 1803-1830s) Osaka School artist.

Ashinuki (fl. c. 1817-1831) Osaka School artist.

Ashisato (fl. c. 1800-1816) Osaka School artist.

Ashitomo (fl. c. 1800-1830) Osaka School artist, pupil of Ashikuni.

Ashiyuki (fl. c. 1814-1833) Osaka School artist, pupil of Ashikuni.

Oban tate-e diptych, each sheet 15 1/4 " x 10 1/2", "Nakumura Utaemon II, Seki Sanjuro and Nakamura Matsue in the roles of the apparition of Hokaibo, Doguya Jinzo and Musume Okumi, in the play Sumida Gawa (Sumida River) performed at the Osaka Kado-za," signed "Gigado Ashiyuki ga," publisher Wataki, dated Bunsei 10 (1827), good impression, moderate color, laid down, wormage, $900-1200.

Ato Sengai (b. 1929) known for use of stencil.

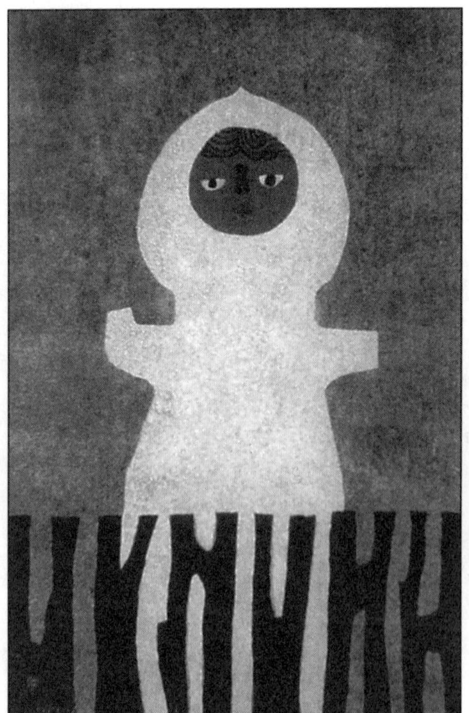

Azechi Umetaro, oban tate-e, approx. 30" x 20", "Shiroi zo," (Figure in White), signed, dated '58 from an edition of 70, very good impression, tape stains on all verso margins $3000-4000.

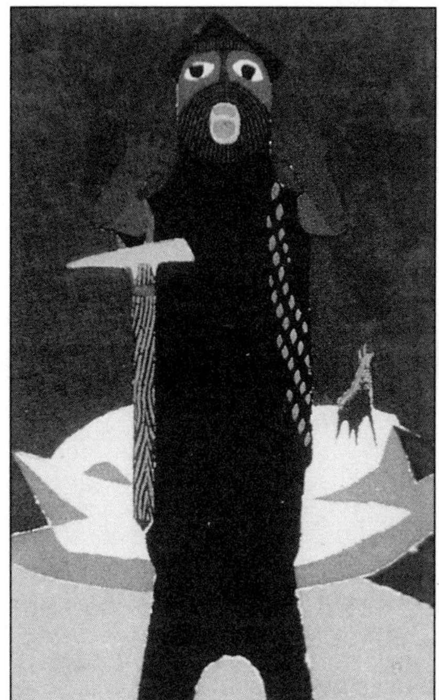

Azechi Umetaro, oban tate-e, 23 1/4" x 14 1/2", "Yama no Sakebi," (Cry on the Mountain) signed and dated '56 from an edition of 30, tape stains on the verso of all the margins, slightly soiled, $2000-3000.

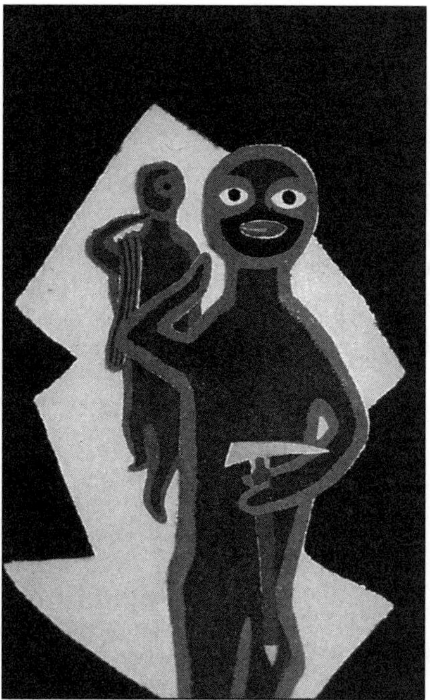

Azechi Umetaro, 28 1/2" x 19", "Yorokobi no Yama," signed in pencil in Roman script "U. Azechi," sealed U and titled in pencil, dated 1955 from an edition of 20, $1500-2000.

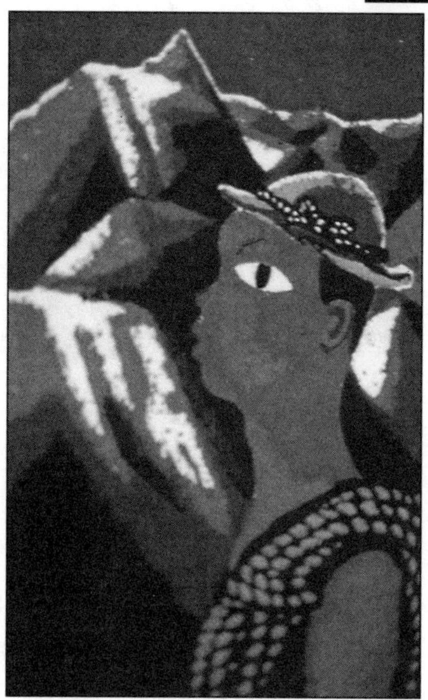

Azechi Umetaro; 16 5/8" x 12 3/8", "Yarigatake," signed in pencil in Roman letters "U. Azechi" and sealed U., dated 1952 from an edition of 50, tape stains on verso, slightly trimmed, moderately toned, $1000-1500.

Ay-O (b. 1931) known for woodblock prints, lithographs, serigraphs,and etchings (editions generally 100).

Azechi Umetaro (1902-) pre WWII prints include landscapes and cityscapes. After WWII his style simplified and mountains and mountaineers contain flat areas of color.

10" x 13" (25. x 33 cm), "Iyo Kanjiizaiji," (Kanjizaiji Temple in Iyo), from the series Shin Nihon Hyakkei (One Hundred Views of New Japan), woodcut, c. 1930s, sealed Ume, tape stains on front and verso, $500-700.

Azuma Kazuo (b. 1910) sometimes signed with "A" in a circle carved into the block.

B

Baba Kashio (b. 1927) known for woodblock prints, lithographs, and etchings, editions of 50.

Baen (fl. c. 1790s-1800s) pupil of Hokusai.

Baido Hosai (1848-1920) also known as Toyokuni IV (but was Toyokuni V), student of Kunisada II, known for war prints, illustrations.

Baien (fl. c. 1819) Osaka School artist.

Baika (fl. c. 1819-1830) Osaka School artist.

Baikei (fl. 1816) Osaka School artist.

Baikosai (fl. c. 1805)

Bairei (1844-1895) designed kacho-e (bird and flower prints).

Baisetsudo (fl. c. 1750s-1760s)

Baldridge Cyrus LeRoy (1889-1975)

Banri (fl. c. 1780s)

Banri ( ) prints of Russo Japanese War published by Narazawa Kenjiro in 1904.

Bartlett, Charles William (1860-1940) born in England, worked for Watanabe Shozaburo in 1916, producing 21 travel prints.

Biho produced Russo Japanese War prints published in 1904 by Matsuki Heikichi.

Bito produced prints of Maiko published by Sastso Shotaro early 1920s.

Bokusen (1736-1824)

Bosai (1752-1826)

Brown Peter Irwin (1903-?)

Buncho (fl. c. 1765-1792)

Buncho II (fl. c. late 18th century)

Bartlett, Charles, oban yoko-e, "Taj Mahal," signed and dated 1916, published by Watanabe, very good impression, good color, slightly toned, tape residue on verso, $500-750.

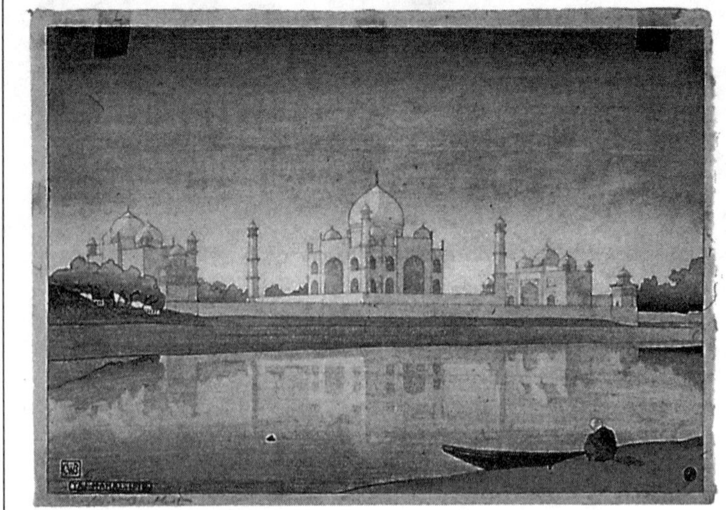

Bunro (fl. 1800-1810) pupil of Buncho.

Bunryusai (fl. mid-18th century) teacher of Eishi.

Buzen (fl. late 18th/early 19th century) Osaka School artist.

C

Capalari Fritz Austrian watercolor painter worked for Watanabe Shozaburo producing 12 prints in 1915, 1918, and 1920.

Charakusai (fl. c. 1810s) Kyoto.

Chikaharu (fl. second half of the 19th century) pupil of Kunichika.

Chikakuni (fl. c. 1821-1823) Osaka School artist, pupil of Ashikuni.

Chikamaro (name used by Kyosai).

Chikanobu (1838-1912) Toyohara Chikanobu, Hashimoto Chikabnobu, pupil of Kunichika.

Chikashige (fl. second half of the 19th century) pupil of Kunichika.

Chinco (1679-1754) pupil of Kiyonobu.

Choki (late 18th/early 19th century)

Chosui (fl. second half of the 19th century) specialized in Surimono.

Chura Obata (1885-1975)

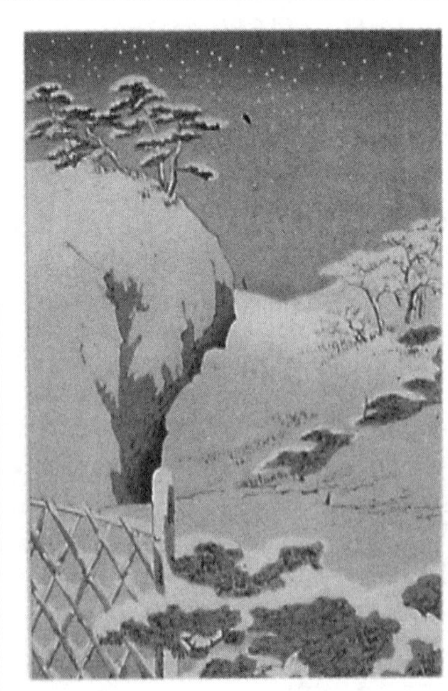
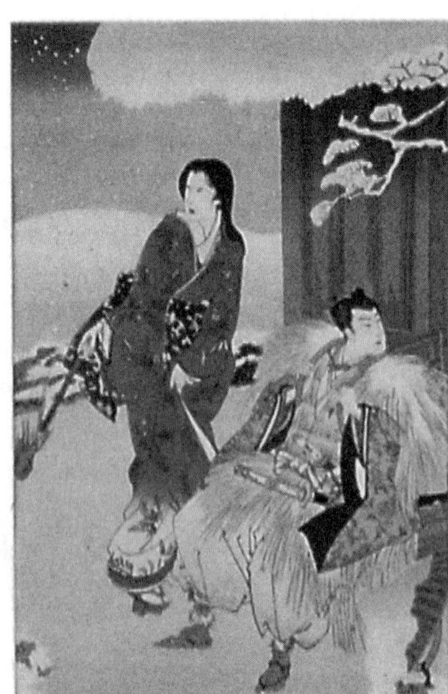
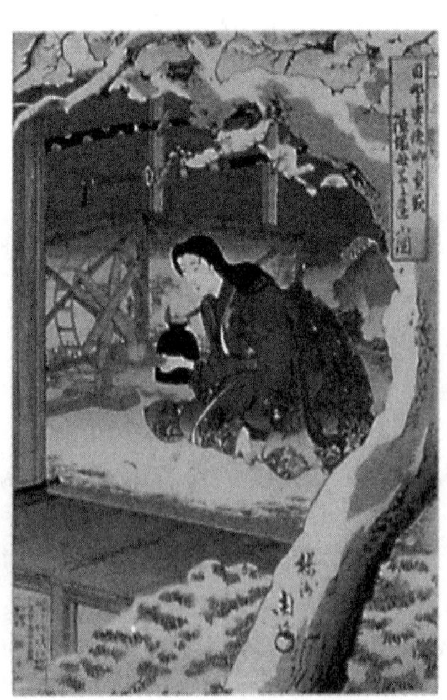

Chikanobu, oban tate-e triptych, "Samurai and Attendants," Meiji period, excellent impression, color, and condition, $1800-2300.

Chikanobu, album with 24 crepe paper prints, each 8" x 10 1/2", "Famous Heroes," Meiji 20 (1887), fine impression, color, and condition, (album)$3500-5500.

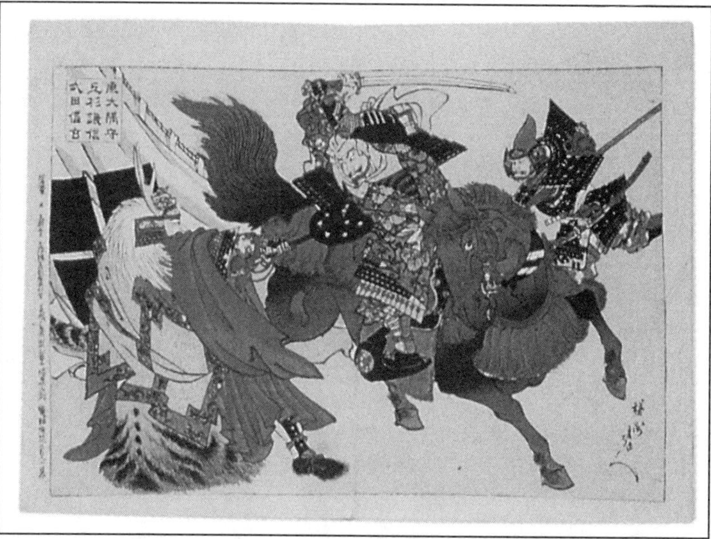

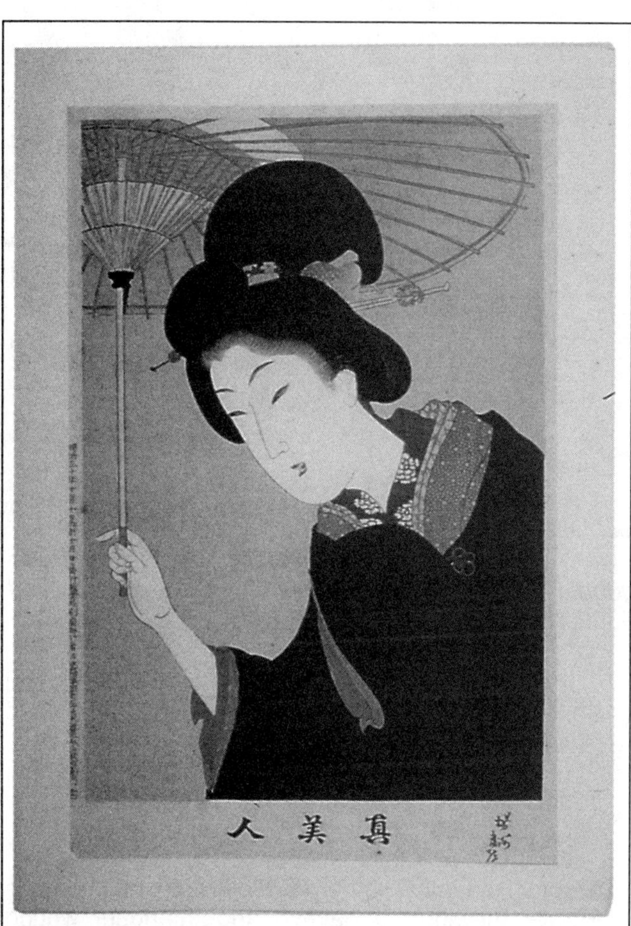

Chikanobu, oban tate-e, "Shin bijin, Bijin with umbrella," Meiji period, very good impression, condition, and color, $350-550.

D

Dobashi Jun (b. 1910) known for woodblock prints, lithographs, and etchings.

Dohan (fl. c. 1710s) Kaigetsudo School.

Doshin (fl. c. 1710s) Kaigetsudo School.

E

Ebikane (fl. c. 1827-1828) Osaka School.

Eiji (fl. c. 1830s-1850s) Osaka School.

Eijiro (1870-1946) published by Nishinomiya Yosaku early 20th century.

Eiju (fl. c. 1830s-1850s) Eisen and Osaka Schools.

Eiko (fl. c. 1790s) pupil of Eishi.

Eiri Chokyosai (fl. c. 1790s/early 1800s) pupil of Eishi.

Eiri Rekisentei (fl. c. 1790s)/(fl. early 19th century) pupil of Eizan.

Eisen (fl. 1790-1848) pupil of Eizan.

Kakemono-e, full-length portrait of a man wearing checked robes and holding a fan, signed "Keisai Eisen ga," published by Tsutaya Kichizo, good impression, faded, torn, rubbed, $1000-1500.

Oban tate-e, "Nihonbashi Nishi Gashi," (The West Bank of the Sumida River by Nihonbashi), a woman in purple kimono holding an umbrella, signed "Keisai Eisen ga," published by Tsutaya Juzaburo, good impression, color, wormage, binding holes, rubbed and slightly soiled, $2500-3500.

Eisen Tomioka (1864-1905) illustrator.

Eishi (1756-1829) Oban tate-e, the courtesan Kisegawa with hand-scroll from the series "Seiro Bijin Rokkasen," (Six Beauties of the Licensed Quarters), signed "Eishi zu," good impression, soiled, trimmed into publisher's seal, stained, backed, $1200-1800.

Oban yoko-e, two bijin and a samurai on a verandah, c. 1788, one sheet from a triptych, soiled, thinning paper, wormage restored, good impression, $1500-2200.

Oban tate-e, center sheet of a triptych of "Clam Digging", signed "Eishi ga," published by Izumiya Ichibei, good impression, moderately faded, soiled, worm holes, backing, $1000-1500.

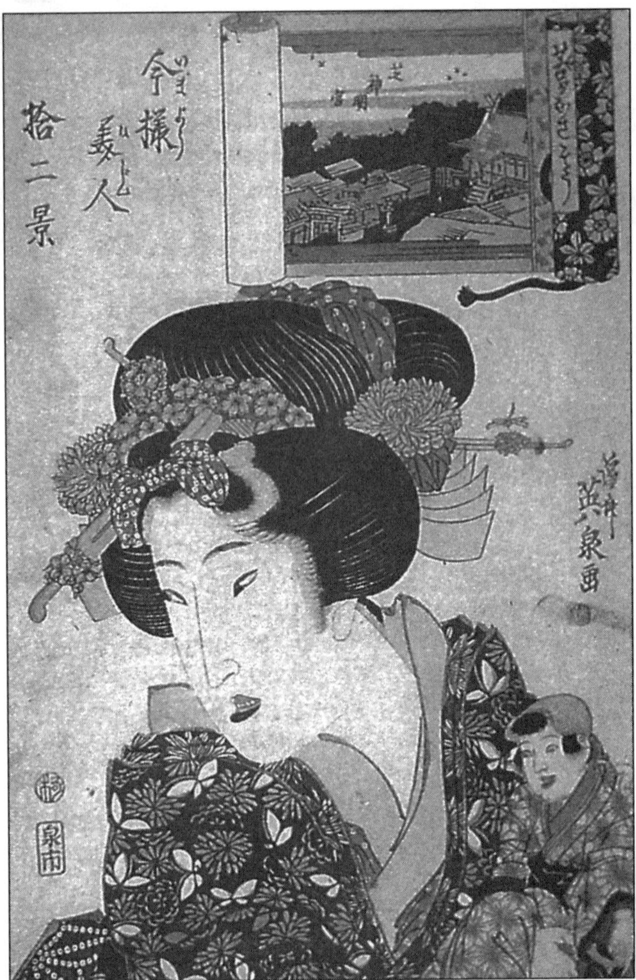

Eisen, oban tate-e 15 1/4" x 10", a bijin okubi-e, "Kuganasaso," (The Carefree Type) sub-title Shiba Shimmei-gu (Shiba Shimmei Shrine), from the series Imayo Bijin Juikei (Twelve modern day beauties), signed "Keisai Eisen ga," published by Izumiya Ichibei, Bunsei 5 (1822), good impression and color, soiled, corners restored, $4500-6500.

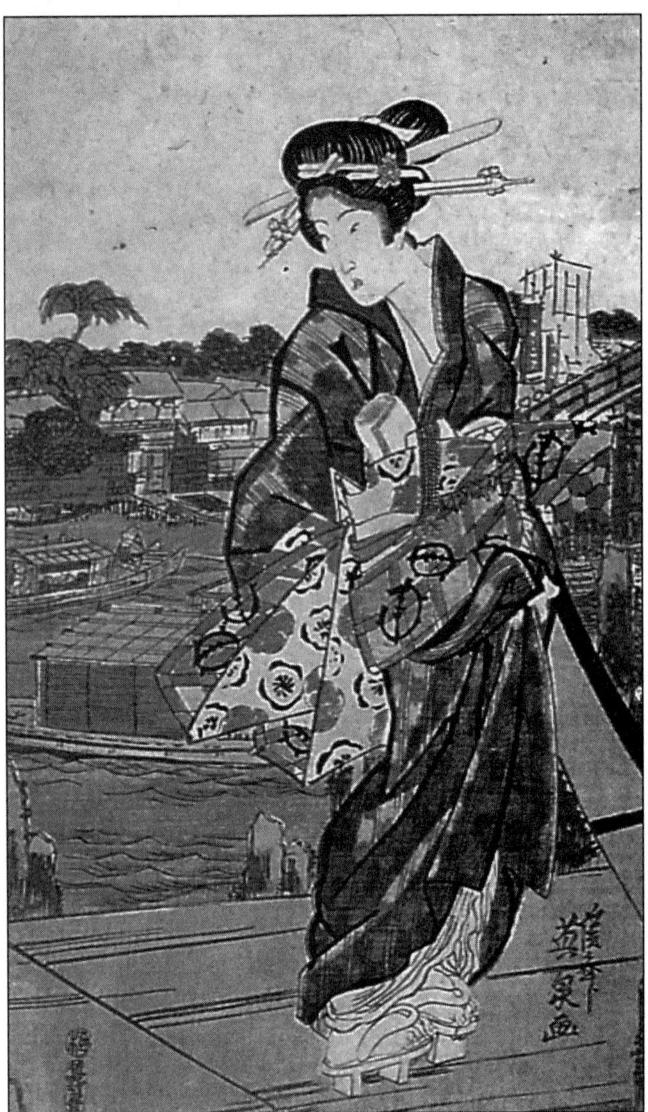

Eisen, oban tate-e, "Bijin on A Dock," kiwame seal, very good impression, good condition, good color, soiled, $300-450.

Eishin (fl. c. 1790-1810s) pupil of Eishi.

Eisho (fl. c. 1790s)

Hashira-e, courtesans after a bath, unsigned but attributed to Eisho, published by Surugaya Hanbei, good impression, stains, rubbed, $2500-3500.

Eishun (fl. c. 1720s) Kaigetsudo School.

Eisui (fl. c. 1790-1823) pupil of Eishi.

Eizan (1787-1867) founder of the Kikugawa style.

Kakemono-e, full-length portrait of a woman in aubergine kimono and green checked obi, blind printing, signed "Eizan hitsu," published by Wakasaya Yoichi, good impression, color and condition, $6000-8000.

Kakemono-e, full length portrait of a woman wearing an orange kimono with red inner robe, gray sash, signed "Kikugawa Eizan hitsu," fine impression, very good color, small hole on lower right, slightly soiled, $4000-5000.

Oban tate-e, approx. 12 1/2" x 8", "Furyu Yusuzumi San Bijin," (Three Fashionable Beauties), signed "Kikukawa Eizan hitsu," published by Yamadaya Shojiro, very good impression, faded in places, small worm holes, laid down , rubbed along edges, trimmed, $2500-4000.

Oban tate-e, triptych, approx. 10 1/4" x 8 1/4", "Furyu Hanami Sugate-e" (Picture of Fashionable Flower Viewing), a daimyo and attendant writing poetry surrounded by bijin viewing cherry blossoms, signed "Kikugawa Eizan hitsu," published by Kawaguichiya Uhei, very good impression, a bit of fading and soiling, edges trimmed and rubbed, repair to some wormage, binding holes, $1200-1800.

Enjaku (fl. c. 1858-1865) Osaka School artist.

Enkyo (1749-1803)

Enshi (fl. c. 1785-1795) pupil of Shunsho.

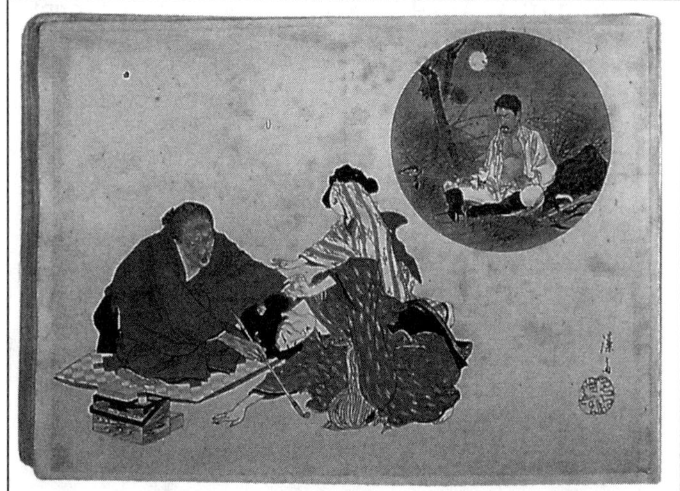

Eisen Tomioka, , oban yoko-e, 11 1/2" x 8 1/2", (Kiyokata Kaburagi, Eisen Tomioka, Kiyochika Kobayashi, Hanko Kajita, Kason Suzuki, Keishu Takeuchi, Chikanobu Yoshu, Toshimine Tsutsui, Toshikata Mizuno), 24 woodblock illustrations for Romantic Novels, fine impressions, very good color and condition, mica, gauffrage, late Meiji period c. 1900, $2500-4500.

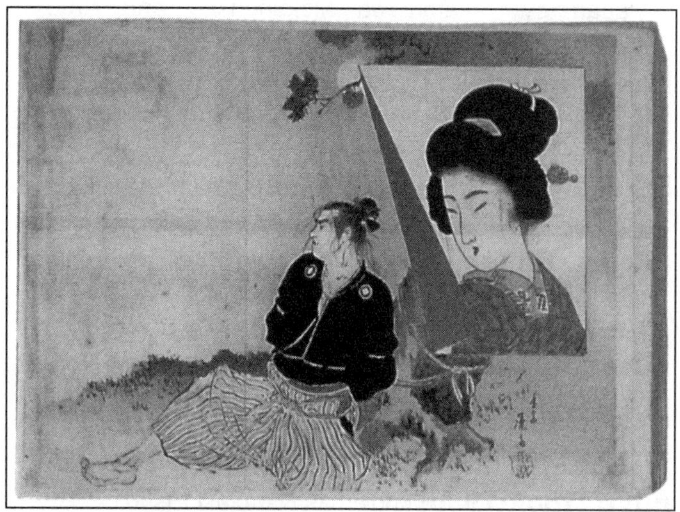

Eisen Tomioka, oban yoko-e, 11 1/2" x 8 1/2", (Kiyokata Kaburagi, Eisen Tomioka, Kiyochika Kobayashi, Hanko Kajita, Kason Suzuki, Keishu Takeuchi, Chikanobu Yoshu, Toshimine Tsutsui, Toshikata Mizuno), 24 woodblock illustrations for Romantic Novels, fine impressions, very good color and condition, mica, gauffrage, late Meiji period c. 1900, $2500-4500.

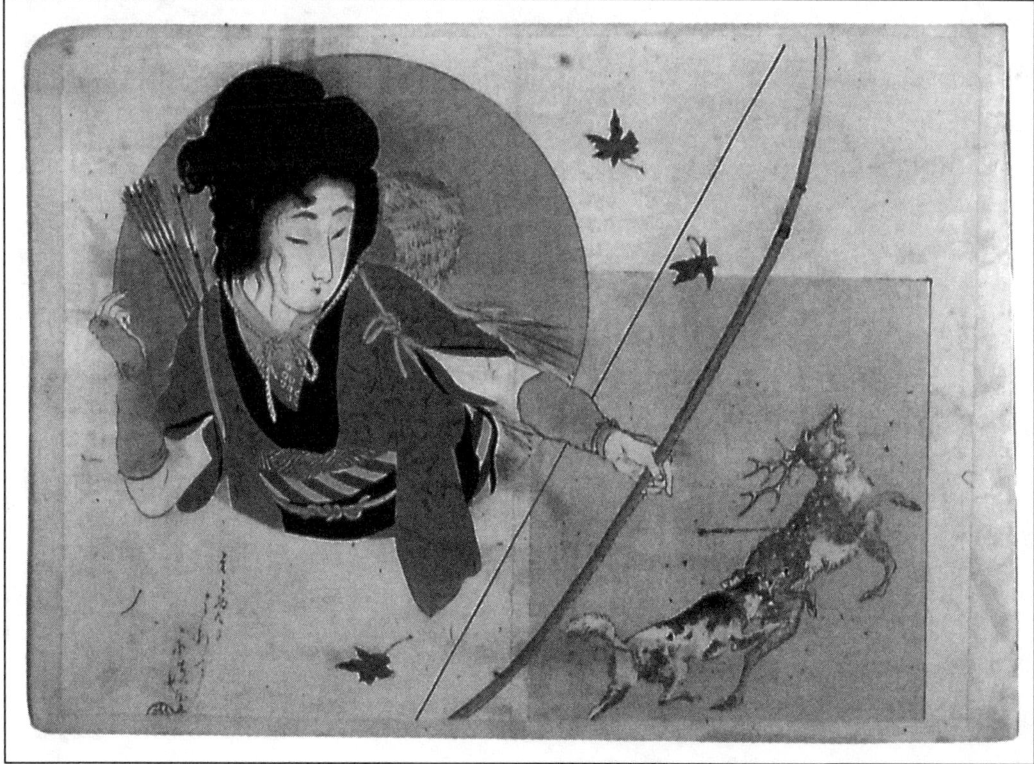

Eisen Tomioka, oban yoko-e, 11 1/2" x 8 1/2", (Kiyokata Kaburagi, Eisen Tomioka, Kiyochika Kobayashi, Hanko Kajita, Kason Suzuki, Keishu Takeuchi, Chikanobu Yoshu, Toshimine Tsutsui, Toshikata Mizuno), 24 woodblock illustrations for Romantic Novels, fine impressions, very good color and condition, mica, gauffrage, late Meiji period c. 1900, $2500-4500.

F

Fujikuni (fl. mid 1820s) Osaka School artist.

Fujimaro (fl. c. 1800s-1810s)

Fujimori Shizuo (1891-1943) sometimes used the signature SIZ on early prints, he produced woodblock illustrations for Dowashu and for newspaper serializations, his works have an impressionist style.

Fujinobu (fl. c. 1750s-1760s) influenced by Harunobu.

Fujita Fumio (b. 1933) known for moku hanga.

Fujita Tsuguharu (Foujita Tsuguji, Leonard Fujita) (1886-1968) changed name to Leonard in 1959, designed etchings and lithographs from 1925. After his death, his moku hanga were published in Japan by Takamizawa Mokuhansha and Kato Hanga Kenkyusho.

Fukita Fujimaki (b. 1926) known for prints with oils over water base pigments, abstract subjects, limited editions.

Furukawa Ryusei (1893-1968) late prints include landscapes, seasonal flowers, still life.

Furuya Taiken student of Kaburagi Kiyokata, prints published by Watanabe Shozaburo in 1922 and 1936.

Fusanobu (fl. c. 1750s-1760) pupil of Shigenaga.

Fusatane (fl. c. 1849-1870) pupil of Sadafusa.

Fuyo (fl. c. 1790s) influenced by Kiyonaga.

Fuyo (1864-1936) known as Narazaki Eisho.

G

Gakutei (c. 1786-1868) pupil of Hokkei.

Gesso Yoshimoto (1881-1936) produced kacho-e and landscapes, published by Nishinomiya and Hasegawa.

Gessai (1784-1864)

Ginko (fl. c. 1874-1897) Sino-Japanese War prints.

Gokyo (fl. c. 1795) pupil of Eishi.

Gosei (fl. c. 1800s-1830s) illustration in Hokusai style.

Goshichi (c. 1776-1831) pupil of Harukawa Eizan, designed surimono and prints in Utamaro style.

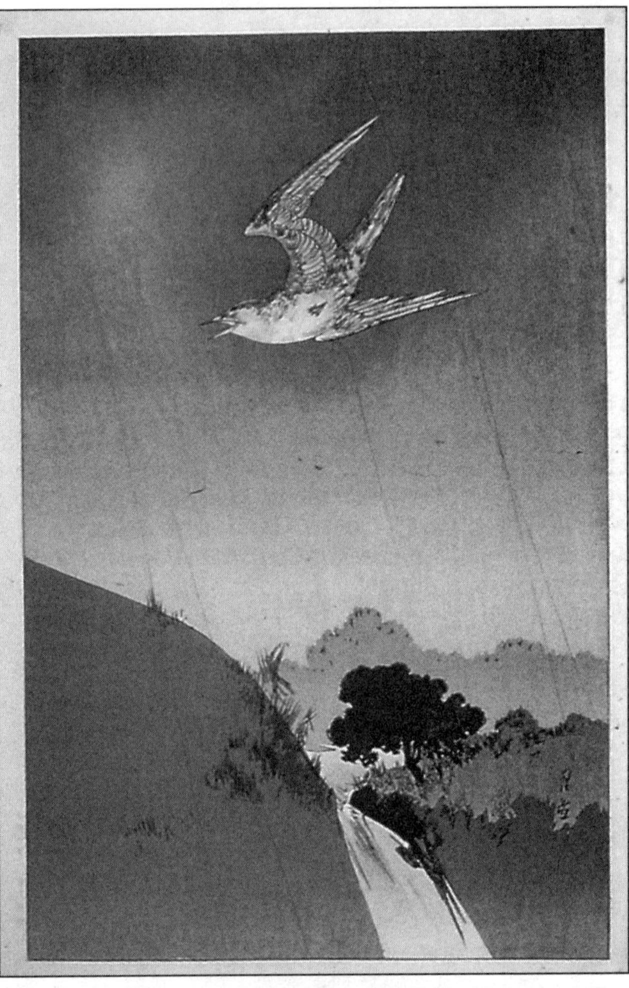

Gesso Yoshimoto, oban tate-e, "Birds in Rainstorm," c. 1930, published by Nishinomiya, fine color, impression, and condition, $400-500.

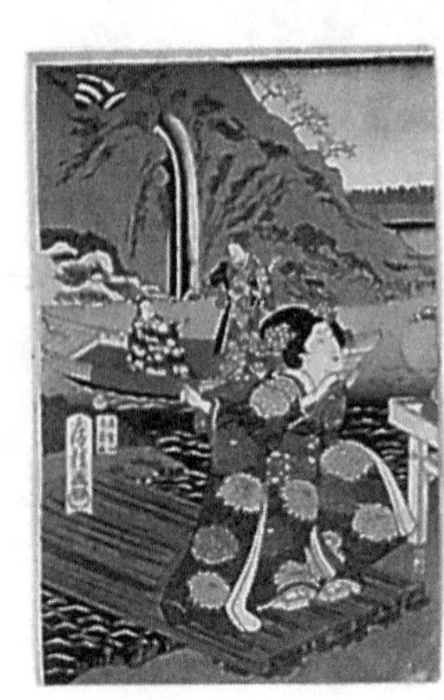
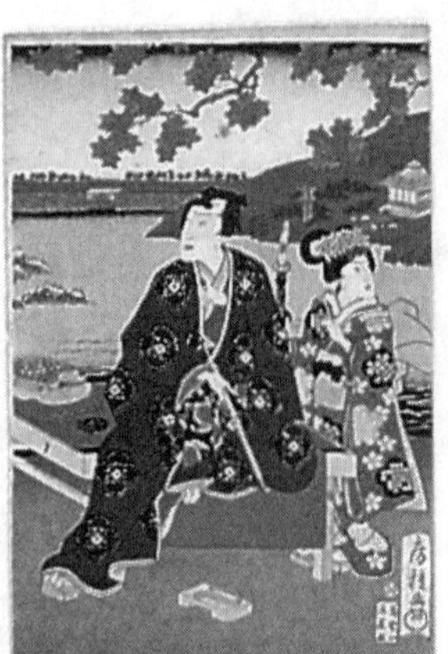
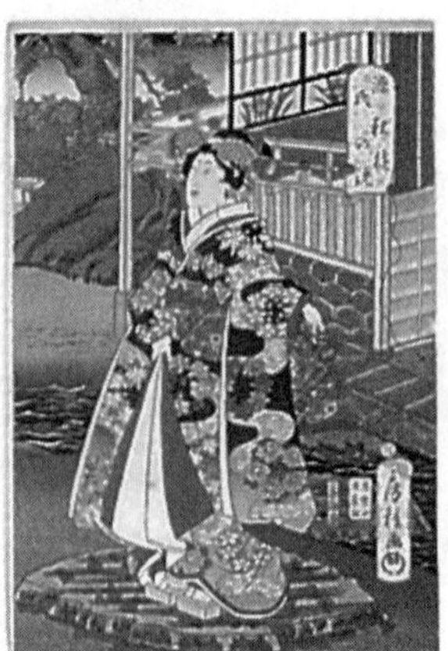

Fusatane, oban tate-e triptych, "Year of the Horse (1858)", fine impression, color, and condition, light paper backing, $1200-1800.

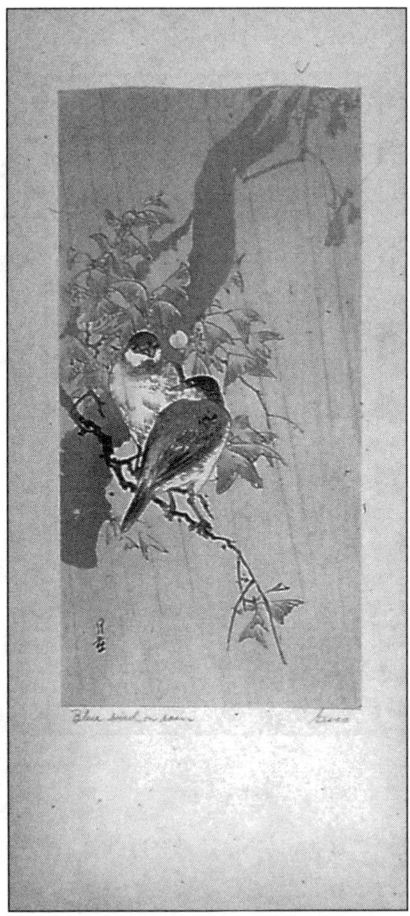

Gesso Yashimoto, tanzaku, original mat, good impression, condition, slightly toned, $100-175.

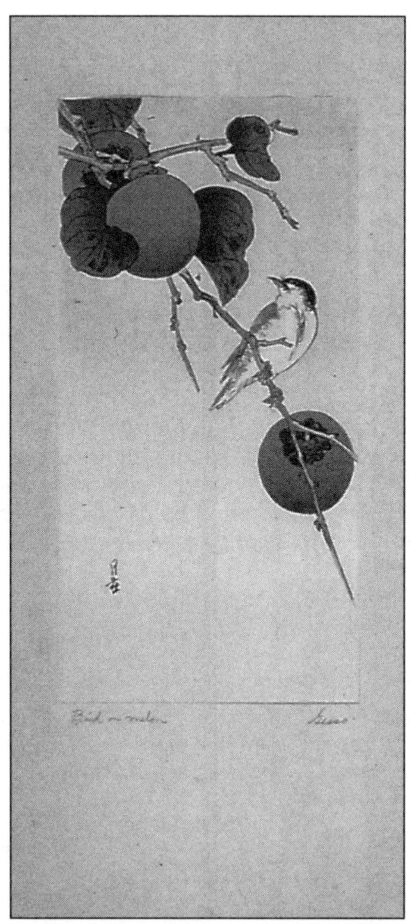

Gesso Yashimoto, tanzaku, original mat, good impression, condition, slightly toned $100-175.

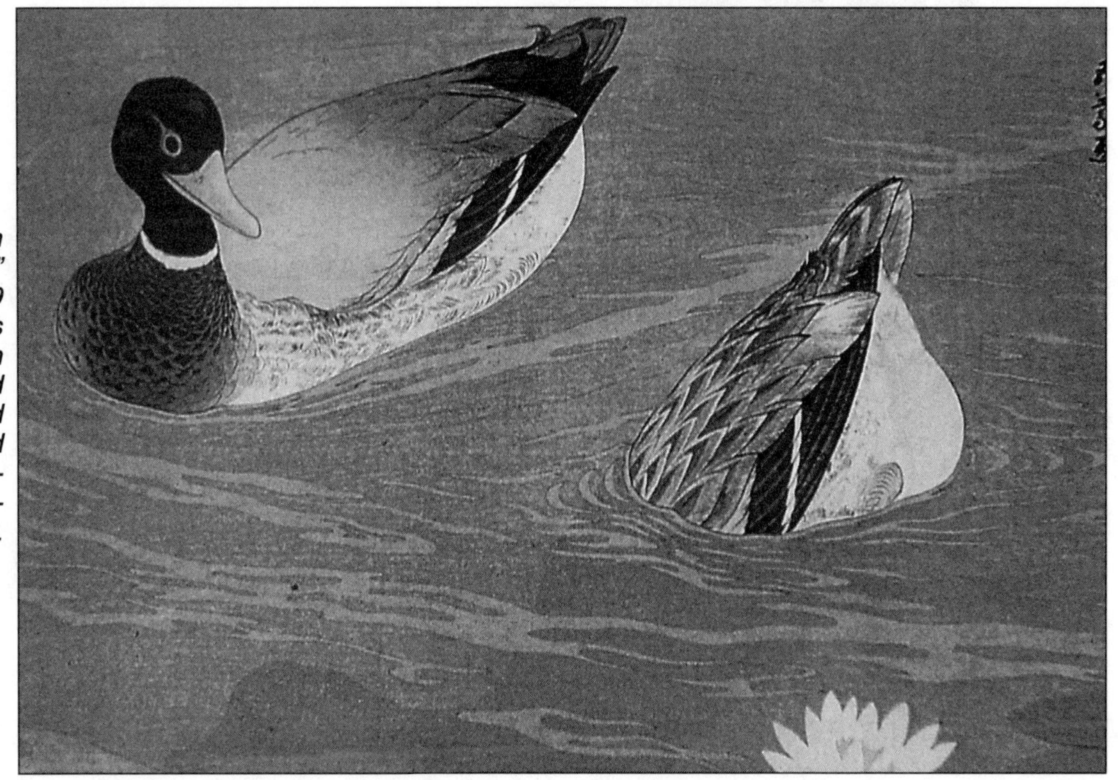

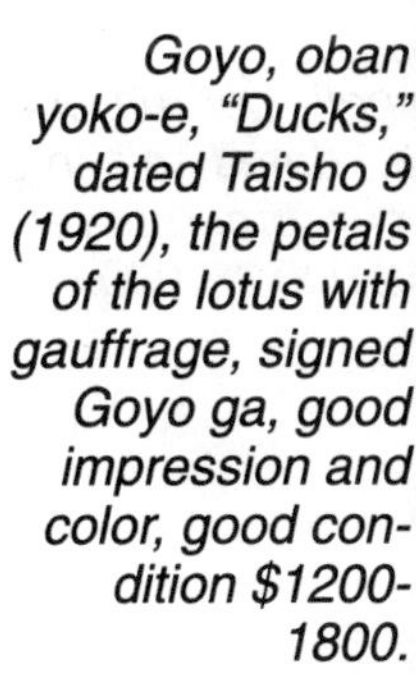

Goyo, oban yoko-e, "Ducks," dated Taisho 9 (1920), the petals of the lotus with gauffrage, signed Goyo ga, good impression and color, good condition $1200-1800.

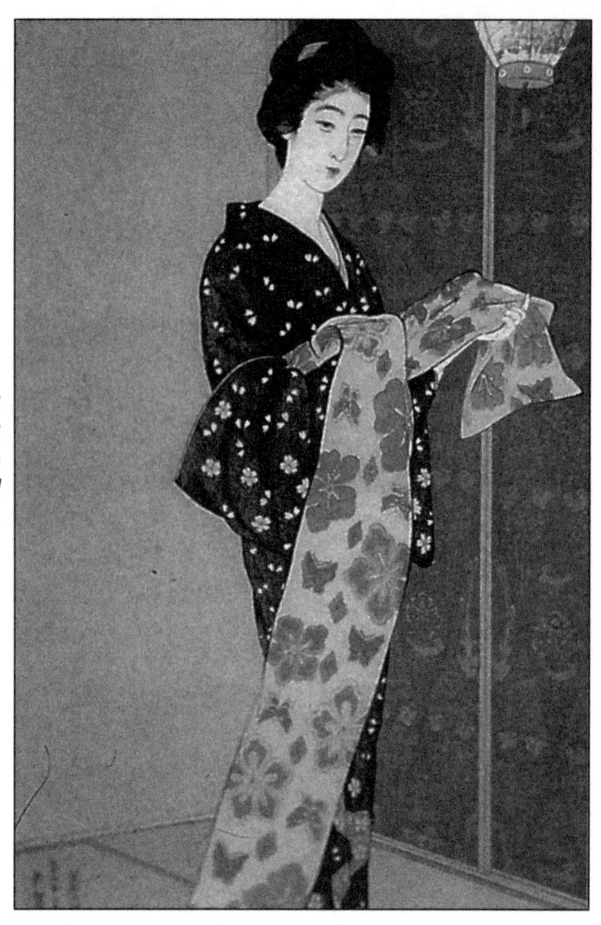

Goyo, nagaban, 22" x 14 1/4", "Kaso no musume," (Young Woman in Summer Clothing), full length portrait of a standing beauty in a gauze kimono holding a patterned obi, signed "Goyo ga," dated Taisho 9 (1920), sealed in red, mica background and mica on obi; fine impression and color, creases, corner crease, minor stains and soiling, slightly rubbed, $5500-9500.

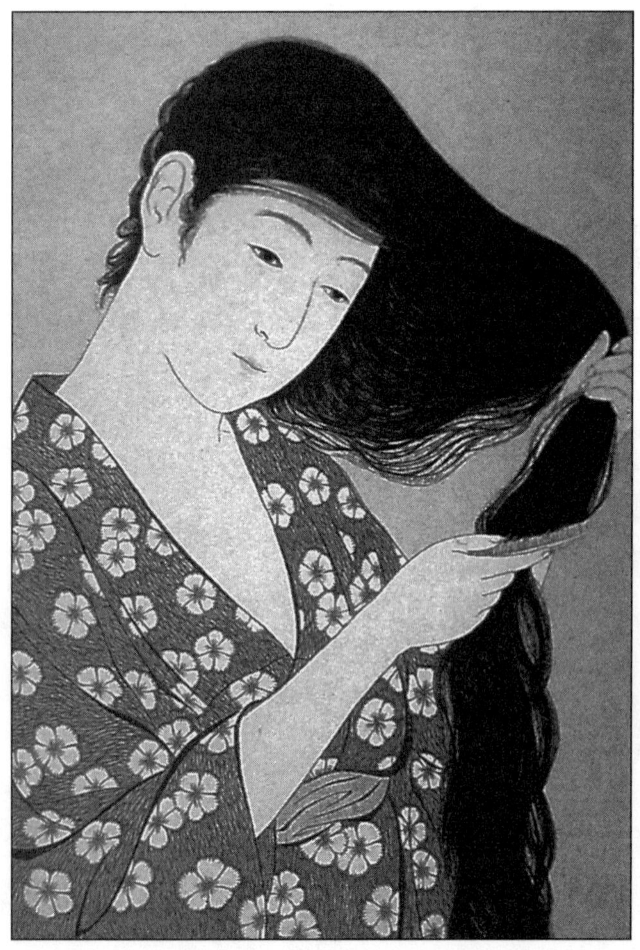

Goyo, dai oban tate-e, 18" x 14", half-length portrait of a woman combing her hair, igned "Goyo ga," dated Taisho 9 (1920), Goyo seal in the image, mica background, very good impression, color, and condition, $12,000-15,000.

Goyo Hashiguchi (Kyoshi) (1880-1921) designed "Bathing" for Watanbe Shozaburo in 1915, produced series of studies of women, total print output of 14 images, some of his designs were created into prints and issued following his death.

15 3/4" x 19 1/2","Yabakei," woodcut, 1918, signed "Goyo ga" and sealed Goyo, dated Dai Taisho 7, stained into image, tears, laid down on cardboard, slightly trimmed, $1500-2000.

Dai oban yoko-e, "Mt. Ibuki in Snow," signed "Goyo ga," dated Taisho 9 (1920), published by Watanabe, from an edition of 100, very good impression, color, and condition, $3000-4000.

Oban yoko-e, "Mandarin Ducks Swimming in a Lotus Pond," signed "Goyo ga," dated Taisho 9 (1920), fine impression, color, and condition, margins slightly trimmed, $3000-4000.

Gyokusen (fl. md. 1830s) Osaka School artist.

Gyokushu (fl. c. 1839s) Osaka School artist.

Gyokuso (fl. c. 1830s)

H

Hagiwara Hideo (b. 1913) known for abstract images, sometimes printed on both sides of the paper.

37 1/2" x 25 1/2", "Ishi no Hanna (Shiro)," (White Stone Flower), woodcut, 1960, signed in pencil and titled in pencil, toned, stained, trimmed, $1500-2000.

34 3/4" x 24 1/2", "Shiro no Genso (1)," (Fantasy in White), woodcut, embossed, mica, signed in pencil, numbered in pencil, signed and dated in English and Japanese, '62, from a series of 50, tape stains on front margins, and verso, slightly toned, slightly trimmed, stain at upper right into image, $2000-2500.

Hamaguchi Kei (b. 1936) known mostly for abstracts from the 1960s-1970s.

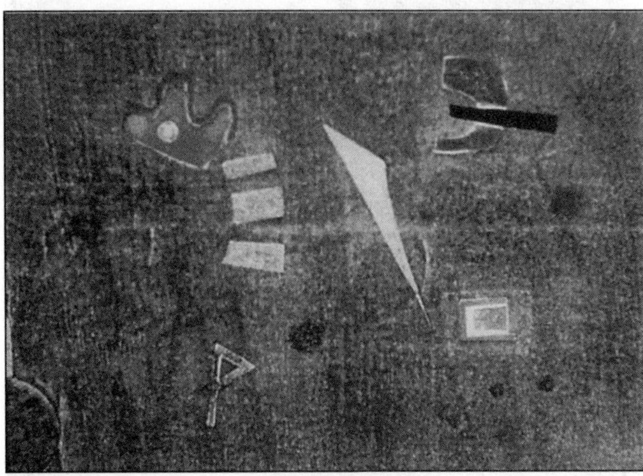

Hagiwara Hideo, woodcut and embossing, title "Yugijo" (1), signed and dated "Hideo Hagiwara '64," from an edition of 50, approx. 28" x 21", framed , toned, and laid down on board, $900-1200.

Hamaguchi Yozo (b. 1909) known for etchings.

Hara Ken (Hara Takeshi) (b. 1942) produced lithographs and serigraphs of abstract images.

Harunobu Suzuki (c. 1724-1780) the first woodblock artist to use color.

Chuban tate-e, two women in an interior, one sleeping under a mosquito net, the other reads a love letter, signed "Harunobu ga," moderate impression, faded, toned, soiled, water stain, $3500-5500.

Chuban tate-e, children performing as shishimai dancers, signed "Suzuki Harunobu ga," good impression, faded, rubbed, creased, tears repaired, $2000-4000.

Hashira-e, from Furyu nana komachi (Fanciful Transformed Versions of the 7 Episodes of the Poetess Komachi), sub-title Oomu (parrot), a poem inscribed in the square box, signed "Harunobu ga," good impression and color, foxing and rubbing, framed and glazed, framed size 30" x 6", $6500-8500.

Harushige name used by Kokan on prints in Harunobu-style.

Hashigawa Kiyoshi (1891-1980) moku hanga, etchings.

4 1/2" x 3 1/2", "French Doll," etching and drypoint, not dated, artist's seal, fine condition, $300-500.

Hashimoto Okiie (b. 1930) woodblock, limited editions.

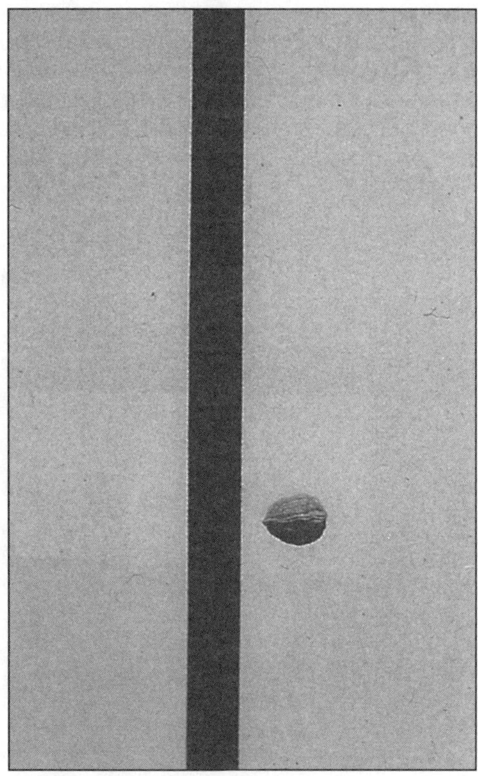

Hamaguchi Yozo, approx. 29 " x 13 3/4", "Kuromi," (Walnut), mezzotint on rives, c. 1959, signed in pencil in Roman script "Hamaguchi," from an edition of 50, tape stains on verso, toned, $3500-5500.

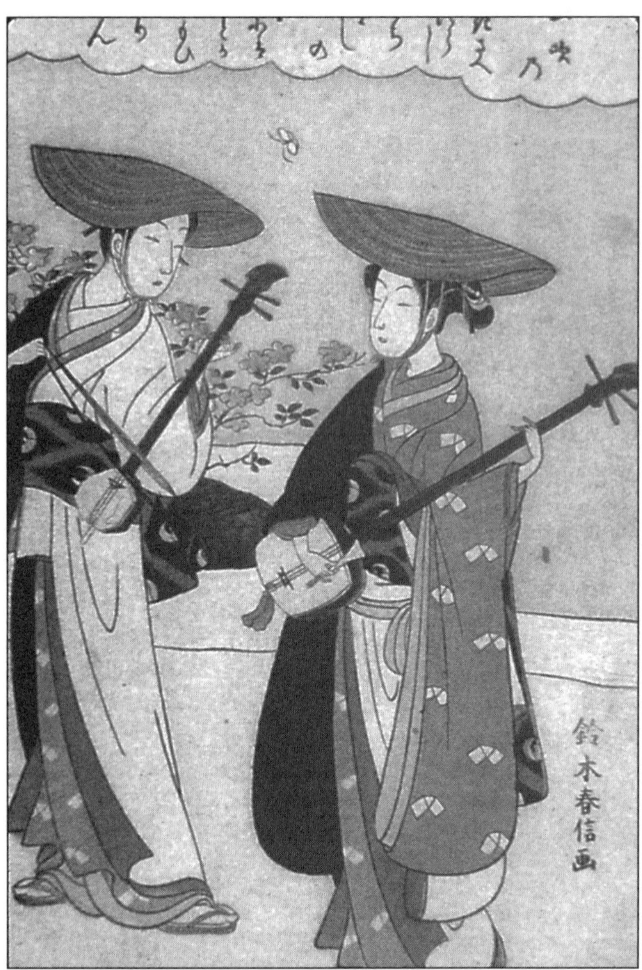

Harunobu, chuban, approx. 11" x 8", A young couple dressed as musicians playing a shamisen and Chinese violin, gauffrage, patterns in their attire with blind printing, signed "Suzuki Harunobu ga," good impression, faded and toned, soiled and stained, $6000-8000.

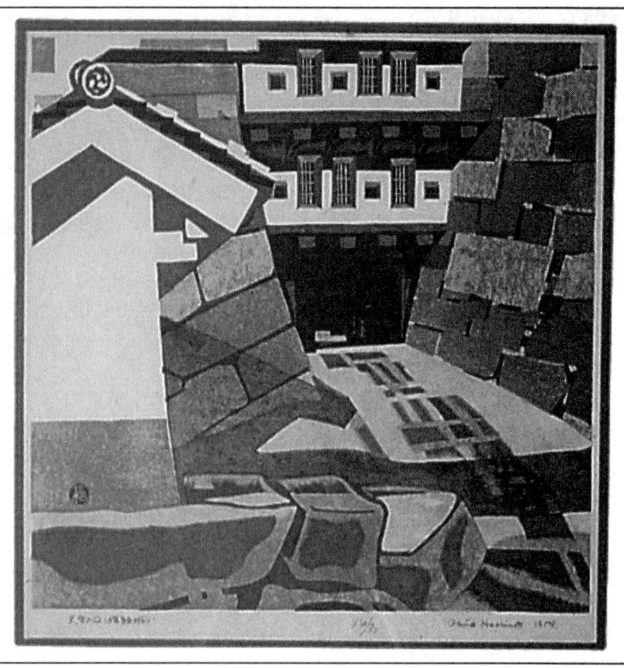

Hashimoto Okiie, dai oban, 16 1/2" x 17 1/2", from an edition of 30, dated 1957, signed on lower margin and sealed "Hashi," very good condition and color, $500-700.

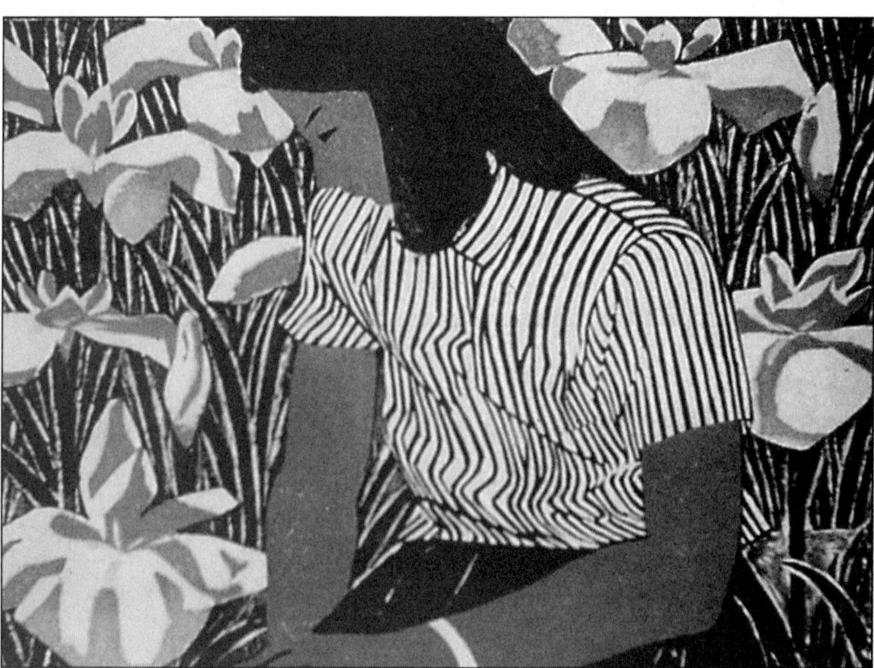

Hashimoto Okiie, "Young woman and Iris," sealed Hashi, c. early 1950s, approx. 15 1/4" x 21 1/4", toned, slightly trimmed, $600-800.

Hasui Kawase (1883-1957)

Kawase Hasui was born Kawase Bunjiro on May 18, 1883, in Shiba, Tokyo, the son of a thread merchant. His mother (by whose second marriage he was the first of ten children) was the daughter of a specialist in the art of inlay and the sister of the famous Meiji period playwright Kanagaki Robun.

At the time of Hasui's youth, Western art and its use of color, light, and perspective were influencing Japan. When he began painting, at age six, it was in the Western-style. At age sixteen Hasui studied Japanese painting under Aoyanagi Bokusen. He had studied for one year when his parents interceded because they wanted him to manage their shop. Attempts to study and paint on his own were blocked because of family pressures. When Hasui was 26 years old the family business went into bankruptcy.

That same year he asked Kaburagi Kiyokata, a well-known artist, to be taken on as his student. Kaburagi Kiyokata had studied woodblock printmaking with Toshikata. Toshikata represented the continuation of a well-known line of student-teacher relationships that dated back through Yoshitoshi, Kuniyoshi, and Toyokuni I to Toyoharu, founder of the Utagawa School of ukiyo-e masters. Kaburagi Kiyokata was known as a Japanese-style genre painter, and he thought Hasui too old to begin an artistic career. After studying in oils and watercolors for two years, with Okada Saburosuke, a Western-style painter, Hasui returned to Kaburagi Kiyokata, who this time accepted him. Over the years Hasui painted subjects ranging from kabuki stage settings to picture postcards to portraits. Kaburagi Kiyokata introduced Hasui to Watanabe Shozaburo. Watanabe was a prestigious print publisher who was looking for a new landscape artist.

Beautiful women and actors were among Hasui's subjects, but his greatest interest was in the landscapes he viewed during his travels. Hasui visited every scenic location in Japan, making detailed sketches that he later developed into designs for his prints. He is known to have said, "I don't sketch subjectively, but objectively. When I sketch, I can omit, but I cannot deceive."

In 1918, Watanabe published Hasui's first prints. He sent Hasui on sketching tours, publishing the prints that resulted. Unlike Hasui's ukiyo-e predecessors, to whom the essence of a print was conveyed by its use of line, Hasui found color and lighting equally important. At this time it was quite popular for the artists to engrave and print their own works. Hasui's prints were produced in the traditional manner by an engraver and a printer. The term "new prints" was coined by Watanabe to describe works by Hasui and several other artists, who combined Western-style art with traditional ukiyo-e.

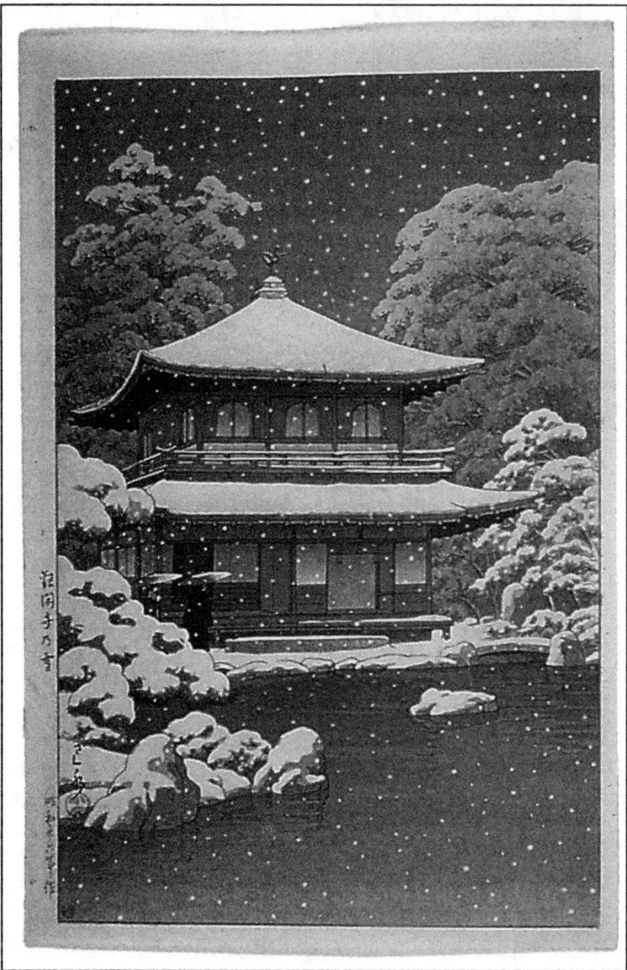

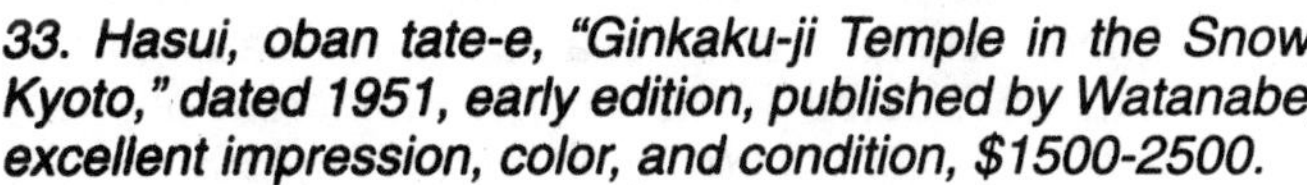

33. Hasui, oban tate-e, "Ginkaku-ji Temple in the Snow, Kyoto," dated 1951, early edition, published by Watanabe, excellent impression, color, and condition, $1500-2500.

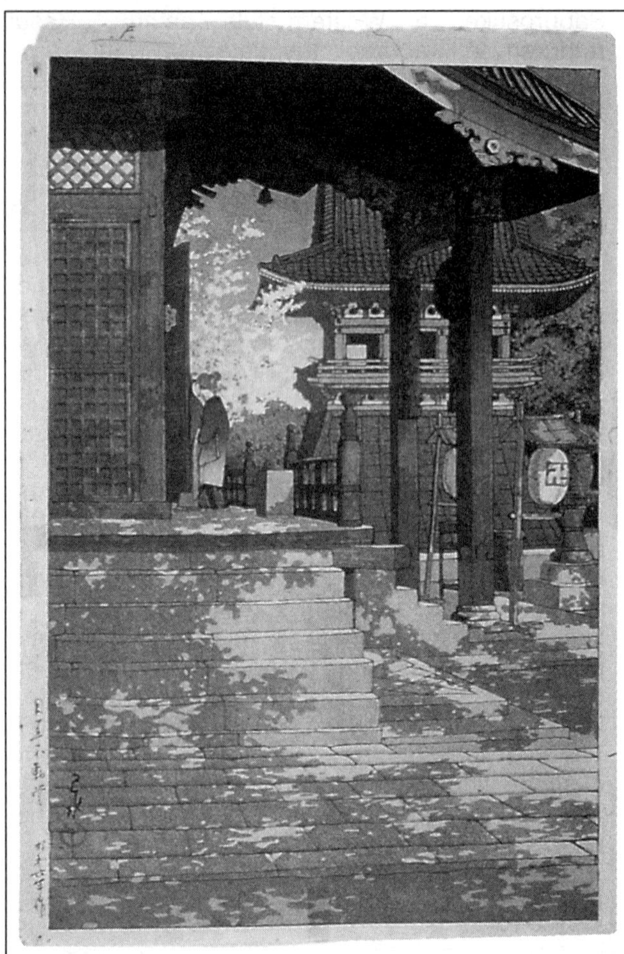

Hasui Kawase, oban tate-e, "Mefuro Fudodo, Tokyo," dated Showa 6 (1931), later edition, published by Watanabe, fine impression, color, and condition, $750-950.

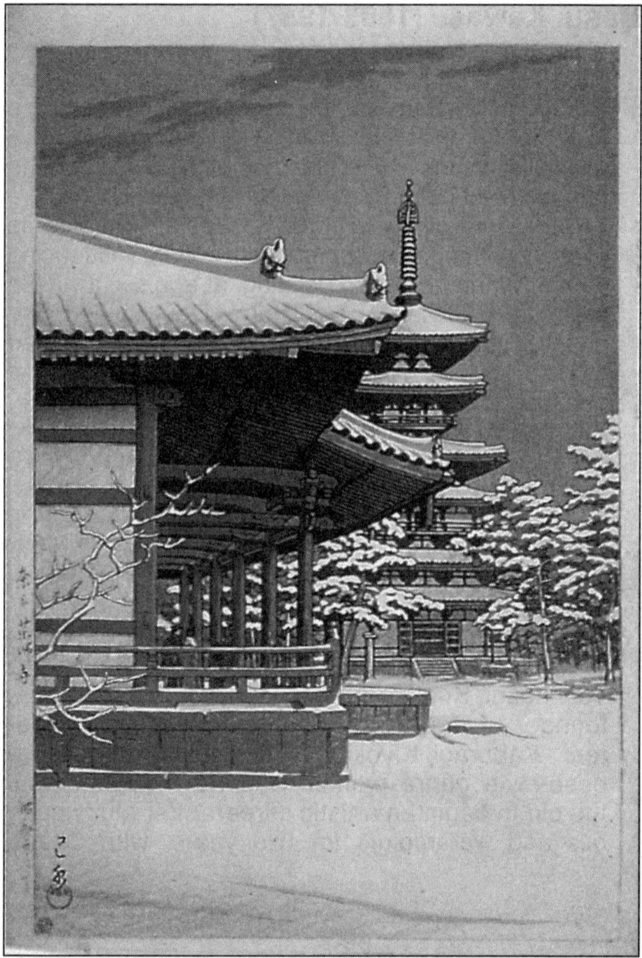

Hasui, oban tate-e, "Temple After the Snow," dated Showa 26 (1951), early edition, fine impression, color, and condition, $1500-2000.

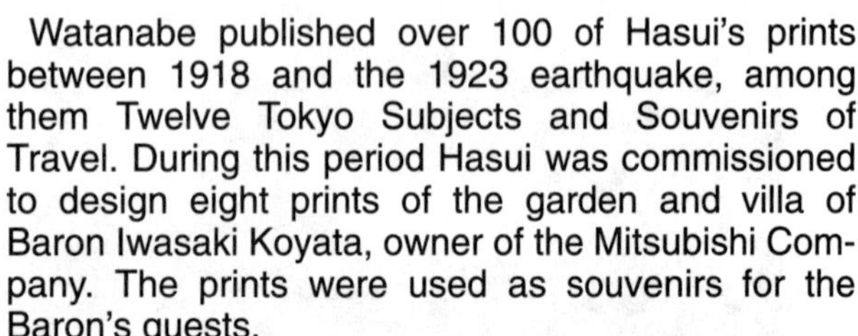

Watanabe published over 100 of Hasui's prints between 1918 and the 1923 earthquake, among them Twelve Tokyo Subjects and Souvenirs of Travel. During this period Hasui was commissioned to design eight prints of the garden and villa of Baron Iwasaki Koyata, owner of the Mitsubishi Company. The prints were used as souvenirs for the Baron's guests.

On Sept. 1, 1923, a cataclysmic earthquake struck Japan leveling portions of Tokyo, including Hasui's home. Fire destroyed all but a few of his prints, including the blocks from which they had been produced and by which they might have been reproduced. Also consumed in the fire were works partially completed, as well as Hasui's sketchbooks. So great was the damage to the extant art of Hasui and others that it took nine years before Watanabe could present them in a major exhibition.

Hasui was traveling and sketching less than two months after the earthquake. His reputation grew as his prints were shown in the West, as well as in domestic exhibitions. During WWII, when print production slowed, Hasui concentrated on paintings. He eventually returned to prints. In 1953 the Japanese government's Committee for the Preservation of Intangible Cultural Treasures, in recognition of the collaborative techniques involved in producing Shin Hanga (New Prints), commissioned Hasui to create a new print titled "Snow at Zojoji Temple" with assistance from other artisans. Narazaki Muneshige carefully documented the process. Hasui was named a Living National Treasure in 1956. He passed away on Nov. 27, 1957.

Oban tate-e, "Ginkaku-ji," (Temple after the Snow), signed "Hasui" and sealed, published by S. Watanabe, dated 1951, very good impression, very good color, very good condition, $1000-1500.

As above, mounted on board, faded, $200-300.

Dai oban tate-e, "Inokashira no Yuki," (Snow at Inokashira Benten Shrine), signed "Hasui" and sealed, published by Watanabe Shozaburo, dated Showa 3 (1928), good impression and color, tape residue on edges, rubbed and creased, stained along top and bottom, $900-1200.

Oban tate-e, "Kintai-Baishi Bridge in Spring Evening, Yamaguchi," signed "Hasui" and sealed, published by S. Watanabe, dated 1947, very good impression, very good color, very good condition, $1800-2200.

Oban tate-e 15 3/4" x 10 1/2", "Mt. Fuji After Snow," published 1932 by Doi, signed and sealed "Hasui," fine color, impression, and condition, posthumous print, $400-600.

Oban tate-e, "Yuki no Kururu Terajimamura," (Nightfall in Snow at Terajima Village), from the series Twelve Views of Tokyo (Tokyo junikei), signed "Hasui" and dated on the image Taisho 9 (1920), published by Watanabe, very good impression, color, and condition, $6500-8500.

"Nightfall in Snow at Terajima Village," as above, very good impression, color, margins trimmed to image, $2500-3500.

Oban tate-e, "Ohasi no Yuki (Edogawa)," (Snowy Bridge Edo River), azuri-e; signed "Hasui," dated Showa 7 (1933), publisher's seal in left margin, moderate condition, toned, trimmed, faded, $800-1200.

As above: fine condition, color, and impression, slightly trimmed, 15 1/2" x 10 1/4", $1800-2800.

Oban yoko-e, "Shiobara Arayu no Aki," (Fall at Arayu Hot Spring in Shiobara), from the series Tabi Miyage dai Isshu "Souvenirs of My Travels-First Series," signed "Hasui" and sealed, dated Taisho 9 (1920), published by Watanabe Shozaburo, good impression and condition, toned margins into image, faded, tape on verso, otherwise good condition, $550-900.

As above, very good impression and color, margins trimmed, tape residue on verso, $1200-1800.

As above, fine condition, fine impression, very good color, $6000-8000.

O-tanzaku tate-e, "Shiobara Hatakudari," (Hatakudari Hotsprings in Shiobara in the Rain), dated Taisho 7 (1918), published by Watanabe Shozaburo, good impression and color, slightly toned and soiled, $7500-15,000.

Dai oban tate-e, "Tsuruoka Hachimangu," (Tsuruoka Hachiman Shrine), signed "Hasui" and sealed, published by S. Watanabe, dated Showa 6, (1931), good impression, good color, soiled and trimmed margins, tape stains at top, $800-1200.

Hidemaro (fl. early 19th century) pupil of Utamaro.

Hikokuni (fl. c. 1821-1824) pupil of Ashikuni.

Henmi Takashi (1895-1944)

Hiroaki (see Shotei)

Hirano Hakuho (1879-1957) signed "Hakuho ga" and sealed Hirano, produced mainly bijin-ga, worked for Watanabe Shozaburo.

Hiratsuka Un'ichi (1895-1997) woodblock, limited editions.

Hirokage (fl. c. 1855-1865) pupil of Hiroshige.

Hirokuni name used by Hirosada until 1847.

Hironobu I (fl. c. 1851-1870)

Hironobu Oda (1888-?)

Hironobu II (fl. 1844-1890) pupil of Hironobu I.

Hirosada (fl. c. 1820s-1860s) pupil of Kunimasu.

Hiroshige (1797-1858)

Through his expression in his art Hiroshige comes closest to representing the sentiment and life of the Japanese people of his time. His prints represent a typical Japanese image of nature.

Hiroshige used planes rather than lines to dominate compositions, as compared to Utamaro, Hokusai, and Sharaku, all of whom emphasized lines. Utamaro expressed the women in his prints by the use of elegant graceful lines rather than planes, which would have suggested swelling volume. Hokusai's expression is found in the clarity of his outlines. Sharaku made use of line for sharp definition. In contrast, Hiroshige's interest appears to be in the aesthetic composition of planes of color. The human figure(s) that appear in most of his prints are anonymous and not specific characters such as famous actors or noted bijin.

Hiroshige was born in 1797, son of an Edo fire warden. In 1811 he entered the studio of Utagawa Toyohiro, and soon took the name Hiroshige. His first published work was as a book illustrator (1818). From c. 1818-1828 he published prints which featured actors, bijin, and warriors. From c. 1831 he began the landscape series that made him so famous: Fifty-three Stations of the Tokaido. Additional famous Hiroshige series include: Famous Views of Japan, Sixty-nine Stations of the Kiso Highway, Eight Views of Lake Biwa, and Famous Views of Kyoto. Among his pupils were Hiroshige II, Shigekatsu, Shigekiyo, and Hiroshige III.

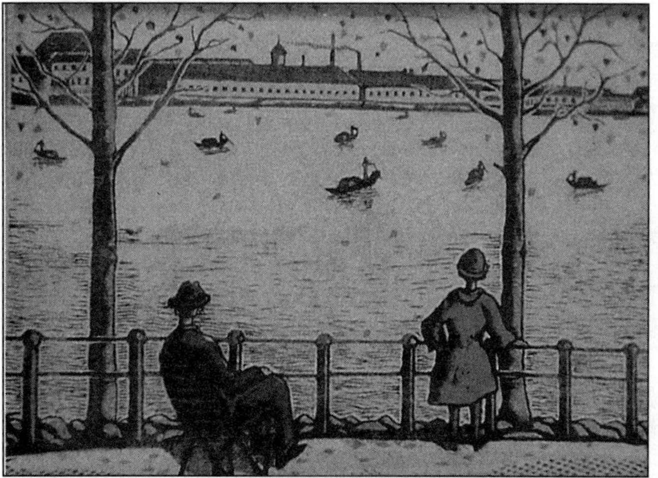

Henmi Takashi, oban yoko-e, 10" x 12 1/2", "Shan'hai Fukei," (View of Shanghai) early 1930s, signed "Nenmi Takashi" and "Takashi" in the block and titled in Japanese, slightly trimmed, slightly toned, and creased, $2000-3000.

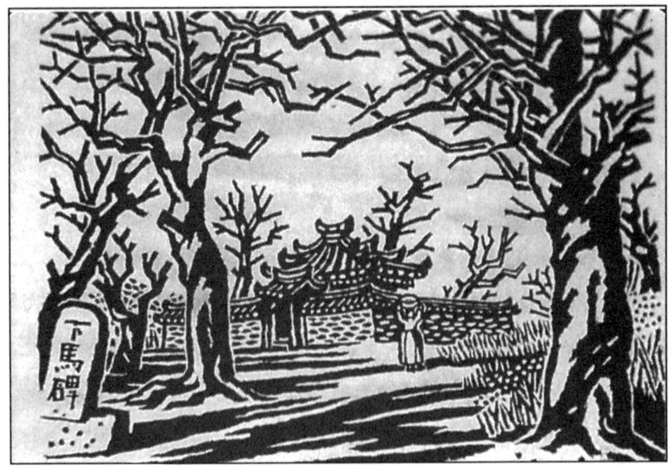

Hiratsuka Un'ichi, oban tate-e, 20" x 27 1/8", "Keirin in Kyongiu," signed in pencil and sealed, from an edition of 30, c. 1930s, good impression, very toned and worn, stained, tape residue on verso, $2000-3000.

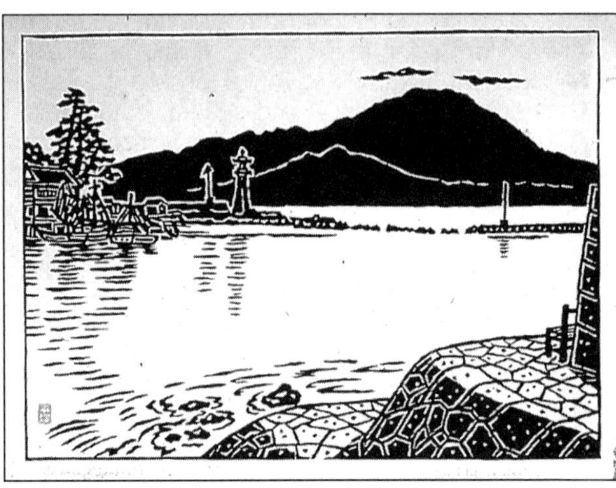

Hiratsuka Un'ichi, dai oban, "Izumo Inonosaki," original folio with title signature and seal, title and signature in pencil on lower margin, seal on lower right margin, and sealed within the image, fine impression, color, and condition, $3500-6000.

Hiroshige II (1829-1869) pupil and adopted son of Hiroshige I, used the name from 1858-1865.

Oban tate-e, "Shinshu Kiso no Yuki," (Snow in the Kiso Gorge in Shinano Province), from the series Shokoku Meisho Hyakkei (One Hundred Views of Famous Places in the Various Provinces), publisher Uoya Eikichi, censor's date seal, aratame, Year of the Goat (1857), very good impression and color, mica on snow, spoiled, wormage, 2 sets of binding holes, one set in the left margin and one set in the left side of the image, $3000-4000.

Oban tate-e, "Suo Iwakuni Kintaibashi," (The Kintai Bridge), from the series Shokoku Meisho Kyakkei (One Hundred Views of Famous Places in the Various Provinces), publisher Uoya Eikichi, censor's date seal, aratame, Year of the Goat (1857), signed "Hiroshige ga," very good impression and color, mica on snow, soiled, wormage, 2 sets of binding holes, one set in left margin and one set in image on left side, $3500-4500.

Hiroshige III (1843-1894) pupil of Hiroshige, took the art name Hiroshige III in 1865.

Hisanobu (fl. c. 1801-1815) influenced by Utamaro.

Hokkei (1780-1850) pupil of Hokusai, specialized in surimono.

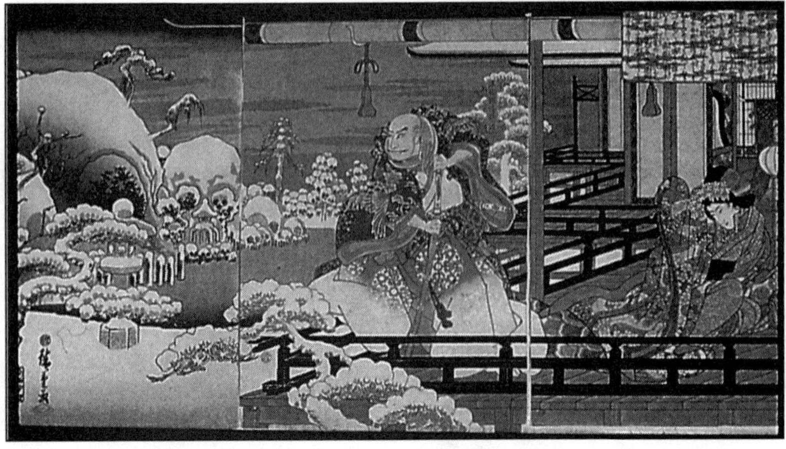

Hiroshige, oban tate-e triptych, "Taira no Kiyomori Kaii o Miru Zu," (Taira no Kiyomori Gazing at Specters in a Snowy Garden), the warrior priest Taira no Kiyomori Nyudo is gazing at the snow in his garden forming into the skulls of his defeated enemies; publisher Ibaya Senzaburo, censor's nanuchi-in Wata (Watanabe) c. 1943-47; signed "Ichiryusai Hiroshige ga" with Hiro seal, very good impression, slightly faded and rubbed, each sheet torn around the edges, $3000-4500.

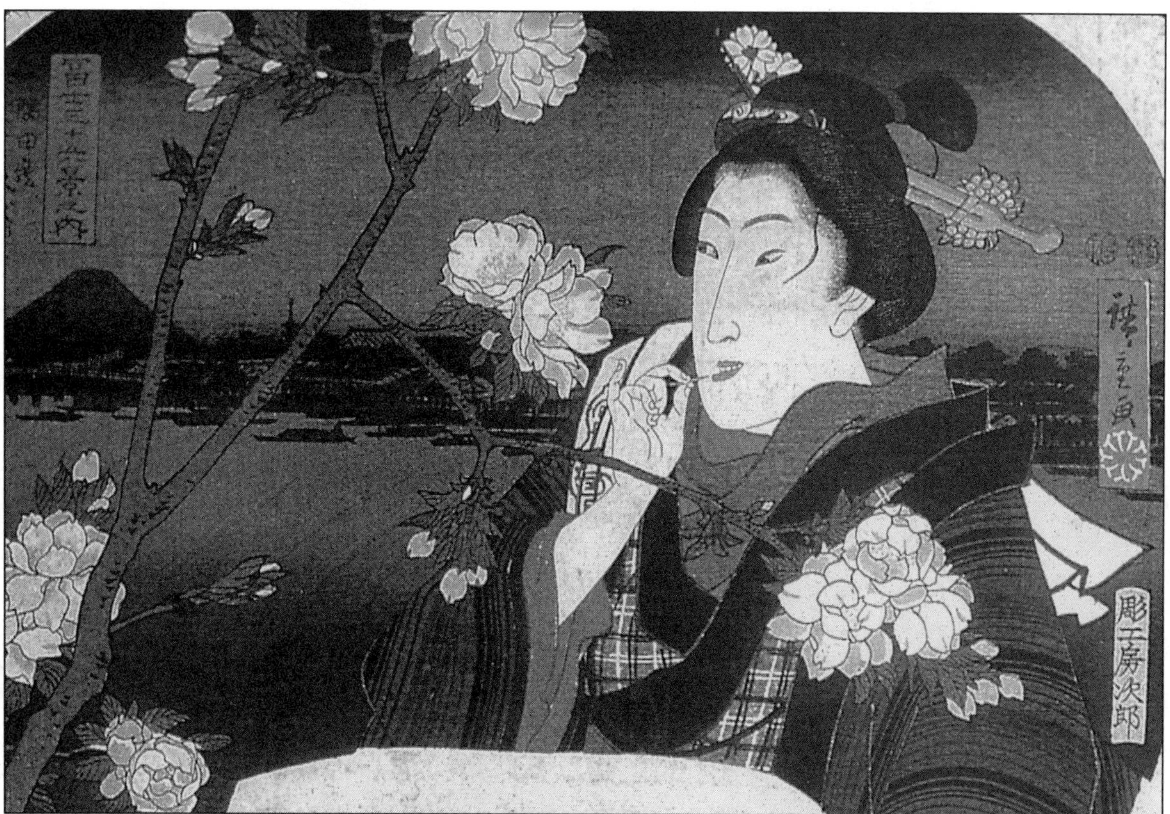

Hiroshige, uchiwa-e, 9 1/4" x 12", "Sumida Tsutsumi Tasogare no Fuji," (Twilight Fuji on the Sumida Embankment) from the series Fuji Sanjurokkei no Uchi (The 36 Views of Mt. Fuji), signed "Hiroshige ga," publisher Marukyodo, very good impression and color, corners restored, wormage restored, $4000-6000.

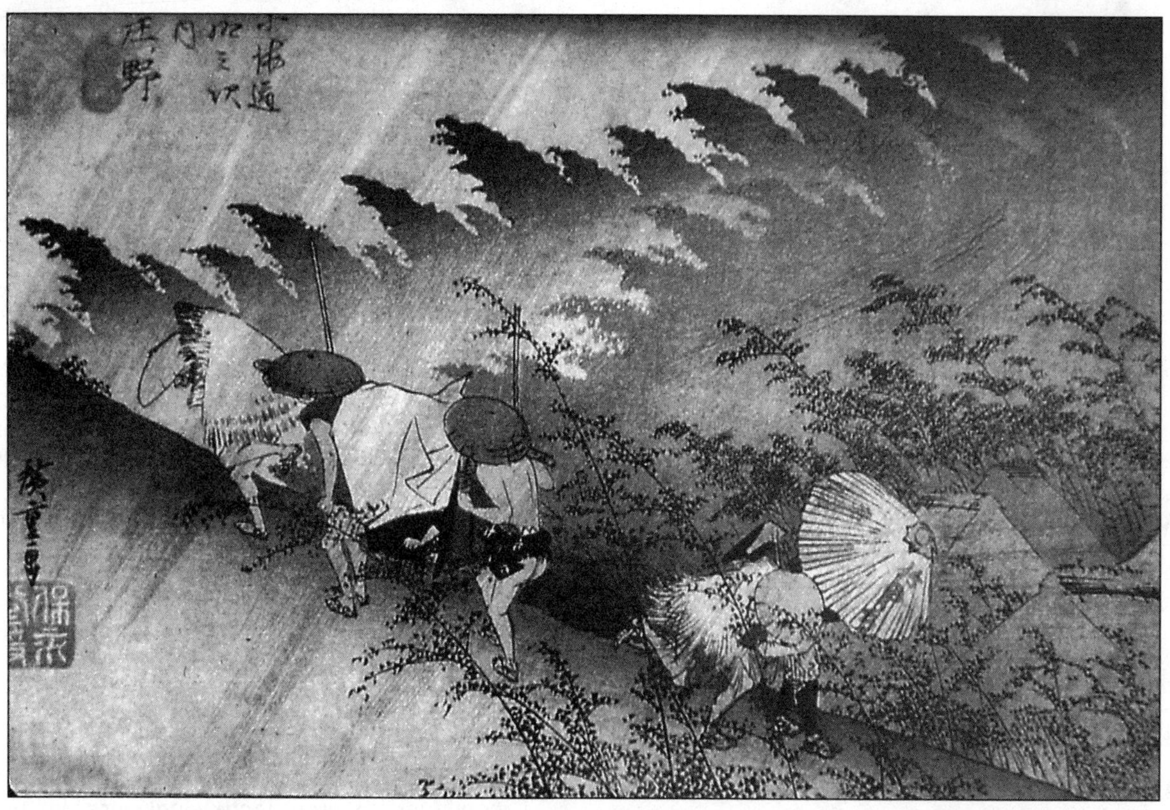

Hiroshige, oban yoko-e, approx. 9 1/4" x 14 1/4", "Shono, Haku-u," (White Rain, Shono) from the series Tokaido Gojusan Tsugi no Uchi (The 53 Stations of the Tokaido), signed "Hiroshige ga," published by Hoeido/Senkakudo, good impression and color, remargined on right side, left margin trimmed, wormage restored, $4500-6500.

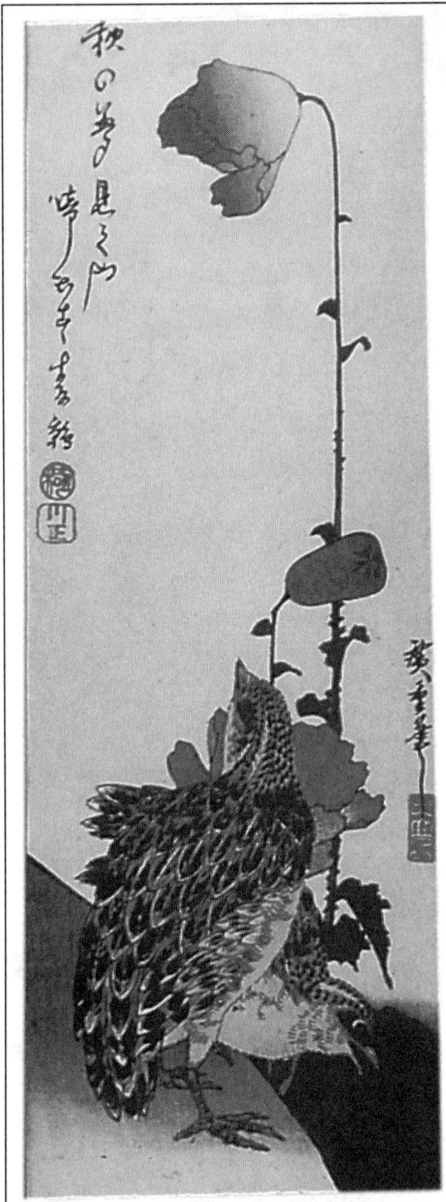

Hiroshige, chu-tanzuku, approx. 14 1/4" x 5", "Quail and Wild Poppies," signed "Hiroshige hitsu" and sealed Ichiruysai, publisher Kawaguchiya Shozo, fine impression and color, minor center fold, $18,000-30,000.

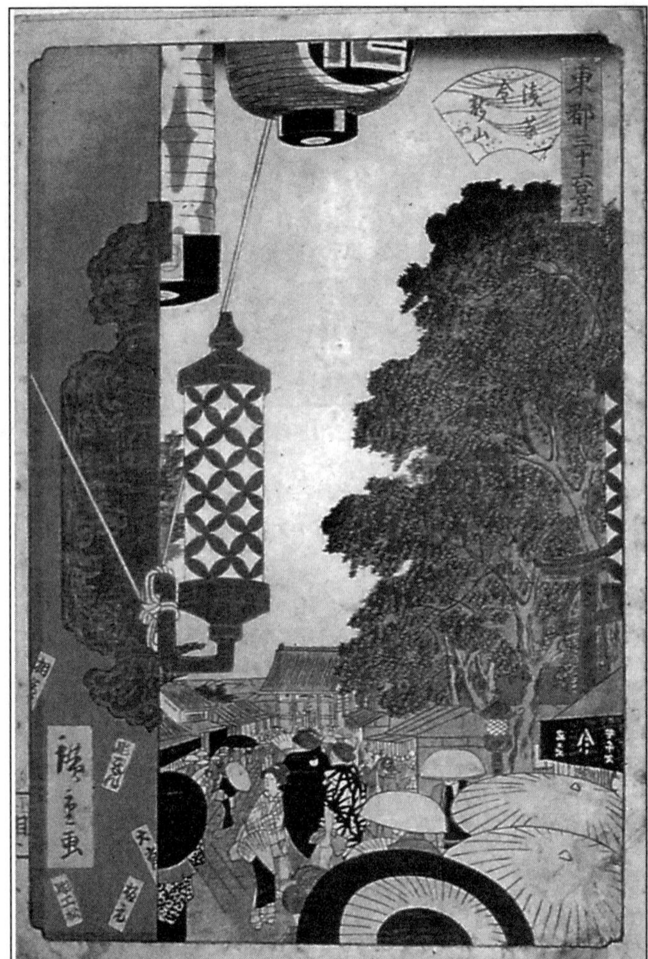

Hiroshige II, oban tate-e, from the series Thirty Six Views of the Eastern Capital, signed "Hiroshige ga," fine impression, color and condition, slightly trimmed right margin, $1200-1800.

Hokuba (1771-1844) produced books, illustrations, and surimono.

Hokuei (early 19th century) pupil of Hokusai.

Hokuga (fl. c. early 19th century) pupil of Hokusai.

Hokugan (fl. c. 1820s) pupil of Yoshikuni.

Hokuichi (fl. c. 1804-1830) pupil of Hokusai.

Hokuju (fl. late 1790s-1820s) pupil of Hokusai.

Hokusai (1760-1849)

Katsushika Hokusai was born in Honjo Wargesui, the son of a family named Kawamura. For a time he became the adopted son of Nakajima Ise, a mirror maker in the service of the shogunate. Although he withdrew from the adoption, Hokusai used the surname Nakajima.

There are many curious anecdotes connected with Hokusai. According to his biography, which he wrote at age 73, he began drawing at age six. He changed his name residence ninety times, and changed his art name many times.

In 1778, Hokusai became a student of the ukiyo-e artist Katsukawa Shunsho and was given the art name Katsukawa Shunro. After Shunso's death in 1792, however, he was expelled from the Katsukawa School. Thereafter he worked on his own to establish himself as an artist, studying the techniques and styles of the Tosa, Kano, and Rinpa Schools of Japanese painting as well as Chinese-style and Western-style painting.

At the beginning of the 19th century, ukiyo-e, while it continued to grow increasingly popular with the public, declined in its expressive power. A tendency toward sterile formalism became particularly marked in the depictions of beautiful women and kabuki

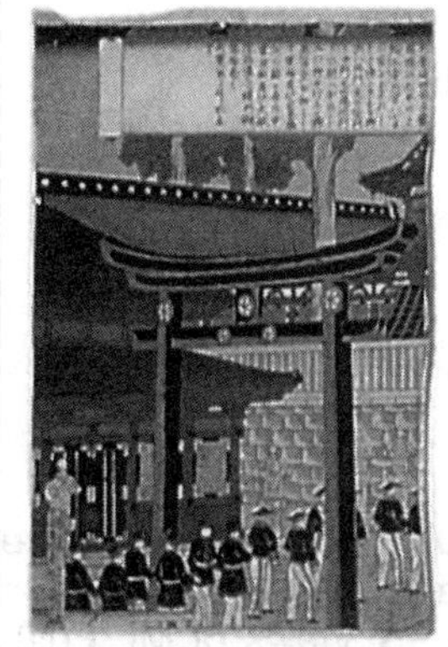
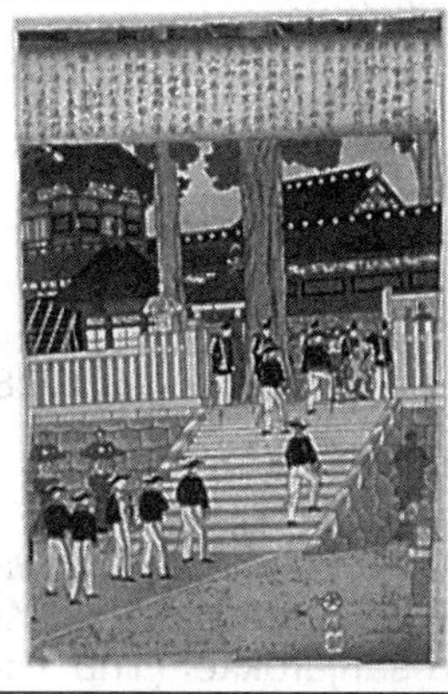
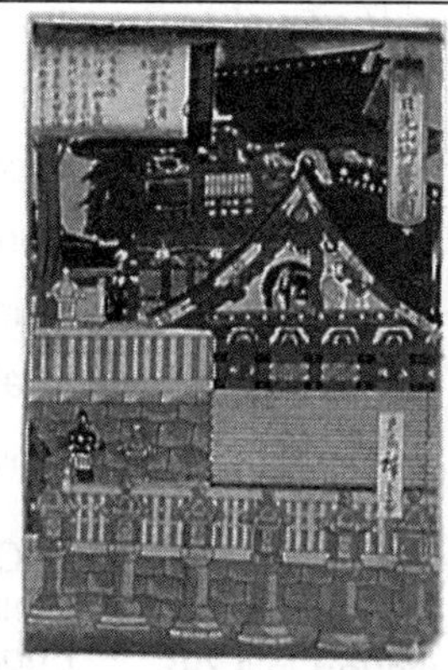

Hiroshige III, oban tate-e triptych, "Nikko, dated Meiji 9 (1876) the date in Arabic numerals, published by Kinaburo Yamamoto, good impression, good color, fair condition, $300-400.

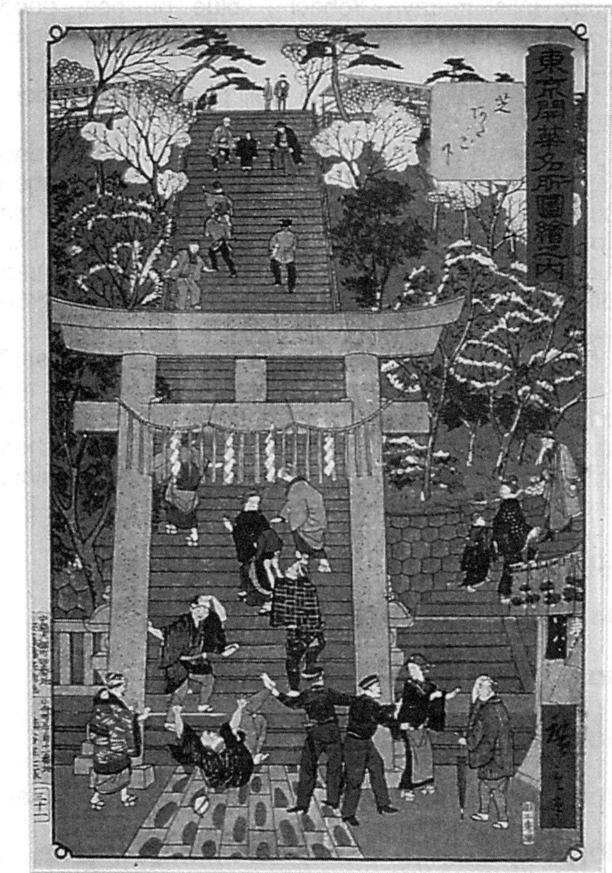

Hiroshige III, oban tate-e, 10" x 14 1/2", fine impression, color , slightly toned, $375-575.

actors, two of the subjects that had been most prominent in ukiyo-e. Appearing on the scene at the right time, Hokusai succeeded through his freshness of observation in opening up whole new areas of treatment in landscape, and bird and flower prints, which greatly extended ukiyo-e style. He worked all his life to develop and change the artistic medium, producing not only single sheet polychrome prints, but illustrations for novels and picture albums as well.

He also produced original paintings that are marked by rich color and vigorous brushwork. In variety of work he is in a class by himself among woodblock print artists. He is especially famous for his set of landscape prints that include various scenes of Mt. Fuji, the set of famous waterfalls, and a set of sea and river scenes.

Hokusai's work influenced artists such as Utagawa Hiroshige and Utagawa Kuniyoshi. He also became known in Europe and his works influenced the development of modern Western painting. Among those who studied with him were Shotei Hokuju, Yanagawa Shigenobu, and Totoya Hokei.

Important Dates in Hokusai's Career

1775	Begins apprenticeship to a woodblock cutter.
1779	Issues his first prints. Art name Shunro.
1780s	Designs many actor prints.
1791	Begins working for the publisher Tsutaya Juzaburo.
1796	Takes the name Sori. For the next ten years designs surimono.
1797	Begins work on his famous wave design.
1799	Changes his name to Hokusai.
1800s	Begins producing various series of Western style prints and albums of views of Edo.
1814	First volume of Hokusai Manga published.
1820	Changes name to Iitsu and keeps the name Hokusai.
1830s.	Publication of Thirty-Six Views of Mt. Fuji.
1833	Publication of series Snow, Moon and Flowers, One Thousand Pictures of the Ocean and True Mirror of Chinese and Japanese-Poems.
1834	Publication of Remarkable Views of Bridges in All Provinces and the first volume of the albumOne Hundred Views of Mt. Fuji.
1835	Publication of the second volume of One Hundred Views of Mt. Fuji and the series One Hundred Poems Explained by the Nurse.
1836-1838	Reduced to poverty, he sells his drawings in the streets.

1842-1843 Third volume of One Hundred Views of Mt. Fuji is published.

1848 Publishes his Picture Book on Coloring (two volumes).

1849 Dies on the eighteenth day of the fourth month.

Hokusai used many art names throughout his career. Some names were used simultaneously with others. His earliest name was Katsukawa Shunro. Works signed with this name, either prefixed by the School name Katsukawa, or short, Katsu, or used alone, date from 1782-1785, 1789, and 1792. Works signed Shunro aratame Gunmatei were issued in 1785 and 1786.

Art names used by Hokusai from 1779-1849

Zewaisai 1781-1782

Gumbatei 1785-1794

Sori 1795-1798

Hokusai Sori 1797-1798

Hokusai 1798-1819

Kako 1798-1811

Fasenkyo Hokusai 1799

Tatsumasa Shinsei 1799-1810

Senkozan 1803

Kintaisha 1805-1809

Gakyojin 1800-1808

Kyukyushin 1805

Gakyo-rojin 1805-1806, 1834-1849

Katsushika c. 1807-1824

Taito 1811-1820

Kyorian Bainen 1812

Raishin 1812-1815

Tengudo Nettetsu 1814

Iitsu 1820-1834

Zen saki no Hokusai Iitsu 1821-1833

Fesenkyo Iitsu 1822

Manji 1831-1849

Tsuchimochi Nisaburo 1834

Hyakusho Hachemon 1834-1846

Fujiwara Iitsu 1847-1849

Oban yoko-e, "Kanagawa Oki Nami Ura," (In the Well of the Great Wave off Kanagawa), from the series Fugaku sanjurokkei (The Thirty Six Views of Mt. Fuji), signed "Hokusai aratame iitsu hitsu," published by Eijudo (Nishimuraya Yohachi), blue outlines, good impression, faded, foxed, restored, tape on verso, $25,000-35,000.

Oban yoko-e, as above, a Meiji period reproduction, $300-500.

Oban yoko-e, a view of farmers working, field, and thatched roofs of a village, the poem of Dainagon Tsunenobu, from the series Hyakunin Isshu Uba ga Etoki (The One Hundred Poems As Told By The Nurse), signed "Zen Hokusai," published by Nishimura Yohachi, good impression, faded, creased, toned, wormage, backed, $1000-1500.

Oban yoko-e, "Tokaido Okazaki Yahagi no Hashi," (Yahagi Bridge at Okazaki on the Tokaido), from the series Wondrous Views of Famous Bridges In All The Provinces, signed "Zen Hokusai iitsu hitsu," published by Nishimuraya Yohachi (Eijudo), fair impression, toned and faded, rubbed, backed, $1000-1500.

Hokusei (fl. c. 1820s) pupil of Shunkosai.

Hokushu (fl. c. 1920s-1930s) pupil of Hokusai.

Hokusui (fl. c. 1854-57)

Hokuto (fl. c. 1835)

Hokuun (fl. early 19th century) pupil of Hokusai.

Horie Ryoichi (b. 1943) moku-han, geometrics.

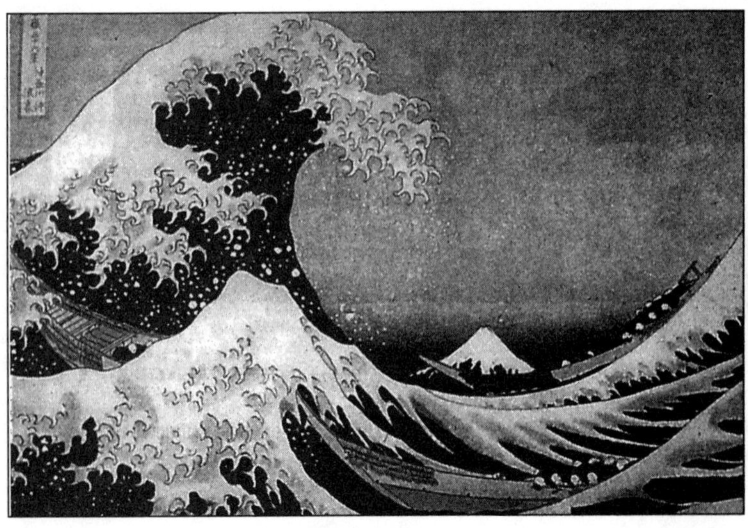

Hokusai, oban yoko-e, 10" x 15", "Kanagawa Oki Nami Ura (In the Well of the Great Wave off Kanagawa) from the series Fugaku Sanjurokkei (The 36 Views of Mt. Fuji), signed "Hokusai aratame Itsu hitsu," publisher Eijudo (Nishimuraya Yohachi), blue outlines, good impression, foxing, faded, tape residue on verso, paper restored, $25,000-35,000.

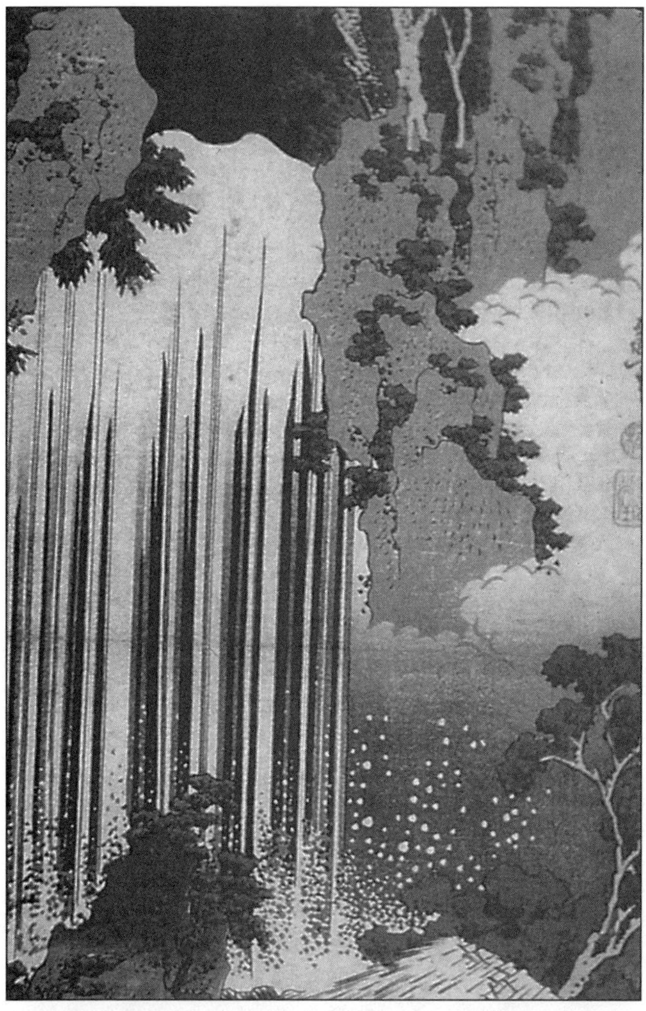

Hokusai, oban tate-e, approx. 14 1/2" x 9 1/8", "Mino no Kuni Yoro no Taki," (Yoro Waterfall in Mino Province) from the series Shokoku Taki Meguri (Journey to the Waterfalls of All the Provinces), signed "Zen Hokusai Itsu hitsu," publisher Mishimuraya Yohachi (Eijudo), very good impression, moderately faded and soiled, centerfold, stains, $3500-6500.

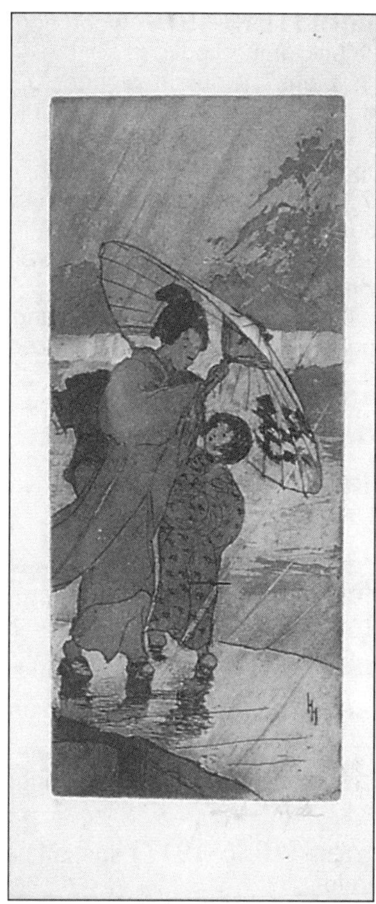

Hyde, Helen, "A Rainy Night," etching and aquatint, 1906, signed and sealed, very fine condition, attached to mat at upper right and left hand corners, $1000-1500.

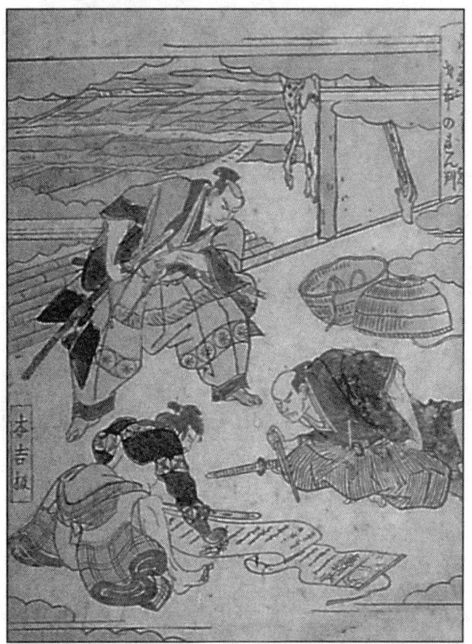

Hokusai, koban from an ehon, early 19th c., mica , very fine impression, color, condition, $500-750.

Hoshi Joichi (1913-1979) wood engraving, stencil, woodblock, limited editions.

"Autumn Light," (Shuko), signed "J. Hoshi" and sealed, dated '78, framed, condition unknown, $700-900.

"Summer Day," signed "Joichi Hoshi" and sealed, dated '77, framed, condition unknown, $700-900.

Dai oban yoko-e, "Yellow Forest," signed and dated "Joichi Hoshi '75," tape on verso, tape on edges, toned, $1000-1800.

"White Tree, Soshun," (Early Spring), signed in pencil and dated '74, framed and glazed, $600-800.

Hosui (fl. c. 1850s) Kyoto School.

Hyakki (d. 1794)

Hyde Helen (1863-1919)

I

Ida Shoichi (b. 1941) serigraphy, lithography, mokuhan.

Ide Gakusui (b. 1899-) moku hanga, kacho-e.

Ido Masao (b. 1945) landscapes and traditional Japanese subjects.

Ikeda Masuo (1934-1997) etching, serigraphy, woodblock.

Ikeda Shoen (1886-1917) she is known for bijinga, illustrator.

Ikeda Terukata (1883-1921) husband of Ikeda Shoen, sometimes signed S. Ikeda.

Ikkei (fl. c. 1870s) pupil of Hiroshige II.

Imao Keinen (1845-1924) specialized in kacho ga.

Inagaki Tomoo (1902-1963) published by Mikumo Mokuhansha in Kyoto during the l950s, woodblock, stencil.

Isai (1821-1880) studied under Hokusai.

Ishii Hakutei (1882-1958) lithography, woodblock prints.

Oban, "Asakusa," from the series Twelve Views of Tokyo (Tokyo junikei), 1910-1916, signed "Hakutei hitsu," soiled, creased, minor wormage, $450-775.

Ishiwata Koitsu (1897-) woodblock prints with Watanabe Shozaburo, later works including combinations of woodblock and stencil, also published by Kato Junji.

Issuisai (fl. c. 1820s-1830s) Kyoto School.

Ito Ben'o (1917-1992) prints with oil pigments, stencil.

Ito Nisaburo published from c. 1910 by Uchida.

Ito Shinsui (1898-1972) prints of beautiful women, landscapes, designated a "Living National Treasure."

Dai oban tate-e, "Kesho Bijin," (A Dressing Beauty), signed and sealed, from a limited edition of 250, published by Katsumura, 1935, good impression, good color, slightly toned, slightly trimmed, $1500-1800.

Dai oban tate-e, "Yoku-go," (After the Bath), from the series The Collection of Modern Beauties, No. 1, signed "Shinsui" and sealed, published by Watanabe, dated Showa 5 (1939), good impression, faded, the verso browned, trimmed, $1000-1500.

Dai oban tate-e "Gifu Chochin," (Gifu Lantern), from the series The Collection of Modern Beauties No. 1, a woman hanging a lantern, signed and sealed "Shinsui ga," published by Watanabe, dated Summer 1930, good impression, good color, slightly trimmed, tape on verso, minor foxing, $2000-3000.

Dai oban tate-e, "Yu no kaori," (Scent of Hot Spring Water), from the series The Collection of Modern Beauties, No. 1, a woman standing on rock drying her feet after a bath, signed and sealed "Shinsui ga," published by Watanabe, dated Showa 5 (1930), good impression, slightly toned and faded, tape stains on verso, $1200-1800.

Dai oban tate-e, "Asa No Yuki," (Snowy Morning), signed and sealed, published by Watanabe, 1939, good impression, good color, good condition, $1200-1800.

See also: Shinsui Ito

Ito Sozan (1884-) kacho prints from 1909.

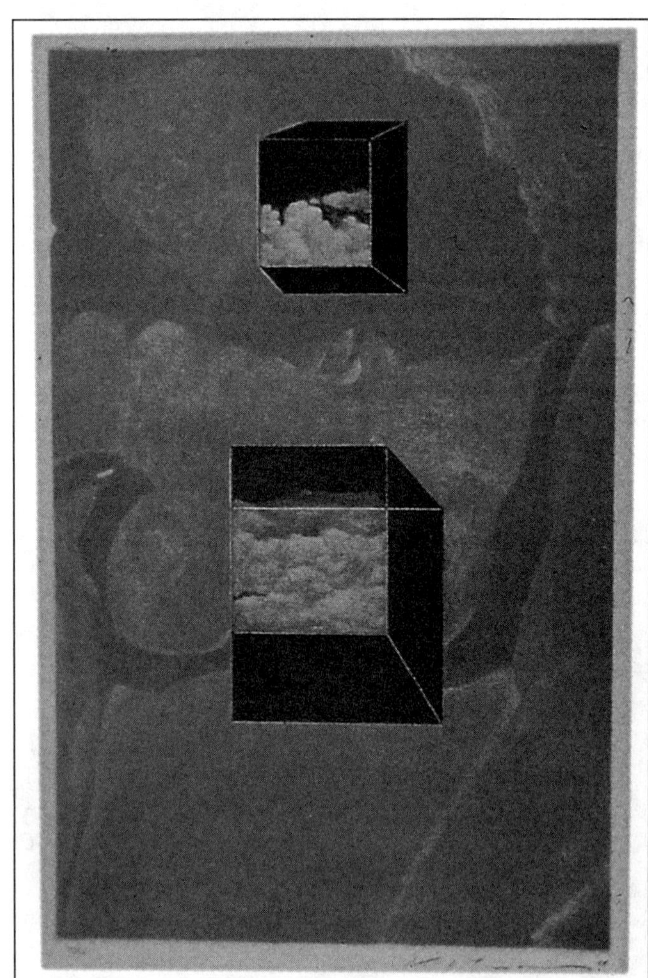

Ikeda Masuo, drypoint roulette and mezzotint, approx. 25" x 18", "Haato no Ichi," (Position of the Heart), dated in pencil in Roman script. "M. Ikeda '69," mat burn, laid down on board, $500-650.

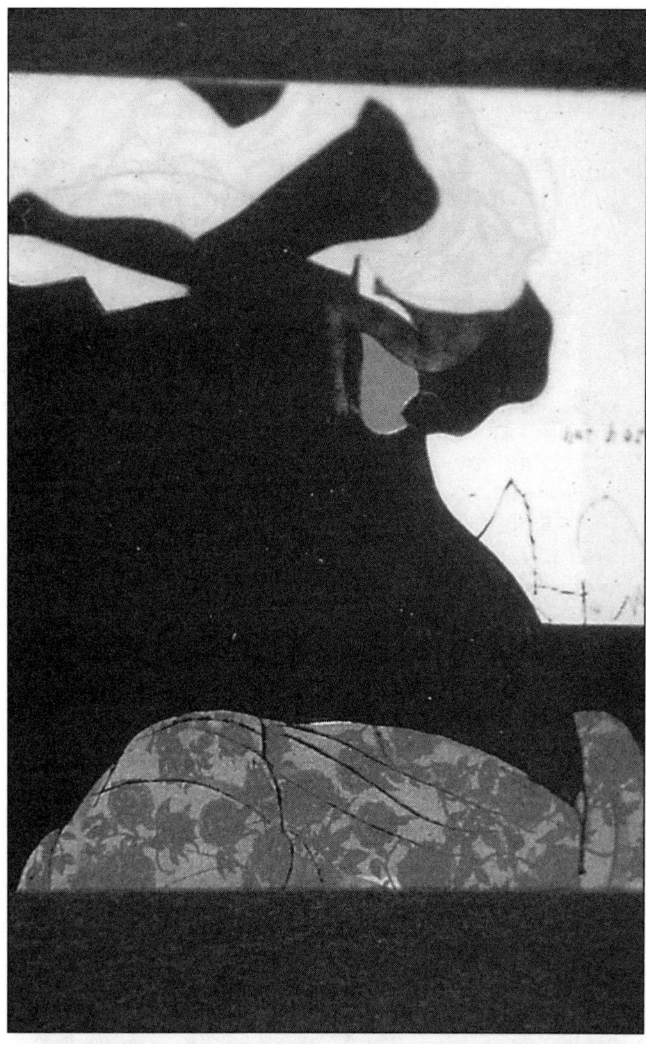

Ikeda Masuo, etching, "Hotto Hatto," (Hot Hat), signed and dated in pencil in Roman script "M. Ikeda '71," from an edition of 50, framed, approx. size 22" x 16 3/4", mat burn, laid down on board, $700-900.

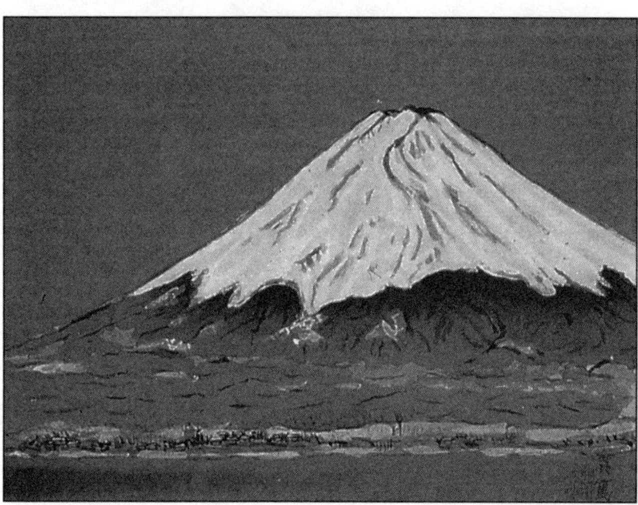

Inagaki Nenjiro, dai oban yoko-e, 20" x 20" (framed size 23" x 23"), Mokumo (publisher), c. 1955, excellent condition, sealed and signed "Mukumo" (the Mikumo Print Shop), $350-475.

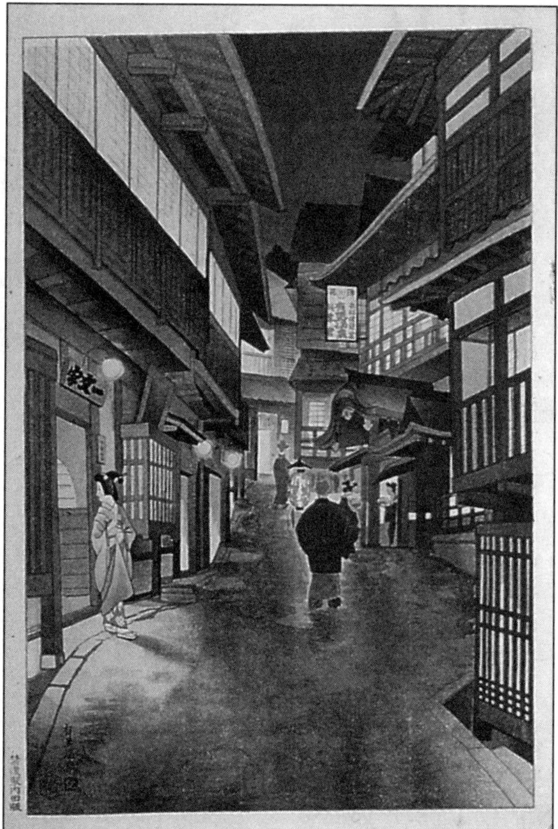

Ito Nisaburo, oban tate-e, "The Inns At Arima Hot Springs," c. 1960, published by Uchida, very good impression, color and condition, $200-375.

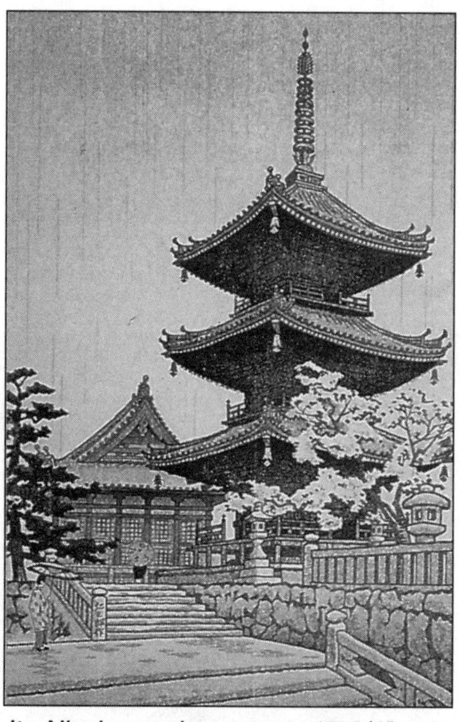

Ito Nisaburo, oban tate-e, 17 3/4" x 11 1/2", "The Pagoda of Kiyomizu Temple, in Kyoto," in original folder, early edition, published by Uchida, c. 1955, fine impression, color and condition, $300-$485.

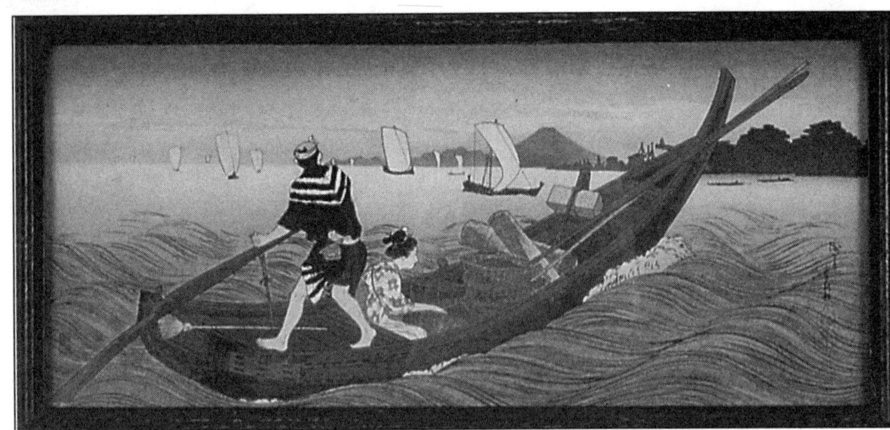

Ishii Hakutei, 5 1/2" x 10", c. 1916, fine color and impression, signed and sealed, $700-950.

Ito Takashi, oban yoko-e, c. 1930s, signed and sealed within image on lower left, right margin trimmed, very good impression and color, $500-750.

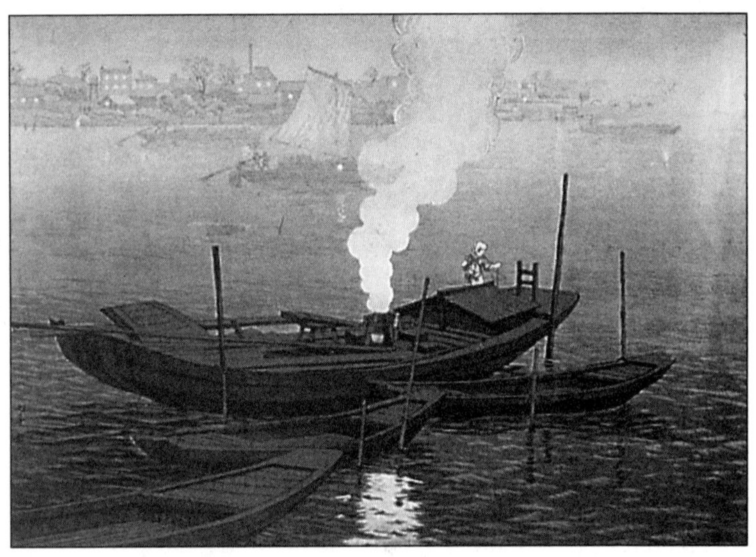

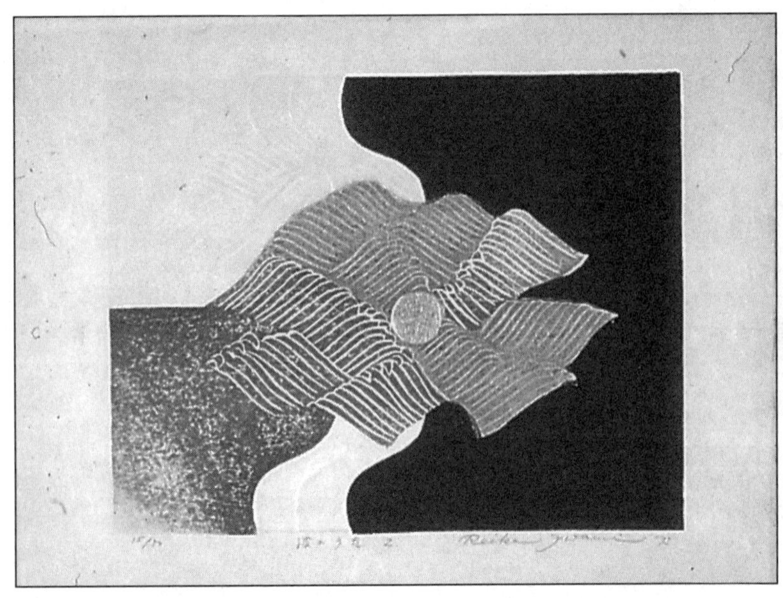

Iwami Reika, oban yoko-e, "Song Of Wave 2," dated 1973 from and edition of 50, mica gauffrage, fine impression, color, and condition, $300-475.

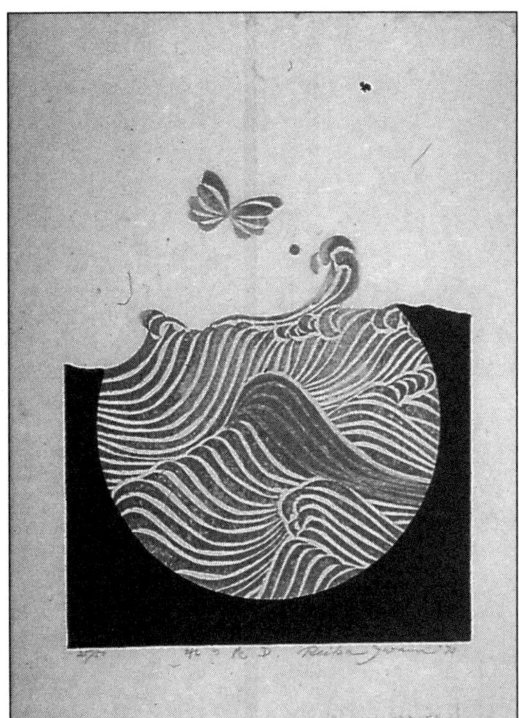

Iwami Reika, oban tate-e, "Water Flower," from and edition of 50, dated 1973, signed on bottom margin in pencil, mica gauffrage, fine impression, color and condition, $300-475.

Ito Takashi (1894-1985) pupil of Kaburagi Kiyokata, landscape prints.

Oban tate-e 15" x 10 1/8", "Dawn At Takegawa," 1932, signed and sealed, fine color and impression, minor tape residue on verso, $900-1200.

Iwami Reika (b. 1927) her prints deal with nature, incorporates use of gold leaf, embossing, and impressions from driftwood, limited editions.

Iwata Sentaro (1901-1974) well known illustrator.

J

Jacoulet Paul (1902-1960)

Paul Jacoulet was born in France on January 23, 1902. That same year his father went to Japan, in response from the Japanese government to the French government for a professor of French to serve as a counselor to the Ministry of Education and teacher at the Imperial University in Tokyo.

The family lived in Tokyo, and Paul was raised in a manner similar to a Japanese boy. He attended Japanese elementary and middle schools. He learned to speak, write and read Japanese. Writing meant mastering the art of calligraphy, which is akin to painting a picture.

Paul Jacoulet loved to draw and preferred to use pen and pencil rather than play with toys. His delicate health kept him from playing boy's games, and he turned his attention toward art. His parents encouraged him and provided him with tutors in Japanese brushwork as well as in Western-style painting, which included pastels and oils.

His tutor for English was the American wife of Yone Noguchi. It was in their home that he became aware of ukiyo-e and Utamaro. It was the human form that always engaged Paul Jacoulet. He returned day after day to copy Utamaro's women and to find the secret of his line. Then he discovered that ukiyo-e could be purchased, and his allowance was spent in this manner. He purchased prints that he studied, compared, and analyzed. Eventually, he accumulated a very fine collection.

As he grew up, he became more intrigued with Japanese culture and kabuki. Many of the kabuki actors became his lifelong friends. The kabuki and the old woodblock prints captured his interest and became part of his world.

In 1920 he took a position as an interpreter with the French Embassy. Although qualified, the work left him little time to pursue painting. The earthquake of 1923 brought him to the conclusion that life had better be lived while it could be, and he left his position. He became a tutor, giving private lessons, which left him time to pursue his love of art.

In 1929 Jacoulet met a boy from Truk, a South Pacific island. The boy's mother was a native of the island and the boy's father was French. The boy was

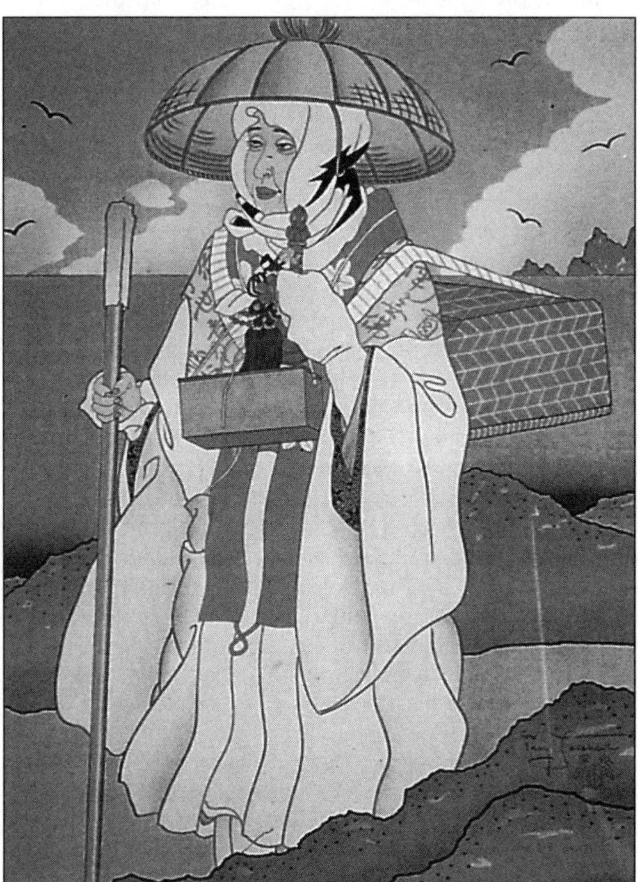

Jacoulet, Paul, dai oban, "Pelerinages D'Automne. Isle De Sado, Japon," (Autumn Pilgrimages. Sado Island, Japan), published July 5, 1952, Ivy seal, carver Maeda, printer Onodera, from and edition of 350, fine color, impression, and condition, $1000-1500.

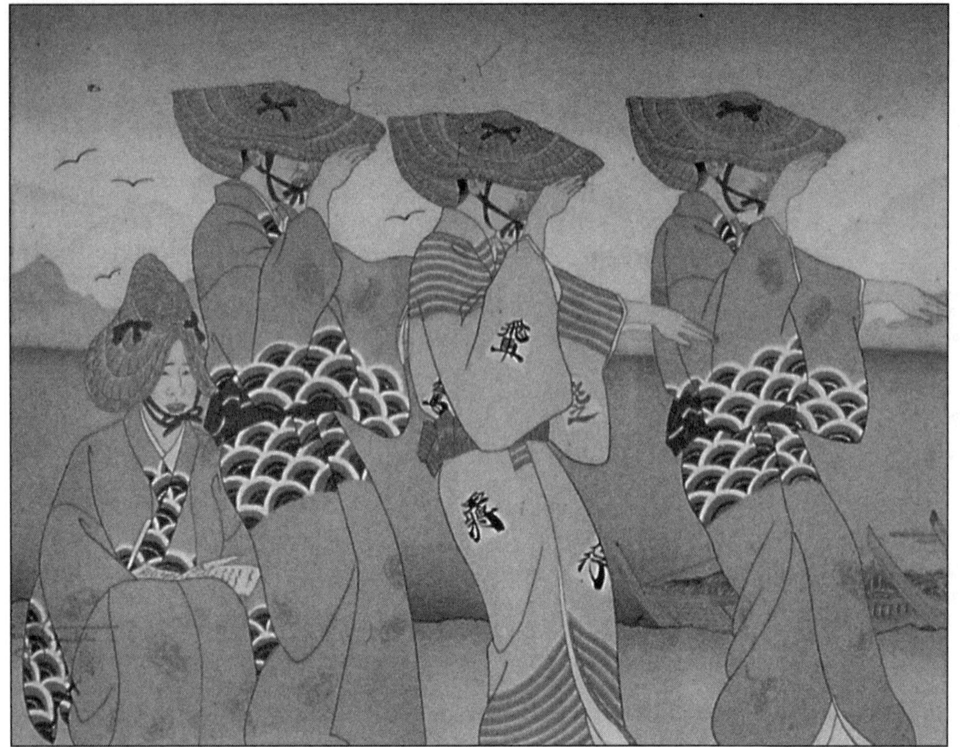

Jacoulet, Paul, dai oban yoko-e, "Danses D'Okesa. Sado, Japon," (Dance Of Okesa. Sado, Japan), published December 4, 1952, Ivy seal, carver Maeda, printer Onodera, the male dancers have pale bluish tinted beards, from an edition of 350 (fewer than 275 impressions), fine impression, color, the margins slightly toned, $1200-1800.

sent to school in Tokyo. Paul befriended him and the result brought an invitation to visit Truk, the first of eight consecutive winters he spent in the South Pacific. Jacoulet was captivated by the islands, and the various cultures amazed him. He picked up the languages easily and was accepted as a friend. He amassed sketches, and this subject matter made him stand out. In 1934, writer Zoe Kincaid persuaded him to show some of his paintings in Tokyo. He had already developed a style of his own, and his friends among print collectors and scholars were quick to recognize that his style was suited to the design of woodblock prints.

In the meantime, his mother remarried and was living in Seoul, Korea. His visits with her resulted not only in his Korean prints, but also in his Manchurian and most of his Chinese designs. In his Manchurian prints, and other even more lavish prints, the technique of woodblock was pushed to the ultimate. In the days of ukiyo-e prints, seven or eight blocks and the keyblock could suffice, however, Jacoulet used as many as 223 blocks. Again and again he challenged his carver and his printer to outdo themselves. He used the finest pigments and the finest paper, which was made to order with a special watermark.

World War II drove him from Tokyo to the mountain resort of Karuizawa. There he lived with his Korean family, two brothers who had been with him since childhood, and the elder's wife and children. In 1949 Jacoulet adopted their three-year-old daughter, Therese. Karuizawa was home for the rest his life. He passed away March 9, 1960 at age 58, due to chronic ill health.

Paul Jacoulet's prints have a richness of texture and color that make them stand apart from other woodblock prints. His works appeal to Orientalists as well as those whose interests are drawn by the Art Modern (Art Deco) movement.

Christmas Cards:

"Decembre, Japon," in original folder with red design on cover, excellent condition, $200-300.

"La Cruche: Mongolie," in original folder with red design on cover, excellent condition, $375-475.

"Le Bonze Errant, Coree," in original folder with yellow design on cover, good condition, $200-300.

"Les Jades: Mandchoukuo," in original folder with red design on carver, excellent condition, $375-500.

As above, toned and faded image, $50-100.

"Longevite," original folder with red design on cover, very good condition, $200-300.

"Pelerinages (Japon)," original folder, toned and browned with mat burn, $45-90.

"Vieil Aino Hokkaido," original folder with green design on cover, very good condition, $300-500.

Dai Oban tate-e

"Fumes De Santal, Mandchuoukuo," (Sandalwood Smoke), signed in pencil, Mitsu-Tomoe seal, carved by Kentaro Maeda and printed by Shunosuke Fujii, published 1948, from an edition of 350, dedicated to King George VI of England, slight toning on reverse, mat adhered to front margins, $2500-3500.

"La Chenille Verte. Coree," (The Green Caterpillar), signed in pencil, Daikoku Mallet seal, carved by Kentaro Maeda, printed by Matashiro Uchikawa, published 1936, edition of 350, good condition, mica rubbed, $800-1200.

"La Geisha Kiyoka, Tokyo," (The Geisha, Kiyoka), signed in pencil lower left, Mandarin Duck seal, carved by Kentaro Maeda, printed by Matashiro Uchikawa, published May 1935, series of 350, fine condition, slight browning on the back, $2000-3500.

"La Peche Miraculeuse. Isu, Japon," (The Miraculous Catch. Izu, Japan), signed in pencil, Boat seal, carved by Maeda, printed by Onodera, published 1939, very good condition, $3500-5500.

"Le Peche Miraculeuse. Isu, Japon," As above but first printing, printer Uchikawa Honda, published 1939, from an edition of 100, very good condition, $4500-6000.

"Le Bonze Errant. Coree," (The Wandering Buddhist Priest. Korea), signed in pencil, Peach seal, carved by Kentaro Maeda and printed by Tetsunosuke Honda, published 1948, from an edition of 250, toned and faded, some foxing, $300-600.

"Le Marie. Seoul, Coree," (The Bridegroom, Seoul, Korea), signed in pencil, Owl seal, carved by Maeda, printed by Uchikawa, from an edition of 100, published 1950, $1800-2500.

"Le Marie. Seoul, Coree," as above, laid down on board and framed, $275-400.

"Le Tabouret De Porcelaine. Mandchuokuo," (The Porcelain Garden Seat), Good Luck Hammer (aka Daikoku's Mallet), carved by Kentaro Maeda, printed by Tetsunosuke Honda, published 1936, toned, faded, slightly trimmed, otherwise good condition, $500-750.

"Les Jades. Chinoise," (Jade Lady), signed in pencil, Boat seal, carved by Kentaro Maeda and printed by Shunosuke Fujii, published 1940, edition of 350, very good condition $2500-3500.

"L'Homme Heureux. Chinois" (The Happy Man), signed in pencil above the Peony seal, carved by Kentaro Maeda and printed by Tetsunosuke Honda, published 1955 from an edition of 350, corners bent, creased , hole restored, lower margin trimmed, good color, $400-600.

"Retour D'Un Banquet. Coree Seoul," (After the Banquet. Seoul, Korea), signed in pencil, Owl seal, carved by Maeda, printed by Onodera Honda, edition of 350, very fine condition, $2500-3500.

"Retour D'Un Banquet. Coree Seoul," As above, laid down on board, trimmed, $500-700.

"Vieillad Au Chapelet Kawadzu," (The Old Man in the Chapel, Mr. Kawada), signed in pencil, Butterfly seal, carved by Kentaro Maeda, printed by Fusakichi Ogawa, published 1940, edition of 300, good color, laid down on board, $300-500.

Jowett Katherine (early 20th century)

K

Kaiseki Jokata produced a set of 12 landscape prints c. 1929.

Kagoshima, Ippei serigraphy, limited editions.

Kagematsu (fl. c. 1830s-1840s) Osaka School.

Kagetoshi (fl. c. 1930s) pupil of Sadakage.

Kaigetsu Doshu (fl. 18th century) Kaigetsudo is a school founded by Ando Kaigetsudo. The following pupils all used the name. Anchi, Doshan, Doshu, Doshin.

Kajita Hanko (1870-1917) illustrator.

Kakihara Toshio (1893-1960) sometimes used KAKI carved in the block, mokuhan.

Kako Watanabe the art name used by the publisher Watanabe Shozaburo.

Kanamori Yoshio (b. 1922) landscapes, limited editions generally 30.

Kanpo Yoshikawa (1894-1979)

Karhu Clifton (b. 1927) woodblock, limited editions.

Kasamatsu Shiro (1898-1992) published by Watanabe Shozaburo, Unsodo, self-published, student of Kaburagi Kiyokata.

Oban tate-e, "Autumn in the Musashi Fields," signed Shiro, dated Showa 32 (1957), very good impression, color, and condition, $1000-1800.

Oban tate-e, "Snow at Red Gate Entrance," signed and sealed, dated 1935, published by Watanabe, very good impression, color, and condition, $1800-2800.

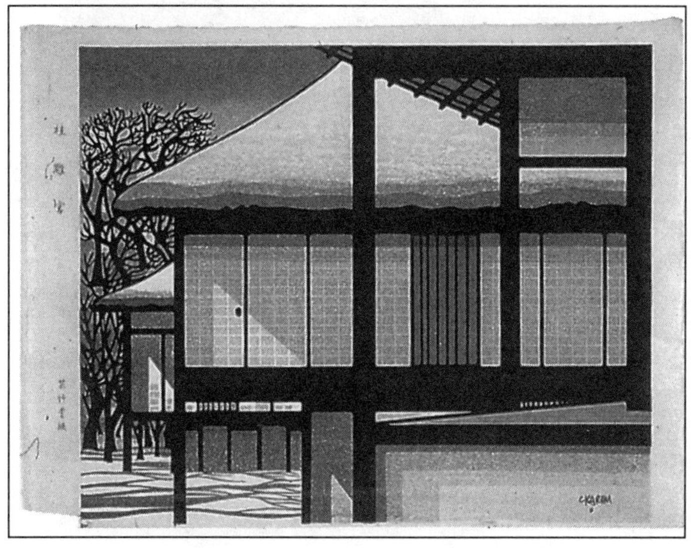

Karhu, Clifton, oban, 12" x 16", "Datsura Rikyu," fine condition, color, and impression, $200-300.

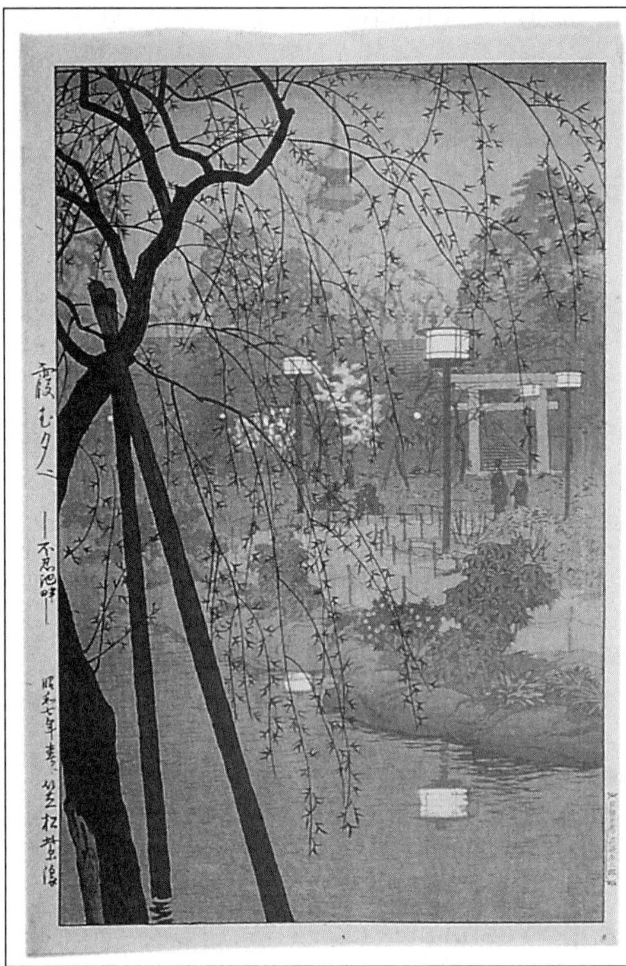

Kasamatsu Shiro, oban tate-e, "Kazumu Yube-Shinobazu Chihan," (Hazy Evening at Edge of Shinobazu Pond), signed and sealed "Shiro," dated Showa 7 (1932), early edition, published by Watanabe, very good impression, color, and condition, $1200-1800.

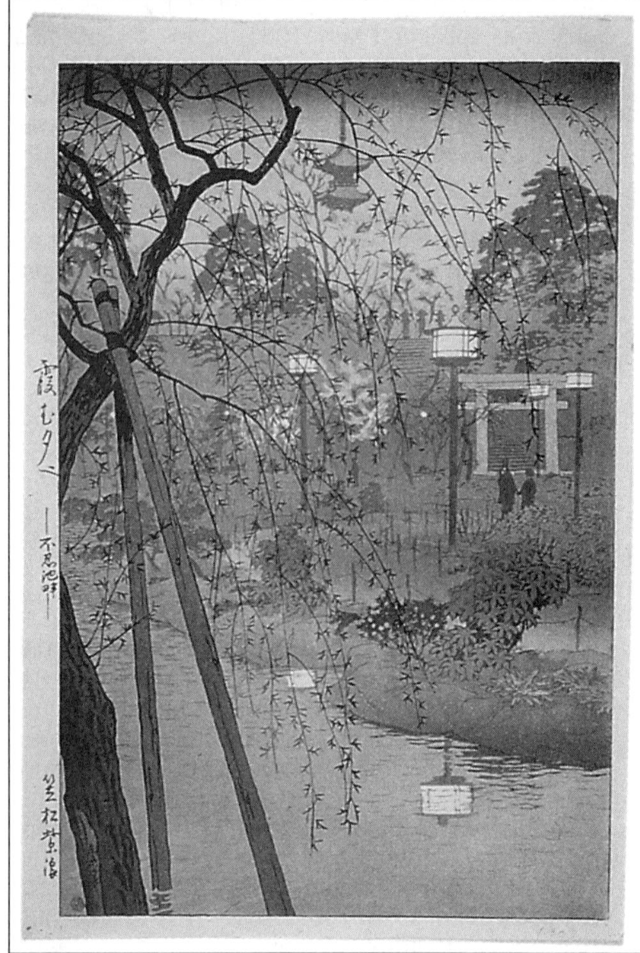

Kasamatsu Shiro, oban tate-e, "Kazumu Yube-Shinobazu Chihan (Hazy Evening at Edge of Shinobazu Pond), signed and sealed "Shiro," dated Showa 7 (1932), later edition with 6mm publisher's seal, published by Watanabe, very good impression, color and condition, $650-850.

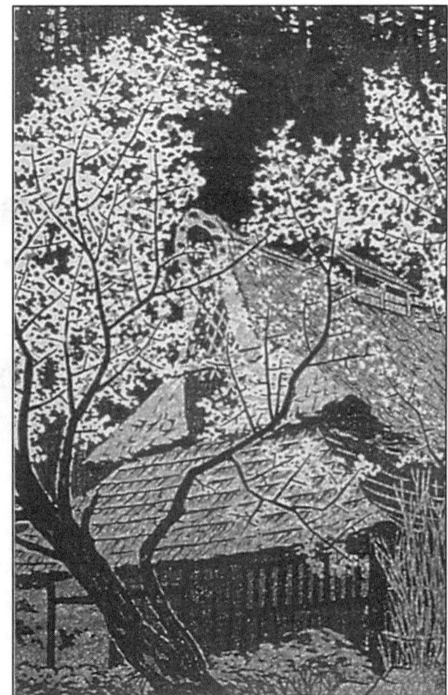

Kasamatsu Shiro, oban tate-e, late edition, published by Unsodo, very good impression, color, and condition, $175-225.

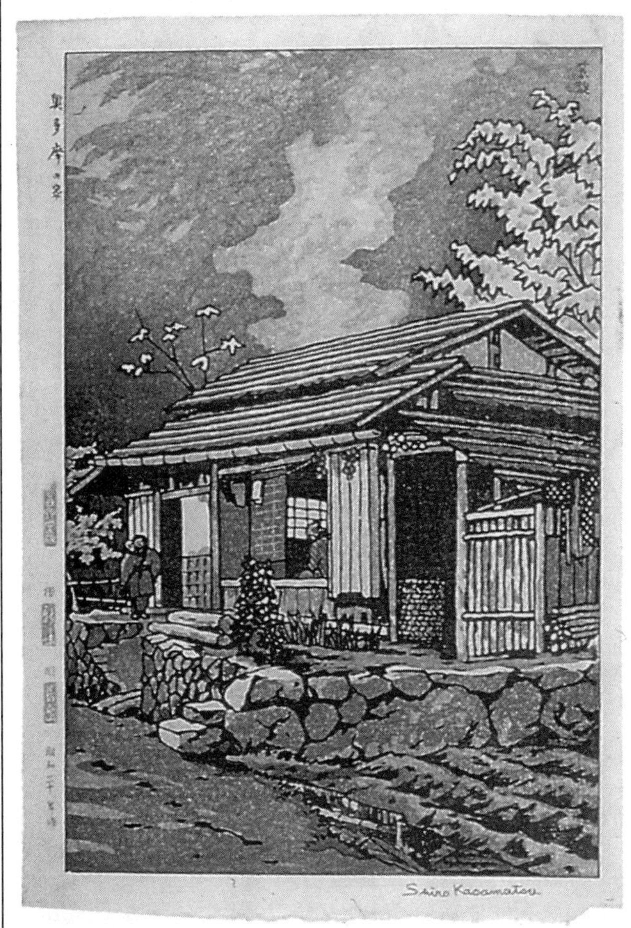

Kasamatsu Shiro, oban tate-e, 10 3/4" x 16", shades of beige , pink and grey, published by Unsodo, dated Showa 30 (1955), signed and sealed in upper right hand corner within image, signed on lower left margin, $900-1200.

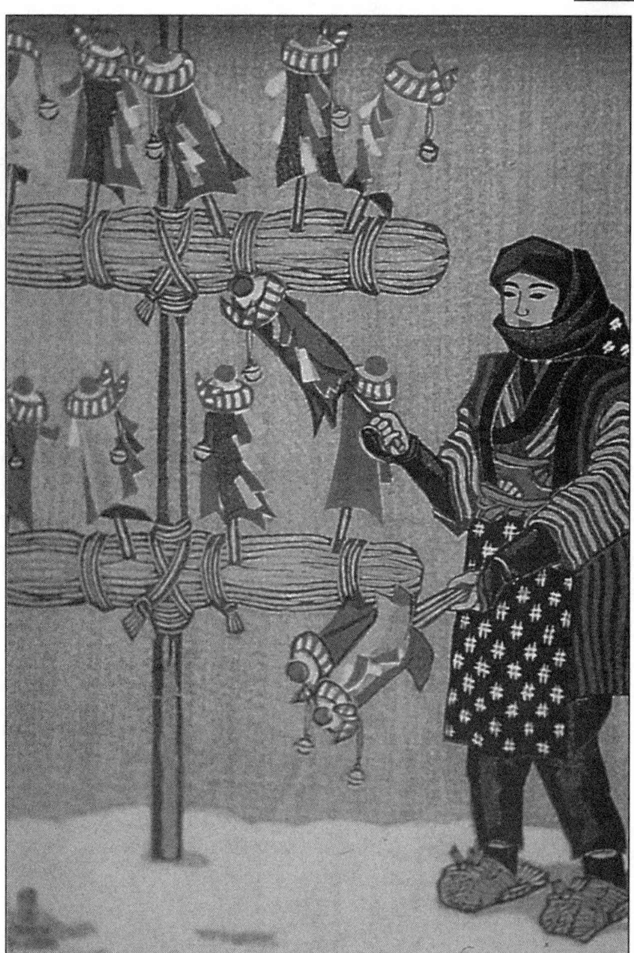

Katsuhira Tokushi oban tate-e, approx. 15 1/2" x 11", "Bonden Uri," (Seller of Bonden), the left margin stamped Suisa Zeneba Guran Bijutsukan shuppin saka 1936 Bonden Uri Showa ju nen (Showa 10 = 1937) with artist's address, and stamped Katsuhira Tokushi Sosaku Hanga, sealed, very good impression and color, stained, tape stains on verso, slightly trimmed, backed, $2500-3500.

Kasamatsu Shiro continued:

Oban tate-e, "Bodhisatva," 1960, from an edition of 100, good impression, color, and condition, margins toned, tape on corners of verso, $400-600.

Oban yoko-e, "Great Lantern at Asakusa Temple," signed and sealed, dated 1934, published by Watanabe, very good impression, color, and condition, $2200-3000.

Oban yoko-e, as above but published posthumously, $350-500.

Oban yoko-e, "Hazy Evening at Shinobazu Pond," signed and sealed, dated 1932, published by Watanabe, framed, faded, mat burn, glue residue on margins, $100-200.

Oban yoko-e, as above, good impression, color, and condition, $800-1200.

Oban yoko-e, approx. 16" x 15 1/4", "Sakura," (Cherry Blossoms), signed and dated 1958, fine condition, color, and impression, $700-900.

Kason Suzuki (1860-1919)

Kato Kiyoharu woodblock, etching.

Kato Kiyomi (b. 1931) lithography, etching.

Katsumoto Fujio (b. 1925) etching, stencil, limited editions.

Katsuhira Tokushi (1904-1971) prints featuring festivals, customs, landscapes, sosaku hanga, sometimes the first character of his given name was carved in the block.

Katsunobu (fl. c. 1716-1735) two artists used this name during the same period of time.

Kawabata Gyokusho (1842-1914) posthumous moku hanga made from his works and published in the early 20th century.

Kawakami Sumio (1895-1972)

Kawanishi Hide (1894-1965) sosaku hanga.

Kawano Kaoru (1916-1965) textured abstracts, limited and unlimited editions.

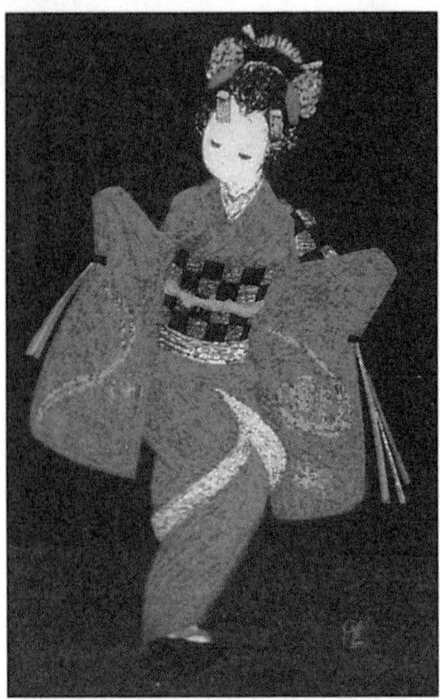

Kawano Kaoru, approx. 11 1/2" x 17", "Dancing Girl," sealed in image, not dated, slightly creased, tape on verso of corners, $350-475.

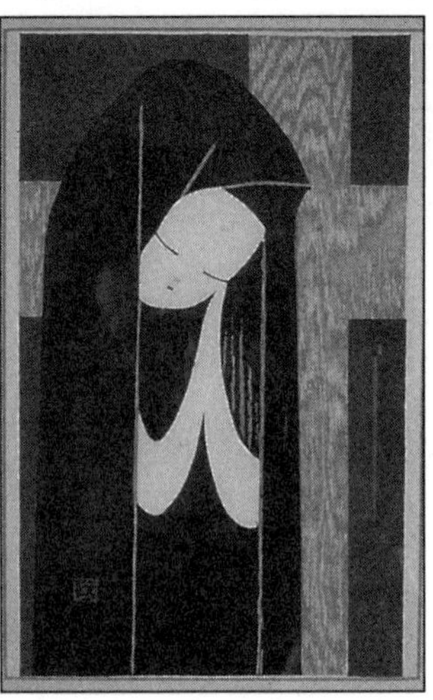

Kawano, oban tate-e, 11 1/2" x 17", "Madonna," fine impression, color and condition, c. 1960, $375-500.

Dai oban, "Dancing Figure," signed in pencil, from an edition of 300, not dated, framed, framed image 20" x 18", not examined out of frame, excellent color, the figure attired in a red kimono, $200-300.

Oban, approx. 11" x 17", "Girl with Yellow Bird," signed, not dated, not numbered, fine condition, $300-400.

Kawazaki Shodo (1889-1973) specialized flower prints, published by Unsodo.

Keishu Takeuchi (1860-1949)

Keith Elizabeth (1887-1956)

Keisai (fl. c.1744-1824)

Kikei (fl. c. 1770s) designed theater programs.

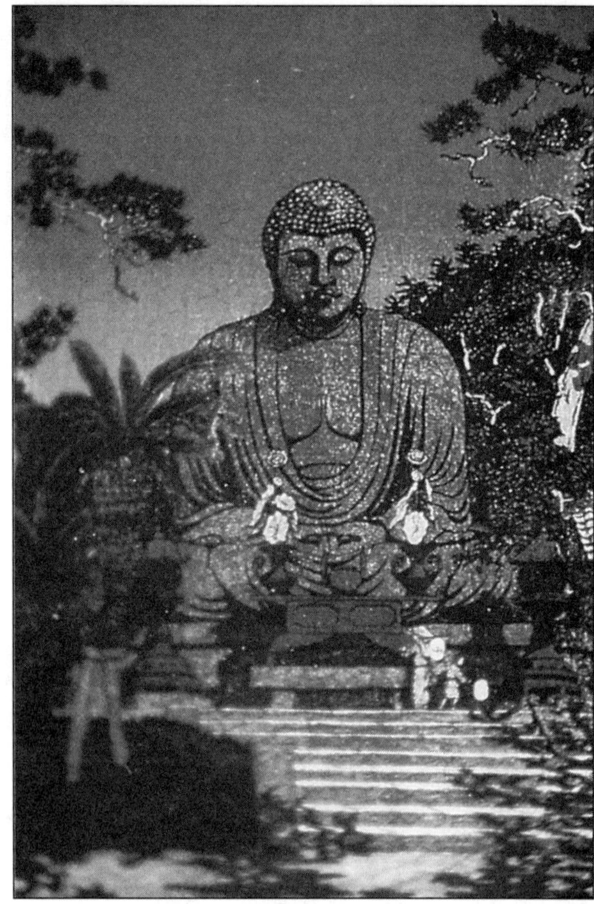

Keith, Elizabeth, oban tate-e, "Kamakura Daibutsu," Taisho 11 (1922), good impression and color, toned, browned on verso, corners attached with tape, $500-600.

Kikuchi Keigetsu (1879-1955) bijin ga.

Kimura Risaburo (b. 1924) lithography, serigraphy, intaglio, limited editions.

Keishu Takeuchi, oban yoko-e, 11 1/2" x 8 1/2", (Kiyokata Kaburagi, Eisen Tomioka, Kiyochika Kobayashi, Hanko Kajita, Kason Suzuki, Keishu Takeuchi, Chikanobu Yoshu, Toshimine Tsutsui, Toshikata Mizuno), 24 woodblock illustrations for Romantic Novels, fine impressions, very good color and condition, mica, gauffrage, late Meiji period c. 1900, $2500-4500.

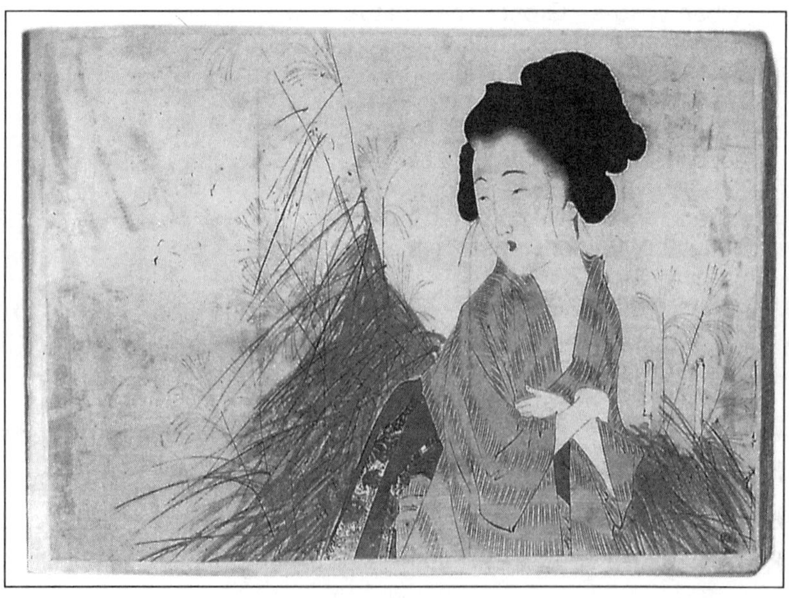

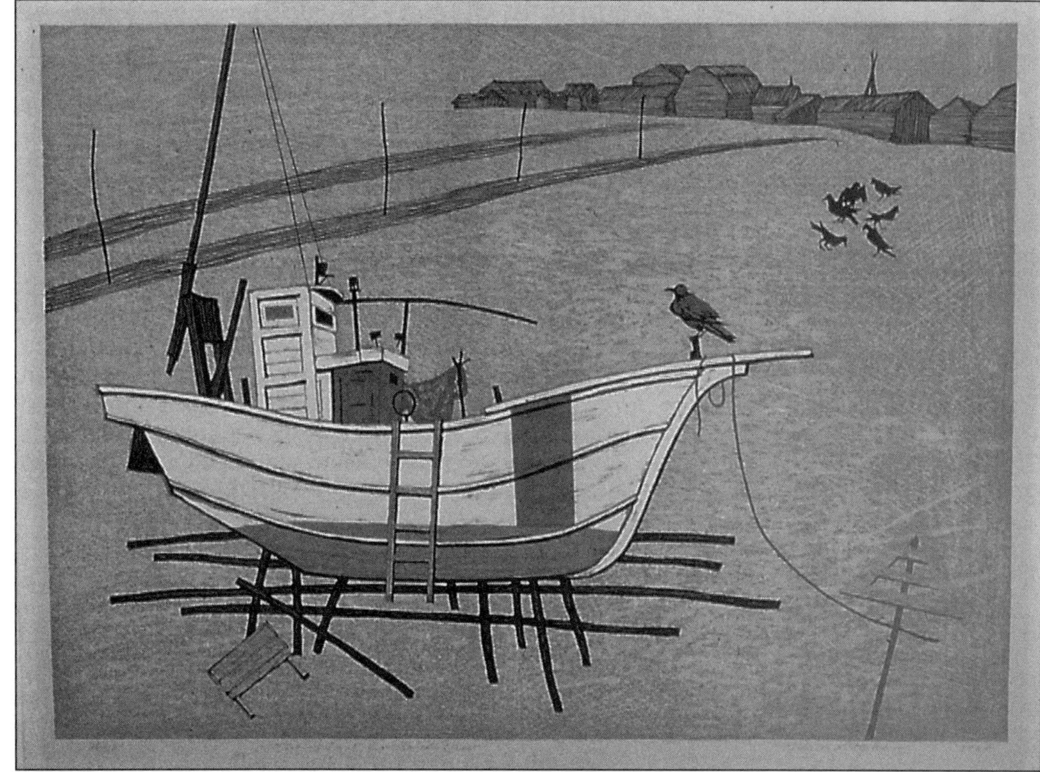

Kitaoka Fumio, dai oban, 23" x 18", "Fishing Boat and Green Crow," from an edition of 120, signed and dated 1969, excellent condition, $800-1200.

Kimura Shigeo (b. 1929) serigraphy, etching.

Kimura Mitsuo (b. 1916)

Kinoshita Tomio (b. 1923) abstracts.

Kitano Tsunetomei (1880-1947) illustrator, bijin ga.

Kitaoka Fumio (b. 1918) moku hanga realism and abstracts, limited editions.

Dai oban, 19" x 24", "Mashuko," (Lake Mashu), signed and dated 1961, from a limited series of 30, slightly trimmed, good impression, and color, $1200-1800.

Dai oban, 14 1/2" x 24", "Maigoya no Rojin," (Old Fisherman in a Net House), signed and dated 1966, from an edition of 50, slightly trimmed, slightly toned in margins, tape on verso, good impression and color, $700-900.

Kitaro (fl. c. 1810s) Kyoto School.

Kiyochika Kobayashi (1847-1915) used Western technique, famous for illuminated prints.

Oban yoko-e; 8" x 10 1/4", "Honcho Dori Yoru (no) Yuki," (Night Snow on Honcho Street), signed "Kobayashi Kiyochika hitsu," published by Fukuda Kumanjiro, dated Meiji 15 (1882), good impression and color, soiling, creased, minor stains, tape on verso along side margins, $1600-2100.

See also: Kobayashi Kiyochika

Kiyohara Hitoshi (1896-1956)

Kiyoharu (fl. c. 1700-1730) pupil of Kiyonobu.

Kiyoharu (fl. c. 1704-1720) follower of Kiyonobu.

Kiyoharu (fl. c. 1820s-1830s) Osaka School.

Kiyohiro(fl. c. 1737-1776) Torii School.

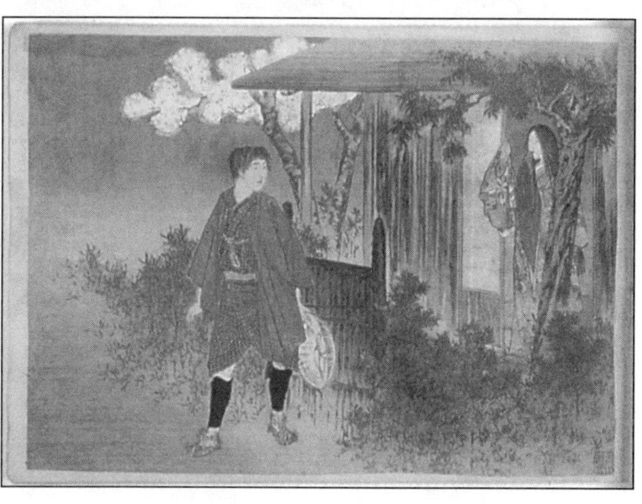

Kiyokata Kaburagi, Eisen Tomioka, Kiyochika Kobayashi, Hanko Kajita, Kason Suzuki, Keishu Takeuchi, Chikanobu Yoshu, Toshimine Tsutsui, Toshikata Mizuno, oban yoko-e, 11 1/2" x 8 1/2", 24 woodblock illustrations for Romantic Novels, fine impressions, very good color and condition, mica, gauffrage, late Meiji period c. 1900 $2500-4500.

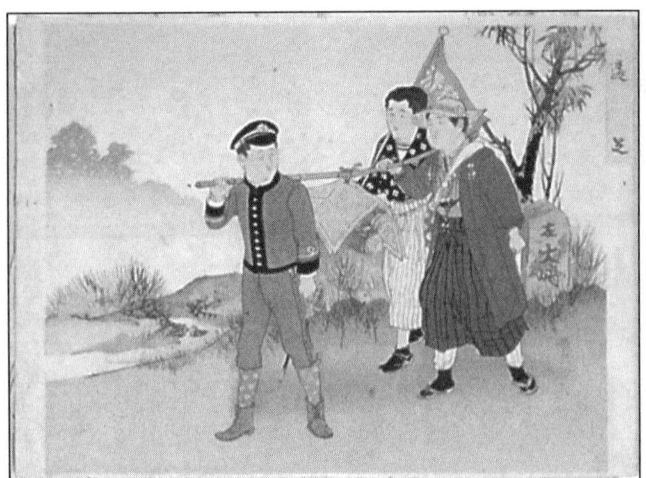

Kiyokata Kaburagi, 10 1/2" x 7", an album of 12 prints, dated 1901, fine impressions, color, and condition, $4000-6500.

Kiyokata Kaburagi (1868-1973) An important 20th century illustrator, moku hanga.

Oban yoko-e, approx. 15 1/2" x 13", "Woman Under a Starry Sky," late Meiji period, sealed Kiyokata, slight toning, good color, and impression, framed, $3000-4000.

Oban tate-e, "A Beauty Kneeling and Holding Blue Cloth," signed "Kiyokata," dated Taisho 12 (1923), good impression and color, laid down on board, slightly foxed, $1500-1800.

Dai oban tate-e, a portrait of a woman standing before a fence and morning-glories, a view of two ships at anchor in the background, signed and sealed, good impression and color, foxing, creased, $1000-1800.

Kiyokuni (fl. c. 1830s-1840s) Torii School.

Kiyomine (1787-1868) Torii School, pupil of Kiyonaga.

Kiyomitsu (fl. c. 1735-1885)

Hosoban, late 18th century, two cranes beneath tree with foliage, good impression, backed (due to thinness of paper), good condition, published by Nishimuraya Yohachi, $350-500.

Kiyomitsu II (1706-1868)

Kiyonaga (1752-1815) pupil of Kiyomitsu I.

Oban tate-e, (this is the left sheet of a diptych) from the diptych "Summer Twilight on the Banks of the Sumida," beauties cooling off on the bank of the river, a woman in a black kimono is seated on a bench, a teahouse waitress and another woman holding an uchiwa are standing beside the seated bijin, ferry boats are off in the distance, very fine impression and color, water stains, center fold, small holes, foxing, and creased, $4500-6500.

Kiyonobu (1664-1729) founder of the Torii School.

Kiyonobu II (1706-1763)

Kiyosada (1844-1901) Torii School.

Kiyoshi Kobayakawa (1896-1948) moku hanga artist, studied with Kaburagi Kiyokata, bijin ga published by Watanabe, Hasegawa, Ensendo; reproductions of his prints published by Takamizawa during the 1950s.

Kiyoshige (fl. c. 1720s-1760s) Torii School, pupil of Kiyonobu I.

Kiyotada (fl. c. 1720-1750) Torii School.

Kiyotada II (fl. c. early 19th century) Torii School.

Kiyotada III (1817-1825) Torii School.

Kiyotomo (fl. c. 1720s-1740s) Torii School, pupil of Kiyonobu I.

Kiyotsune (fl. c. 1757-1779) Torii School.

Kobayashi Asaji (1898-1939)

Kiyokata,Kaburagi Eisen Tomioka, Kiyochika Kobayashi, Hanko Kajita, Kason Suzuki, Keishu Takeuchi, Chikanobu Yoshu, Toshimine Tsutsui, Toshikata Mizuno , oban yoko-e, 11 1/2" x 8 1/2", 24 woodblock illustrations for Romantic Novels, fine impressions, very good color, and condition, mica, gauffrage, late Meiji period c. 1900 $2500-4500.

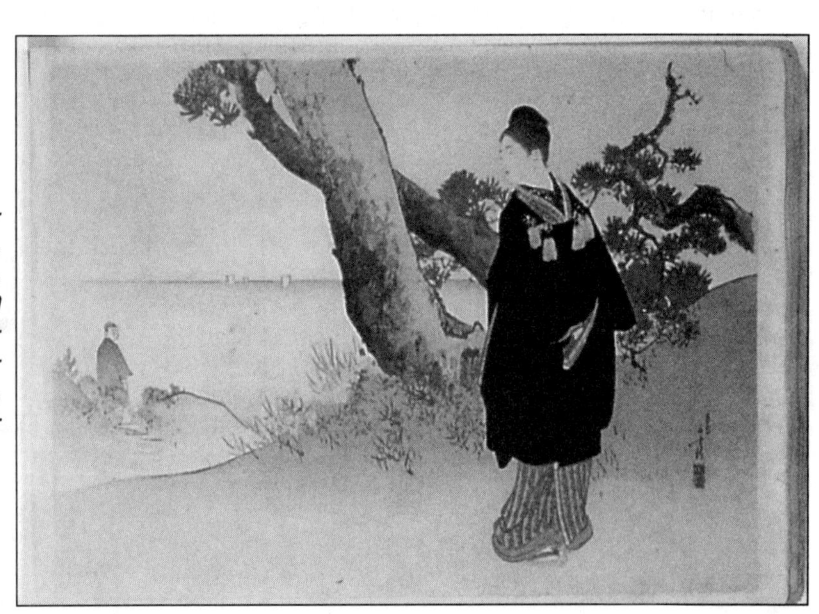

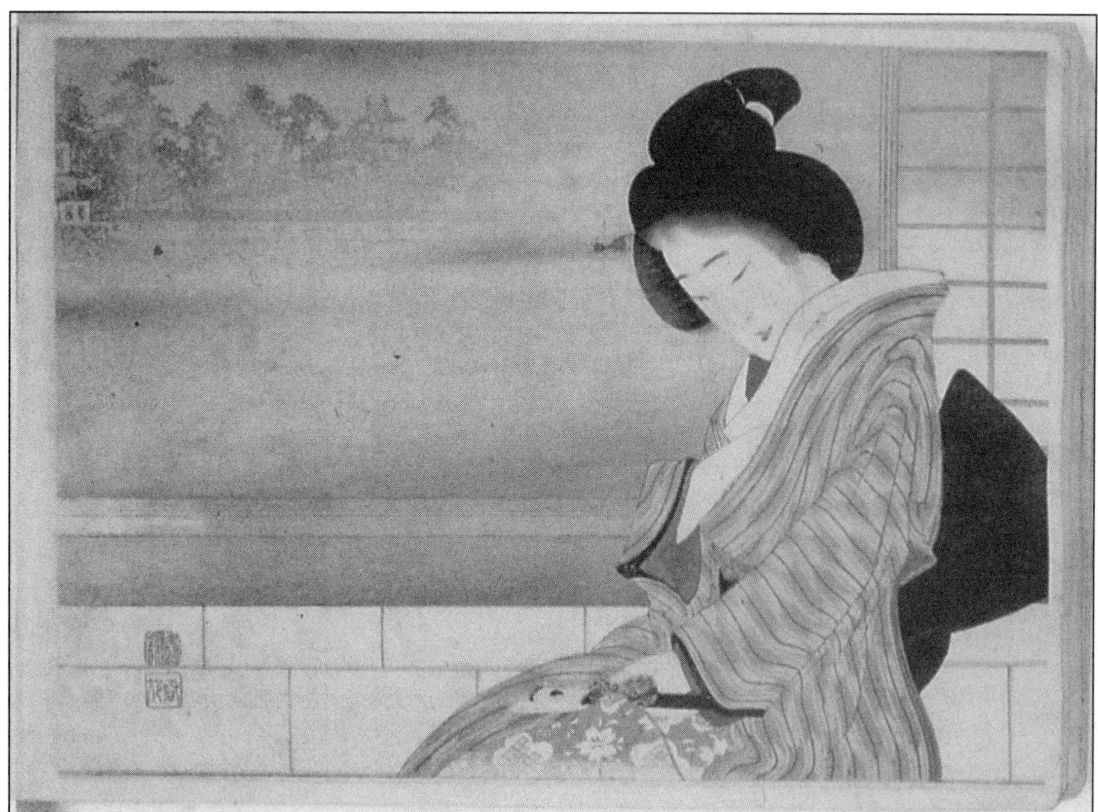

Kiyokata Kaburagi, Eisen Tomioka, Kiyochika Kobayashi, Hanko Kajita, Kason Suzuki, Keishu Takeuchi, Chikanobu Yoshu, Toshimine Tsutsui, Toshikata Mizuno, oban yoko-e, 11 1/2" x 8 1/2", 24 woodblock illustrations for Romantic Novels, fine impressions, very good color, and condition, mica, gauffrage, late Meiji period c. 1900 , $2500-4500.

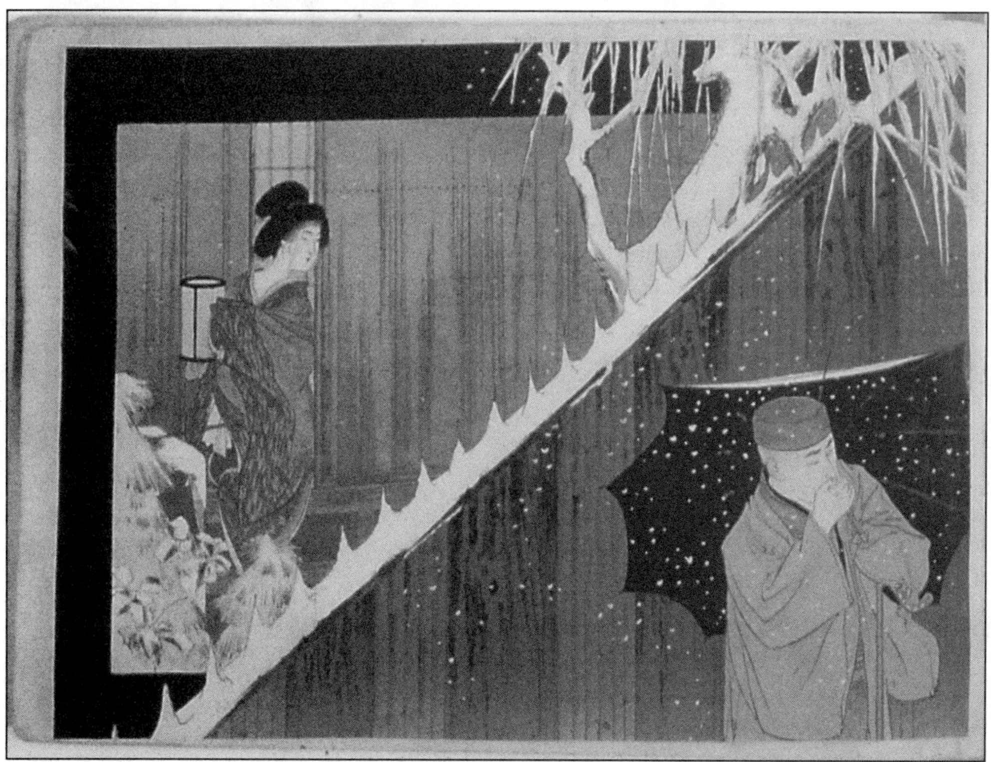

Kiyokata, Kaburagi Eisen Tomioka, Kiyochika Toshimine Kobayashi, Hanko Kajita, Kason Suzuki, Keishu Takeuchi, Chikanobu Yoshu, Tsutsui, Toshikata Mizuno, oban yoko-e, 11 1/2" x 8 1/2", 24 woodblock illustrations for Romantic Novels, fine impressions, very good color and condition, mica, gauffrage, late Meiji period c. 1900 , $2500-4500.

Kiyokata Kaburagi, Eisen Tomioka, Kiyochika Kobayashi, Hanko Kajita, Kason Suzuki, Keishu Takeuchi, Chikanobu Yoshu, Toshimine Tsutsui, Toshikata Mizuno, oban yoko-e 11 1/2" x 8 1/2", 24 woodblock illustrations for Romantic Novels, fine impressions, very good color and condition, mica, gauffrage, late Meiji period c. 1900, $2500-4500.

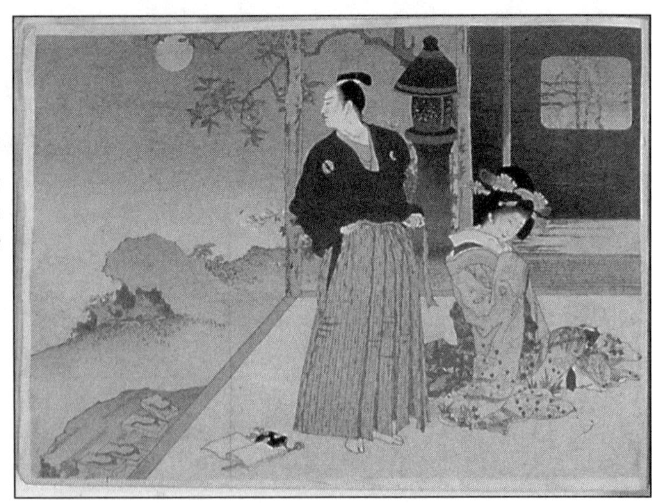

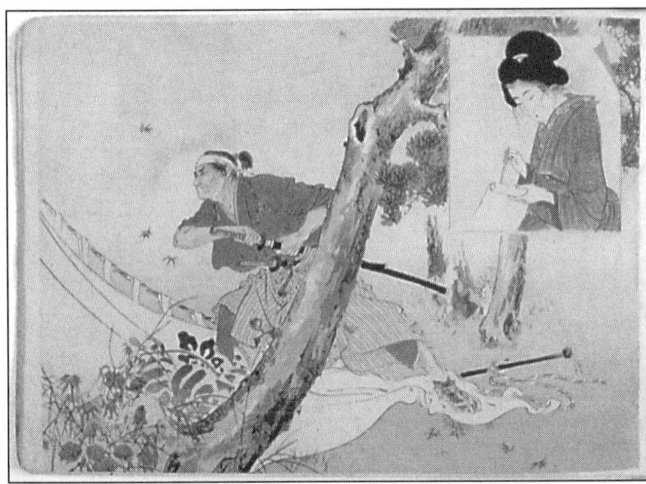

Kiyokata Kaburagi, Eisen Tomioka, Kiyochika Kobayashi, Hanko Kajita, Kason Suzuki, Keishu Takeuchi, Chikanobu Yoshu, Toshimine Tsutsui, Toshikata Mizuno, oban yoko-e, 11 1/2" x 8 1/2", 24 woodblock illustrations for Romantic Novels, fine impressions, very good color and condition, mica, gauffrage, late Meiji period c. 1900, $2500-4500.

Kiyokata Kaburagi, Eisen Tomioka, Kiyochika Kobayashi, Hanko Kajita, Kason Suzuki, Keishu Takeuchi, Chikanobu Yoshu, Toshimine Tsutsui, Toshikata Mizuno, oban yoko-e, 11 1/2" x 8 1/2", 24 woodblock illustrations for Romantic Novels, fine impressions, very good color, and condition, mica, gauffrage, late Meiji period c. 1900, $2500-4500.

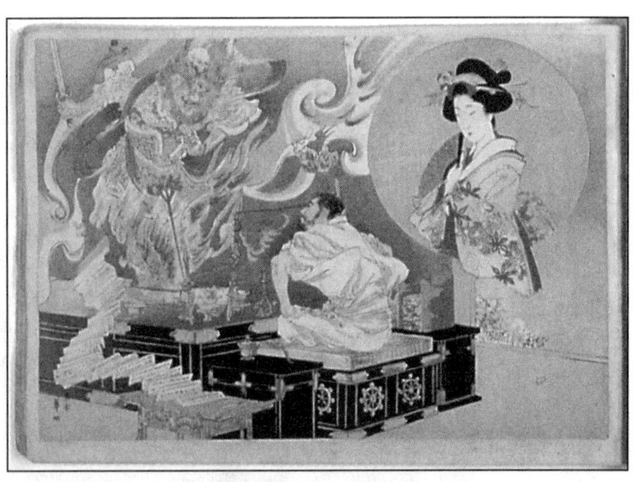

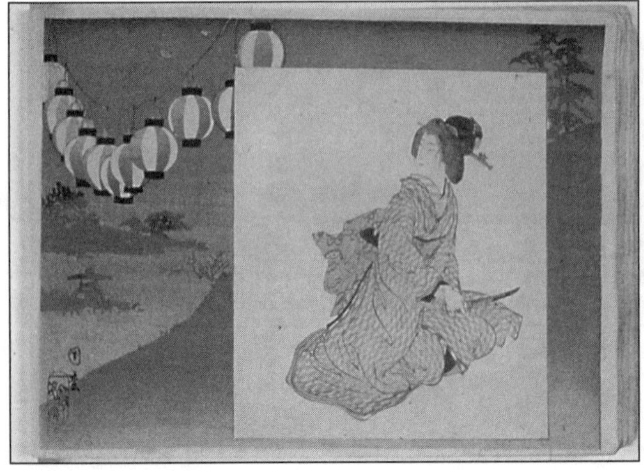

Kiyokata Kaburagi, Eisen Tomioka, Kiyochika Kobayashi, Hanko Kajita, Kason Suzuki, Keishu Takeuchi, Chikanobu Yoshu, Toshimine Tsutsui, Toshikata Mizuno, oban yoko-e, 11 1/2" x 8 1/2", 24 woodblock illustrations for Romantic Novels, fine impressions, very good color and condition, mica, gauffrage, late Meiji period c. 1900, $2500-4500.

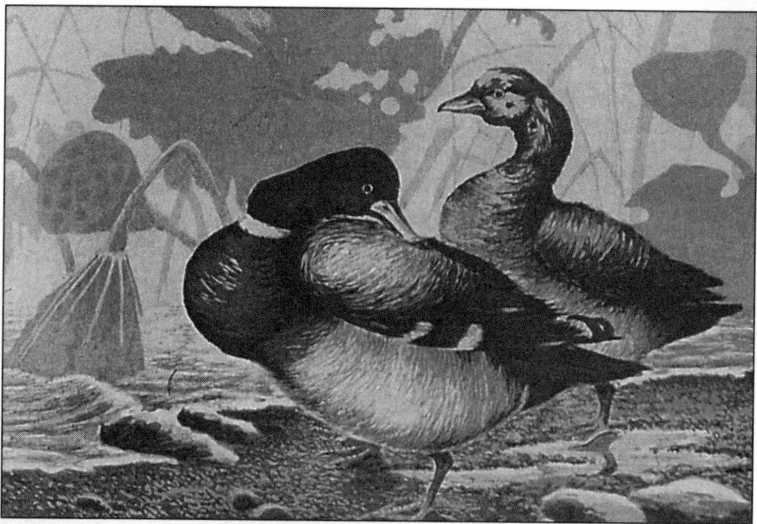

Kiyochika oban yoko-e, 10 1/4" x 15", "Ducks and Withered Lotus," signed Kobayashi Kiyochika ga, dated Meiji 11 (1878), publisher Matsuki Heikichi, very good impression and color, moderately toned, corners restored, $7000-9000.

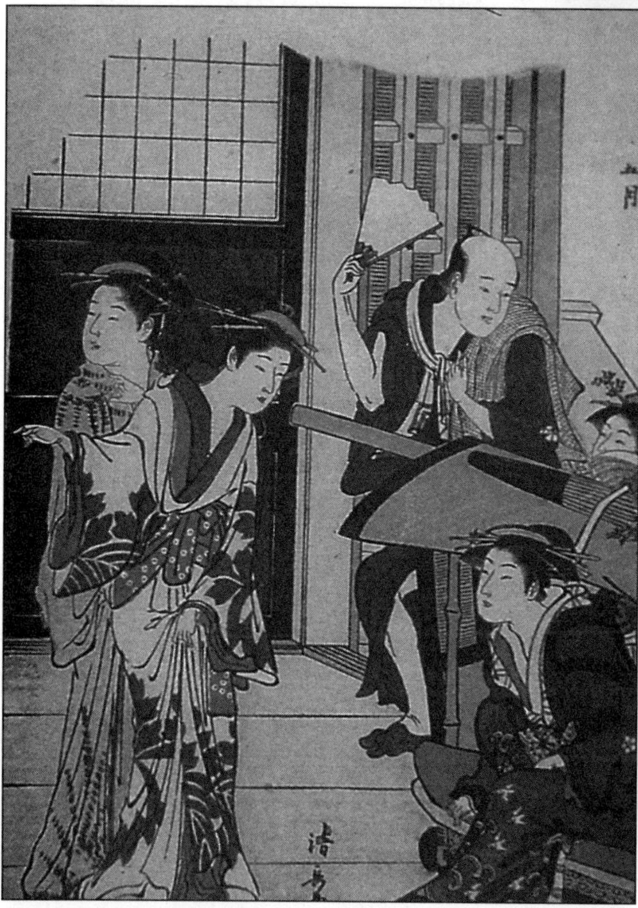

Kiyonaga, chuban, approx. 10" x 7", "Gogatsu," (Fifth Month), from the series Minami Juniko (Twelve Months in the South), signed "Kiyonaga ga," good impression and color, worm holes restored, slightly rubbed, $3500-5500.

Kobayashi Kiyochika (1847-1915) Russo-Japanese war prints, Sino-Japanese war prints, illuminated prints, landscapes.

Oban yoko-e, "Toranomon Yukei," (Evening View of Toranomono), signed "Kobayashi Kiyochika," published by Fukuda Kumanjiro, dated Meiji 13 (1880), very good impression, color, right margin trimmed, dirt spots, $2000-3000.

"Ochanomizu Hotaru," (Fireflies At Ochanomizu), signed and published by Matsuki Heikichi, very good impression and color, slightly trimmed, $1800-2500.

Oban yoko-e, "Kawasaki Gekkai," (Moon and Sea at Kawasaki), signed "Kobayashi Kiyochika hitsu" and published by Fukuda Kumanjiro, dated Meiji 10 (1877), good impression, color, and condition, $1500-2500.

Oban yoko-e, "Sumida Gawa Yoru," (Night at the Sumida River), two figures in silhouette on the riverbank, signed "Kobayashi Kiyochika" and published by Fukuda Kumanjiro, dated Meiji 10 (1877), very good impression and color, margins trimmed, dirt spots, $1500-2500.

Oban yoko-e, "Horidome hanka no Zu," (View of Flourishing Horidome), signed "Kobayashi Kiyochika hitsu," published by Fukuda Kumajiro, dated Meiji 10 (1877), very good impression, color, and condition, $4000-7000.

Kobayashi Kiyomitsu (active late 1920s-1930s)

Kobayashi Tokusaburo (1884-1949) moku hanga, still life, figures, fish, landscapes.

Kochoro (1848-1920) Utagawa School (became Kunisada III in 1889).

Kogan Tobari (1882-1927)

Kogyo Terazaki (1866-1919) Russo-Japanese war, mokuhan, bijin ga, kacho.

Kogyo Tsukioka (1869-1927) specialized in prints of Noh Drama.

Oban tate-e, "Kami," (Spirit), from the series Nogaku Hyakuban (One Hundred No-plays), an actor in the role of the spirit of a deceased person, fine impression, color, and condition, $300-500.

Oban tate-e, two actors from the series Nogaku Hyakuan (One Hundred No-plays), set on a yellow background, signed and sealed "Kogyo," dated 1900, fine impression, color, and condition $300-500.

Oban tate-e, "The Spider Monster," (No-play Tsuchigumo), from the series Nogaku Hyakuban

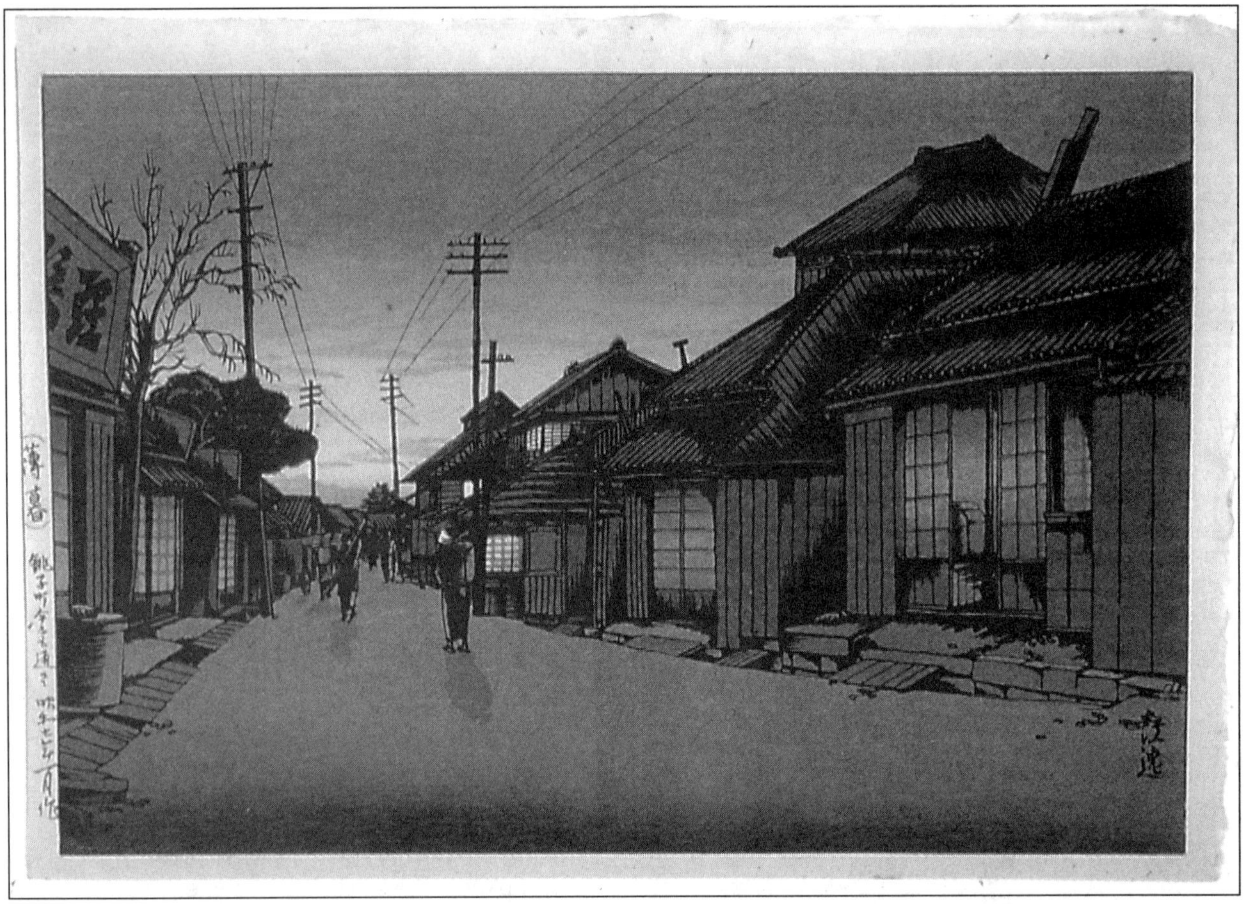

Koitsu Ishiwata, oban yoko-e, "Hakubo, Twilight," (A Street in Choshu), signed and sealed "Koitsu," dated Showa 7, later edition, published by Watanabe, fine condition, impression, and color, $775-900.

"One Hundred No-plays", signed and sealed "Kogyo," published by Matsuki Keikichi, dated 1899, fine impression, color, condition, $300-450.

Koho Shoda (1871-1946)

Koito Gentaro (1887-1978) moku hanga.

Koitsu Ishiwata (b. 1897- ?)

Koitsu Tsuchiya (1870-1949)

Oban tate-e, 15 1/2" x 10", "Rain at Kofukuji Temple, Nara," published posthumously, dated Showa 12 (1937), fine impression, color, and condition, $400-500.

Koizumi Kishio (1893-1945) moku hanga.

Kokan (1747-1818) first to produce copperplate engravings.

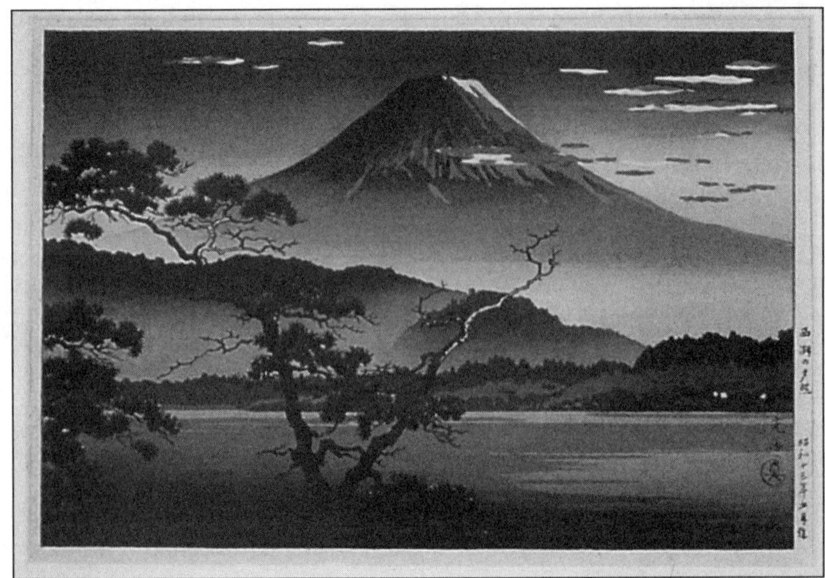

Koitsu Tsuchiya, oban yoko-e, 10 1/2" x 15 1/2", "Mt. Fuji at Sunset," dated Showa 13 (1938), posthumous print, $300-425 .

Koka Yamamura (1885-1942)
Oban tate-e, okubi-e (bust portrait) of the actor Oneoe Matsusuke, signed "Koka ga," sealed Hana, published by Watanabe Shozaburo, very good impression, good color, slightly faded, minor holes restored, $3500-5000.

Kokyo Russo-Japanese war prints published by Matsuki Heikichi (1904).

Konen Uehara (1887-1940)

Konobu (fl. c. 1867-1880s) son of, and pupil of, Sadanobu I, became Sadanobu II.

Komura Settai (1887-1904) illustrator, published posthumously by Adachi Toyohisa.

Kon Junzo (1893-1944) moku hanga, lithography, etchings.

Koryusai (fl. c. 1764-1788)

Kosei (fl. c. 1860)

Koson Ohara (Shoson Ohara) (1877-1945) under the name Koson produced Russo-Japanese war prints, and kacho-e, changed name to Shoson in 1912 when he painted, also used the name Hoson on prints published by Sakai Kawaguchi, published by Watanabe, Nishinomiya, Daikikuya et al., known for kacho hanga.

Oban tate-e, "Geese Amongst Water Reeds on a Black Ground," signed "Koson," published by Watanabe, dated 1928, from an edition of 300, good impression, color, and condition, $800-1200.

Hosoban, "Goose Landing in the Water," signed "Koson," and sealed, fine impression, color, and condition, $700-900.

Oban tate-e, "Two White Herons Flying Past Bamboo," signed and sealed "Shoson," published by Watanabe, good impression, color, and condition, $800-1200.

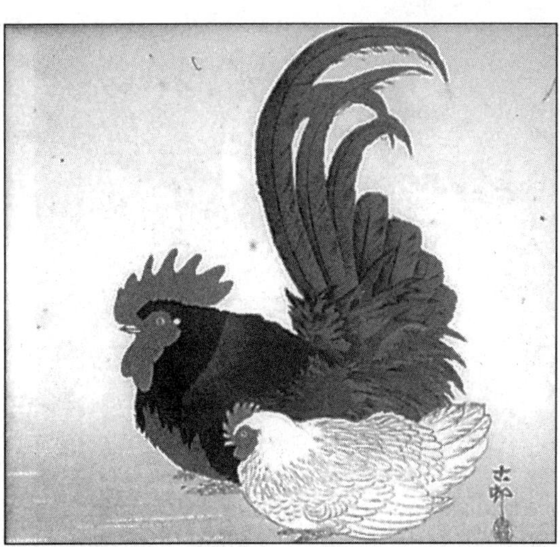

Koson Ohara, shishiban, 9 1/2" x 9" (framed size 12" x 12"), "Cockerel and Hen," c. 1920s, fine impression, slightly toned, $300-500.

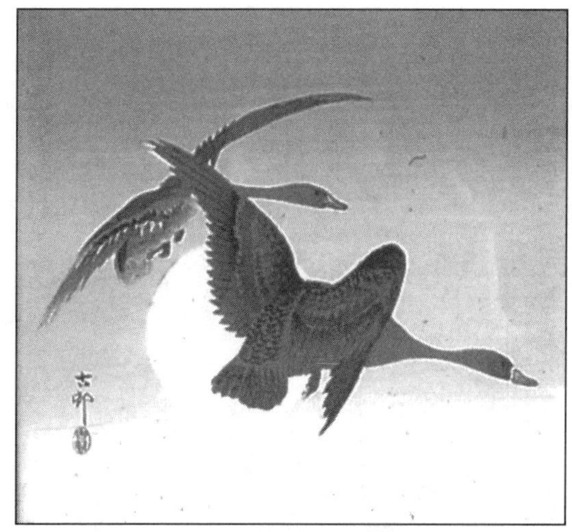

Koson Ohara, shishiban, 9 1/2" x 9" (framed size 12" x 12"), "Flying Geese," c. 1920s, fine impression, slightly toned, $300-500.

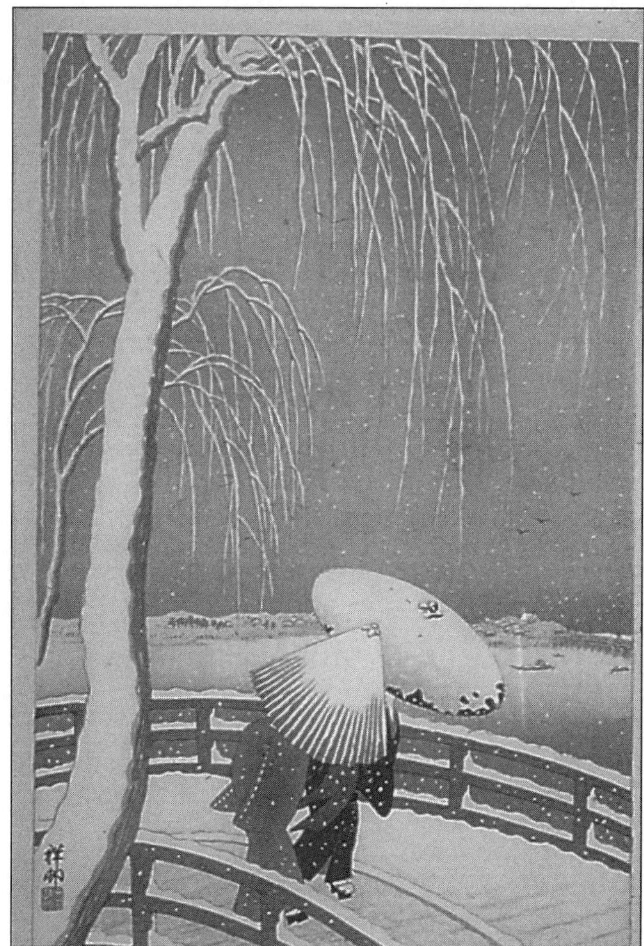

Koson Ohara, oban tate-e, 9 1/2" x 14 1/2", dated 1927, published by Watanabe, fine impression, color, and condition, $2000-3000.

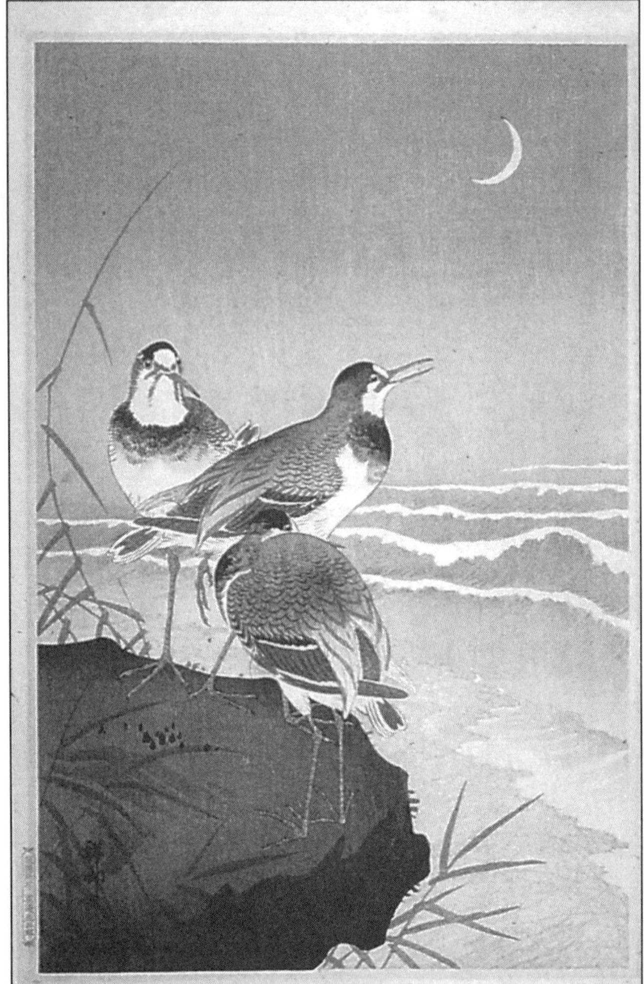

Koson Ohara, oban tate-e, "Water Fowl and Moon," published by Watanabe, c. 1930, early edition, very good color, impression and condition, $2800-3800.

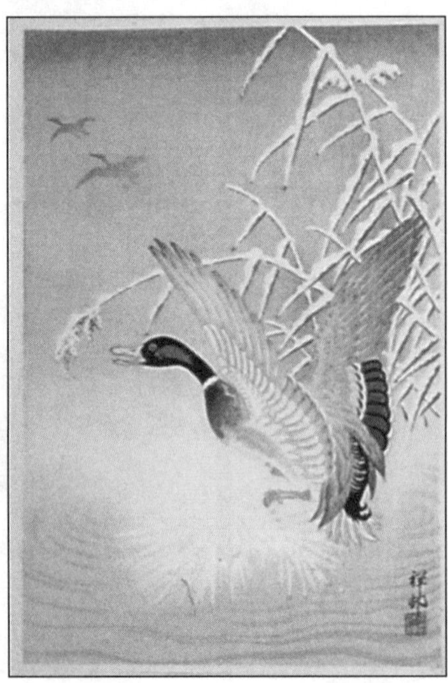

Koson Ohara, chuban, "Geese on Snowy Day," c. 1920, fine impression, color, and condition, $500-775.

Kotondo Torii (1900-1976) bijin ga, 7th generation of the Torii family, designed 21 prints between 1929-1934.

Dai oban tate-e, "Asa Negami," (Morning Hair), a portrait of a beauty resting her chin on a pillow, mosquito netting serving as the background, signed and sealed, from a series of 100, very good impression, color, and condition, $15,000-18,000.

As above, faded, foxing, verso browned, tape residue on verso, $1500-1800.

Dai oban tate-e, "Ame," (Rain), signed "Kotondo ga," published by Sakai and Kawaguchi of Tokyo, dated 1929, good impression, good color, and condition, $1500-2000.

As above, very good impression, very good color, very fine condition, $4000-6000.

Kotozuka Eiichi (b. 1906) landscapes, flowers, published by Uchida, Unsodo.

Kuniaki (1835-1888) Yokohama School, pupil of Kunisada.

Kunichika (1835-1900) pupil of Chikanobu and Kunisada.

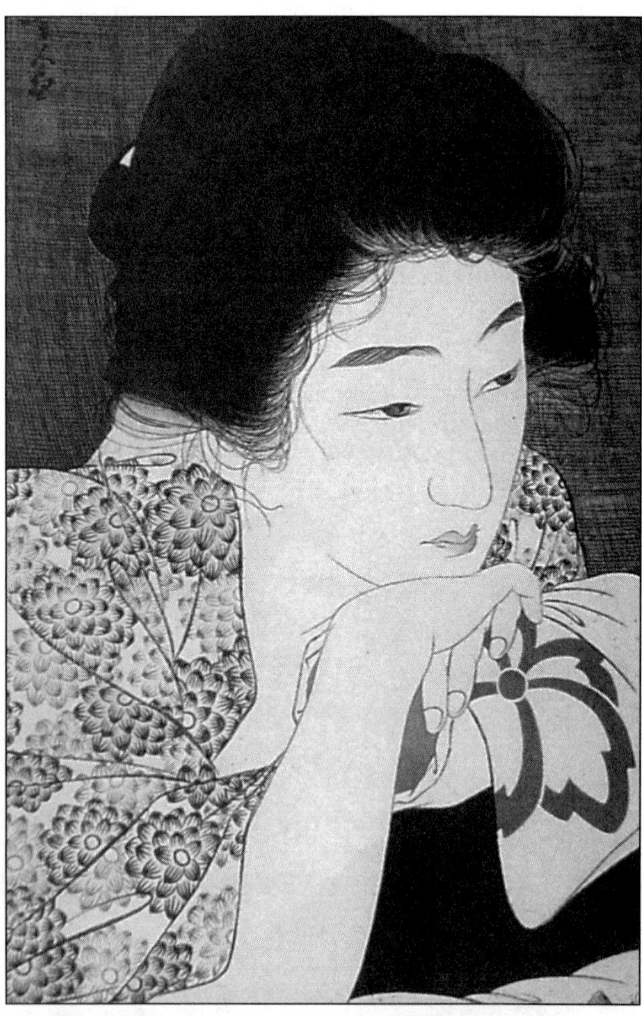

Kotondo Torii, dai oban tate-e, 18 1/2" x 11 5/8", "Asa Negami" (Morning Hair), signed "Kotondo ga," circa 1930, good impression and color, slight foxing in margins, slightly trimmed, tape residue on verso, tape stains on margins, $7000-10,000.

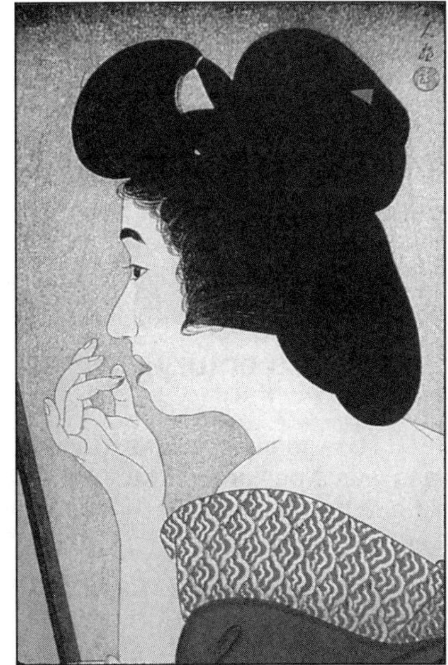

Kotondo Torii, dai oban tate-e, approx. 18 3/4" x 11 1/2", "Kuchi Beni," (Rouge), signed "Kotondo ga" with Torii seal, publisher Ikeda, c. 1930, very good impression and color, slightly trimmed, tape on verso, $5500-8500.

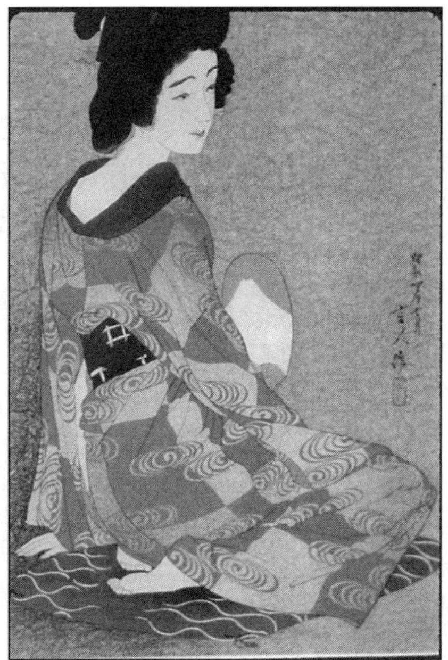

Kotondo Torii, dai oban tate-e, 18 3/4" x 12 1/8", "Nagajuban," (Underrobe), a bijin with a fan, signed "Kotondo saku," sealed Kotondo, Showa 4 (1929), published by Kawaguchi and Saki, from an edition of 200, very good impression and color, creases at corners and horizontal crease, slightly toned, $4000-5000.

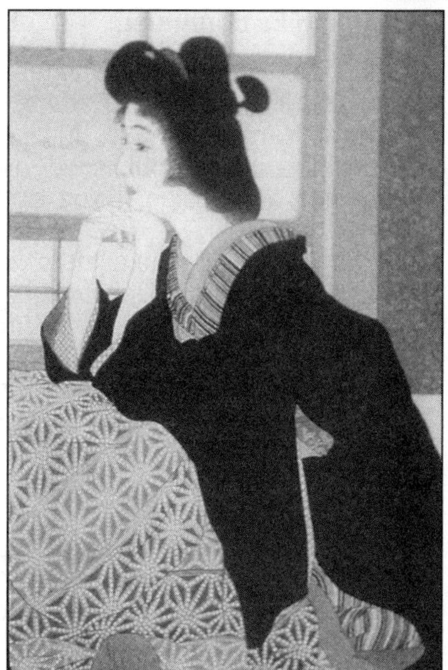

Kotondo Torii, dai oban tate-e, 18 3/4" x 12 1/4", "Yuki," (Snow), a woman in black robe seated at a kotatsu, snow outside visible through the window, signed "Kotonodo ga," dated Showa 4 (1929), published by Kawaguchi and Sakai, from an edition of 200, fine impression and color, the reverse browned, tape stains on verso, $1200-1800.

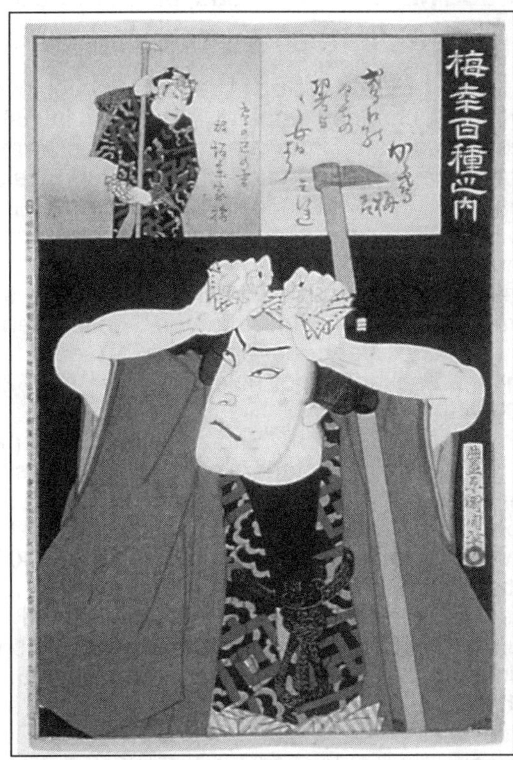

Kunichika, oban tate-e, "The Actor Onoe Baiko," from the series A Hundred Scenes with Baiko, published by Fukuda Kunajiro, 1893, signed Toyohara Kunichika hitsu, with Toshidama seal, excellent impression, condition, and color, $275-400.

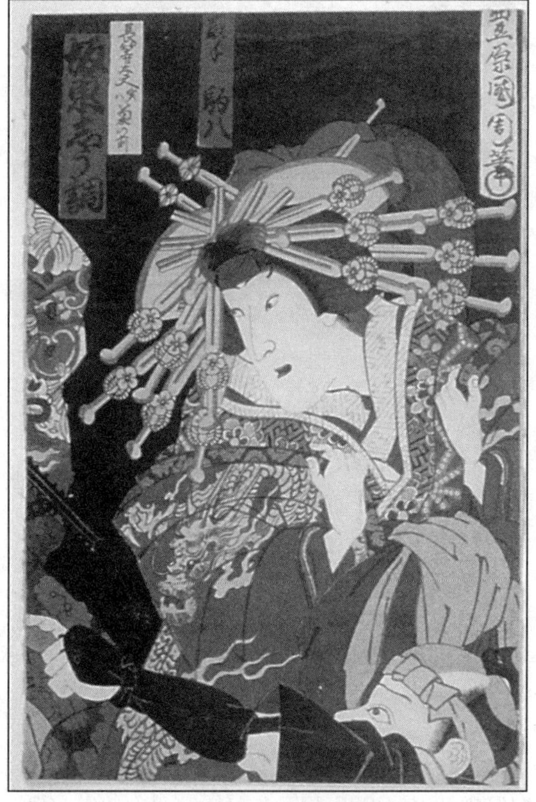

Kunichika, oban tate-e (center sheet of a triptych), actors, c. 1880, fine impression, color, trimmed into image, $100-150.

Kunichika continued:

Okubi-e, Kawarazaki Gonnosuke (Ichikawa Danjuro IX), in the role of Daroku, from the play Nani Oboshi Kanagaki Fude, Meiji 2 (5/1869), signed "Kunichika hitsu," published by Gusokuya Kahei, very fine impression, color, and condition, $3000-5000.

Triptych showing the actor Ichikawa Sadanji I in the role of the otkodate Danjuro Bozu Sankichi from the series Haiyu otokodate den (actors as chivalrous men), signed "Toyohara Kunichika hitsu," published by Akiyama Buemon, dated Meiji 27 (1894), very good impression, color, trimmed, binding holes, backed, $800-1300.

Triptych of Ichikawa Danjuro IX in the role of Komatsu Shigemori, from the series Shijuhachijo Kenja Koseki (48 Wise Men), signed "Oju Toyohara Kunichika hitsu," published by Sasaki Toyokichi, dated Meiji 23 (1890), very good impression, color, backed, slightly trimmed, foxing, $700-1200.

Triptych from Tales of Genji, Prince Genji with objects floating in a bowl for good luck, oban, signed "Kunichika ga," published by Kiya Sojiro, dated 1862, good impression, color, and condition, $1200-1800.

Triptych, oban, Ichikawa Danjuro as Uesugi Kenshin and Nakamura Shikan as Wada Masayuki from the series Tosei Komei Kagami (A Famous Mirror of Modern Times), signed, published by Kurata Tasuke, dated Meiji 15 (1882), good impression, water stains (red pigment blurred and smeared overall), otherwise good condition, $200-300.

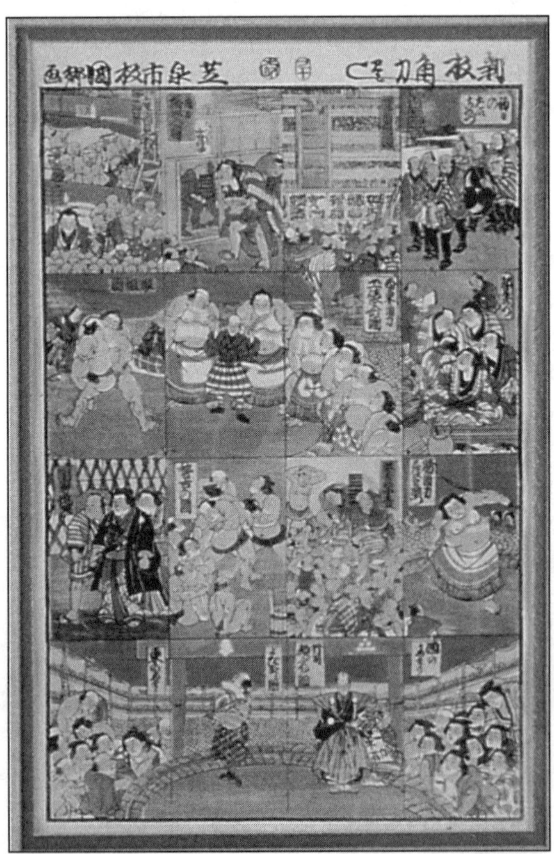

Kunimatsu, oban tate-e, 10" x 14 3/4", dated year of the snake 1857, a Sumo (wrestling) match with 16 vignettes, fine impression, color, and condition, $900-1200.

Kuniharu (1803-1839) pupil of Toyokuni II.

Kunihiro (fl. c. 1815-1843) pupil of Toyokuni II.

Kunihisa II (1832-1891) Yokohama School.

Kunikage (fl. c. 1831) Osaka School.

Kunikazu (fl. c. 1849-1867) pupil of Kunisada.

Kunikiyo (fl. c.mid-19th century) Utagawa School, pupil of Toyokuni I.

Kunimasa (1773-1810) Utagawa School, pupil of Toyokuni I. Kunimasa was a designer of Kabuki portraits, especially okubi-e (facial depiction with strong mask-like lines and coloring).

Kunimatsu (fl. c. mid-late 19th century) pupil of Toyokuni I, Utagawa School.

Kunimitsu (fl. c.1801-1818) Utagawa School

Kunimori (fl. c. 1820s-1830s) pupil of Toyokuni II.

Kunimori II (fl. c. 1850s) pupil of Kunisada.

Kunimune (fl. c. 1818) Utagawa School.

Kunimune II (fl. c. 1825-1844) Utagawa School.

Kuninaga (d. 1829) Utagawa School.

Kuninao (1793-1854) Utagawa School.

Kuninobu (fl. c. 1820s-1830s) pupil of Toyokuni.

Kuninobu (fl. c. 1860s) pupil of Kunisada.

Kunisada I (1786-1865) Utagawa School, pupil of Toyokuni I, changed name to Toyokuni III in 1844.

Aiban uchiwa-e, from the series Furyu Yami No Kaori (Elegant Perfume of the Dark), signed "Konomi ni oji Toyokuni ga," published by Kojimaya Jubei, good impression, toned, soiled, wormage, trimmed, $300-500.

Kakemono, Japanese woman walking in the snow, signed "Kochoro Kunisada ga," published by Sanoya Kihei, very good impression, faded, toned, trimmed, backed, minor holes on lower left, $2000-3000.

Oban tate-e, triptych, "Shoka Nairan Shuken Zu," (A View of the Interior of a Brothel), signed "Kunisada ga," published by Tsuruya Kinsuke, very good impression and color, wormage restored, trimmed, toned from old mat/framing, $800-1200.

Oban tate-e, a hero with tattoos, from the series Kinsei Suikoden (Modern Suikoden), signed "Toyokuni ga," published by Ise, good impression, soiled, stained, wormage, creased, backed, $150-225.

Oban tate-e, Choryo on a dragon, from the series Battle Tales of the Han and Chu, signed "Oju Gototei Kunisada ga," published by Nishimuraya Yohachi, good impression and color, trimmed, backed, and toned into image from old mat, $300-550.

Oban yoko-e, okubi-e, the actor Sawamura Sojuro IV from the series Yakusha Hanjimono (Actor Puz-

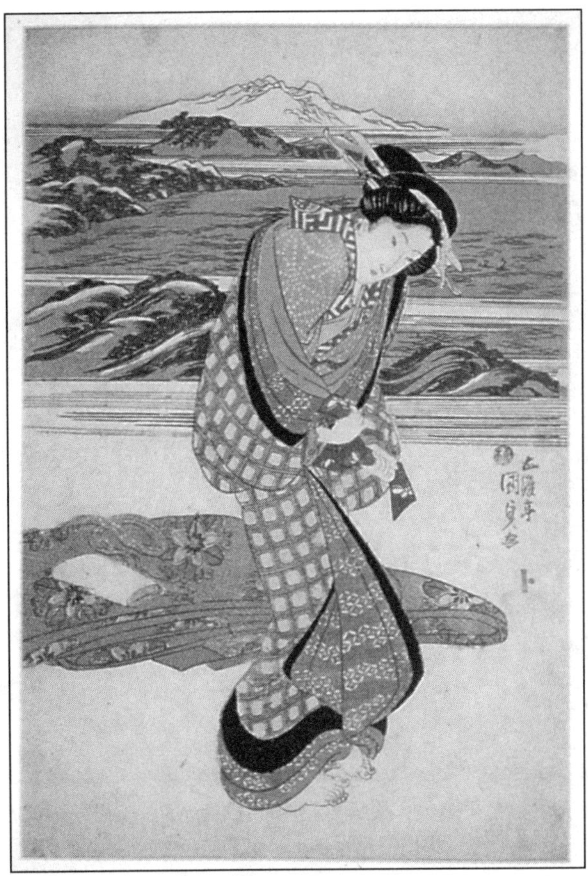

Kunisada, oban tate-e, "Japanese Beauty at the Seaside," kiwame seal, fine impression and color, slightly soiled, $550-750.

zles), signed "Gototei Kunisada ga," published by Nishimuraya Yohachi, good impression and color, wormage restored, rubbed, and soiled, $3500-5500.

Oban yoko-e, beauties at the gate to a villa in the snow, signed "Gototei Kunisada ga," good impression, faded, center crease, binding holes, minor wormage, $300-500.

Oban yoko-e, two women and Ariwara no Narihira walking a bridge in a garden of irises, signed "Kochoro Kunisada ga," published by Yamaguchiya Tobei, good impression, faded, creases, torn corners restored, soiled, trimmed $200-275.

Oban yoko-e, 19 3/4" x 14 1/4", "Gonin Otoko," (The Five Chivalrous Men), Ichikawa Ebizo Vi as Kaminari Shokuro, Ichikawa Danjuro VIII as Gokuin Senemon, Seki Sanjuro III as An no Keibyoye and two other actors as Karigane Bunshichi and Hotei Ichiemon, signed "Toyokuni ga," censor's seal, two nanuchi-in, Mera and Watanabe, publisher Hamadaya Tokubei, dated Kaei 5 (1852), good impression and color, trimmed, center crease, minor rubbing, $800-1200.

See also: Toyokuni III

Kunisada II (1823-1880) pupil of Kunisada, used this name from 1846-1870, Utagawa School.

Ehon Shunga, 8 7/8" x 6 1/2", "Sumida Gawa No Yuki," (Snow at the Sumida River), unsigned c. 1865, the text interspersed with color as well as black and white diptychs, very good impressions, good color (minor ink transfer on sumi-e prints), soiled, wormage, $1000-2000.

Kunisada III (1848-1920) pupil of Kunisada II, began using this name in 1889.

Kunishige name used by Shigeharu.

Kuniteru (1808-1876) Utagawa School, pupil of Kunisada.

Kuniteru II (1829-1874) pupil of Kunisada.

Kunitomi (early-19th century) pupil Toyokuni II.

Kunitora (fl. c. 1810s-1830s) Utagawa School, pupil of Toyokuni I.

Kunitoshi (fl. c. 1847-1899) Utagawa School, pupil of Kunisada.

Kunitsugu (1800-1861) pupil of Toyokuni.

Kunitsuna (1805-1868) Utagawa School, pupil of Toyokuni I.

Kunitsuru (fl. c. 1830s) Utagawa School, pupil of Toyokuni II.

Kuniyasu (1794-1861) Utagawa School, pupil of Toyokuni I.

Kuniyoshi (1794-1834) Utagawa School, pupil of Toyokuni.

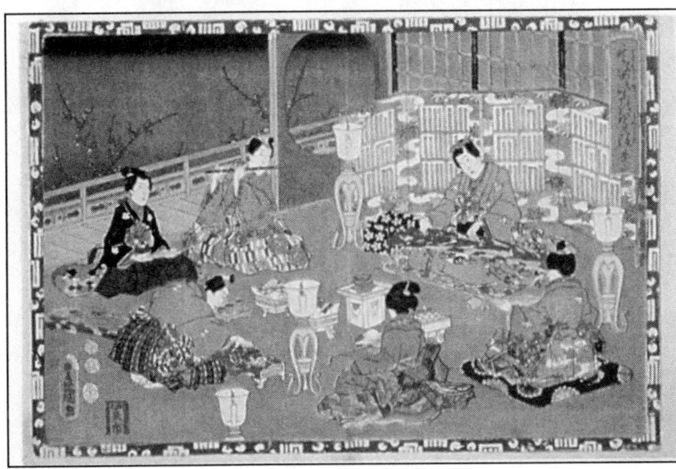

Kunisada, oban yoko-e, from Tale of Genji, signed "Ichiyosai Toyokuni ga," published by Izumiya Ichibei, c. 1860, good impression, color, and condition, center crease, backed, $200-375.

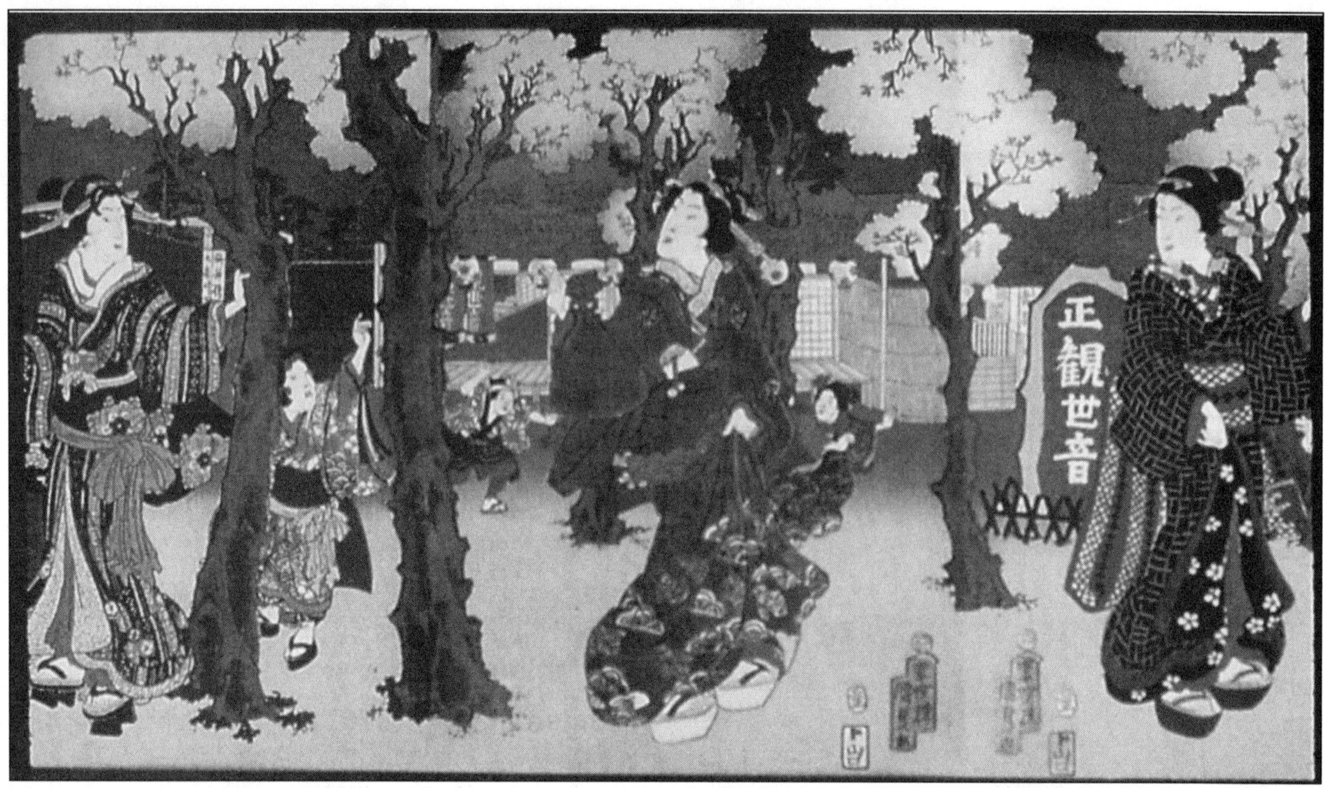

Kunisada II, oban tate-e triptych, "Asakusa Okuyama, Sakura Hanazakari no Zu," (Cherry Blossoms at Okuyama Asakusa), signed "Kunisada ga," publisher Yamaguchiya Tobei, dated first month of 1857, very good impression and color, $1500-2500.

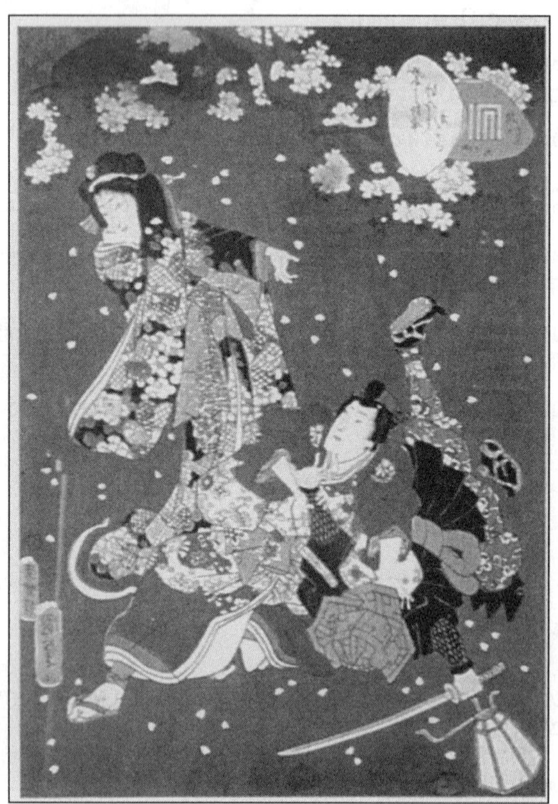

Kunisada II, oban tate-e, 9 1/2" x 13 1/4" (framed size 12" x 16"), from the series Tale Of Genji, chapter 46, dated 11 month year of the snake (1857), good impression, very good color, $350-550.

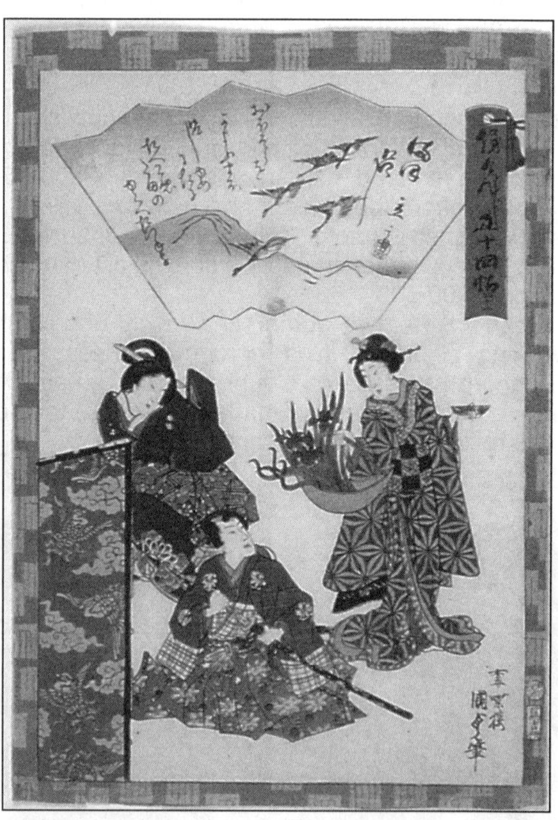

Kunisada II, oban tate-e, from Tale of Genji chapter 50 Azumaya, fine impression, color and condition, $275-475.

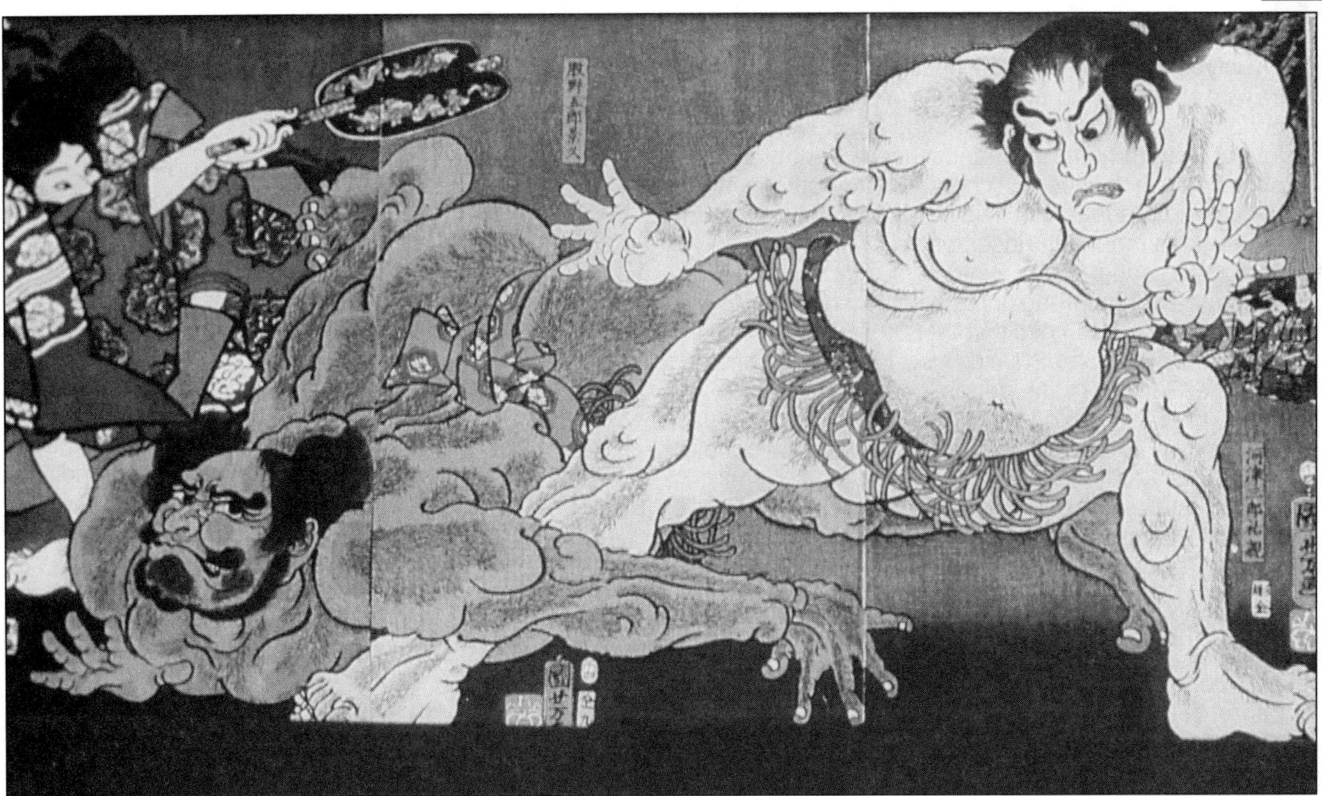

Kuniyoshi, oban tate-e triptych, each sheet 14 3/4" x 10 1/4"; "Akazawayama o-Zumo," (Great Sumo Match at Mt. Akazawa), the wrestler Kozu Saburo Hirochika defeating Matano Goro Kagehisa while Minamoto no Yoritomo observes the match, signed "Ichiyusai Kuniyoshi ga," published by Maruya Kyushiro, very good impression and color, some wormage throughout, $6500-8500.

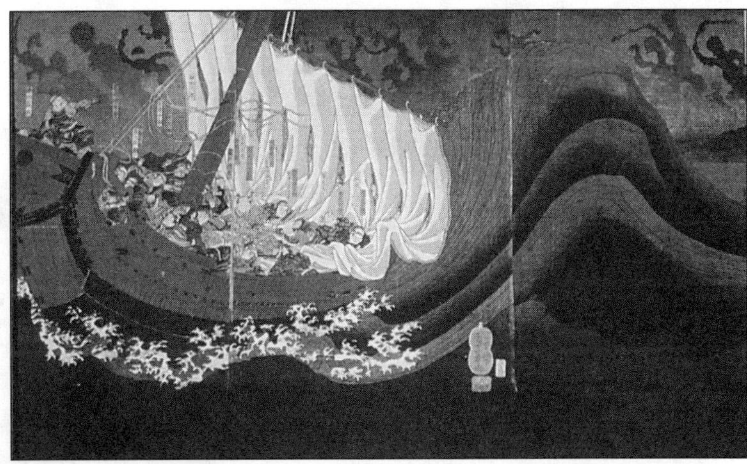

Kuniyoshi, oban tate-e triptych, overall 28" x 13 3/4", "Taira Ghosts at Daimotsu Bay," signed "Ichyusai Kuniyoshi ga," publisher's seals Enshuya Hikobei and Hama, censors seals Fuku and Muramatsu, very good impression and color, trimmed, right side of center sheet and left side of right sheet trimmed (they do not line up), $3000-5000.

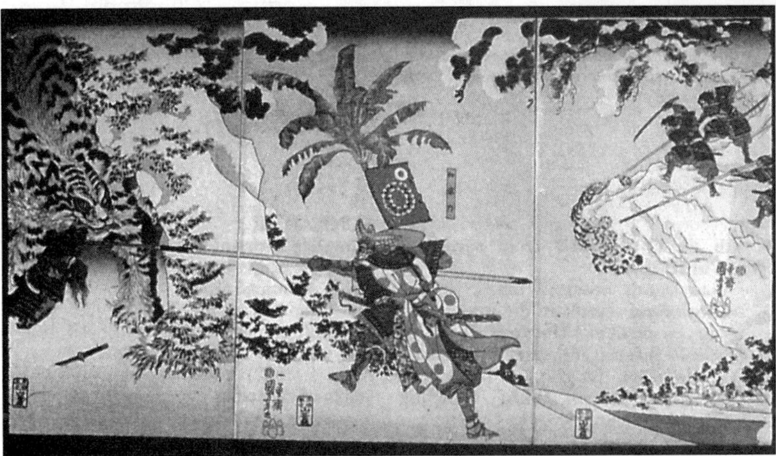

Kuniyoshi, oban tate-e triptych, "Watonai Tora Gari no Zu," (Watonai Hunting Tigers), censor's nanushi-in, Murata (c. 1846), published by Yamashitoya Jimbei, signed "Ichiyusai Kuniyoshi ga" with Yoshikiri mon, very good impression and color, minor creases, minor rubbing and soiling, $2000-3500.

Kuniyoshi continued:

Kuniyoshi's forte was the historical print and portrayals of fierce vigorous figures. Amongst his contributions were satire, lampooning the overbearing feudal government, and landscapes. Variety in his prints was achieved by changing proportions and colors (e. g., a lake, ricefield, or clouds in the center ground and mountain ridges behind with a high horizon) and suggesting movement. He had many pupils, each name beginning with "Yoshi." The foremost of these was Yoshitoshi (1839-1892).

Oban tate-e, "Omi Shimidzu no Kwanja Yoshitaka and the Rat," from the series The Sixty Odd Provinces of Japan, signed, published by Yawata-ya Sakujiro, c. 1845, good impression, color, and condition, $800-1200.

Oban tate-e, "Kokusempu Riki Destroying the Gate to the Hakuryojin Temple with an Ax," from the series Tsuzoku Suikoden Goketsu Hyakuhachinin no Hitori (The Hundred and Eight Heroes of the Popular Suikoden), signed "Ichiyusai Kuniyoshi ga," published by Kagaya Kichiemon, good impression and color, wormage restored, backed with heavy paper, $800-1200.

Oban tate-e, "Shin-Ohashi Kyoka no Chobo," (The View Beneath the Shin Ohashi Bridge), form the series Toto Fujimi Sanjurokkei (Thirty Six Views of Mt. Fuji from the Eastern Capital), signed "Ichiyusai Kuniyoshi ga," published by Marataya Jirobei, good impression, center crease, margins trimmed into seal, wormage, backed, $3000-4000.

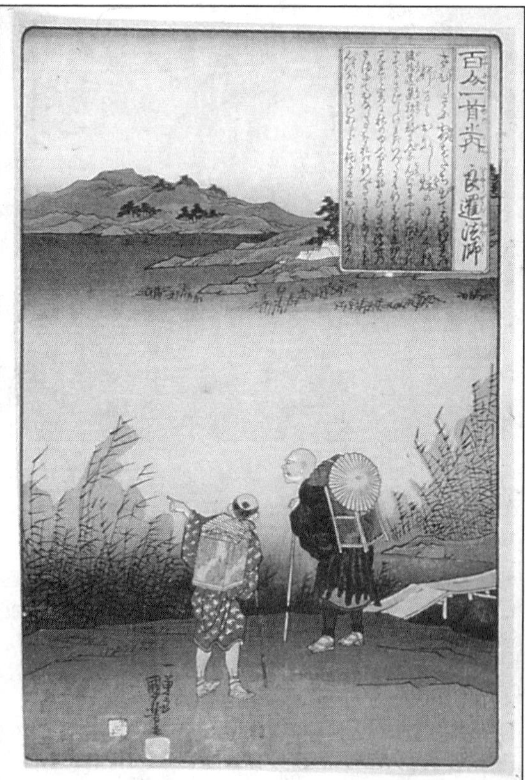

Kuniyoshi, oban tate-e, from the series The Hundred Poems by the Hundred Poets, signed "Ichyusai Kuniyoshi ga," Ebisuya Shoshichi publisher, good impression, color and condition, $400-550.

Oban yoko-e, "The Heavenly Weaver," from the series Nijushiko Doji Kagami (A Mirror for Children of the Twenty Four Paragons of Filial Piety), signed "Ichiyusai Kuniyoshi ga," published by Wakasaya Yoichi, good impression, faded, wormage, binding holes, top margin trimmed, $800-1200.

Oban yoko-e, "Saijun Attacked By Robbers," from the series Morokoshi Nijushiko (The Twenty Four Chinese Paragons of Filial Piety), signed "Ichiyusai Kuniyoshi ga," published by Izumiya Ichibei, good impression and color, margins trimmed, wormage, $800-1200.

Kuroda Shigeki (b. 1953)

"Etching on Arches," not dated, signed in pencil, from a series of 50, approx. size 30" x 22", fine condition, $1500-2500.

Kyoden (Masanobu) (1761-1816) pupil of Shigemasa.

Kyosai (Gyosai) (1831-1889) pupil of Kuniyoshi.

Kyosen (fl. c. 1760s)

Kyosui (fl. c. 1740s) Masanobu-style.

Kyosui (1816-1867)

L

Lum Bertha (1879-1954)

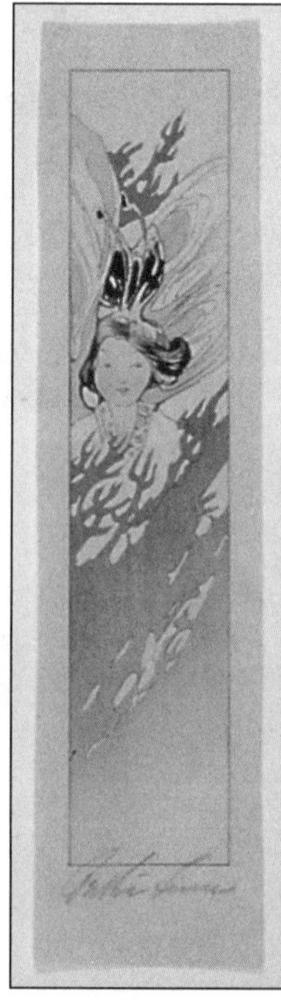

Lum, Bertha, "Christmas Fairy," signed "Bertha Lum," fine impression, color, and condition, $1500-2500.

M

Mabuchi Toru (1920-1994) plates sometimes composed of many small pieces of thin wood adhered to produce a mosaic effect.

Maedo Masao (1904-1974) landscapes, frequently used the first kanji of his given name as a seal.

Maedo Seison (1885-1977) studied with Kajita Hanko, subjects include Mt. Fuji and flowers.

Maeda Toshiro (1904-1990) surrealist linoleum prints, moku hanga.

Maekawa Sempan (1888-1960) woodblock hanga artist, usually signed prints with one or more of the kanji for his name but also used the first three letters of Sempan.

Dai oban approx. 21" x 16 1/4", "Girl From a Fishing Village," not dated, seal to right of image, fine color, impression, and condition, $2500-3500.

Dai oban, approx 18" x 13", "Red Fan," (woman holding a red fan) on a blue ground, some mica intact, signed but not dated but probably early 1950s, fine color and impression, $3000-4000.

Dai oban, approx. 17" x 13 1/4", "Pipe," (seated man holding a pipe), signed in pencil, fine color, impression, and condition, except for tape residue on verso, $1500-2500.

Maki Haku (b. 1924) limited editions, deeply embossed designs.

Maruyama Banka (1867-1942) although a watercolorist, he did woodcut illustrations.

Maruyama Hiroshi (b. 1953) prints from the 1970s include bands of color across dark backgrounds.

Masafusa (fl. c. 1740s) Osaka School.

Masakazu (d. 1886) pupil of Kunisada II.

Masakuni (fl. c. 1820) pupil of Yoshikuni.

Masanobu (fl. c. 1770s) Harunobu-style.

Hosoban, benizuri-e, a young woman practicing calligraphic skills, (1716-1735), published by Okumuraya Gwenroku, good impression, faded, tears on edges, wormage restored, $2000-3000.

Masanobu (fl. 1850s) pupil of Kunimasu.

Masanobu Okumura (1686-1784)

Masatsugu (fl. c. 1765-1880) pupil of Hidenobu.

Masayoshi (1784-1824) pupil of Shigemasa.

Masuda Yoichi etching.

Matsubara Naoko (b. 1937) her prints deal with American and Japanese subjects.

Matsubara Tatsuo (1941) serigraphy.

Masuharo (fl. c. 1850s) pupil of Kunimasa.

Matsumoto Akira (1936) woodblock, intaglio, serigraphy, limited editions.

Matsubashi Keigetsu (1876-1963)

Matsumoto Akira (b. 1936) woodblock, intaglio, serigraphy.

Matsutani Takesada (1937) serigraphy, lithography, intaglio, etching, limited edition.

Migata Toshihide (1863-1925)

Oban tate-e, from the series Bijin Junishi (Beautiful Women for the 12 Months), 9th month, a woman gazing at the falling maple leaves, signed "Toshihide," published Akiyama Buemon, dated Meiji 34 (1901), very good impression, color, and condition, $1000-1500.

Okubi-e, Ichikawa Danjuro IX in the role of Benkei, from Danjuro juchaiban, oban tate-e, published by Sasaki Toyo, dated Meiji 26 (1885), very good impression, color, and condition, $600-900.

Triptych, Ichikawa Danjuro VIII as Kato no Kiyomasa, from the series Taiko Gunki Chosen no Maki (Military Exploits of Hideyoshi), signed and sealed, published by Sasaki Toyokichi, dated Meiji 24 (1891), good impression, color, right sheet trimmed, some toning, foxing, $800-1200.

Miki Suizan (1887-1957)

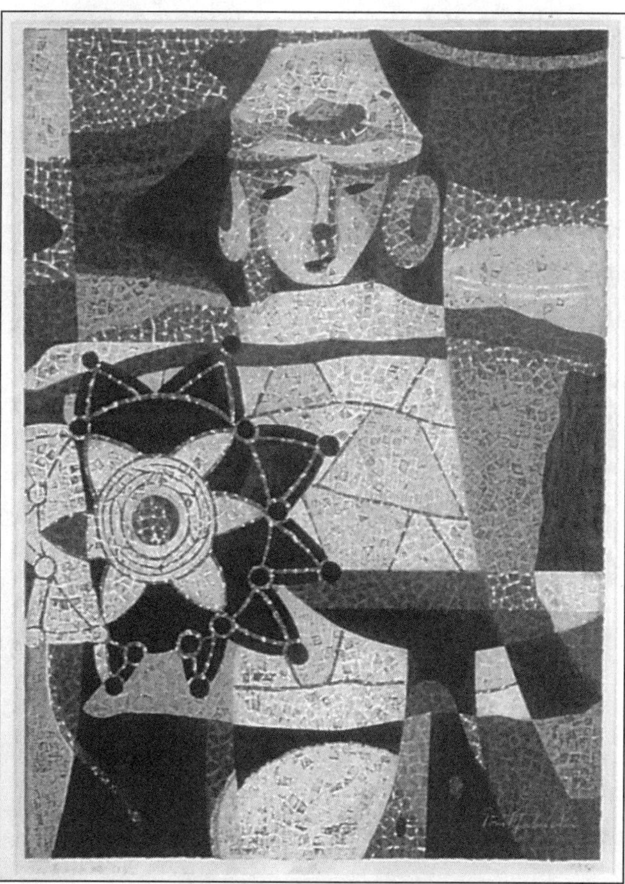

Mabuchi Toru, "Zosen-jo Akibi," (Dockyard in the Autumn), from an edition of 30, signed and sealed with penciled title, very fine condition, $900-1200.

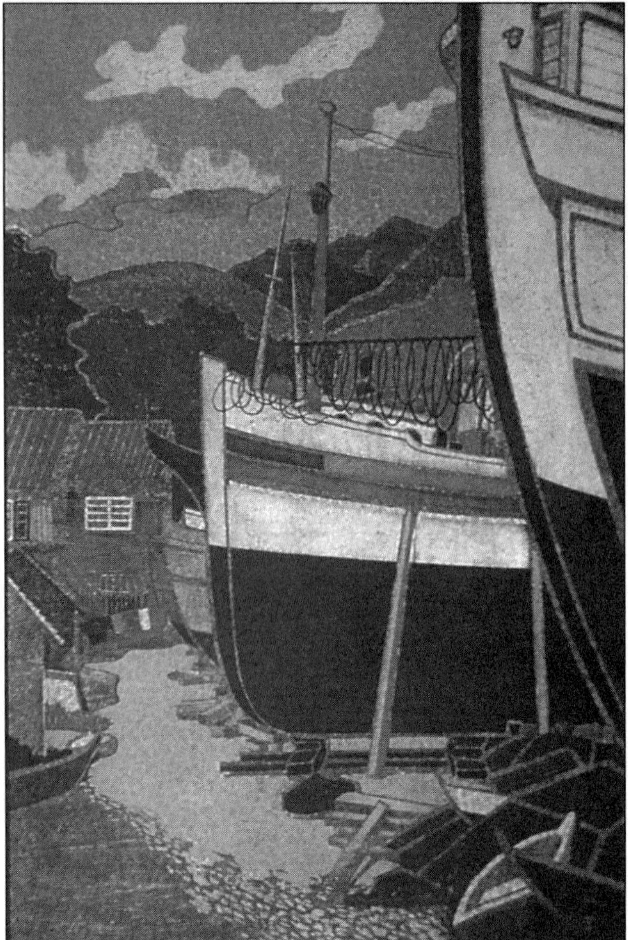

Mabuchi Toru, dai oban tate-e, 17" x 23", "Haniwa (1)," from an edition of 100, dated 1960 and signed Toru Mabuchi, excellent condition, $900-1200.

Minko (fl. c. 1760s)

Mitsui Eiichi lithography, limited editions.

Mitsunobu (fl. c. 1730s-1760s) pupil of Sukenobu.

Miyagawa Shuntei (1873-1914)

Mizufune Rokushu (1912-1980) woodblock, limited editions.

Mori Yoshitoshi (1898-1992) stencil, limited and unlimited editions.

"Akazaya," signed "Y. Mori," and sealed, dated '77, good condition, $275-475.

35" x 27", "Fudo Myo-o," (Warrior with Battle Fan), signed in pencil, dated '81, from an edition of 50, good condition, $900-1200.

"Yoichi No Ninoya," signed "Yoshitoshi Mori," and sealed, dated '71, good condition, $300-500.

Morita Tsunetomo (1881-1933)

Moromasa (fl. c. 1712-1772) Hishikawa School.

Moronobu (fl. c. 1618-1694)

Munakata Shiko (1903-1975) woodcut, woodblock, etching.

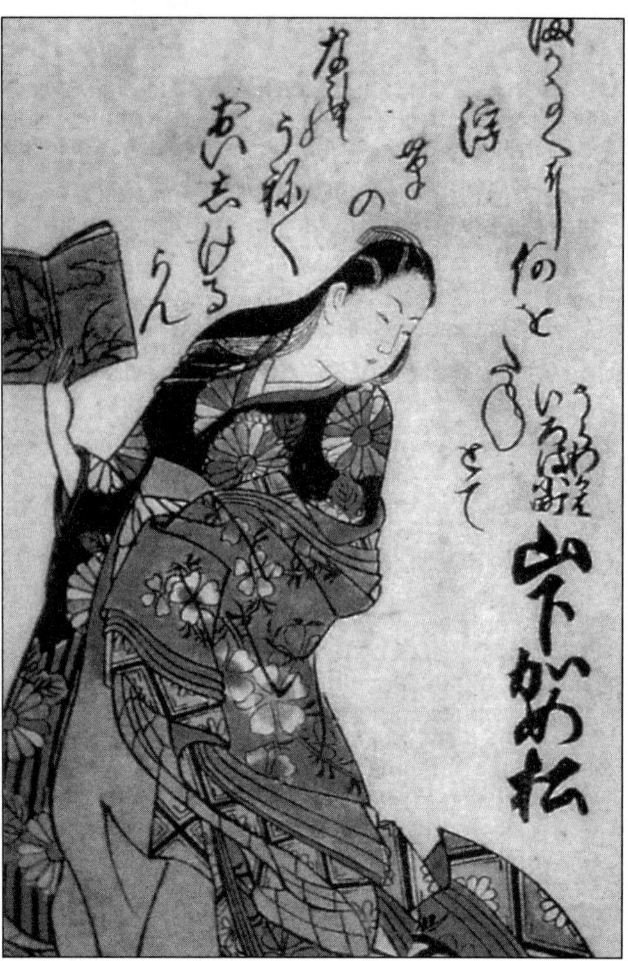

Masanobu Okumura, hosoban, 12 3/4" x 6", sumizuri-e with hand applied color, the actor Yamashita Kamekichi as a beauty in an elegant robe holding a book, signed "Nihon gako Okumura Masanobu seihitsu," publisher Okumura Genroku, good impression and color, minor toning, restored worm holes, $3500-4500.

"Becoming Buddha," sumizuri-e and color, signed and sealed, good condition, $3000-4000.

"Fireflies on a Summer Evening," sumizuri-e and color, a woman wearing a yukata passing on a stone bridge along a bamboo fence, a poem of fireflies above, from the series Utautaban Gasaku no Uchi, Hotaru-zoe, signed in pencil and sealed, dated 1956, laid down, framed, toned, $3000-4000.

17" x 12 7/8", "Fish, Flower, Buddha," signed in pencil and sealed, dated 1957, sumizuri-e (black and white), tape on verso, foxing, toned, trimmed, $2000-3000.

11 5/8" x 8 7/8", "Fudo Myo-o no Saku," (fudo Myo-o), signed in pencil lower right in Japanese "Shiko," and in roman script "Munakata," sealed upper right Setsujo shimo-o kuwau-sumizuri-e woodblock print with hand applied color, $3000-4000.

13" x 16" "On the Beach," sumizuri-e (black and white), from the series The Story of the Cormorant, signed and sealed, trimmed, slightly toned, foxed, tape on verso, $2500-3500.

Munehiro (fl. c. 1846-1867) pupil of Hirosada.

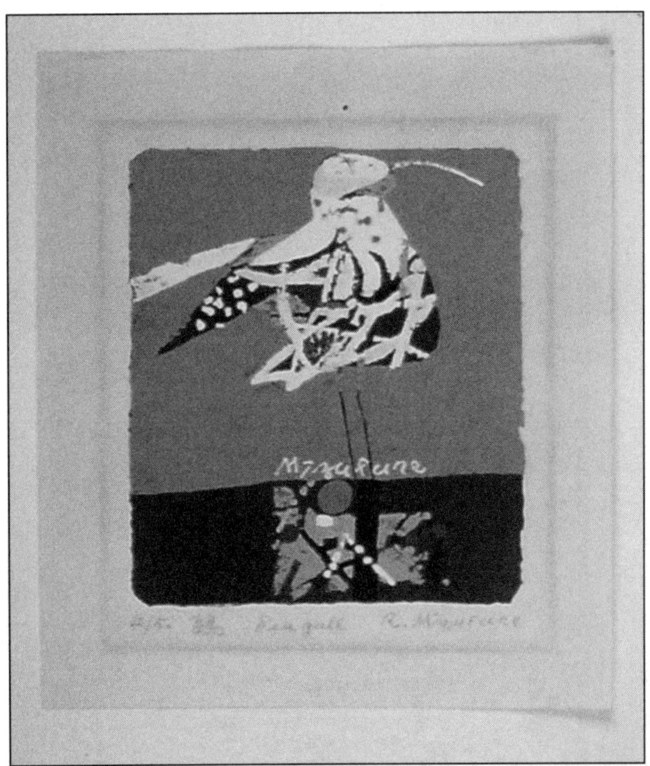

Mizufune, 8 3/4" x 9 3/4", "Seagull," from an edition of 50, signed in pencil on lower margin and within image, very good condition, $1000-1500.

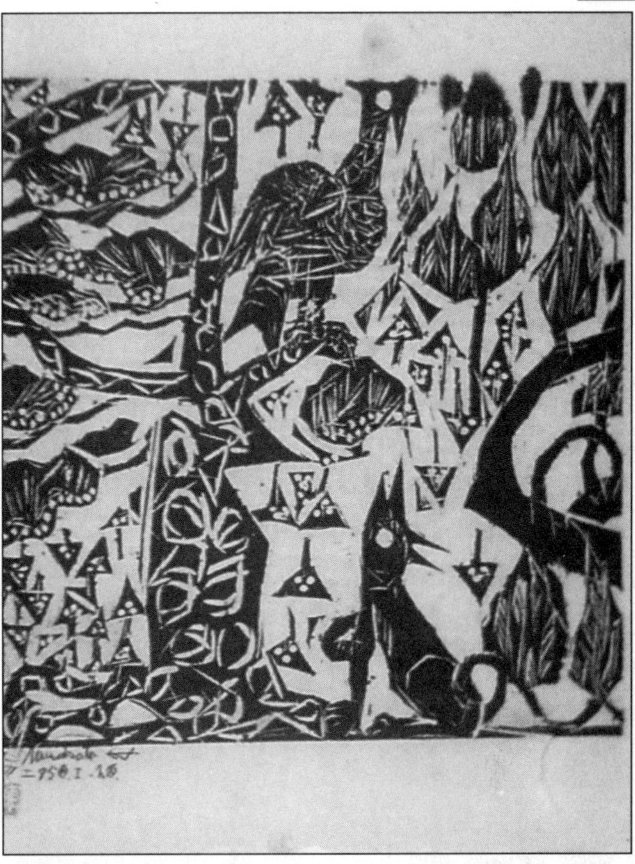

Munakata Shiko, woodcut, approx. 23 1/4" x 22", "Hinoki Matsu no Saku," (Cypress and Pine), 1958, signed in pencil in Japanese "Shiko" and "Munakata" in Roman script, sealed Muna, tape stains, slightly toned, $3500-5500.

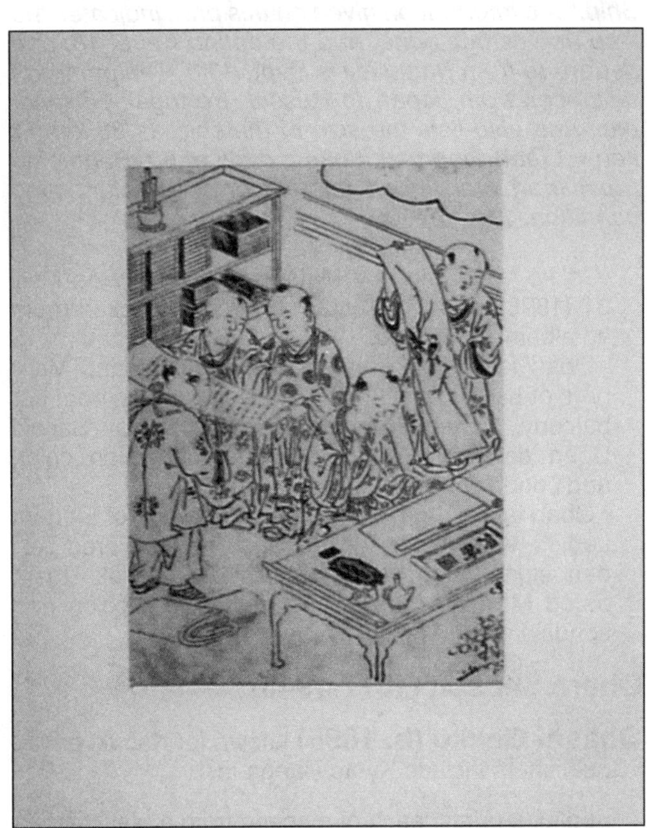

Morikuni, koban from ehon, sumizuri-e, karako in their study room, c. 1735, fine impression and condition, $375-500.

N

Nagahide (fl. c. 1804-1848)

Nagakuni (fl. c. 1814-1820s)

Nagai Iku( )

Nagai Kazumasa (b. 1929) woodblock, zinc relief, stencil.

Nagase Yoshio (1891-1978) woodblock, lithography, serigraphy, etching, stencil.

Nishijima Katsuyuki (b. 1945)

Nishimura Goun (1877-1938)

Nishimura Hodo (fl. c. 1930s)

Nobuharu (fl. c. 1832) pupil of Sadanobu.

Nobuhiro (fl. c. 1839) pupil of Sadamasa.

Nobumasa (fl. c. 1832-1848)

Nobumitsu (fl. c. 1850s)

Nobusada (fl. c. 1823-1832) pupil of Shigenobu.

Noda Kyuho (1879-1971)

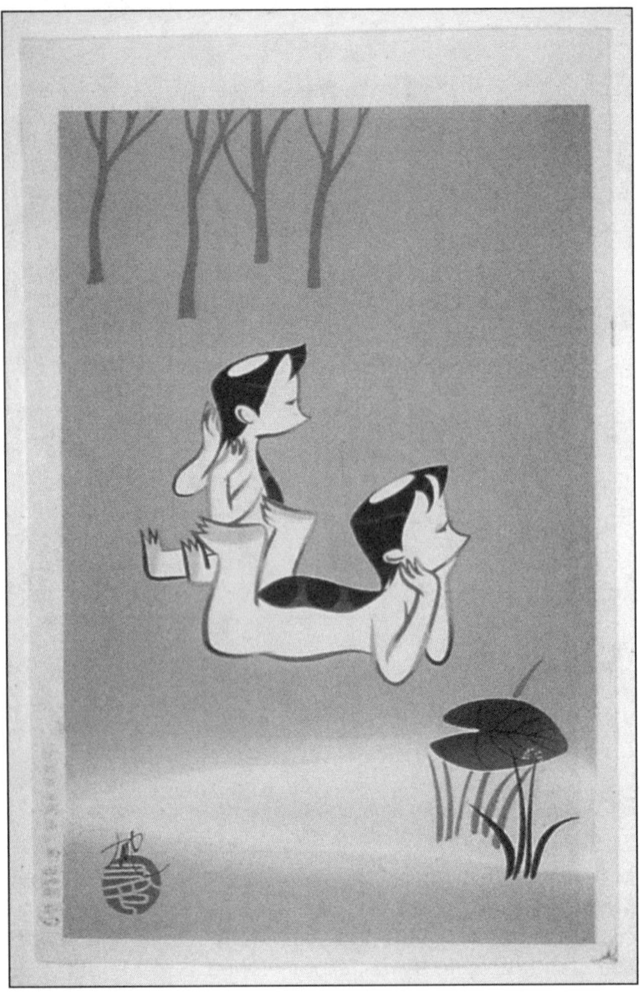

Nagai Iku, oban tate-e, mythological spirits, published by Kyoto Hanga-In, c. 1956, fine impression, color, and condition, slightly toned margins, $125-185.

Noda Tetsuya (b. 1940)

Woodcut with mica and silk-screen (serigraphy) on Japanese paper, approx. 24" x 29", "Diary Feb 10th,"signed and dated in pencil, '68, excellent condition, $2000-3000.

Woodcut with mica and silk-screen (serigraphy) on Japanese paper, approx. 24" x 24", "Diary May 3rd," signed and dated in pencil, '68, from a series of 20, framed, (not viewed out of frame), fine condition as visible, $1000-1800.

Nouet Noel published by Doi c. 1930.

O

Oda Kazuma (1881-1956)

Oda Mayumi (1941-) serigraphy, stencil, limited editions.

Ogata Gekko (1859-1920)

Oban tate-e, "Koshikawa Baien," (Plum Blossom Garden at Koshikawa), from the series Fujin Fuzoku Ga (Modern Images of Elegant Women), signed

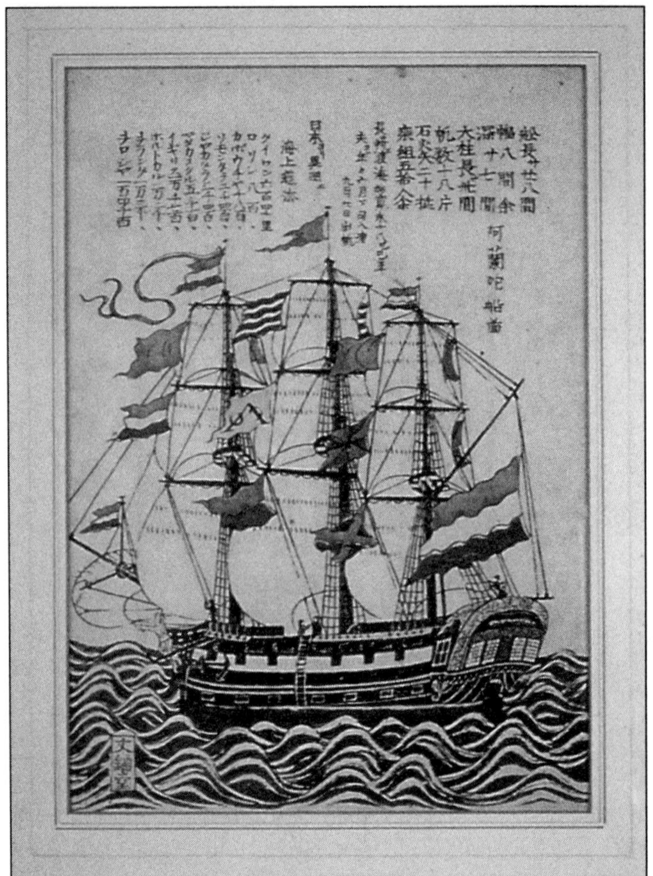

Nagasaki (artist unknown), oban tate-e, "Dutch Ship," the information given on this print indicates the ship arrives late June, and the dating Kanei 18, and departure from Nagasaki is Sept. 20th. The print lists distances from Japan to Russia, Portugal, Holland, etc., and also lists the size of the ship as 28 ken (1 ken =6 feet), and that it has a crew of 50, Bunmeido (publisher), very good impression and color, good condition, $1000-1500.

"Gekko," published by Matsuki Heikichi, dates Meiji 31 (1898), good impression and color, backed (from an album), $350-550.

Oban tate-e, from the series Customs and Manners of Ladies, a woman watches fireworks from her balcony, signed and sealed, published by Sasaki Ugen, dated Meiji 24 (1891), fine impression, color, and condition, $300-500.

Oban tate-e, from the series A Selection of Elegant Ladies, two women looking at a snow-covered garden, signed and sealed, published by Sasaki Ugen, dated Meiji 24 (1891), fine impression, color, and condition, $300-500.

Ohara Shoson (1877-1945)

Ohashi Gekko (b. 1895) known for Kabuki prints, publishers include Kyoto Hanga-in.

Folio, 6 prints, each of a scene from a play, perfect condition, approx. 9" x 9", published, $600-850.

Okada Koichi (b. 1907) studied with Ishii Hakutei.

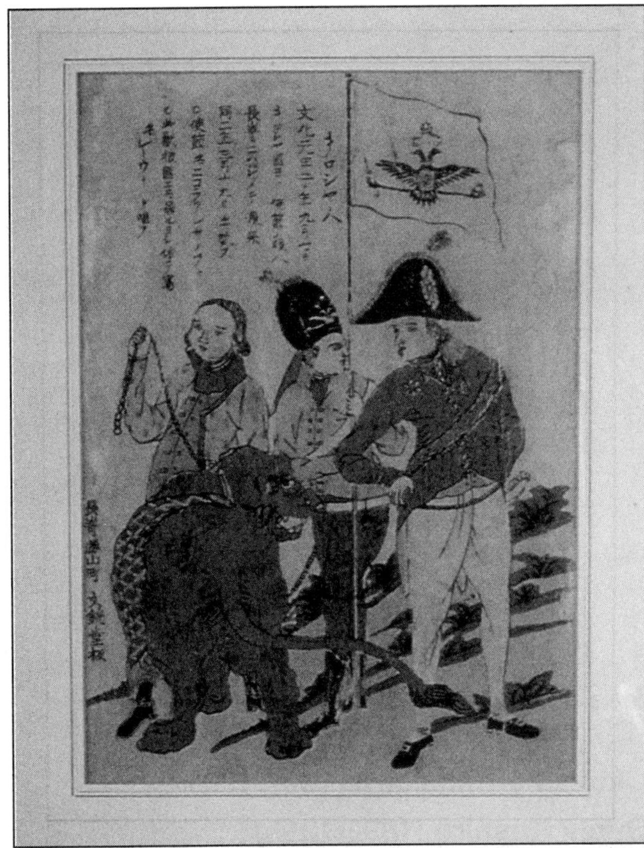

Nagasaki (artist unknown), oban tate-e, "Russian Delegates To Nagasaki," Bunkindo (publisher), the print states first arrival Bunka 1 (1804) and the Delegate's name Nicholai Lesanotzu, departure is given as Bunka 2 (March 19th), good impression, fair color, faded, tones, tears repaired, $600-800.

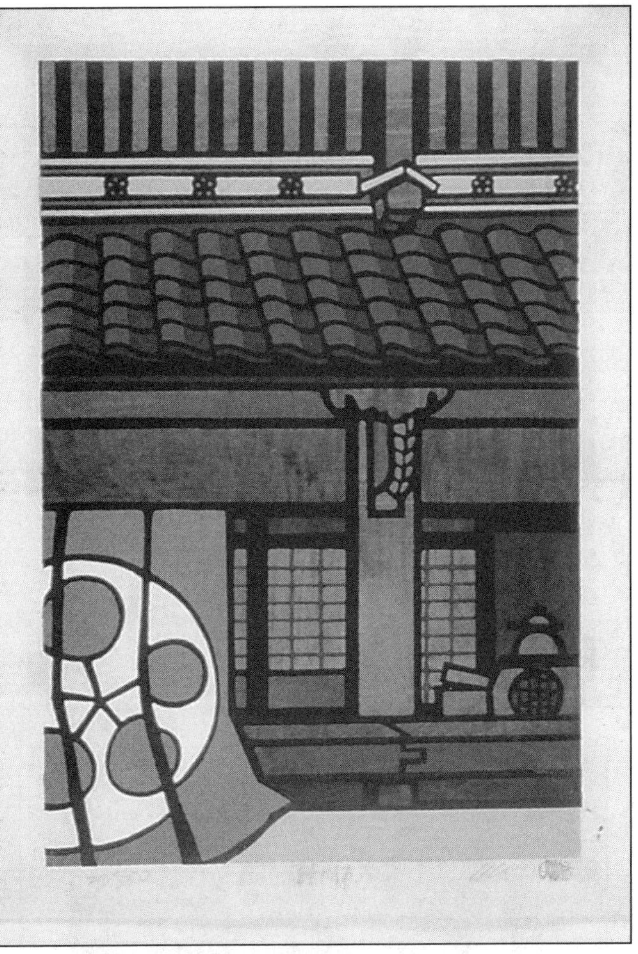

Nishijima Katsuyuki, oban, 2" x 18", from an edition of 500, excellent condition $150-200.

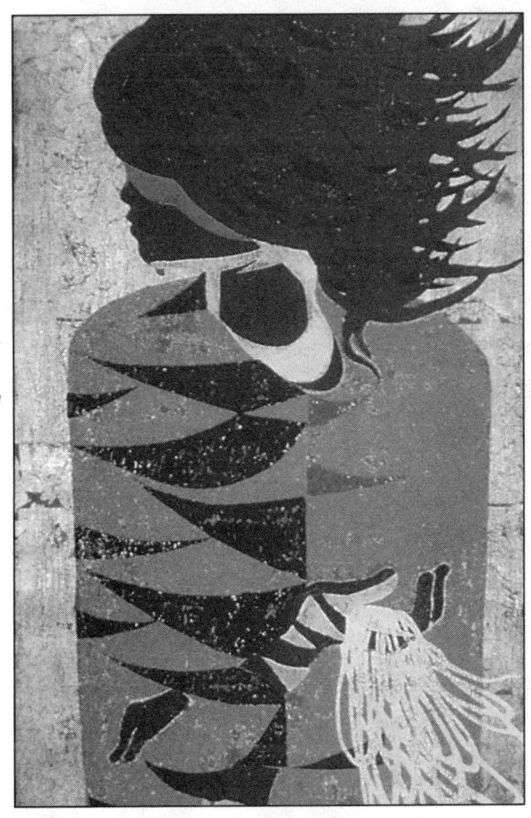

Nakayama Tadashi, woodcut with metallic powder, 25" x 16 1/2", "Akai Fuku," (Wind, Red Clothes), signed and dated in pencil in Roman script "T. Nakayama," sealed, dated 1957, slightly trimmed, tape stains on verso of all margins, margins slightly toned, $400-500.

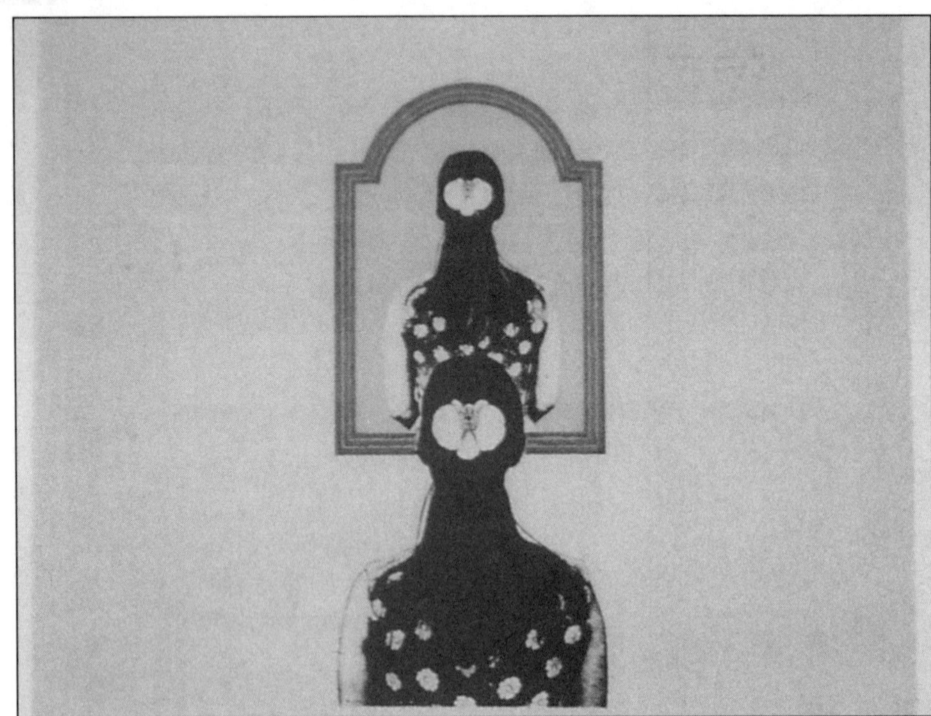

Noda Tetsuya, woodcut and silk-screen on Japanese paper, "Diary: July 1st," approx. 22" x 22" framed, signed and dated in pencil in Roman script "T. Noda '69," toned and laid down on board, $900-1200.

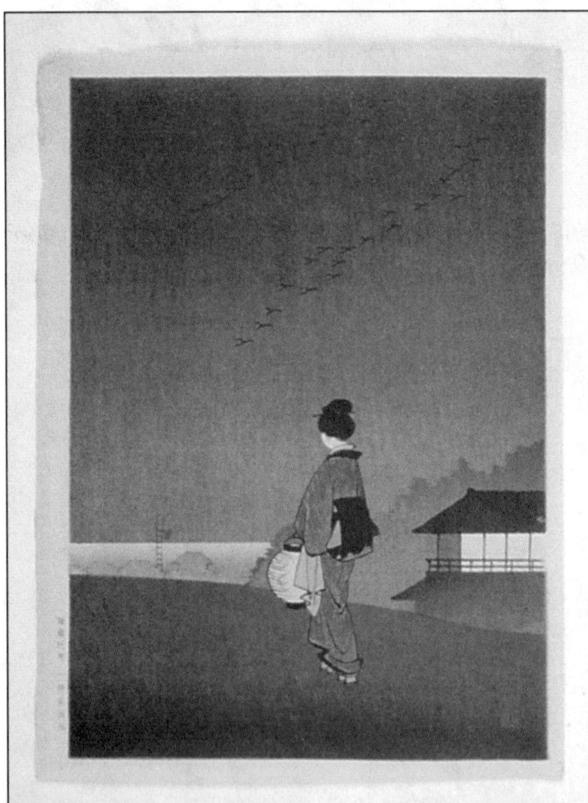

Nishiomiya (publisher), 9" x 10", illuminated night view of lady walking with lantern, c. 1920, fine condition, color and impression, stamped on the back with publisher's name and address, (unsigned) $200-275.

Okamoto Shinjiro (b. 1933) woodblock, serigraphy, limited editions.

Okamoto Shogo (b. 1920) etching, limited editions.

Okuyama Gihachiro (1907-1981)

Onchi Koshiro (1891-1955)

Ono Bakufu (1888-1976) one of the founders of Kyoto Hanga-in.

Ono Tadashige (1909-1990)

Orlik Emil (1870-1932)

Osencho (early-19th century)

Ota Gako (1892-1975)

Ota Masamitsu (Ota Gako)

Ouchi Makoto (b. 1926) stencil.

Ouchi Seiho (1898-1981)

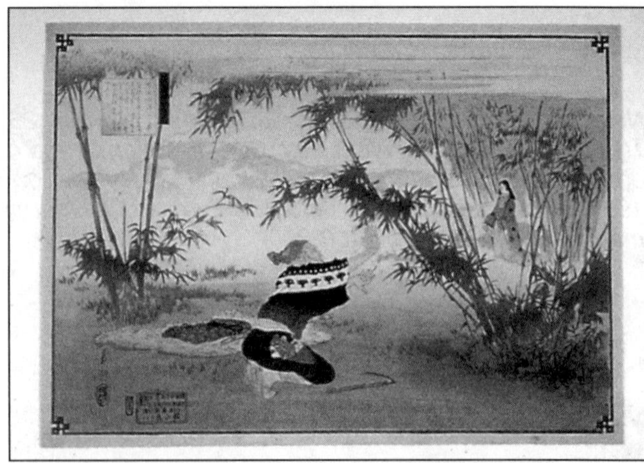

Ogata Gekko, oban yoko-e, "Taketori Monogatari," dated Meiji 23 (1888), very good impression, color, and condition, $175-285.

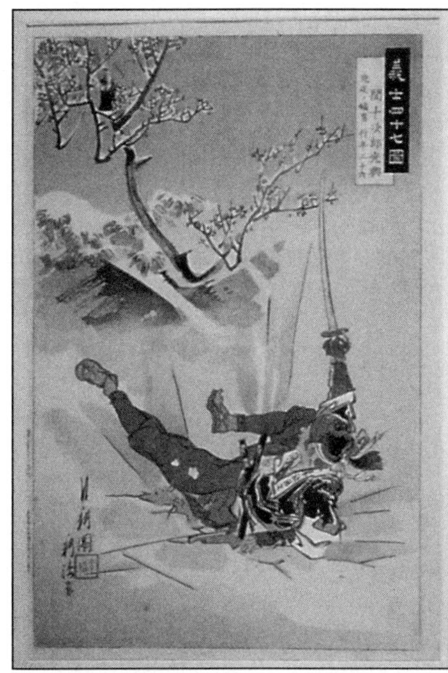

Ogata Gekko, oban tate-e, from the series The 47 Loyal Retainers, fine color, condition, and impression, $950-1250.

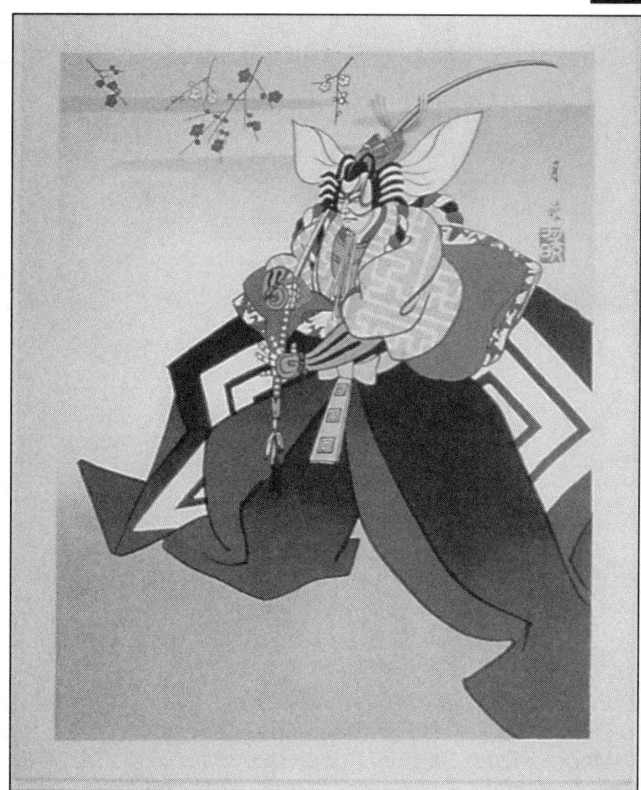

Ohashi Gekko, 9 1/4" x 11 1/4", "Kabuki Explanation and Stories, Series 1," a scene from Shibaraku, one of the 18 best plays which was first staged by danjuro Ichikawa under the name of Kauemon Fuwa in the 10th year of Genroku 1667, from a folio of 6 prints, published by Kyoto Hanga In Co. 1954, fine impressions, color, and condition, $600-850.

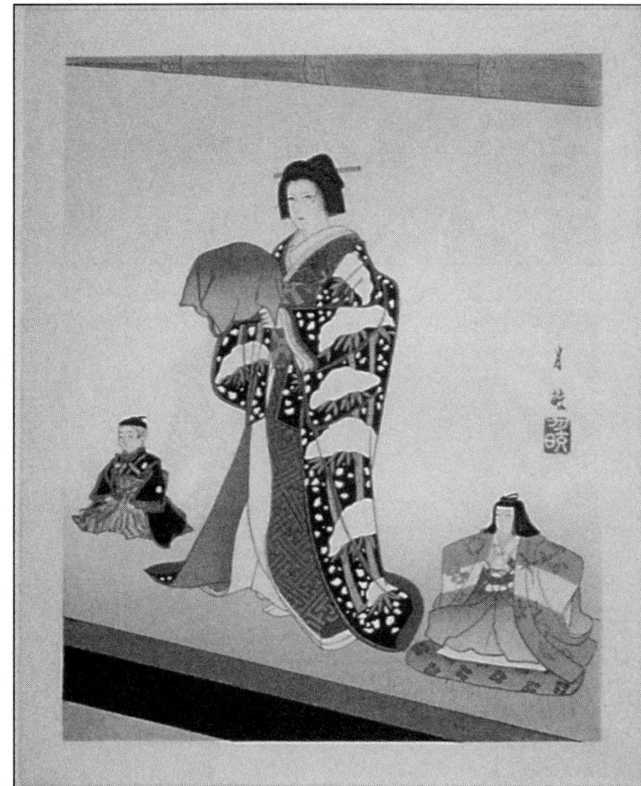

Ohashi Gekko, 9 1/4" x 11 1/4", "Kabuki Explanation and Stories, Series 1," a scene from Meiboku Sendai Hagi, from a folio of 6 prints, published by Kyoto Hanga In Co. 1954, fine impressions, color, and condition, $600-850.

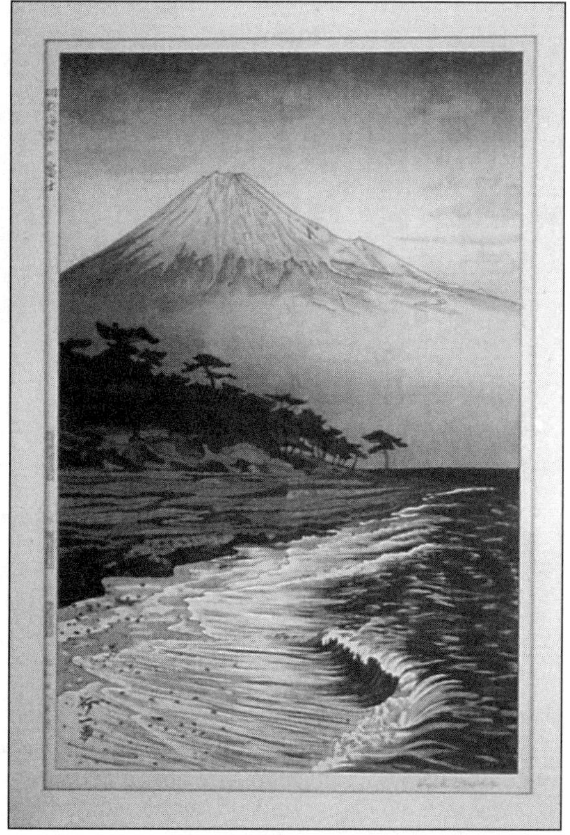

Okada Koichi, oban tate-e, "Mt. Fuji at Sunset," from a series entitled 12 Views of Japan, signed and sealed, dated Showa 29 (1954),early edition, published by Unsodo, excellent impression, color, and condition, $1800-2500.

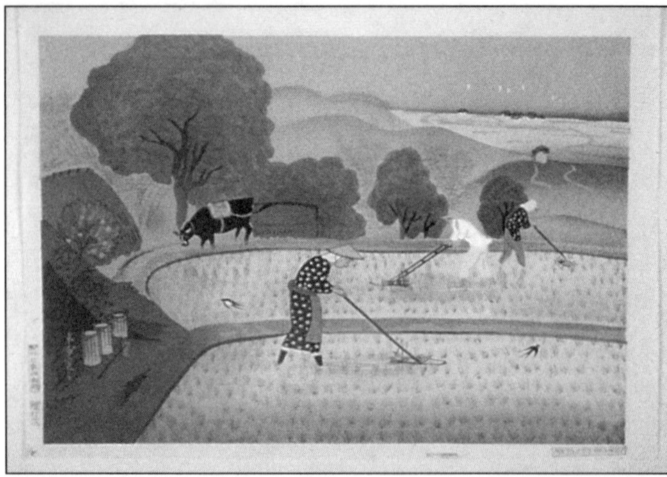

Ohno Bakufu, oban yoko-e, "Farming," printed by Kyoto Hanga-In , 1952, fine impression, color and condition, $375-500.

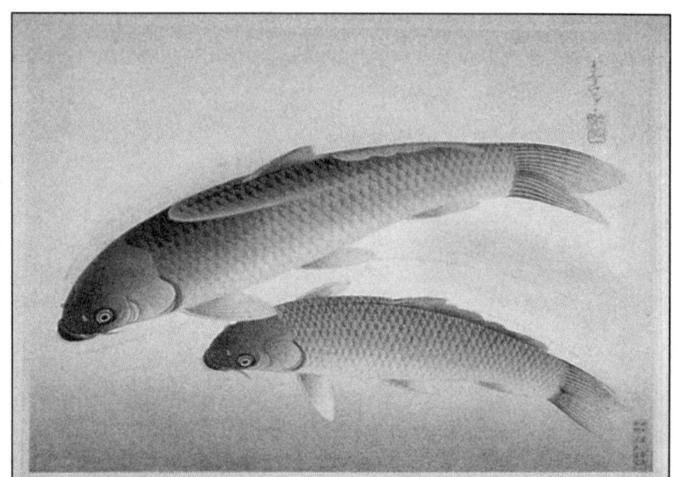

Ohno Bakufu, dai oban yoko-e, "Koi," (Carp), in original folio from the series Familiar Fishes Of Nippon, Vol. 2 No. 1 Magoi (True Carp), Supervisor Sanzo Wada, Artist Bakufu Ohno, September, 1938, fine condition, color, and impression, $1000-1500.

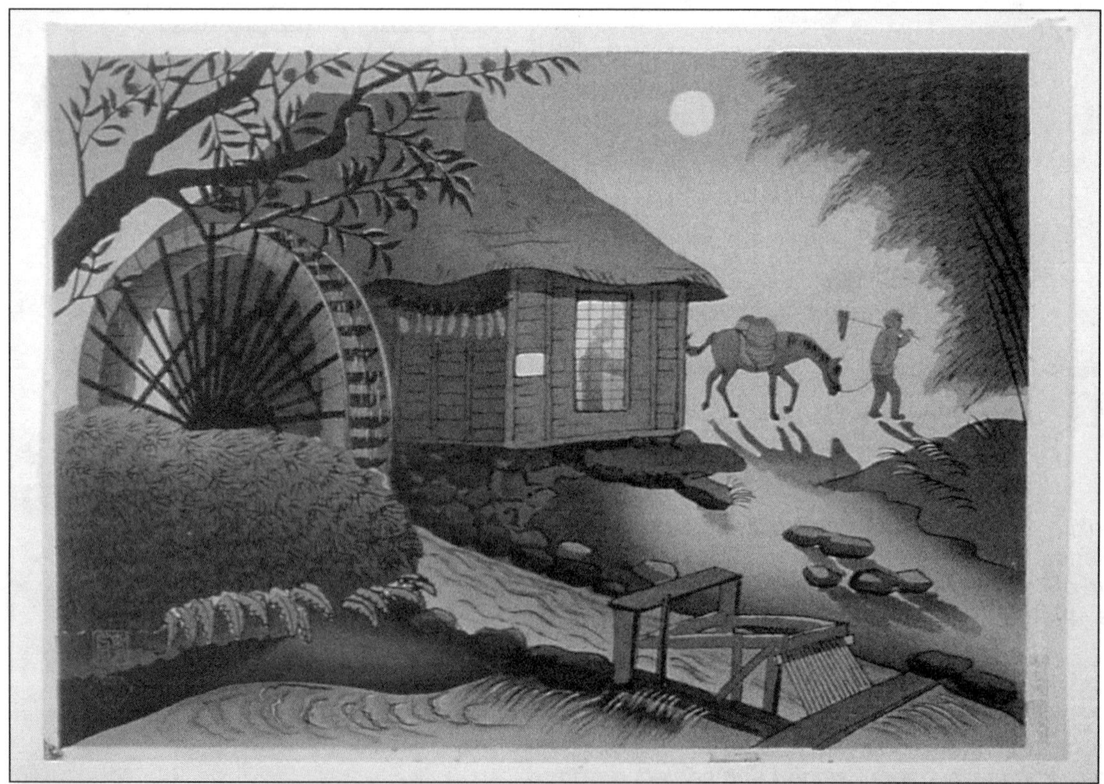

Ohno Bakufu, oban yoko-e, "Farmer and Mule," illuminated scene, published by Kyoto Hanga-In, 1952, fine color, impression, and condition, $375-500.

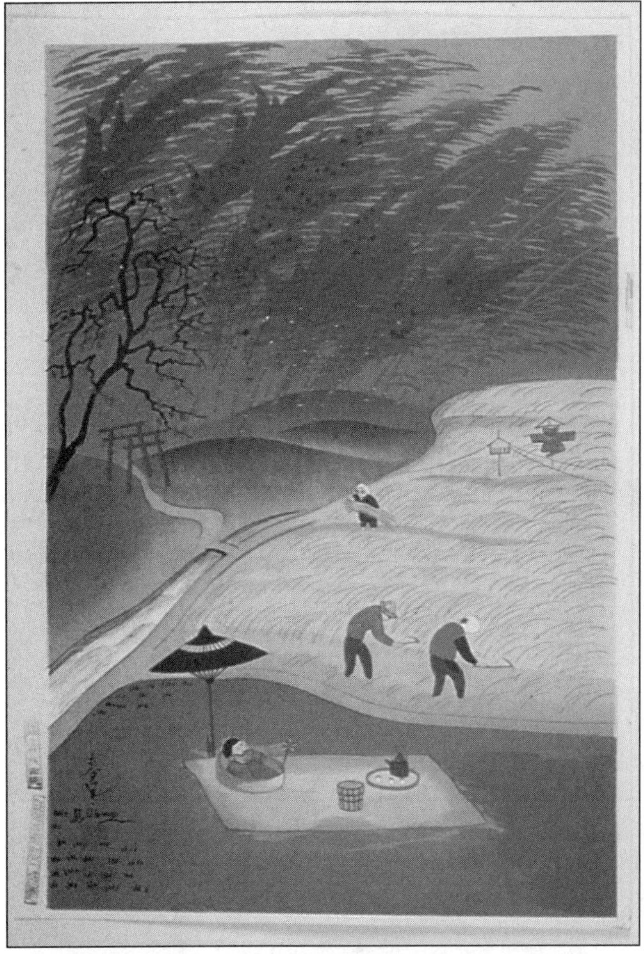

Ohno Bakufu, oban tate-e, "Farming," printed by Kyoto Hanga-In, 1952, fine impression, color and condition, $375-500.

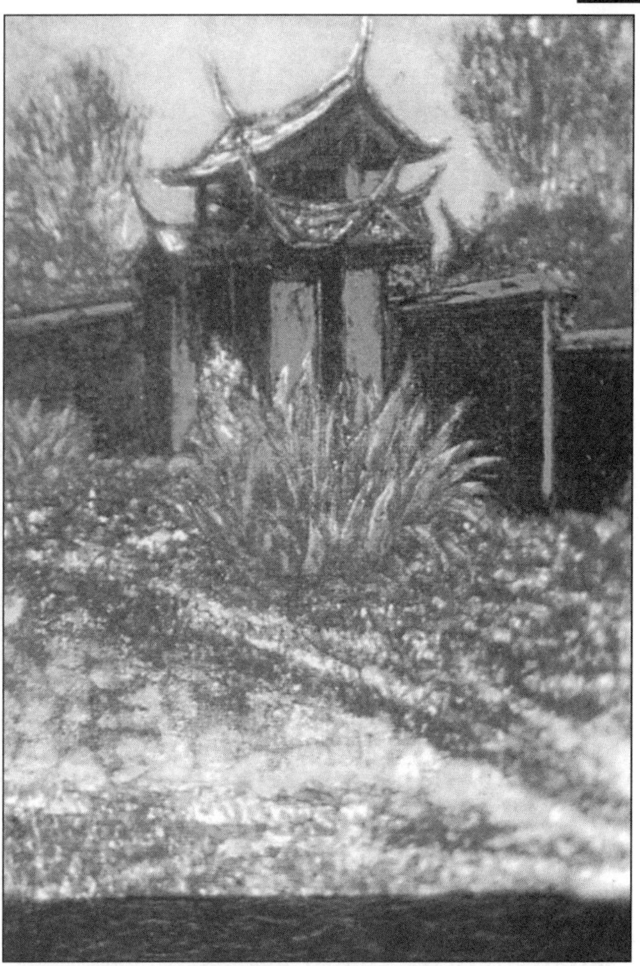

Onchi Koshiro, oban tate-e, approx. 18 1/4" x 14 1/2", "Tainan Koshibyo Sokumon," (Side Gate of Confucian Temple in Taiwan), c. 1936, signed in ink in Japanese, sealed Ko, titled in ink in the image, tape residue and stained along the edges of the margins, small tear in lower margin, creased, $5000-7000.

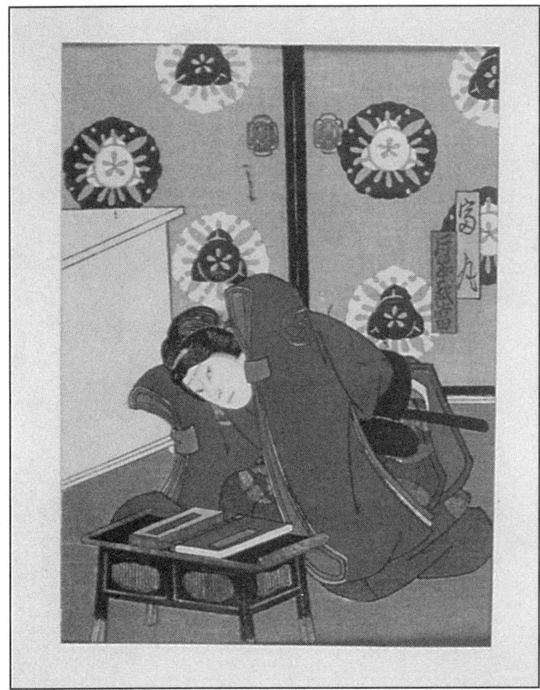

Osaka School (artist unknown), koban, "Kitaoka Gado as Tomimaru," unsigned, c. 1830 , fine impression , color, and condition, $175-225.

R

Raizan Negoro (1887-?)

Rankosai (fl. c. 1805)

Reizan (fl. c. 1871)

Riko (fl. c. 1820s)

Ryukuko (fl. c. 1800s) Utamaro style.

Ryukosai (1772-1816) founder of the Osaka School.

Ryunsai (fl. c. 1788) follower of Kiyonaga.

Ryuson Ogura (fl. c. 1880s) Kiyochika-style.

S

Sadafusa (fl. c. 1825-1850) Utagawa School, pupil of Kunichika.

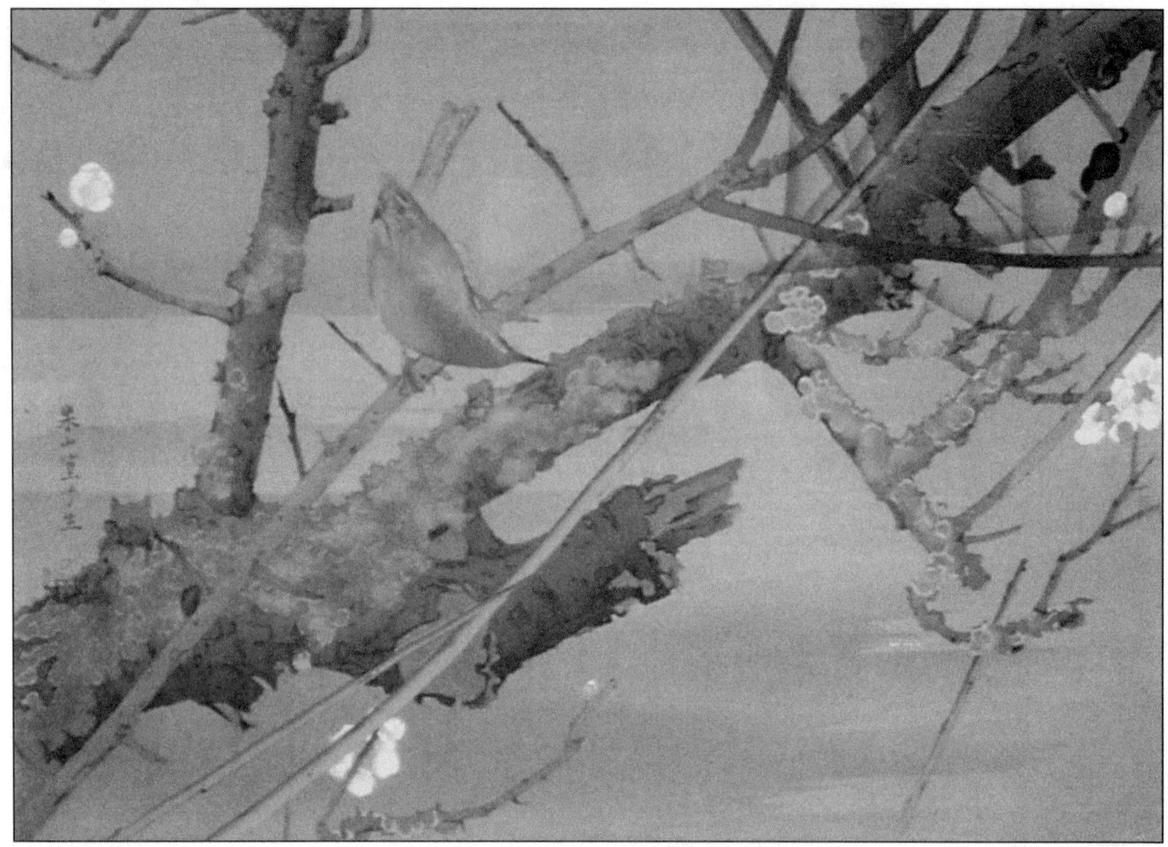

Rakuzan, dai oban yoko-e, 18" x 24", from a limited edition of 150, signed and sealed and titled in pencil, excellent impression, color, and condition, $700-950.

Sadaharu (fl. c. 1830-1844) Osaka School.

Sadahide(1807-1873) Utagawa School, pupil of Kunisada.

Sadahiro (fl. c. 1825-1875) Osaka School.

Sadahiro II (fl. c. 1864-1876) student of Hirosada.

Sadakage (fl. c. 1820s-1830s) Utagawa School, pupil of Kunisada.

Sadamasa (fl. c. 1830s-1840s) Osaka School, pupil of Sadanobu.

Sadamasu II (fl. c. 1830s) pupil of either Kunisada or Kunimasu.

Sadanobu (fl. c. 1730s) worked in Masanobu-style.

Sadanobu (1809-1879) Osaka School.

Sadanobu II (fl. c. 1846-1886) son of Sadanobu.

Sadanobu Hasegawa III (1881-1963) son of Sadanobu II.

Sadataka (fl. c. 1830s) Edo School.

Sadatora (fl. c. 1817-1830s) Utagawa School, pupil of Kunisada.

Sadatsugu (fl. c. 1835-1839) pupil of Kunisada.

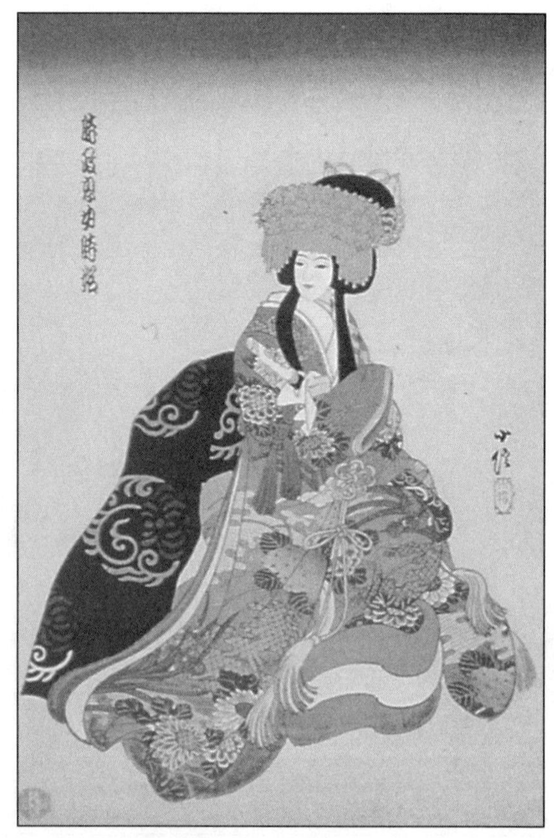

Sadanobu III, oban tate-e, "Bunraku," c. 1955, early edition, right side of diptych, published by Uchida, fine impression, color, and condition, $175-300.

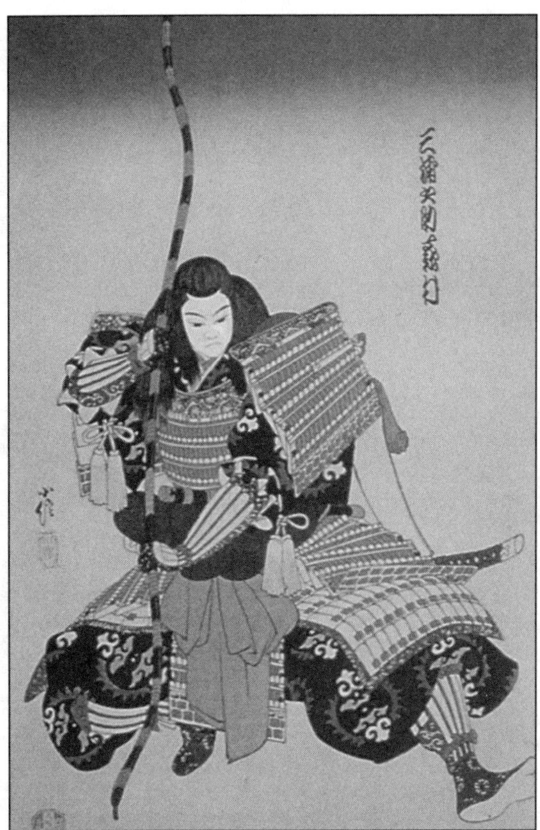

Sadanobu III, oban tate-e, "Bunraku," c. 1955, early edition, left side of diptych, published by Uchida, fine impression, color, and condition, $175-300.

Sadayoshi (fl. c. 1760s) (fl. c. 1850s) (fl. c. 1837-1860s) all Osaka School.

Oban tate-e, "Sawamura Tokiwa as Taruya Osen," dated Tenpo 13 (1842), signed "Kaishuntei Sadayoshi ga," with seal, publisher Wataki, good impression and color, and good overall condition, $700-900.

Sadayuki (fl. c. 1830-1840s) pupil of Sadamasu.

Saito Ioe (1881-1965) woodblock print illustrations pre-WWII.

Saito Kiyoshi (1907-1997)

Kiyoshi Saito was born in 1907, in Sakamoto, Fukushima prefecture. He moved to Otaru in Hokkaido at age five. Later he was an apprentice to a sign painter. From an early age he operated a successful sign painting business in Ataru. He studied drawing with Narita Gyokusen in Otaru. Infatuated with the art world, he sold his business and moved to Tokyo in 1932. He studied Western-style painting at the Hongo Painting Institute. He exhibited oil paintings with Kakujitsukai, Nikakai, Kokugaki, and Tokokai. In 1936, he exhibited with Nihon Hanga Kyokai. Having acceptance of moku hanga in the print division of Kokugakai in 1937 brought about his desire to produce woodblock prints.

In the 20th century, Japanese print makers learned of the Western manner of working, wherein the artist drew, chiseled, and printed himself. Today, many Japanese woodblock prints are created in this manner, with the only major difference being that Japanese artists work with blocks of wood generally cut along the grain rather than across the grain. The mental approach of the modern print artist differs from the Western attitude in that the Japanese artist carves with brush strokes in mind. The graphics created in Japan since World War II have been termed "Creative Prints," and it is in Creative Prints that Saito is an acknowledged master.

Saito was as steeped in the Western tradition of art as he was in the Oriental. In fact, he named Munch and Gauguin amongst his strongest influences. He stated, "It was only through Gauguin that I began to appreciate the qualities of ukiyo-e, and especially those created by Sharaku."

In 1938, at the invitation of Ono Tadashige, he joined Zokei Hanga Kyokai. In that same year, he began the Winter in Aizu series, a group of prints of the snow country in which he lived as a child. He first exhibited his Aizu prints in 1942 under wartime conditions in the upstairs gallery of a brush and paper store. In 1943, he worked with the Asahi Newspaper Company. A chance meeting with Onichi Koshiro at the Asahi office led to an invitation to Ichimokukai and membership, from 1944, in Nihon Hanga Kyokai. In 1946 and 1947, shortly after the war ended, he exhibited with Hiratsuka Un'ichi and Kawanishi Hide in a new gallery opposite the Imperial Hotel in Tokyo. At that show he sold his first prints. In 1948, he exhibited at the Salon Printemps, an exhibition sponsored by Americans as a benefit for Japanese artists. Perhaps part of his success was a postwar phenomenon. In the late 1940s and early 1950s, foreigners, mostly Americans, traipsed through Japan visiting temples, trying the tea ceremony, and trying to comprehend the significance of the rock garden and other elements of traditional Japanese culture. Saito's bold, graceful, simplified expression strengthened their experiences and helped make sense of stone lanterns, tiny shops, temple paths, and whatever it was that Japanese meant at that period in time. His designs were uncomplicated harmonies of lines, spaces, and the peacefulness of soft hues (greens, rusts, shades of black, shades of gray, etc.).

In 1951, he received first prize at the first biennial exhibition of the Modern Art Museum of Sao Paulo, Brazil. Due to the late arrival of the Japanese for the exhibition his print was in competition against Japanese oil paintings and nihon ga. This award to a woodblock print in an international exhibition awakened the Japanese art establishment which had been indifferent to moku-hanga. Saito also won a major prize at the international competition at Ljubljana in 1956. In 1956, he visited the United States. From that time his works were widely exhibited throughout the United States and Europe.

In the 1960s Saito generally worked from several blocks for each print (a different block for each color). He also produced many prints from a single block. Since he could only print one color at a time, he had to lift his paper carefully so it would not shift after each printing. While an unconventional method, its satisfaction lay in the fact that he was

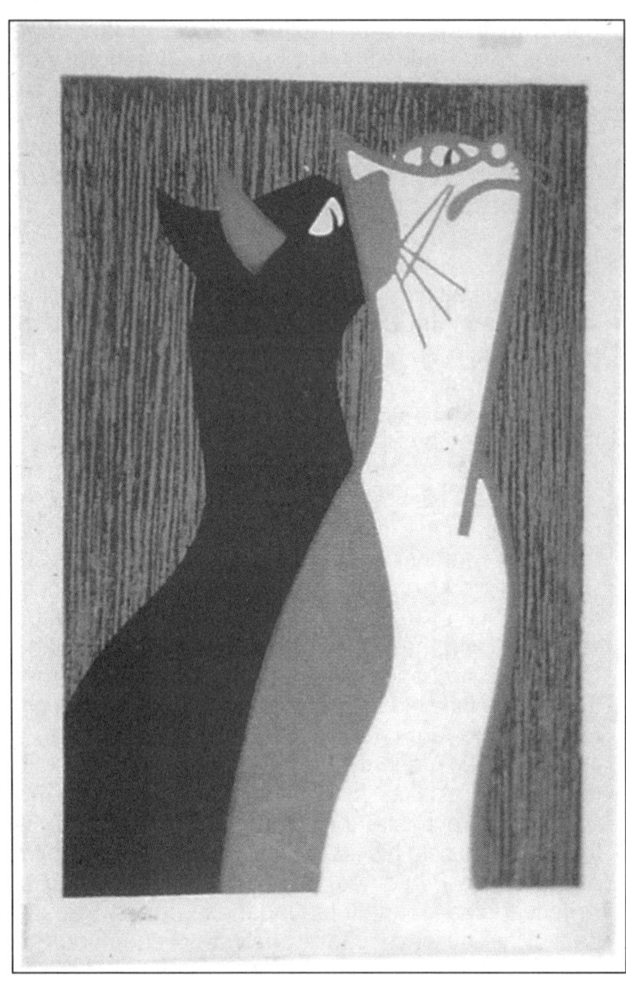

Saito Kiyoshi, oban tate-e, 15 1/2" x 10 1/4", "Steady Gaze," signed in pencil, very good impression, slightly trimmed, tape stains on verso, $1200-1800.

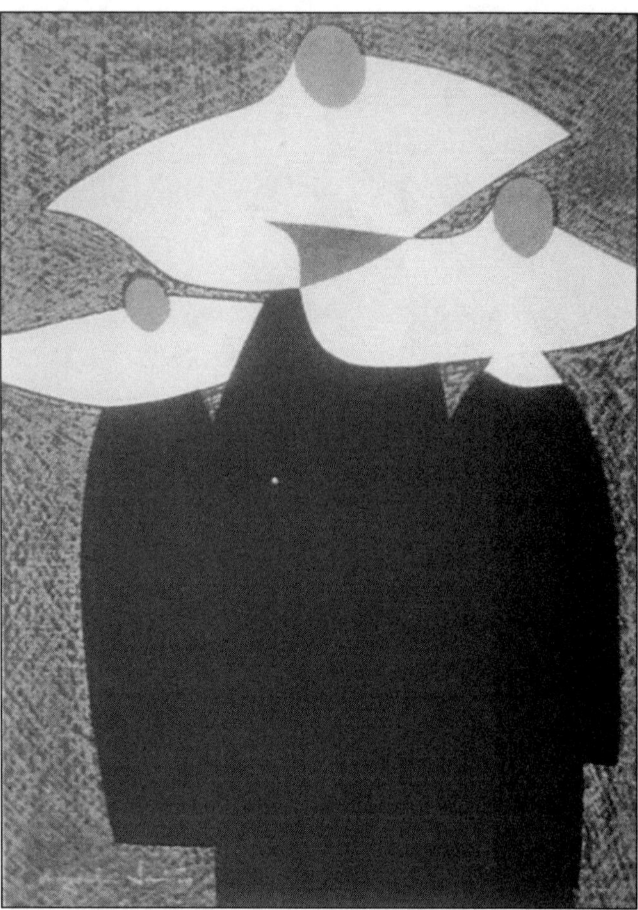

Saito Kiyoshi, woodcut, 26 1/2" x 21 1/4", "Meditation Paris 1960," from an edition of 80, signed in white ink within the image, signed and titled on lower margin, toned, tape stains, $5500-7500.

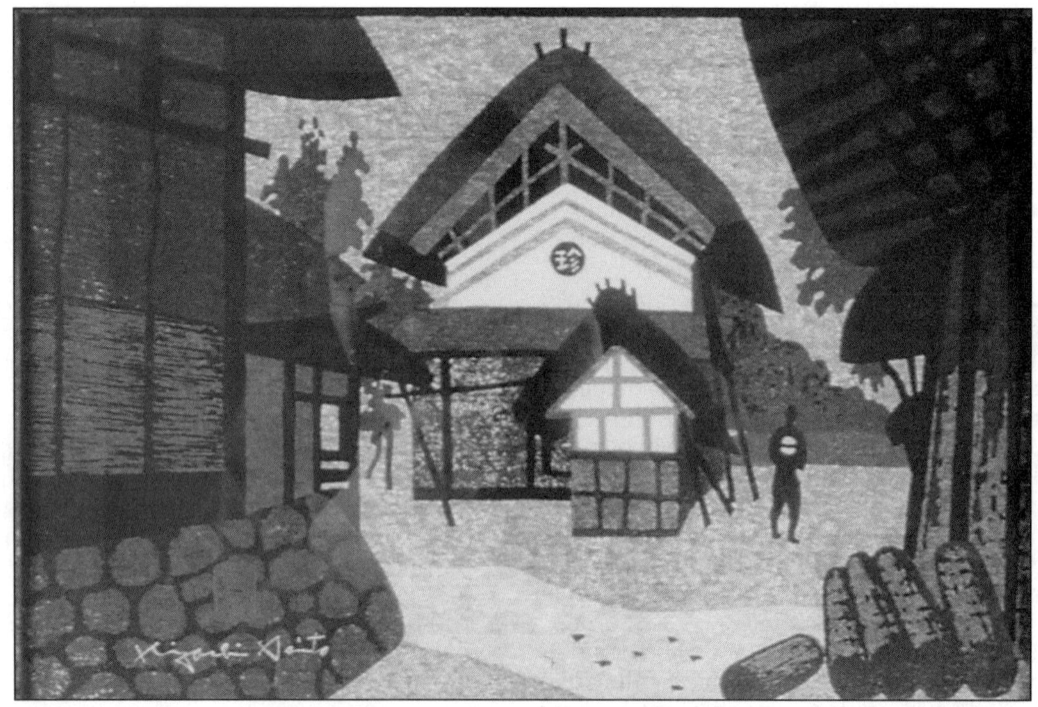

Saito, oban yoko-e, 17" x 11 1/2", signed and sealed in image, c. 1965, fine impression, color, (margins folded under to fit frame), $375-575.

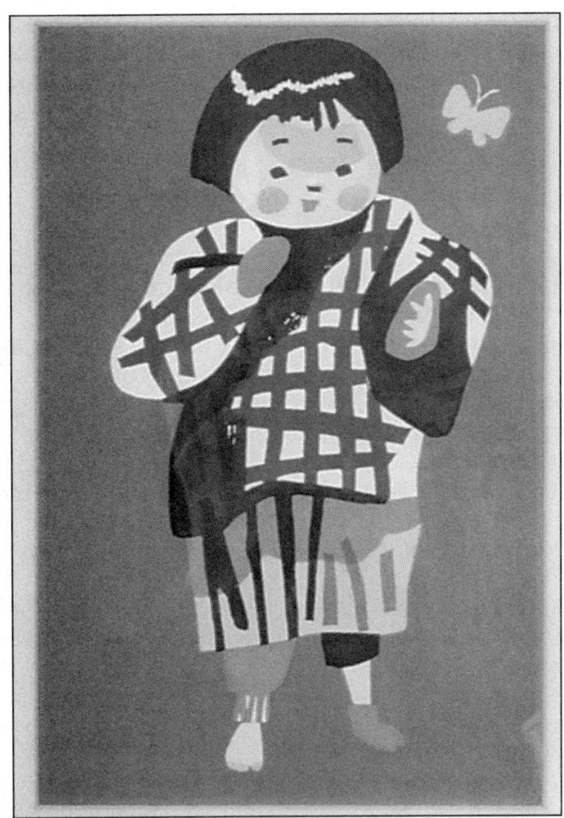

Saito Kiyoshi, oban tate-e, 11 1/2" x 17", "Girl with Butterflies,"c. 1960, very good condition, color, and impression, $450-600.

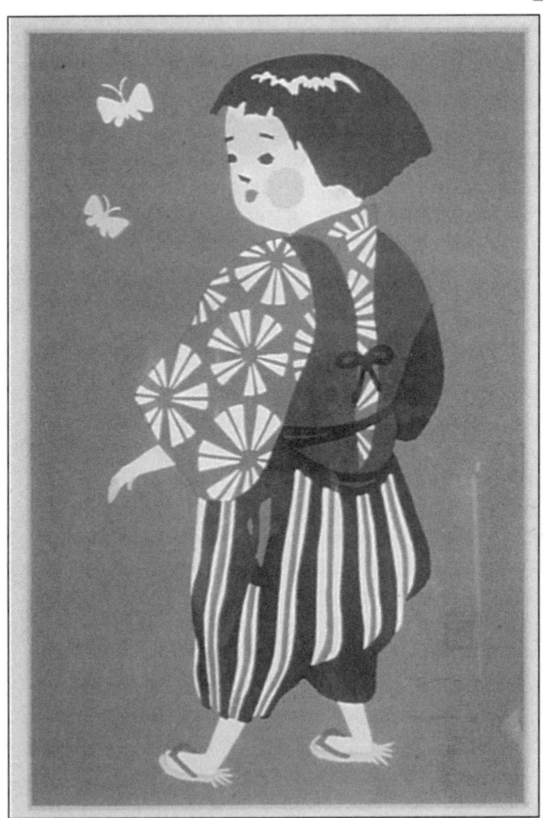

Saito Kiyoshi, oban tate-e, 11 1/2" x 18", "Boy with Butterflies," c. 1960, very good condition, color, and impression, $450-600.

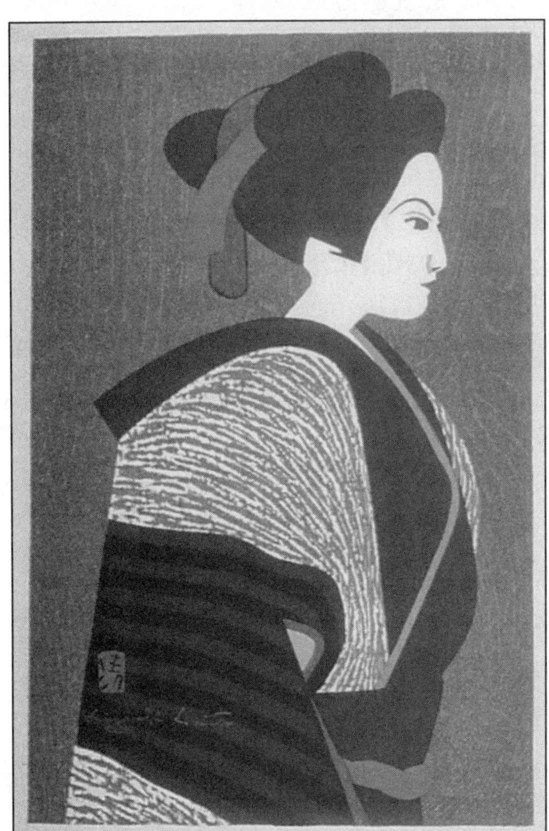

Saito Kiyoshi, oban tate-e, 11 1/2" x 17", "Maiko," c. 1960, signed and sealed Saito, fine impression, color, and condition, $1000-1500.

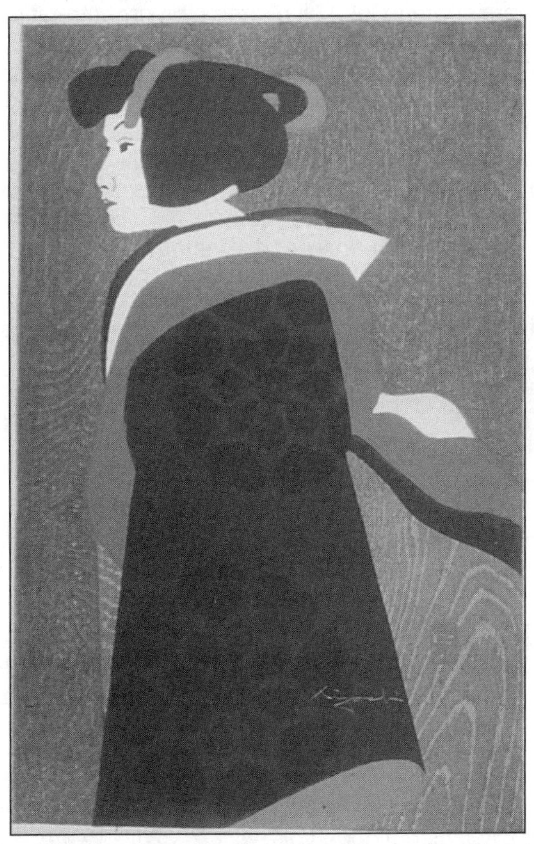

Saito Kiyoshi, oban tate-e, 11 1/2" x 17", "Maiko," c. 1960, signed and sealed Saito, fine impression, color, and condition, $1000-1500.

Saito Kiyoshi continued:

able to gain depths of tone that were difficult to achieve when using a different block for each color. He worked with Katsura cherry and plywood. The choice of wood varied depending on the type of grain needed for his subject and composition. His choice of paper was kizuki hoso, which was generally used for ukiyo-e.

In *Modern Japanese Prints: An Art Reborn* by Oliver Statler, Saito is quoted as follows, "I am amused—and a little annoyed—by people who talk about some of my effects as though they were happy accidents. These people seem to think we modern artists let our medium control us. I scheme and work and sweat over my prints. Making a woodcut is much too strenuous to let accidents determine result."

Saito's mastery of the woodblock medium is easily recognized. By being self-taught, his creative prints were not bound by a teacher's rules. Many times he allowed woodgrain to lend power to his works; other times he rejected grain, laying color on color on color so that the richness and texture of the pigment provided the surface excitement.

From the *Washington Post and Times Herald*, July 28, 1957, "In his best prints, Saito can combine extreme simplicity with a force and vigor that are a delight to the eye. He is a fine example of an Oriental artist who, while studying the techniques and ideas of the West, still retains the expression and character of his homeland. This is an achievement particularly among modern Oriental artists, many of whom seem to lose all of their own great traditions in absorbing the art of the West."

Time, September 7, 1959, "The most popular of the moderns, Kiyoshi Saito has achieved a success almost worthy of the top ukiyo-e artist." In 1955, he exhibited 67 of his pieces in the United States, and in a grand gesture gave them all to the University of Michigan. In debt, like most of his contemporaries, to Western influence and Western audience, Saito lately visited ancient Kyoto to recapture special Japanese qualities he feels his work lacks, ruefully muses: "We have lost our Japanese origin. I keep on going to Kyoto to rediscover them." But to a Western eye, his origins are unmistakable and inimitable.

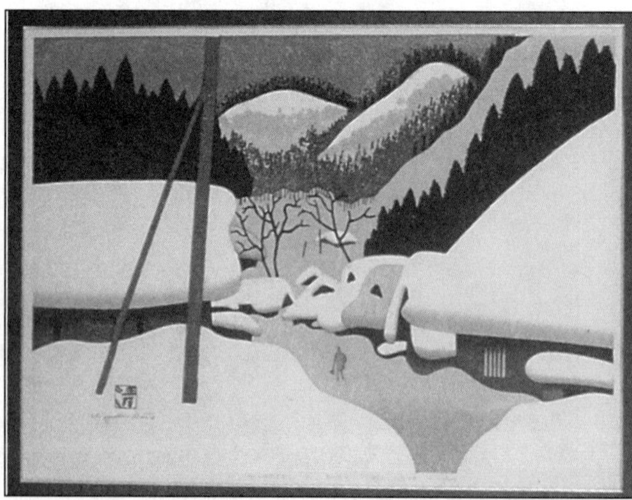

Saito Kiyoshi, dai oban yoko-e, 17" x 23", "Winter In Aizu (33)," title and number in lower margin,from an edition of 100 dated 1978, fine impression, color, and condition $3500-5500.

Dai oban tate-e, "Maiko, Kyoto," series L, 1966, signed in white ink, very good impression, color, and condition, $3500-4500.

Dai oban tate-e, "Iyacko-in Kyoto," 1966 from an edition of 50, signed and sealed, good impression, color, and condition, $1500-2500.

Oban tate-e, 23 1/2" x 18", "Maiko Kyoto," series F, from a limited edition of 200, dated 1961, signed in white ink "Kyoshi Saito," with red seal, very good impression, color, and condition, $3000-5000.

Oban tate-e, 23" x 18", "Maiko Kyoto," series J, 1961, from a limited edition of 300 signed in black ink "Kiyoshi Saito," with red Kiyo seal, good impression and color, slightly trimmed and toned, $2000-3000.

Oban yoko-e, "White Horse," unlimited edition, signed and sealed, good impression, color, and condition, $300-500.

Oban yoko-e, "Snow in Aizu," signed and sealed, good impression, color, and condition, light paper backing, $600-900.

Oban yoko-e, "Teahouse," unlimited, signed and sealed, good impression, color, and condition, $300-500.

Dai oban tate-e, "Maiko, Kyoto," series L, 1966, signed in white ink, very good impression, color, and condition, $3500-4500.

Dai oban tate-e, "Iyacko-in Kyoto," 1966 from an edition of 50, signed and sealed, good impression, color, and condition, $1500-2500.

Oban yoko-e, "White Horse," unlimited edition, signed and sealed, good impression, color, and condition, $300-500.

Saito Ryo (b. 1941) serigraphy, limited editions.

Sakamoto Koichi (b. 1932) etching, limited editions.

Sasajima Kihei (1906-1993) woodblock, limited editions.

"White Road," embossed, signed in pencil, from an edition of 50, $1200-1600.

Sato Hiroshi (b. 1923) semi -abstract images.

Seiho Takeuchi (1864-1942)

Seiko (fl. 1810s-1820s) Osaka School.

Seiko early 20th c., kacho-e.

Seitei Watanabe (1851-1918)

Sekijo (fl. ca 1800-1807)

Sekino Jun'ichiro (1914-1988) etching, lithograph, woodblock, limited editions.

Seimiya Hitoshi (1886-1969)

Seimiya Noabumi (b. 1917)

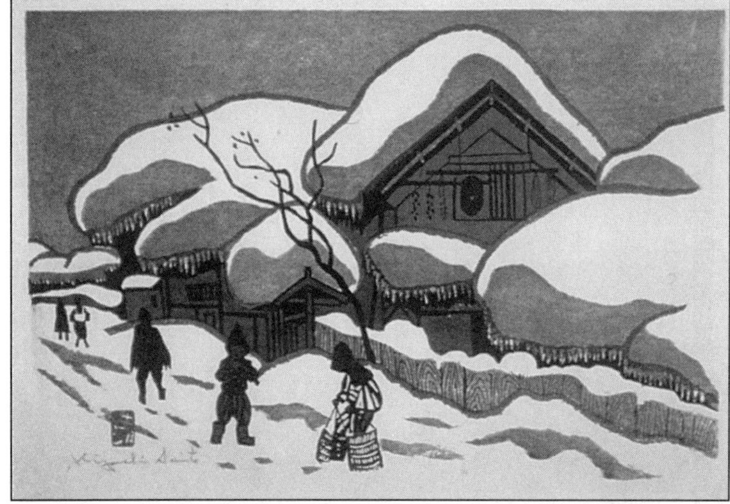

Saito Kiyoshi, oban yoko-e, 15 1/2" x 11", "Aizu," original folder, "Hand Carved And Printed By Mr. Saito", attached to back of the print is the Saito label-"self-carved self-printed K. Saito" with his seal, c. 1948, fine impression, color, condition, center crease, $2000-3000.

Saito Kiyoshi, oban yoko-e, "Aizu," c. 1960, (sealed on back of print), signed and sealed within image, fine impression, color, and condition, $1000-1500.

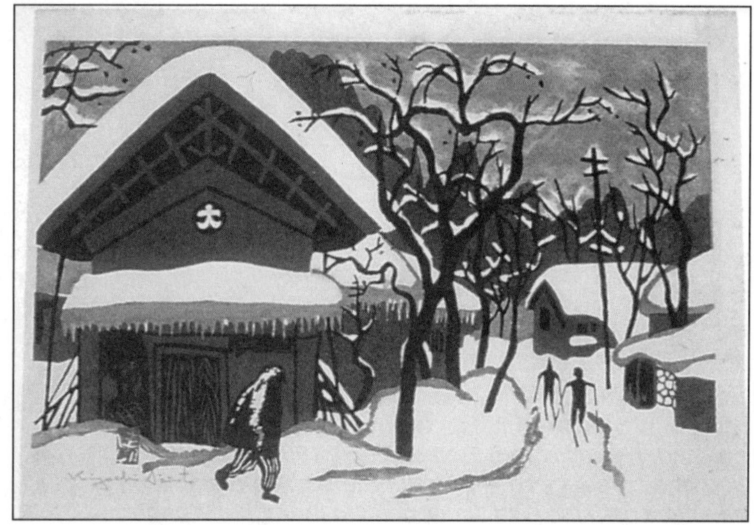

Senman (fl. ca. 1820s) Osaka School.

Sharaku (fl. 1784-1785)

Sharaku Toshusai produced 145 prints of kabuki actors during 1794 and 1795. All of his prints were published by Tsutaya Juzaburo, the same publisher who assisted Utamaro in becoming a leader in the depiction of beautiful women. Departing from the idealized depictions of actors that had been conventional, Sharaku's images were highly expressive by being somewhat exaggerated. He captured a balance between the actors face and the face demanded by the role. Because he declined to depict the popular actors of the time in an idealized form, he angered the fans of kabuki and his works met with rejection, and he withdrew from ukiyo-e. His prints are divided into four categories:

Most prized is a series of 28 prints dated 5th month of 1794.

The second period consists of 38 prints from the 7th and 8th months of 1794.

The third period consists of 64 prints dated the 11th month of 1794.

The fourth period consists of 15 prints dating 1795.

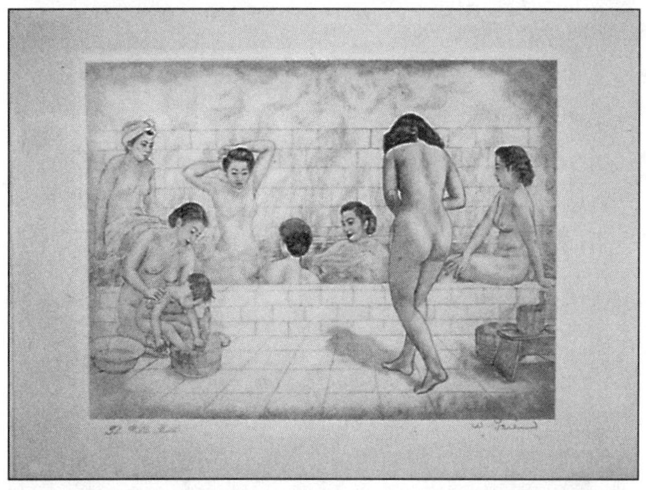

Seiler Willy, etching, 12 1/2" x 15 1/4", "The Public Bath," from a limited edition of 180, (when new this sold for $3.90), c. 1955, $175-225.

Shibakuni (fl. 1821-1826) pupil of Yoshikuni.

Shibuya Eiichi (b. 1928) etching, limited editions.

Shigefusa ((fl. c. 1740s-1760s)

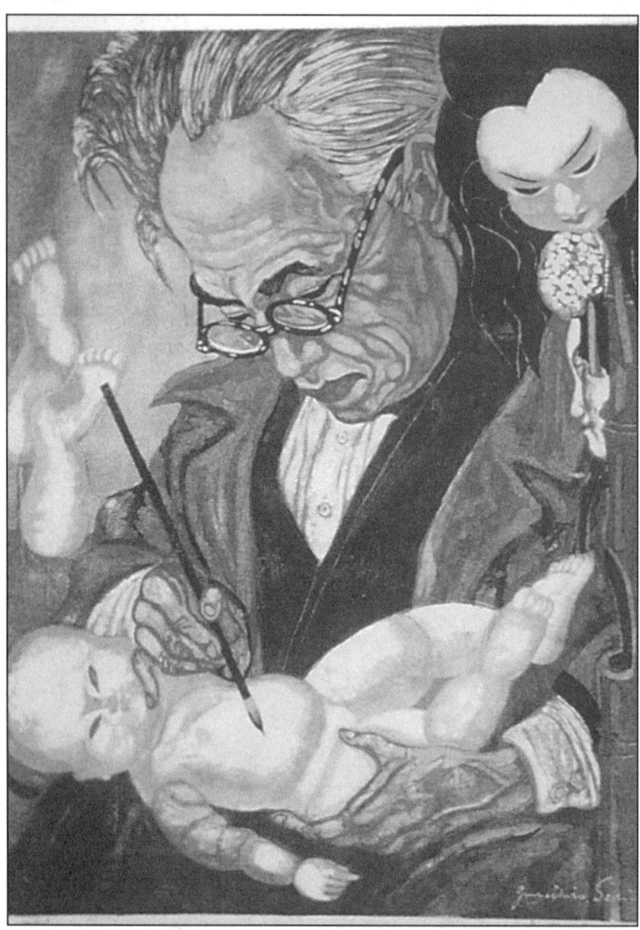

Sekino, oban tate-e, approx. 10 1/4" x 24", "The Doll Maker," signed in white ink in Roman script "Jun. Sekino" and in pencil "Junichiro Sekino," 1956 from an edition of 30, very good impression, foxing, tape stains on all edges of verso with stains coming through the paper, $4000-6000.

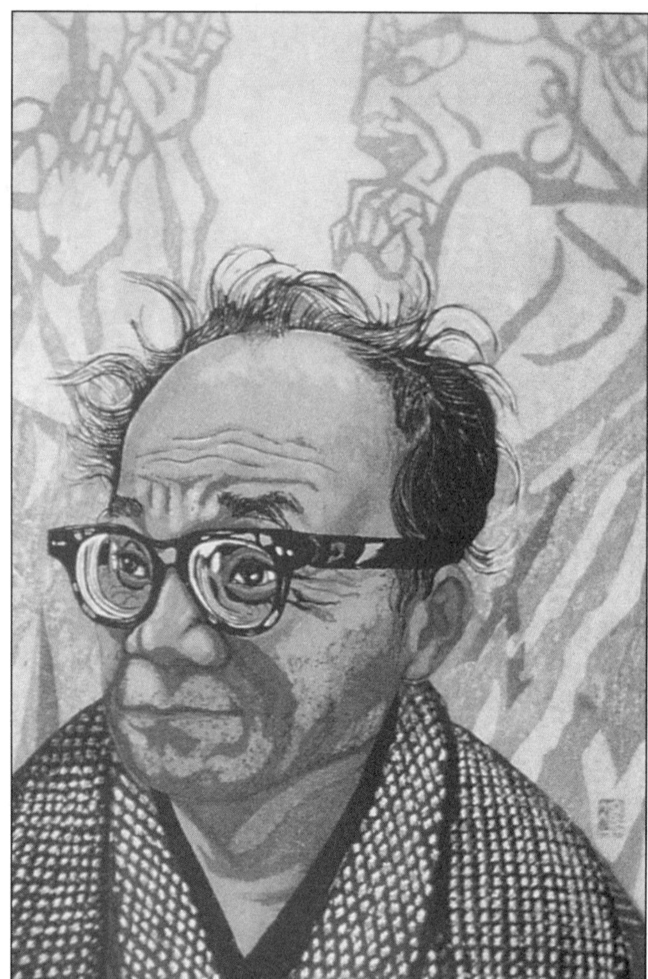

Sekino Jun'ichiro; 30" x 24 5/8", portrait of Munakata Shiko, c. 1968, signed in pencil in Roman script "Jun. Sekino," form an edition of 118, sealed Jun, $2500-3500.

Sekino Jun'ichiro, approx. 21 1/2" x 26 1/4", "Eiza to Matsuomaru," (Eiza and Matsuomaru), signed in pencil in Roman script "Junichiro Sekino," sealed Jun in the image, from and edition of 30, very toned, soiled, and foxed, $800-1200.

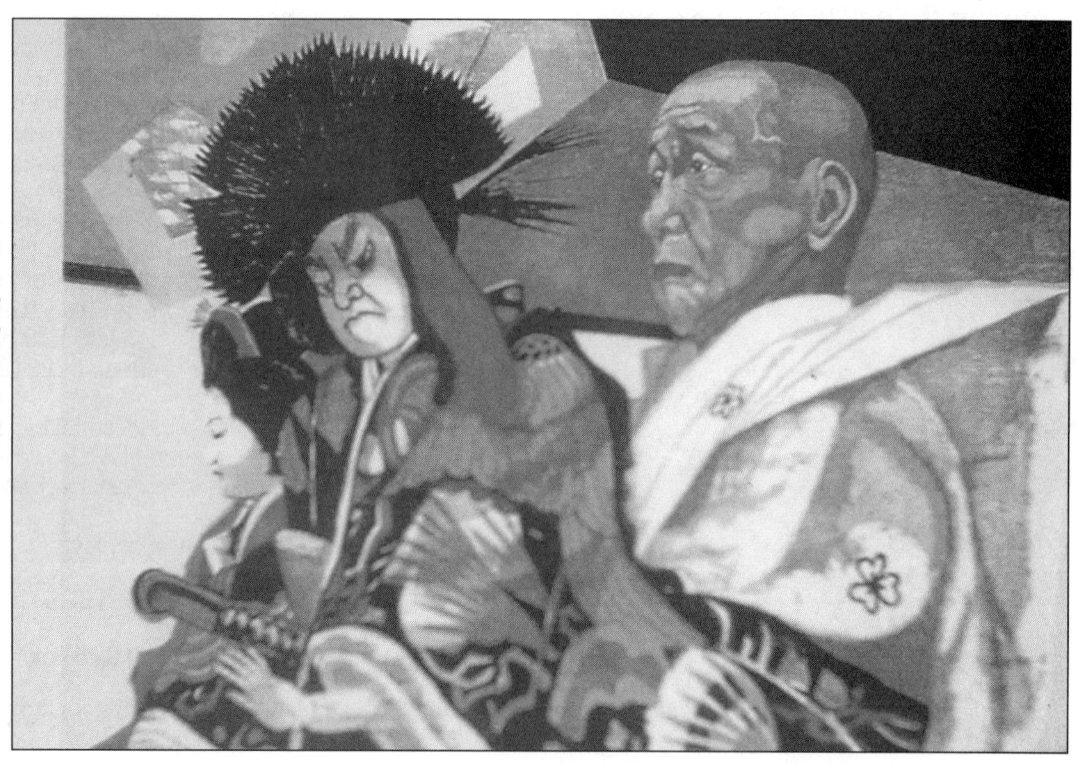

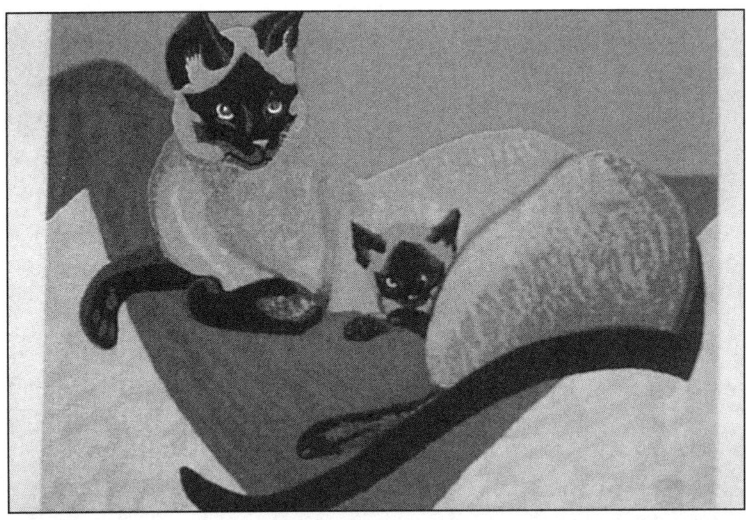

Sekino Jun'ichiro, approx. 16 3/4" x 21 1/2", "Siamese Cats," 1960, from an edition of 100, signed and dated in pencil, good overall condition, $2500-3500.

Shigefusa II (fl. c. 1850) Osaka School.

Shigeharu (1803-1853) pupil of Shigenobu.

Shigehiro (fl. c. 1865-1878) Osaka School.

Shigemaro (fl. c. 1816) Osaka School.

Shigemasa (1739-1830)

Shigenaga (fl. c. 1697-1756)

Shigenao (fl. 1824-1841) Osaka School, became Nobukatsu in 1829.

Shigenobu (fl. c. 1716-1736) Torii-style/(fl. 1720-1740), Masanobu-style/(fl. c. 1724-1735), Nishikawa-style/(fl. c. 1764-1779), Harunobu- style/(1787-1832) pupil of Hokusai.

Shigenobu II (fl. 1820s) pupil of Shigenobu/ name used by Hiroshige II.

Shikan (fl. c. 1778-1838) name used by Nakamura Utaemon III.

Shikimaru (fl. c. 1810) pupil of Tsukimaro.

Shima Seien (1893-1970) bijin-ga prints.

Shima Tamami (b. 1937)

Shimamaryu (fl. c. 1830) Osaka School.

Shinogawa Takumi (b. 1908) stencil, woodblock, limited editions.

Shinoda Toko (b. 1913) lithograph.

Lithograph, "Wood Sprite," from an edition of 70, signed and dated "Toko Shinoda '69, very good condition, $1500-2500.

Shinsui Ito (1898-1972) famous for prints of beautiful women and landscapes.

Shiseki (1712-1786) Nagasaki School.

Shodo Kawarazaki (1889-1973) flower prints.

Shodo bijin-ga.

Shokosai (fl. c. 1795-1809) one of the founders of the Osaka School.

Shotei Takahashi (aka Hiroaki) (1871-1945)

Shoun Yamato (1870-1965)

Shucho (fl. c. 1790s-early 1800s) pupil of Buncho.

Shuho Yamakawa (1898-1944) noted for bijin-ga.

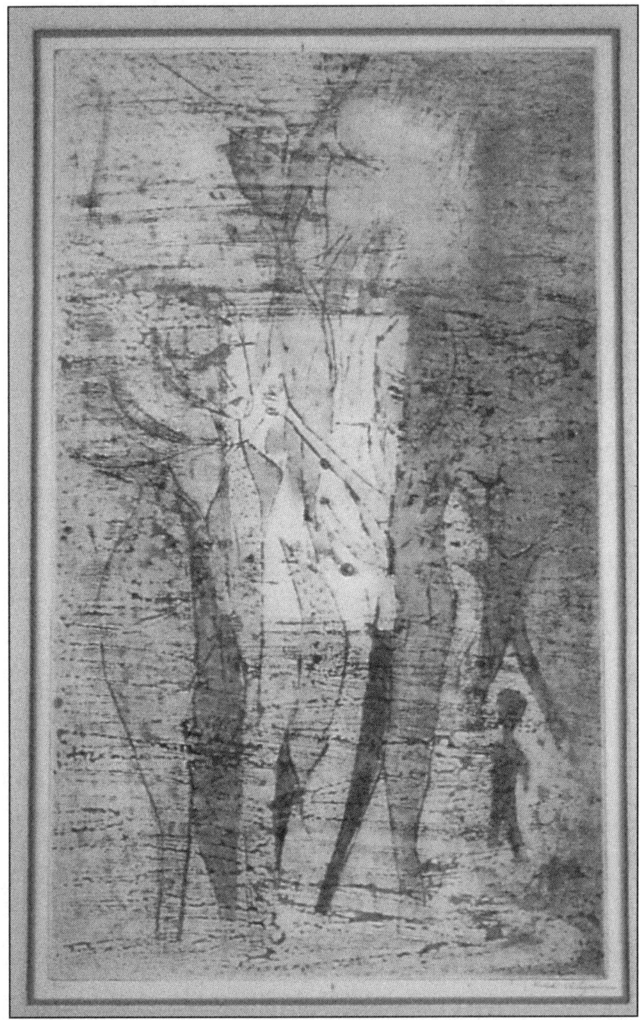

Shibuya Eiichi, etching, 15 1/4" x 24 1/2", from an edition of 50, excellent condition, $400-600.

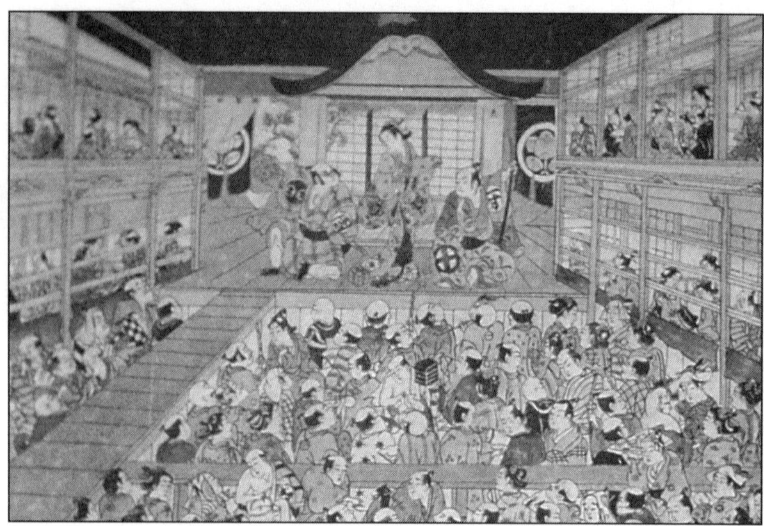

Shigenaga, dai oban yoko-e, approx. 13 1/4" x 17 1/2", a perspective print of the interior of Ichimuraza theater, publisher Izutsuya San'emon, trimmed, faded, creased, backed, $2000-3000.

Shujin (fl. c. 1858-1861) pupil of Hiroshige, kacho-e.

Shuncho (fl. ca. 1815-1823) pupil of Shunkosai.

Shuncho Gajuken (fl. c. 1820s) Osaka School.

Shuncho Katsukawa (fl. c. 1780-1795) pupil of Shunkosai.

Shundo (fl. c. 1780-1792) pupil of Shunsui and Shunco.

Shunei (fl. c. 1810s-1820s) Osaka School.

Shunei (1762-1819) pupil of Katsukawa Shunsho, leader of the Katsukawa School.

Shunjo (fl. c. 1830s) Osaka School.

Shunju (fl. 1828-1829) Osaka School, pupil of Hokuei.

Shunkei (fl. c. 1840) Osaka School.

Shunkin (fl. c. 1862) Osaka School.

Shunko name used by Hokushu from 1810-1818.

Shunko (1743-1812) pupil of Shunsho, Katsukawa School.

Shunko II name used by Shusen (1762-1830) after 1812.

Shunkyo (fl. c. 1914) Osaka School.

Shunkyo (fl. c. 1800s) pupil of Shunsho and Shuntei.

Shunman (1757-1820) pupil of Shigemasa.

Shunpo (fl. c. 1820s) Osaka School.

Shunsei (fl. c. 1820s) Osaka School, pupil of Shunshi.

Shunsen (1762-c. 1830) Katsukawa School, pupil of Shunei.

Shunsen (fl. c. 1780-1790s) Katsukawa School, pupil of Shunsho.

Shunsen Natori (1886-1960) noted for actor portraits.

Okubi-e, Bando Hikosaburo as Matsuo in the play Sugawa wearing a white kimono decorated with pine; sealed Natori, signed "Shunsen," published by S. Watanabe, good condition, $500-700.

Okubi-e, Ichikawa Uzaemon XI, oban tate-e, mica ground, signed and sealed, published by Watanabe, c. 1920s, good condition, $700-900.

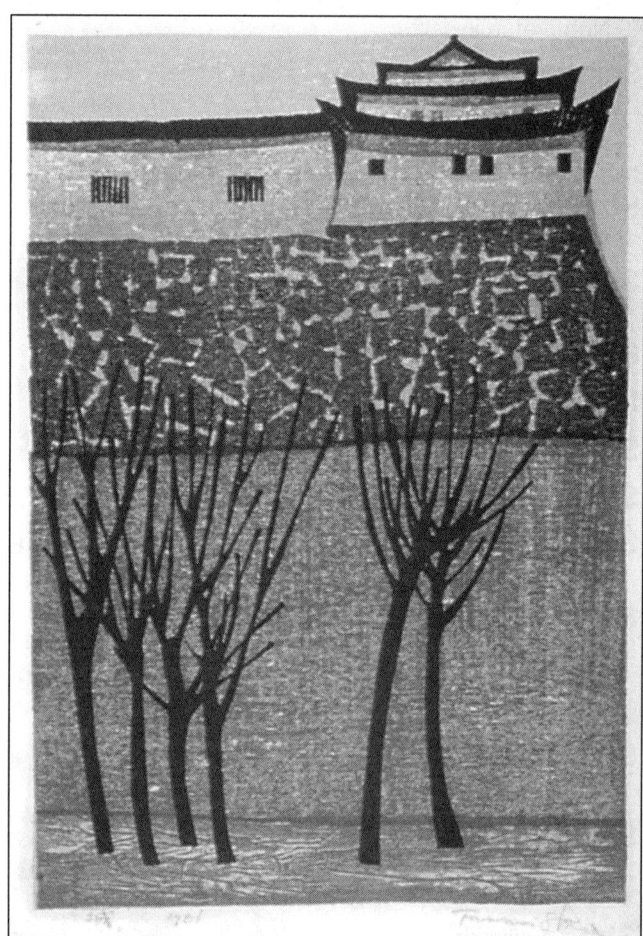

Shima Tamami, oban tate-e, "Castle," dated 1961, signed on lower margin, fine impression, color, and condition, $400-600.

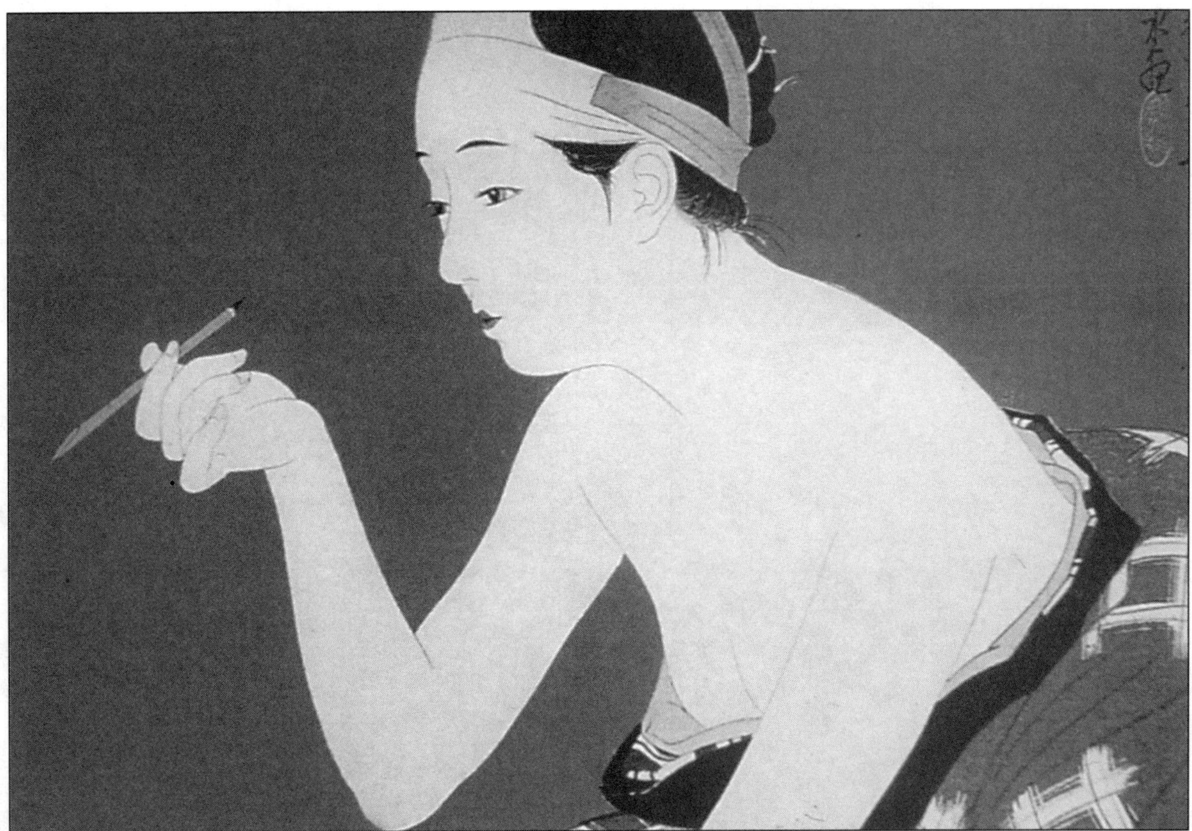

Shinsui Ito, dai oban yoko-e, an actress applying sumi to her eyebrows with a brush, red ground, signed "Shinsui ga," sealed Shinsui, published by Watanabe, dated Showa 3 (1928), very good impression and color, good overall condition, $7000-9500.

Shinsui Ito, oban, "Taikyo," (Woman in Red Robe), a woman in a red nagajuban, dated Taisho gonen shichigatsu shi-hitsu (July 1916, preliminary brush), published by Watanabe, from an edition of 150, signed "Shinsui' with seal, very good impression, print browned overall, $5000-8000.

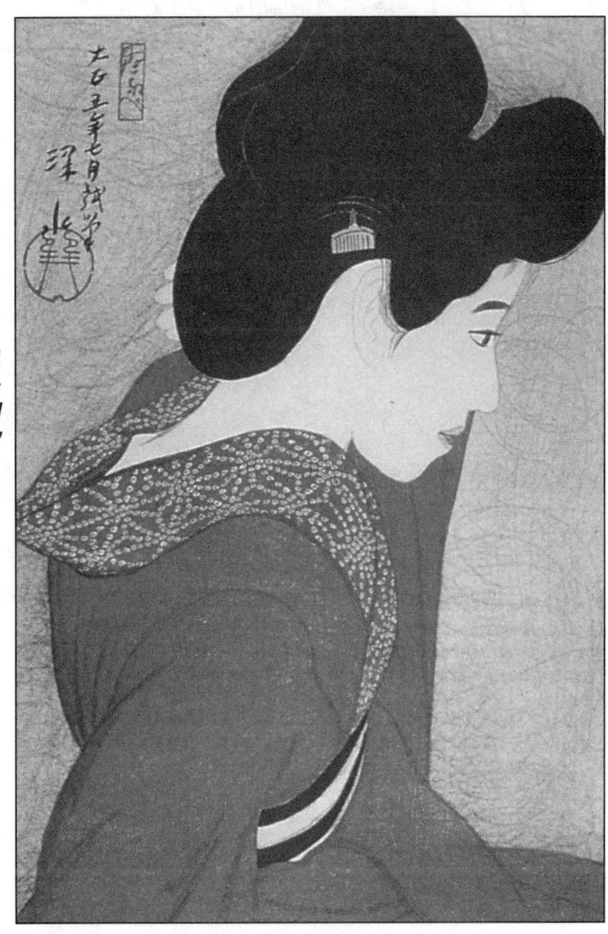

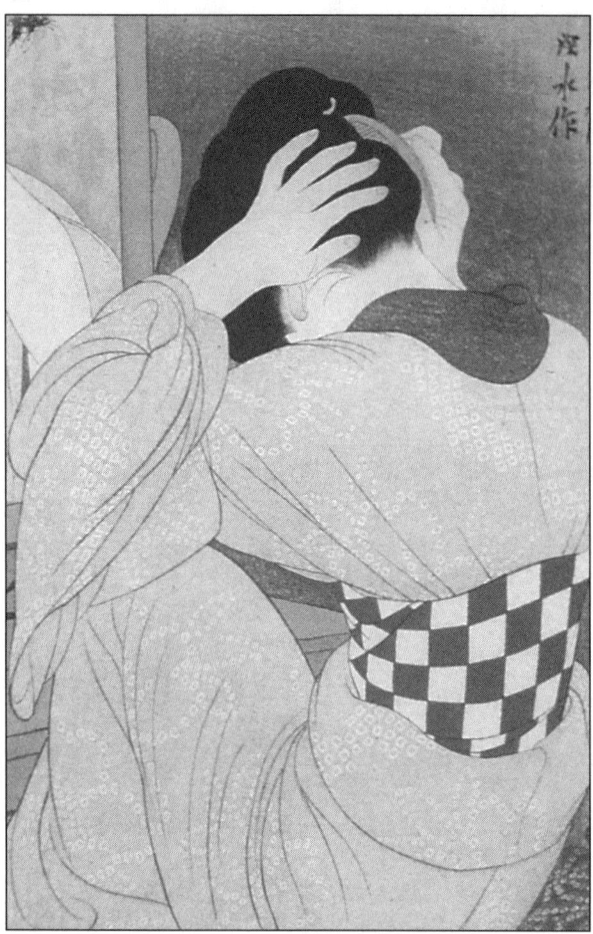

Shinsui Ito,dai oban tate-e, "Datemaki no Onna," (Woman with Under-Sash), a woman in a pink kimono with under-sash seated before a mirror putting a comb in her hair, signed "Shinsui saku," dated Taisho 10 (1921) from a limited edition of 200, published by Watanabe, good impression and color, slightly toned, mica rubbed, slightly soiled, $4000-6000.

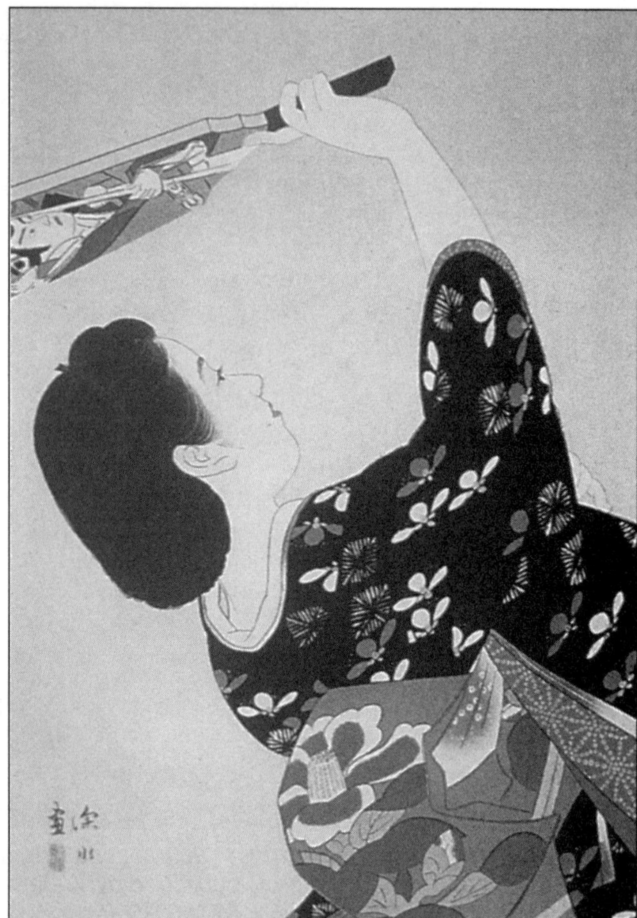

Shinsui Ito, oban tate-e, approx. 17 1/4" x 11", "Gendai Binjinshu Dai Nishu: Hitomi," (Second series of Modern Beauties: Pupil of the Eye), signed "Shinsui ga," dated 1936, publisher Watanabe, very good impression and color, mica rubbed, $6500-9500.

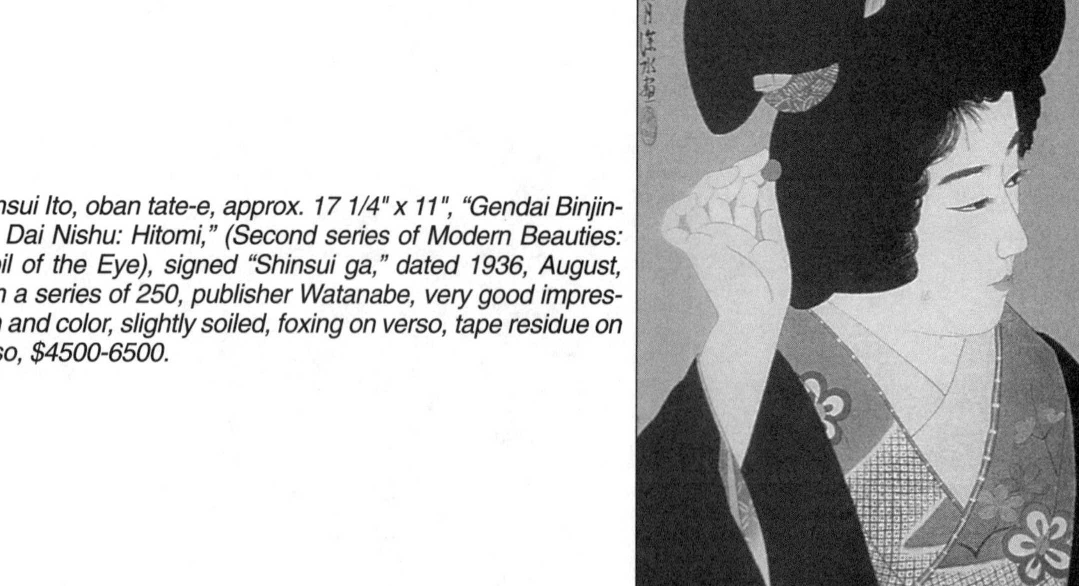

Shinsui Ito, oban tate-e, approx. 17 1/4" x 11", "Gendai Binjinshu Dai Nishu: Hitomi," (Second series of Modern Beauties: Pupil of the Eye), signed "Shinsui ga," dated 1936, August, from a series of 250, publisher Watanabe, very good impression and color, slightly soiled, foxing on verso, tape residue on verso, $4500-6500.

Shinsui Ito, four panel table screen with calendar, a woodblock print on each panel, the 2 prints of Bijin by Shinsui Ito, the calendar year is 1936, all original, print size 5" x 3", fine color, each print laid down, the panels are silk brocade, $750-1275.

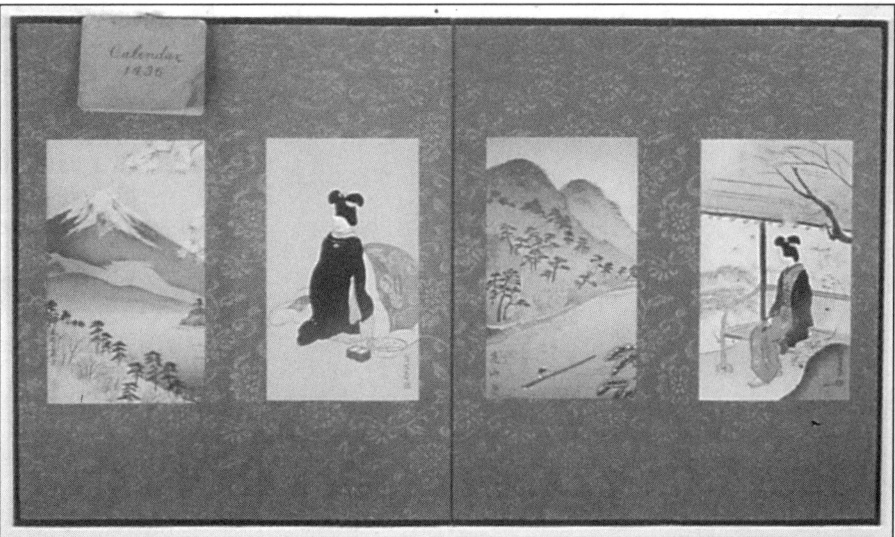

Shunsen Natori continued:

Okubi-e, Nakamura Tomijuro IV as a dancing kamuro, oban tate-e, dated Showa 27 (1952), good condition, slightly toned, $450-600.

Shuntei (1770-1820) Katsukawa school.

Shuntoku(fl. c. 1820s) Katsukawa School.

Shunyo name used by Hokei from 1813-1818.

Shun' Yosai go of Hokkei.

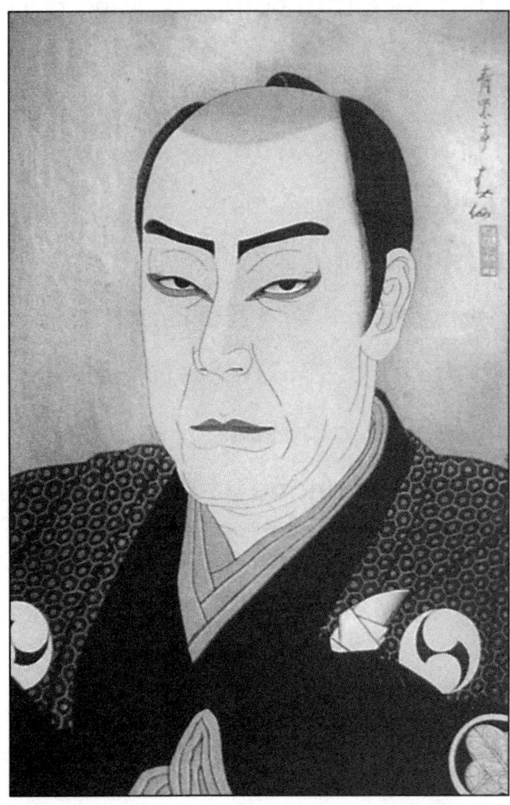

Shunsen Natori, oban tate-e, "Bando Jusaburo III as Oboshi Yuranosuke,"published by Watanabe, dated Showa 27 (1952), good overall condition, glue stains on verso along edges, $1500-2500.

Shunzan (fl. c. 1827-1829) Katsukawa School, pupil of Shunsho.

Simon, T. Frederick (Simon, T.F.) ( )

Sora Mitsuaki (b. 1933)

Sozan Ito (1884-?) kacho-e.

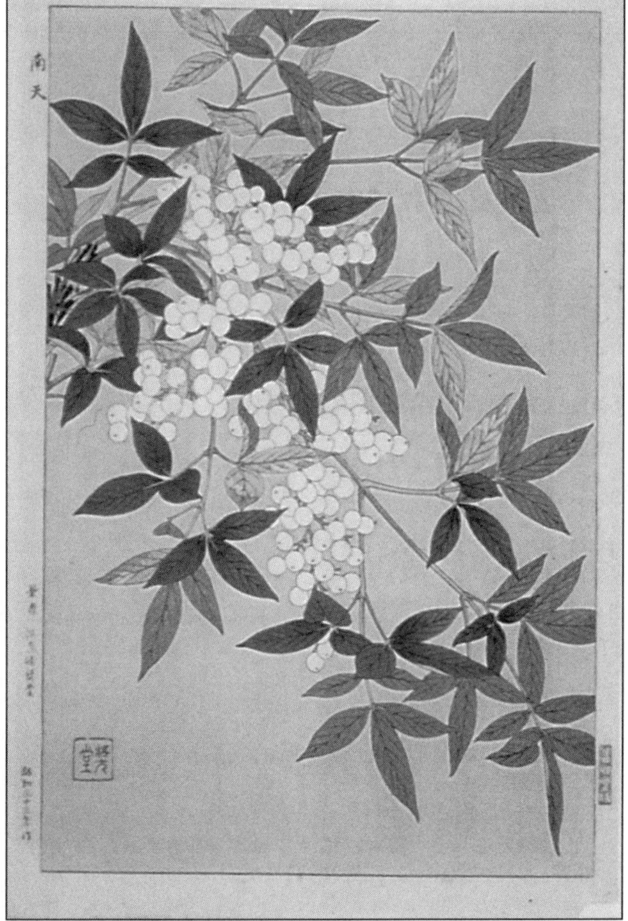

Shodo Kawarazaki, oban tate-e, 15 1/2" x 10 3/4", "Berries and Foliage," early edition print 1958, fine color, condition, and impression, $175-275.

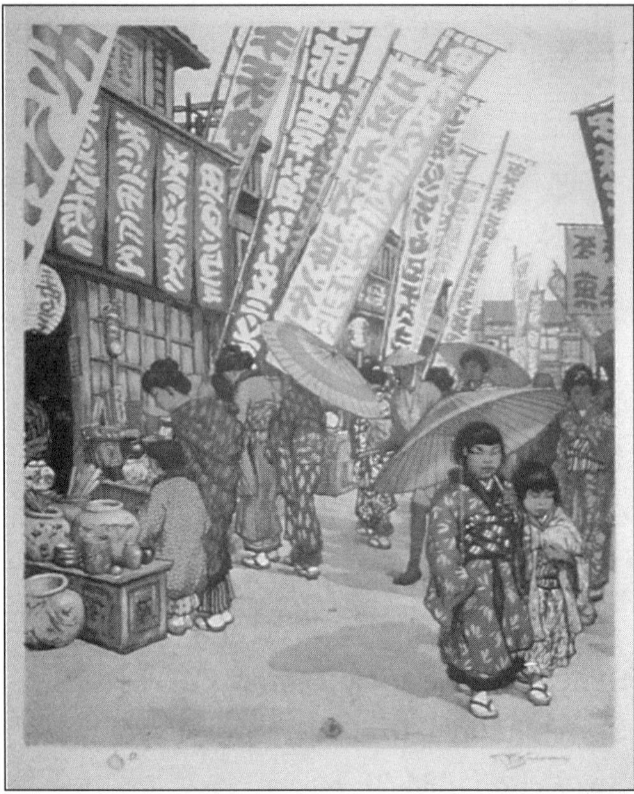

Simon, T.F., dai oban tate-e, "Scene of Tokyo," c. 1930, signed in pencil and sealed, and sealed in print, (Japanese paper with kiku mon water mark), excellent color, impression, and condition, $700-1000.

Suizan Miki (1887-1957)

Sukenobu (1671-1751) member of the Kyoto School.

Suzuki Hiroshi (b. 1933) landscapes.

Suzuki Kason (1860-1919) illustrator, ukiyo-e.

Suzuki Shonen (1848-1918)

T

Tadakiyo (1875-1941)

Taito II (fl. c. 1810-1853) pupil of Hokusai (Hokusai was Taito I).

Tajima Hiroyuki (1911-1984) illuminescent prints.

Takahashi Hiroaki (see Shotei)

Takehisa Yumeji (1884-1934)

Takeuchi Seiho (1864-1942)

Tamakuni (fl. 1823) Osaka School.

Tanaka Kyokichi (1892-1915)

Tanaka Ryo (1884-1974)

Tanaka Ryohei (b. 1933) etching, limited editions.

Terauchi Manjiro (1890-1964)

Terazaki Kogyo (1866-1919)

Terushige (fl. c. 1715-1725) Katsukawa School.

Toboragi Kogan (1882-1927)

Tokuriki Tomichiro (b. 1902)

Tomihari Hiroshi (b. 1936)

Tomikuni (fl.c. 1821-1822) Osaka School.

Tominobu (fl. mid. 18th century) Miyagawa School.

Tomoka Eisen (1864-1905)

Tomoyuki (fl. c. 1850s) Osaka School.

Torii Kiyomitsu (Torii IX) (b. 1938)

Torii Kiyotada (Torii VII) (1875-1941)

Torii Tadamasa (see Ueno Tadamasa)

Torin I (fl. late 18th century) founder of the Tsutsumi School.

Torin II (fl. c. 1789-1801)

Torin III (c. 1743-1820)

Toshihide (see Migata Toshihide)

Toshikata (see Mizuno Toshikata)

Toshinobu (fl. c. 1717-1750) pupil of Masanobu.

Toshinobu (fl. c. 1857-1886) pupil of Yoshitoshi.

Toshiyoshi (fl. c. 1890s)

Toyohara Chikanobu (1838-1912) (Hashioto Chikanobu, aka Yoshu Chikanobu), pupil of Kunichika.

Toyoharu (1735-1825) founder of the Utagawa School.

Toyohide (fl. c. 1839-1841) Osaka School.

Toyohiro Utagawa (1763-1828) Toyohiro's work is delicate and soft, detached and wistful. He was Hiroshige's teacher.

Toyohisa (fl. c. 1801-1818) Utagawa School, pupil of Toyoharu.

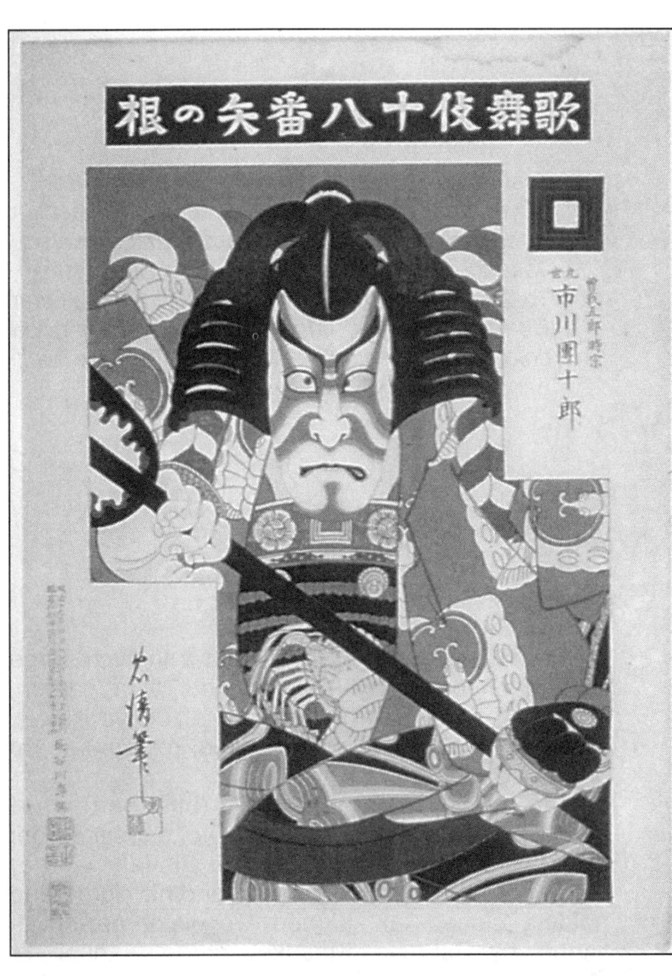

Tadakiyo, oban tate-e, from the series Kabuki Juhachiba, 18 plays, seal Garaku, dated Meiji , fine impression, color, and condition, $1000-1500.

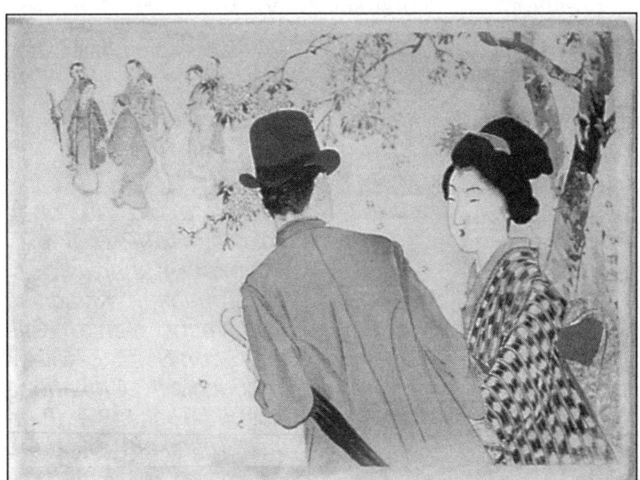

Takeuchi Keishu, oban yoko-e, 11 1/2" x 8 1/2" (Kiyokata Kaburagi, Eisen Tomioka, Kiyochika Kobayashi, Hanko Kajita, Kason Suzuki, Keishu Takeuchi, Chikanobu Yoshu, Toshimine Tsutsui, Toshikata Mizuno), 24 woodblock illustrations for Romantic Novels, fine impressions, very good color and condition, mica, gauffrage, late Meiji period c. 1900, $2500-4500.

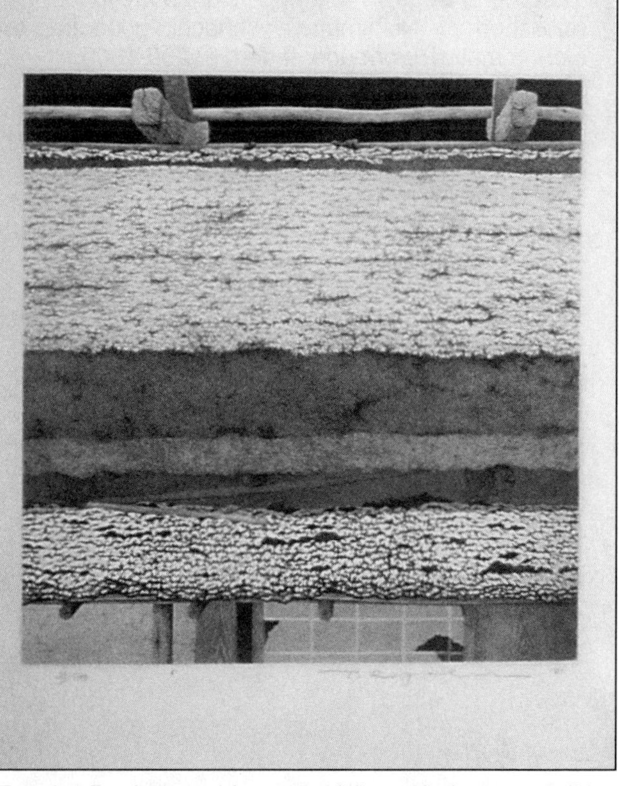

Tanaka Ryohei, etching, 18 1/4" x 19", from an edition of 100, dated 1981, excellent condition, $450-650.

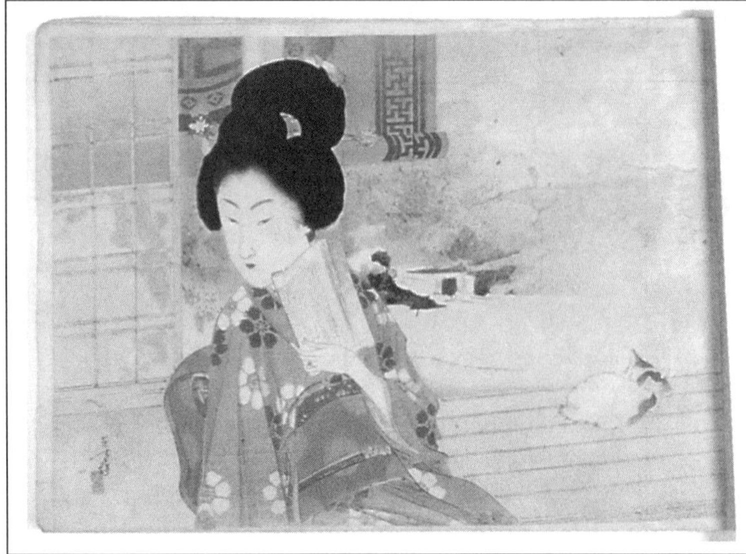

Toshimine Tsutsui, oban yoko-e, 11 1/2" x 8 1/2", (Kiyokata Kaburagi, Eisen Tomioka, Kiyochika Kobayashi, Hanko Kajita, Kason Suzuki, Keishu Takeuchi, Chikanobu Yoshu, Toshimine Tsutsui, Toshikata Mizuno), 24 woodblock illustrations for Romantic Novels, fine impressions, very good color and condition, mica, gauffrage, late Meiji period c. 1900, $2500-4500.

Toyohisa II (fl. c. 1830s)

Toyokuni I (1769-1825) Utagawa School, pupil of Toyoharu.

Apprenticed to Toyoharu at an early age, Toyokuni began his work with figures of women. As he progressed, his work showed the influence of Shensho, Kiyonaga, and Utamaro. He borrowed color schemes and designs from these artists. His actor prints of the late 18th century/early 19th century, as well as pillar prints and triptychs, are considered his best works. Among his students were Kuimasa, Kunisada, and Kuniyoshi.

Aiban tate-e, double portrait of actors Ichikawa Yaozo and Segawa Kikunojo, signed "Toyokuni ga," published by Nishimuraya Yohachi, good impression, trimmed, wormage, faded, $1200-1800.

Oban tate-e, a single sheet from a triptych, three women on a verandah looking out at a garden, signed "Toyokuni ga," published by Izumiya Ichibei, good impression and color, backed, restored at top corners, $500-700.

Oban tate-e, 13" x 9", okubi-e (bust portrait) of Ichikawa Danjuro VI as Arajishi Otokonosuke from the play Omiura Date no Nebiki. His left hand at the base of the hilt of his sword and his right hand holding closed fan, signed "Toyokuni ga," published by Tsuruya Kinsuke, dated Kansei 11 (1799), very good impression, good color, trimmed, wormage, laid down, rubbed, soiled, two creases, $3500-5500.

Oban yoko-e, "Furyu uki-e Megurosan no zu," (Fashionable Perspective View of Mt. Meguro),

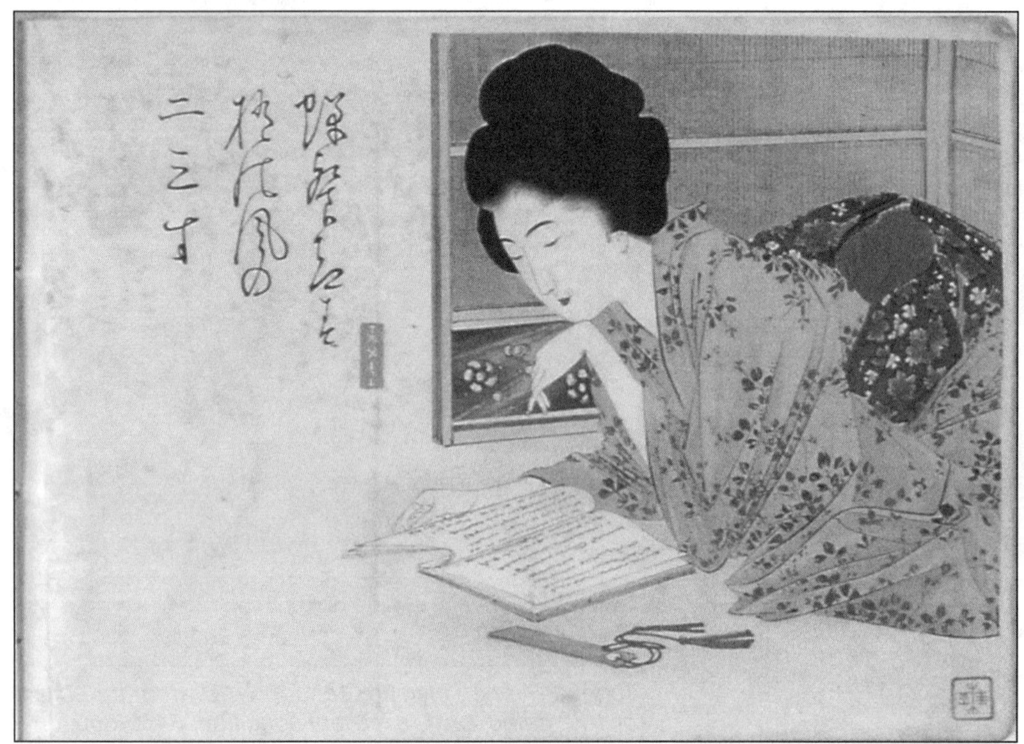

Toshikata Mizuno, oban yoko-e, 11 1/2" x 8 1/2", (Kiyokata Kaburagi, Eisen Tomioka, Kiyochika Kobayashi, Hanko Kajita, Kason Suzuki, Keishu Takeuchi, Chikanobu Yoshu, Toshimine Tsutsui, Toshikata Mizuno), 24 woodblock illustrations for Romantic Novels, fine impressions, very good color and condition, mica, gauffrage, late Meiji period c. 1900, $2500-4500.

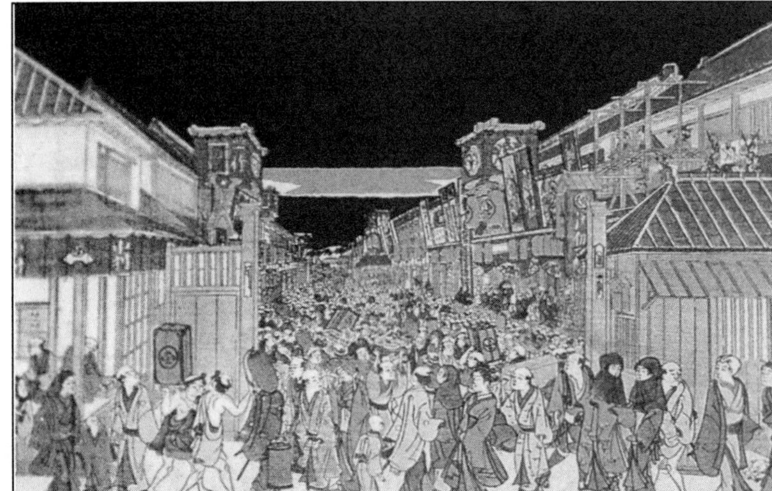

Toyoharu, oban yoko-e, 9 3/4" x 15", "Night View of the Theater District at Sakaicho," published by Nishimura-ya, signed "Utagawa Toyoharu ga," good impression, very good color, good overall condition, $3500-5500.

signed "Utagawa Toyokuni," published by Izumiya Ichibei, good impression and color, binding holes, minor wormage, $1000-1500.

Oban yoko-e, Courtesans (Takihime and Takihashi), late 18th c., published by Izumiya Ichibei, good impression, moderately faded, some foxing, $600-850.

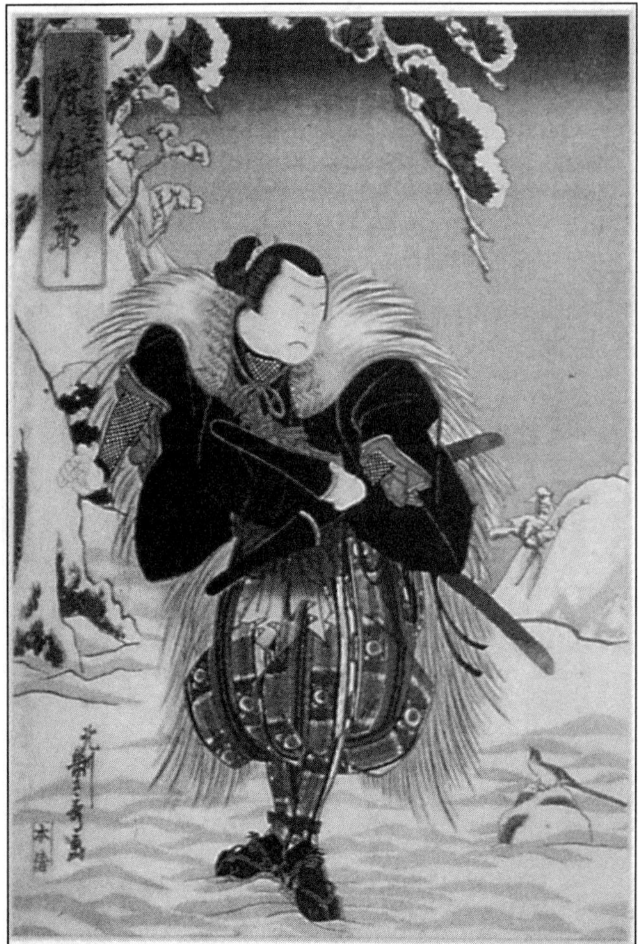

Toyohide, oban tate-e, 10 14" x 14 1/4", an actor in the role of Rashi Kanzaburo, c. 1840, very good impression, color, slightly trimmed, $375-675.

Oban yoko-e diptych, actors Ichikawa Danjuro and Iwai Hanshiro, early 19th c., (Bunka period 1804-1820), fair impression, toned, trimmed, wormage restored, foxing, $200-300.

Toyokuni II (1777-1835) pupil of Toyokuni I, used the name Toyokuni II from 1825.

Oban yoko-e, "Kamakura Banso," (Evening Bell, Kamakura), from the series Meisho Hakkei (Eight Views of Famous Places), signed "Toyokuni Hitsu," sealed Utagawa, published by Iseya Reihi, good impression, faded and toned, foxing, soiled, center crease, scotch tape residue on verso, $800-1200.

Toyokuni III (Kunisada I) took the name in 1844, pupil of Toyokuni I (his name is always enclosed).

Gototei Kunisada entered the studio of Toyokuni I at age 15. After a short apprenticeship, he began producing bijin ga, actor prints, and occasional landscapes. Supported by management and publishers, his works were soon acclaimed by the print buying public. Some print connoisseurs believe his best works were produced early in his career under the name of Gototei (Gosoki). His bijin ga are realistic depictions of daily life. He created some innovation in a series of okubi-e by showing mirrored women's faces in various attitudes. In 1833, he began to sign his work Kodoro Kunisada, and upon Toyokuni's death, he was in turn briefly named Toyokuni II, and finally Toyokuni III. A number of his students perpetuated the Utagawa School. These artists' names were all prefixed "Kuni". Among his best pupils were Toyoharu Kunichika and Yoshu Chikanobu.

See Also Kunisada

Toyokuni IV (Baido Hosai)

Toyomasa (fl. c. 1770-1780) pupil of Toyonobu I.

Toyonobu I (1711-1785) (fl. 1770-178)/ (?-1886) Utagawa School, pupil of Kunihisa.

Toyoshige II (fl c. late 1800s) Yokohama School..

Tsuchiya Koitsu (1870-1949)

Oban tate-e, "Two Beauties at Yosuya," dated 1936, signed and sealed, published by Doi, good impression, color, and condition, $650-950.

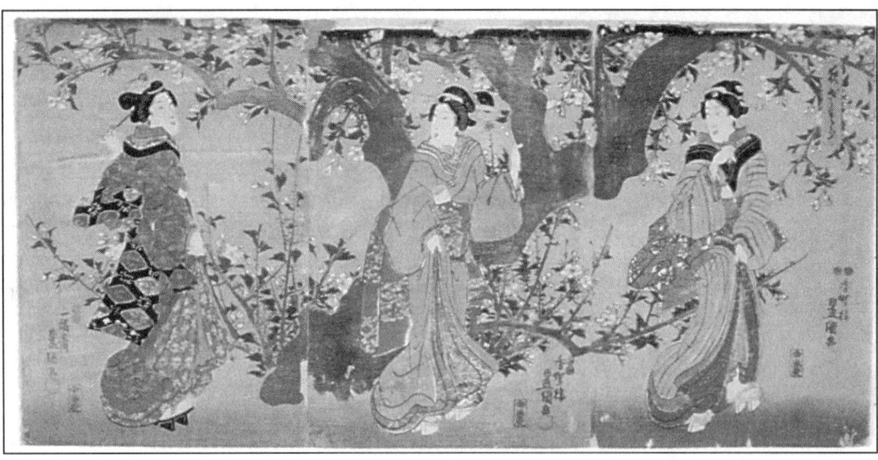

Toyokuni III, oban tate-e triptych, 1847-1848, "Bijin Under Flowering Cherry Trees," very good impression, good color, fair condition , soiled, $250-350.

Oban yoko-e, "Fishing with Cormorants at Night," 1940, signed and sealed, published by Doi, good impression, color, and condition, $600-900.

Oban yoko-e, as above, a posthumous print, $200-300.

Oban yoko-e, "View of Mt. Fuji," dated 1933, signed and sealed, dated 1933, good impression, color, and condition, $600-900.

Tsuchiya Rakuzan (b. 1886-?) kacho-e.

Tsukimari (fl. c. 1800s-1820s) Kitagawa School, pupil of Utamaro.

Tsukioka Kogyo (1869-1927) famous for Noh Drama prints.

Tsuruya Kokei (b. 1946) actor prints.

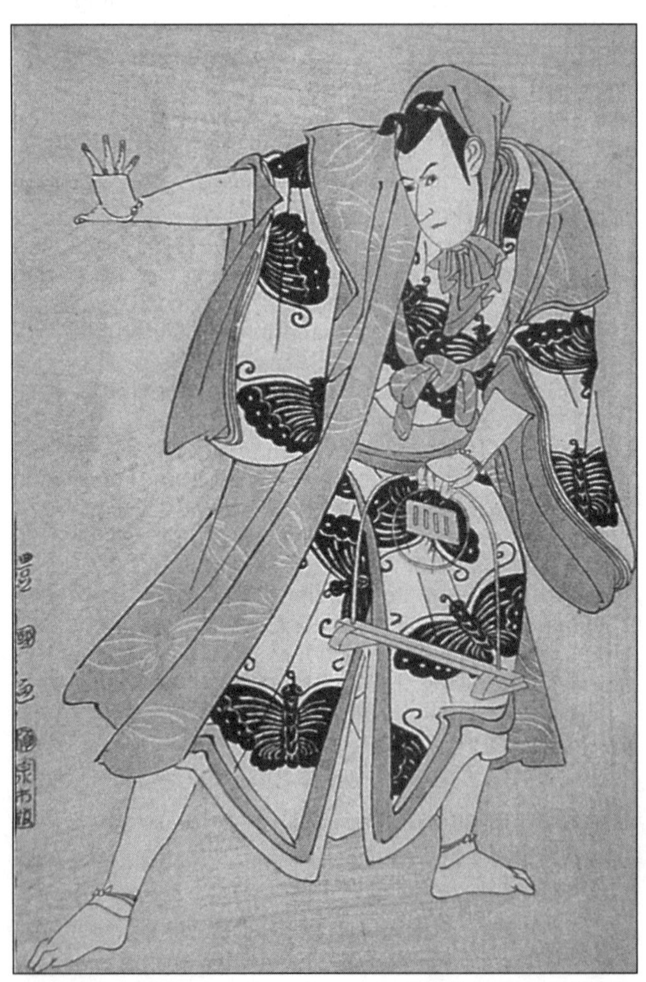

Toyokuni I, oban yoko-e, approx. 15" x 10", "Ichikawa Yaozo III in the role of Soga No Goro," signed "Toyokuni ga," publisher Izumiya Ichibei, kiwame seal c. 1794, good impression, slightly faded and soiled, horizontal crease line, corners restored, $3000-4500.

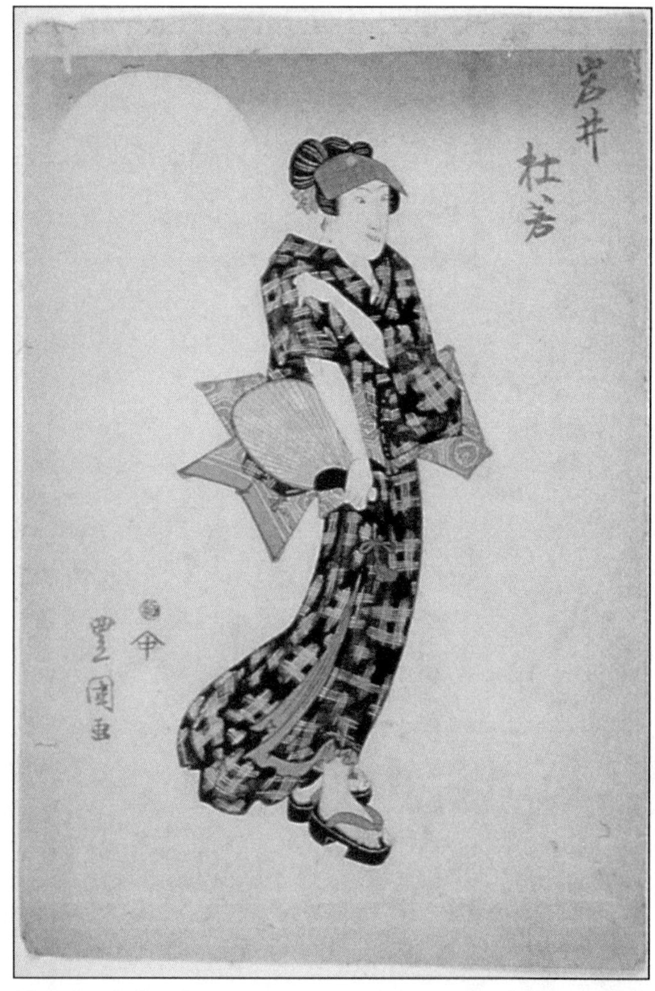

Toyokuni II, oban tate-e, actor, very good impression and color, slightly soiled, rubbed and worm holes restored, $500-700.

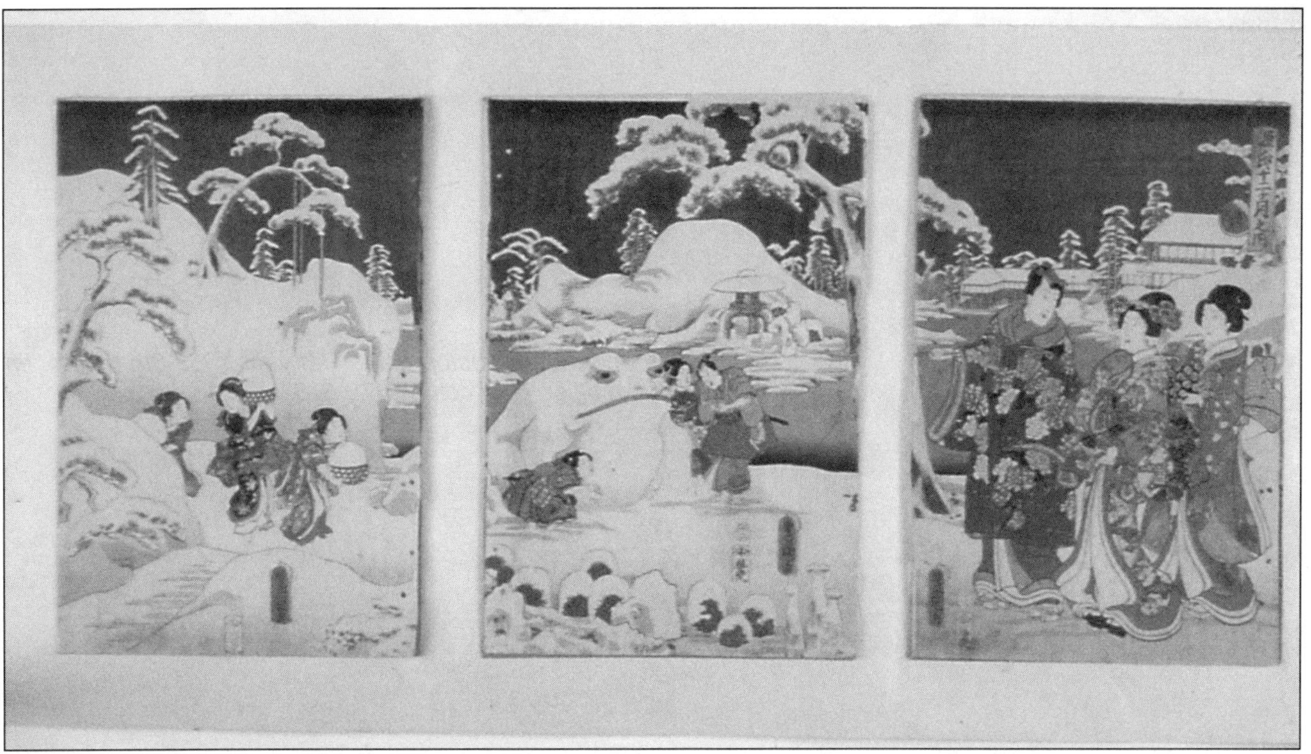

Toyokuni III, oban tate-e triptych, "Playing In The Snow," dated second month of year of the Horse (1858), very good impression, color, and condition, $2500-3500.

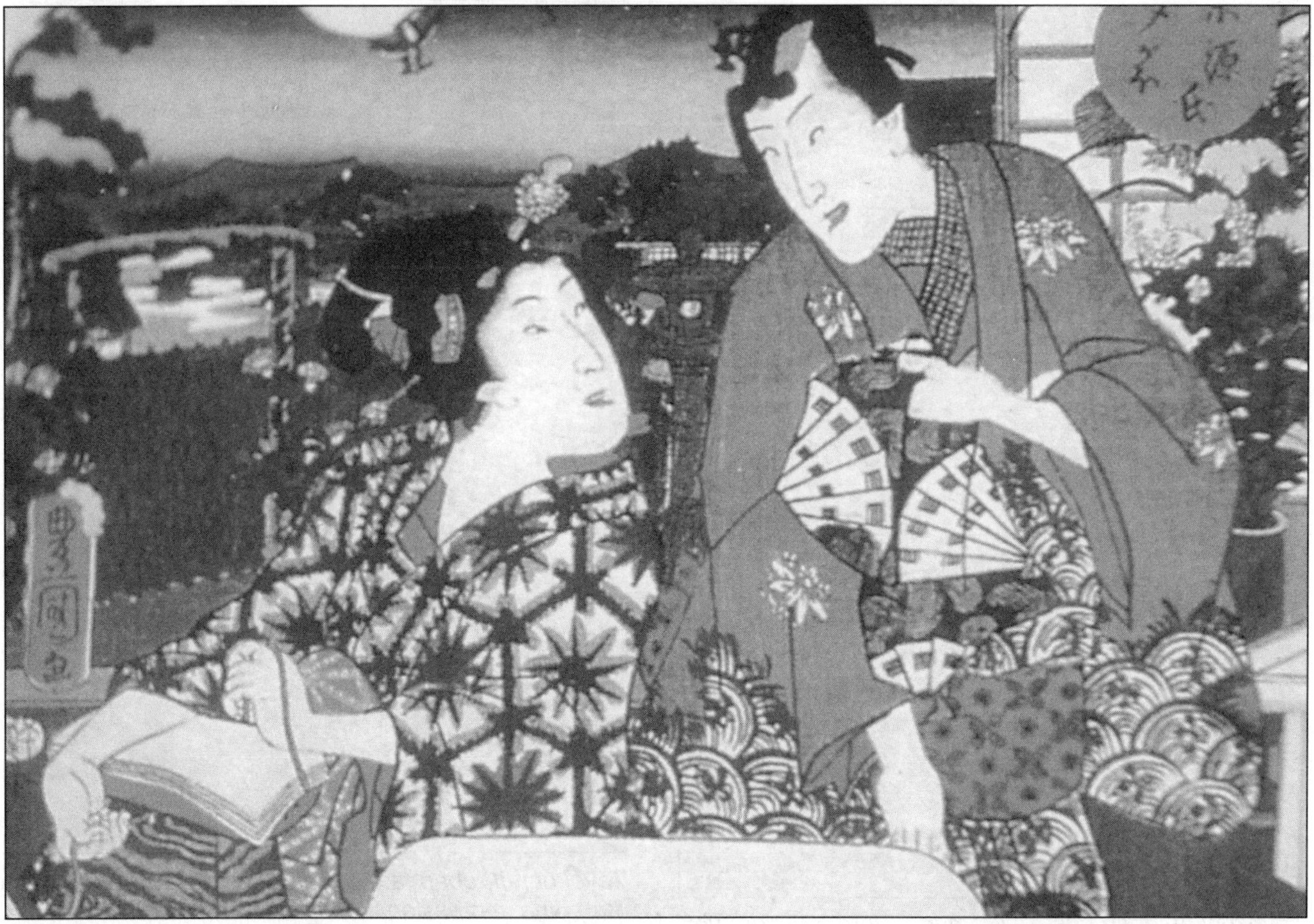

Toyokuni III (Kunisada), uchiwa-e, from the series Zuma Genji (Genji from the Eastern capital), signed "Toyokuni ga," publisher Enshuya Matabei, c. 1858, very good impression and color, minor wormage, corners creased, $3500-5500.

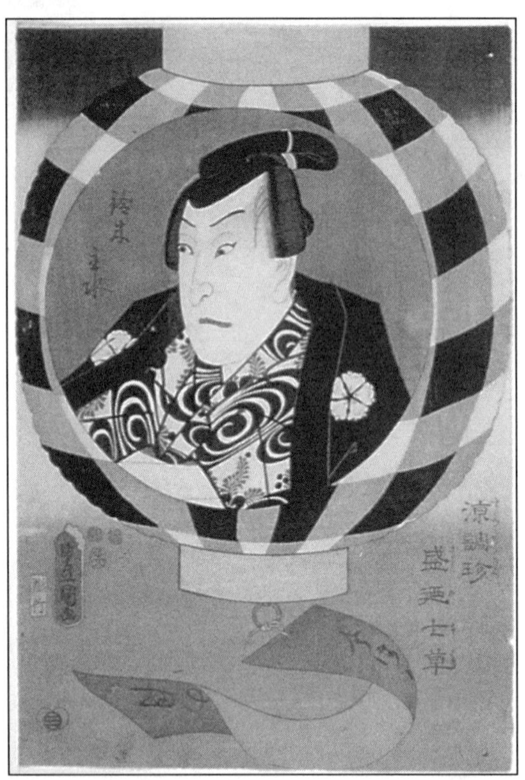

Toyokuni III, oban tate-e, actor, dated Rat year 1852 8th month, fine impression, condition, and color, $475-675.

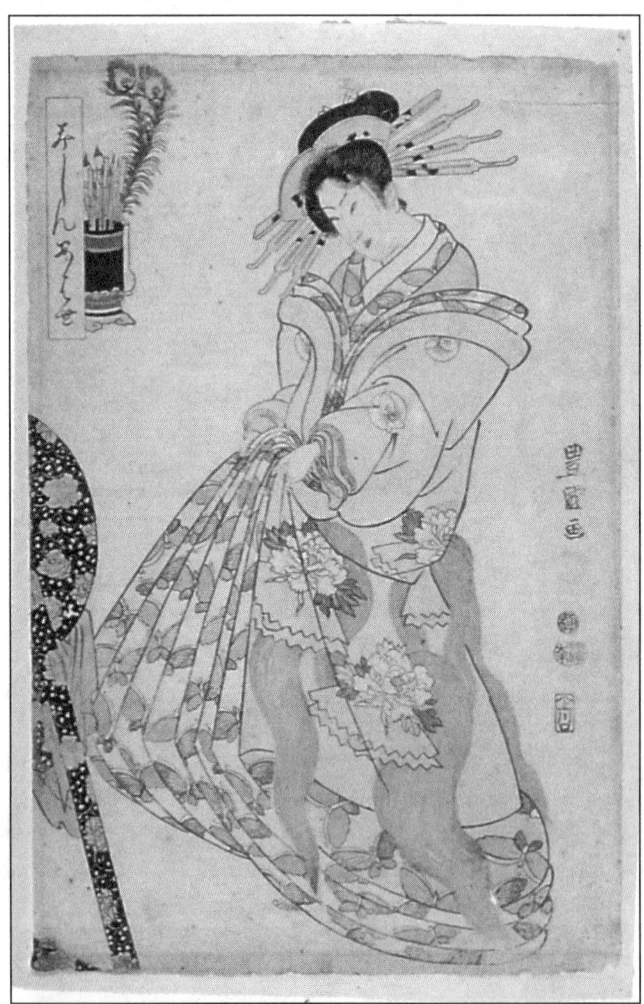

Toyokuni III, oban tate-e, "Woman Before a Mirror," very good impression, faded, toned, soiled, rubbed corners, center crease, $100-175.

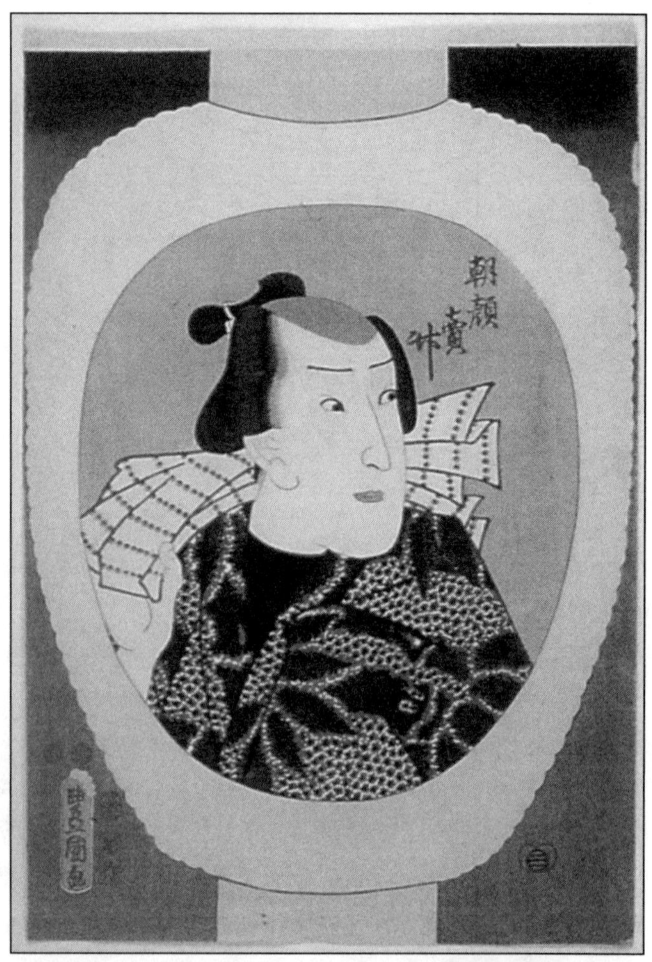

Toyokuni III, oban tate-e, actor, dated 1852 (year of the Rat), fine impression, condition, and color, $475-675.

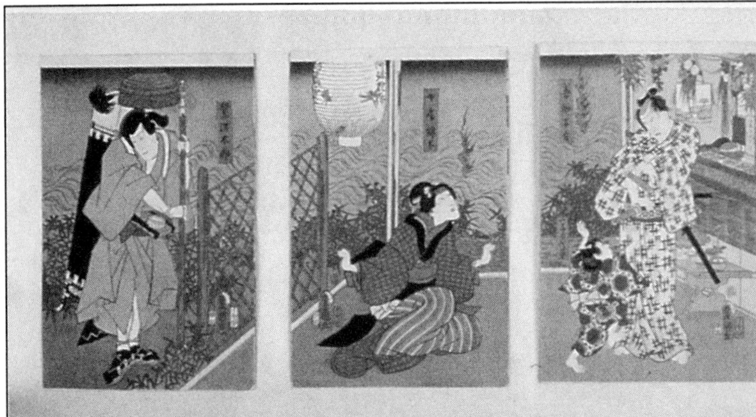

Toyokuni III, oban tate-e triptych, the image of actors has illuminated lanterns, dated 1859 (year of the goat), fine impression, color, and condition, $2500-3500.

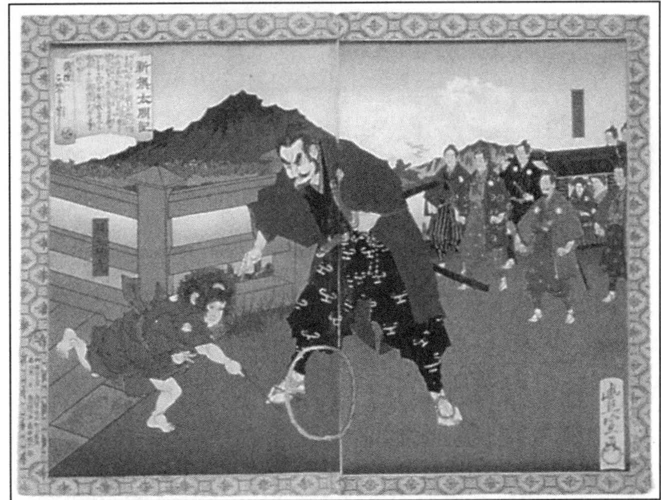

Toyonobu, oban tate-e diptych, from the series A New Edition of Hideyhoshi's Story, dated Meiji 16 (1883), fine impression, color and condition (backed with Japanese paper), $475-775.

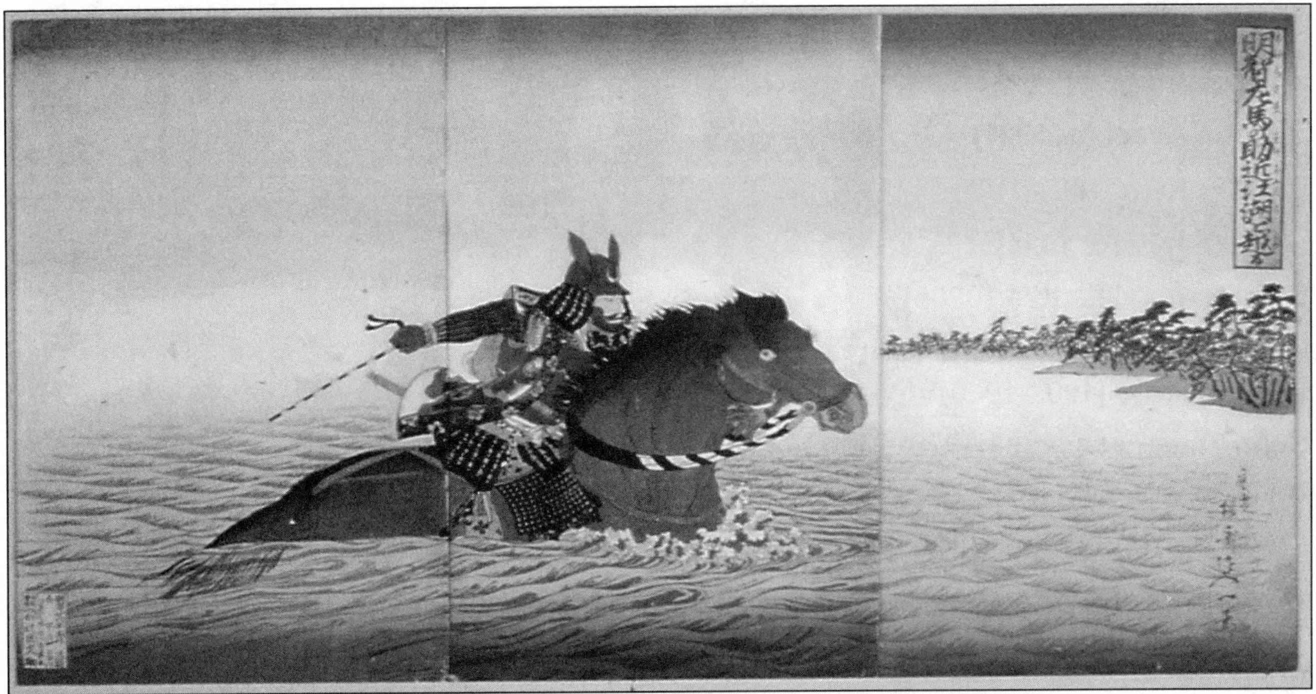

Toyonobu, oban tate-e triptych, 10" x 15", "Samurai on Horseback Crossing a Lake," Meiji period, very good impression, slightly soiled, backed, toned, some bleeding of color, $500-700.

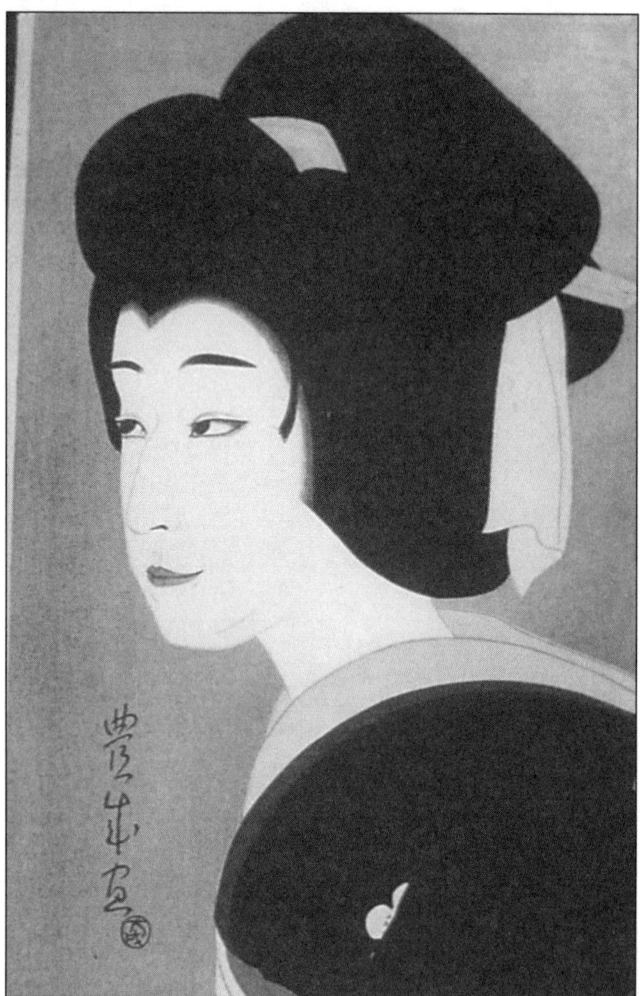

Toyonari, oban tate-e, "Sawamura Sonosuke as Umekawa," dated Taisho 11 (1921) good condition, soiled, holes restored, $1200-1800.

U

Uchima Ansei (b. 1921)

Ueda Fujo (b. 1899-?)

Ueda Gagyu (b. 1921)

Ueda Ryuichi (active 1930s)

Uemura Shoko (b.1904-?) kacho-e.

Ueno Makoto (1909-1980)

Ueno Tadamasa (1904-1970)

Umehara Konen (1878-1940)

Umehara Yosoji (active 1930s)

Umekuni (fl. c. 1823-1826) Osaka School, pupil of Yoshikuni.

Umemura Shoen (1875-1949)

Umenara Ryuzaburo (1888-1986)

Unno Mitsuhiro (1939-1979)

Unsen (fl. c. 1870s)

Urushibara Mokuchu (1888-1953)

Utagawa Kokunimasa (1874-1944)

Utagawa Kunimatsu (1855-1944)

Utakuni (1777-1806) Kamigata School.

Utamaro (1754-1806)

Kitagawa Utamaro was an ukiyo-e artist of the late Edo period. In his youth he studied under a painter of the Kano school named Toriyama Sekien and, adopting the element Toyo from his teacher's personal name, Toyofusa, he embarked on an artistic career under the name Utagawa Toyoaki. He published a number of works — actor prints and illustrations for books under this name. His earliest known work bearing his signature is dated 1775. It is the illustrated text of a play. In 1782, at the age of 29, he changed his name to Kitagawa Utamaro and began his artistic activity in earnest.

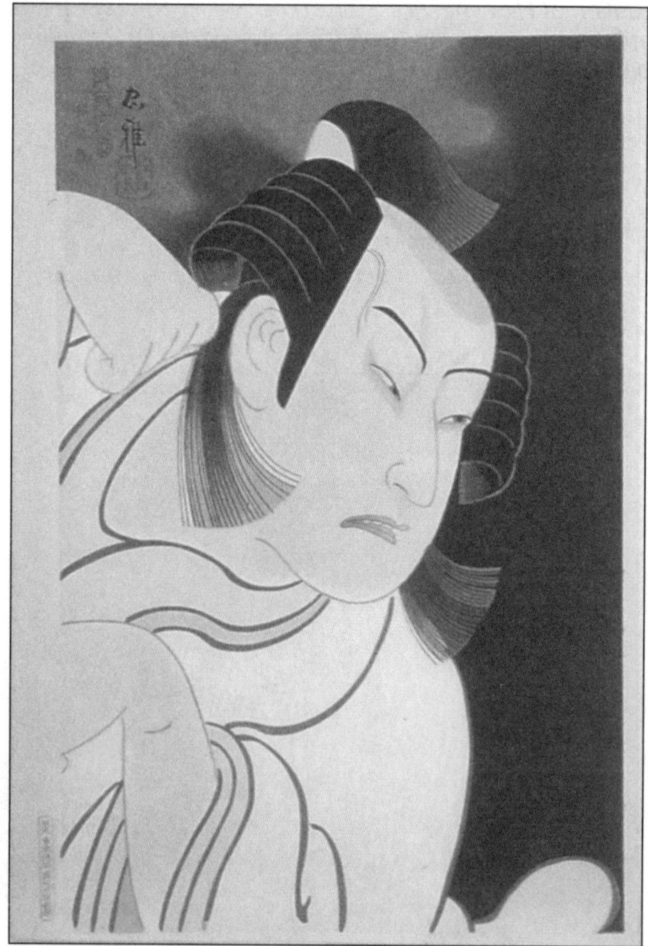

Ueno (Torii) Tadamasa, dai oban , An actor wearing a white kimono in the role of a fox, with kitsune no kuma (make-up lines representing the fox), from the series Eighteen Classical Types of Make-Up for the Kabuki, published by Watanabe, fine impression, color, and condition,$1000-1500.

His style in the early period of his career was heavily influenced by that of older ukiyo-e artists such as Katsukawa Shunso, Torii Kiyonaga, and Kitao Shigemasa. With the beginning of the Temmei era (1781-1789), he began experimenting with new methods of delineation that would produce a more realistic rendering of the subject to be represented. These efforts resulted in works such as ehon.

Mushierami (1787), Shiohi no Tsuto, and Momo Chidori, albums of brilliant polychrome prints, presented detailed representations of various animals and plants. With these he established himself as an artist of the first rank. These picture albums were all brought out by the publisher Tsutaya Juzaburo (known as Tsutaju for short), an indication of the important role that this publisher played in assisting Utamaro on the road to success.

With the beginning of the Kansei era (1789-1801), Utamaro began producing a number of half-length portraits of women known as bijin okubi-e, in which the figure almost fills the picture surface. These polychrome prints on a mica ground are extremely beautiful. The women are depicted with great care and perception, representing a wide variety of temperaments, social classes, and ways of life. Revealing subtle inner states of mind, these prints are a far cry from the highly idealized, impersonalized, and expressionless beauties that were typical of earlier ukiyo-e art.

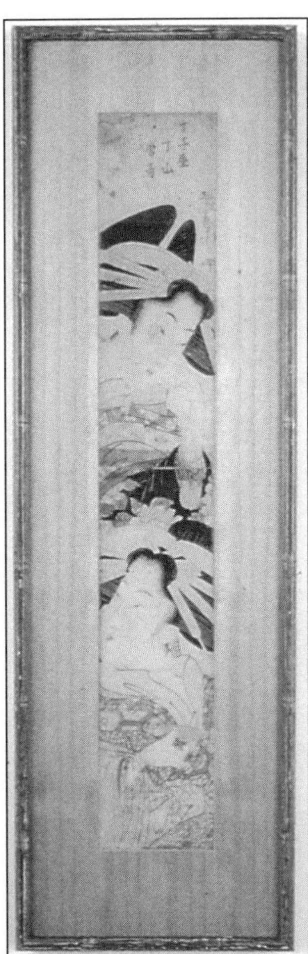

Utamaro, hashira-e, 23 1/2" x 4", "Bijin," very good impression, fair color, rubbed, soiled, $700-950.

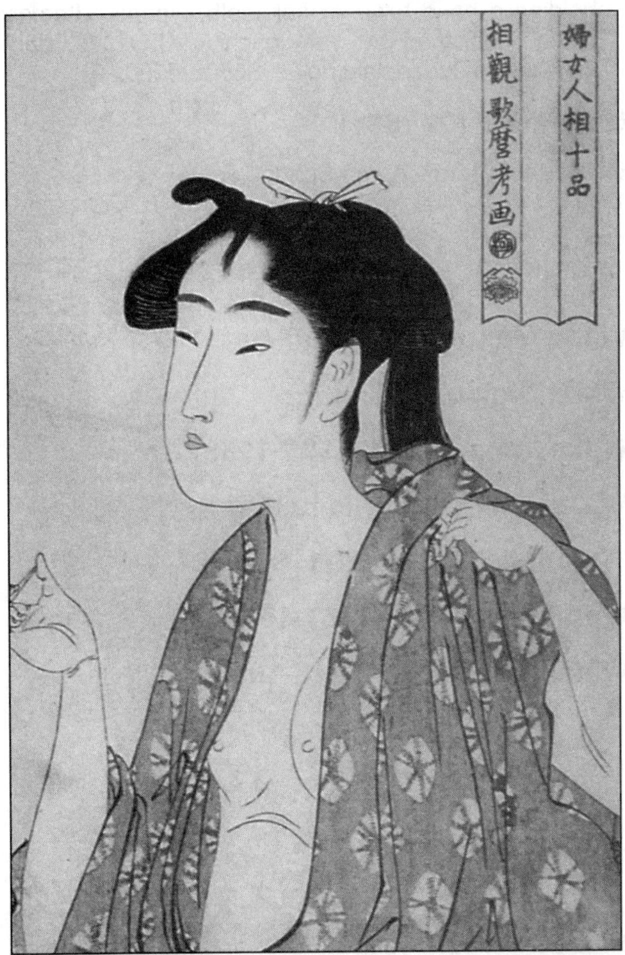

Utamaro, oban tate-e, approx. 14 1/4" x 9 3/4", half-length portrait of a woman smoking, the pipe in her right hand, from the series Fujo Ninso Juppan (Ten Types of Women's Physiognomy) signed "Sokan Utamaro koga," publisher Tsutaya Juzaburo, white mica background, good impression, moderately toned, moderately faded, several vertical creases, worm holes restored, corners restored, $30,000-45,000.

The year 1790 was pivotal for Utamaro in several respects. In the 5th moon of the year the government instituted a reform and attempted to curb the publication of ukiyo-e, which it regarded as conducive to frivolity and immorality. In the 8th moon of that year a woman very closely connected to Utamaro died. From this time on he only published pictures of women.

With the publication of such commemorative series of prints as Kasen Koi no Bu and Fujo Ninso Juppin (renamed while in process of publication Fujin Sago Jittery), Utamaro became the undisputed leader of the artists specializing in prints of beautiful women. In 1797, when the publisher Tsutaya Juzaburo died, Utamaro was besieged by requests for work from the various publishing houses in Edo. In his later years he turned out works with such rapidity that the quality declined somewhat.

In 1804 he published some prints based upon a historical work, the *Taikoki,* that was among the books interdicted by the government. As a result, he was imprisoned for three days and condemned to wear war chains on his hands for 50 days. The *Taikoki* was a set of prints which showed Hideyoshi amusing himself with his five concubines. This greatly offended the

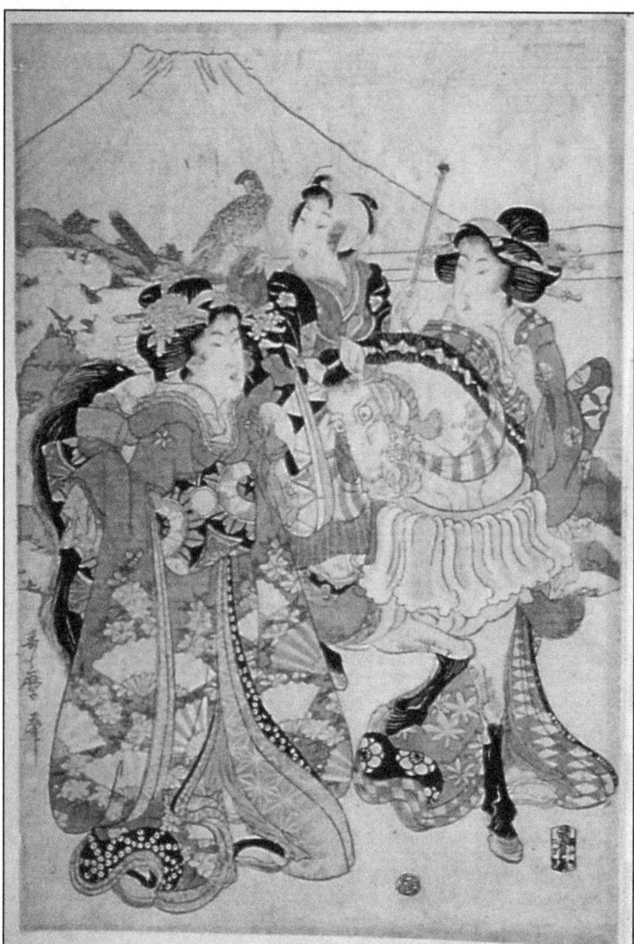

Utamaro, oban tate-e, an interesting print with falcon, rider on horseback, Mt. Fuji in the background, very good impression, faded but retaining some good color, laid down on Japanese paper, $1000-1800.

Utamaro continued:

Tokugawa government, which considered the work an indirect gibe against it. This was the final blow to Utamaro's pride. Defeated and rejected, he gave up his battle against the trends of the age. With nothing more to live for, he died in obscurity two years later.

Oban tate-e, an okubi-e (portrait) of the courtesan Tagasode of the Daimonjiya, from the series Seiro nana komachi (The 7 Komachi of the licensed quarters), signed "Utamaro hitsu," and sealed Honkei and published by Sensa, good impression, slightly faded and soiled, some wormage, first edition (the flesh lines are black, and the yellow ground is gray, and the Honkei seal removed in the later edition), $18,000-25,000.

Oban tate-e, "Nakadaya," (The Nakadaya Tea House), signed "Utamaro hitsu," published by Yamaguchiya Chusuke, good impression, toned, soiled, restored along edges and corners, $1000-1500.

Oban tate-e, a bijin holding a bucket, signed "Utamaro hitsu," dated 1805, publisher Iwai-ya, good impression, faded, backed, soiled, $1000-1500.

Oban tate-e, "Feeding the Silk Worms," from the set Joshoku Kaiko Tewaza-kusa (Silkworm Culture-Handiwork of Women), signed "Utamaro hitsu," published by Tsuruya Kinsuke, good impression, faded, stained, soiled, backed, $1000-1500.

Oban tate-e, single sheet from a triptych, courtesan dancing, "Seven Drunken Shojo," signed "Utamaro suichu hitsu," good impression, faded, soiled, stained, holes, $400-600.

Oban tate-e, a bust portrait of Okita of the Naniwaya holding a hand towel in her teeth, signed "Utamaro hitsu," published by Yamaguchiya Chusuke, good impression, faded, laid down, $3500-5500.

Utamaro II (?- 1831)

Utatora (?) Yokohama School.

W

Wada Makoto (b. 1939)

Wada Sanzo (1883-1968)

Wakayama Yasoji (1903-1983)

Watanabe Kenkichi (1930s)

Watanabe Nobukazu (1874-1944)

Watanabe Seitei (1851-1918)

Watanabe Sadao (1913-1996)

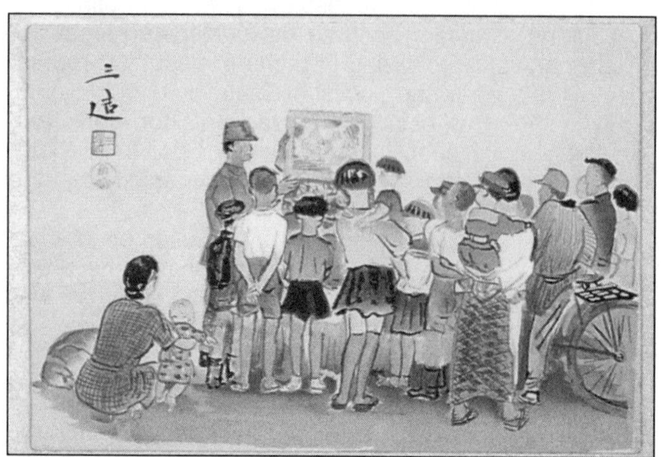

Wada Sanzo, oban yoko-e, 16" x 11 1/2", "The Lesson," published Kyoto Hanga In Co. Ltd., 1952, signed and sealed "Sanzo," fine condition, impression, and color, $375-500.

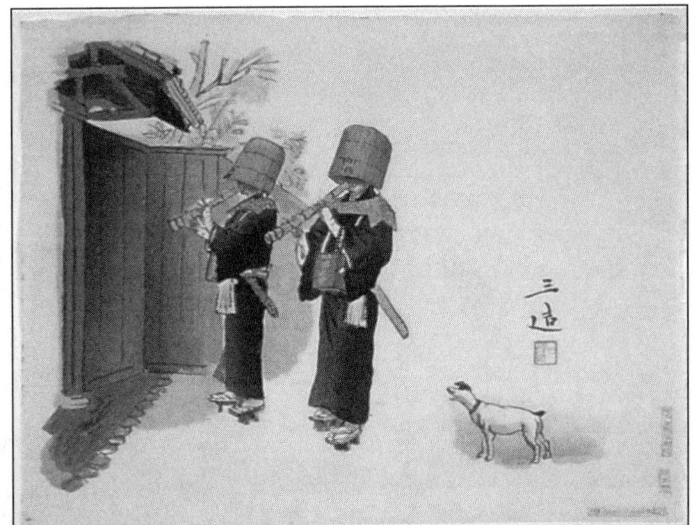

Wada Sanzo, oban yoko-e, "Beggars," published by Kyoto Hanga -In, dated 1952, signed and sealed "Sanzo," fine impression, color, and condition, $375-500.

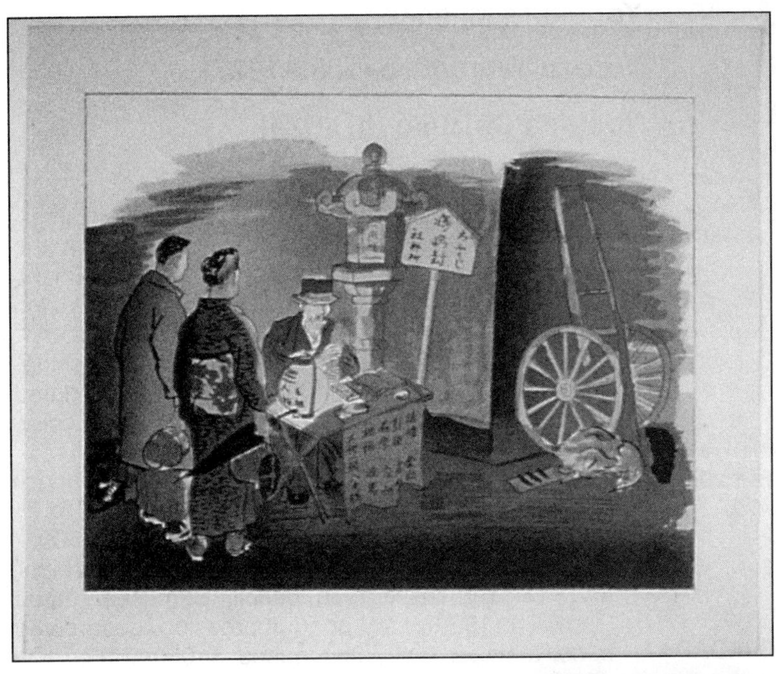

Wada Sanzo, oban yoko-e, 11 1/4" 9 1/2", "The Fortune Teller," c. 1952, from an album of loose prints (also published in larger size as individual prints), published by Kyoto Hanga In, fine condition, color and impression, album $800-1200.

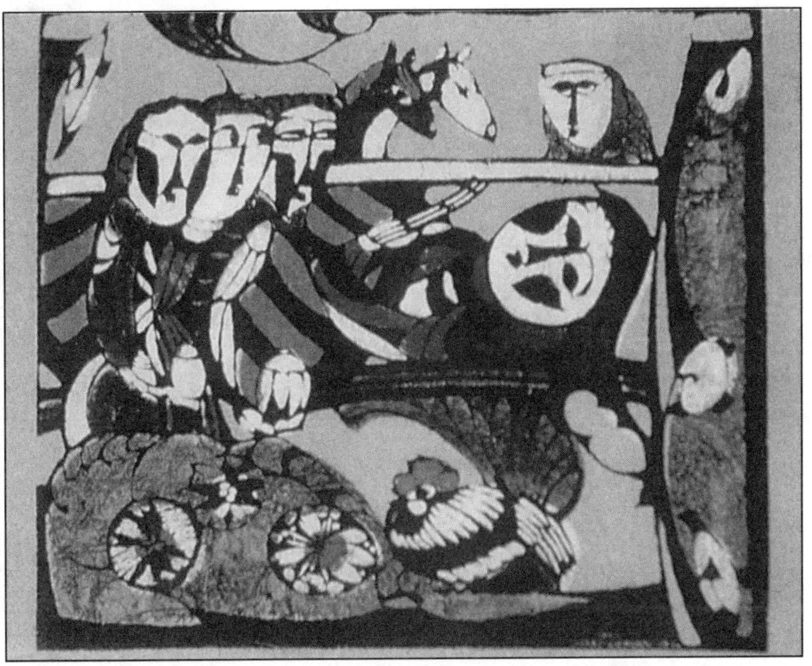

Watanabe Sadao, untitled stencil with brushed pigments, 23" x 32", signed in Roman letters "Sadao Watanabe", from an edition of 50, not dated, tape on verso, $350-500.

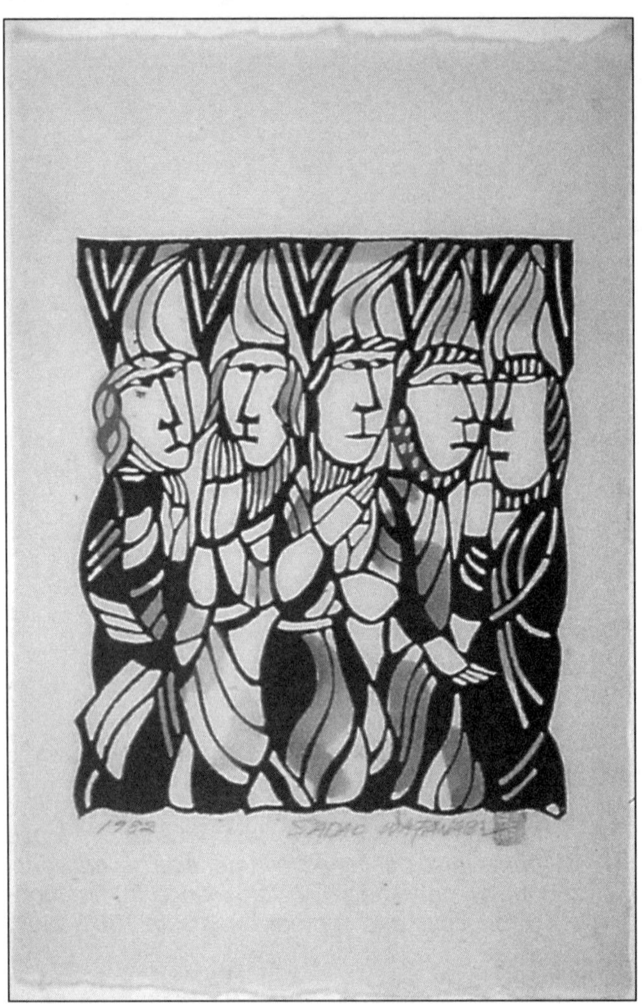

Watanabe Sadao, 12" x 16 1/2", stencil, religious subject, signed and sealed, unlimited edition, $250-400.

Y

Yamada Basuke signed his prints YAMADA BASKE

Yamada Shoun I (b. 1901-?)

Yamada Shoun II (b. 1925)

Yamakawa Shuho (see Shuho)

Yamaguchi Gen (1903-1976)

Yamaguchi Susumu (1897-1982)

Yamamoto Kanae (1882-1945)

Yamamato Shoun (1870-1965)

Yamamura Koka (see Yamamura Toyonari)

Yamamura Toyonari (1885-1942)

Yamashita Shintaro (1881-1966)

Yasui Sotaro (1888-1955)

Yonekura Masakane (b. 1934) bijin ga

Yorozu Tetsugoro (1885-1927)

Yoshida Chizuko (b. 1924)

Yoshida Hiroshi (1876-1950)

Dai oban yoko-e, approx. 23" x 29" "Fujiyama--First Light of the Sun," signed "Yoshida" in brush and "Hiroshi Yoshida" in pencil, jizuri seal, dated Taisho 15 (1926), fine impression, good color, minor foxing in margins and image, slightly toned, $6000-8000.

Dai oban yoko-e, "Sea of Cloud," signed "Yoshida" and "Hiroshi Yoshida" in pencil, jizuri sea, dated Showa 3 (1928), very good impression, good color, minor toning in margins, creases, $4000-6000.

Oban tate-e, "Study of a Nude," signed in pencil "Hiroshi Yoshida," jizuri seal, dated Showa 2 (1927), good impression, color and condition, $1000-1500.

Dai oban yoko-e, "Sea of Cloud," signed "Yoshida" and "Hiroshi Yoshida" in pencil, jizuri sea, dated Showa 3 (1928), very good impression, good color, minor toning in margins, creases, $4000-6000.

Oban tate-e, "Study of a Nude," signed in pencil Hiroshi Yoshida, jizuri seal, dated Showa 2 (1927), good impression, color and condition, $1000-1500.

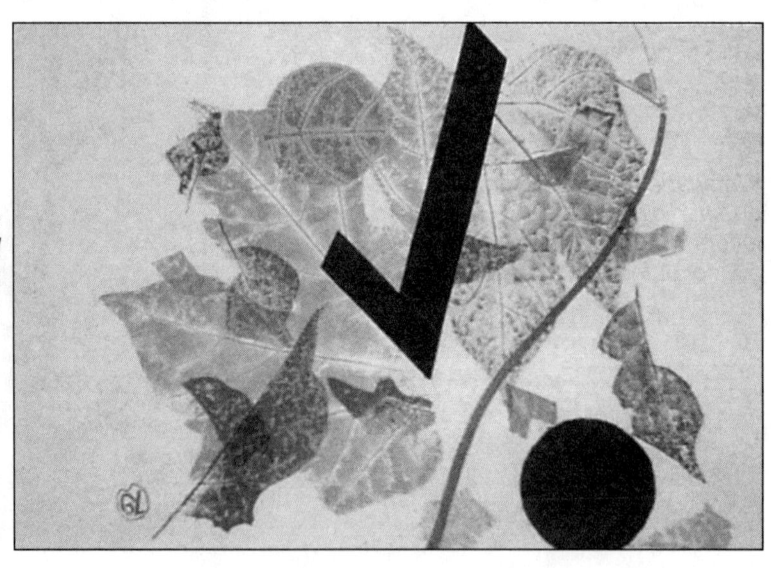

Yamaguchi Gen, approx. 15" x 15", c. late 1940s, "Poetry of Early Autumn, Leaves and String," signed in pencil Roman script "Gen Yamaguchi" and monogram GY, from an edition of 50, framed $2000-3000.

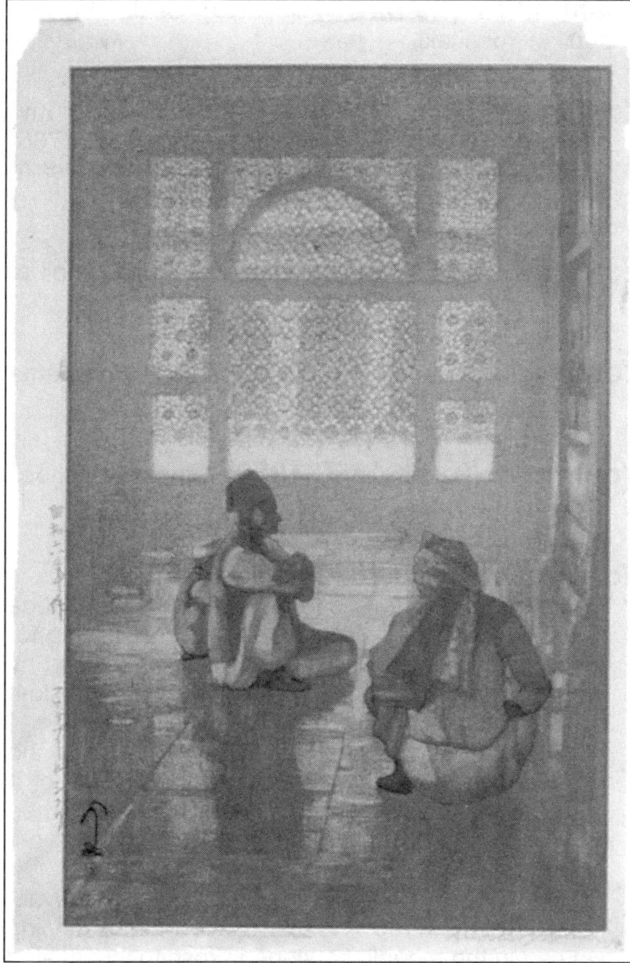

Yoshida Hiroshi, oban tate-e, "A Window at Fatehput-Sikri," dated Showa 6 (1931), very good impression, color, and condition, $600-950.

Oban tate-e, "Himeji Castle, Evening," dated 1926, jizuri seal, good impression, toned, browning on verso, $400-700.

Oban tate-e, "Singapore," jizuri seal, dated 1931, very good impression, good color, good condition, $800-1200.

Yoshida Hodaka (1926-1995) etching, woodblock, intaglio, serigraphy, lithograph, limited editions.

Yoshida Masaji (1917-1981) woodblock, etching, stencil, limited editions.

Yoshida Masazo (1907-1974) etching, limited editions.

Yoshida Toshi (1911-1995) woodblock, lithograph, etching.

Yoshikawa Kanpo (1894-1979)

Yasuji (1864-1889) pupil of Kiyochika.

Yoshiku (1833-1904) Utagawa School, pupil of Kuniyoshi.

Yoshiharu (1828-1888) Utagawa School, pupil of Kuniyoshi.

Yoshikazu (fl. 1850-1870) Yokihama School, pupil of Kuniyoshi.

Yoshikuni (1855-1903) Kyoto, pupil of Yoshiume.

Yoshikuni (fl. c. 1803-1840) Osaka School, pupil of Ashikuni.

Yoshimine (fl. c. 1855-1875) Osaka School, pupil of Yoshiume.

Yoshida Hodaka, oban, 10 1/4" x 15 1/4", "Narrow Street," signed and dated in pencil in lower margin, 1957, fine condition, color, and impression, $900-1500.

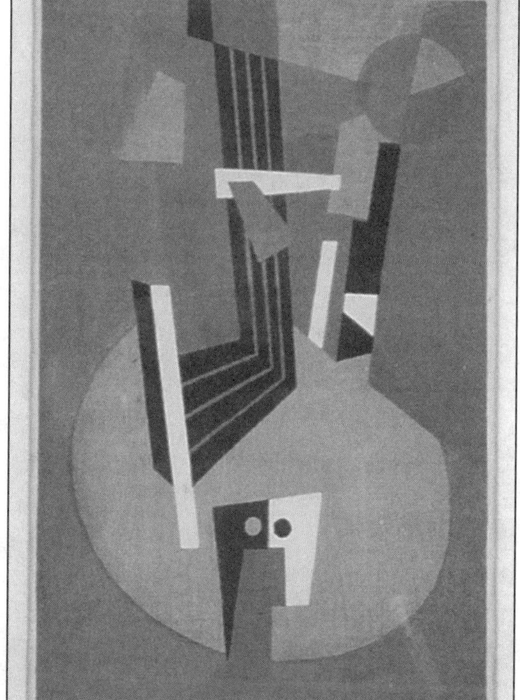

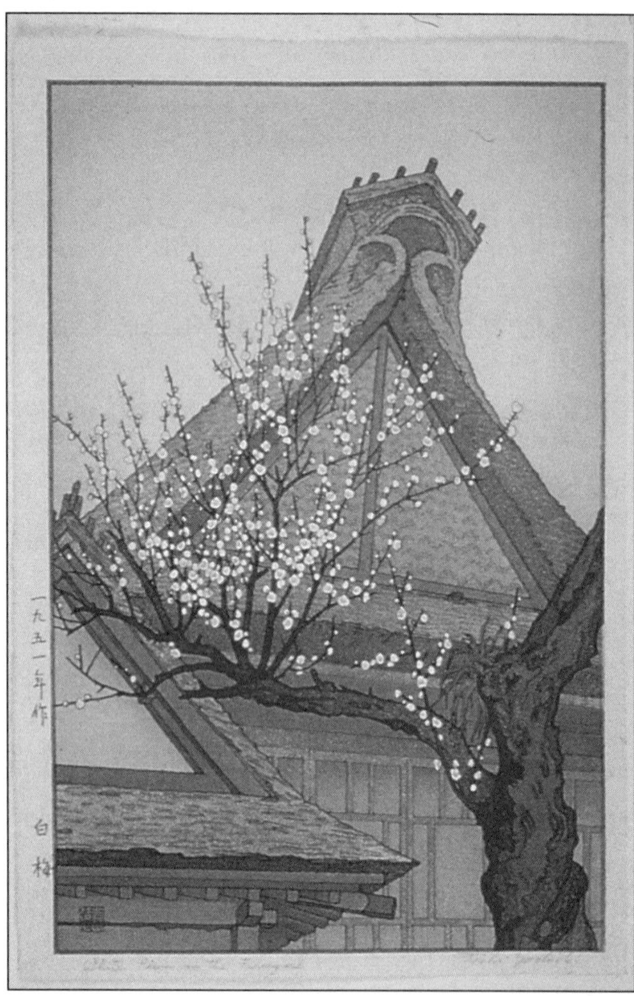

Yoshida Toshi, oban tate-e, 16" x 10 3/4", "White Plum in the Farmyard," dated 1951, early edition, sealed in the image lower left, artist signed in pencil in lower margin, fine impression, color, and condition, $1000-1500.

Yoshimitsu (fl. c. 1873-1880) Osaka School, pupil of Yoshitaki.

Yoshinobu (fl. c. 1730s-1740s) follower of Kiyonobu/(fl. 1745-1758), pupil of Shigenaga/(fl. 1765-1770), follower of Harunobu/(fl. c. 1840s), Osaka School/(1848-1864), pupil of Kuniyoshi.

Yoshitaki (1841-1899) Kamigata School, pupil of Yoshiume.

Yoshitomi (fl. c. 1850s-1870s) Yokohama school, pupil of Kuniyoshi.

Yoshitora (fl. c. 1850-1880) Utagawa School, pupil of Kuniyoshi.

Yoshitoshi (1839-1892) pupil of Kuniyoshi.

Chuban from the series Yoshitoshi Ryakuga (Sketched by Yoshitoshi), Empress Jingu fishing for a cat, signed and sealed "Yoshitoshi," published by Funazu, dated 10/5/1882, very good impression, color and condition with blind printing, $400-600.

Chuban, same series as above, "Kaika no Daruma," the zen priest Daruma as the client of a courtesan, signed "Yoshitoshi," seal Taiso, published by Funazu, dated 15/5/1882, very good impression, color, and condition, $500-700.

Oban tate-e, "The Moon of the Oban Festival," from the series 100 Aspects of the Moon, dancing women in the moonlight, signed "Yoshitoshi," sealed Taiso, published by Akiyama Buemon, dated 1886, good impression, color, and condition, $800-1200.

Oban tate-e, as above, water stains, blurred pigments, $100-200.

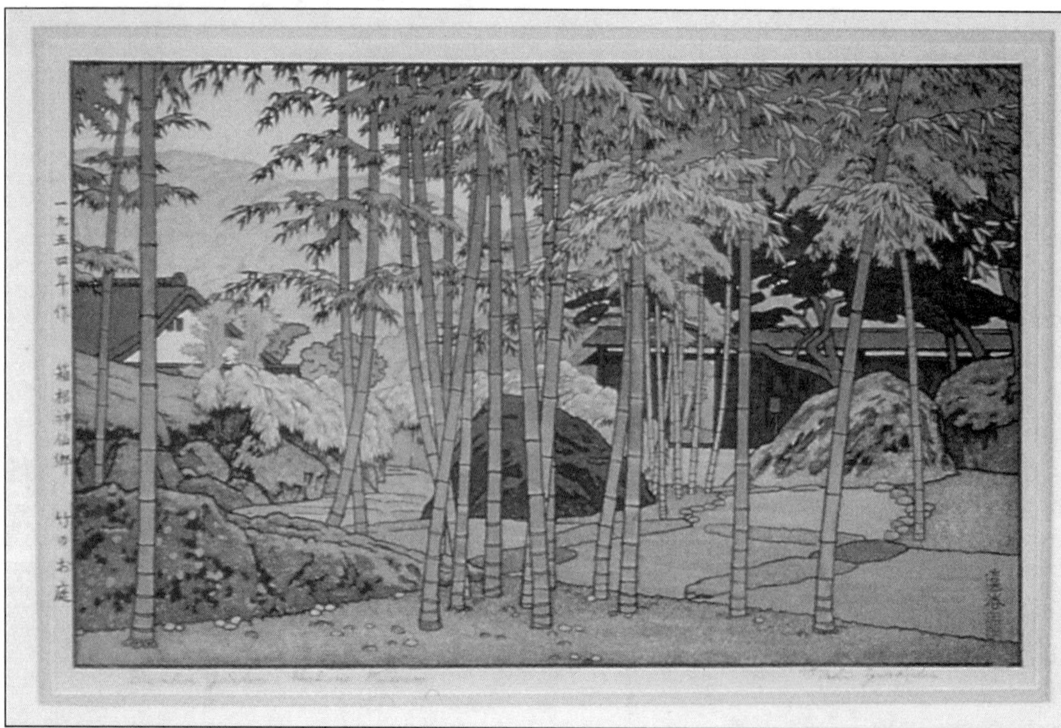

Yoshida Toshi, oban yoko-e, 10" x 15 1/2", "Bamboo Garden, Hakone Museum," signed and sealed, dated 1954, early edition, excellent condition, color, and impression, $800-1200.

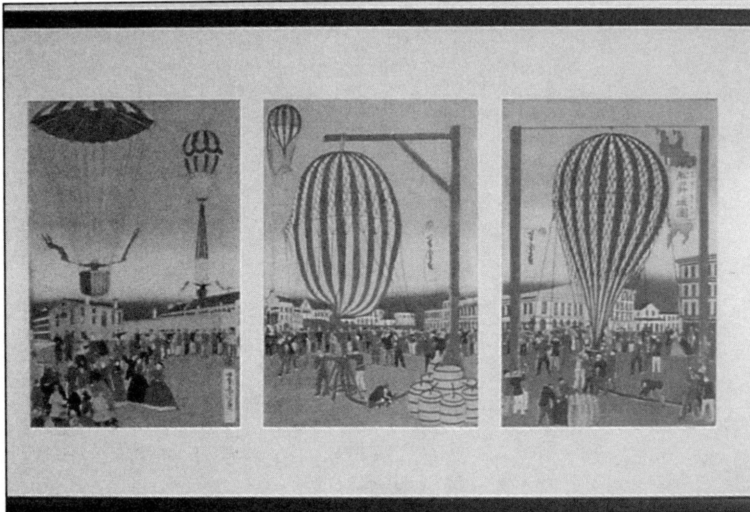

Yoshitora, oban tate-e triptych, each panel 10" x 15", "View of Balloons Ascending," c. 1884, good color and impression, stained, creases on right side of left panel and left side of center panel, $1200-1600.

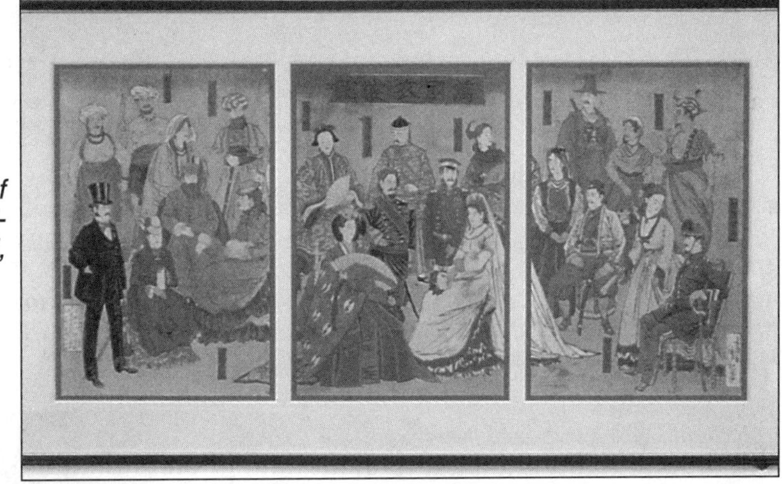

Yoshitora, oban tate-e triptych, "Mirror of Many Country's Costumes," dated Meiji period, good impression, toned, soiled backed, faded, $500-750.

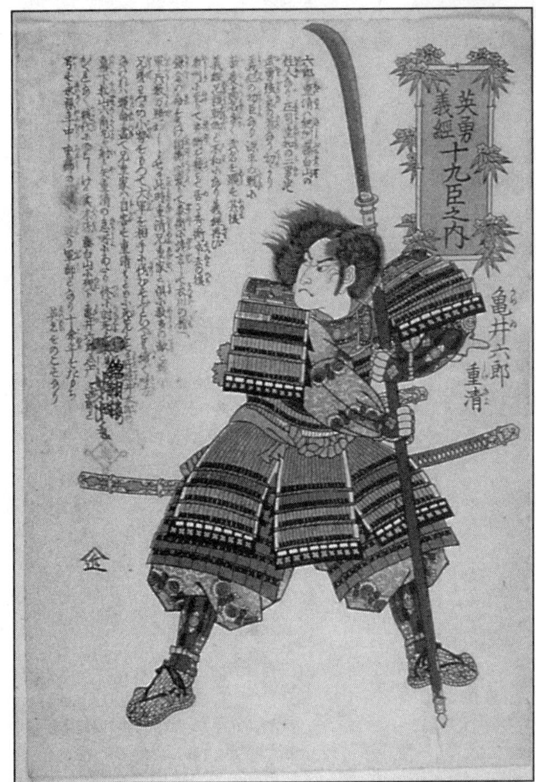

Yoshitora, oban tate-e, from the series Chushin Gishi Meimei Den (Biographies of the Individual Loyal Retainers), excellent condition, color, and impression, $1000-1500.

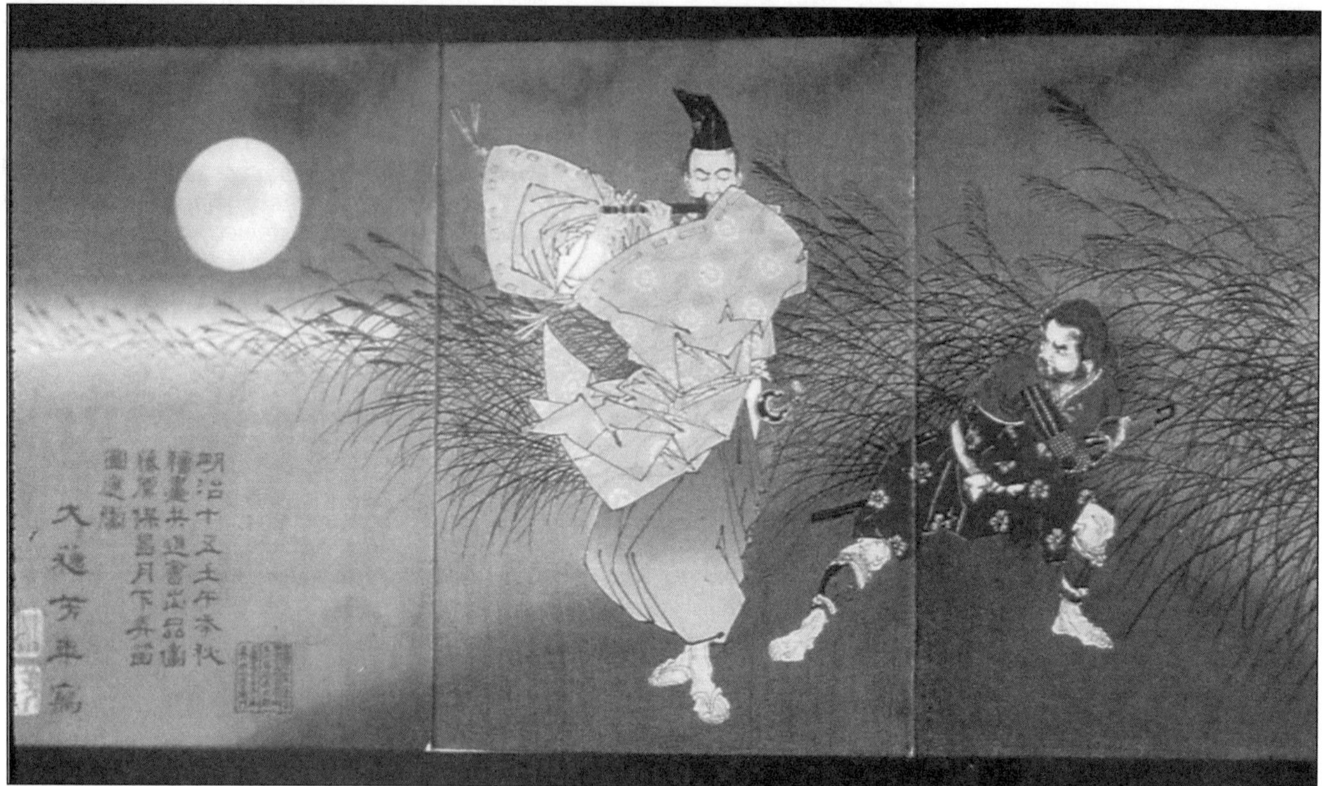

Yoshitoshi, oban tate-e triptych, overall size 14 7/8" x 29 1/2", "Fujiwara Yasumasa Gekka Roteki Zu," (Fujiwara Yasumasa Playing the Flute in the Ichihara Moor), depicting one of Minamoto raiko' retainers, Hirai (Fujiwara) Yasumasa, playing the flute on a moonlit night and the robber Hakamadare Yasusuke sneaking up behind him and about to strike with his sword; dated Meiji 16 (1883), publisher Akiyama Takememon, signed Taiso Yoshitoshi and sealed, very good impression and color, slightly stained, slightly trimmed, margins toned and worn, $3500-5500.

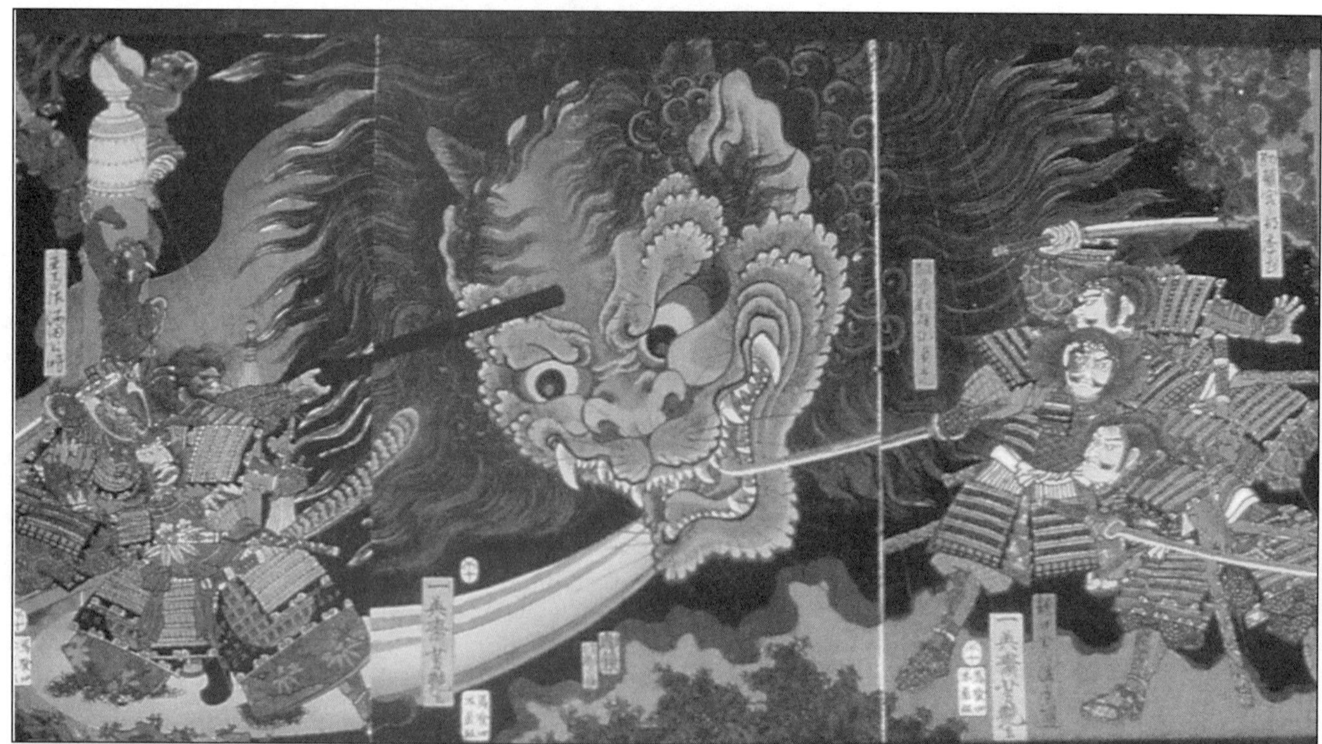

Yoshitsuya, oban tate-e triptych, each sheet approx. 14" x 10", "Oeyama Shuten Taiji," (Slaying the Drunken Demon of Oeyama), Minamoto no Yorimitsu slaying the huge demon in a storm, the demon's eyes with black lacquer, signed "Ichieisai Yoshitsuya ga," published by Kiya Sojiro, very good impression and color, margins with binding holes, slightly trimmed, $2000-3000.

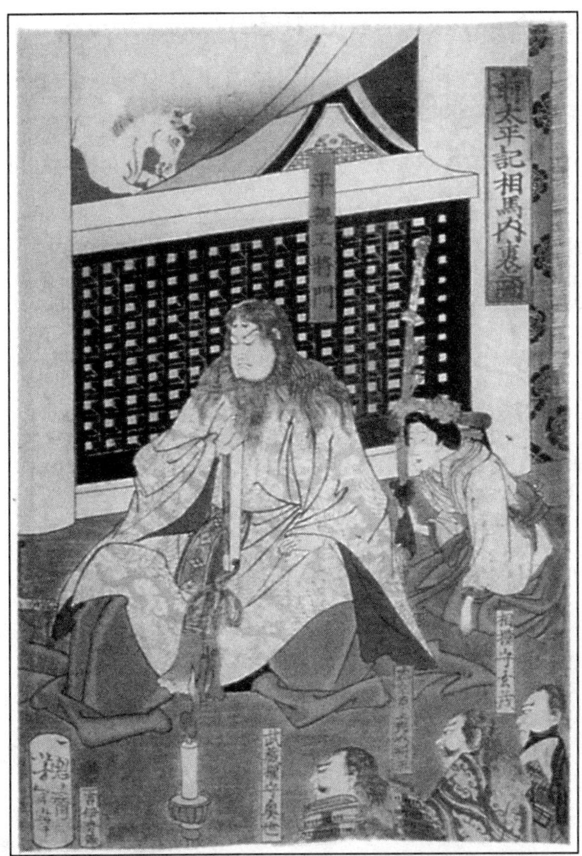

Yoshitoshi, oban tate-e, an early Yoshitoshi print, slightly trimmed, very good color, fine impression, $300-400.

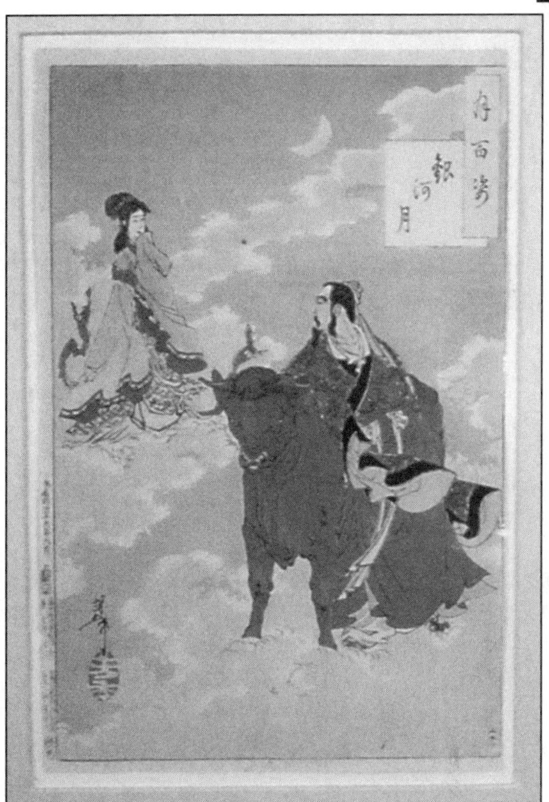

Yoshitoshi, oban tate-e, "The Oxherdsman and the Weaving Girls' Rendezvous at Ama-no-gawa, the Milky way from Tsuki Hyaku Sugata," fine impression, color, and condition, $900-1250.

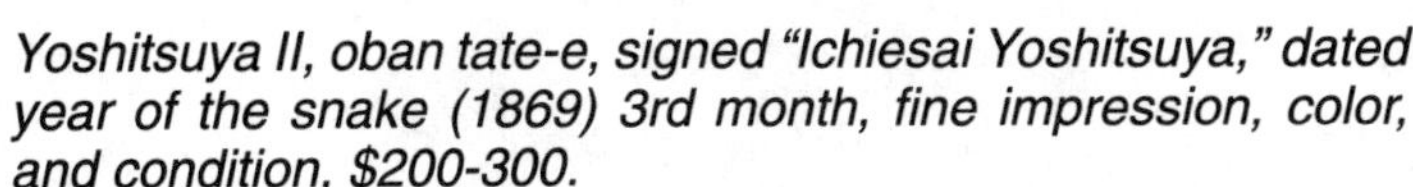

Yoshitsuya II, oban tate-e, signed "Ichiesai Yoshitsuya," dated year of the snake (1869) 3rd month, fine impression, color, and condition, $200-300.

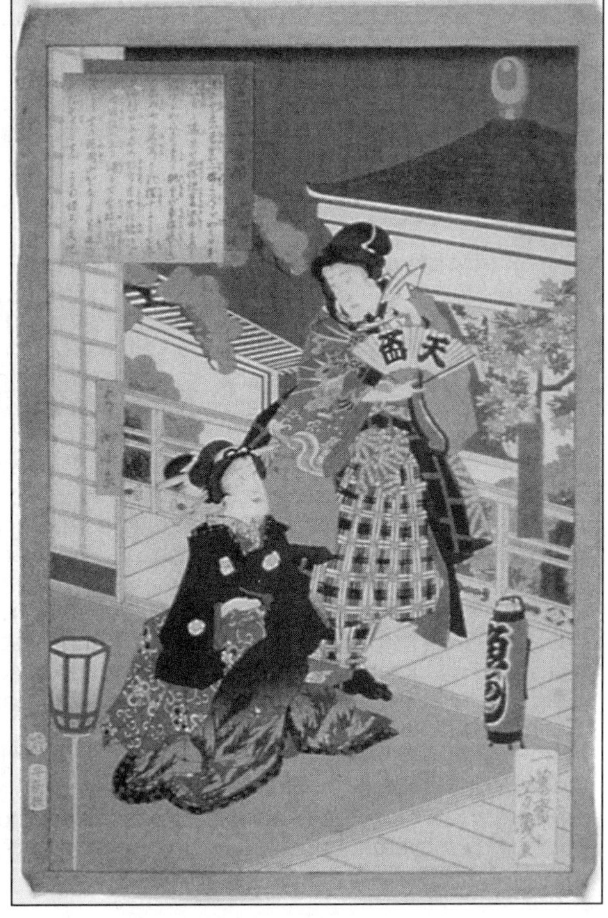

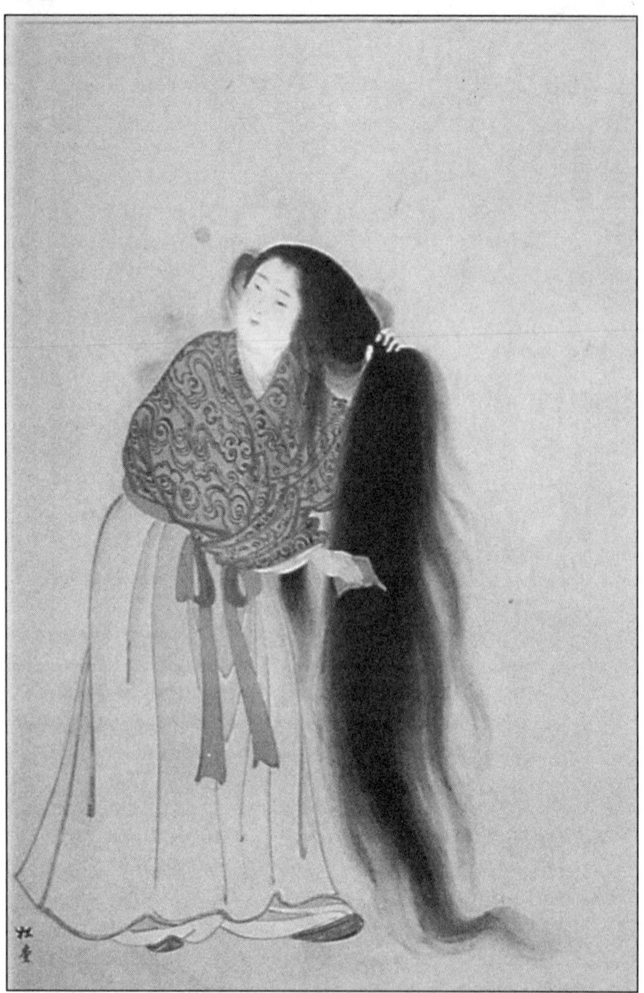

Yukawa Shodo, oban tate-e, "Korean Beauty Combing Her Hair," from the series One Hundred Beauties, Past and Present, signed and sealed "Shodo," dated 1903, fine impression, condition, and color, $1000-1500.

Yoshitoshi continued:

Oban tate-e, Saimyoji Tokiyori Nyudo standing in the snow, holding his hat, from the series A Mirror of Famous Japanese Generals, signed and sealed, published by Shojiro Runazu, dated 1878, good, impression, color, and condition, $600-900.

Oban tate-e, "Okigatsukiso Meiji Nenkan Saikunno Guzoku," from the series Thirty Two Aspects of Women, a woman opening a lit paper lantern, signed "Yoshitoshi," published by Tsunashima Kamekichi, good impression, color, and condition, $800-1000.

Oban tate-e, a No actor holding a long staff, from the series One Hundred Aspects of the Moon, signed "Yoshitoshi," published by Akiyama Buemon, dated Meiji 20 (1887), good impression, color, and condition, $800-1200.

Oban tate-e, "Faith in the Third Day Moon-Yukimori," from the series One Hundred Aspects of the Moon, 1886, signed "Yoshitoshi," seal Taiso, published by Akiyama, good impression, color, and condition $650-850.

Yoshitoyo I (fl. 1840-1860) Osaka School.

Yoshitoyo II (fl. c. 1890s-1900) Osaka School, son of Yoshimine.

Yoshitsuga (fl. c. 1830s) Osaka School, pupil of Sadayoshi.

Yoshisuya I (1822-1866) pupil of Kuniyoshi.

Yoshisuya II (fl. c. 1870s)

Yoshiyuki (1835-1879) pupil of Yoshiume.

Yukawa Shodo (1868-?) bijin ga.

Yukimaro (1797-1856) Kitagawa School, pupil of Tsukimaro / (fl. 1780-1790) Kitagawa School, pupil of Utamaro.

Yurakusai name used by Nagahide.

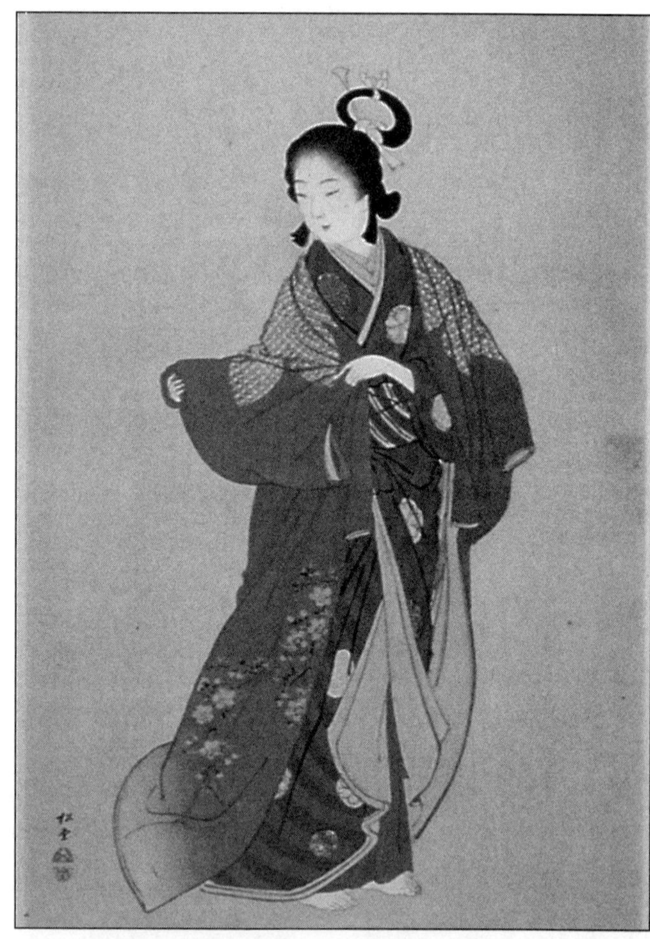

Yukawa Shodo, oban tate-e, bijin, her kimono enhanced with hand painted flowers, from the series One Hundred Beauties, Past and Present, signed and sealed "Shodo," dated 1903, fine impression, condition, and color, $1000-1500.

Z

Zeshin Shibata (1807-1891) Edo Shijo School

Amano Kunihiro, dai oban tate-e, 15 1/2" x 23", "Enclosure," from an edition of 30, dated 1965, signed, excellent condition, $1000-1500.

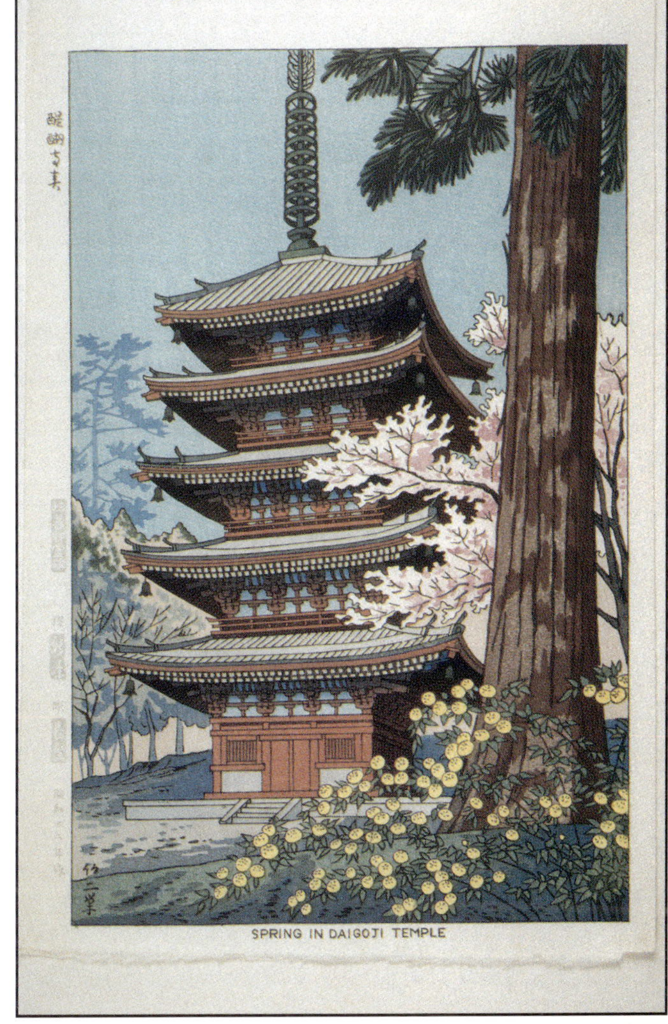

Asano Takeji oban tate-e, 16" x 11 1/4", title on lower margin "Spring In Daigoji Temple," signed "Asano," publisher Unsodo, dated Showa 26 (1951) early edition, fine impression, color, and condition, $450-650.

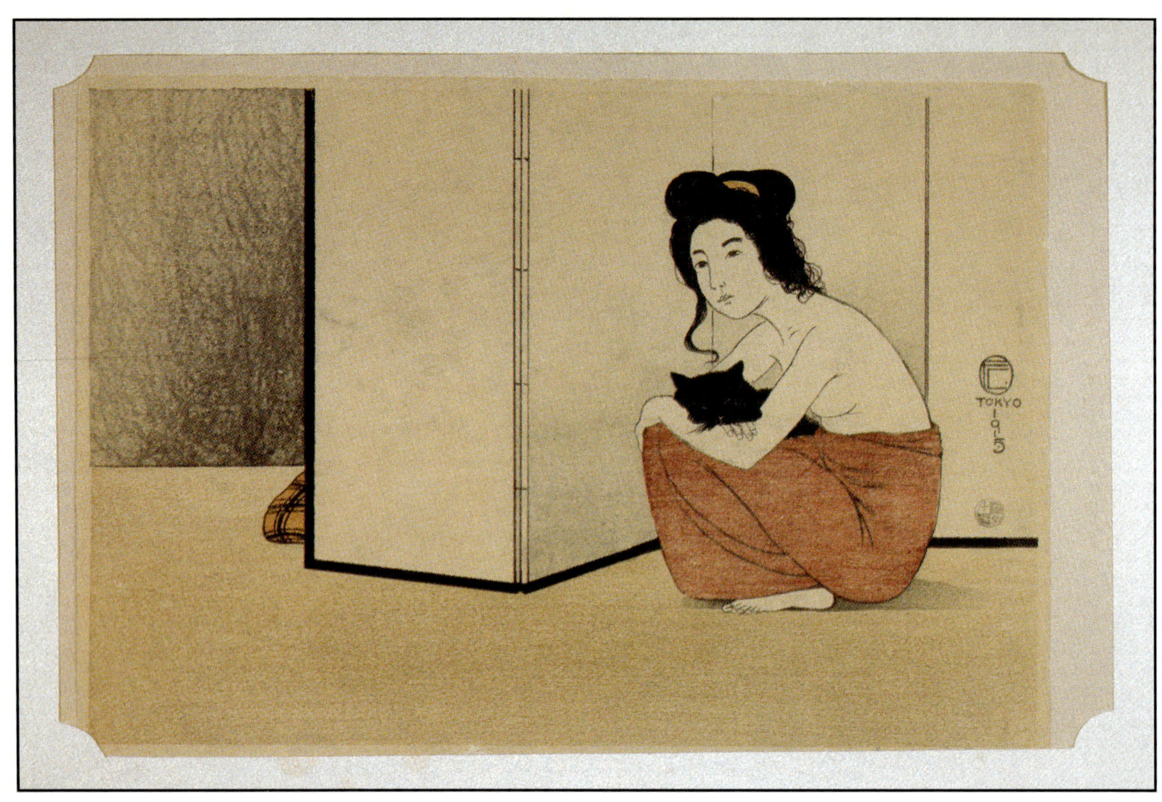

Capelari, Fritz, oban yoko-e, 12 1/2" x 8 1/4", Semi nude, published 1915 by Watanabe, signed and sealed and dated "Fritz Capelari," very good color and impression, lower margin trimmed, $1000-1500.

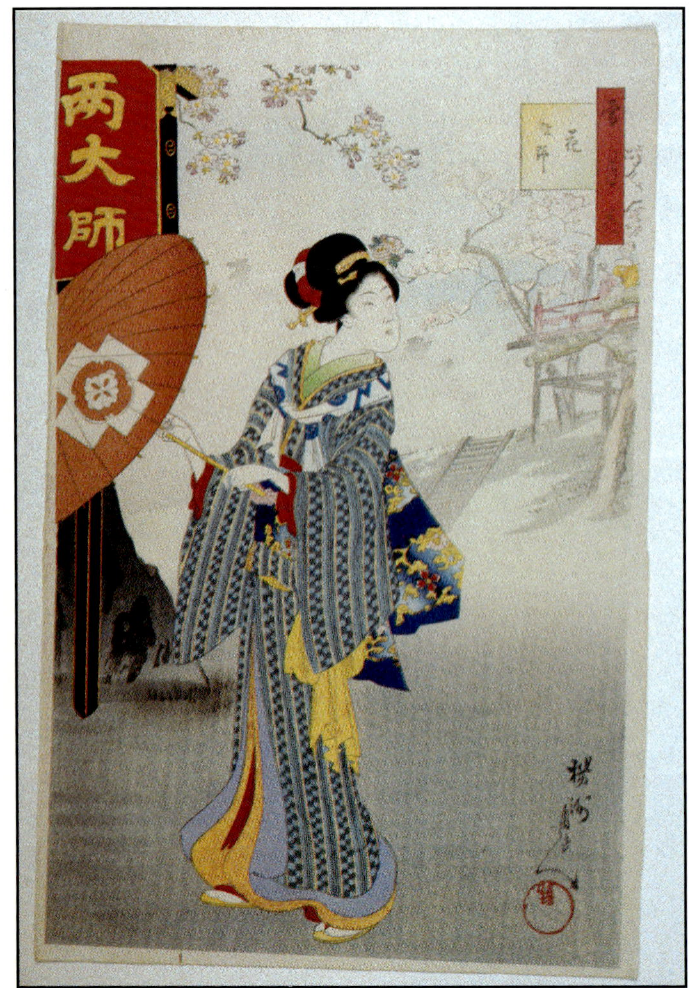

Chikanobu, oban tate-e, "Bijin," dated Meiji 31 (1897), fine impression, condition, and color, $375-575.

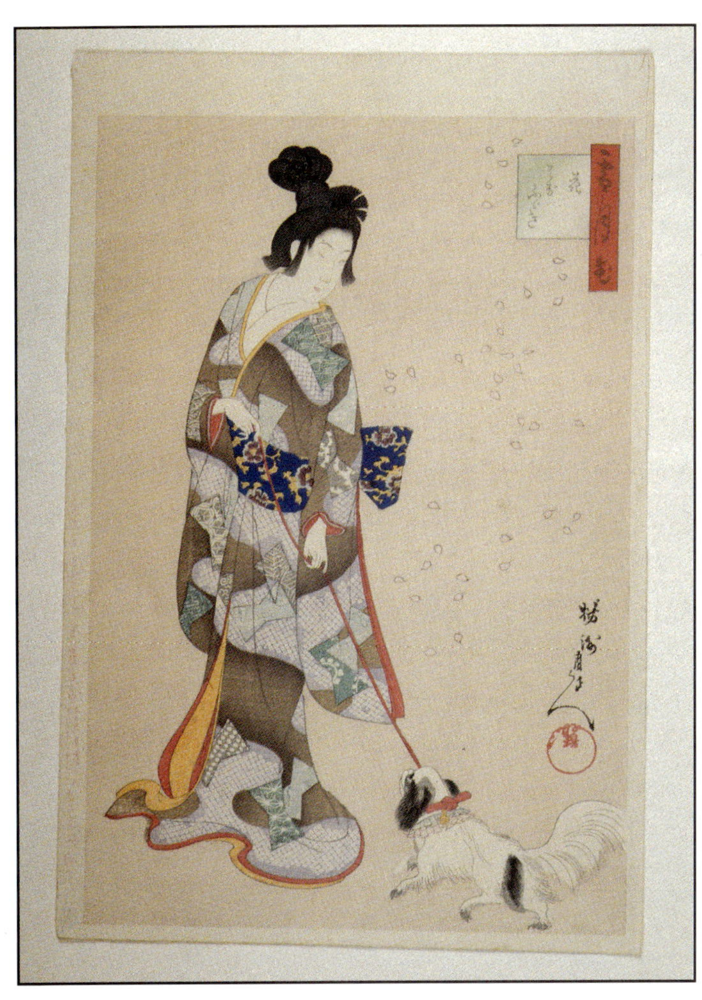

Chikanobu, oban tate-e, "Bijin and Her Dog," dated Meiji 31 (1897), fine impression, condition, and color $500-700.

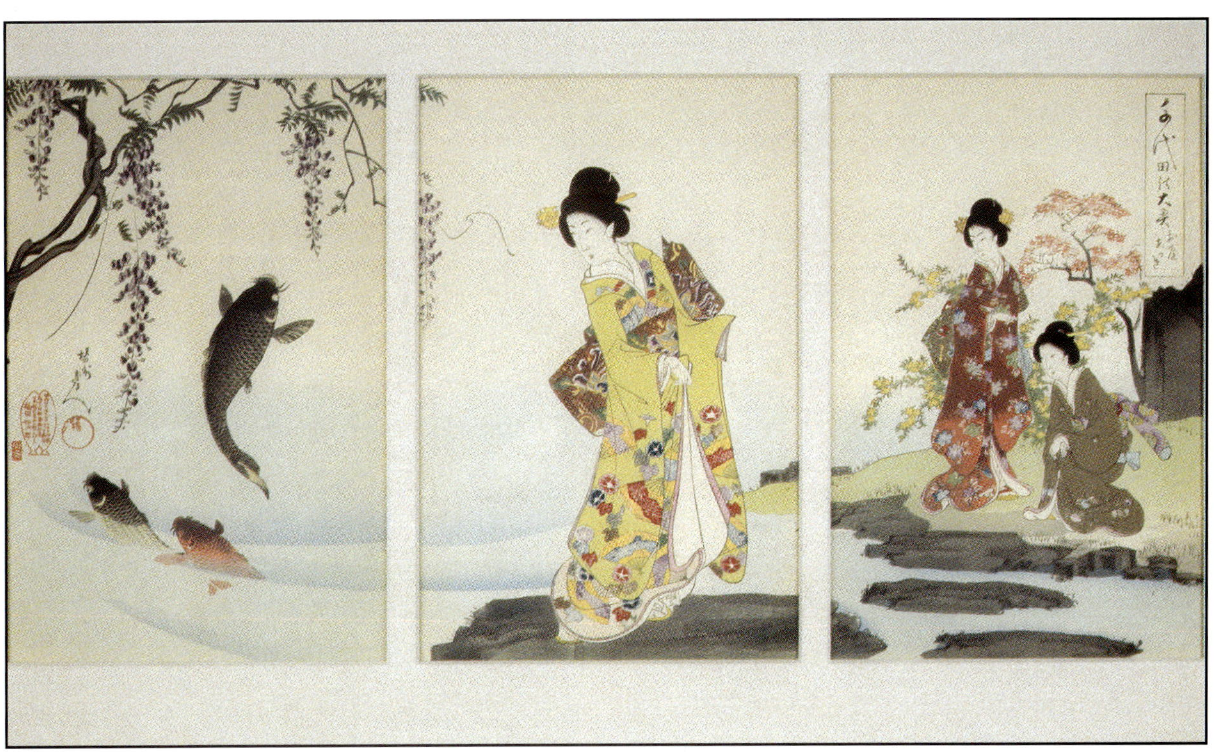

Chikanobu, oban tate-e triptych, "Bijin and Koi," dated Meiji 29 (1896), very fine impression, color, and condition, $1800-2300.

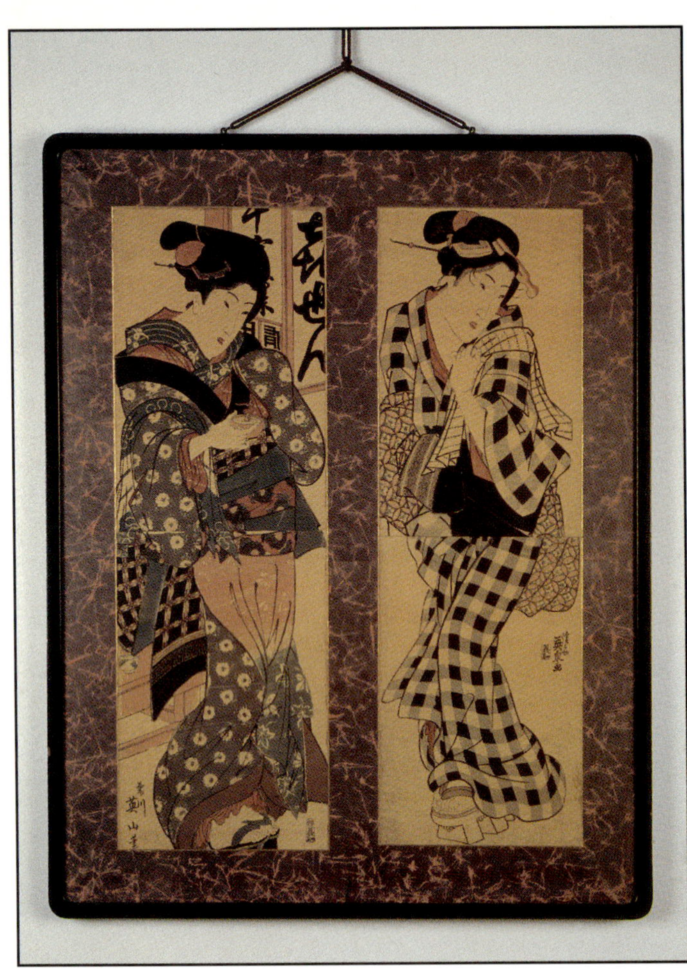

Eizen and Eisen, kakemono-e, a panel with two kakemono-e of bijin, fine impression, very good color and condition, slightly soiled, $3000-5000 each.

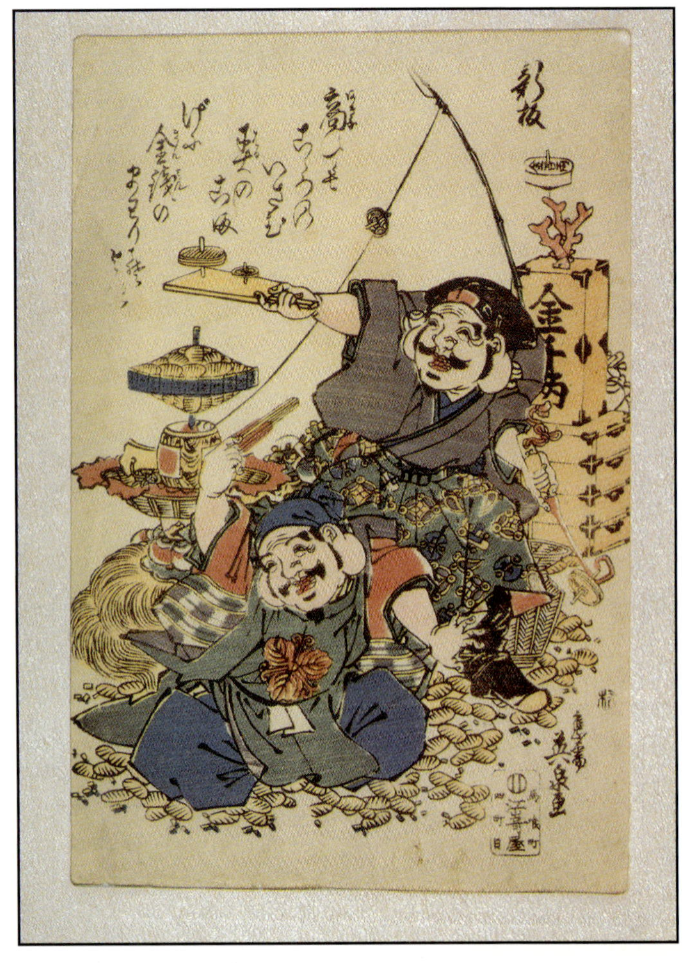

Eisen, oban tate-e, "Daikoku and Ebisu," fine impression and color, corners rubbed, slightly soiled, $400-650.

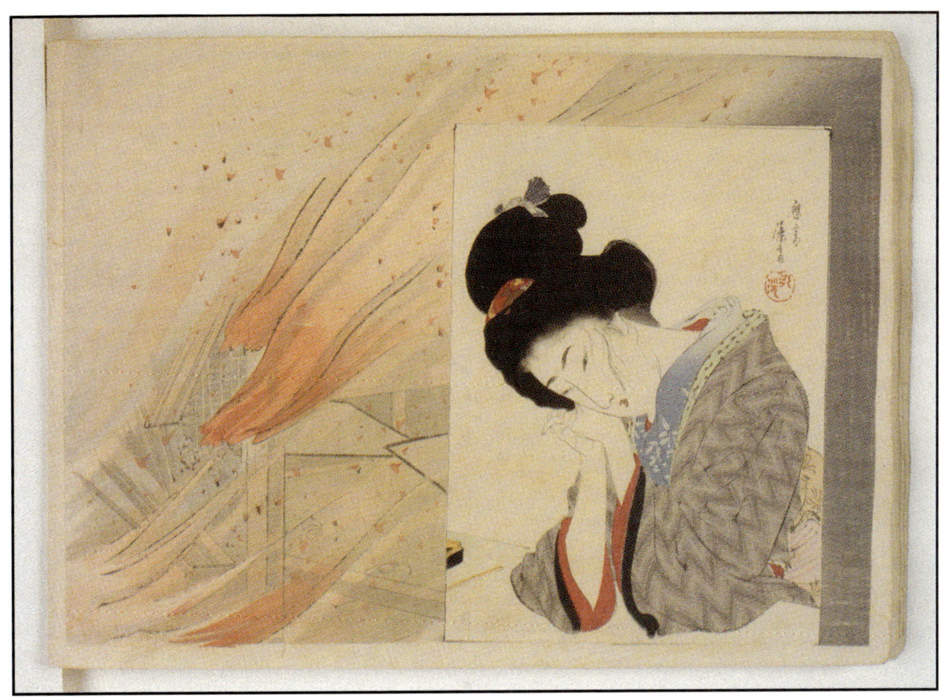

Kiyokata Kaburagi, Eisen Tomioka, Kiyochika Kobayashi, Hanko Kajita, Kason Suzuki, Keishu Takeuchi, Chikanobu Yoshu, Toshimine Tsutsui, Toshikata Mizuno, oban yoko-e 11 1/2" x 8 1/2", (Eisen Tomioka signed upper right oju Mosai (on request Mosai) with artist's seal Eisen), 24 woodblock illustrations for Romantic Novels, late Meiji period c. 1900, fine impressions, very good color and condition, mica, gauffrage, $2500-4500.

Eizan, oban tate-e, "Bijin With Biwa in the Snow," kiwame seal, very good impression, good color, toned and slightly soiled, backed, $375-485.

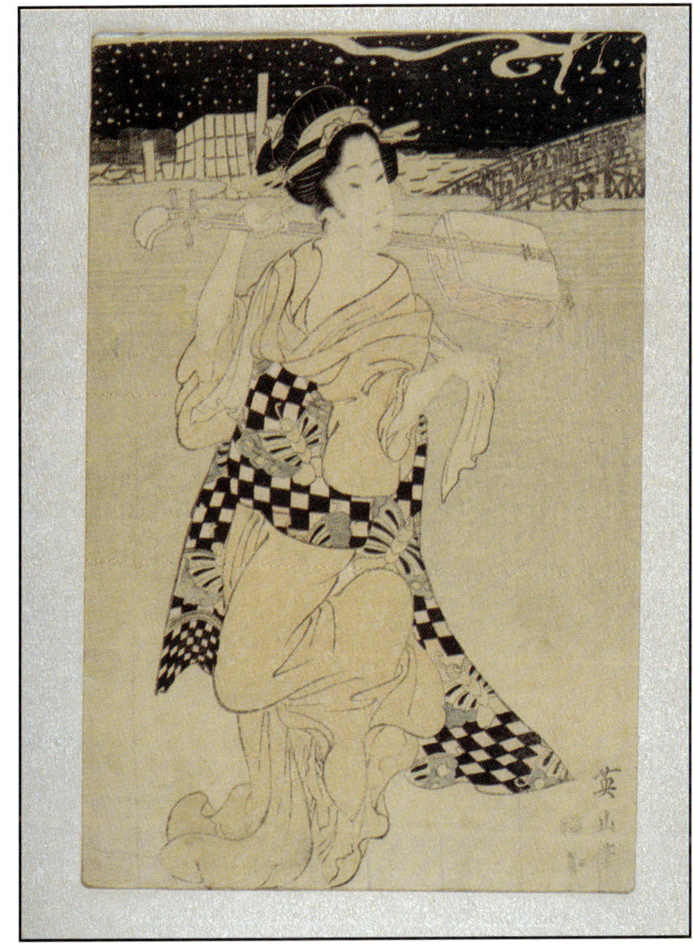

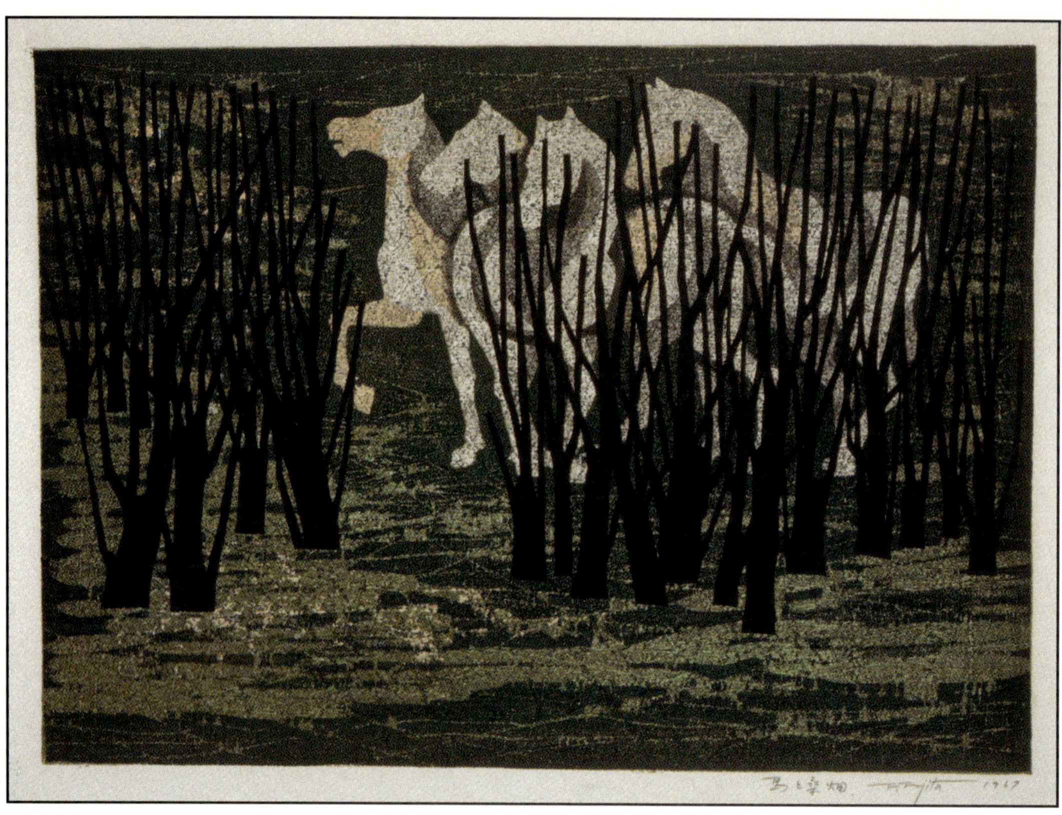

Fujita Fumio, oban yoko-e, "Horses Amongst Trees," signed and dated 1967, fine impression, color, and condition, $250-375.

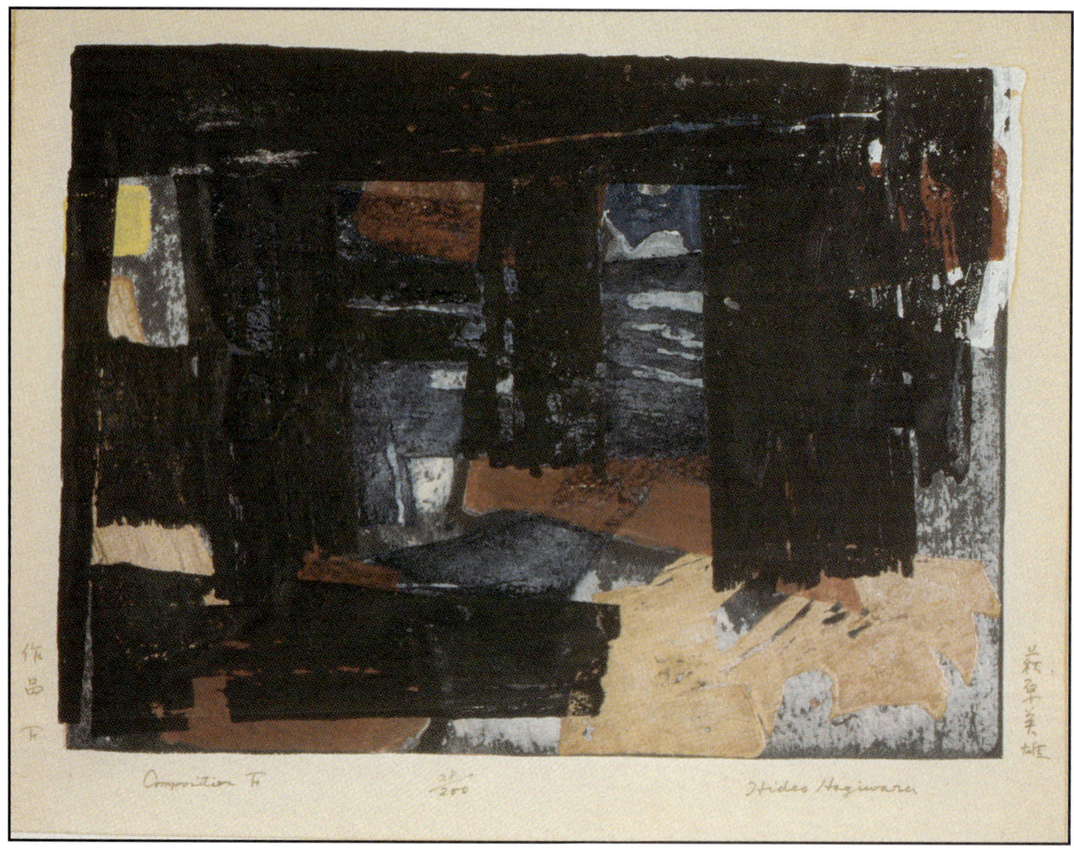

Hagiwara Hideo, oban yoko-e, "Composition F," from an edition of 200, fine condition, color, and impression, $1000-1800.

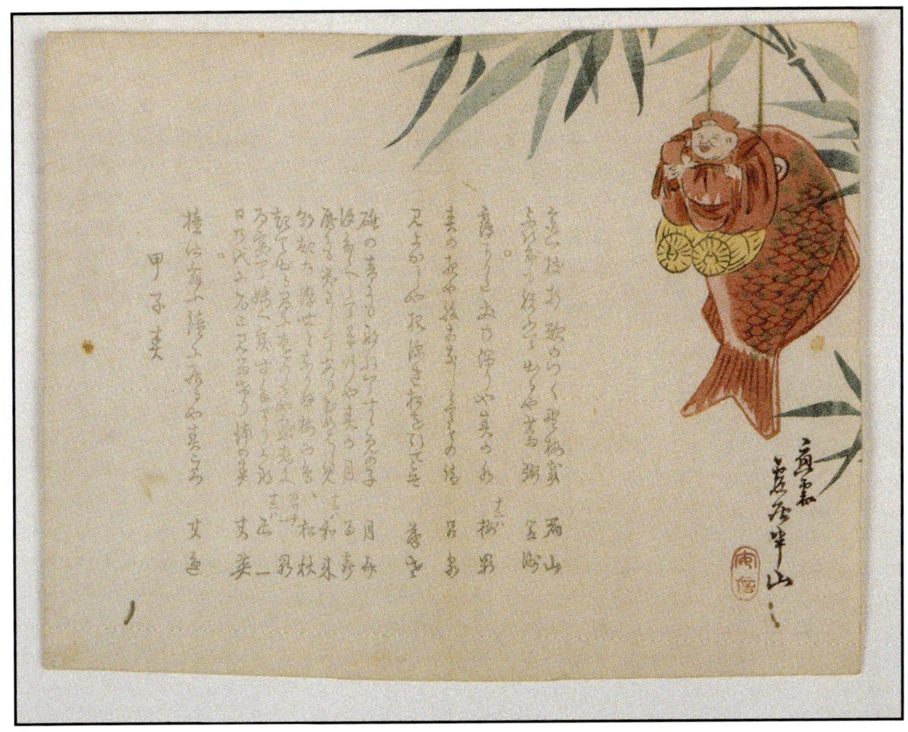

Hanzan, surimono, "Daikoku and Fish," c. 1860, very fine impression, very good color, three creases, two tiny worm holes (mirror image), $450-750.

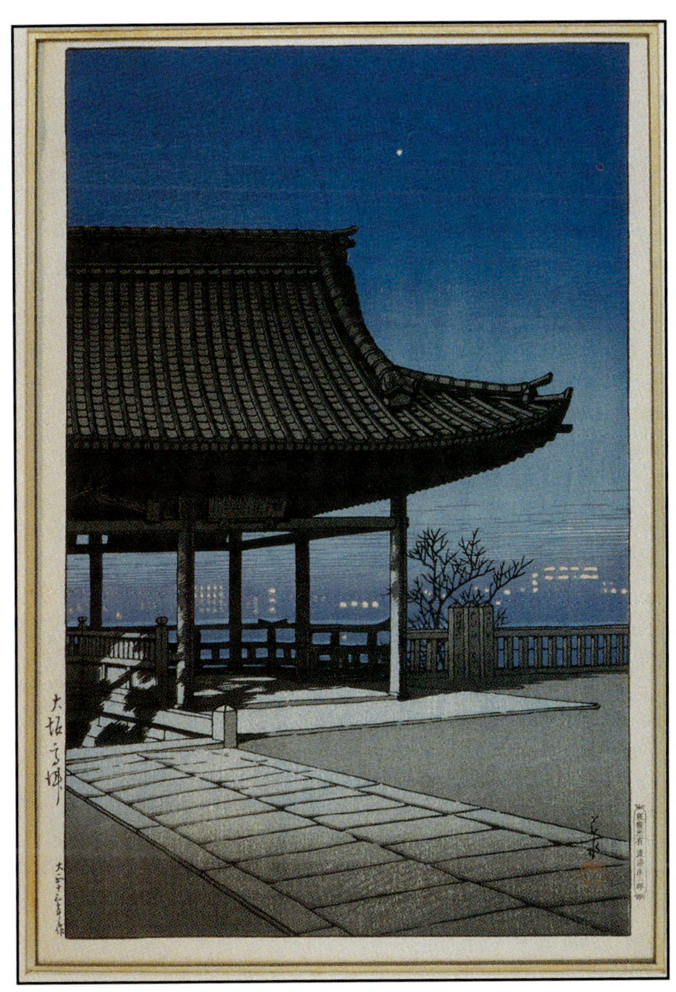

Hasui, oban tate-e, "Kozu, Osaka," dated Taisho 13 (1924), published by Watanabe, fine impression, color, and condition, $5500-7500.

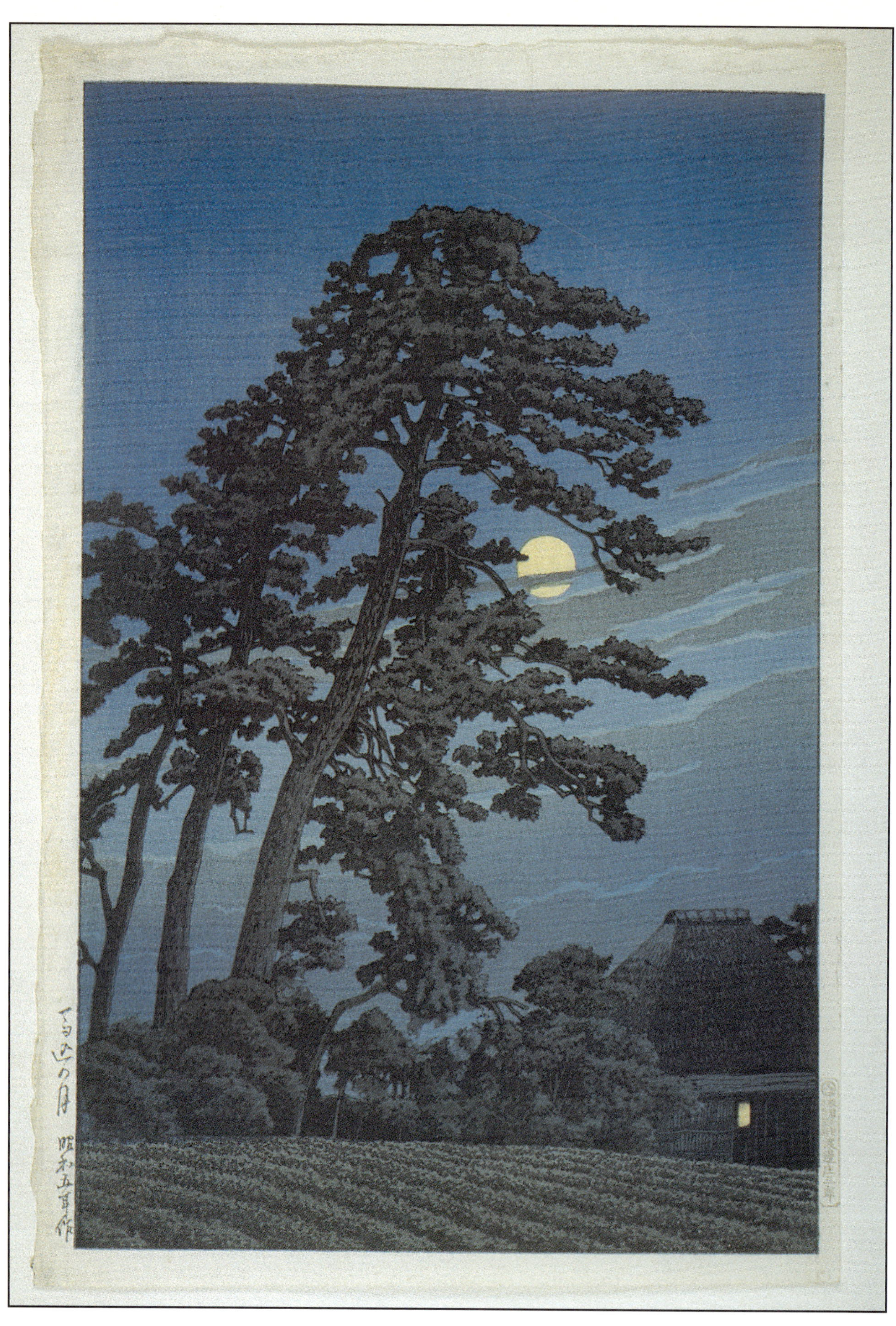

Hasui, oban tate-e, 15 1/4" x 10 1/4", "Moon At Magome," dated Showa 5 (1930), early edition, published by Watanabe, excellent condition, color, and impression, $3500-5500.

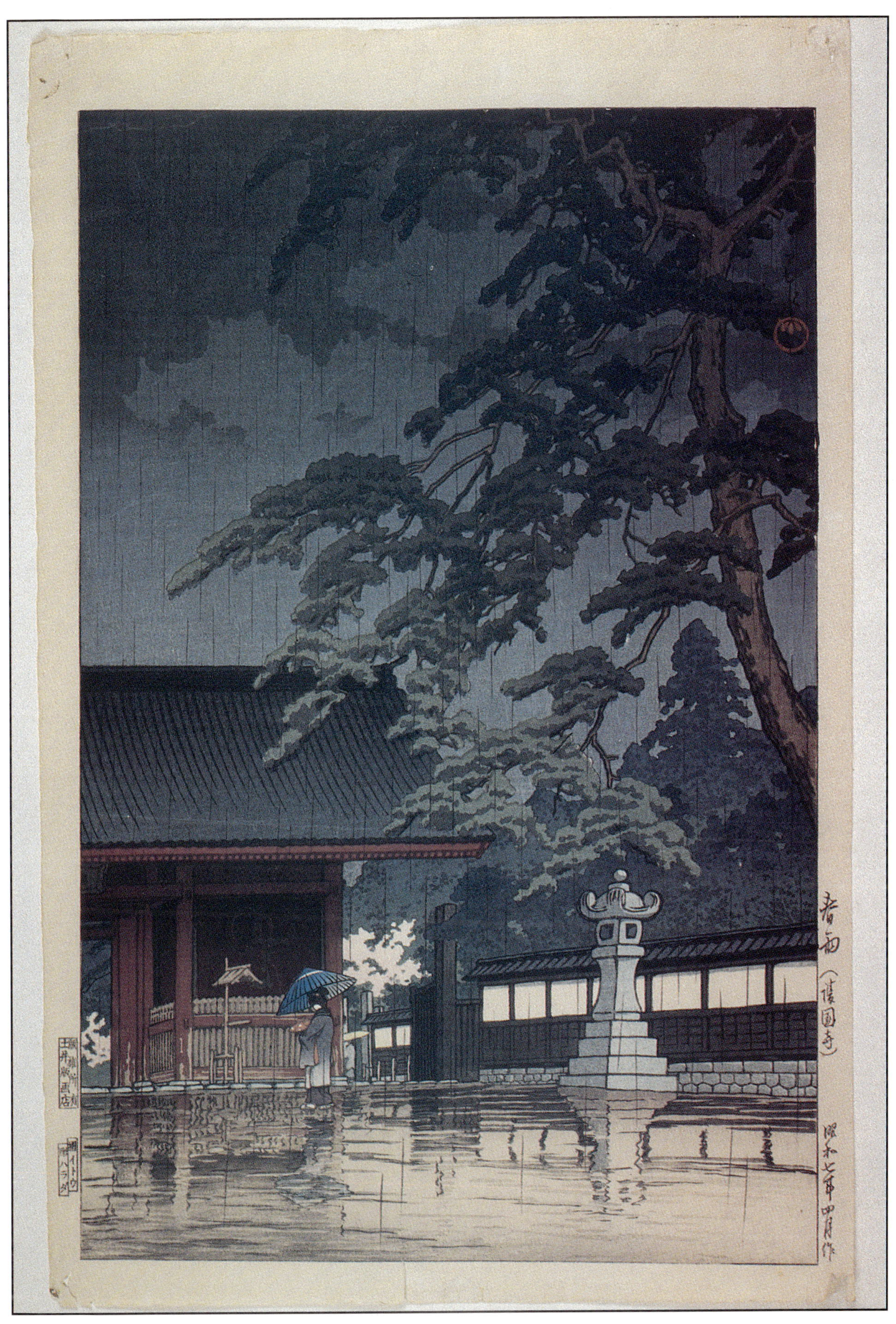

Hasui Kawase, oban tate-e, "Spring Rain At Gokokuji Temple," dated Showa 7 (1932), early edition, published by Doi, very good impression, toned, foxed, tape residue on verso $300-450.

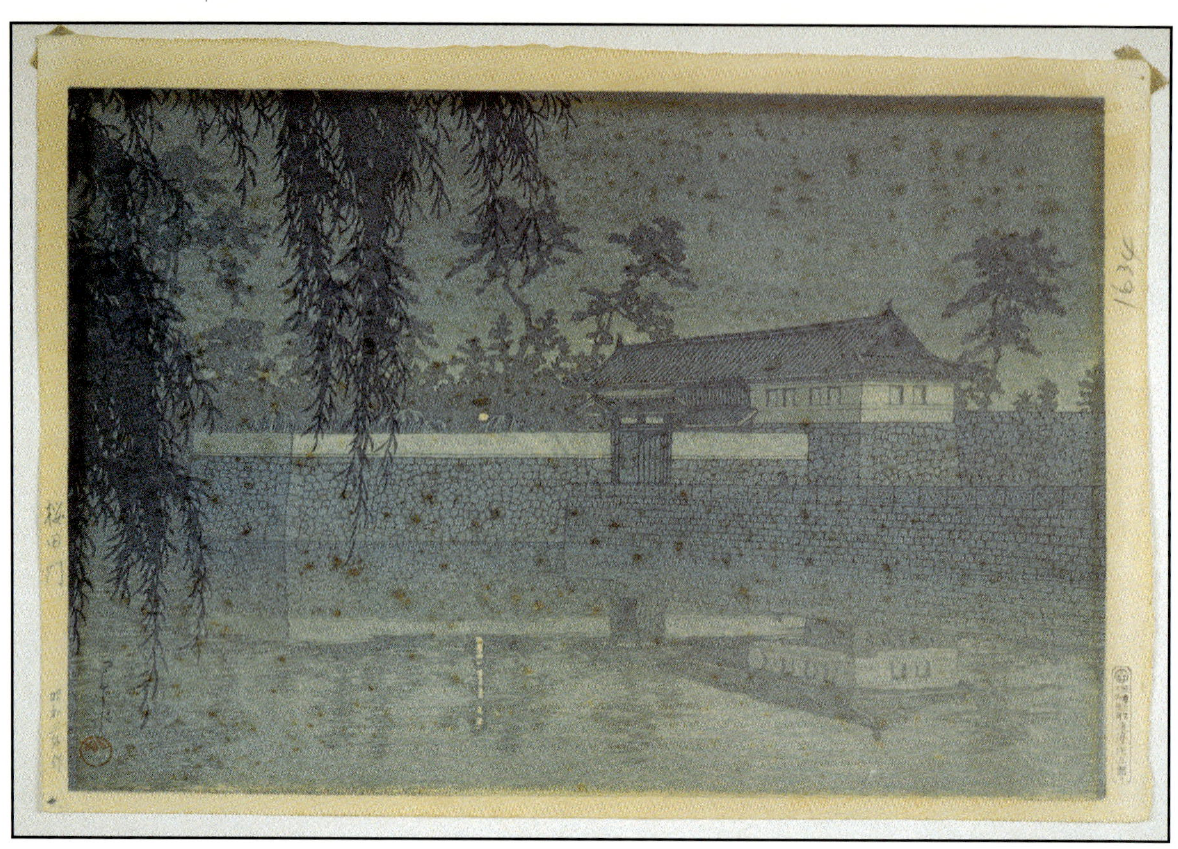

Hasui Kawase, oban yoko-e, azuri-e, early edition published by Watanabe, faded, toned, foxed, mat burn, verso browned, verso with tape residue, $100-150.

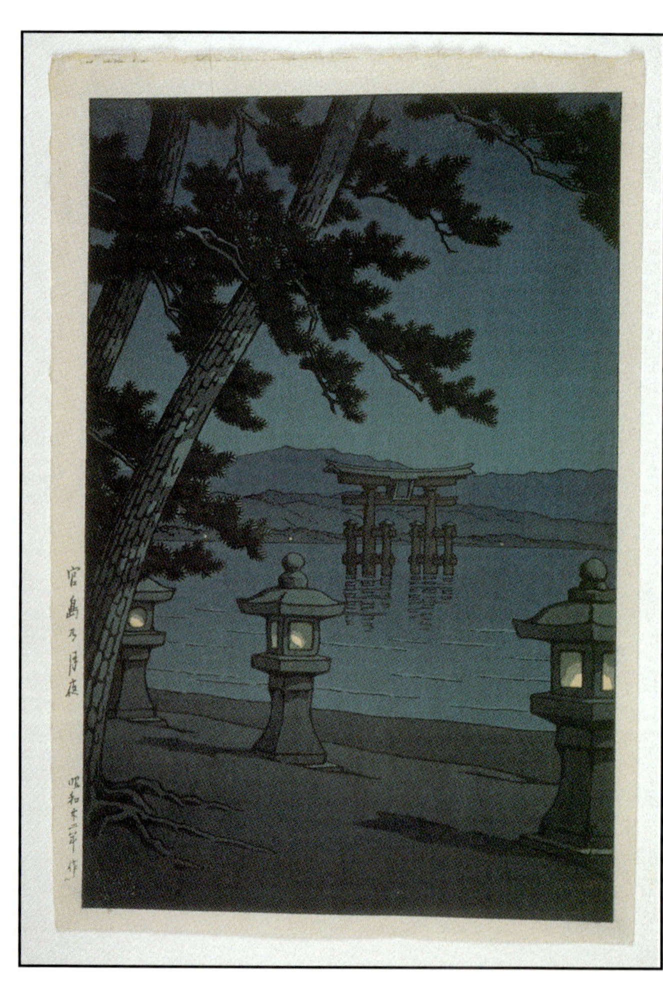

Hasui Kawase, oban tate-e, "Stone Lanterns at Miyajima Shrine," dated Showa 22 (1947), early edition, published by Watanabe, fine impression, color, and condition, $1000-1500.

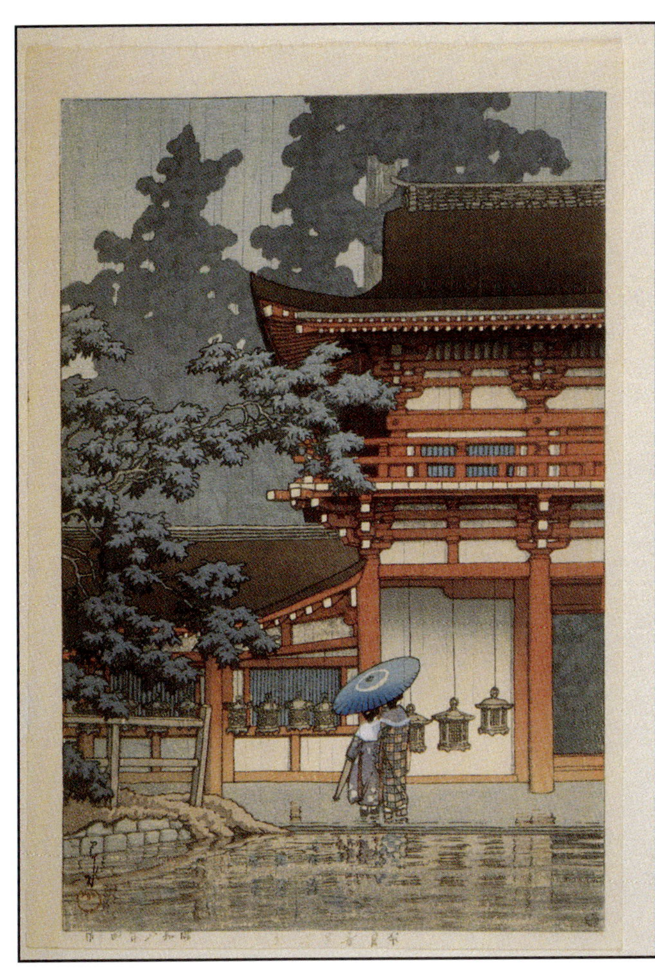

Hasui Kawase, oban tate-e, "Kasuga Shrine in Nara," dated Showa 8 (1933), later edition, 6mm Watanabe seal, fine impression, color, and condition, $800-1200.

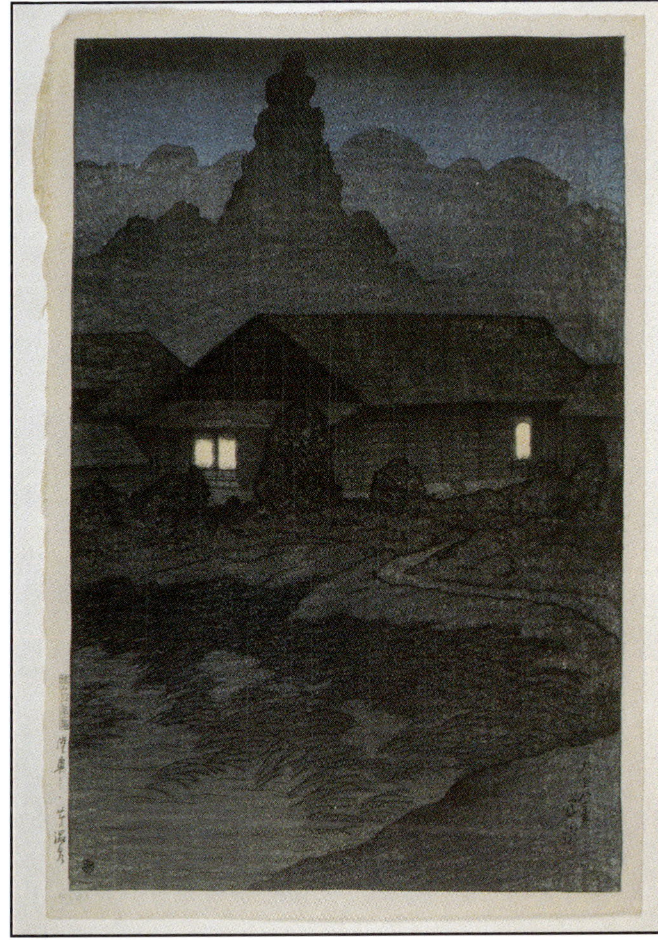

Hasui Kawase, oban tate-e, "Tsuta-Onsen Spa, Aomiri," dated Taisho 8 (1919), published by Watanabe, fine color, impression, and condition, $6500-8500.

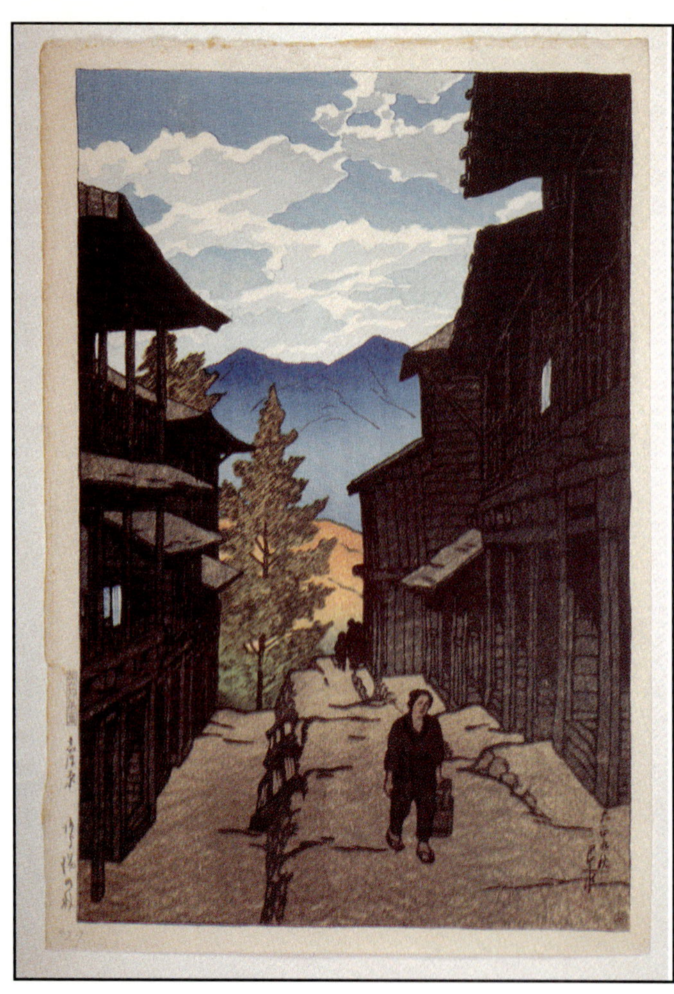

Hasui Kawase, oban tate-e, "Arayu in Autumn Shiobara," dated Taisho 9 (1920), published by Watanabe, fine color, impression, and condition, $6500-8500.

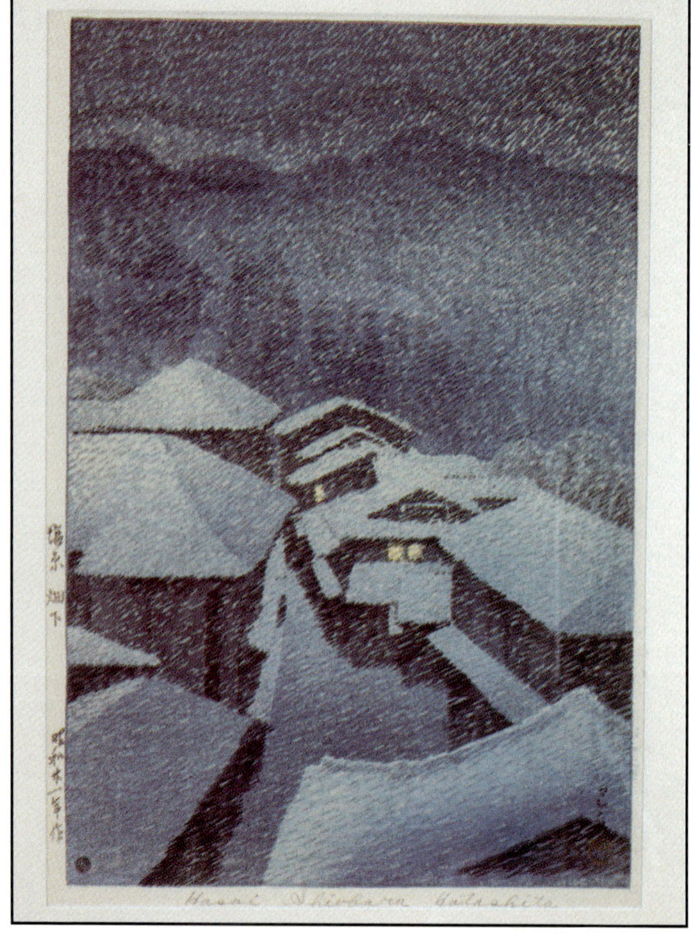

Hasui Kawase, oban tate-e, "Hatori, Shiobara," (Snow Storm at Shiobara), signed and sealed within the image, published by Watanabe, dated 1946, fine impression, condition, and color, $3500-5500.

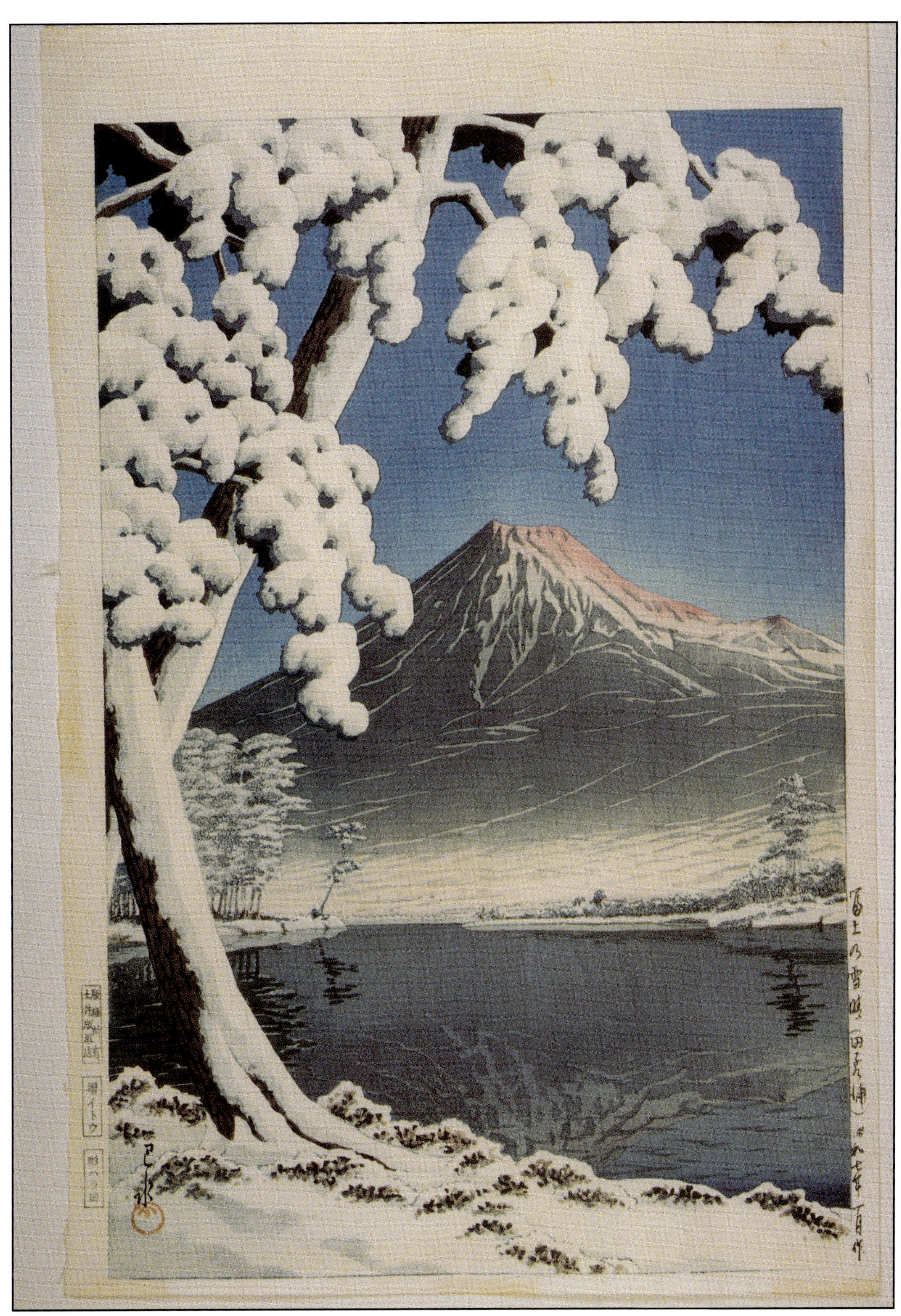

Hasui Kawase, oban tate-e, 15 3/4" x 10 1/2"; "Mt. Fuji After Snow," published 1932 by Doi, early edition, signed and sealed Hasui, fine color, impression and condition, $2500-3500.

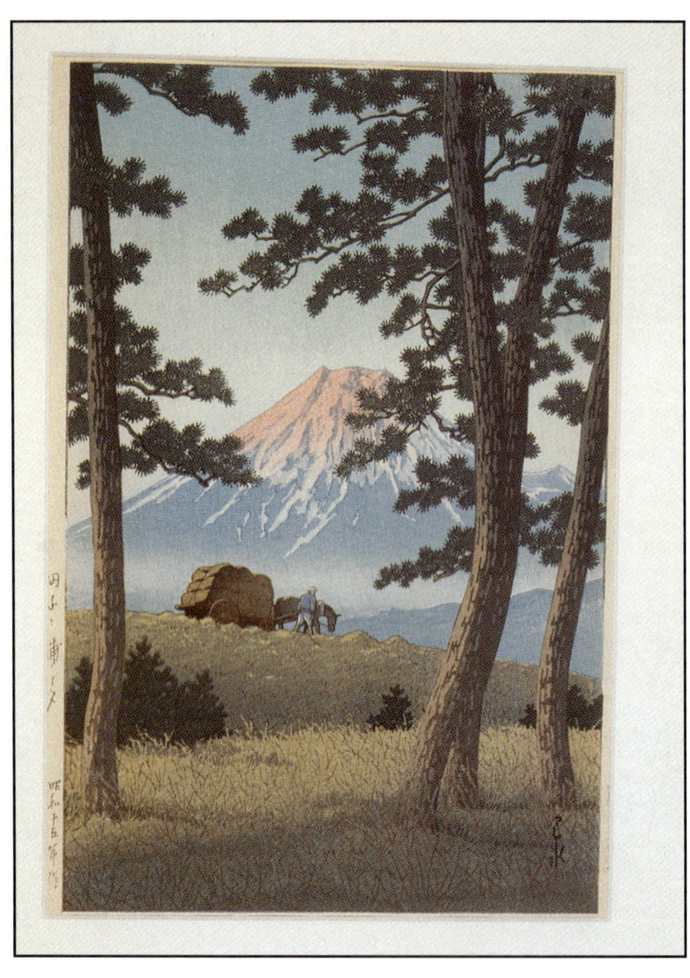

Hasui, oban tate-e, "Evening At Tago No Ura," dated Showa 15 (1940), signed and sealed Hasui (Kawase), published by Watanabe, fine impression, color, and condition, $2500-3500.

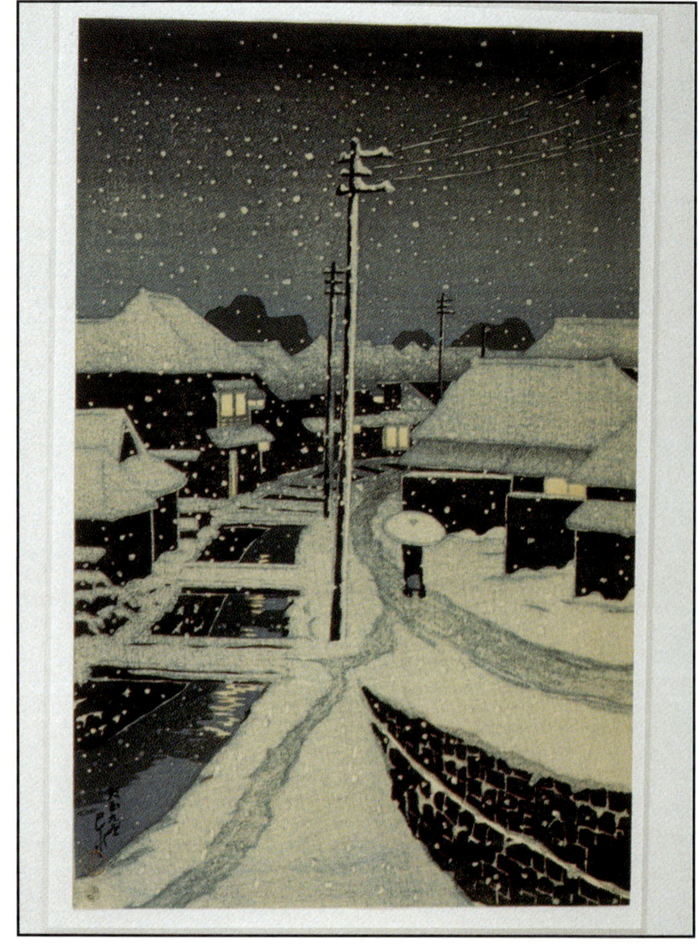

Hasui, oban tate-e, "Terajima Village in a Snowy Twilight, Mukojima, Tokyo," signed and sealed Hasui, fine impression, color, and very good condition, margins trimmed, dated 1920, $2550-3500.

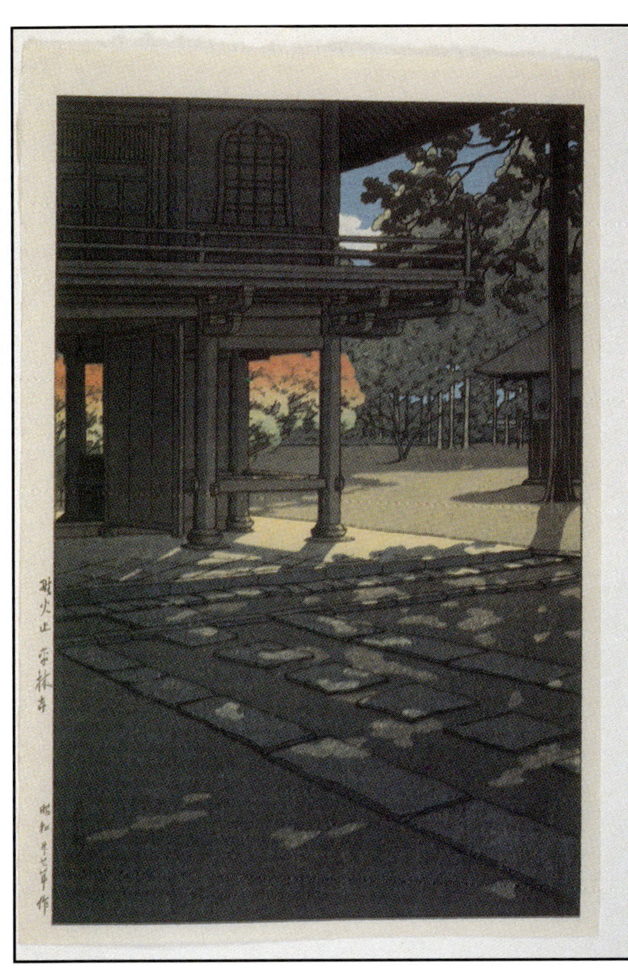

Hasui Kawase, oban tate-e, "Nobidome Heirin-ji Temple, Saitama," dated Showa 27 (1952) early edition, publisher Watanabe, fine impression, color, and condition, $1200-1800.

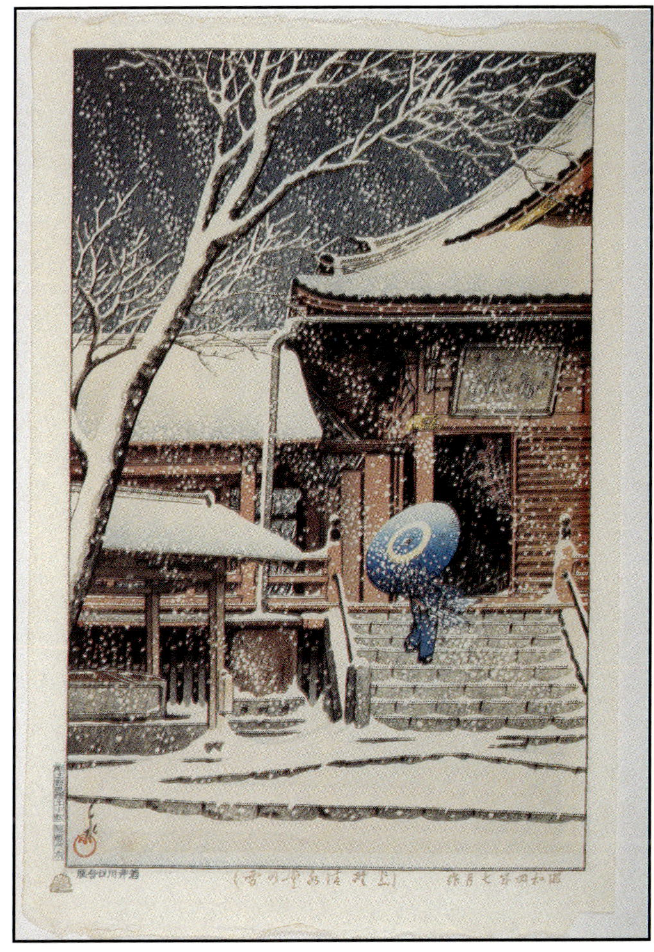

Hasui Kawase, oban tate-e, "Ueno Kiyomizudo In Snow," dated Showa 4 (1929), from a limited edition of 350, limited edition seal on back with Hasui seal, published by Sakai/Kawaguchi, fine impression, color, and condition, $8500-12000.

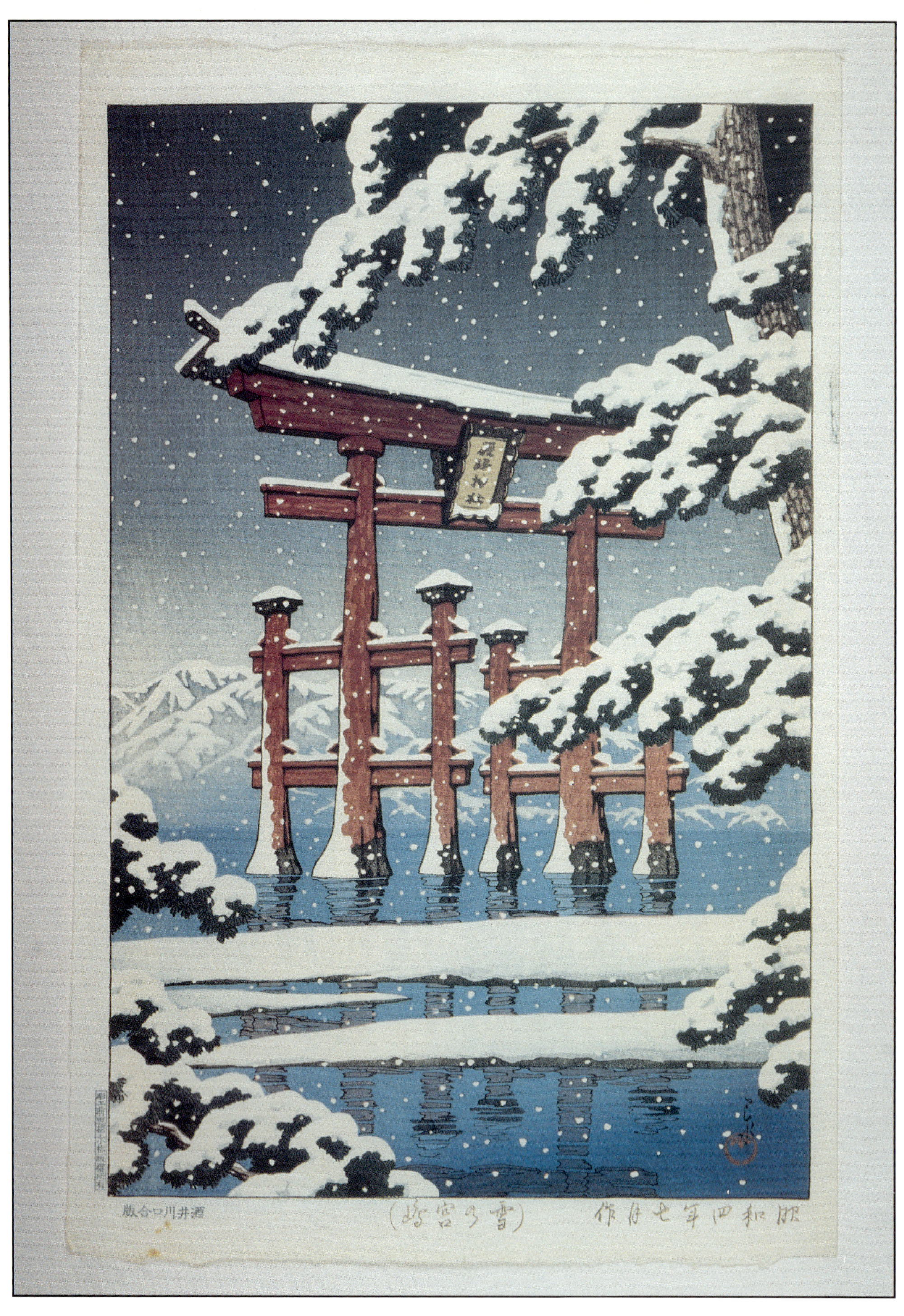

Hasui Kawase, oban tate-e, "Snow At Miyajima," dated Showa 4 (1929), from a limited edition, published by Sakai/Kawaguchi, fine impression, color, and condition, $5500-8500.

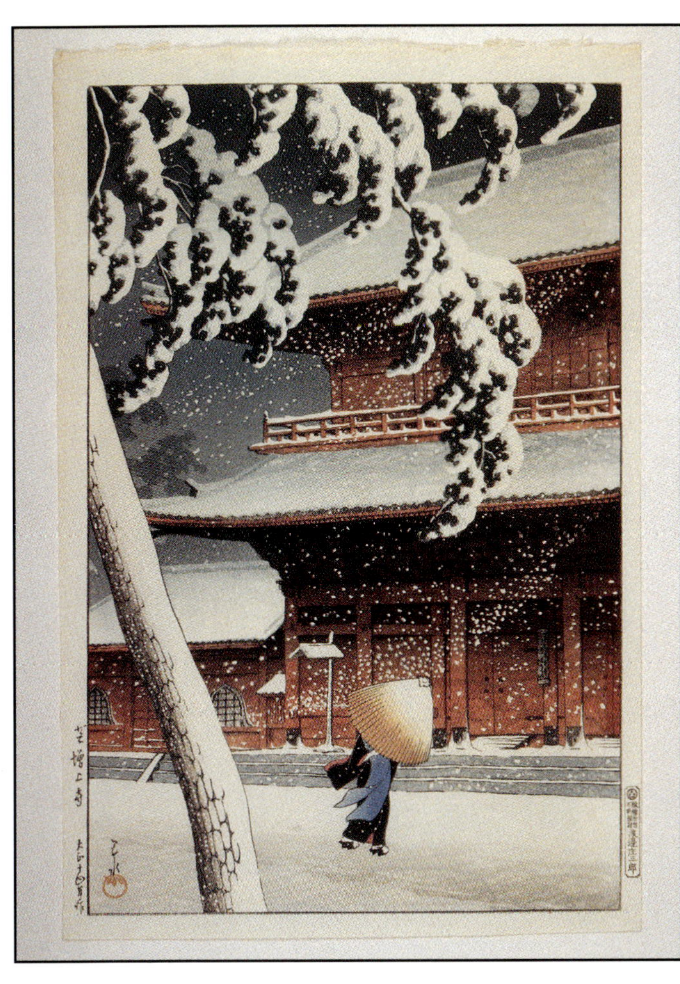

Hasui Kawase, oban tate-e, "Zojo-ji Temple, Shiba," dated Taisho 14 (1925), printed 1931, published by Watanabe, fine impression, color, and condition, $5500-7500.

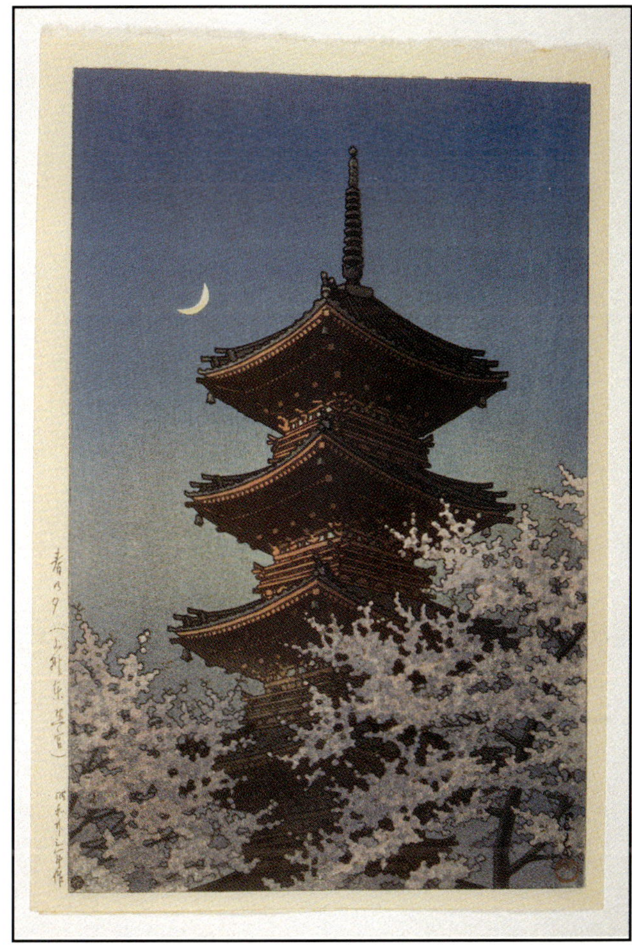

Hasui Kawase, oban tate-e, "Ueno Park, Tokyo," dated Showa 23 (1948),early edition, published by Watanabe , fine impression, color, and condition, $900-1200.

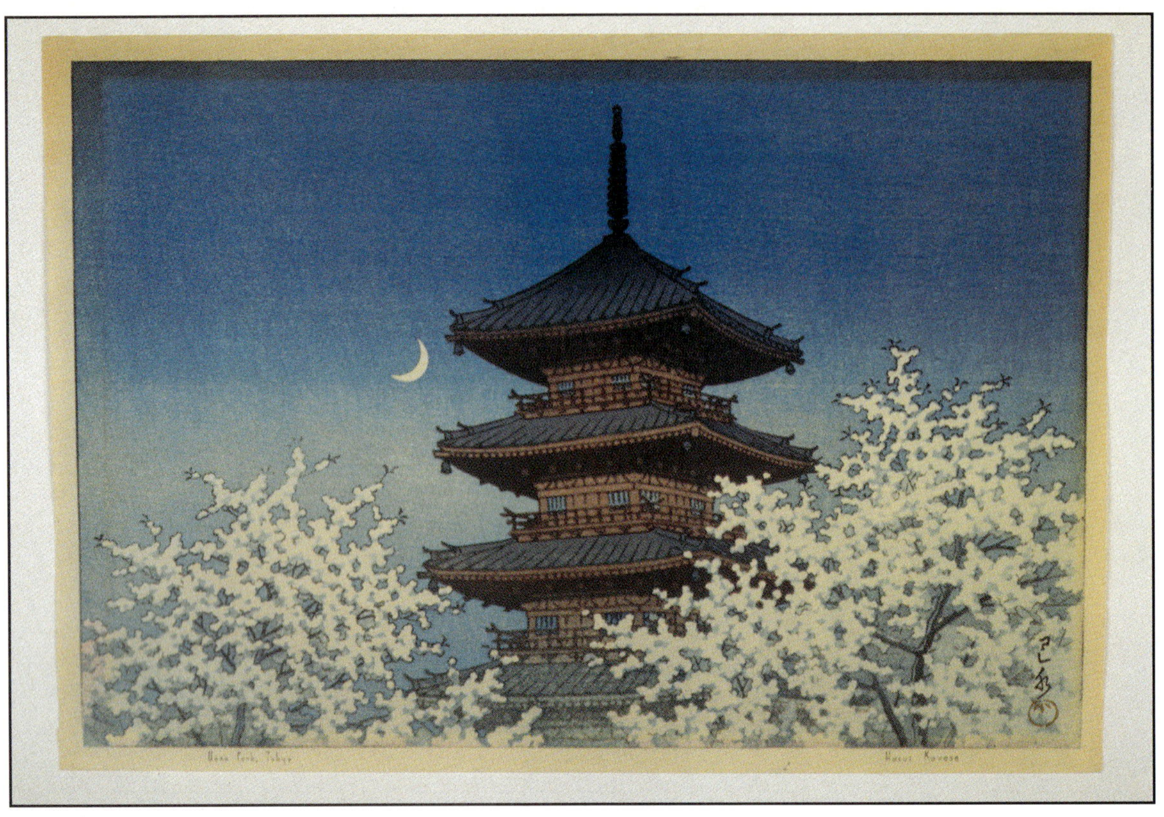

Hasui Kawase, oban yoko-e, "Ueno Park, Tokyo," March 1952, title and print artist on lower left margin; a calender print commissioned by Pacific Transport Lines, Inc., 1952, toned, $100-150

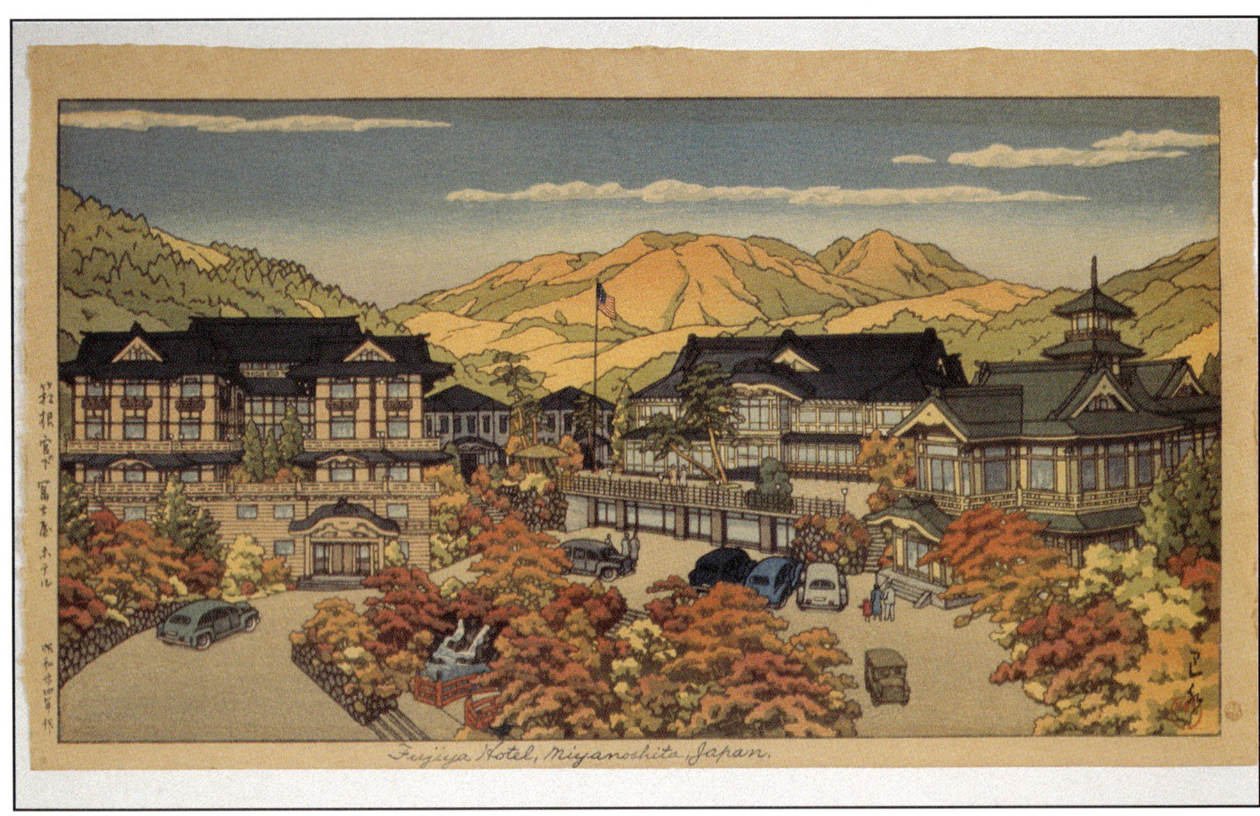

Hasui Kawase, Oban yoko-e, 16 1/2" x 9", "Fujiya Hotel, Miyanoshita, Japan," published by Watanabe, dated Showa 24 (1949), an unusual print with western vehicles, army jeep, American Flag and western figures (an autumnal scene), fine impression, slightly toned, very good color, Watanabe 6mm seal (red) in lower right margin, $1500-2200.

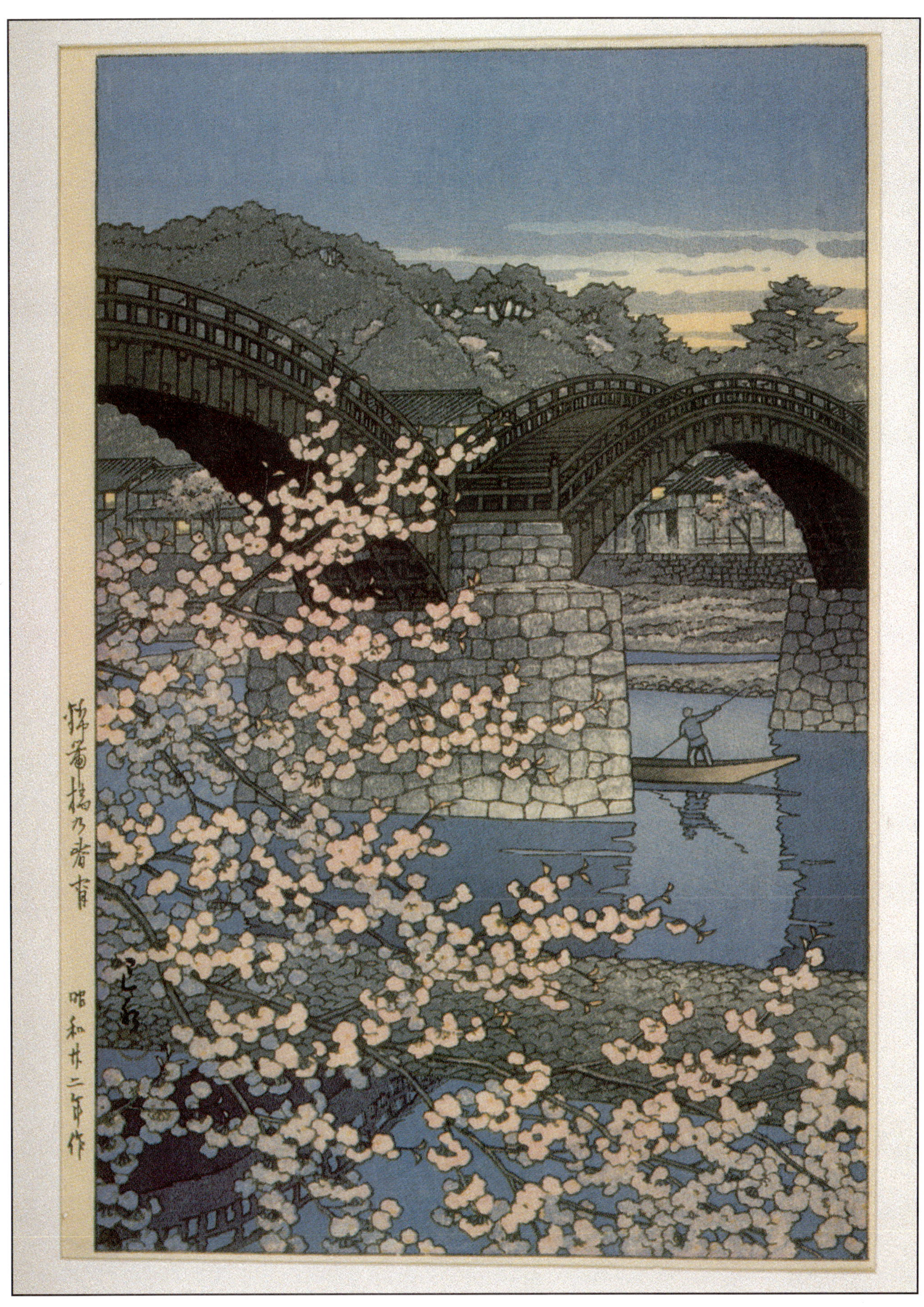

Hasui Kawase, oban tate-e, "Kintai-Bashi Bridge in Spring Evening, Yamaguchi," dated Showa 22 (1947), early edition, published by Watanabe, fine impression, color and condition, $1500-1800.

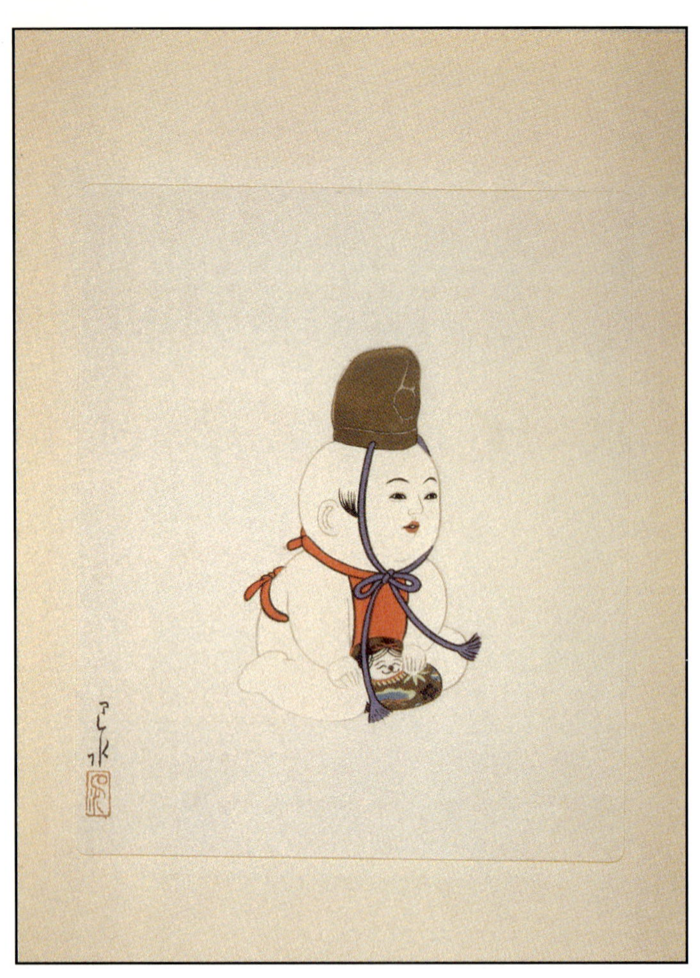

Hasui, shishiban, "Ningyo (doll) With Cat," from a series of dolls produced for the Japanese Woodblock Print Assoc. 1936, signed and sealed "Hasui," in original folio marked #10, fine impression, condition ,and color with mica, $750-1200.

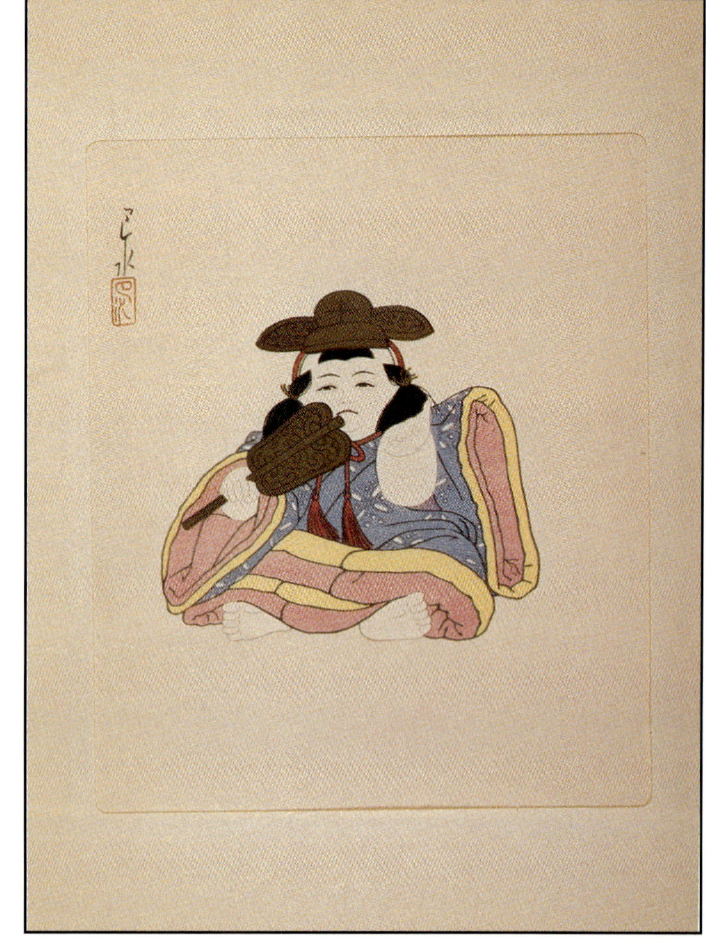

Hasui, shishiban, "Ningyo (doll) With Fan and Sack," from a series of dolls produced for the Japanese Woodblock Print Assoc. 1936, signed and sealed "Hasui," in original folio marked #17, fine impression, condition, and color, with mica, $750-1200.

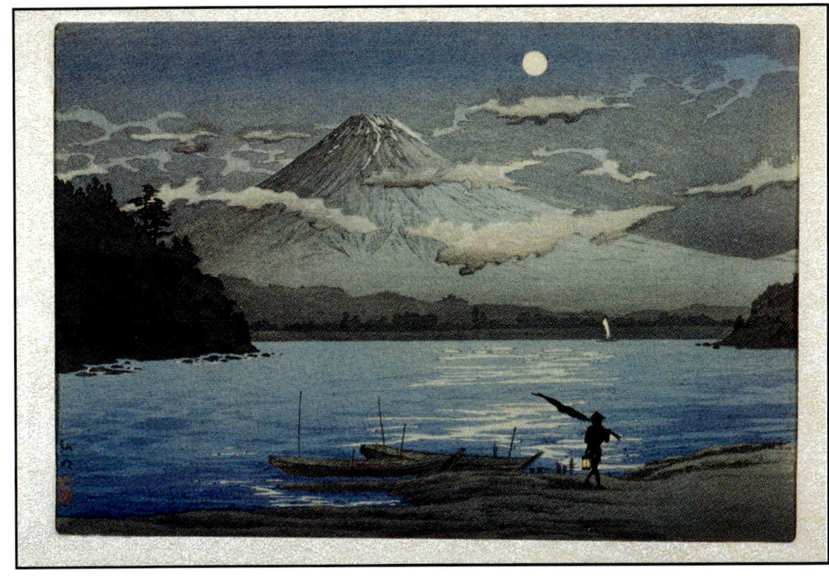

Hiroaki Takahashi (Takahashi Shotei) oban yoko-e, 15 1/2" x 10 1/4", "Mt. Fuji in the Moonlight," published by Fusui Gabo, (act. 1930s) early edition, fine impression, color, and condition, $1000-1500.

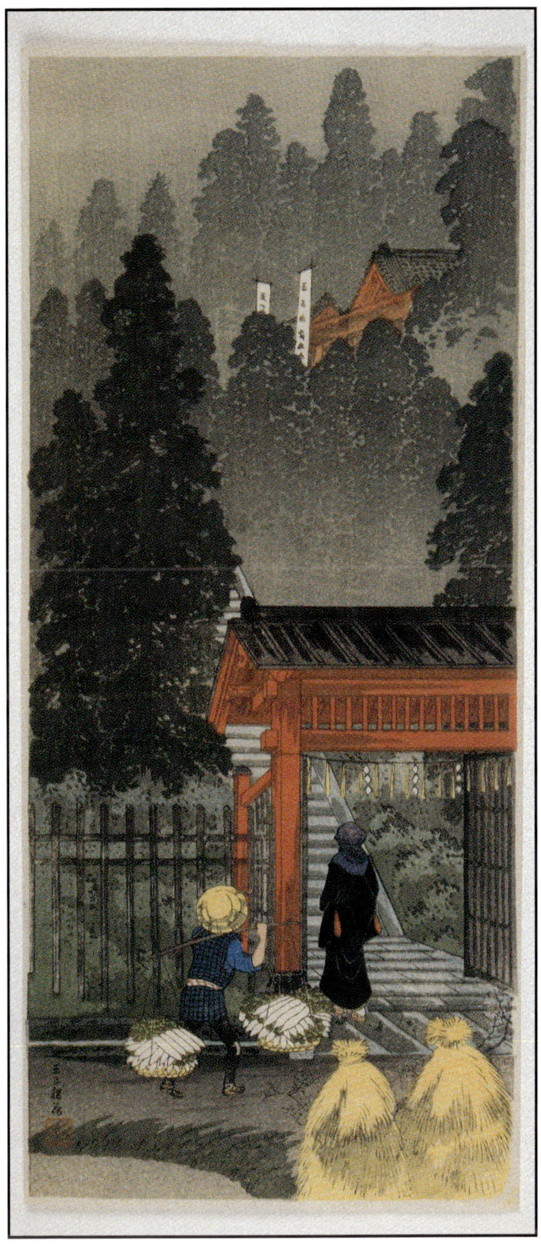

Hiroaki Takahashi (Takashi Shotei), tanzanku, "Daikon Vender," c. 1920, fine color, impression, and condition, $775-975.

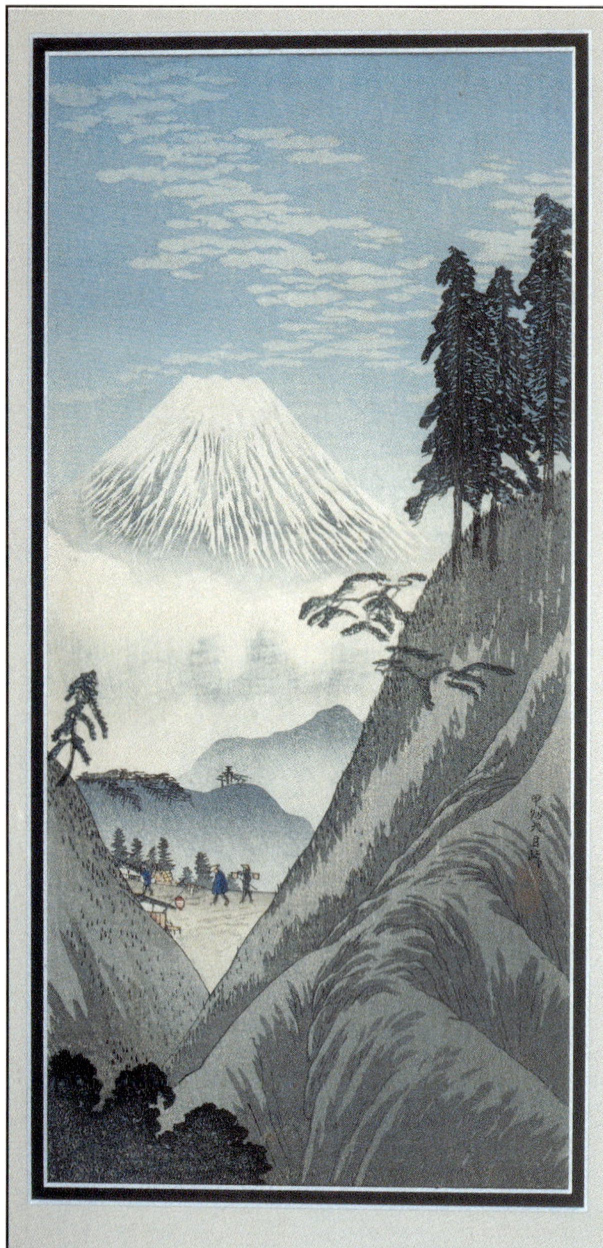

Hiroaki Takashi (Takashi Shotei), tanzanku, "Mt Fuji," c. 1920, fine color, impression, and condition, $775-975.

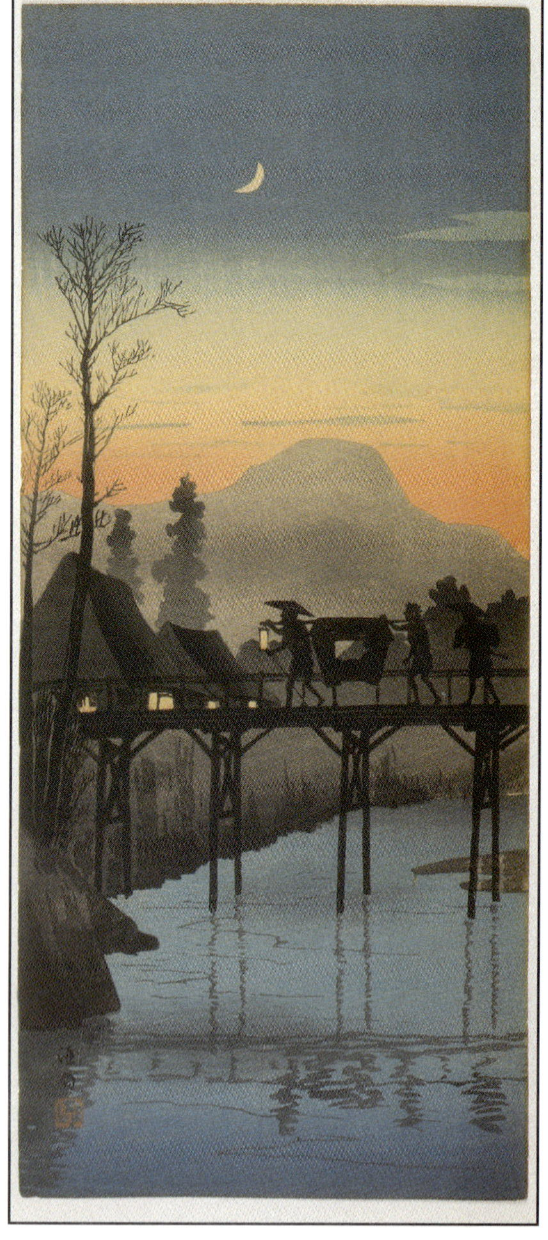

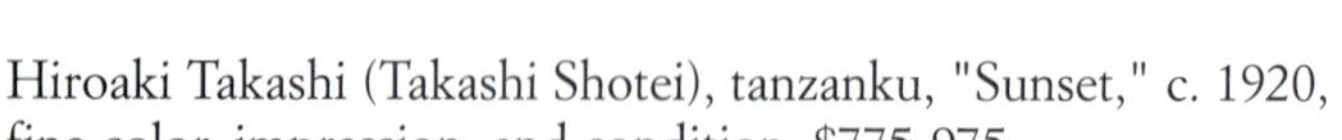

Hiroaki Takashi (Takashi Shotei), tanzanku, "Sunset," c. 1920, fine color, impression, and condition, $775-975.

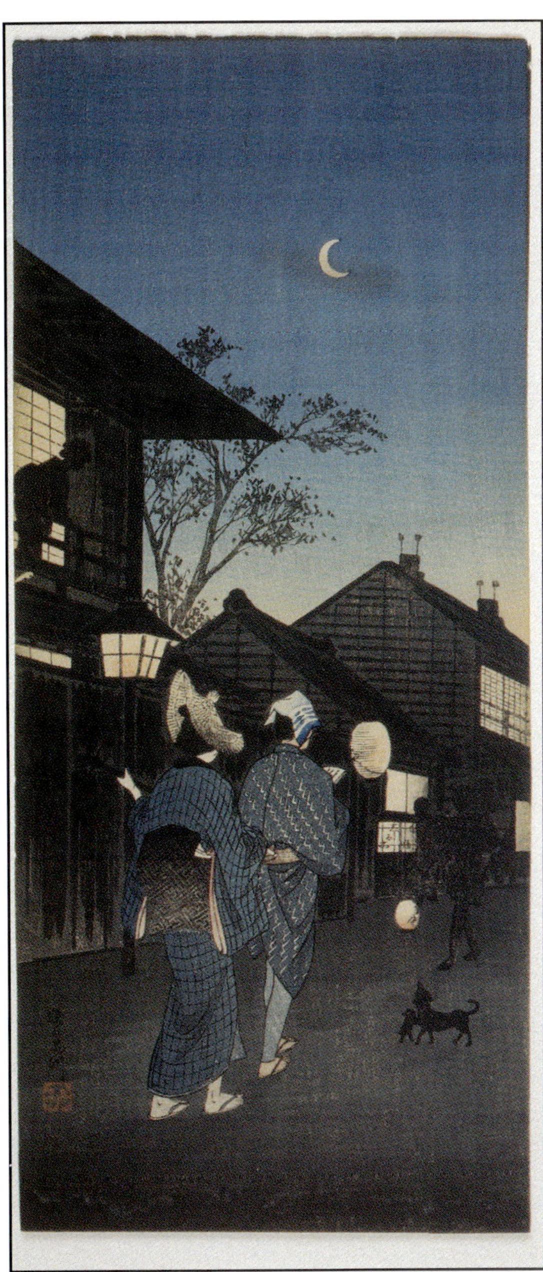

Hiroaki Takashi (Takashi Shotei), tanzaku, "Musicians Walking Home at Sunset," c. 1920, fine color, impression, and condition, $775-975.

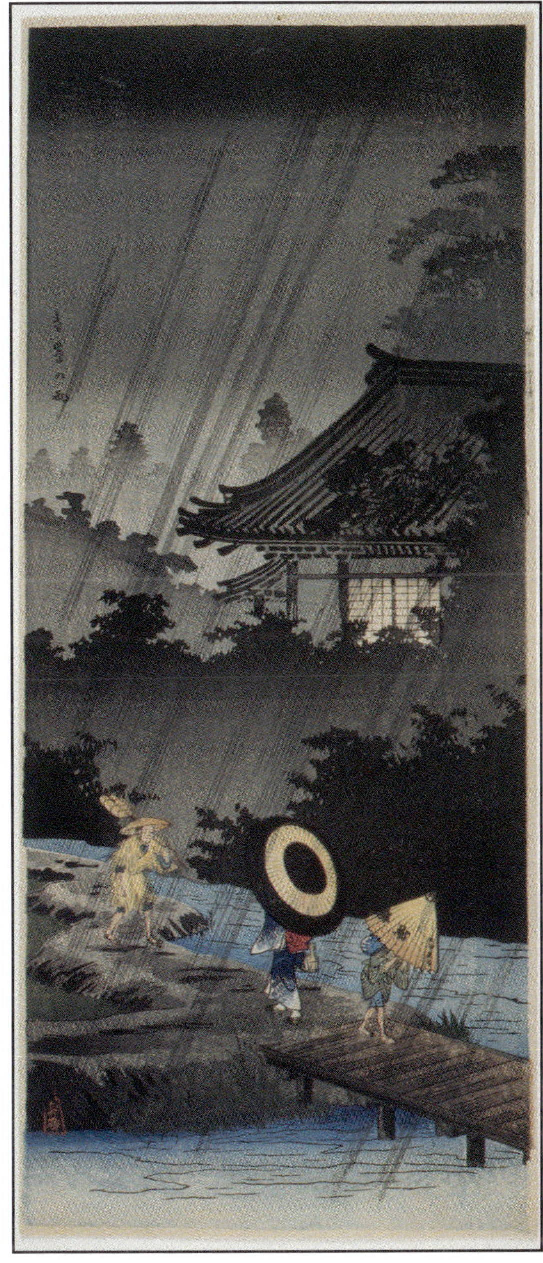

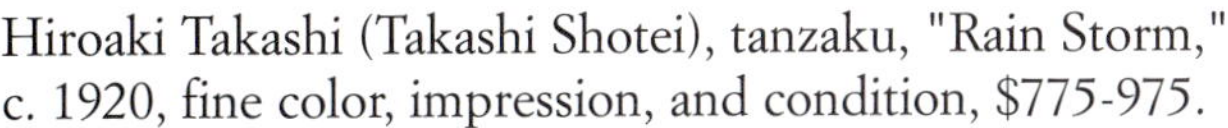

Hiroaki Takashi (Takashi Shotei), tanzaku, "Rain Storm," c. 1920, fine color, impression, and condition, $775-975.

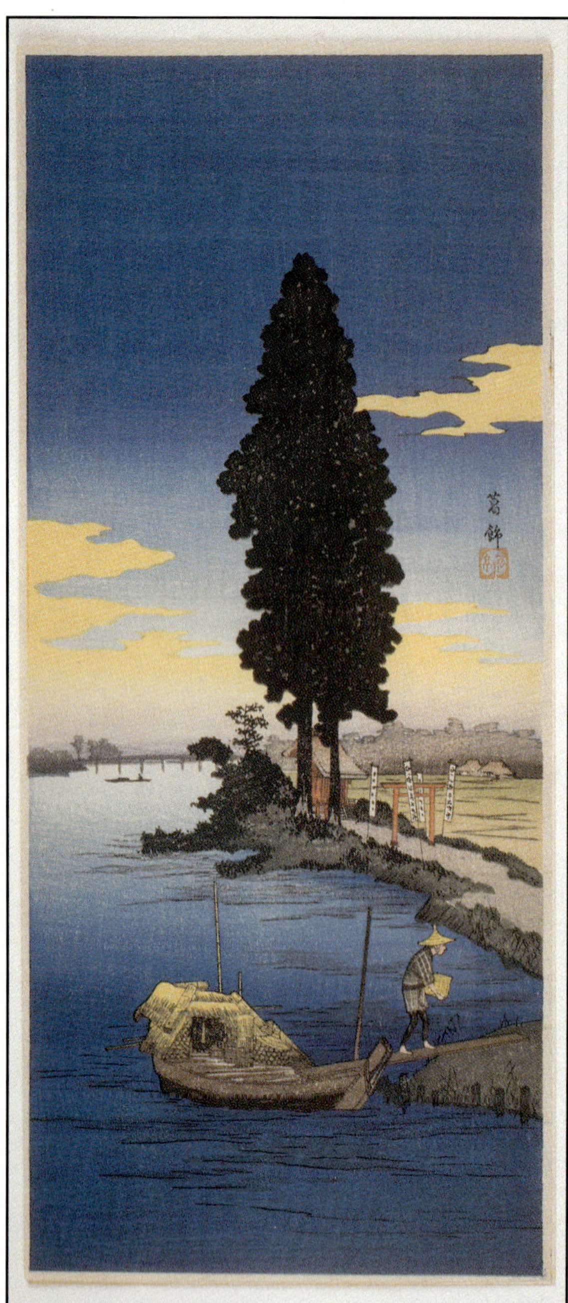

Hiroaki Takashi (Takashi Shotei), tanzaku, "Lake in the Evening," c. 1920, fine color, impression, and condition, $775-975.

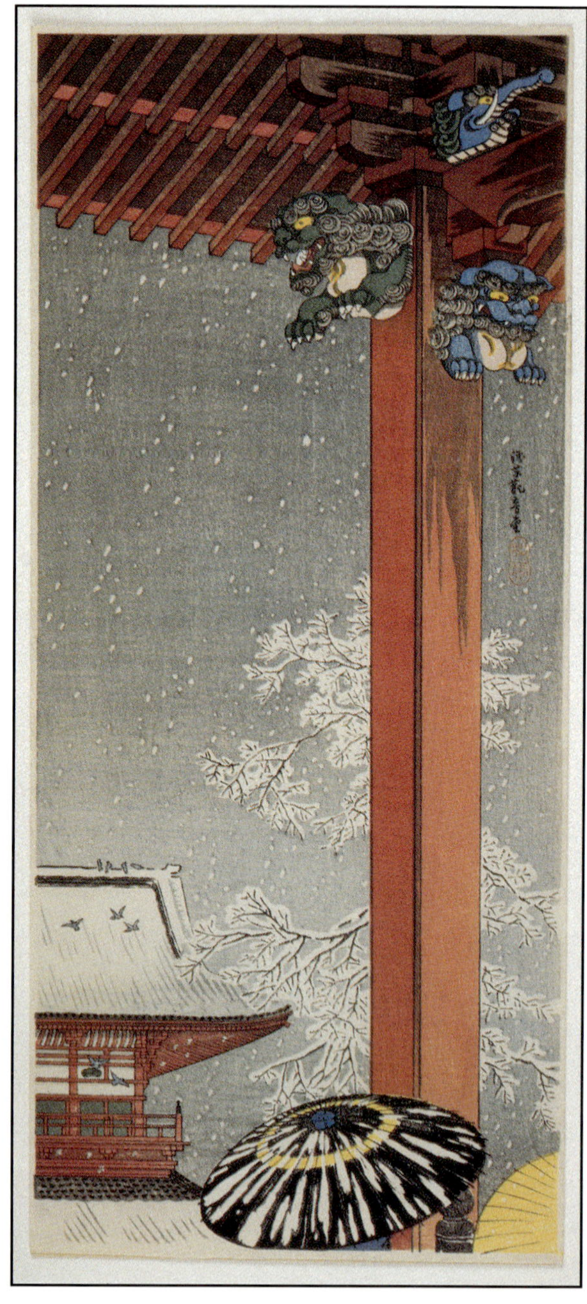

Hiroaki Takashi (Takashi Shotei), tanzaku, "Temple in Asakusa," c. 1920, fine color, impression, and condition, $775-975.

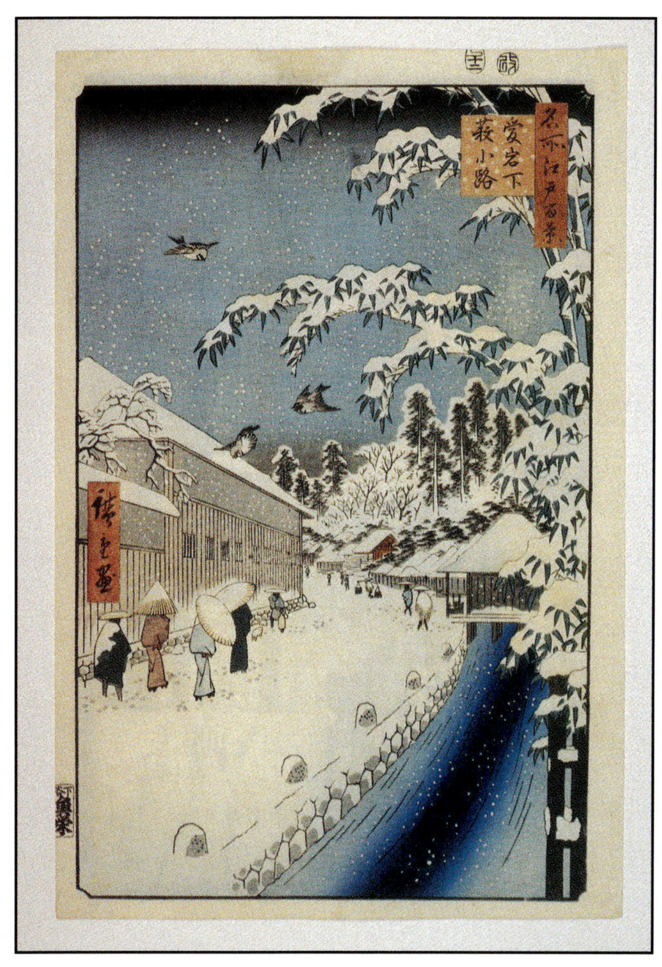

Hiroshige, oban tate-e, 14" x 9 1/2", "Atagoshita Yabukoji," (Yabukoji Street at Atagoshita), from the series Meisho Edo Hyakkei (One Hundred Famous Places in Edo), signed "Hiroshige ga," published by Uoya Eikichi, dated 12/1857, fine impression, color, and condition, binding holes in right margin, $9,000-12,000.

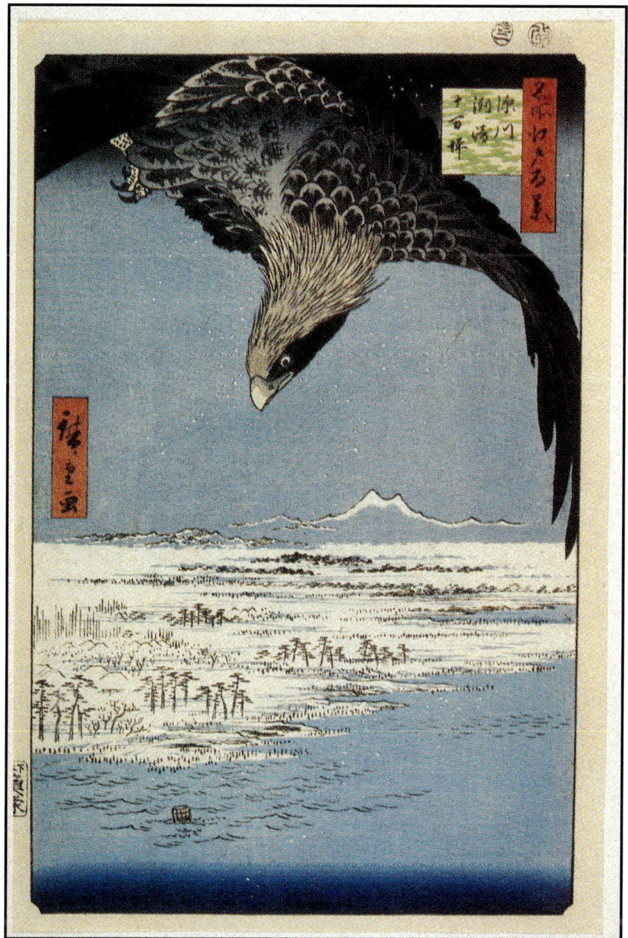

Hiroshige: oban tate-e, 14" x 9 1/2", "Fukagawa Susaki Jumantsuho," (The 10,000 Acre Plain at Suzaki, Fukagawa), from the series Meisho Edo Hyakkei, (One Hundred Views of Famous Places in Edo), signed Hiroshige ga, published by Uoya Eikichi, fine impression, color, and condition, the left margin slightly trimmed, $35,000-45,000.

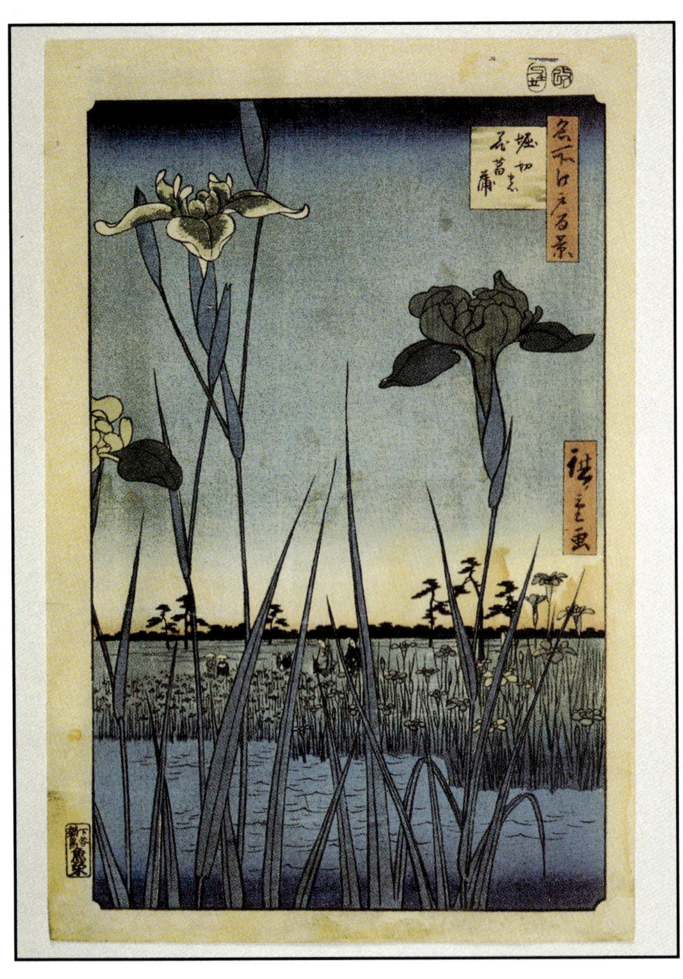

Hiroshige, oban tate-e, 15" x 10", "Horikiri no Hanashobu," (Iris Flowers at Horikiri), from the series Edo Meisho Hyakkei, (One Hundred Views of Famous Places in Edo), signed "Hiroshige ga," published by Uyoa Eikichi, fine impression, very good color, some stains and soiling, $3000-4000.

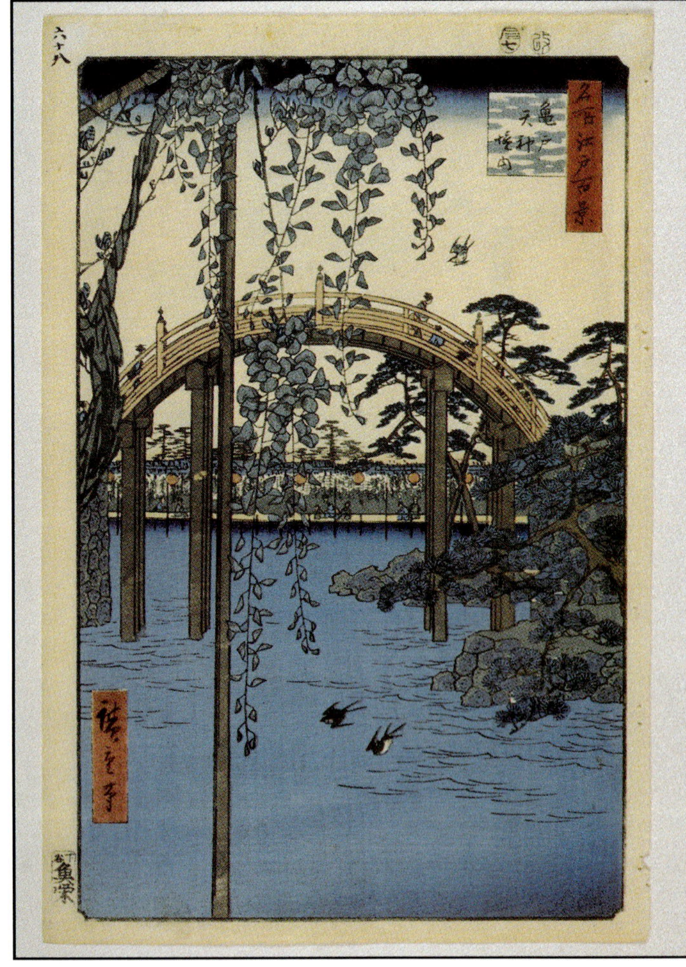

Hiroshige, oban tate-e, 14" x 9 1/4"; "Kameido Tenjin Shrine," Snake 5 (1857), from the series Meisho Edo Hyakkei (One Hundred Views of Famous Places in Edo), signed "Hiroshige ga," published by Uoya Eikichi, fine impression, very good color, binding hole in right margin, $6000-9000.

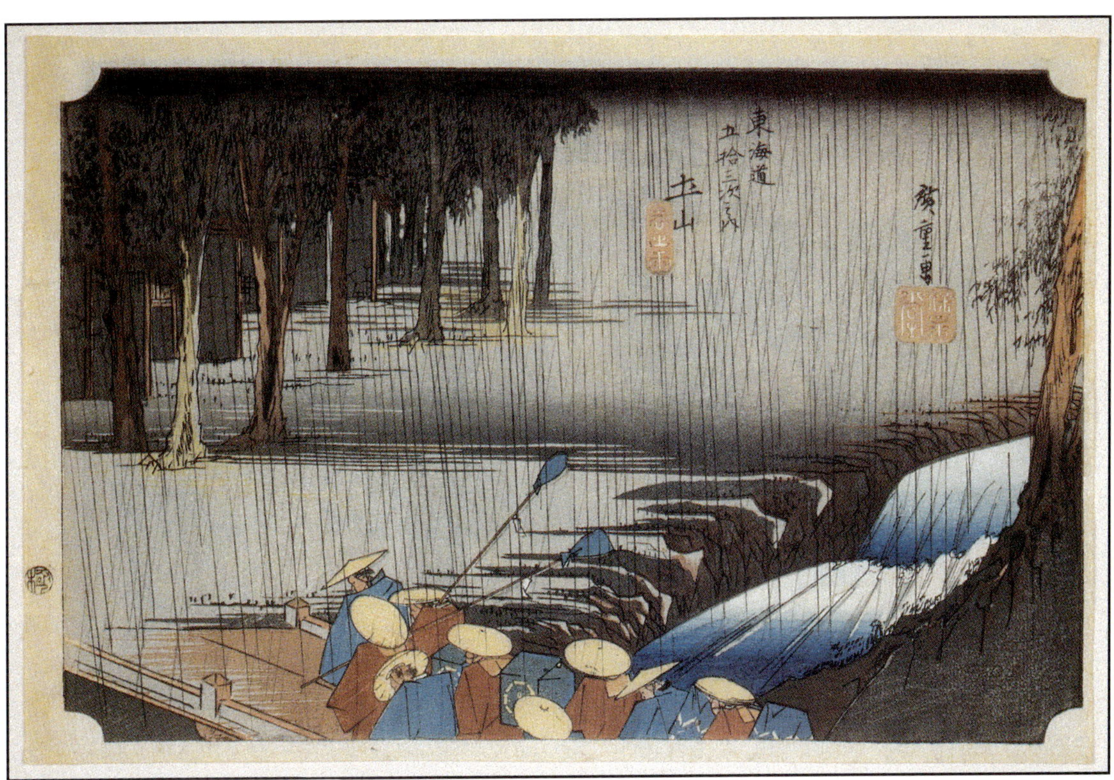

Hiroshige, oban yoko-e, 14 1/4" x 9 1/2"; "Tsuchiyama, Haru no Ame," (Spring Rain, Tsuchiyma, Station 50), from the series Tokaido Gojusan Tsugi no Uchi (The Fifty Three Stations of the Tokaido), a first state, fine impression, color, and condition, the right margin trimmed, $12,000-18,000.

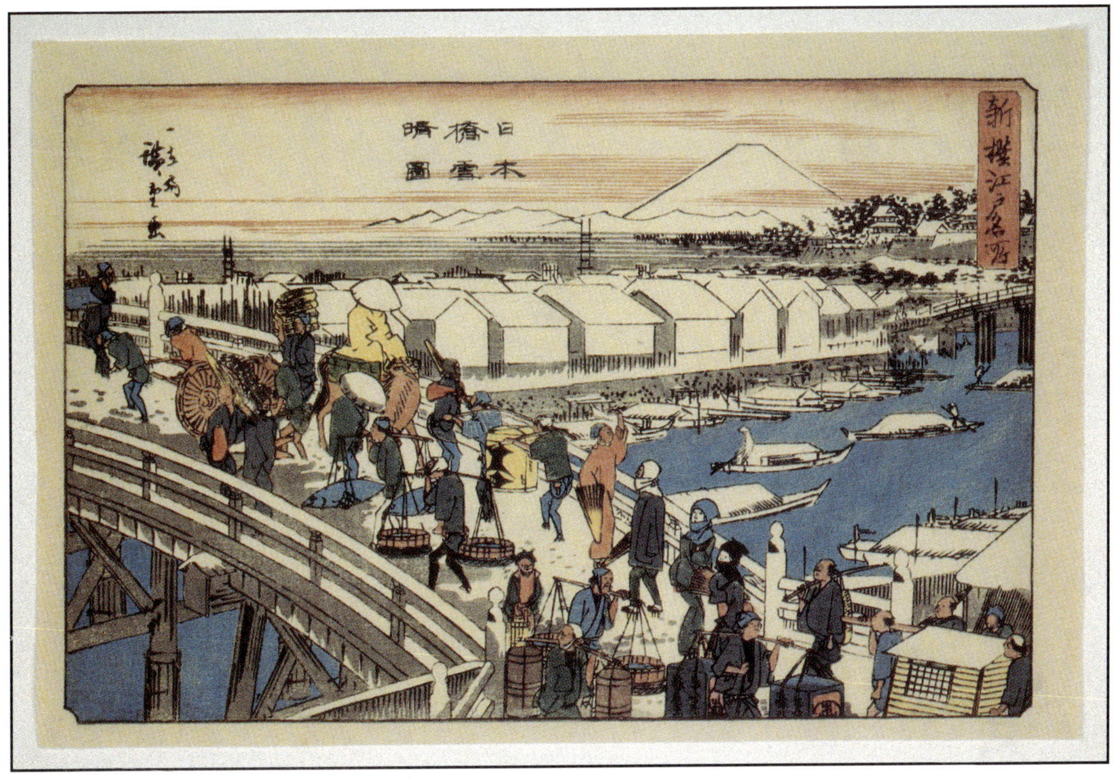

Hiroshige, oban yoko-e, 14" x 9 1/2", "Nihombashi Sekkei no Zu," (Nihombashi in the Morning After Snow), from the series Shinpan Edo Meisho, signed "Ichiryusai Hiroshige ga," good impression and color, margins trimmed to border, remargined, $1000-1500.

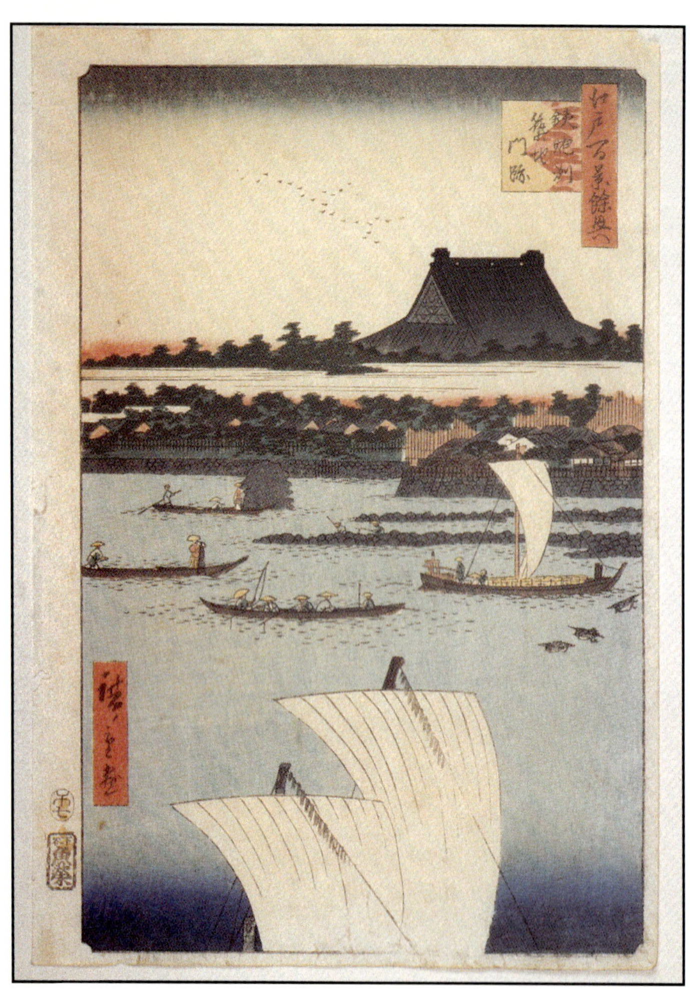

Hiroshige, oban tate-e, 15" x 10", "Mitsumata, Wakare no Fuchi," (Farewell Deep at Mitsumata), from the series Edo Meisho Hyakkei, (One Hundred Views of Famous Places in Edo), signed "Hiroshige ga," published by Uyoa Eikichi, fine impression, very good color, $5000-7000.

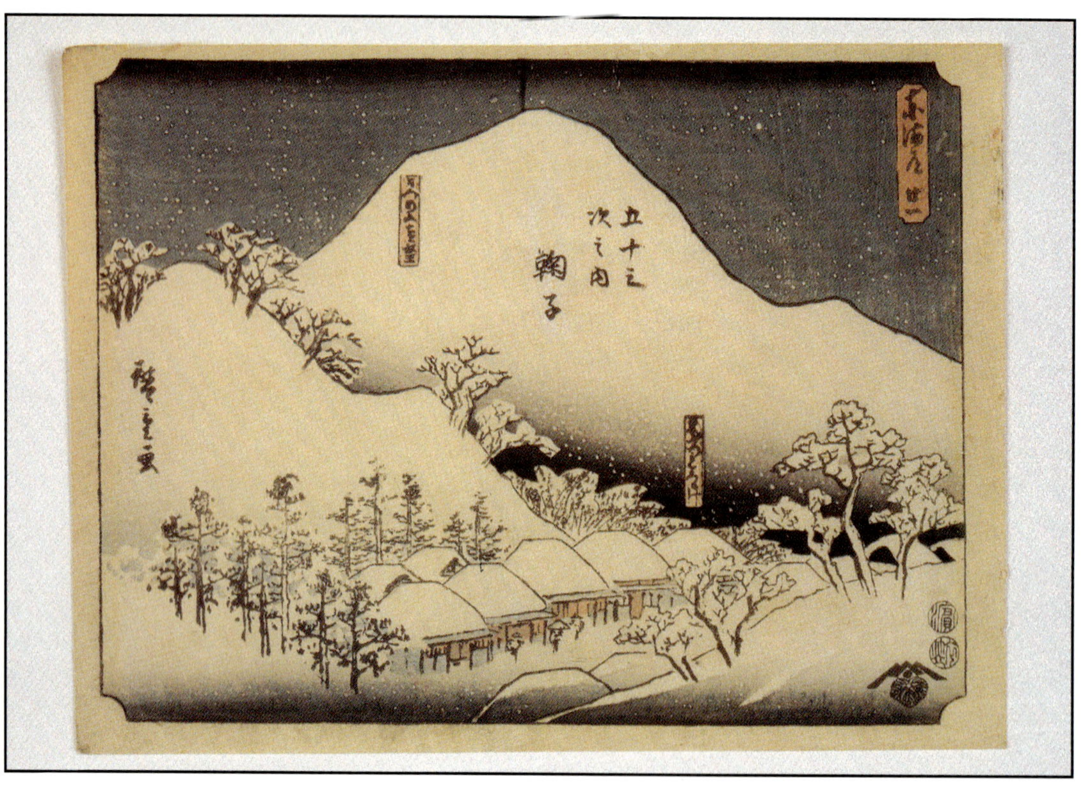

Hiroshige, chuban, "Mariko," from the series The Fifty-three Stations of the Tokaido, c.1847-48, fine impression, color, and condition, $2200-3000.

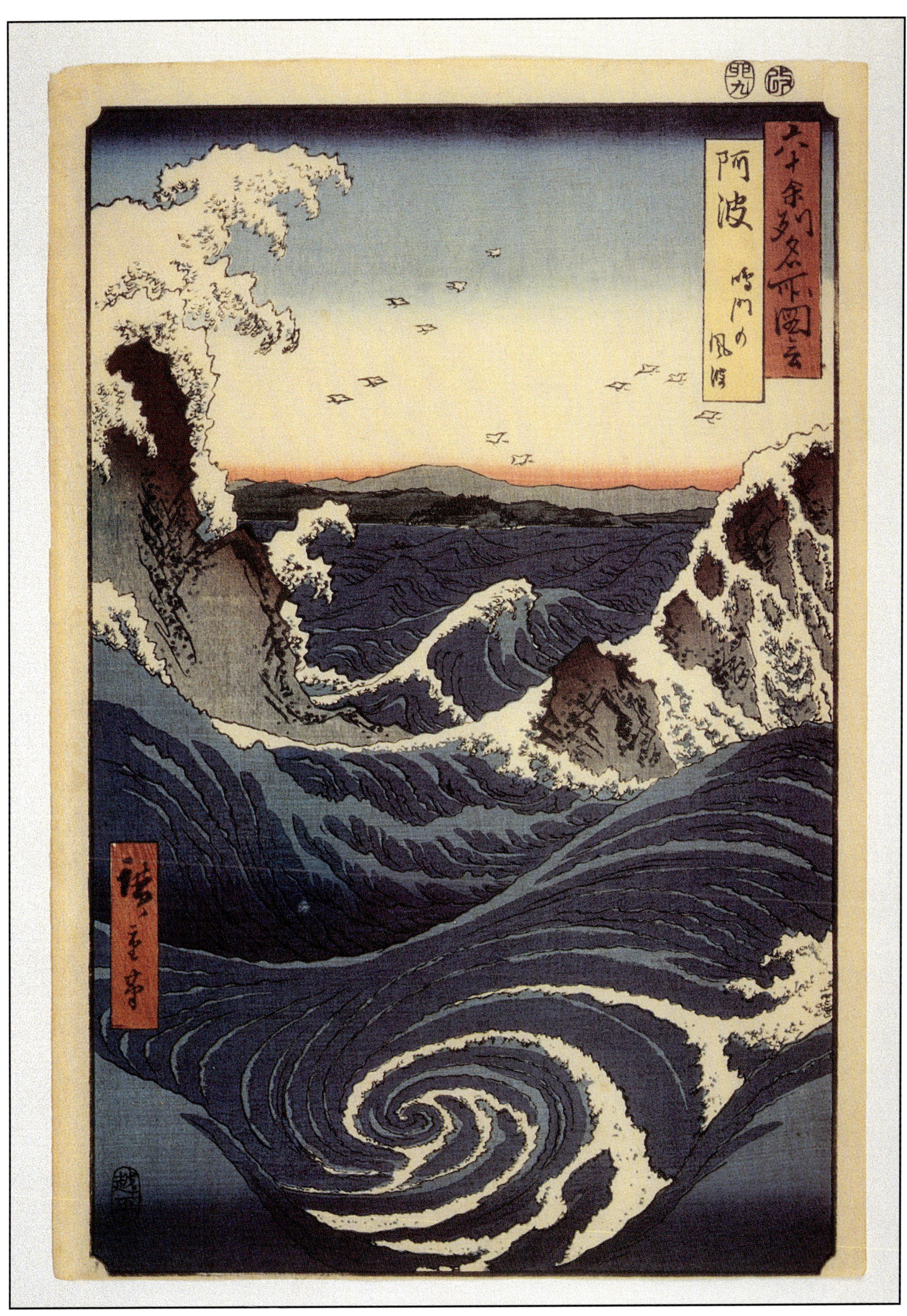

Hiroshige, oban tate-e, 14" x 9 3/4", "Haruto no Fuha," (Whirlpool at Naruto), Awa province, from the series Rokujuyoshu Meisho Zu (Pictures of Famous Places in the Sixty-Odd Provinces), signed "Hiroshige hitsu," published by Koshimuraya Heisuke, fine impression and color, lower margin trimmed, $12,000-15,000.

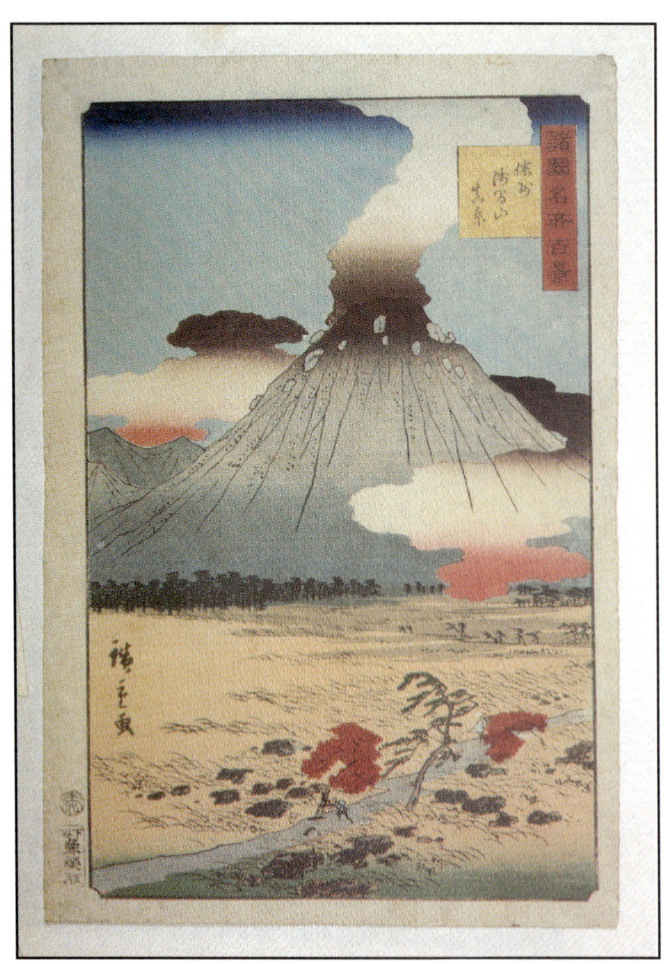

Hiroshige II, oban tate-e, "Volcano" from the series Shokoku Meisho Hyakkei (One Hundred Famous Views of the Province), publisher Uoei (Uoya Eikichi), fine impression, very good color, and condition, $3000-4500.

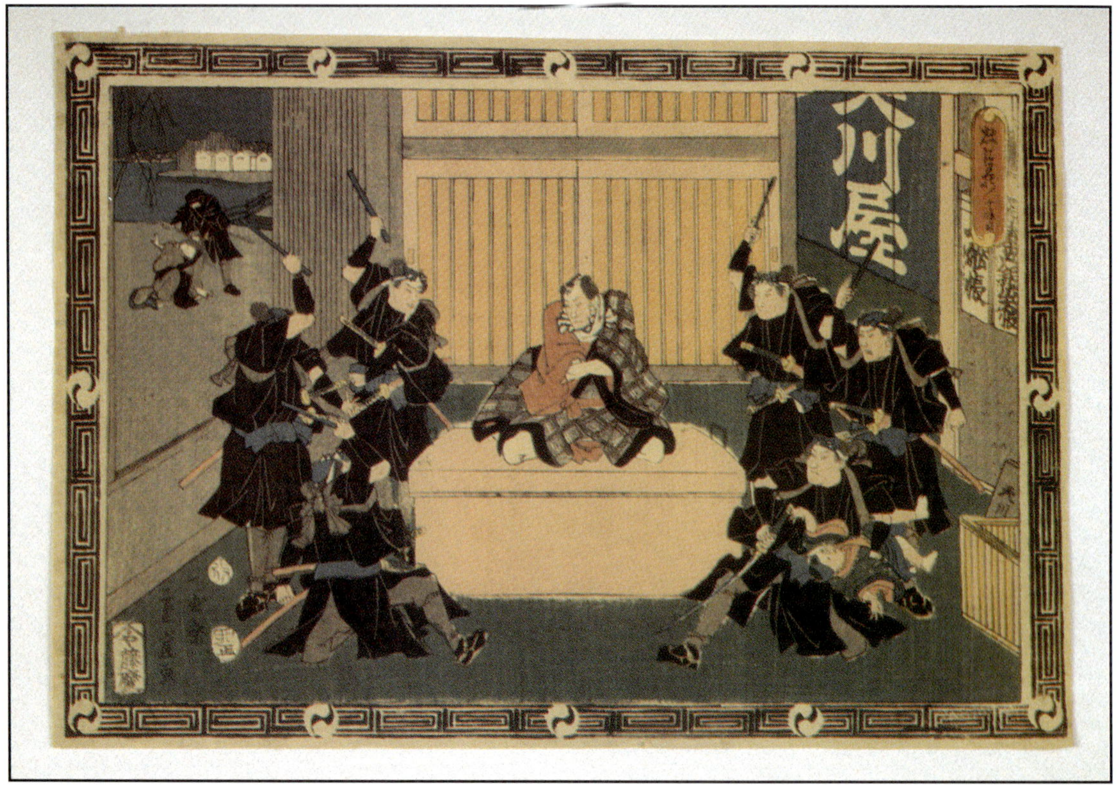

Hiroshige II, (Shigenobu), oban yoko-e, 1855 (Year of the Hare) from the series Chushingura, very good impression, color, and condition, $900-1200.

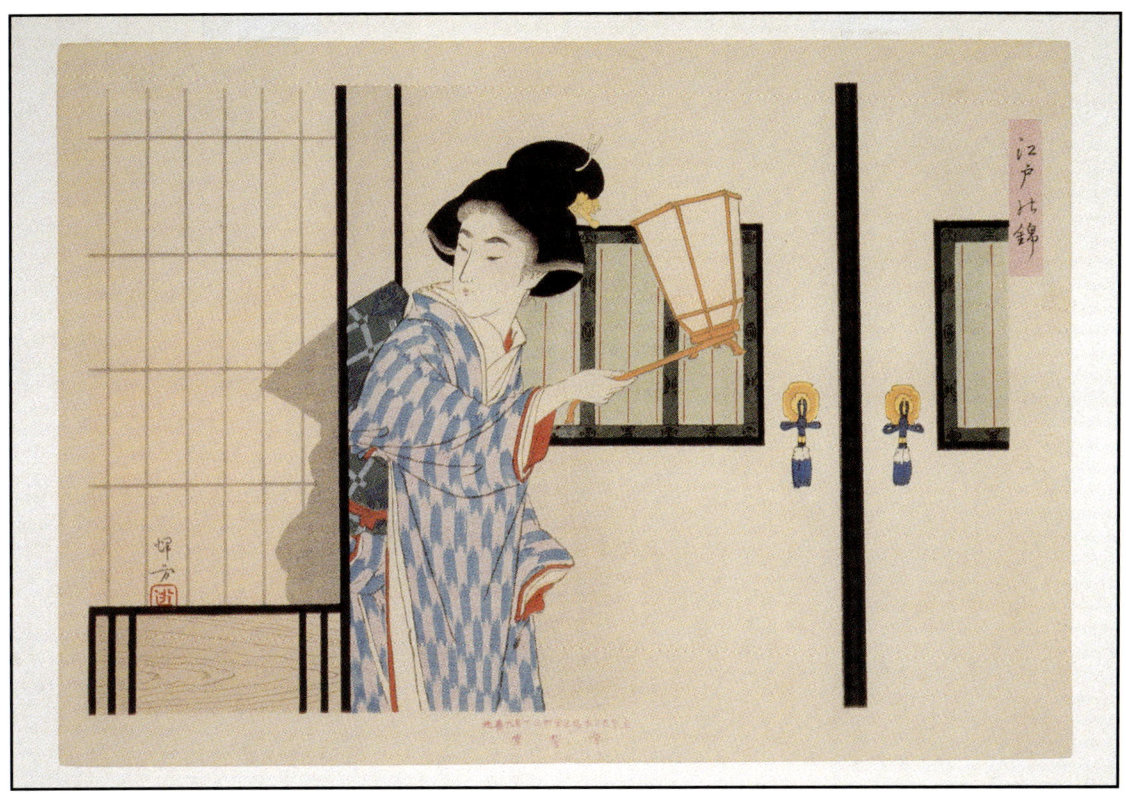

Ikeda Terukata, kachi-e, c. 1905, illuminated scene with mica, fine condition, color and impression, center crease, and backing, $450-750.

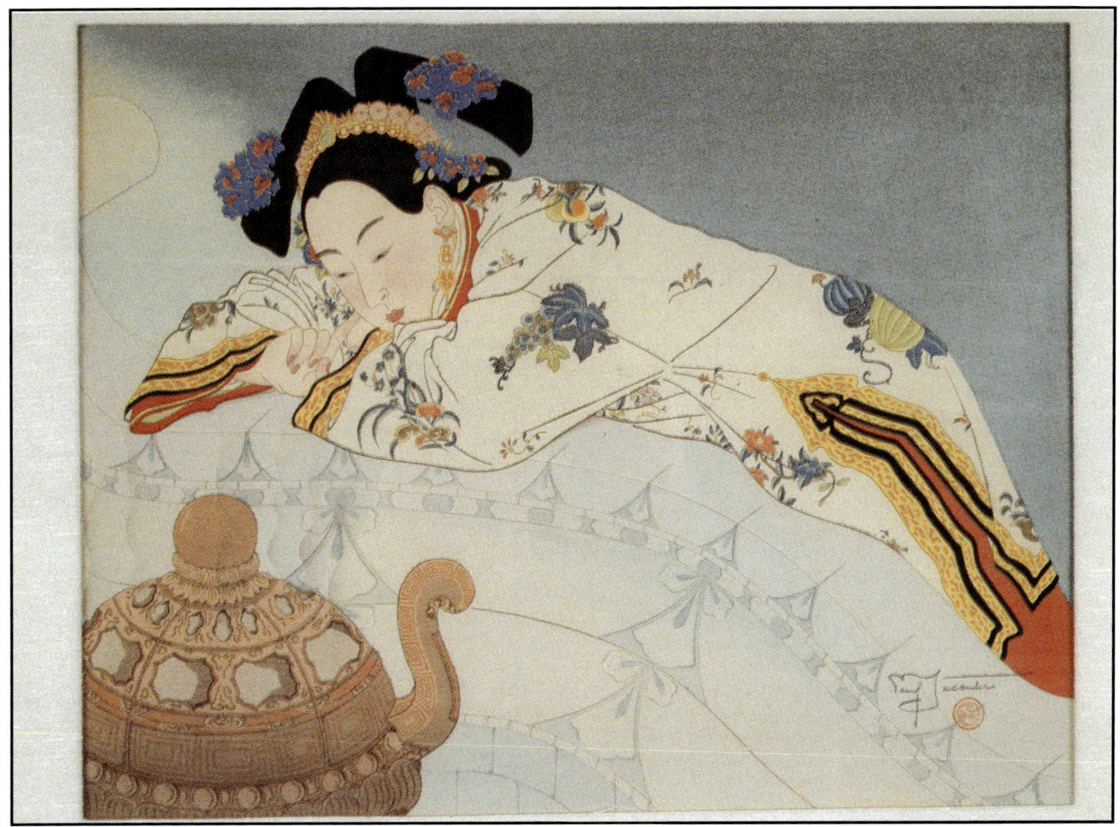

Jacoulet, Paul, dai oban, Fumes De Santal. Mandchoukuo (Sandal Smoke) published December 25, 1948, Mitsu-Tomoe seal, Carver Maeda, Printer Dujii from an edition of 150 (this edition has silver metallics and gauffrage on the gown), fine condition and color, $2000-3000.

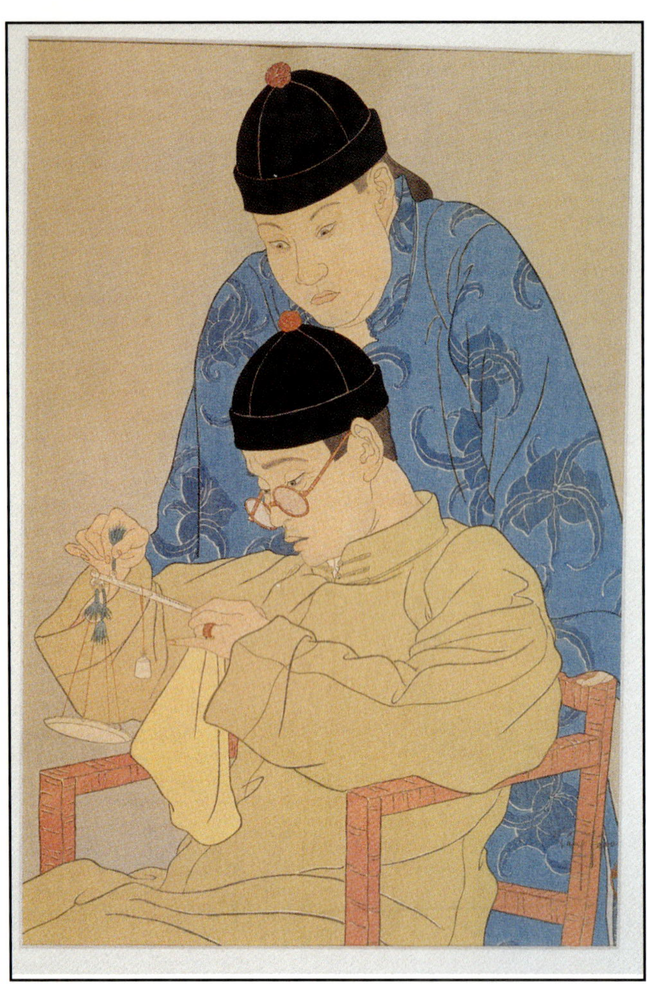

Jacoulet, Paul, dai oban tate-e, "La Balance Chinois", (The Scale,) signed in pencil lower right above tea jar seal, seals of the carver, Kentaro Maeda and printer Fusakichi Ogawa in lower right margin, from an edition of 350, published 5 February 1939, very good impression, color, slightly toned, $850-1000.

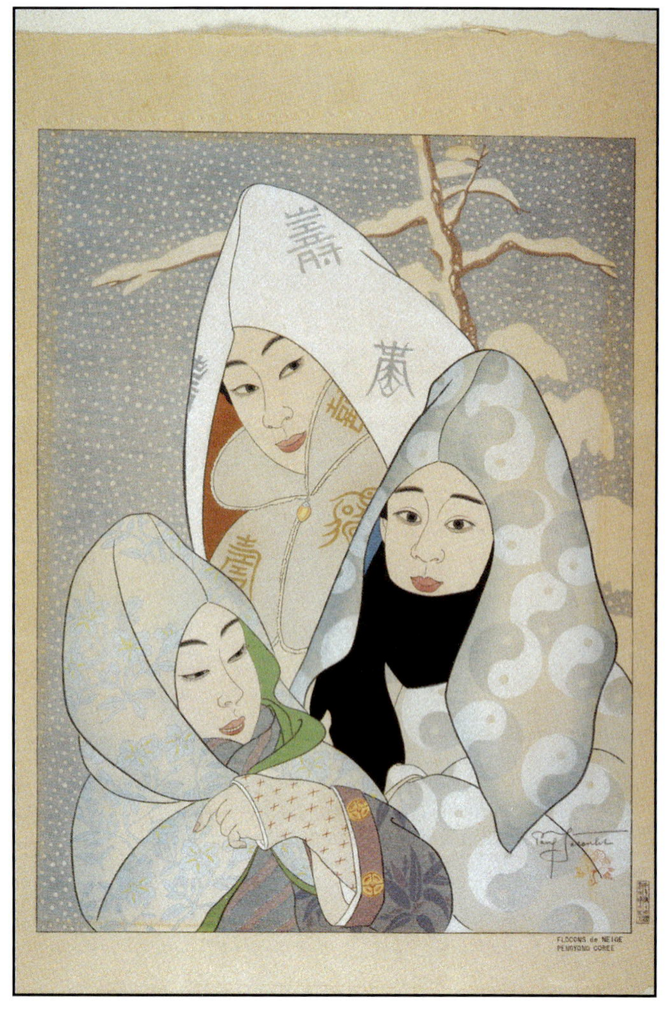

Jacoulet, Paul, dai oban tate-e, "Flocons De Neige. Pengyong Coree," (Snowflakes. Peng-Yong, Korea), dated 1956, from an edition of 350, peony seal, fine condition, color, and impression, $4500-6500.

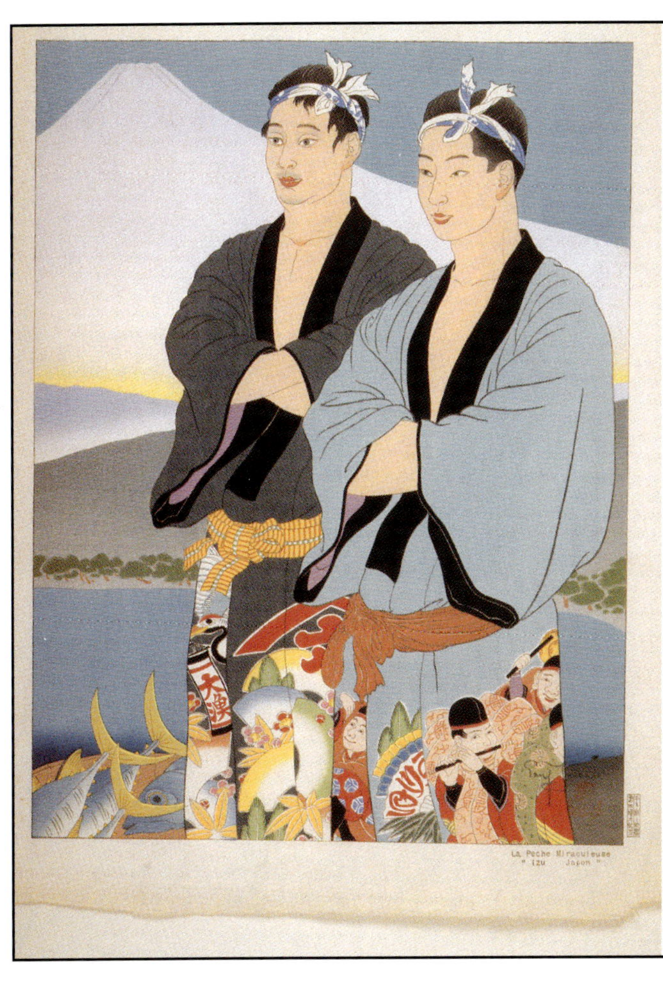

Jacoulet, Paul, dai oban tate-e, "La Peche Miraculeuse, Izu, Japon," (The Miraculous Catch. Izu, Japan), dated 1939, from an edition of 150, boat seal, fine impression, color and, condition, $3000-4500.

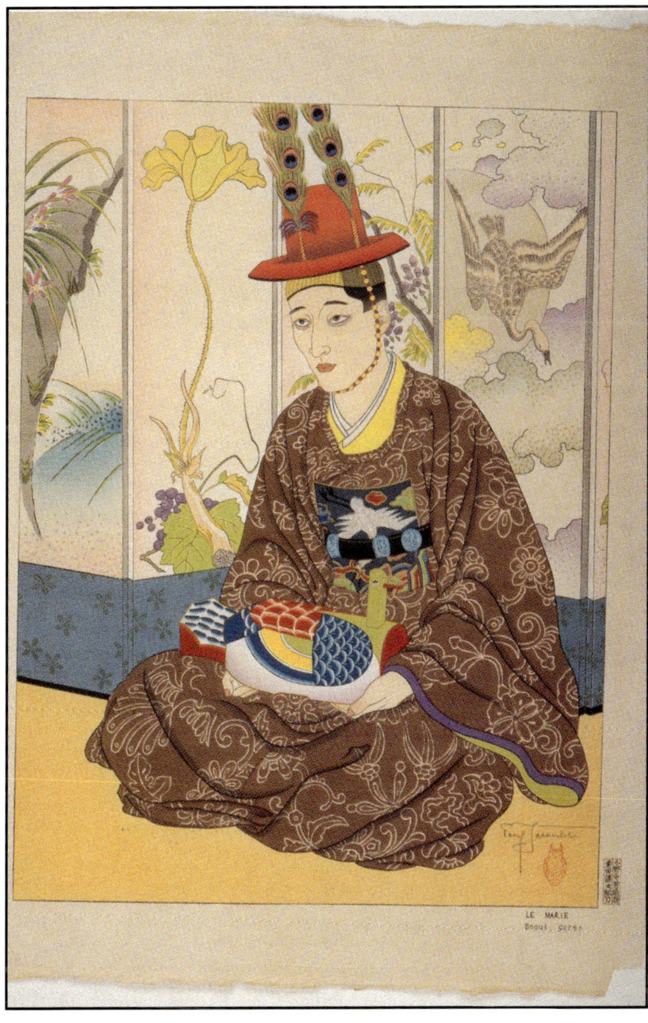

Jacoulet, Paul, dai oban tate-e, "Le Marie. Seoul, Coree," (The Bridegroom. Seoul, Korea), published 1950, owl seal, from an edition of 250, fine impression, color, slightly toned, $1000-1500.

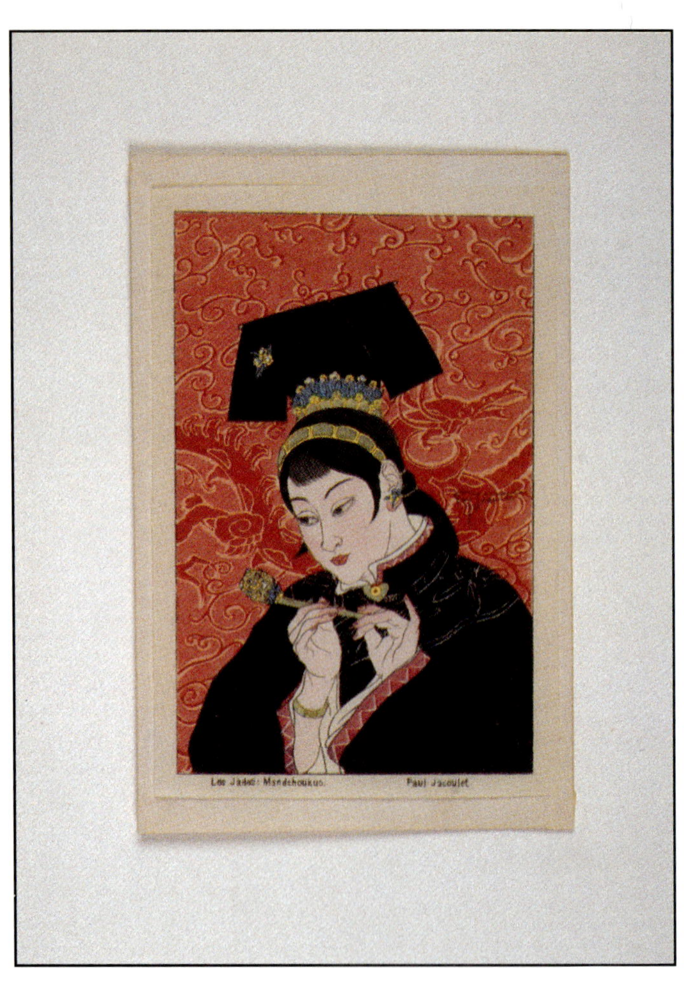

Jacoulet,Paul, christmas card in original folder, "Les Jades, Chinoise," (Jade Lady, Chinese), greeting on folder, yellow design on cover, fine condition $375-500.

Jacoulet, Paul, dai oban tate-e, "Les Jades, Chinoise," (Jade Lady, Chinese), dated 1940, boat seal, from an edition of 250, fine condition, color, and impression, $2500-4500.

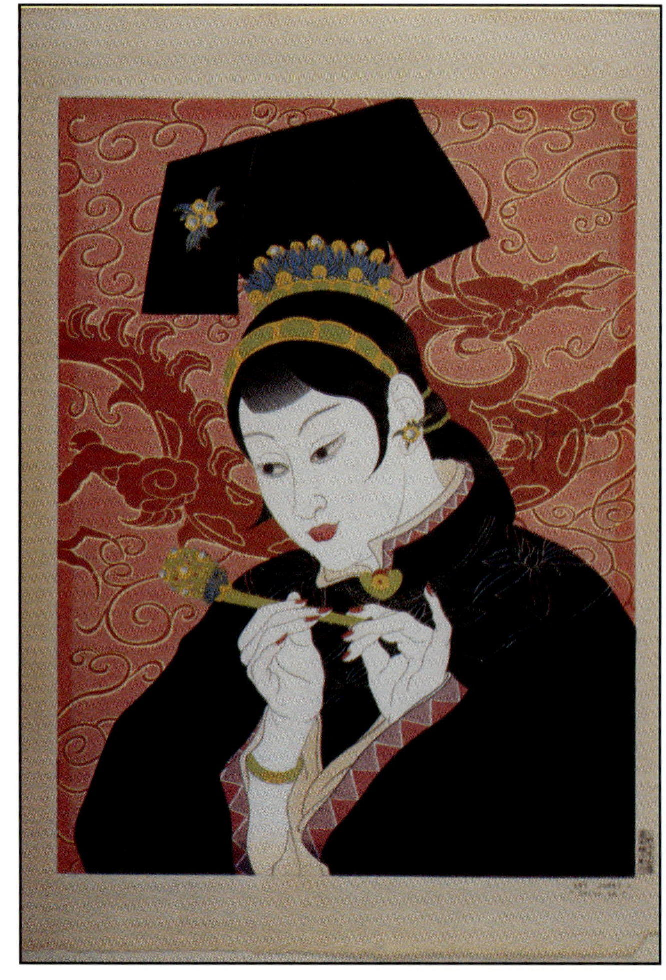

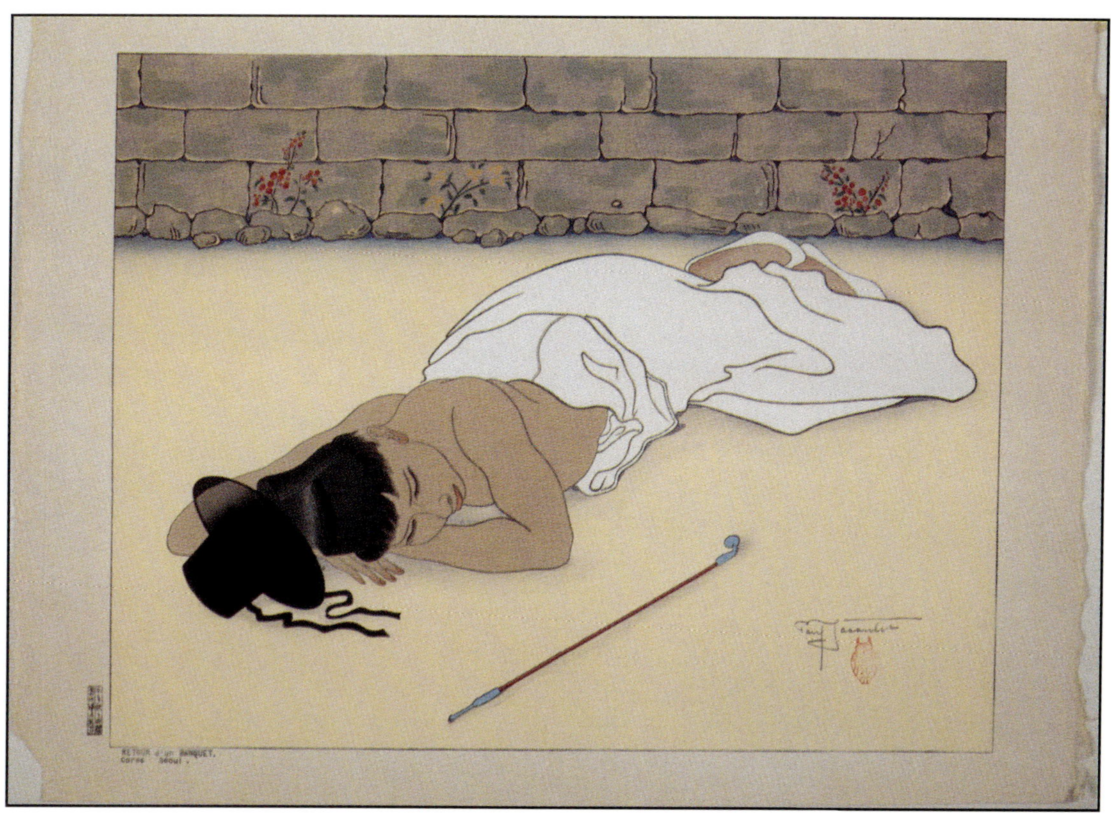

Jacoulet,Paul, dai oban yoko-e, "Retour D'Un Banquet, Coree Seoul," (After The Banquet, Seoul, Korea), dated 1951, owl seal, from an edition of 350, fine impression, color, and condition, $2500-3500.

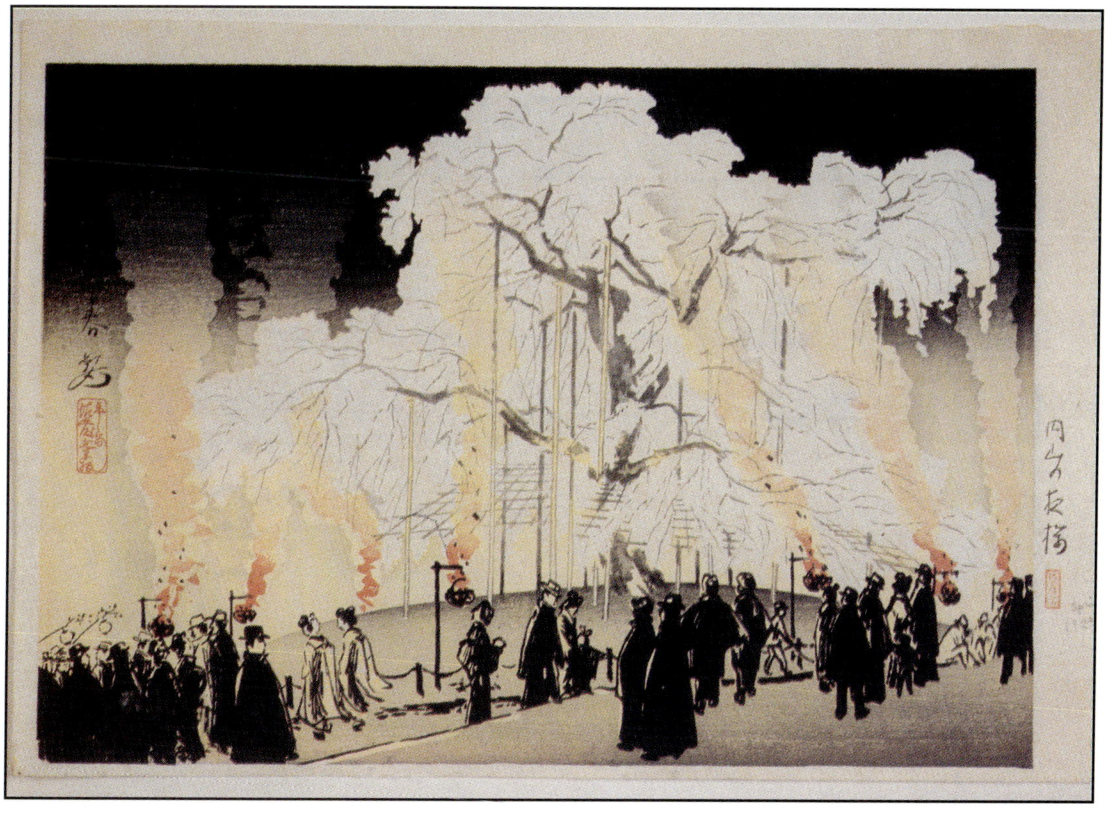

Kampo Yoshikawa oban yoko-e, "Cherry Blossom Viewing in Maruyama," dated within the image Spring 1925, published by Sato Shotaro, signed "Kampo," fine impression, color, and condition, $1200-1800.

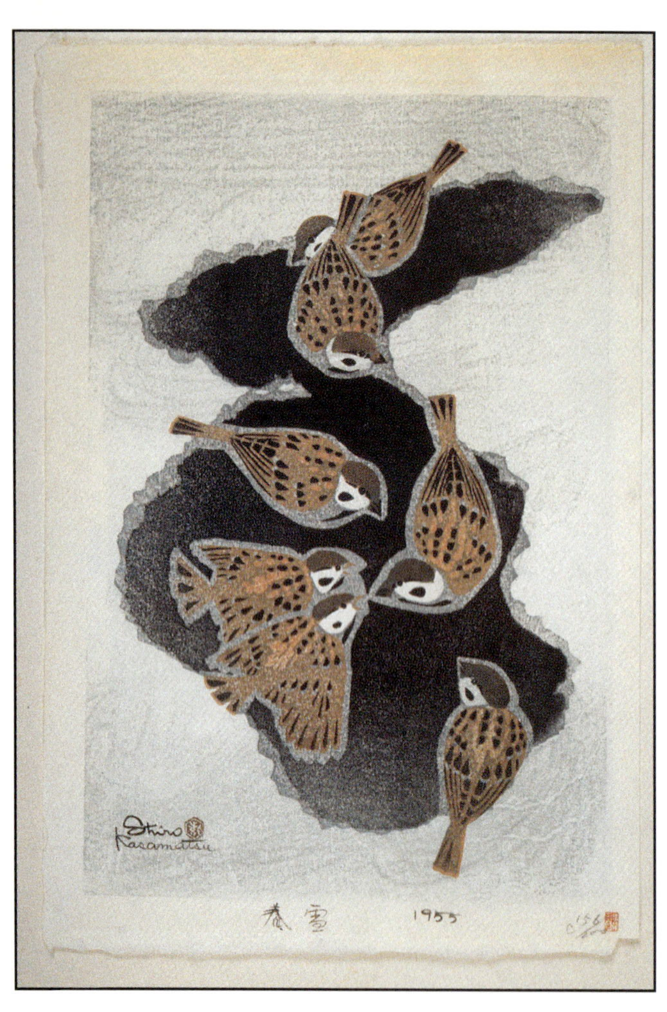

Kasamatsu Shiro, oban tate-e, 16 1/4" x 11 1/4", "Sparrows," from a limited edition of 200, signed and sealed in lower right within image, dated 1955, fine impression, color, and condition, $900-1200.

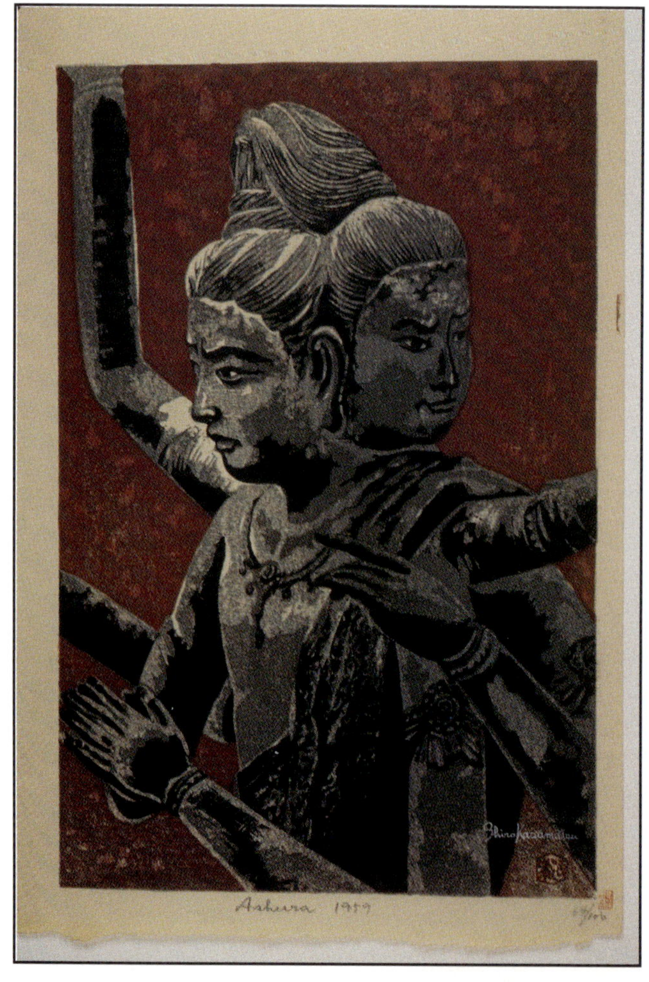

Kasamatsu Shiro, oban tate-e, "Ashura," 1959, from an edition of 100, signed and sealed within image, fine impression, condition, and color, $750-1200.

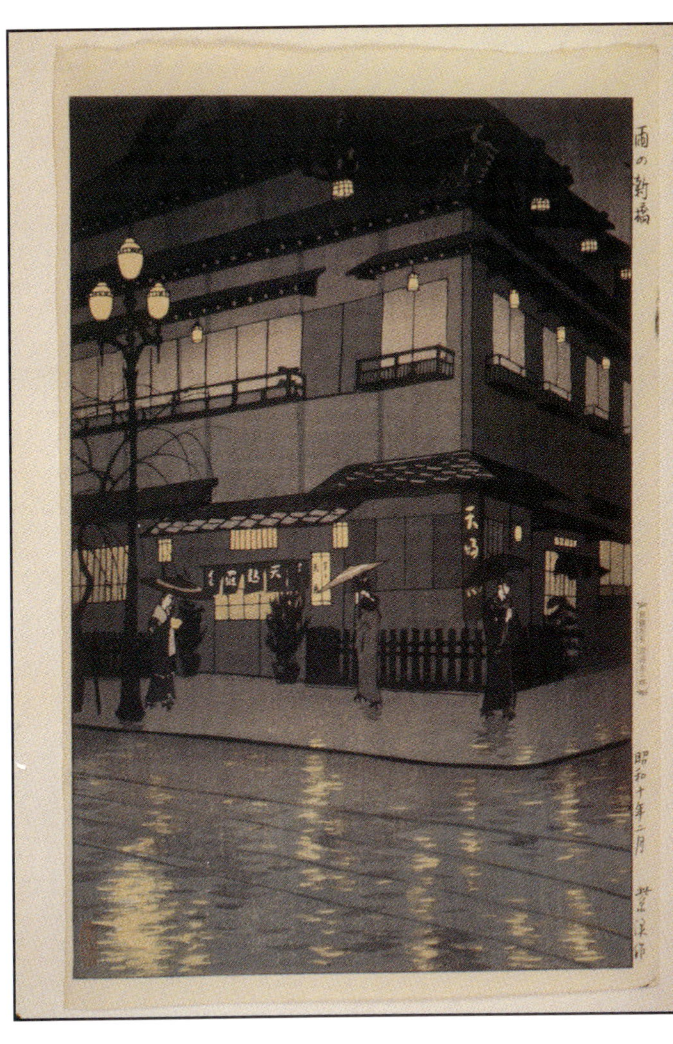

Kasamatsu Shiro, oban tate-e, "Evening Rain," early edition, dated Showa 8 (1933), illuminated print, published by Watanabe, fine impression, color, and condition, $1500-2200.

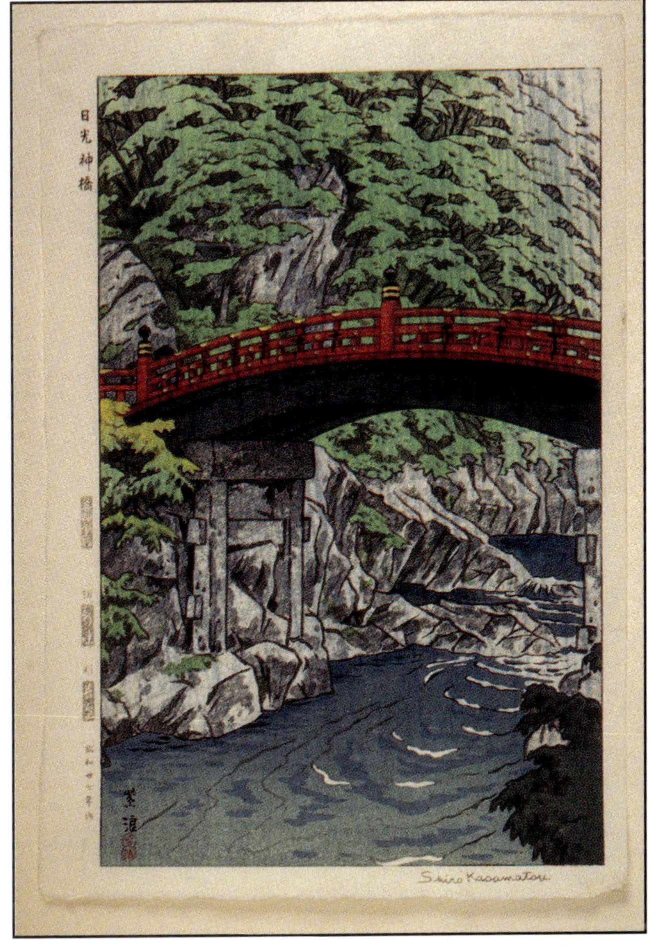

Kasamatsu Shiro, oban tate-e, 16" x 11", "Sacred Bridge in Nikko," early edition, dated Showa 27 (1952), published by Unsodo, very good color, impression, and fine condition, $1000-1500.

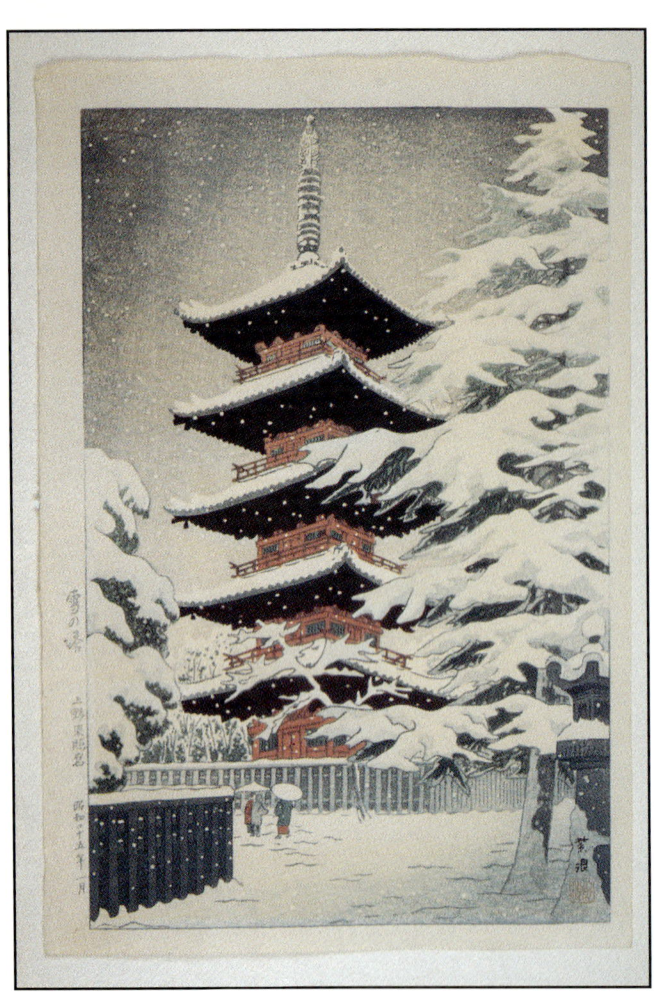

Kasamatsu Shiro, oban tate-e, 15 3/4" x 10 3/4", "Toshogu In Ueno," dated Showa 29 (1954), signed and sealed in the lower left of the image, self published, fine condition, color, and impression, $1000-1500.

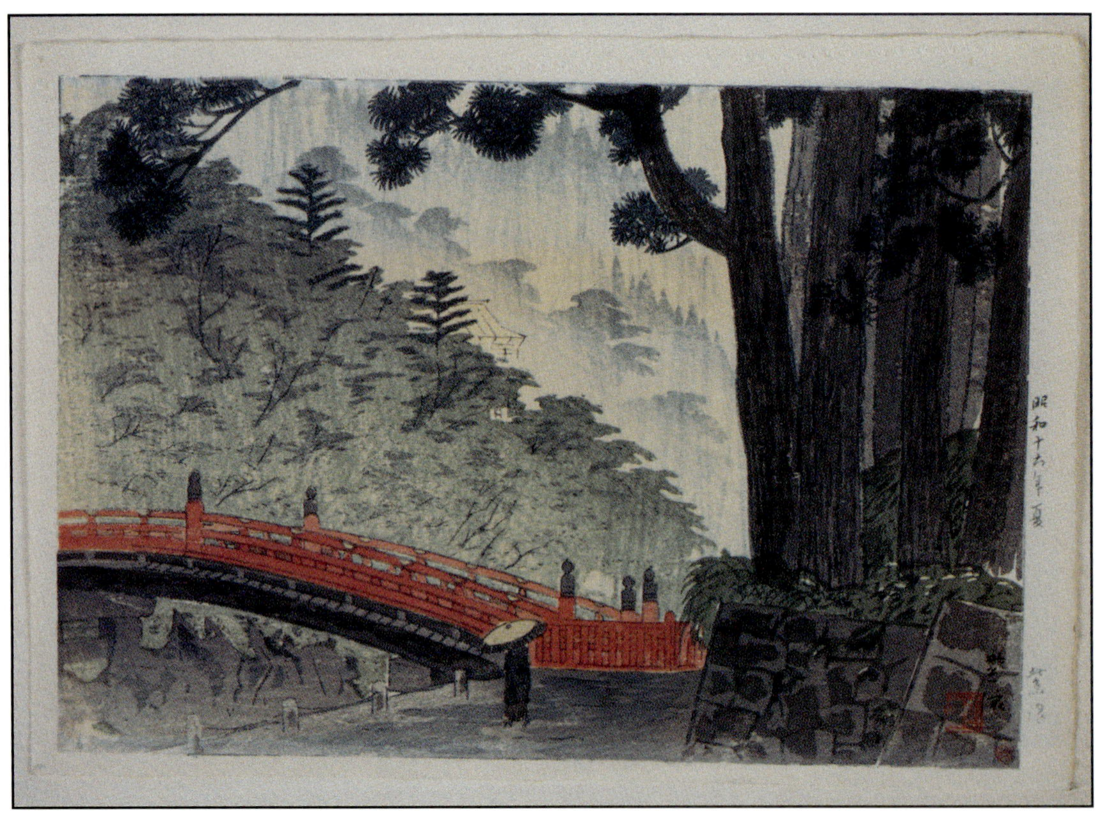

Kasamatsu Shiro, oban yoko-e, 15 1/2" x 10 3/4", "Sacred Bridge at Nikko," published by Watanabe (1946), early edition, fine impression, color, and condition, $800-1200.

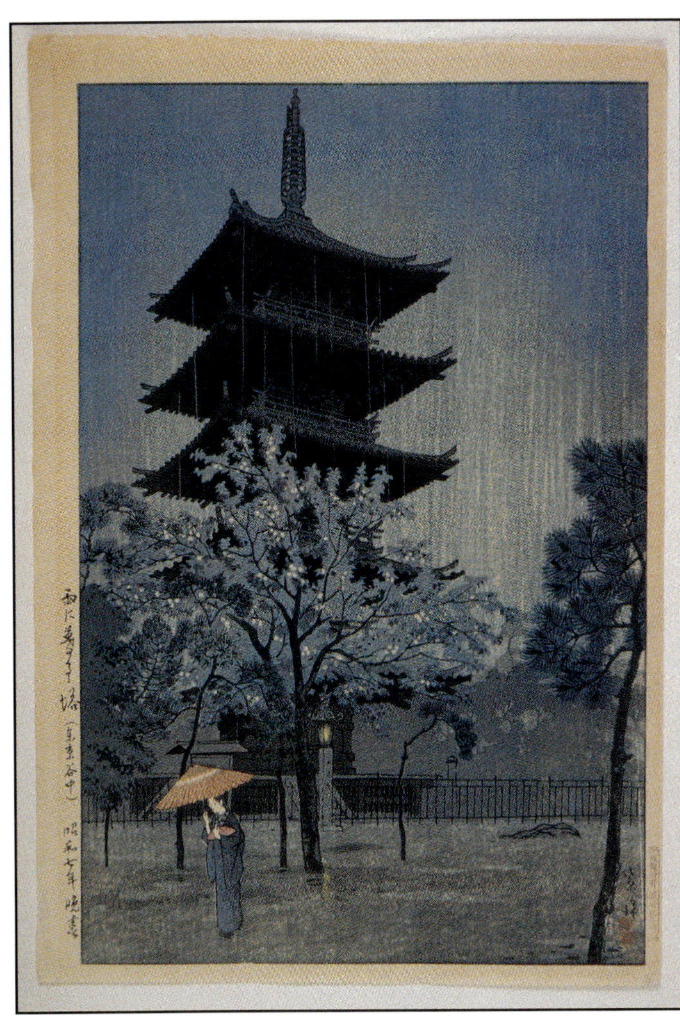

Kasamatsu Shiro, oban tate-e, "Tokyo Yachu," dated Showa 7 (1932), published by Watanabe, early edition, fine impression, condition, and color, $1200-1800.

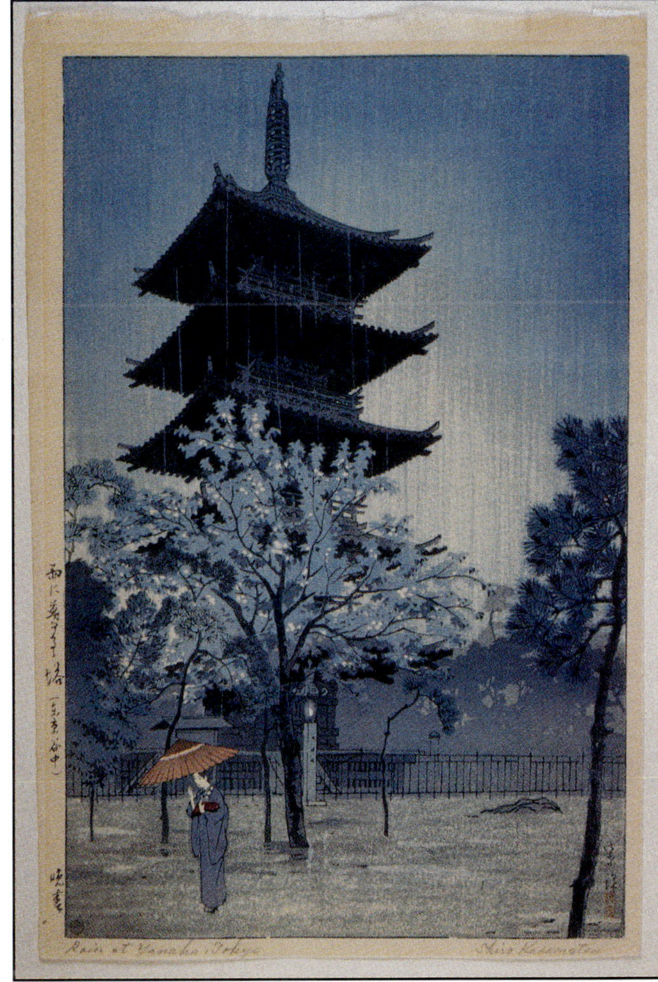

Kasamatsu Shiro, oban tate-e, "Tokyo Yachu," dated Showa 7 (1932), published by Watanabe, later edition (the color is much deeper with tones of violet blue, which differs from the lighter tones of blue in the early edition) fine impression, condition, and color, $750-1200.

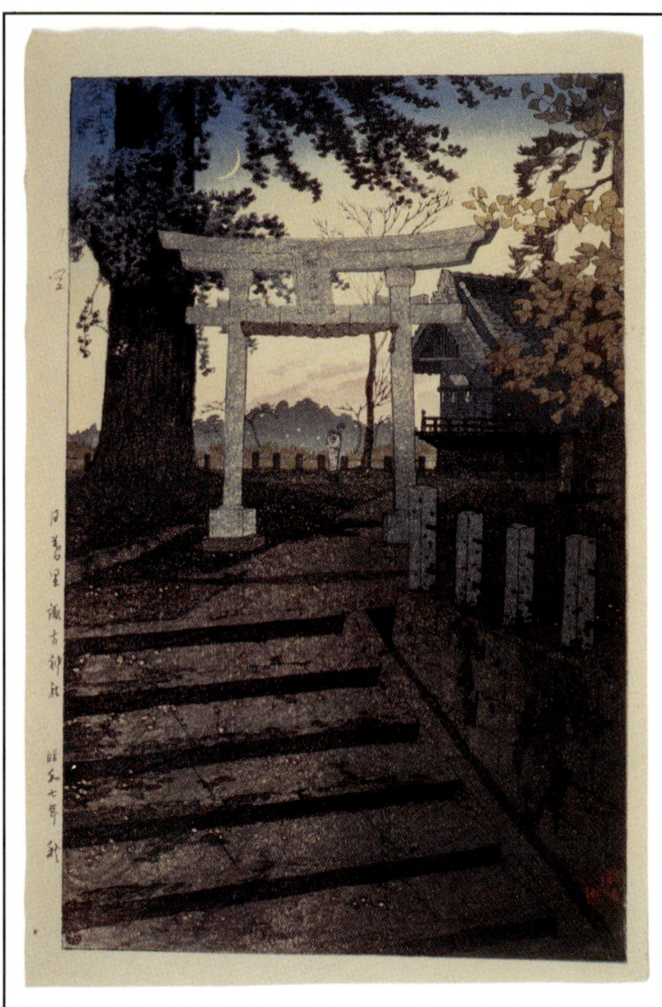

Kasamatsu Shiro, oban tate-e, "The Suwa Shrine at Nippori at Sunset," published by Watanabe (6mm seal), fine impression, color, and condition, $800-1200.

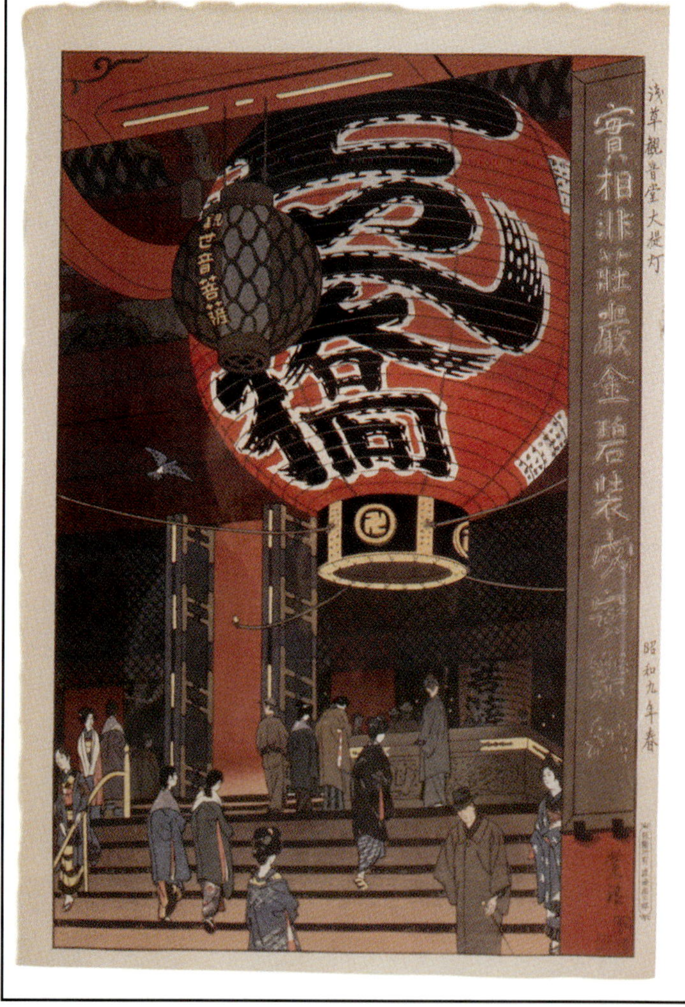

Kasamatsu Shiro, oban tate-e, "The Great Lantern at the Asakusa Kannodo," published by Watanabe, dated Showa 9 (1934), early edition, excellent impression, condition, and color, $2000-3000.

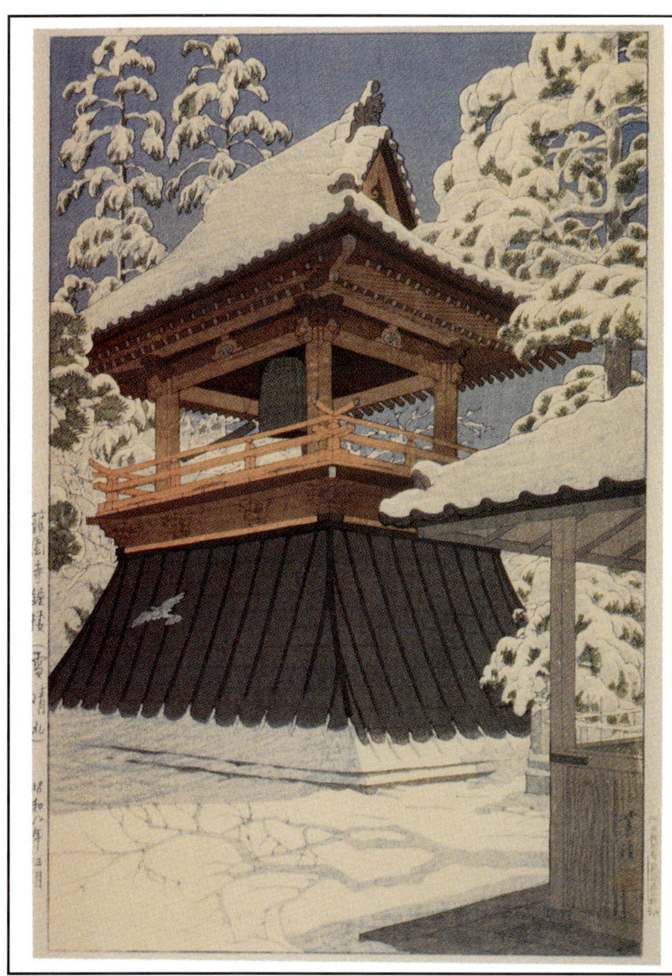

Kasamatsu Shiro, oban tate-e, "Temple in Snow," dated Showa 8 (1933), signed and sealed "Kasamatsu Shiro," published by Watanabe, early edition, blue outlines, fine impression, color, and condition, $1500-2000.

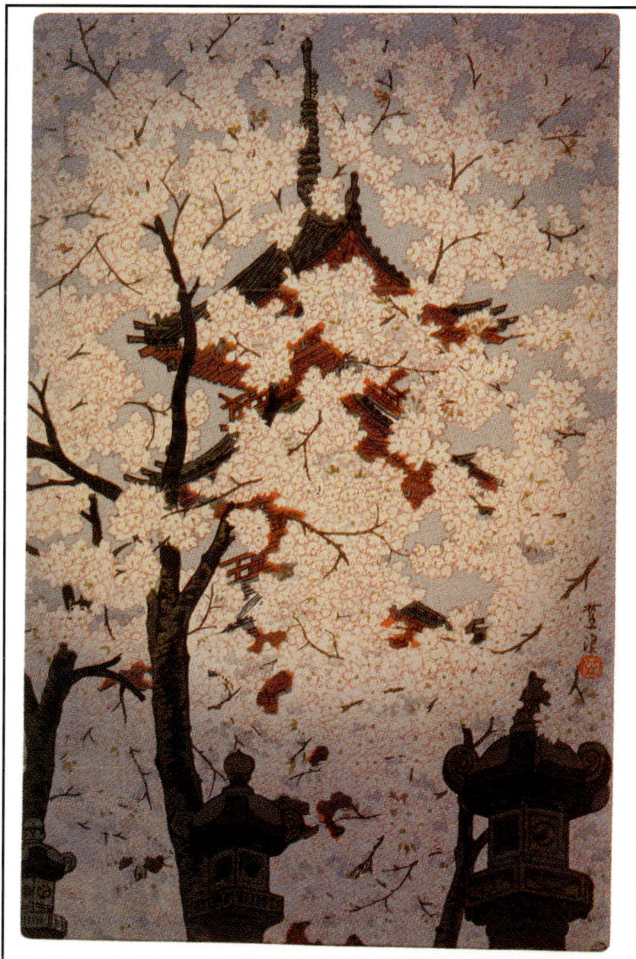

Kasamatsu Shiro, oban tate-e, "Pagada At Yanaka, Ueno, Under Rain," dated Showa 10 (1935), published by Watanabe, fine impression, color, and condition, $900-1200.

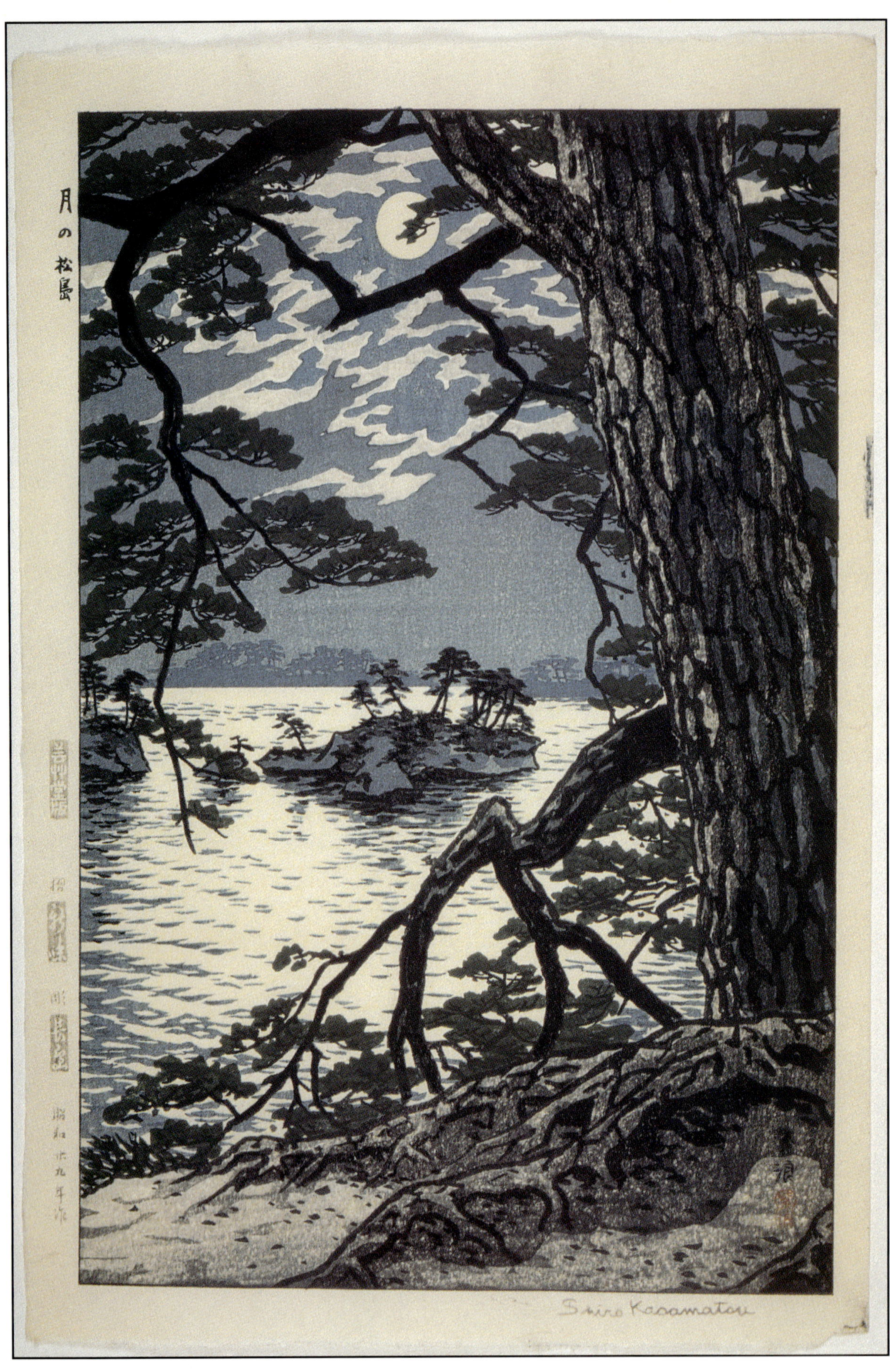

Kasamatsu Shiro, oban tate-e, "Lake and Moon," dated Showa 29 (1954), published by Unsodo, early edition, signed and sealed in image in lower left, signed on lower margin, fine impression, color, and condition, $750-950.

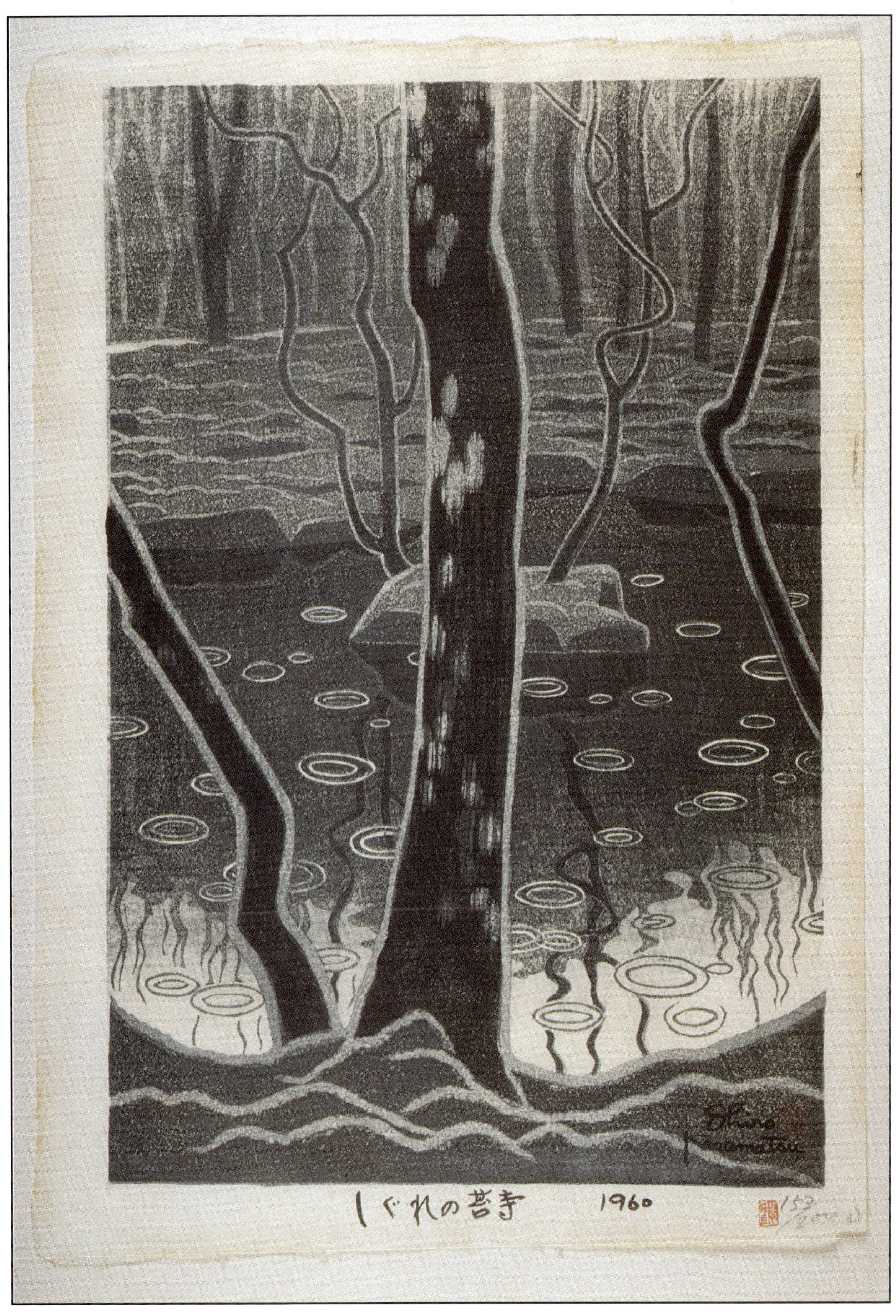

Kasamatsu Shiro, oban tate-e, 16" x 11 1/4", "Forest," from a limited edition series of 200, dated 1960, signed and sealed in lower left within image, very good impression, color, and condition, minor tape residue on edges of back margins, $700-950.

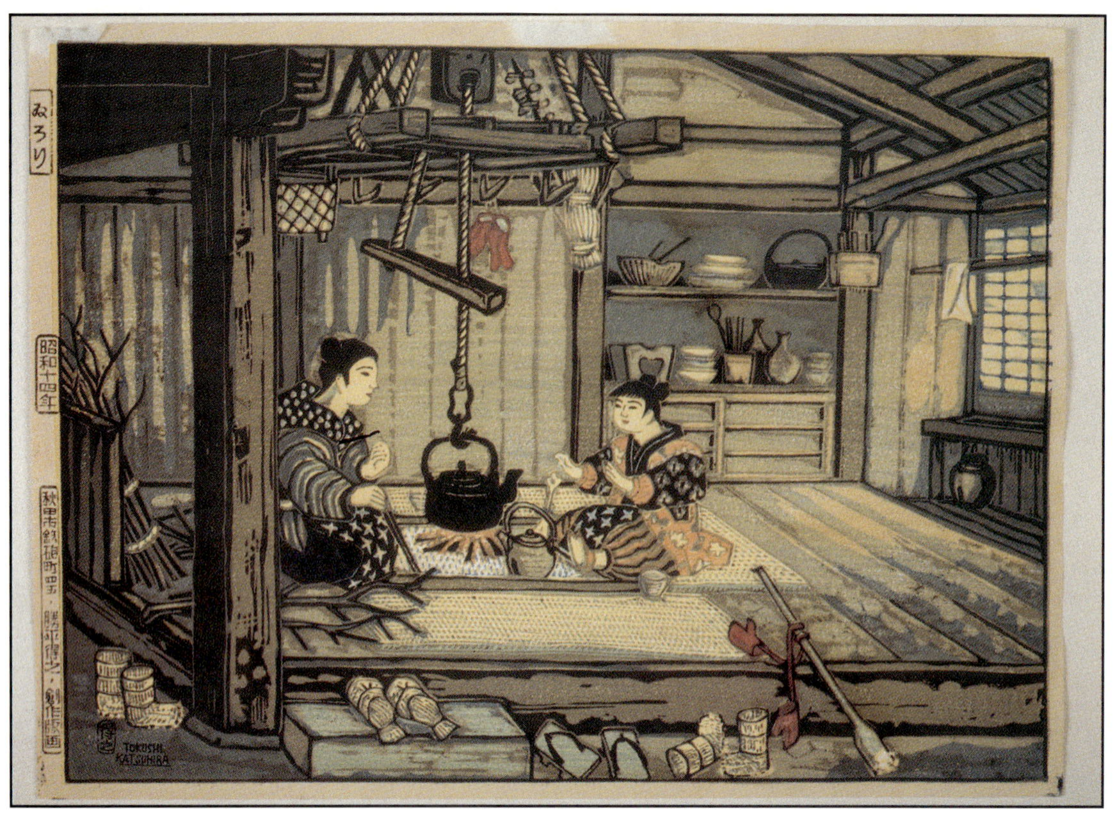

Katsuhira Tokushi, oban yoko-e, dated Showa 14 (1939), signed and sealed with image in lower left, signed and sealed in left margin, self carved, self printed, fine condition, impression, and color, $3500-5500.

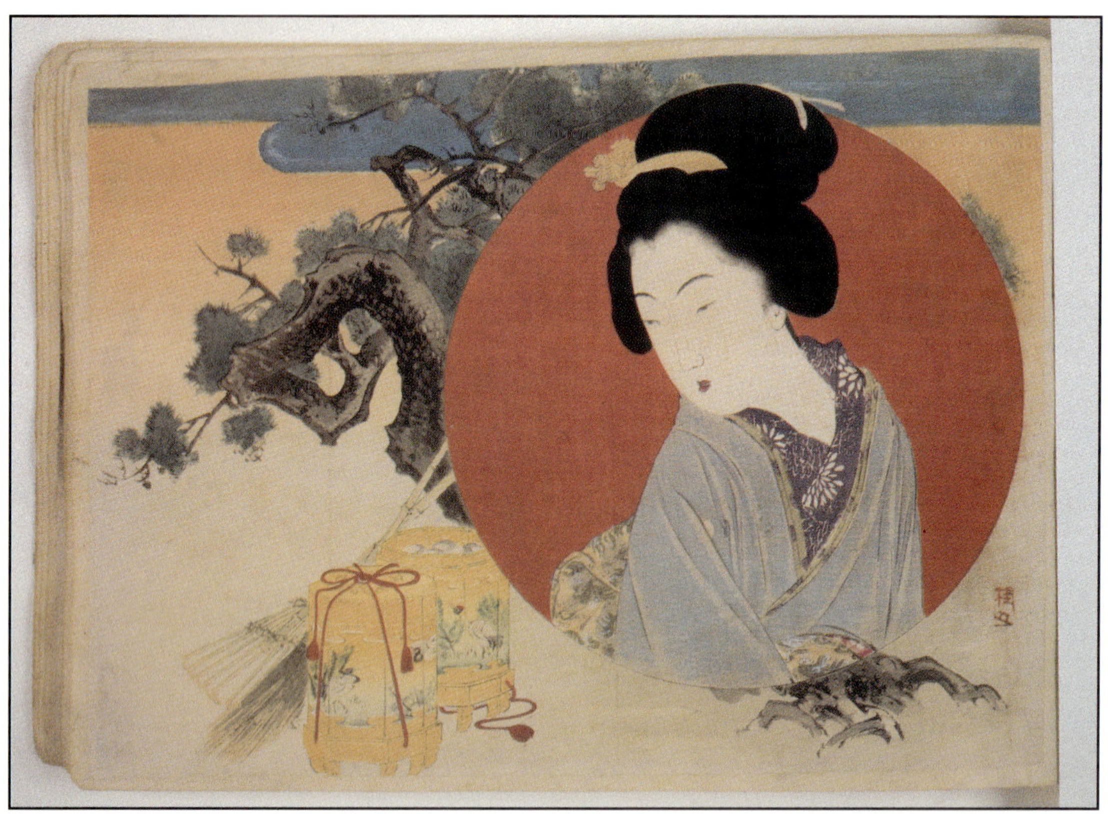

Kiyokata Kaburagi, Eisen Tomioka, Kiyochika Kobayashi, Hanko Kajita, Kason Suzuki, Keishu Takeuchi, Chikanobu Yoshu, Toshimine Tsutsui, Toshikata Mizuno, oban yoko-e, 11 1/2" x 8 1/2" (Keishu Takeuchi), 24 woodblock illustrations for Romantic Novels, late Meiji period c. 1900, fine impressions, very good color and condition, mica, gauffrage, $2500-4500.

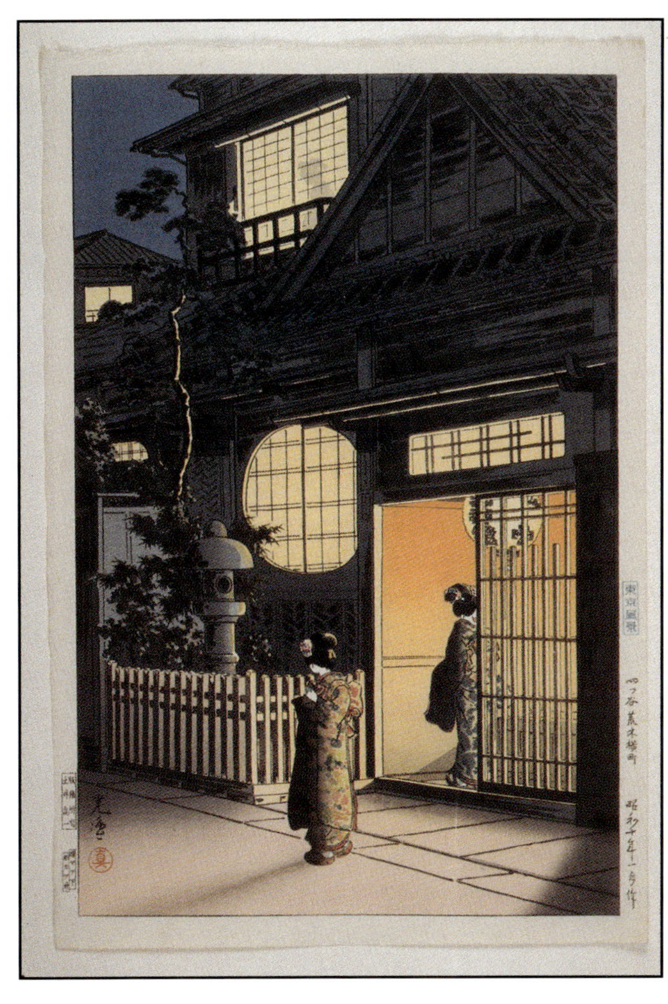

Koitsu Tsuchiya, oban tate-e, 15 3/4" x 10 1/2", "Yotsuya," Showa 8 (1935), early edition (with illumination in shades of yellow), published by Watanabe, fine impression, color, and condition, $1000-1500.

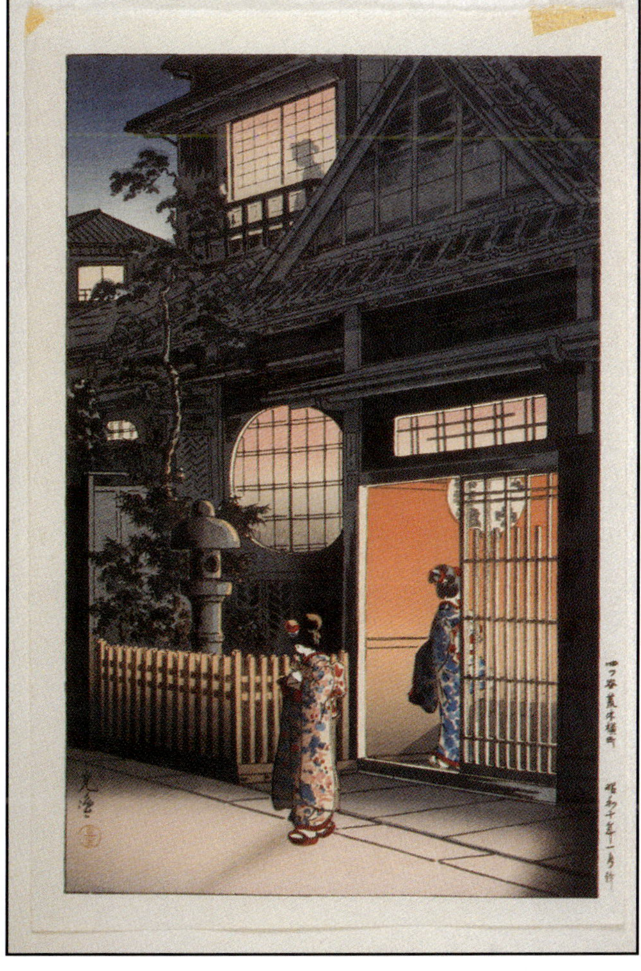

Koitsu Tsuchiya, oban tate-e, 15 3/4" x 10 1/2", "Yotsuya," Showa 8 (1935), posthumous edition, published by Watanabe, excellent condition, (this print has a deeper coloring and more use of the paper to show illumination than the early edition), $325-475.

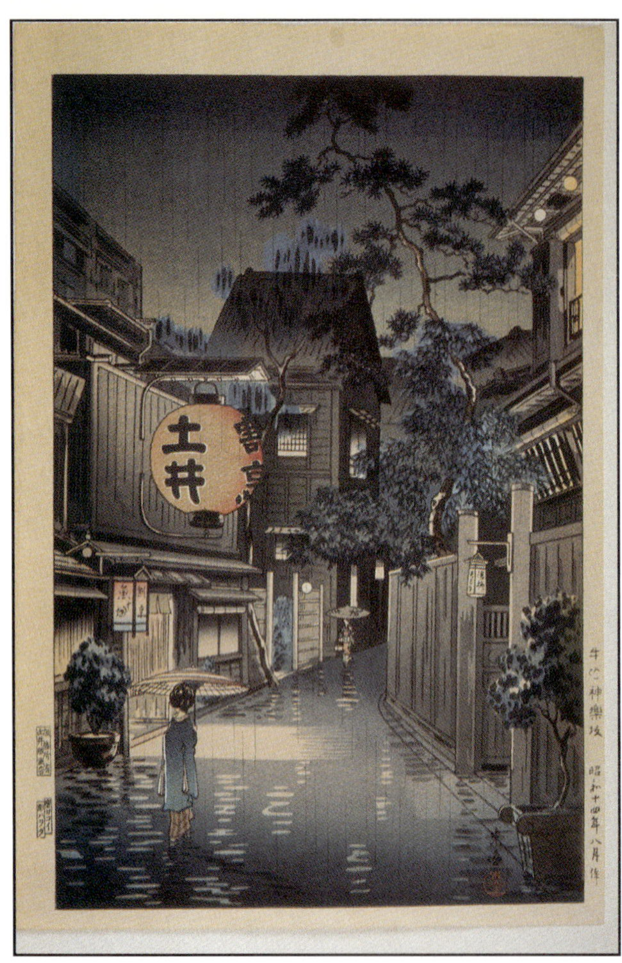

Koitsu Tsuchiya, oban tate-e, 16 3/4" x 11 1/2", "Jinrakuzaka at Ushigome," published by Doi, dated Showa 14 (1939), early edition, signed and sealed "Koitsu" within the image in lower right, fine impression, faded, paper toned from old mounts, $200-300.

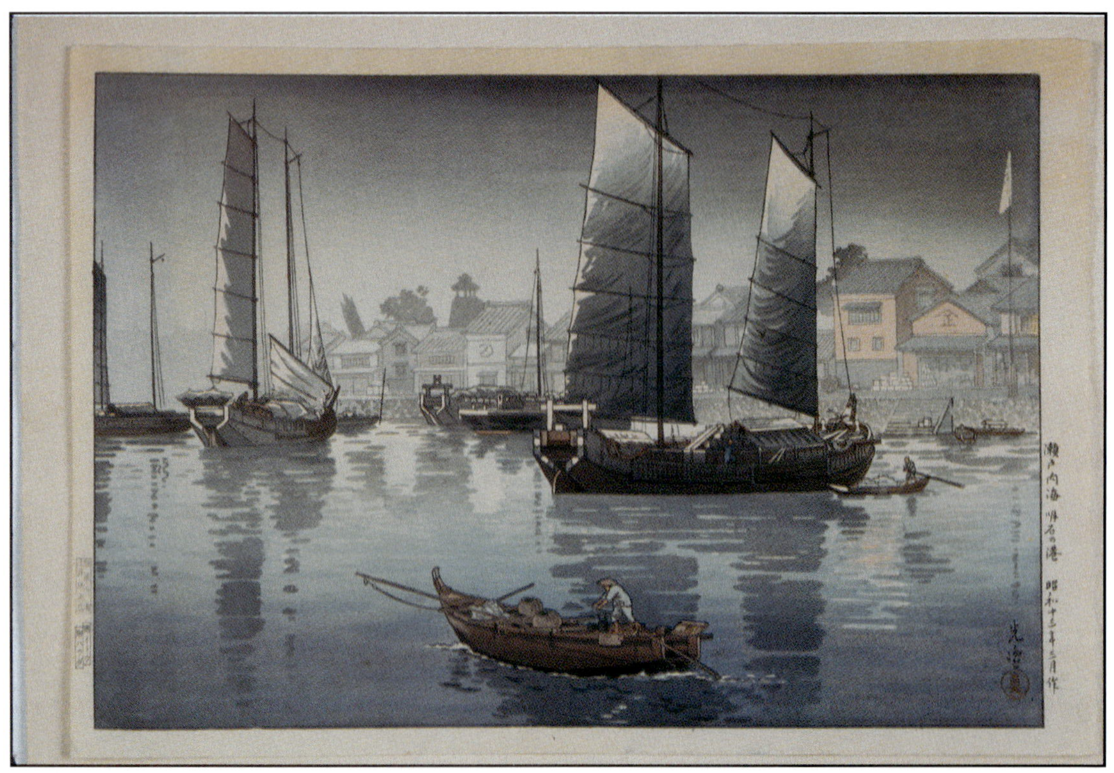

Koitsu Tsuchiya, oban yoko-e, 16 3/4" x 11 1/4" "Akashi Harbor, Seto Inland Sea," published by Doi, dated Showa 13 (1938) early edition, fine condition, color, and impression, $1000-1500.

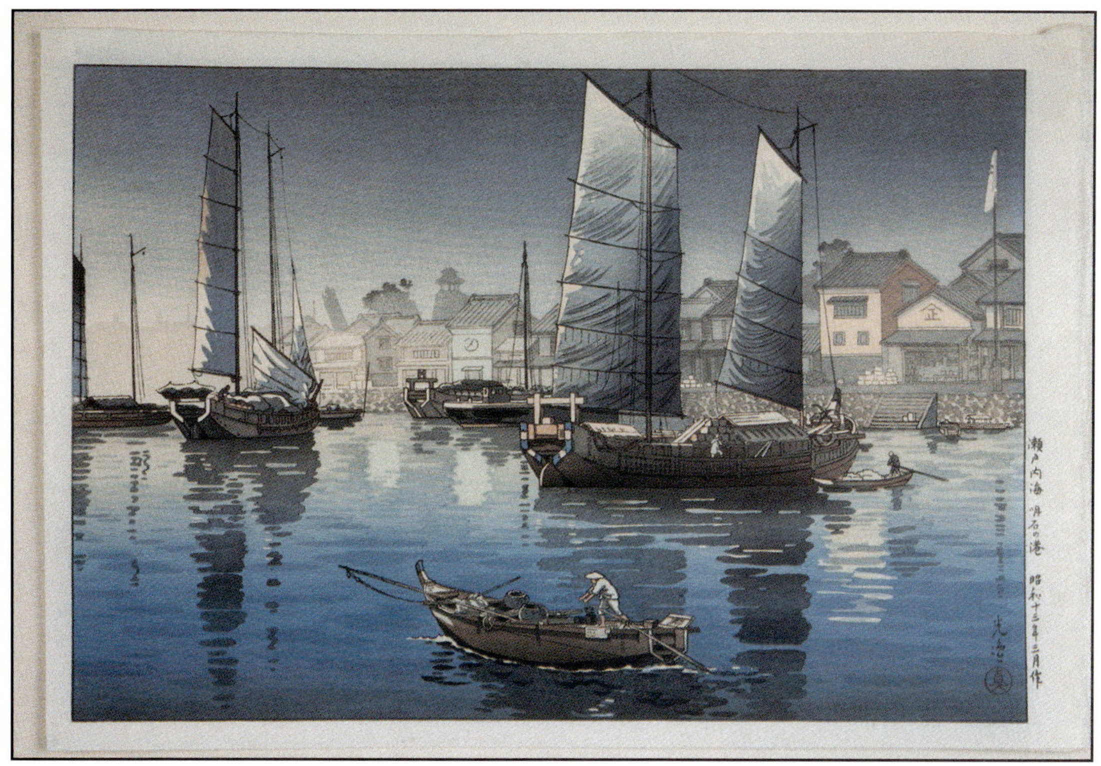

Koitsu Tsuchiya, oban yoko-e, 17" x 11 1/4" "Akashi Harbor, Seto Inland Sea," dated Showa 13 (1938), fine condition, fine color (not as intense as the early edition), and impression, posthumous (printed from original blocks), $350-450.

Koitsu Tsuchiya, oban tate-e, 16 3/4" x 11 1/4", "Rain at Kofukuji Temple, Nara," published by Doi, dated Showa 12 (1937), early edition, signed and sealed "Koitsu" lower left within image, fine impression, color, and condition, $1500-2500.

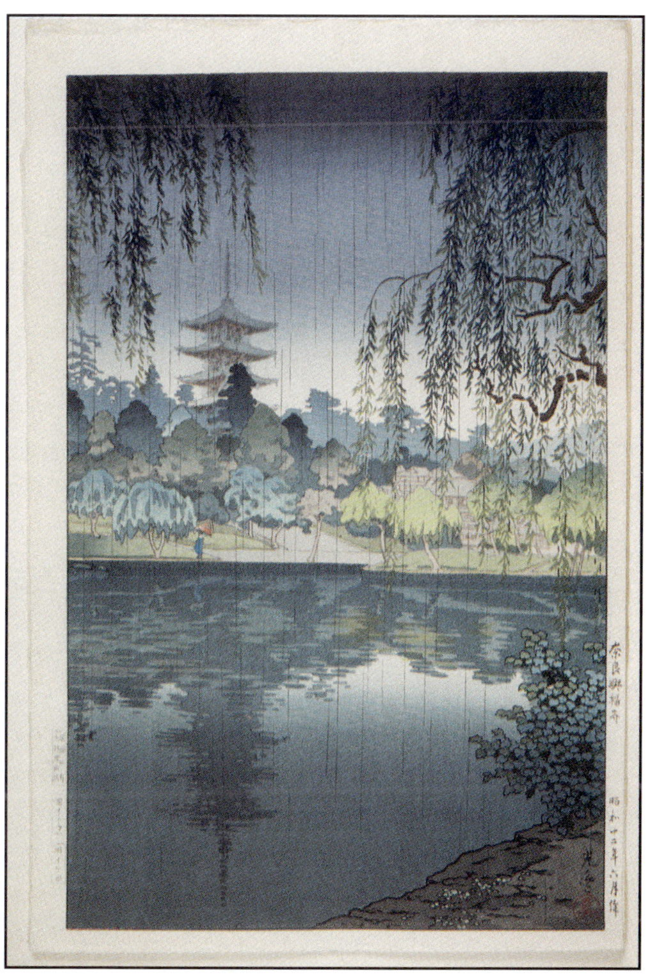

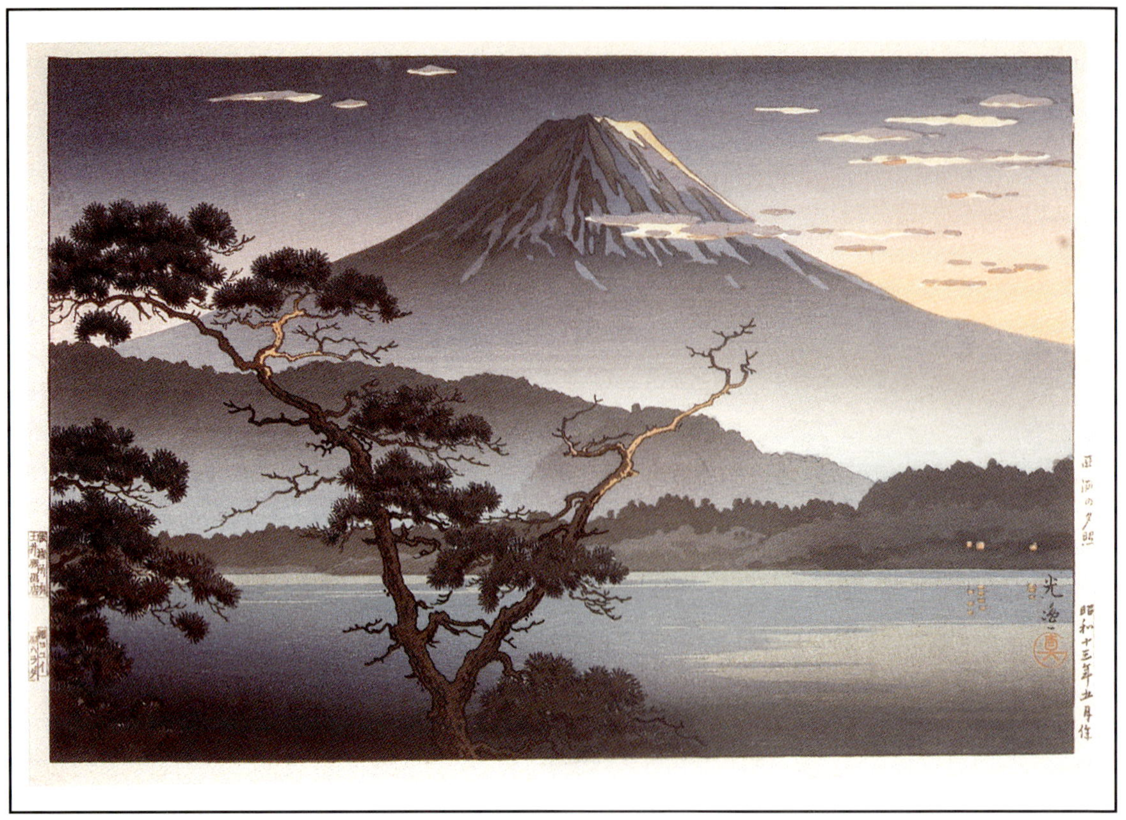

(Cover) Koitsu Tsuchiya, oban yoko-e, 10 1/2" x 15 1/2", "Mt. Fuji at Sunset," dated Showa 13 (1938), early edition, fine impression, color, and condition, $1500-2200.

Koitsu Tsuchiya, oban tate-e, "Bridge in Rain," dated Showa 8 (1933), published by Doi, early edition, fine impression, color, and condition, $1200-1800.

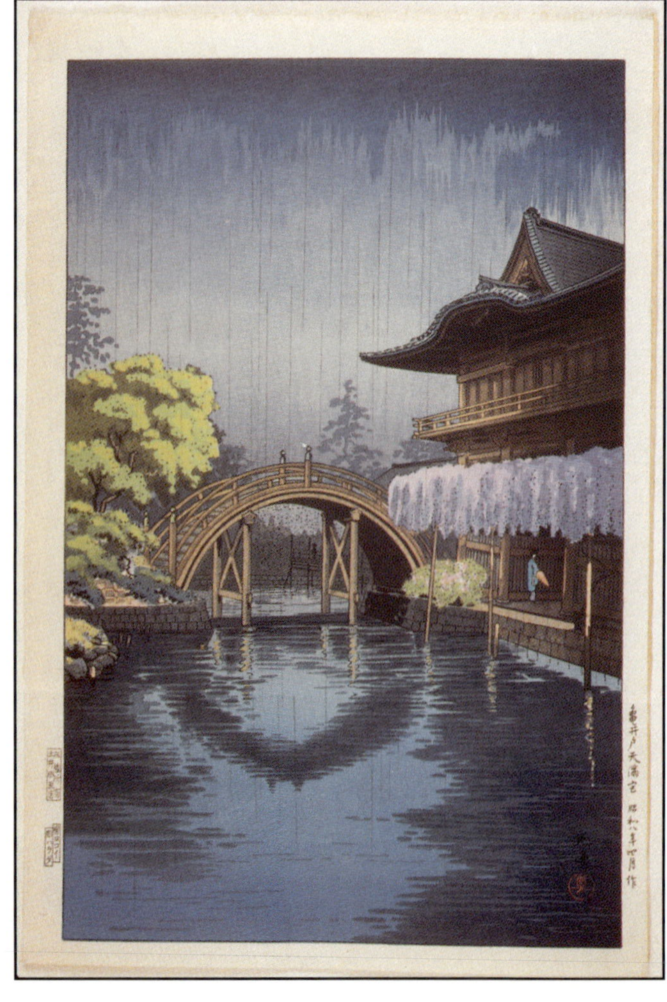

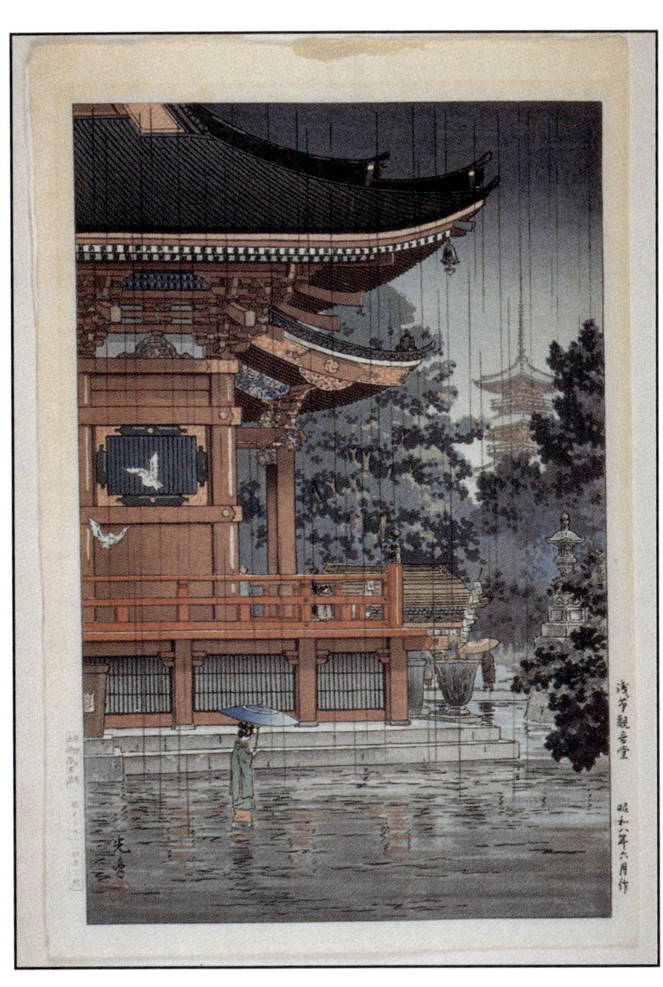

Kotisu Tsuchiya, oban tate-e, "Pagoda in Rain," dated Showa 8 (1933), published by Doi, early edition, fine impression, very good color, slightly toned margins, $750-1000.

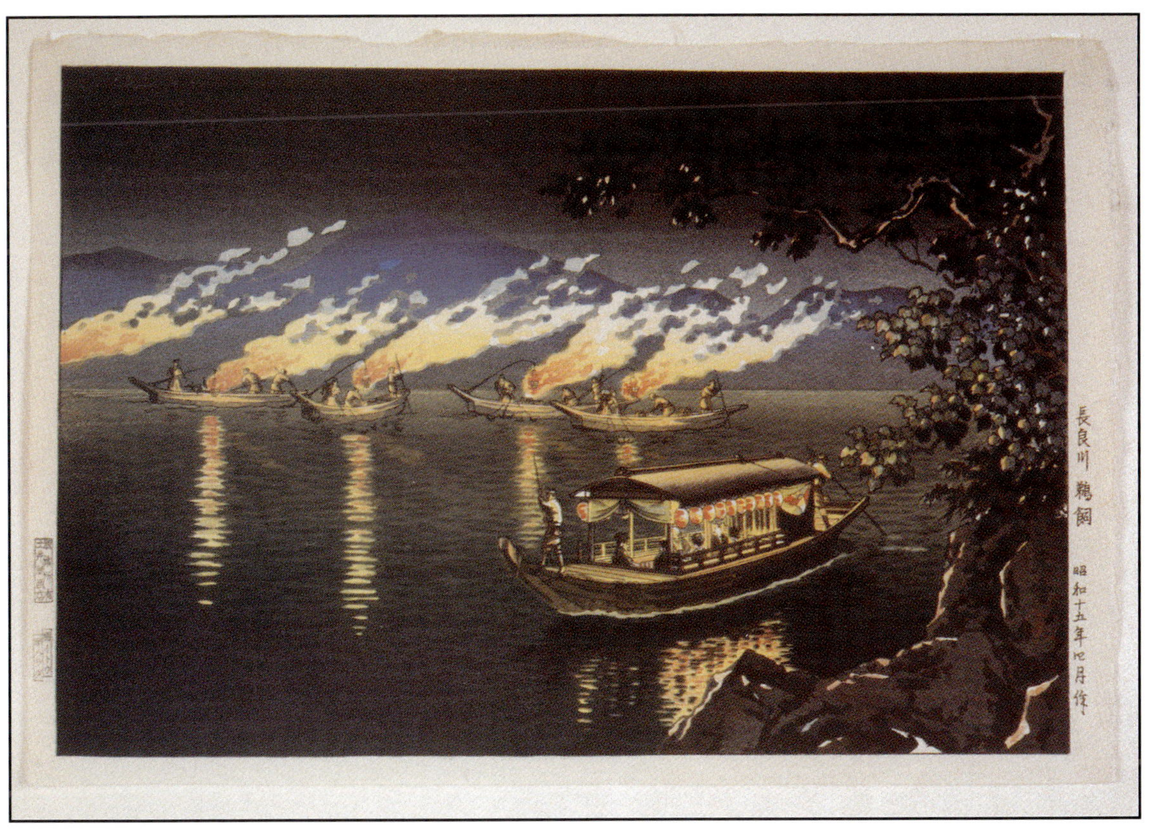

Koitsu Tsuchiya, oban yoko-e; "Fishing with Cormorants," dated Showa 15 (1940), early edition, signed and sealed "Koitsu," published by Watanabe, fine impression, color, and condition, $950-1250.

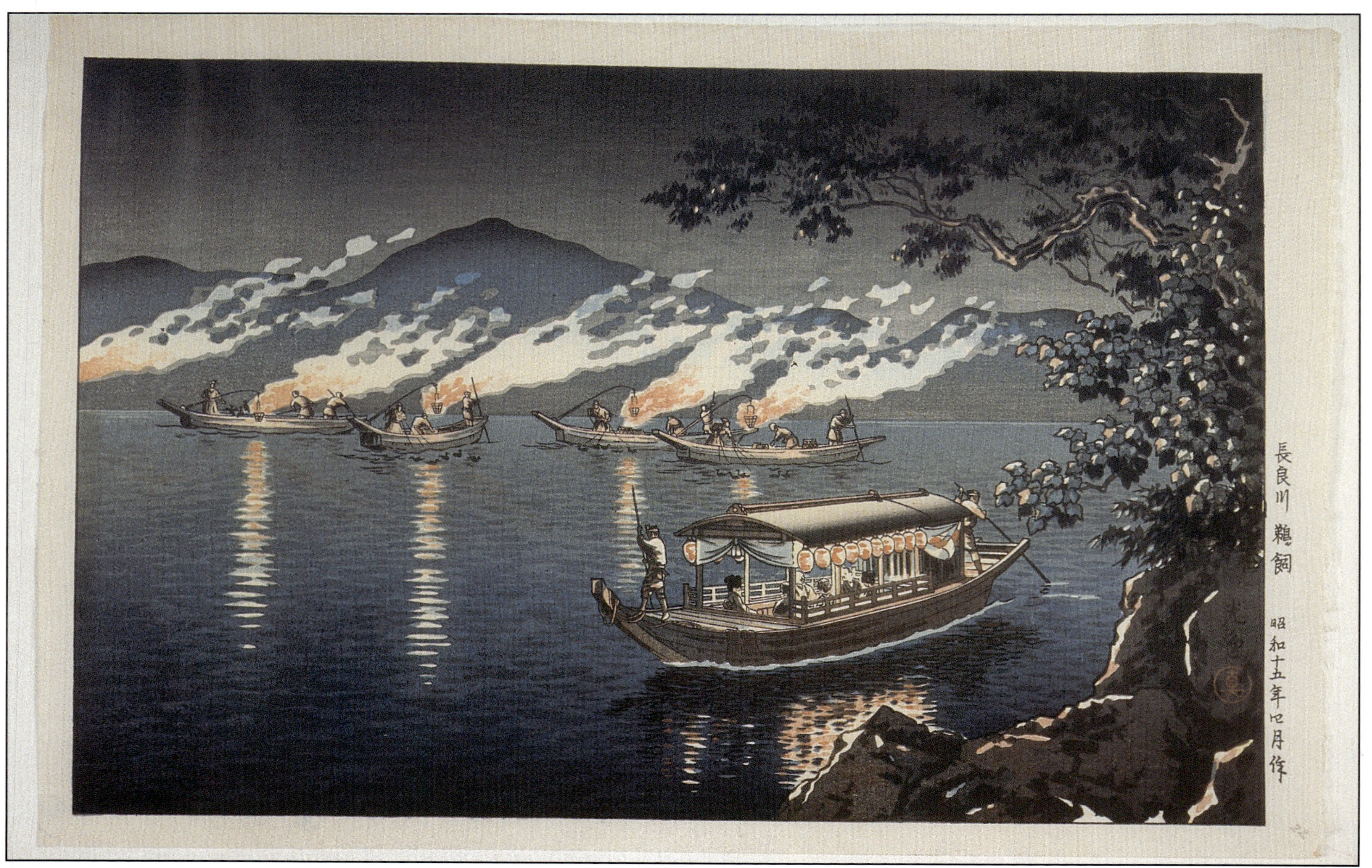

Koitsu Tsuchiya, oban yoko-e, "Fishing with Cormorants," dated Showa 15 (1940), signed and sealed "Koitsu," published by Watanabe, fine impression, color (this posthumous print is lacking the bright hues of the flames), and condition, a posthumous print, $300-400.

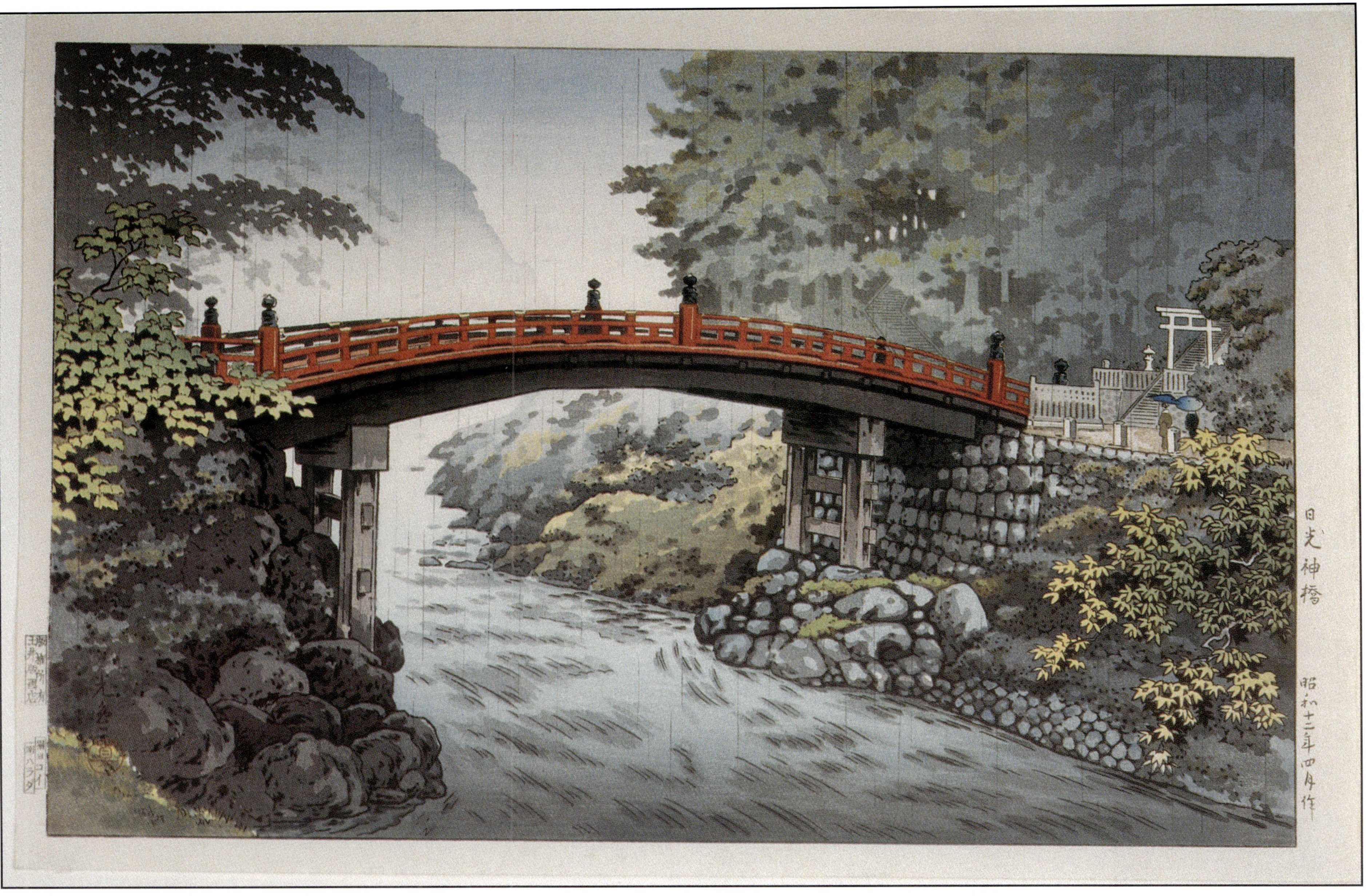

Koitsu Tsuchiya, oban yoko-e, 16 1/2" x 11 1/4", "Sacred Bridge In Nikko," dated Showa 8 (1933), early edition, publisher Doi, fine impression, color, and condition, $1200-1800.

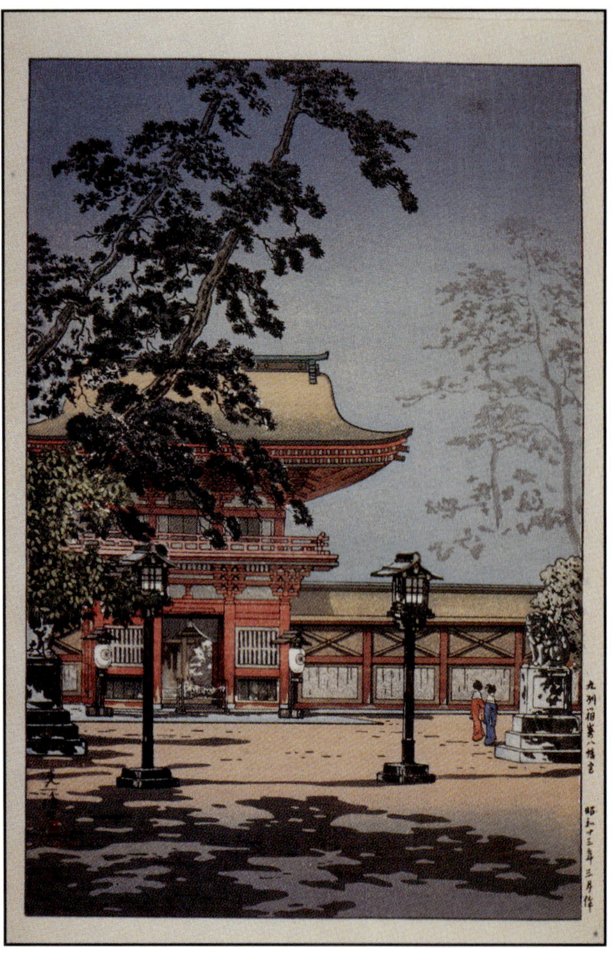

Koitsu Tsuchiya, oban tate-e, dated Showa 13 (1938), posthumous printing, fine color, impression, and condition, $225-350.

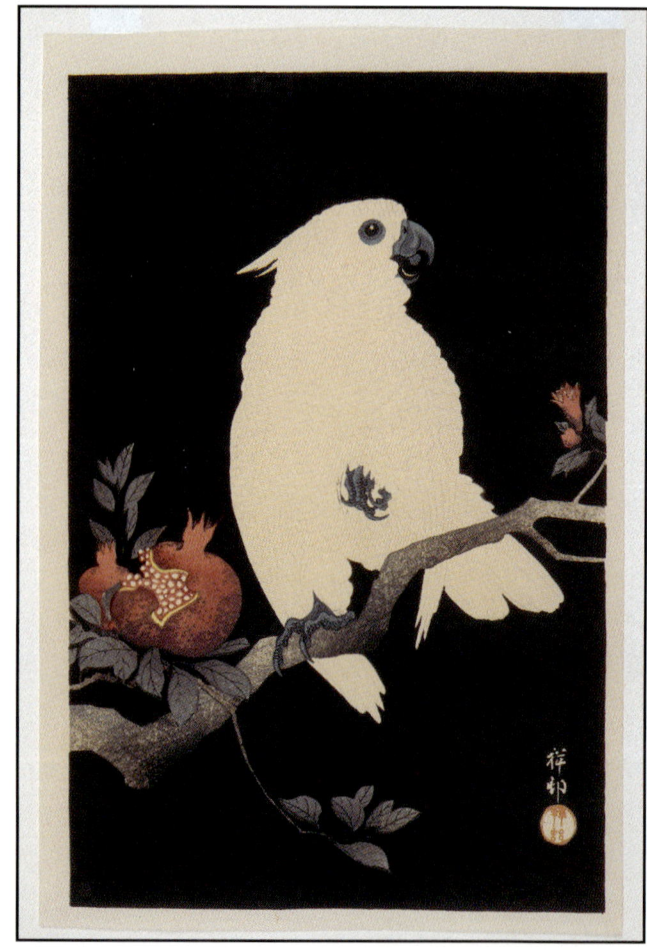

Koson Ohara, oban tate-e, "Parrot on Pomegranate Tree," Showa 5(1930), published by Watanabe, later edition, fine condition, color, and impression, $775-975.

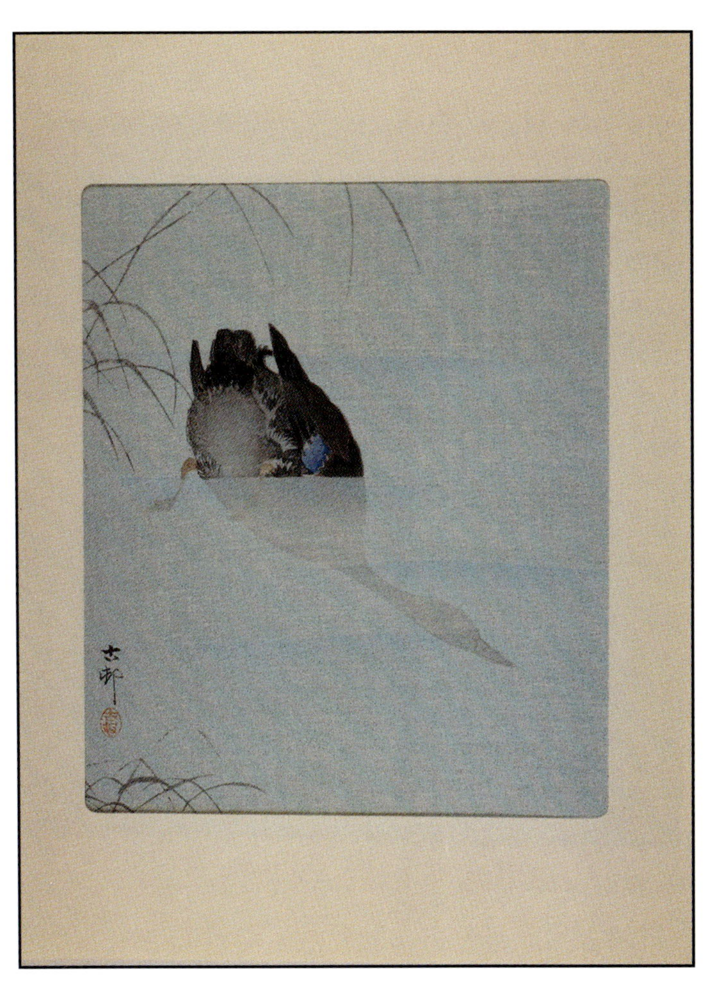

Koson Ohara, shishiban, "Duck Underwater," c. 1920s, original folio with states on the back " Imported Japanese Prints Made By Hand From Cherrywood Blocks On Mulberry Paper," published by Shima Art Company Inc. New York And Tokyo, Print #21, fine condition, color, and impression, $475-675.

Kotondo Torii, dai oban, "Bijin Adjusting Hairpin," from a limited edition, fine impression, color, and condition, $12,000-18,000.

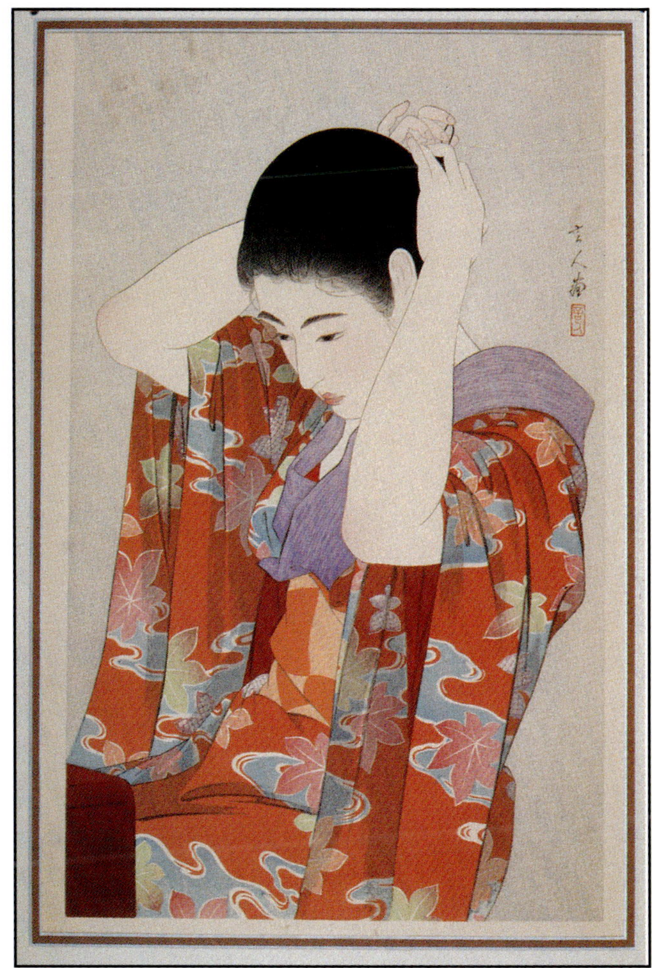

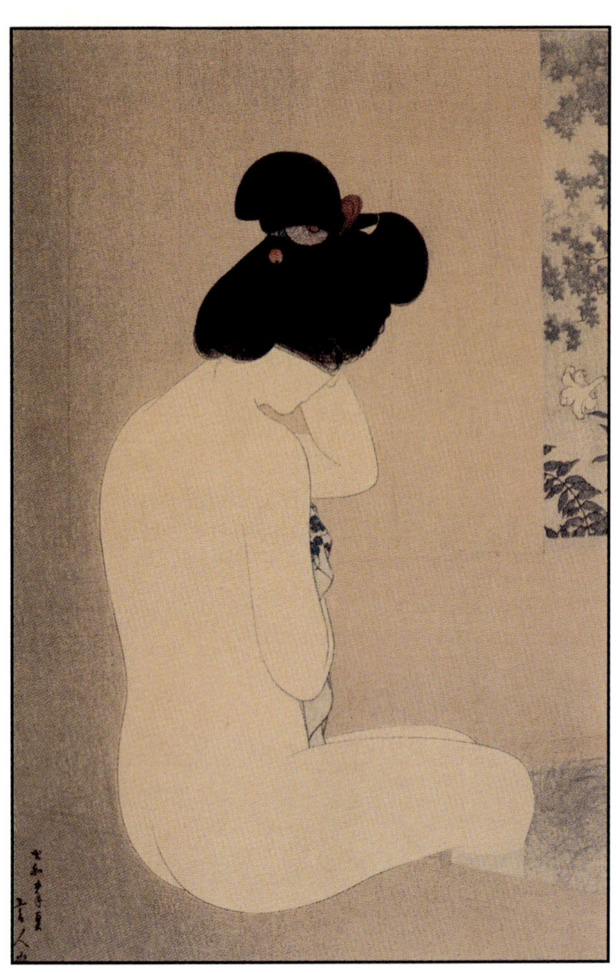

Kotondo Torii, dai oban tate-e, "Hot Spring," published by Sakai/Kawaguchi, from a limited edition, fine impression, faded, toned, mat burn in margins, $900-1200.

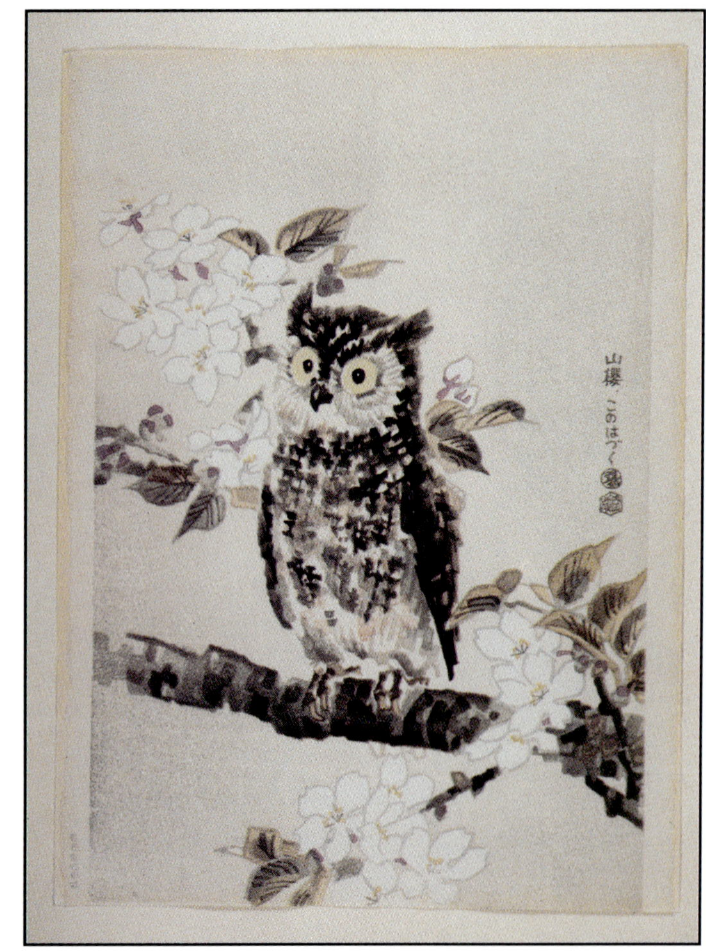

Kotozuka, oban tate-e, "Owl On Flowering Branch," c. 1955, published by Uchida, fine color, impression, $375-475.

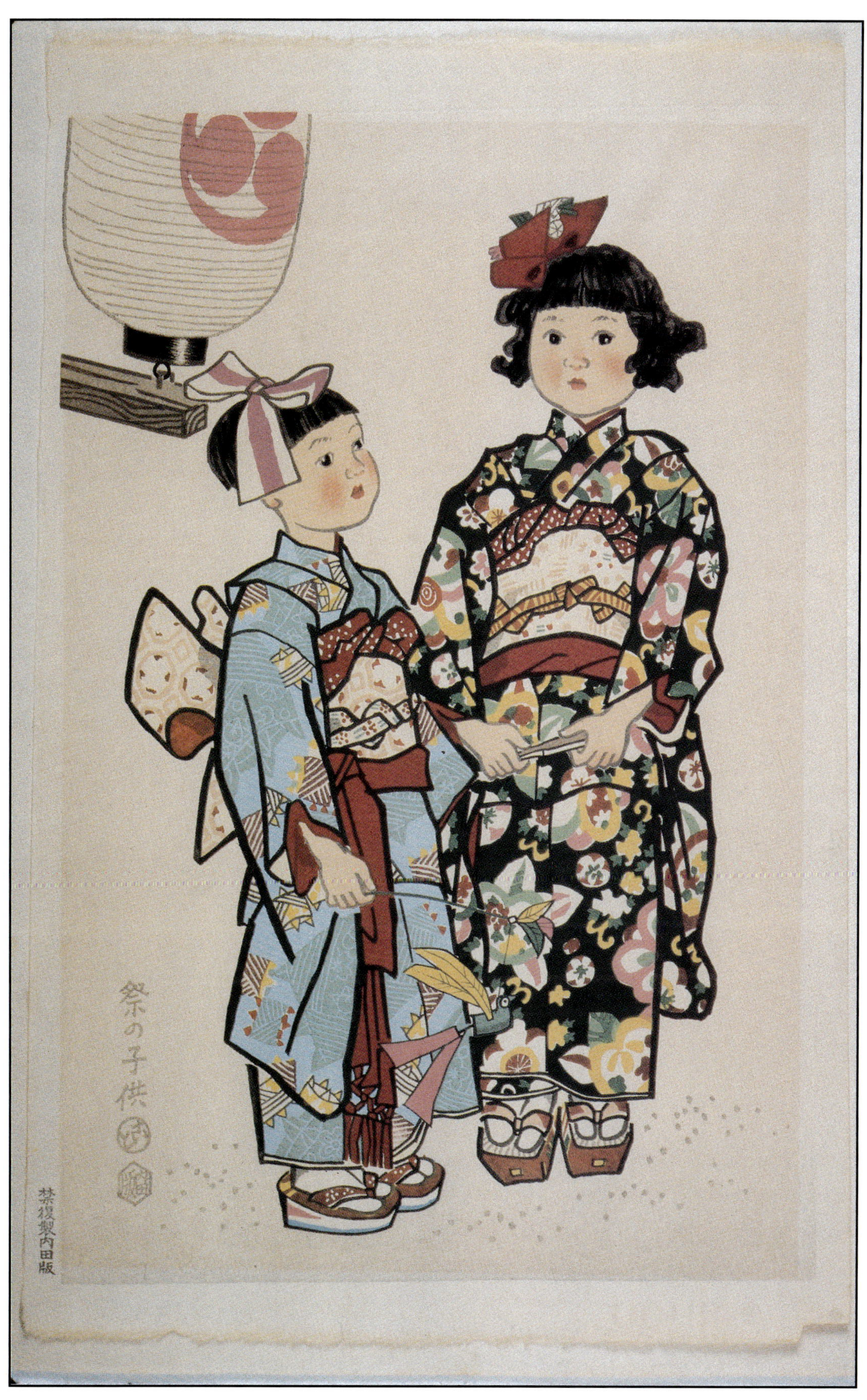

Kotozuka Eiichi, oban tate-e, 17 1/2" x 11 1/2", "The Children on Festival," c. 1955, early edition, published by Uchida, fine impression, color, and condition, $375-500.

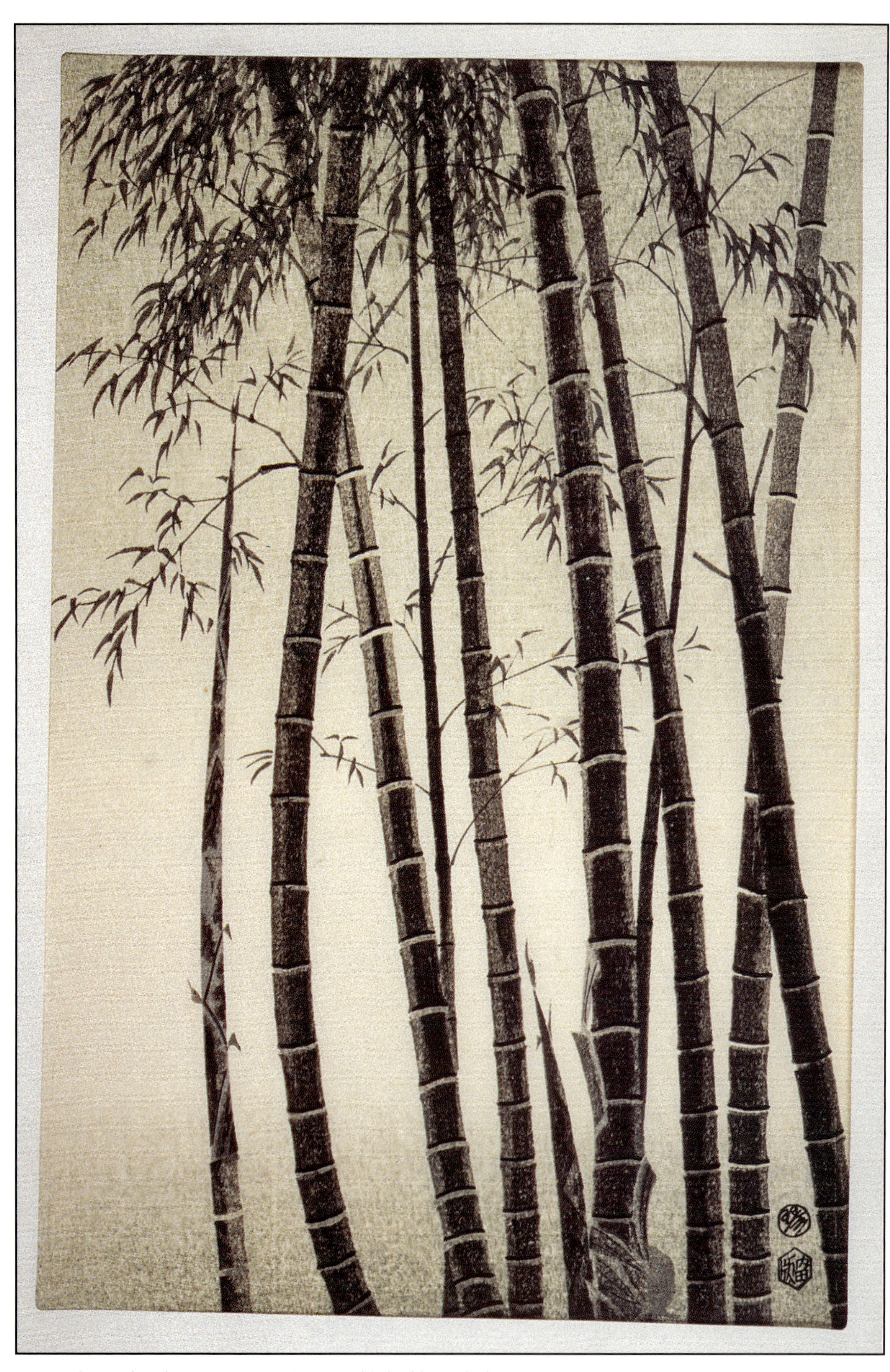

Kotozuka Eiichi, oban tate-e, "Bamboo," published by Uchida, c. 1960, $175-285.

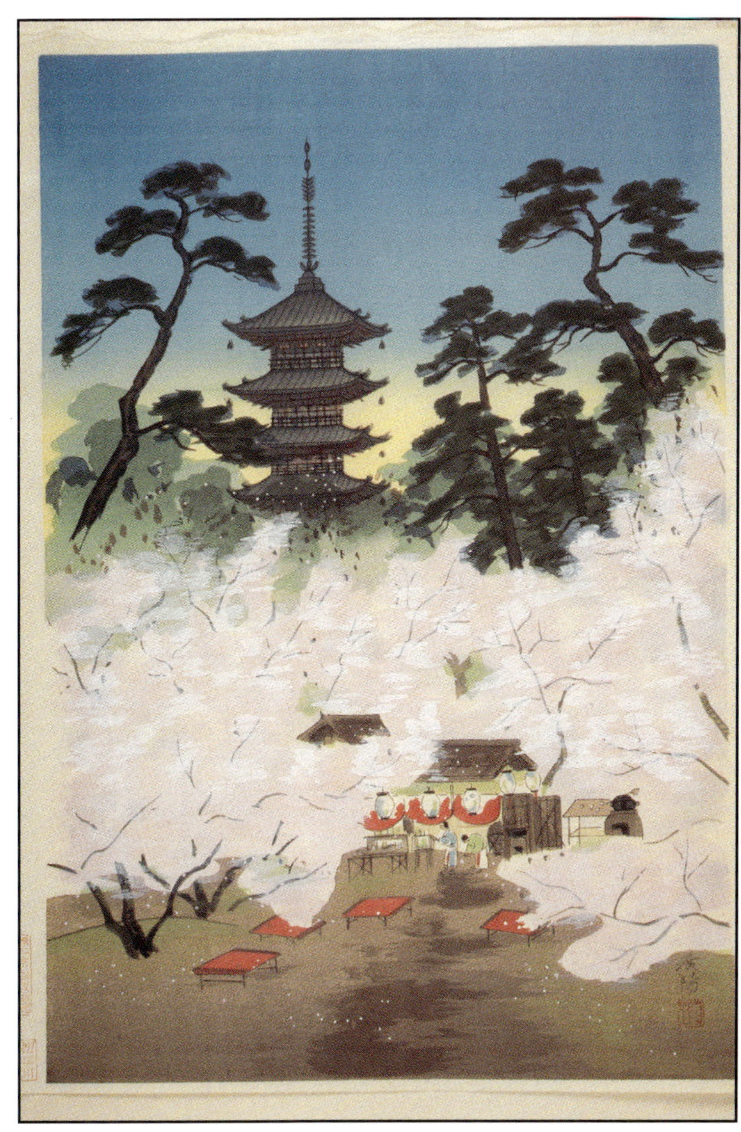

Koyo Omura, oban tate-e, "Cherry Blossoms," published by Kyoto Hanga-In, c. 1952, fine impression, color, and condition, $125-185.

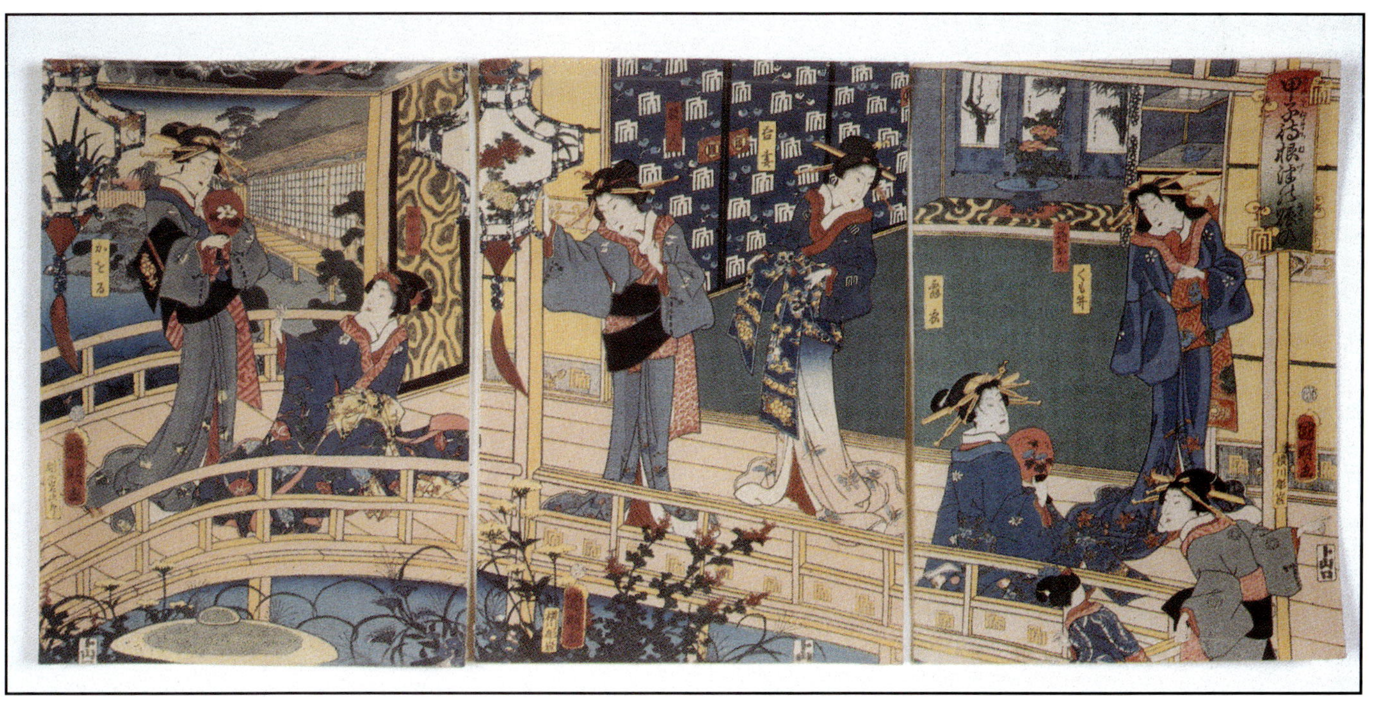

Kuniaki, koban triptych, crepe paper, from Tale of Genji, fine condition, color, and impression, $450-750.

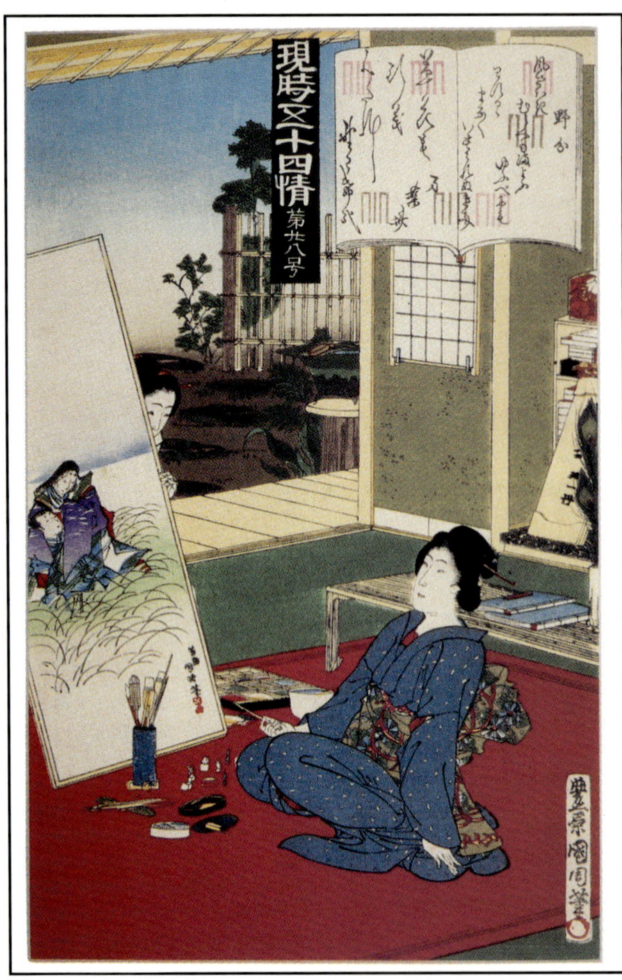

Kunichika, oban tate-e, 14 3/4" x 9 1/2" from Tale of Genji chapter 28 Nowaki, c. 1880, fine impression, color, and condition, $675-975.

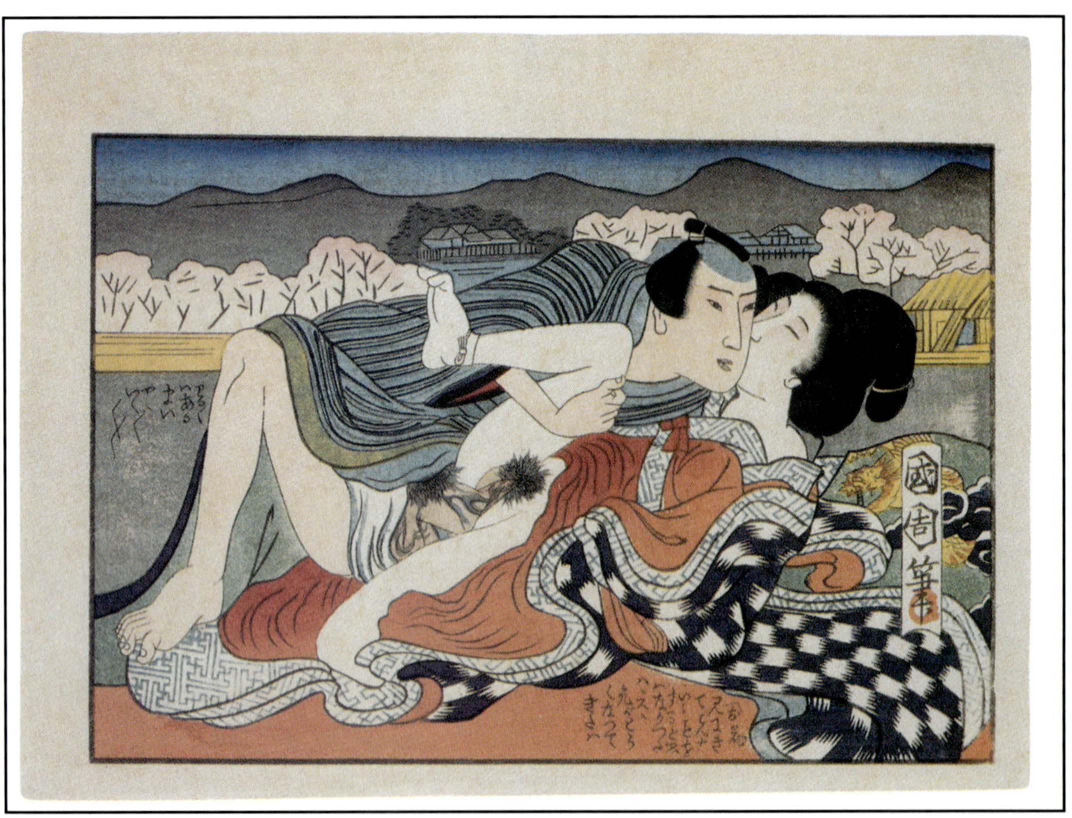

Kunichika, 10" x 7", Shunga (erotica), signed and sealed within image, fine impression, condition, and color, $700-900.

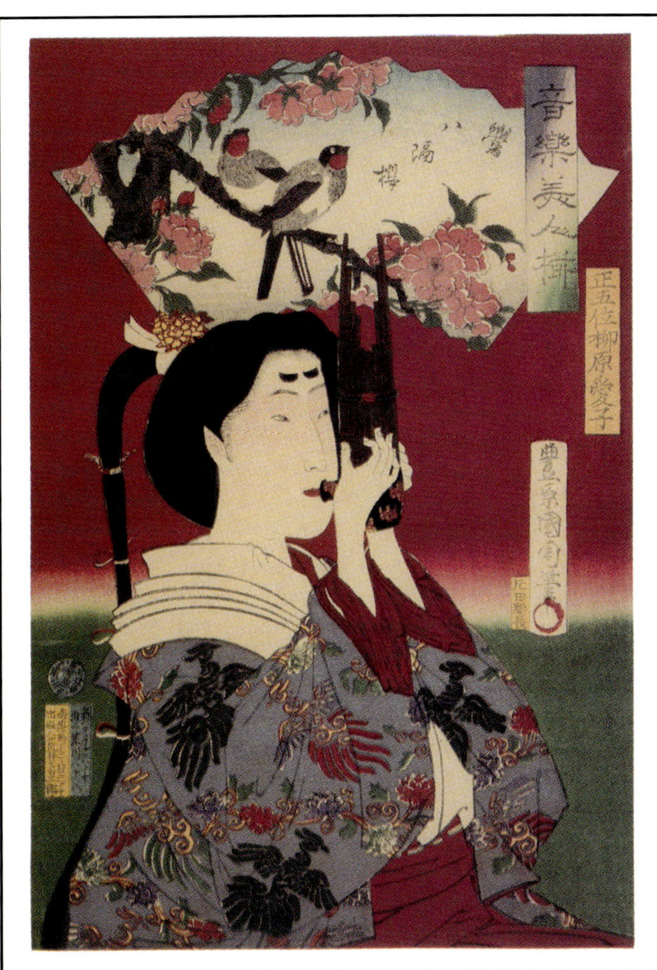

Kunichika, oban tate-e, "Beauty and Sho" (musical instrument), dated Dec. 1878, fine impression, color, and condition, $1000-1500.

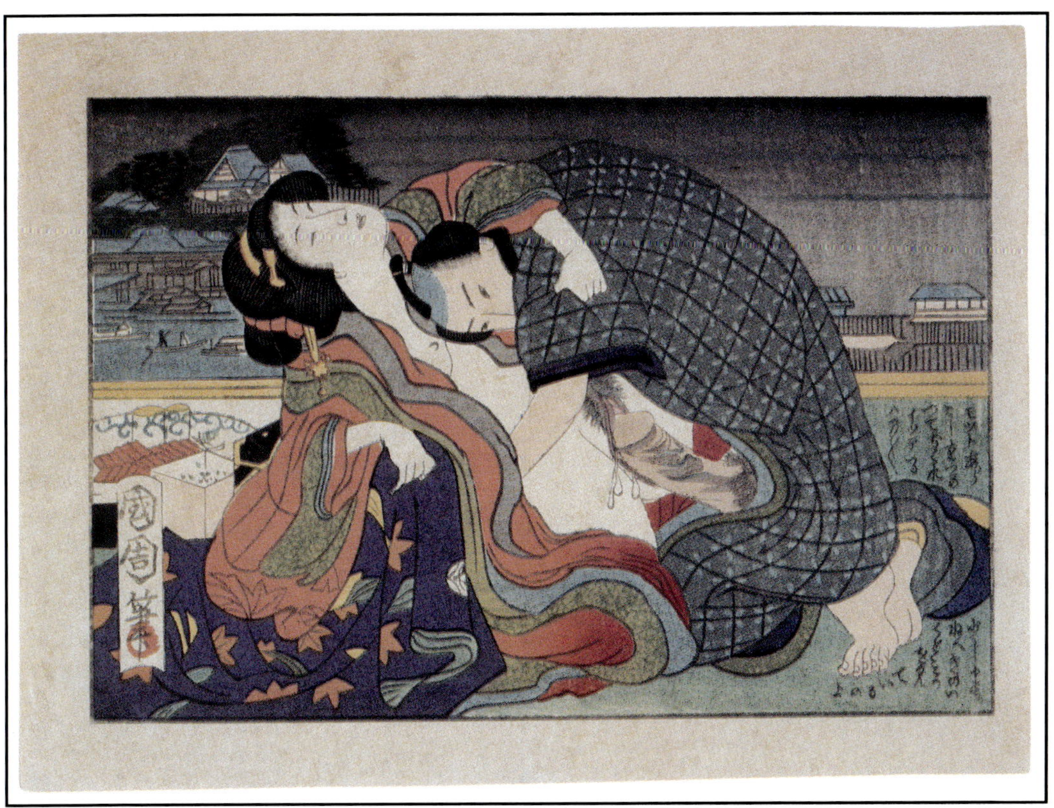

Kunichika, 10" x 7", Shunga (erotica), signed and sealed within image, fine impression, condition, and color, $700-900.

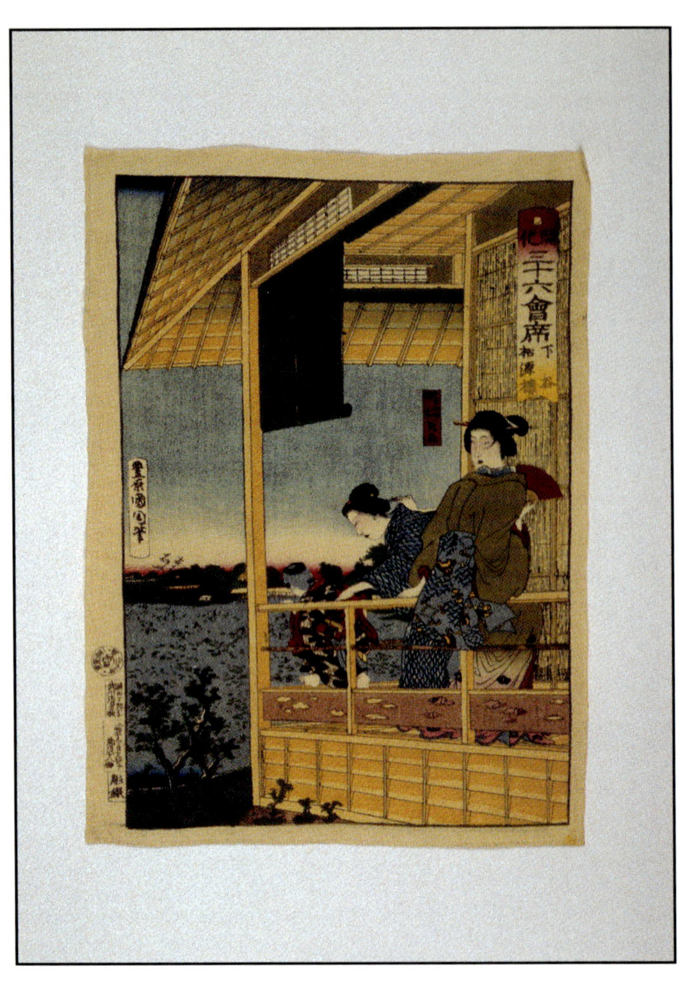

Kunichika, chuban, crepe paper, dated Meiji 11 (1878), fine impression, color, and condition, $275-485.

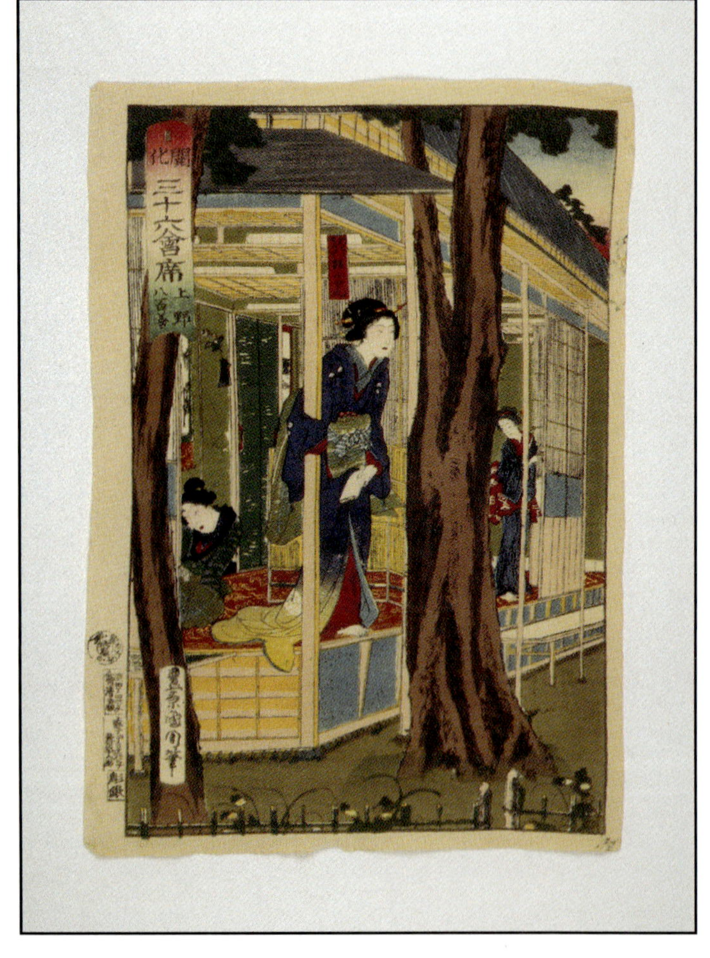

Kunichika, aiban, crepe paper, dated Meiji 11 (1878), fine impression, color, and condition, $375-500.

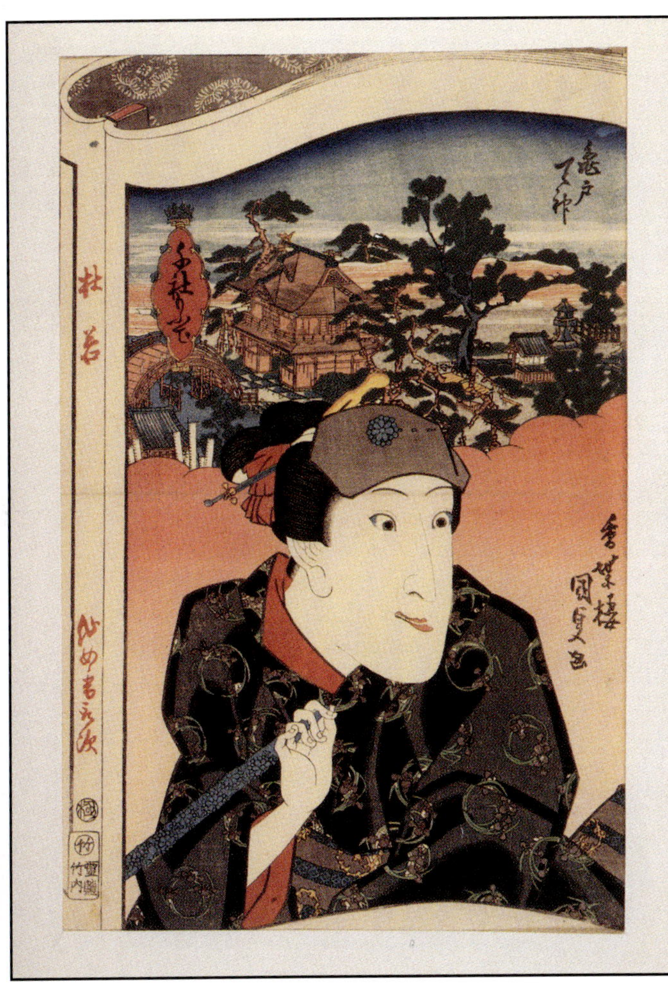

Kunisada, oban tate-e, 14 1/2" x 10", an onnagata with scenic background from the series Senjoko Toritsugi (Make-up Powder), signed "Kohoro Kunisada ga," Takeuchi Magohachi publisher, c. 1833, very good impression and color, slightly trimmed on left, a smudge above lip, center crease, $750-950.

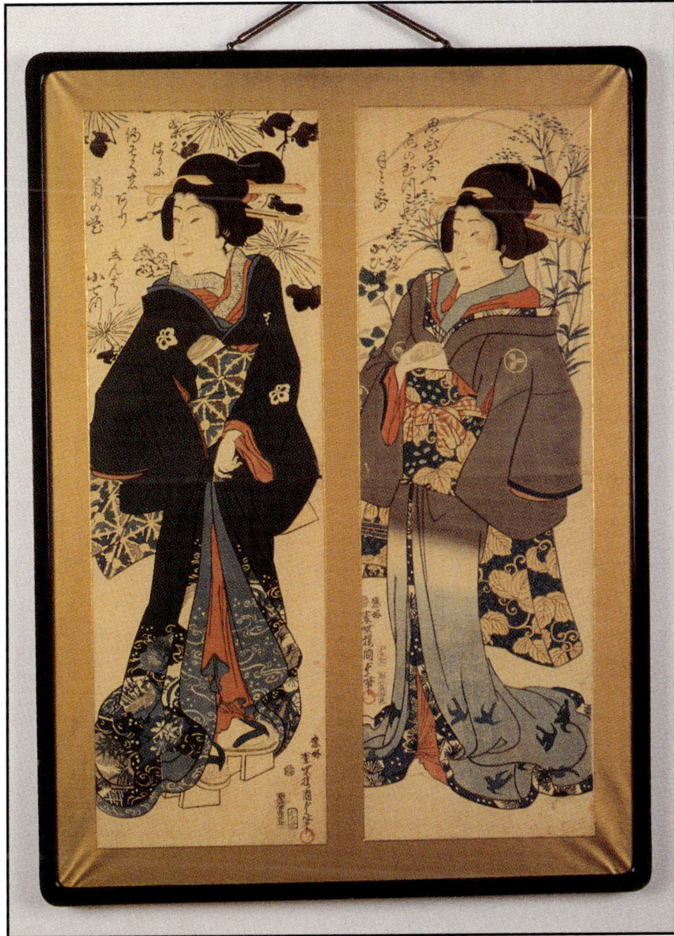

Kunisada, kakemono-e, a panel with two kakemono-e of bijin, fine impressions, color, slightly soiled, $3500-5500 each.

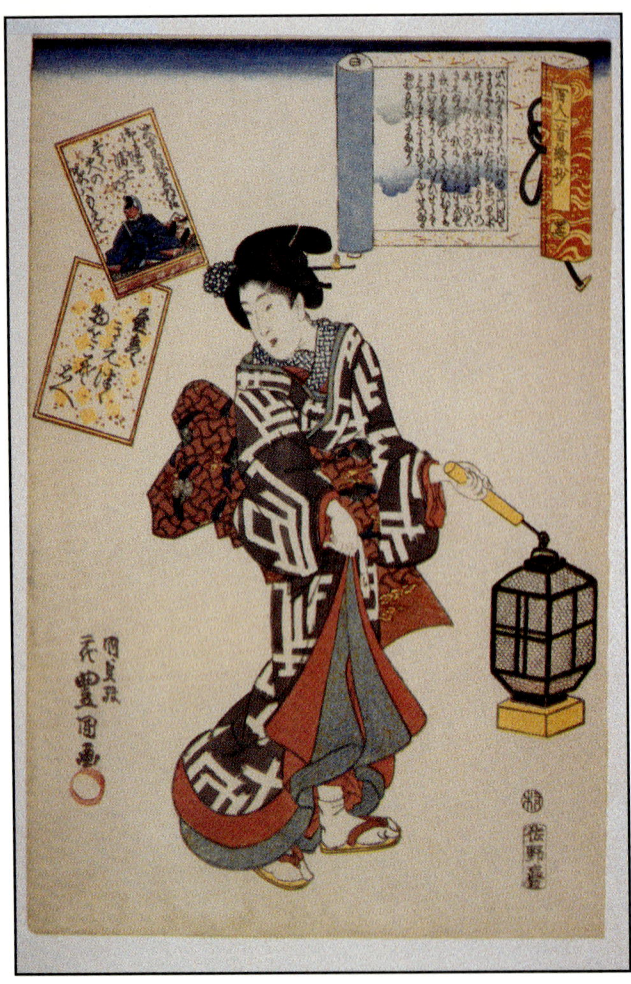

Kunisada (Toyokuni III), oban tate-e, a beauty holding a lantern, with playing cards on the left, from the series Hyakunin Isshu Kaisho, (A Selection of Pictures Matched to One Hundred Poems, one by each poet), signed "Kunisada aratame nidaime Toyokuni ga," with Toshidama seal, kiwame seal, published by Sanoya Kihei (This print dates 1844 and has both names -Kunisada and Toyokuni III), very good impression, condition, and color, $900-1500.

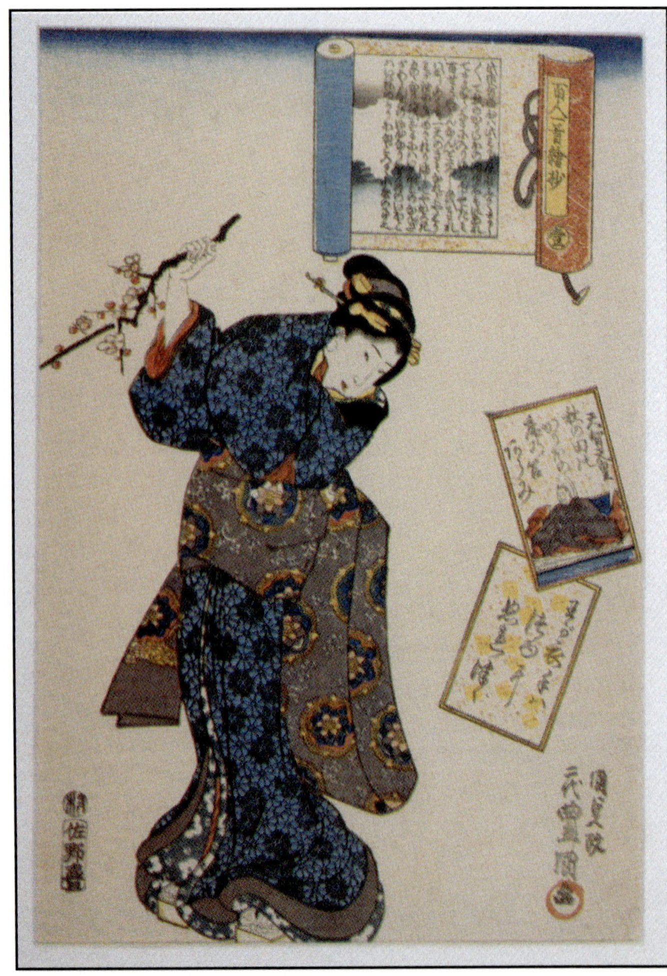

Kunisada (Toyokuni III), oban tate-e, a beauty holding a flowering branch, with playing cards on the left, from the series Hyakunin Isshu Kaisho, (A Selection of Pictures Matched to One Hundred Poems, one by each poet), signed "Kunisada aratame nidaime Toyokuni ga," with Toshidama seal, kiwame seal, published by Sanoya Kihei (This print dates 1844 and has both names -Kunisada and Toyokuni III), very good impression, condition, and color, $900-1500.

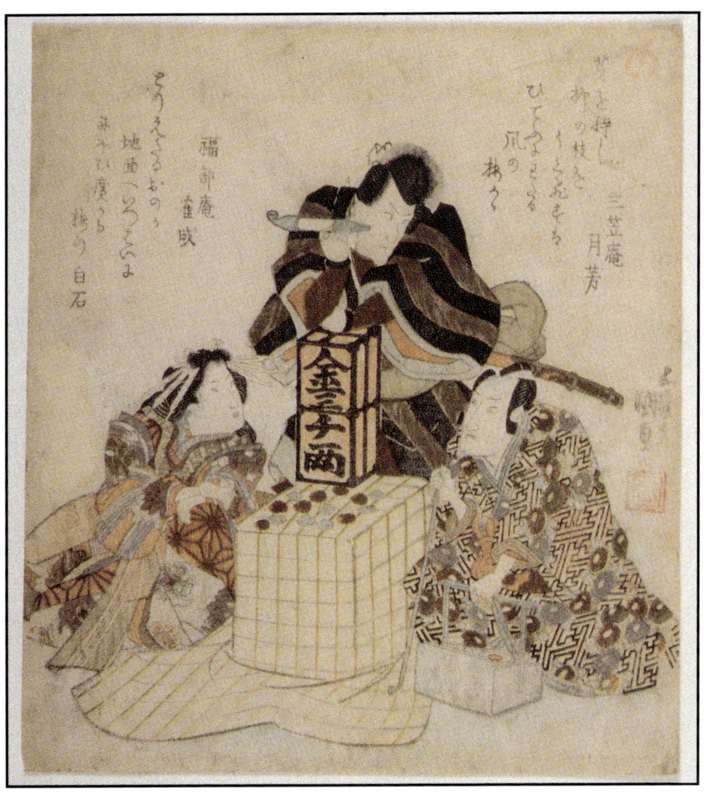

Kunisada, surimono, three actors, one with a long pipe, one with a short pipe, two engaged in playing go, signed "Gototei Kunisada," c. 1829-1842, fine impression, very good color, slightly rubbed, $2500-3500.

Kunisada II, oban tate-e, Genji, fine impression, very good color, trimmed left and right margins, $300-500.

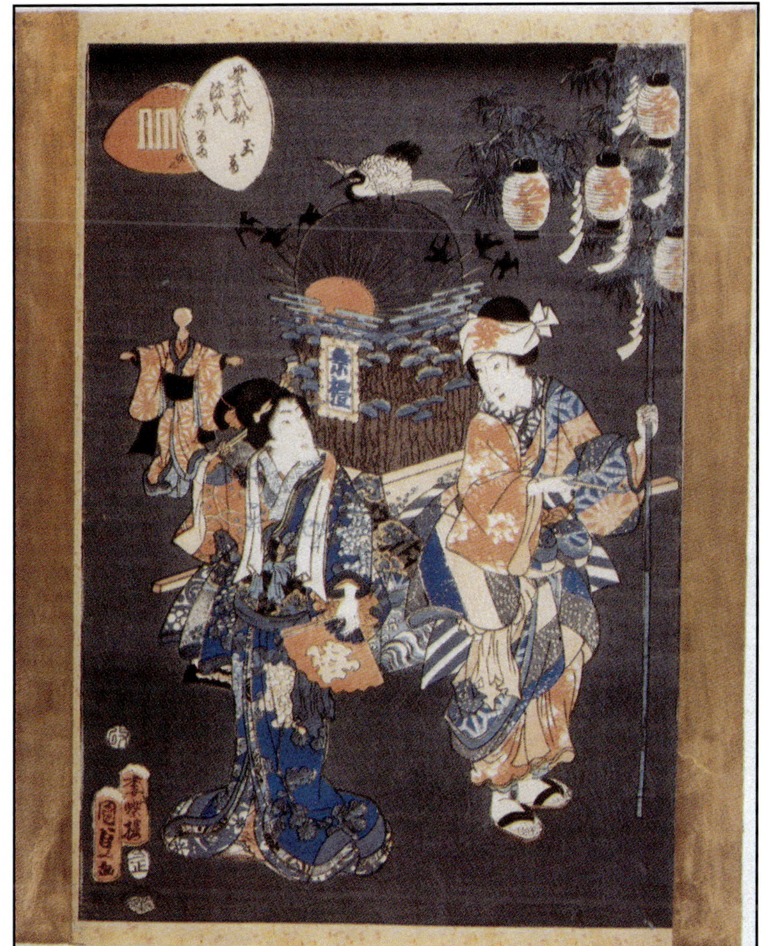

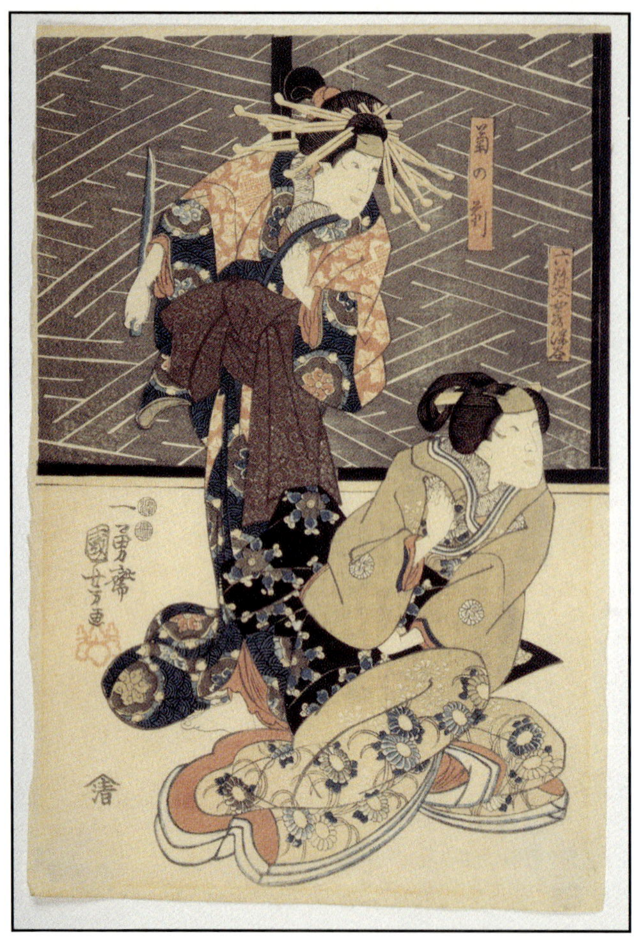

Kuniyoshi, oban tate-e, Actors, c. 1849-1853, fine impression, toned, faded, mat burn, soiled, $150-225.

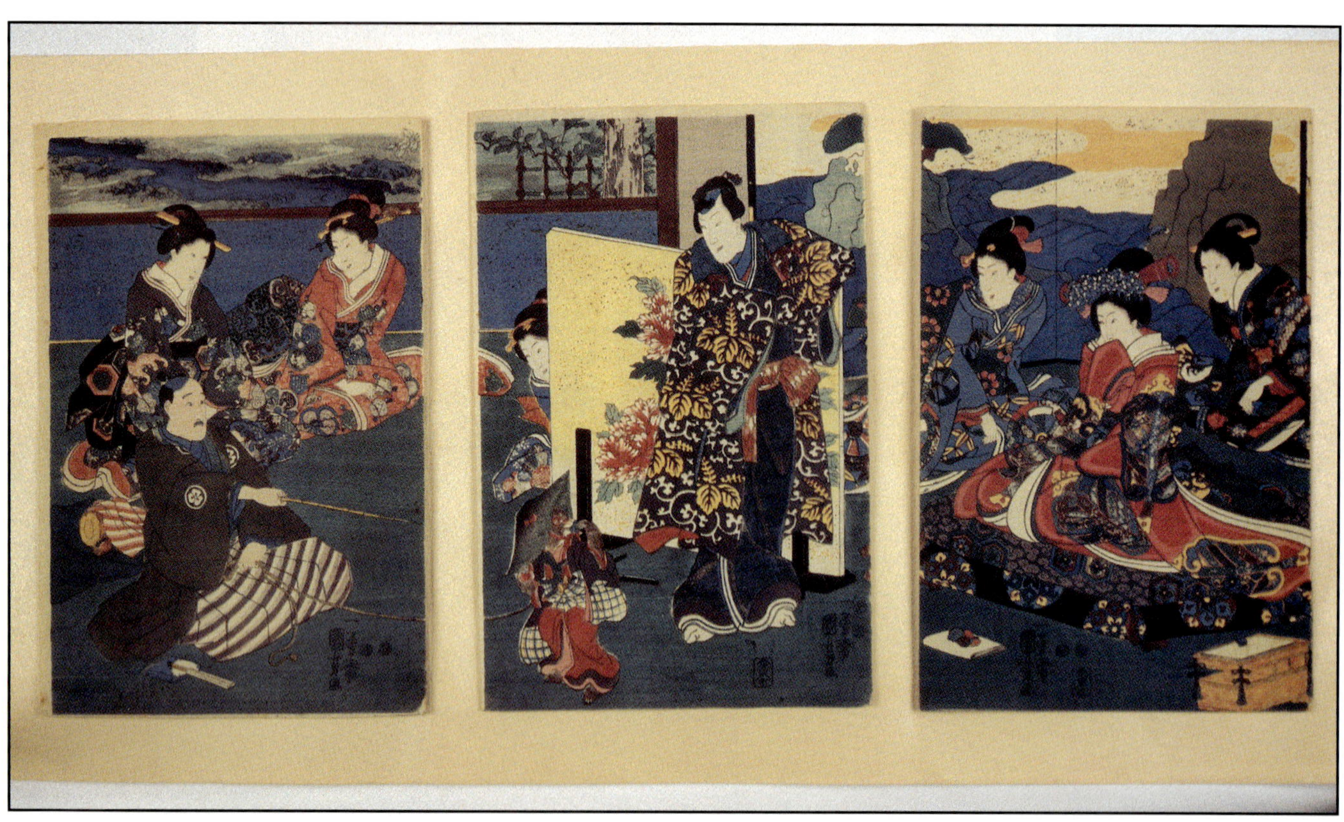

Kuniyoshi, oban tate-e triptych, "Spring Party," (entertainment with Monkey Trainer and his monkey), c.1851-1853, fine impression, color, and condition, $2500-3500.

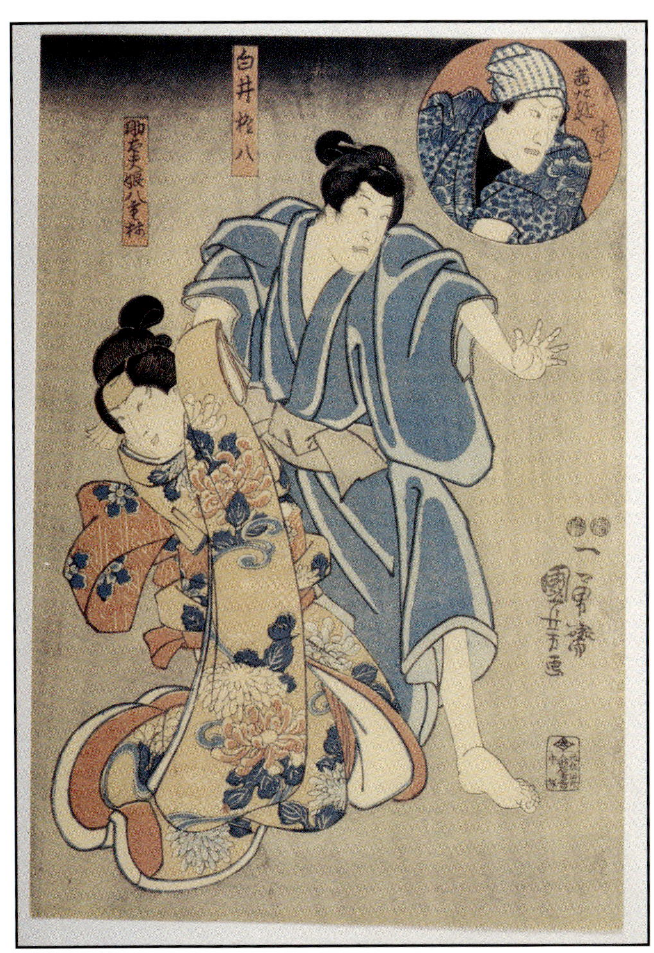

Kuniyoshi, oban tate-e, 13 1/2" x 9 1/4", kabuki scene, dated 1853 (year of the ox), very good impression, good color, binding holes, paper backing, $275-400.

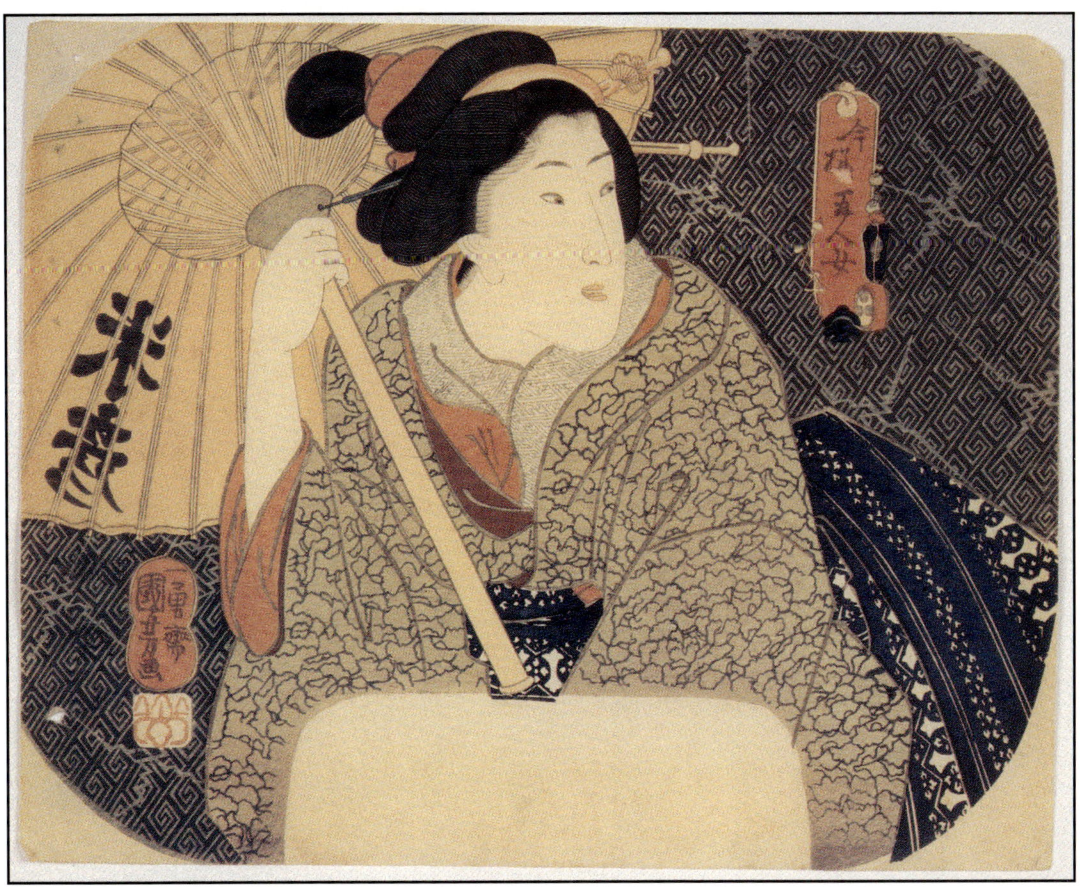

Kuniyoshi, aiban uchiwa-e, 11 1/2" x 9", bijin with umbrella, fine impression, color, and condition, binding holes on left, $5500-7500.

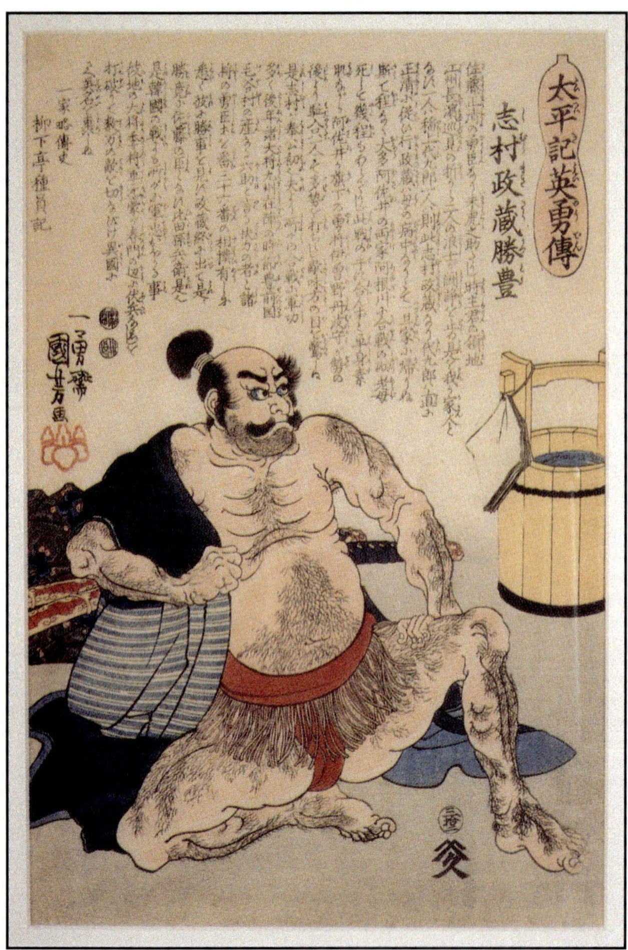

Kuniyoshi, oban tate-e, "Taibeiki Yeiyu Den," (Heroic Stories of the Taibeki, the Taikeiki is "Chronicle of Great Peace"), Shimura Masazo Katsutoyo seated and stripped to his loincloth, a kimono over one shoulder, his swords, a bucket of water and paper towels behind, Yamamoto-ya Heikichi publisher, censor Mura-Murata, c. 1848-49, fine impression, condition, and color, $1000-1800.

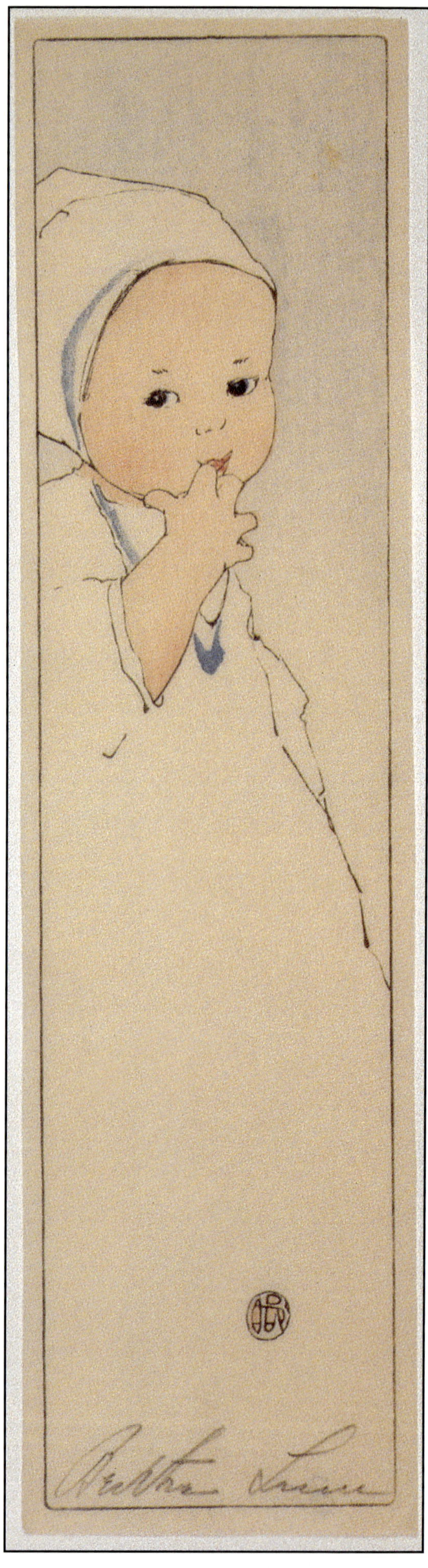

Lum Bertha, "Baby," signed in pencil and sealed, fine impression, condition, and color, $1500-1800.

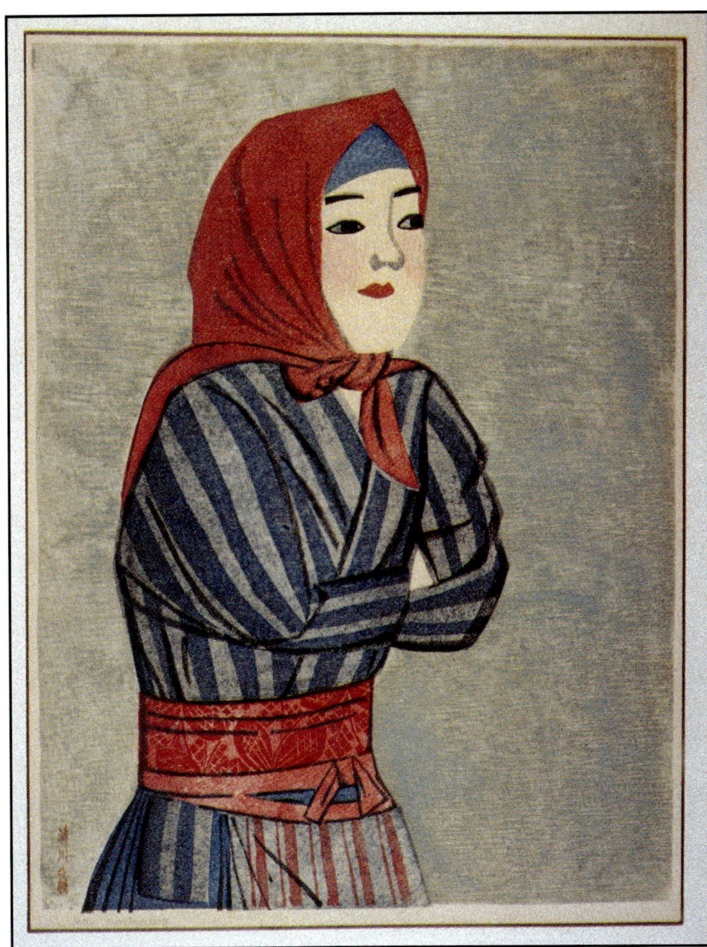

Maekawa Senpan, dai oban, woman with red kerchief, signed and sealed, c. 1950, very good impression, color, and condition, $3500-5500.

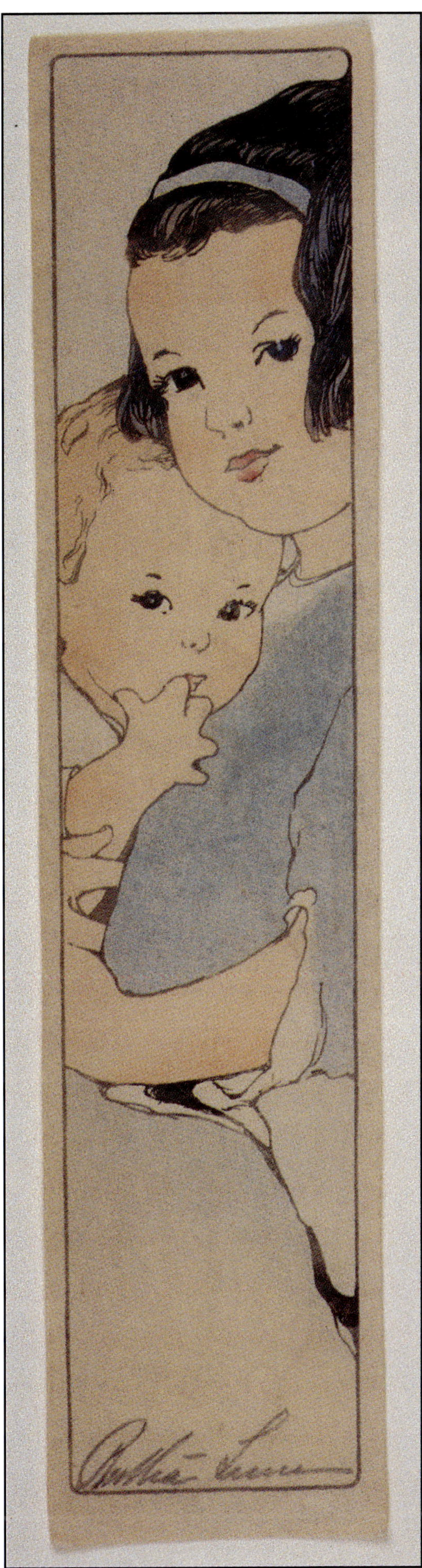

Lum, Bertha, "Little Sisters," 12" x 7", signed and sealed, 1912, fine impression, color, and condition, $1500-2500.

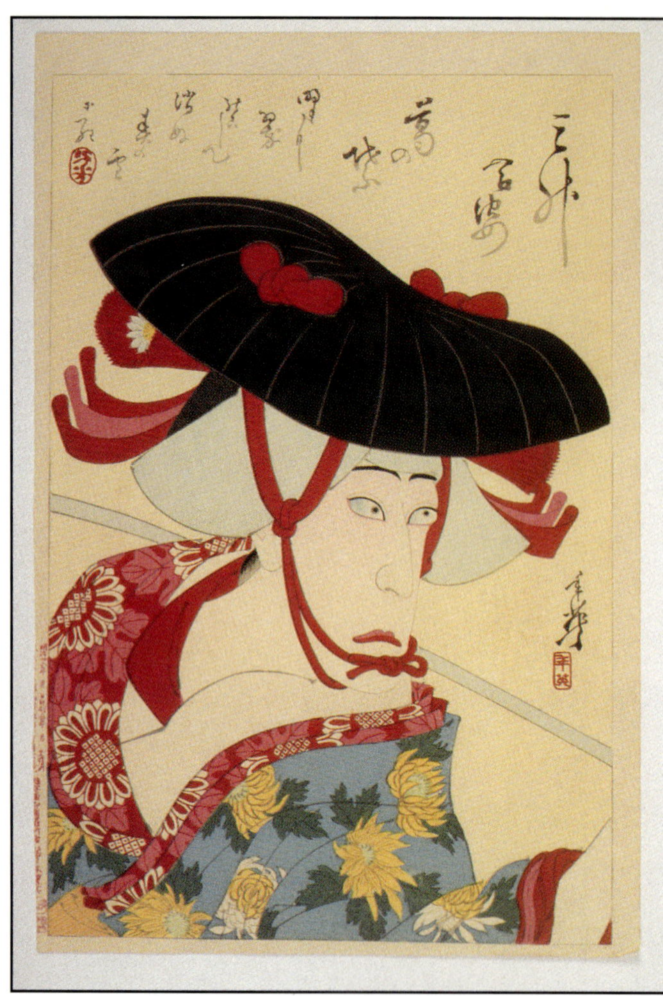

Migata Toshihide, oban tate-e; from the series Sanshogo Sugata, dated Meiji 26 (1894), signed and sealed "Toshihide (Migata)," fine impression, color, very good condition, $900-1200.

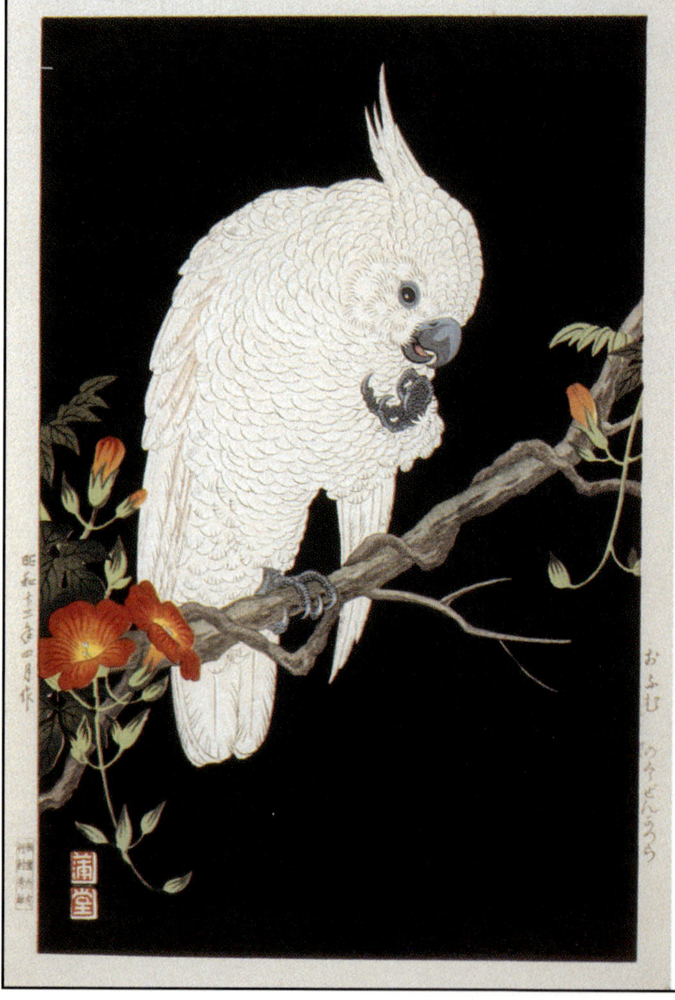

Nishimura, Hodo, oban tate-e, "Omu," (Parrot), published by Takemura Hideo, May 1938, excellent condition, color, and impression, $750-1000.

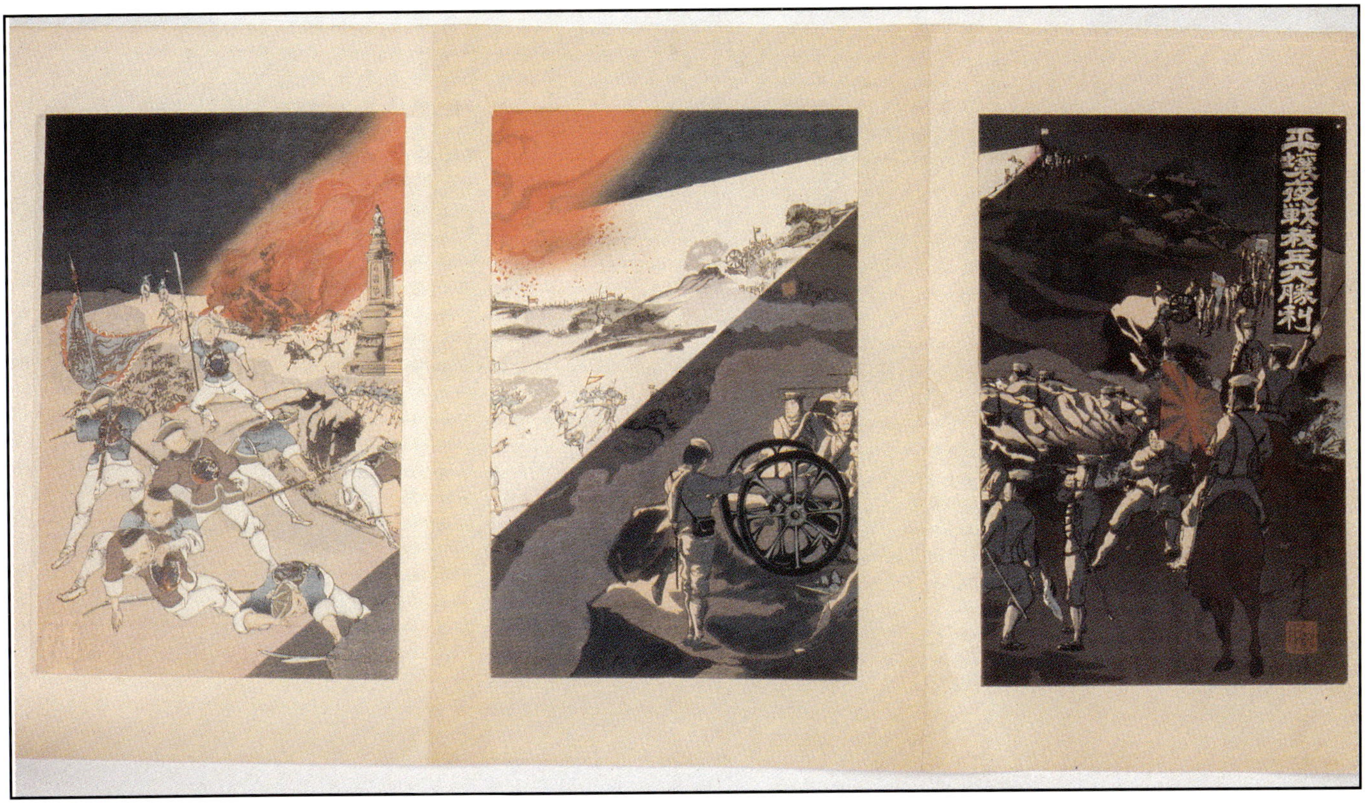

Nobukazu, oban tate-e triptych, "Sino-Japanese War," dated Meiji 30 (1897), mica, illuminated, fine impression, color, and condition, $1000-1500.

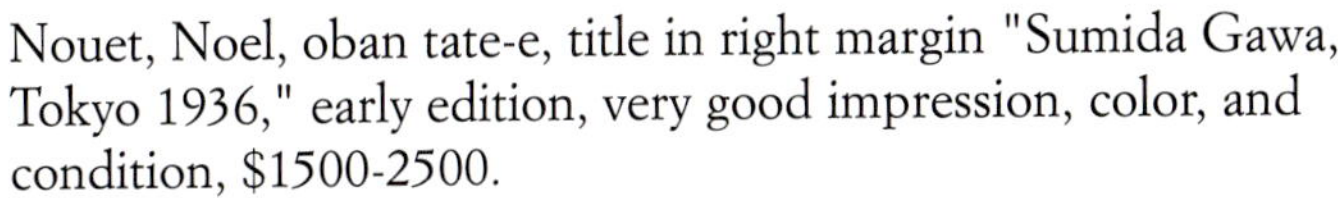
Nouet, Noel, oban tate-e, title in right margin "Sumida Gawa, Tokyo 1936," early edition, very good impression, color, and condition, $1500-2500.

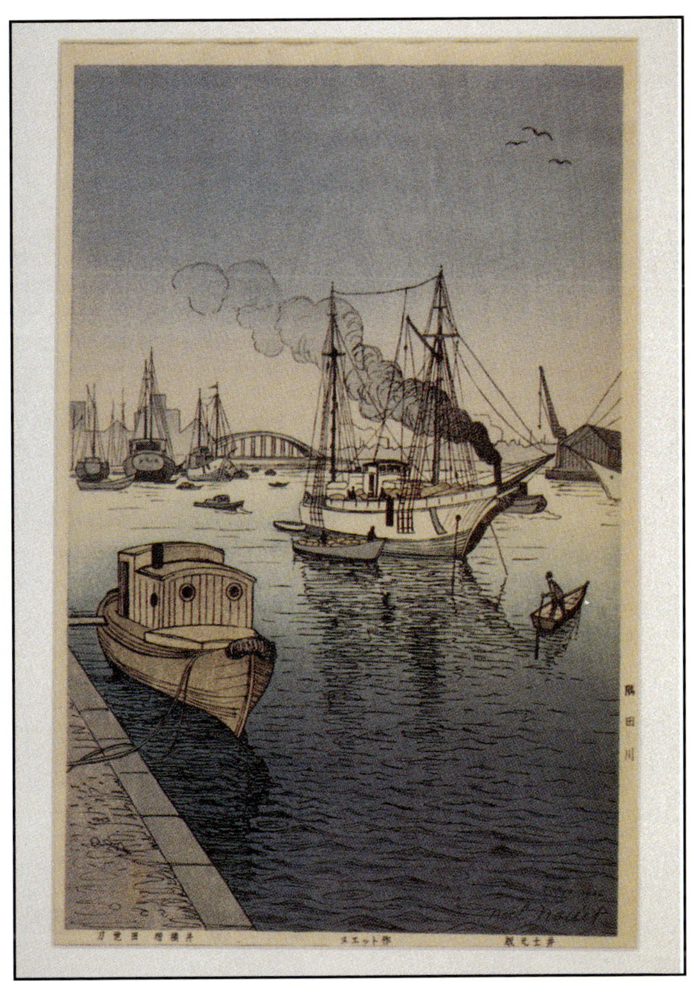

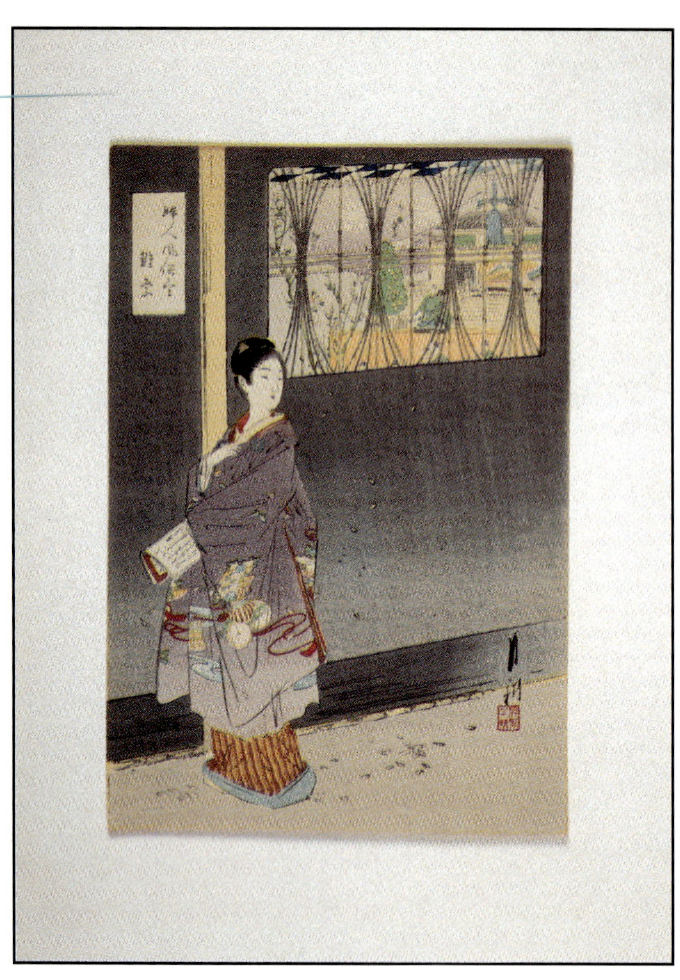

Ogata Gekko, chuban (crepe paper), bijin, dated Meiji 21 (1888), fine condition, color, and impression, $275-375.

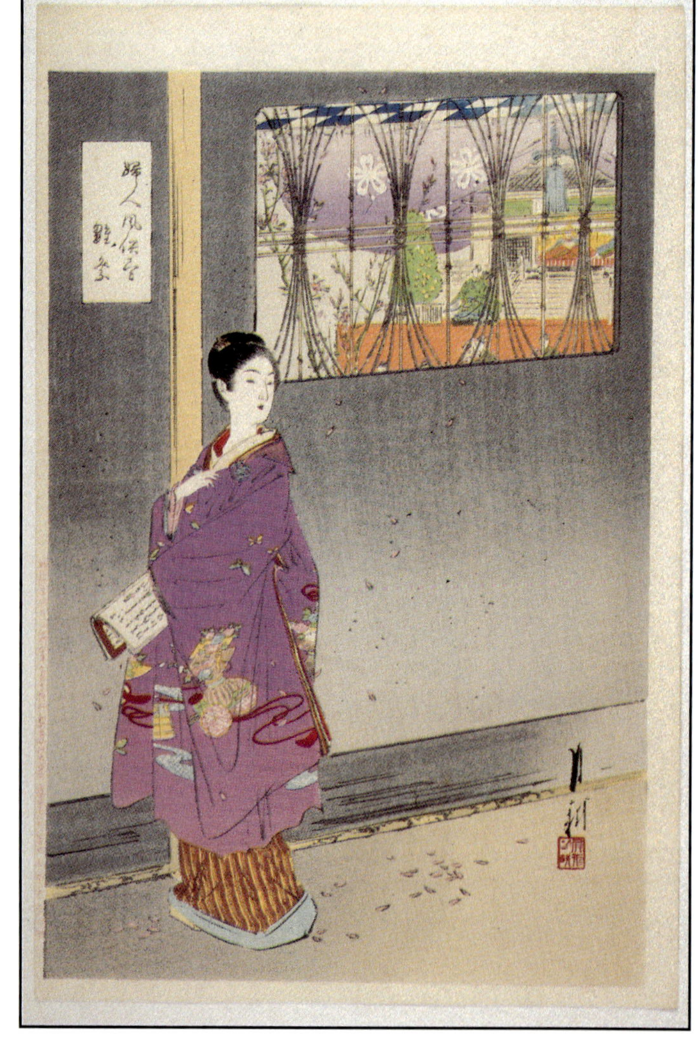

Ogata Gekko, oban tate-e, bijin, dated Meiji 21 (1888), fine condition, color, and impression, $375-475.

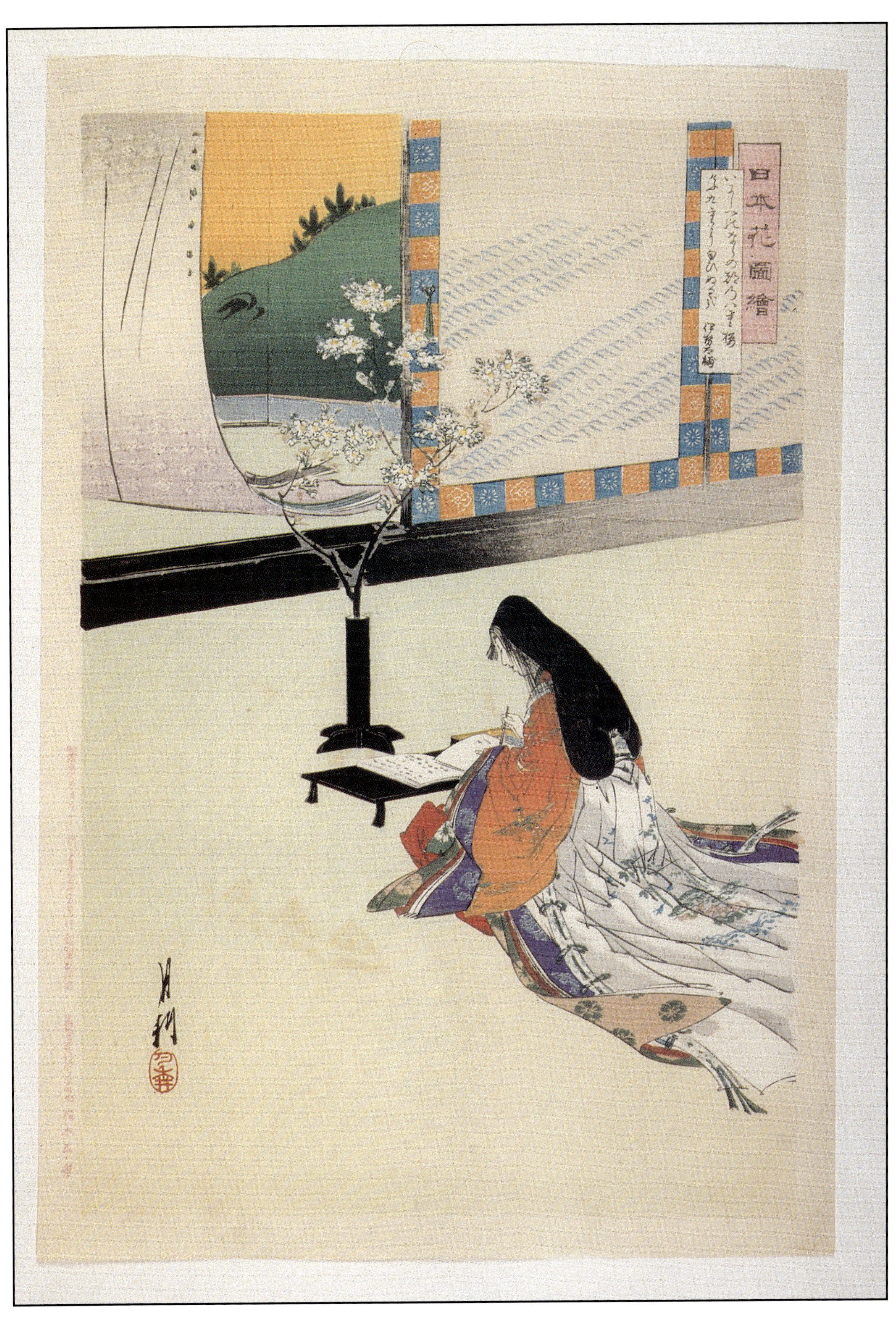

Ogata Gekko, oban tate-e, Calligraphy, dated Meiji 22 (1889), signed and sealed "Gekko," mica, fine impression, condition, and color, $225-300.

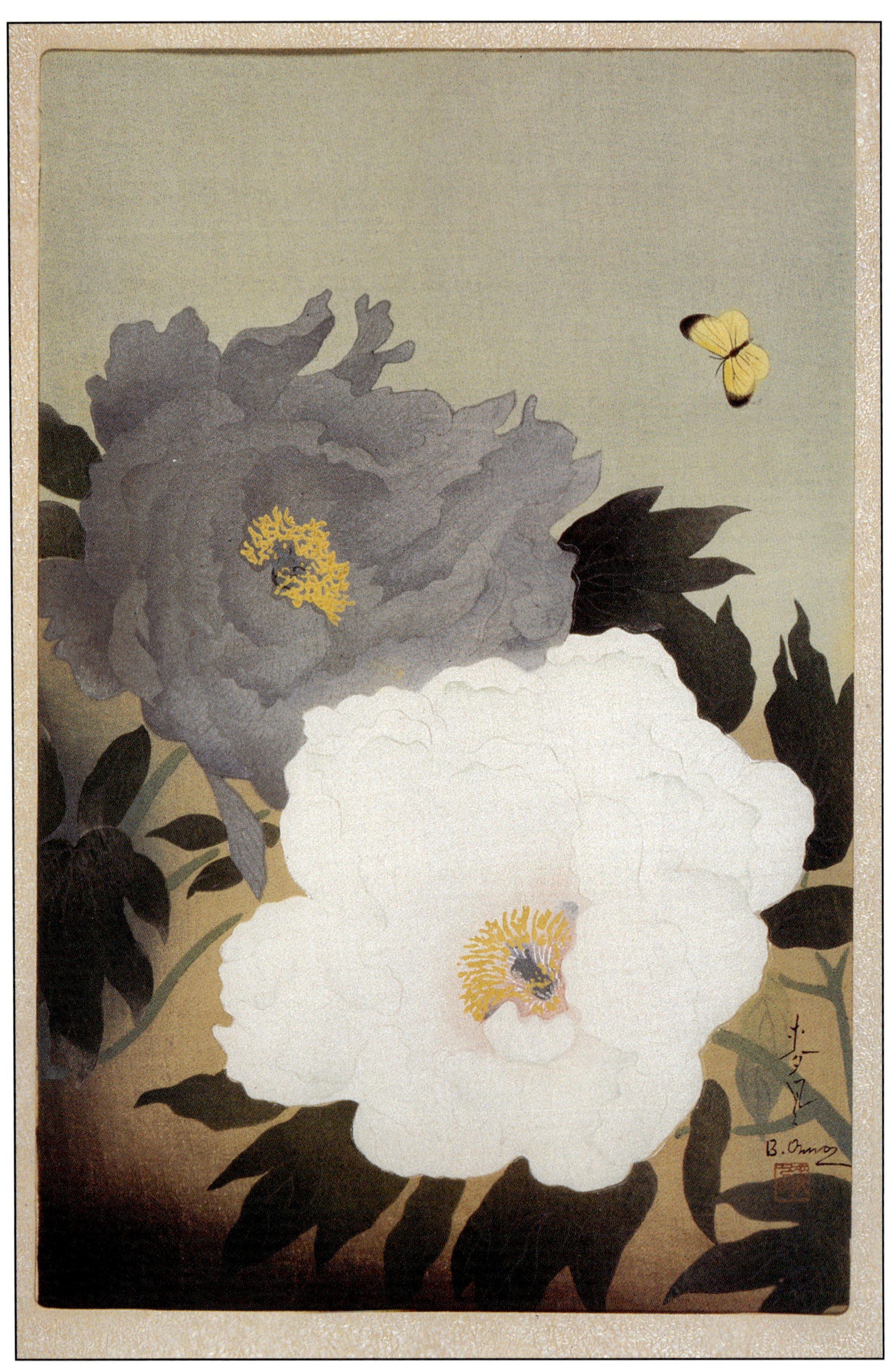

Ohno Bakufu, oban tate-e, "Camilla," printed by Kyoto Hanga-In, 1950, fine color, impression, and condition, $375-550.

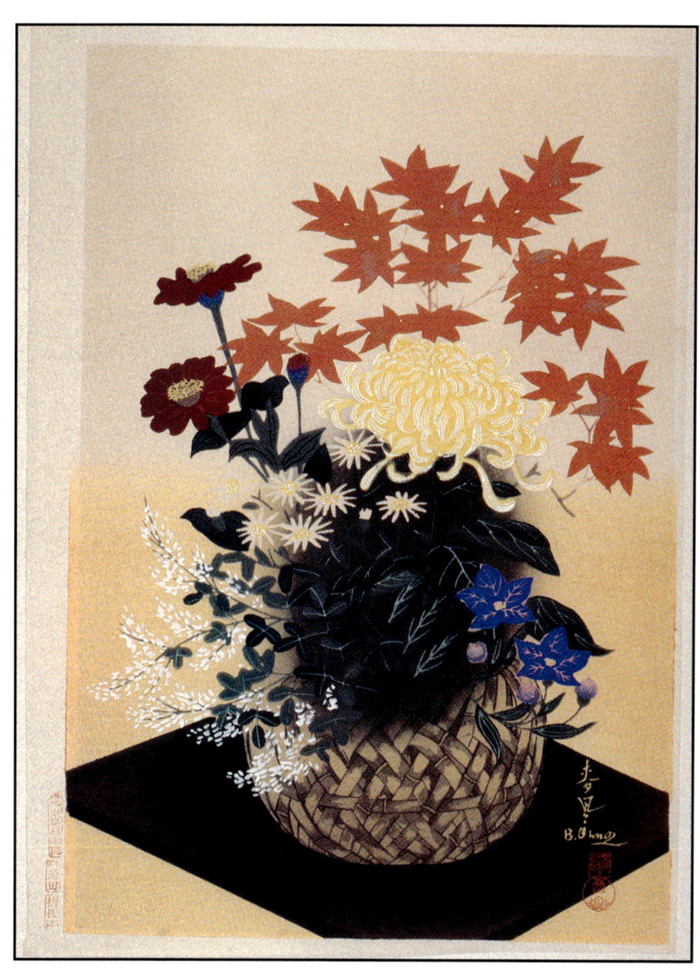

Ohno Bakufu, oban tate-e, flowers in basket with hand-painted embellishments, published by Kyoto Hanga-In, c. 1952, fine condition, impression, and color, $375-500.

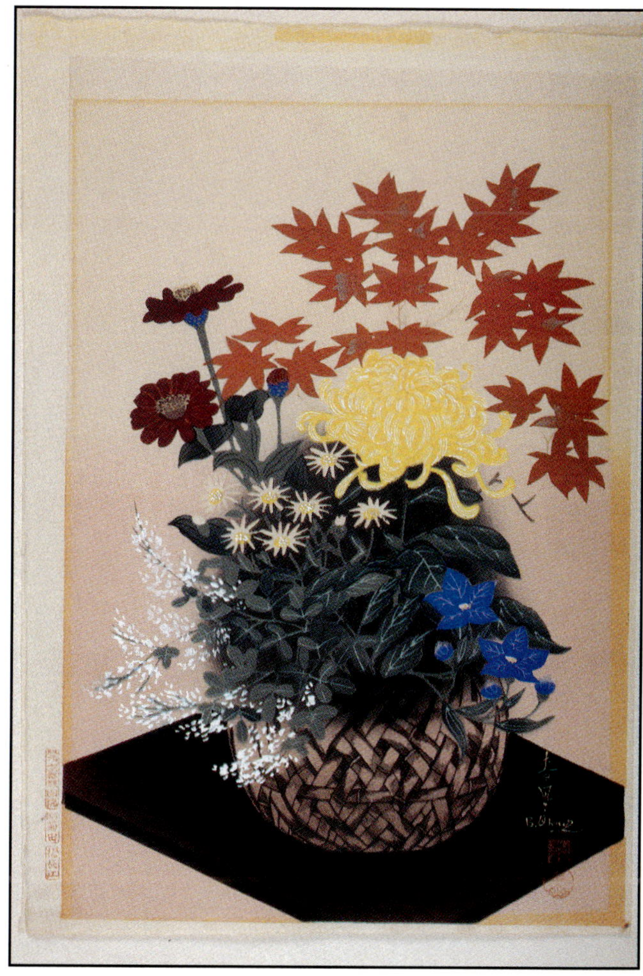

Ohno Bakufu, oban tate-e, flowers in basket with handpainted embellishments, published by Kyoto Hanga-In, c. 1952, very good impression, good color, mat burn on margins, toned, $75-125

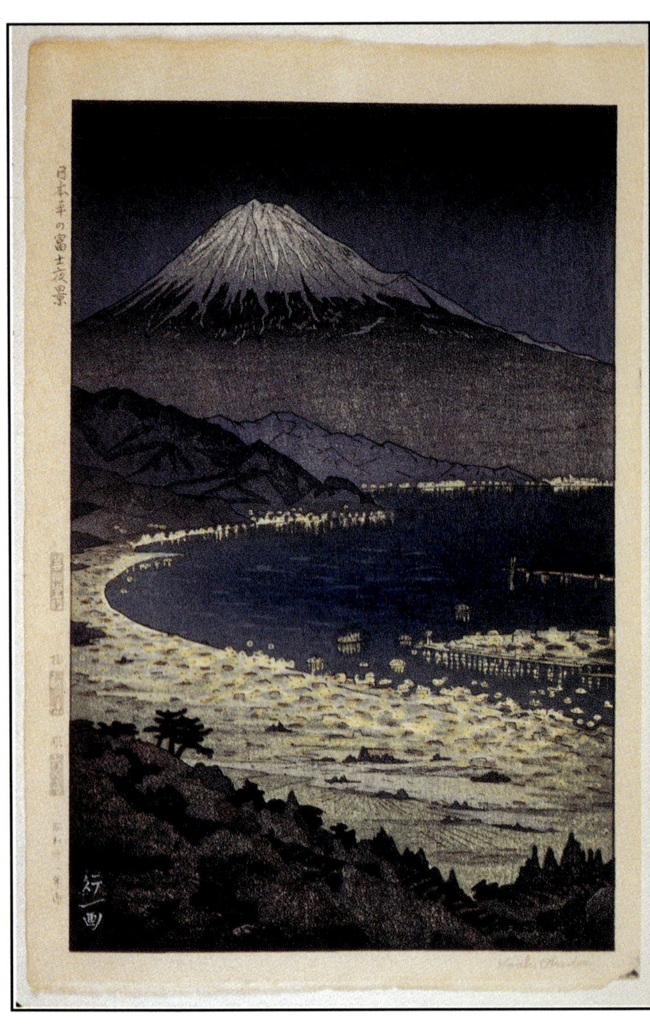

Okada Koichi, oban tate-e, 16" x 10 3/4", "Night View of Mt. Fuji," from the series 12 Views of Japan, published by Unsodo, dated Showa 21 (1956), signed in pencil "Koichi Okada" in lower right margin, signed and sealed in lower left within image, fine impression, color, and condition, paper slightly toned, $1800-2500.

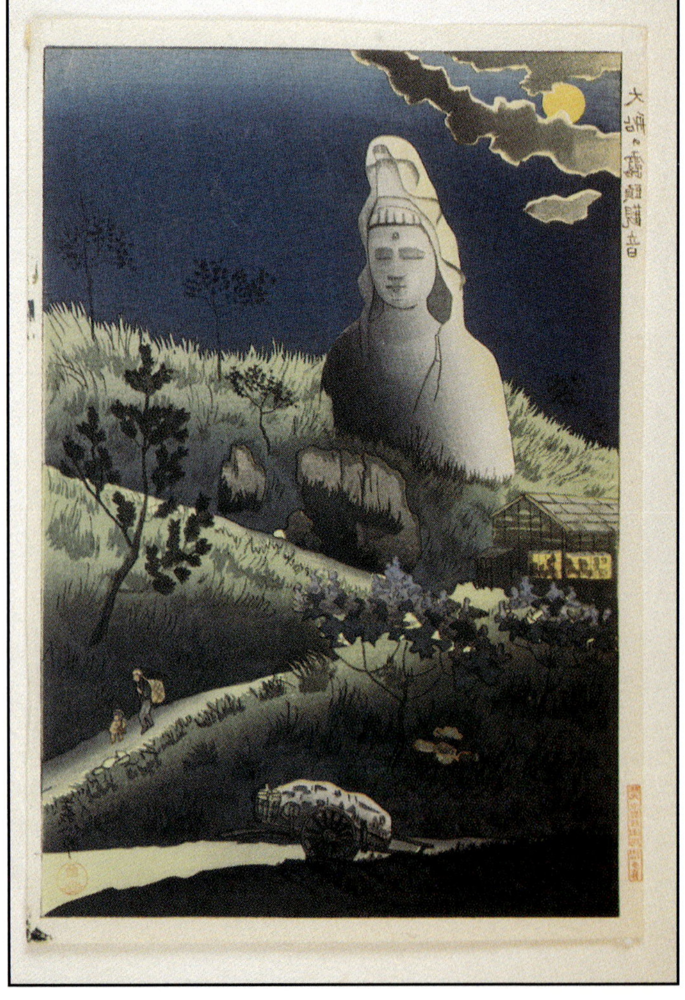

Okuyama Gihachiro, oban tate-e, 16 1/4" x 11 1/4", c. 1950, signed and sealed lower right within the image, published by Kyoto Hanga In, fine impression, color, and condition, $700-950.

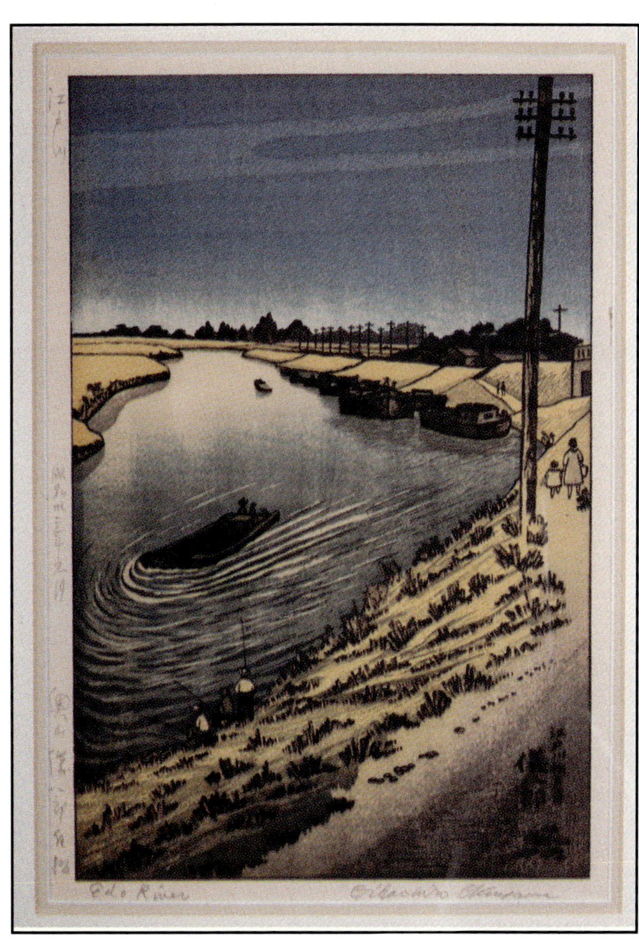

Okuyama Gihachiro, oban tate-e, 10 1/2" x 15 1/2", "Edo River," dated Showa 22 (1947), signed and sealed lower right within image, dated and titled in pencil, signed in pencil, fine impression, color, and condition, $900-1200.

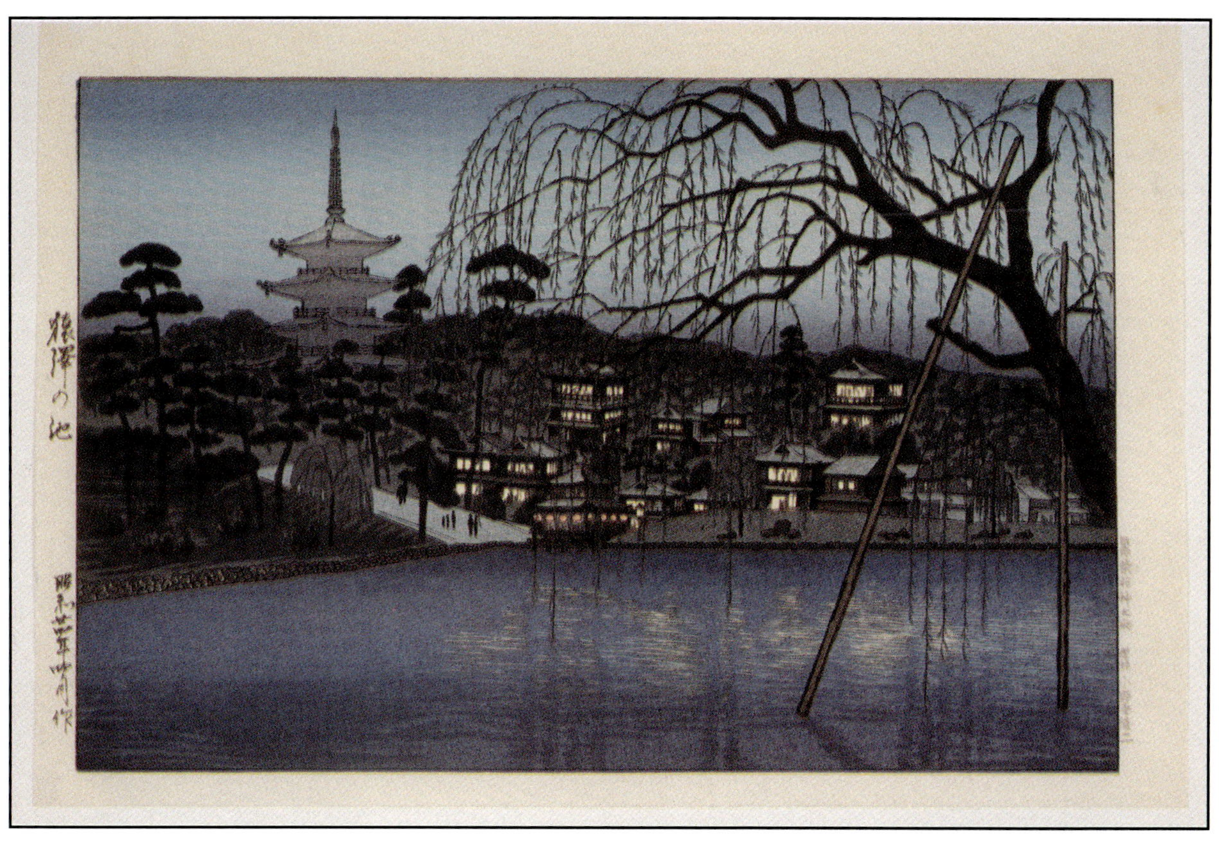

Okuyama Gihachiro, oban yoko-e, "Willow and Pond at Night," dated Showa 24 (1949), jizuri seal and signature in right hand margin (self published), fine condition, color, and impression, $550-850.

Ota Gako (Masamitsu Ota), oban tate-e, actor as Wisteria Maiden, dated Showa 18 (1943), published by Watanabe, fine condition, color, and impression, $1500-2500.

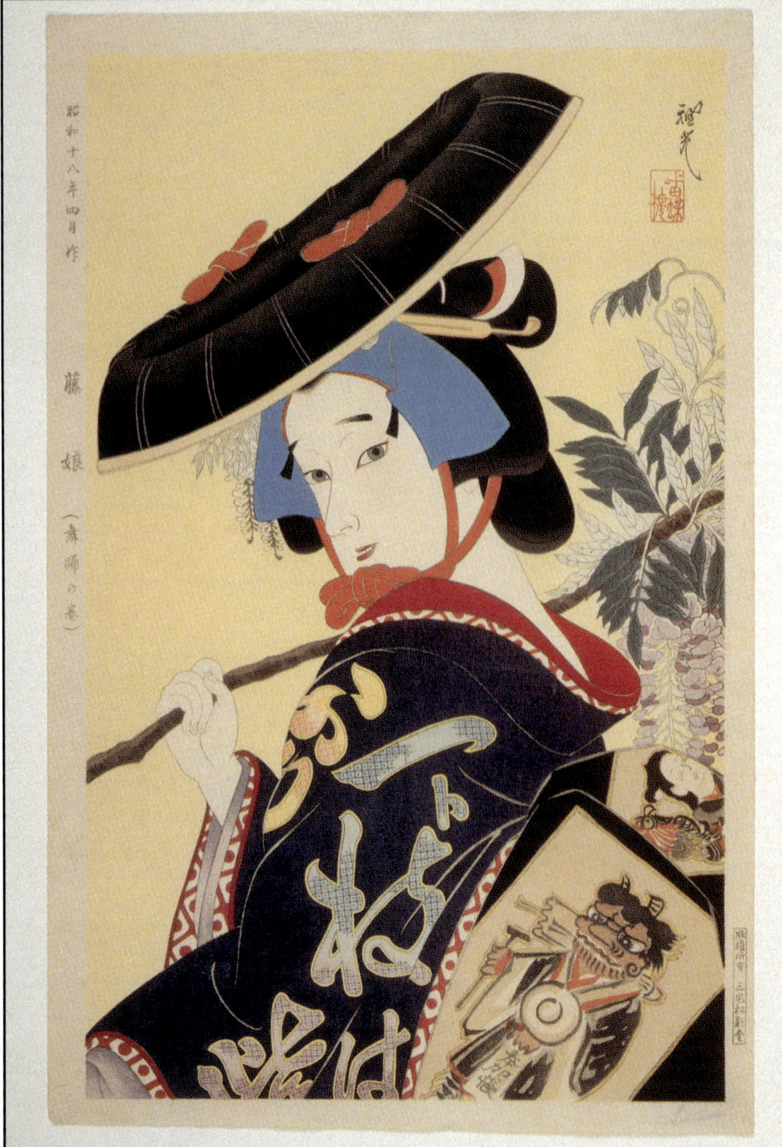

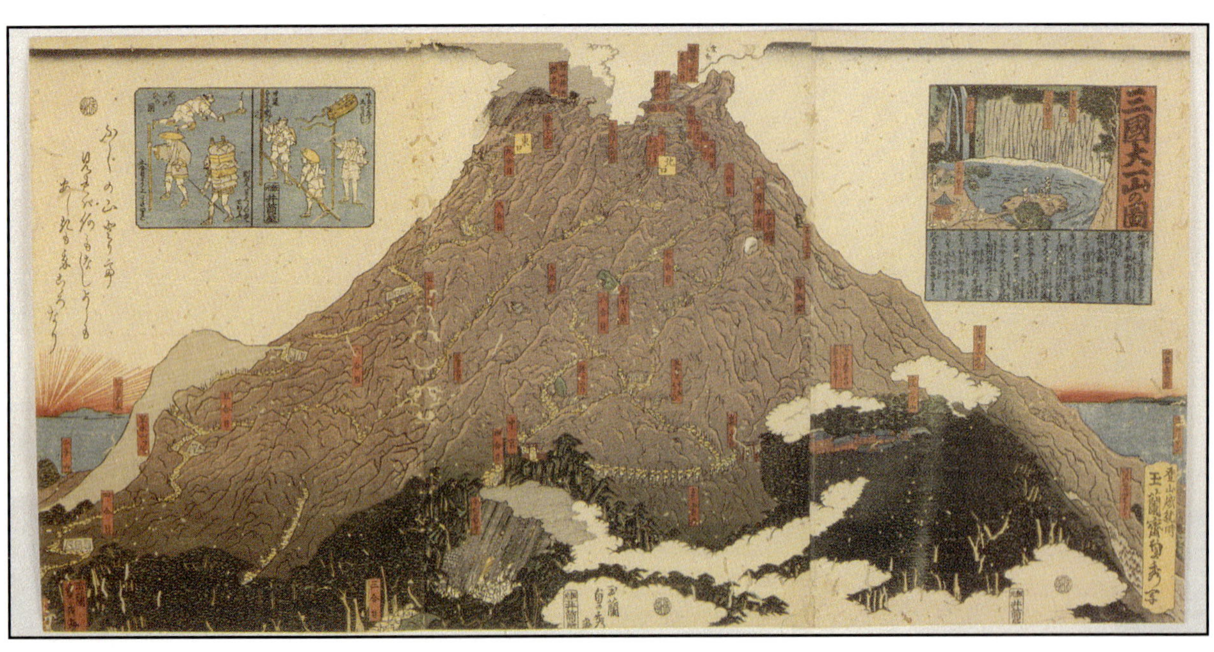

Sadahide, oban tate-e triptych map, backed to cover worm holes, slightly trimmed, very good color and impression, $900-1500.

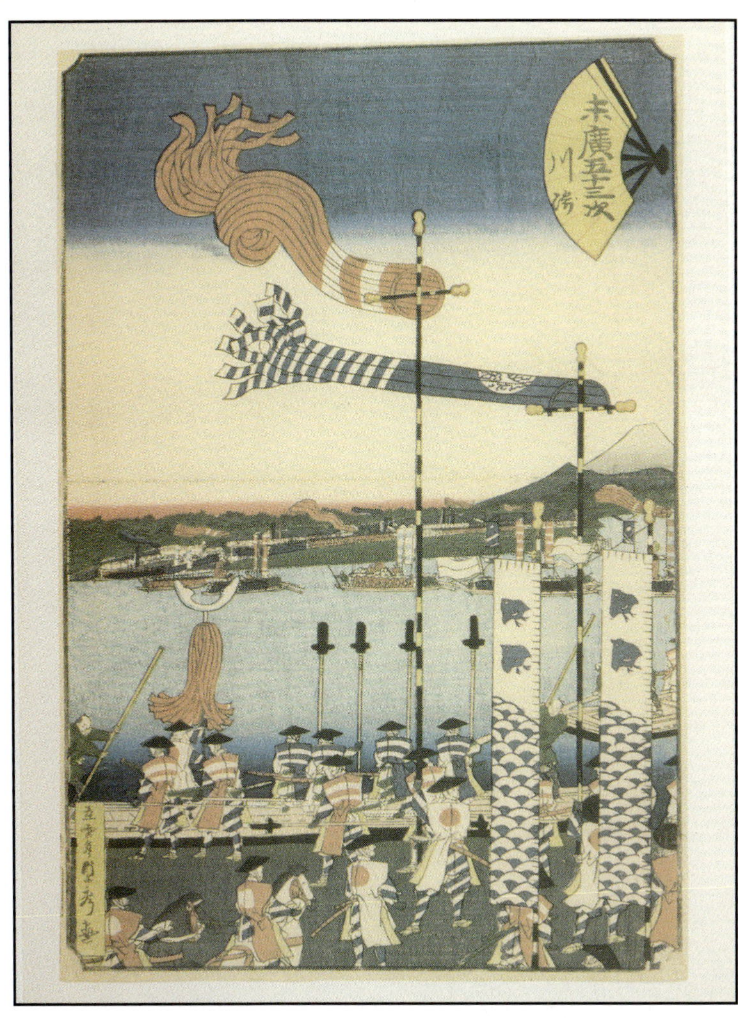

Sadahide, oban tate-e, fine impression and color, trimmed to edge of image, $175-225.

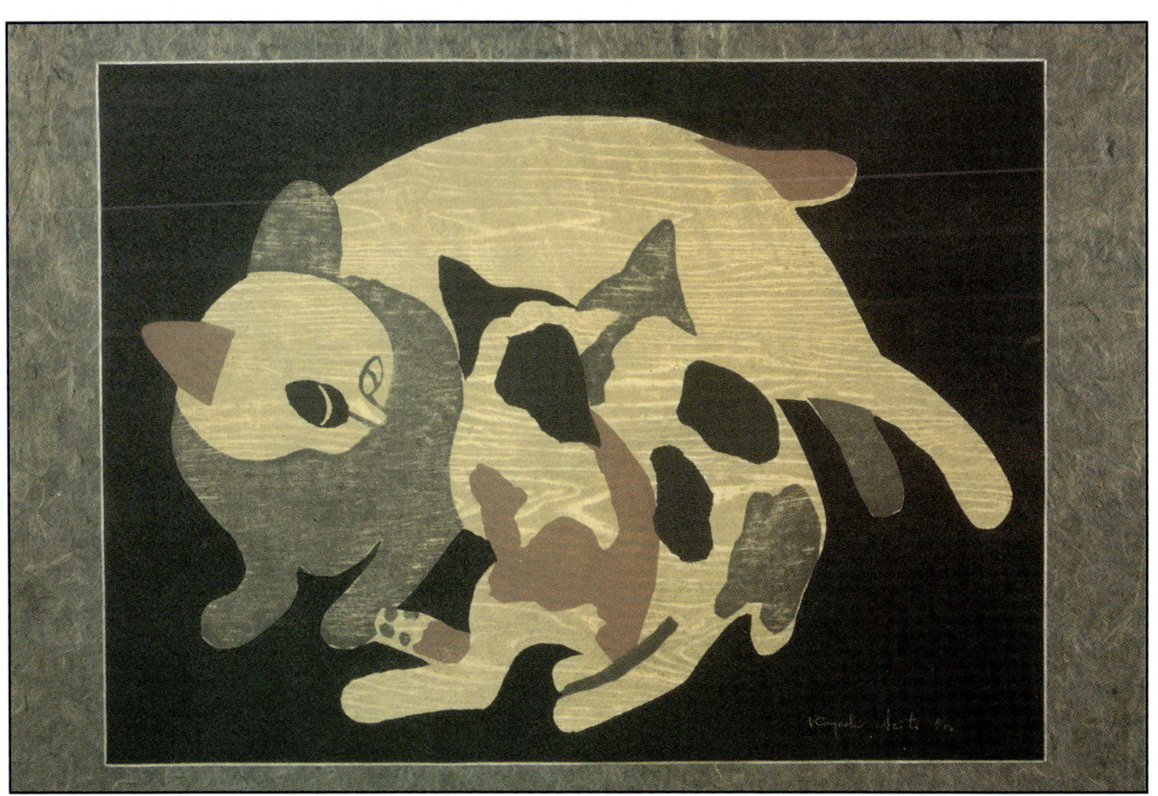

Saito Kiyoshi, dai oban, left side of a two panel screen, screen size 38" x 57 1/2", Untitled (Caress (A)), signed and sealed, numbered 5/50, c. 1954, screen, $5000-7000.

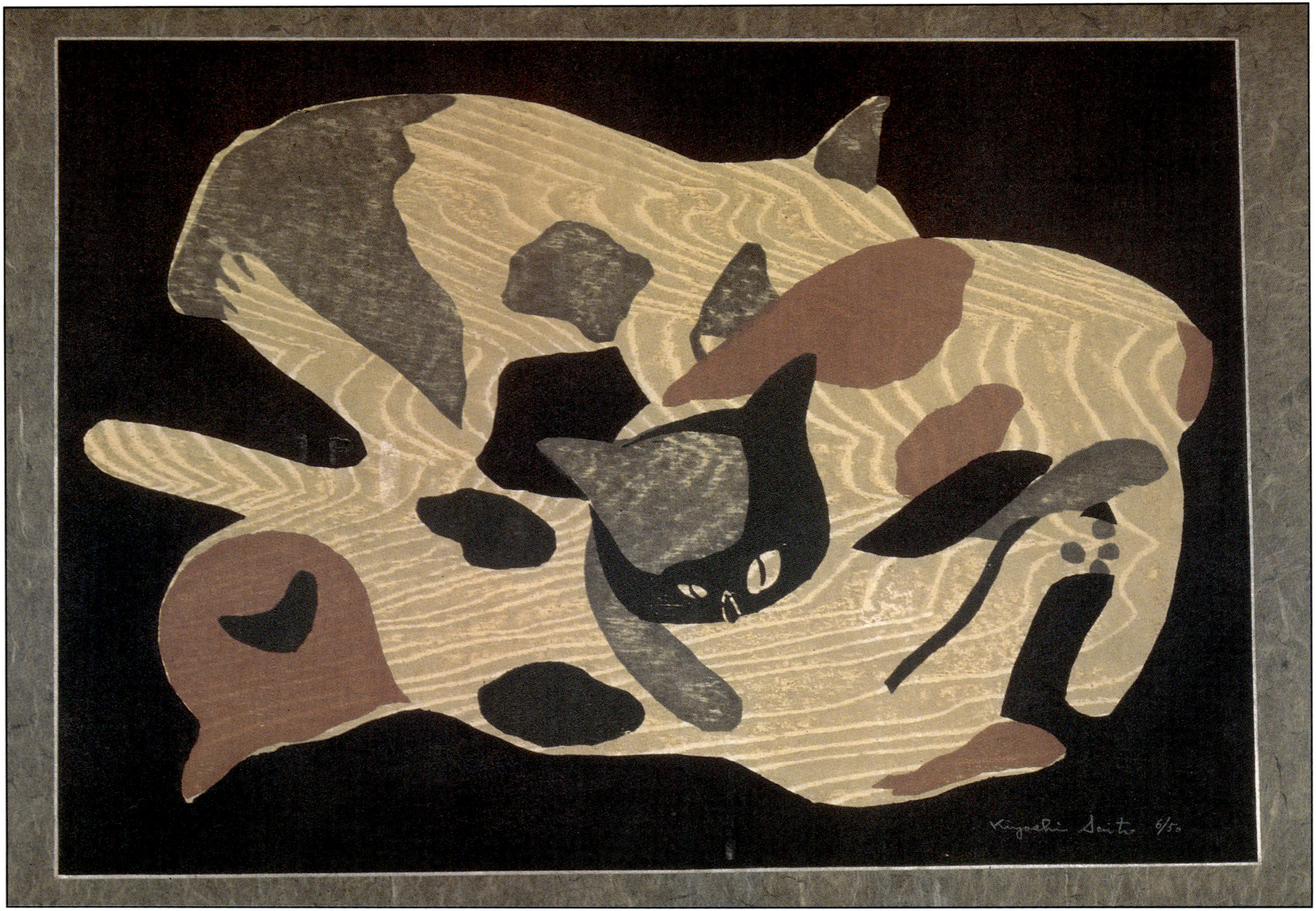

Saito Kiyoshi, dai oban, right side of a two panel screen, screen size 38" x 57 1/2", Untitled (Caress), signed and sealed, numbered 6/50, c. 1954, screen, $5000-7000.

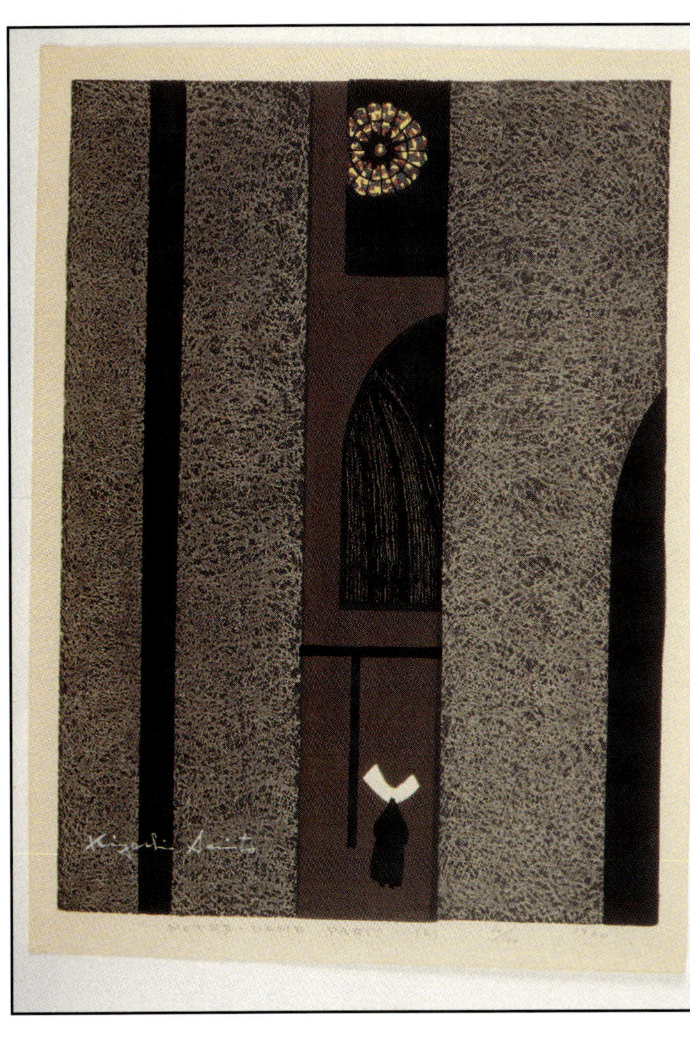

Saito Kiyoshi, dai oban 22" x 16 1/4", "Notre-Dame Paris (A)," 1960 from an edition of 120, signed and sealed, $5500-7500.

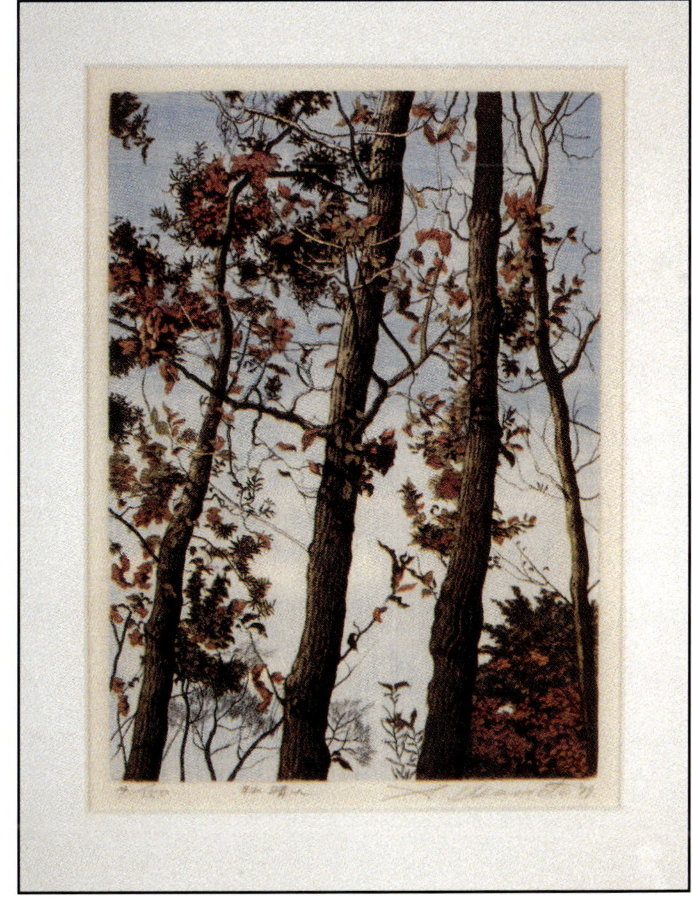

Sakamoto, etching, 10" x 8", edition of 150, dated 1979, fine condition, color, $250-375.

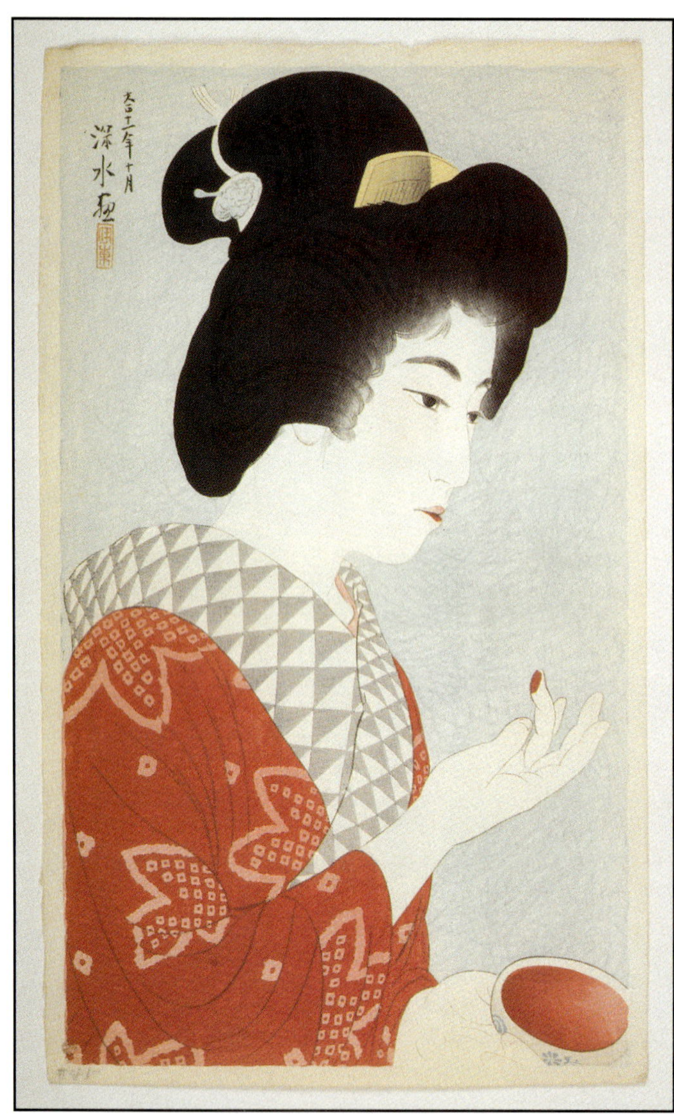

Shinsui Ito, dai oban tate-e, woman applying lipstick, signed "Shinsui ga," dated Taisho 11 (1922), published by Watanabe, fine impression, color, and condition, $9000-15,000.

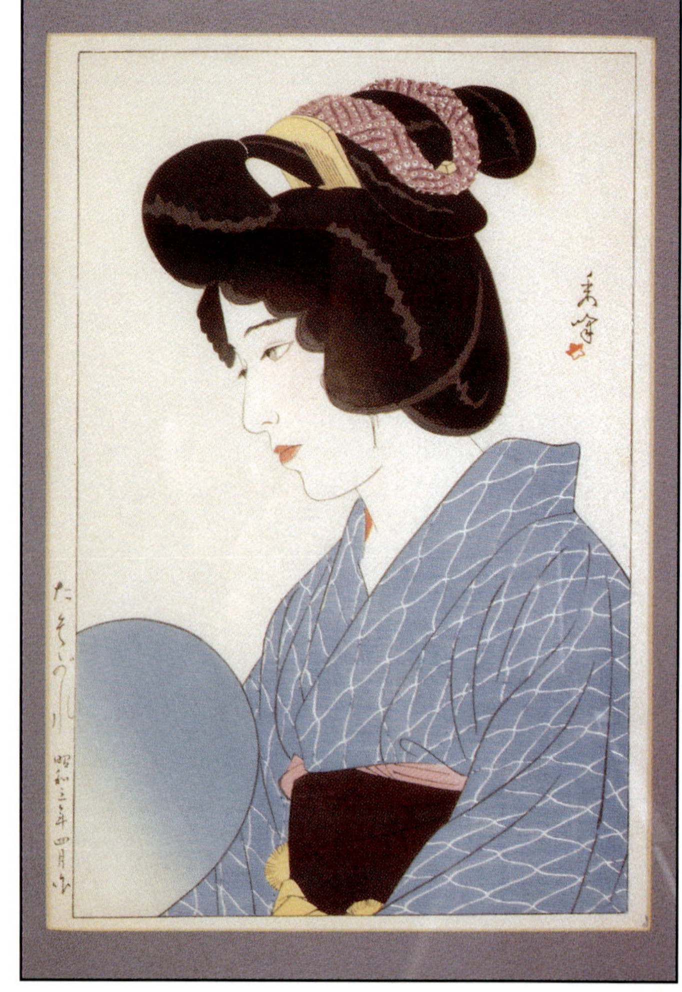

Shuho Yamakawa, oban tate-e, "Beauty With Fan," signed "Shuho" above leaf pattern seal, dated Showa 3 (1928), publisher Bijutsusha, fine impression, color, and condition, $1200-1800.

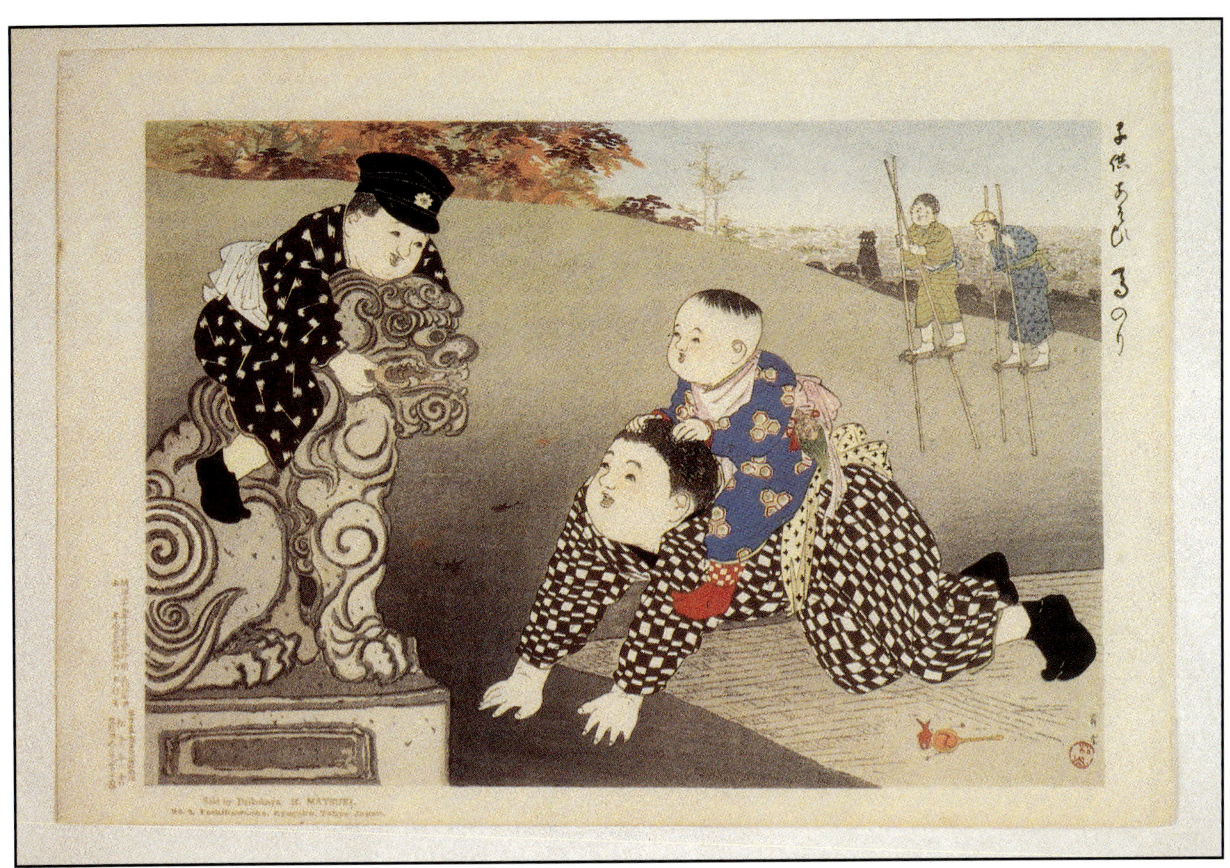

Shoun, oban yoko-e, "Boy's At Play," dated Meiji 39 (1906), sold by Daikokuya, H. Matsuki (on lower margin), fine impression, color, and condition, $1200-1800.

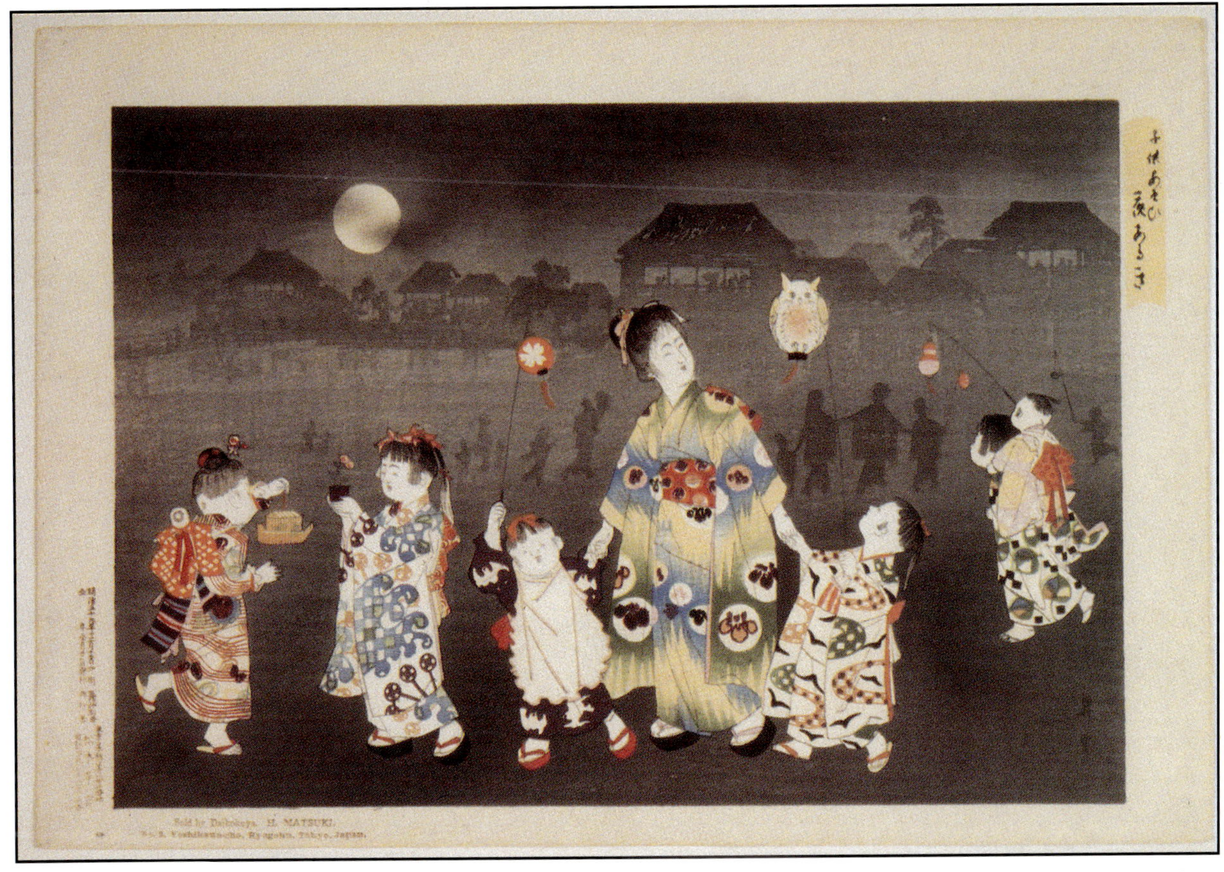

Shoun, oban yoko-e, "Girls with Illuminated Lanterns," dated Meiji 39 (1906), sold by Daikokuya, H. Matsuki (on lower margin), mica, fine impression, color, and condition, $1200-1800.

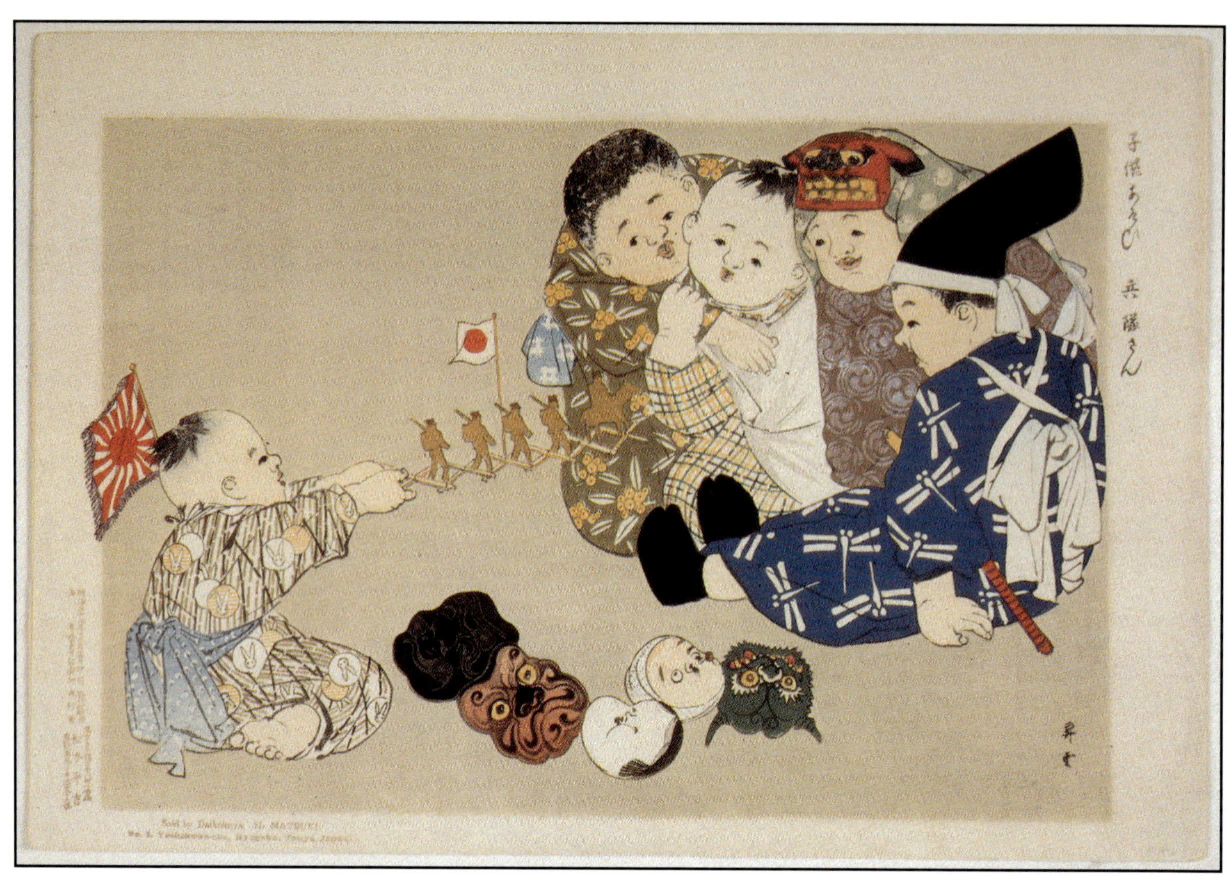

Shoun, oban yoko-e, "Boys Playing with Paper Dolls in the Form of Japanese Soldiers," dated Meiji 39 (1906), sold by Daikokuya, H. Matsuki (on lower margin), fine impression, color, and condition, $1200-1800.

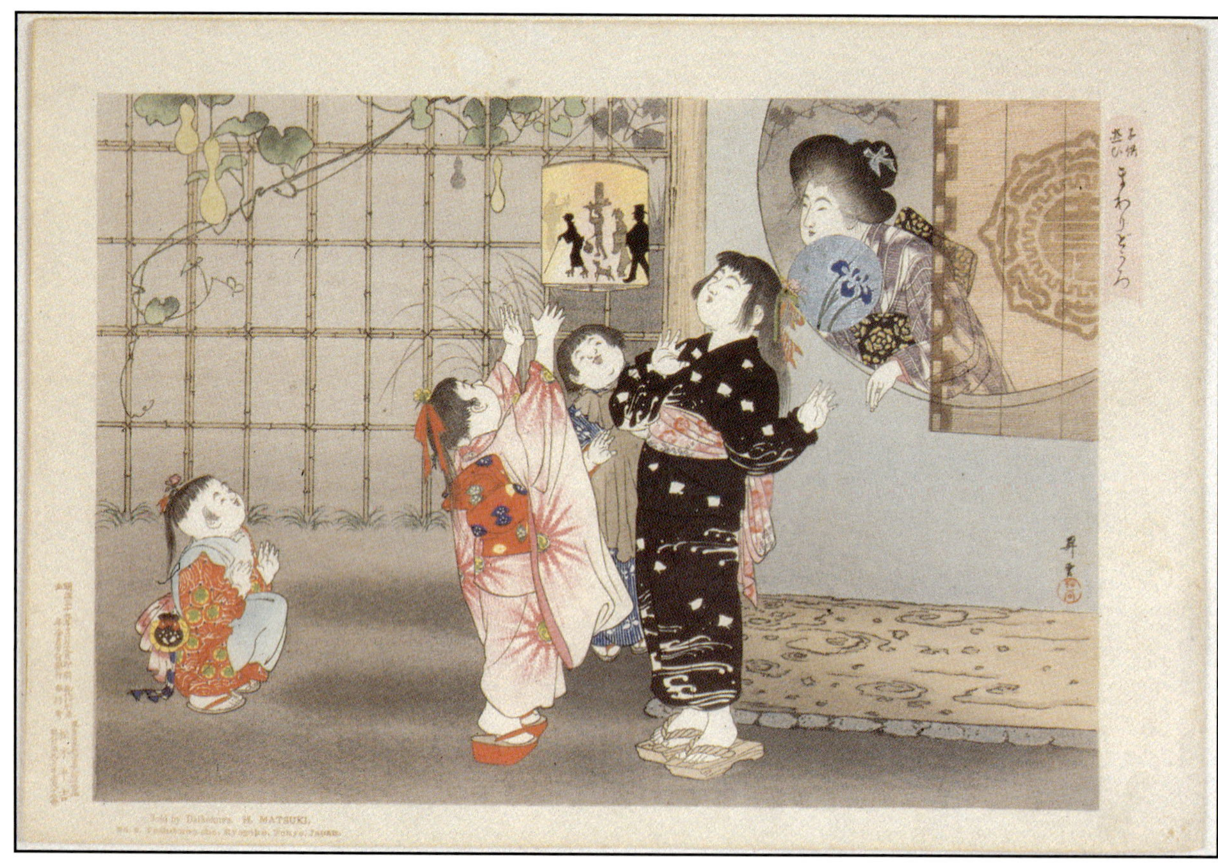

Shoun, oban yoko-e, "Girls Looking at Illuminated Lantern with Designs of Figures Including a Westerner Wearing a Top Hat," dated Meiji 39 (1906), sold by Daikokuya, H. Matsuki (on lower margin), mica, fine impression, color, and condition, $1200-1800.

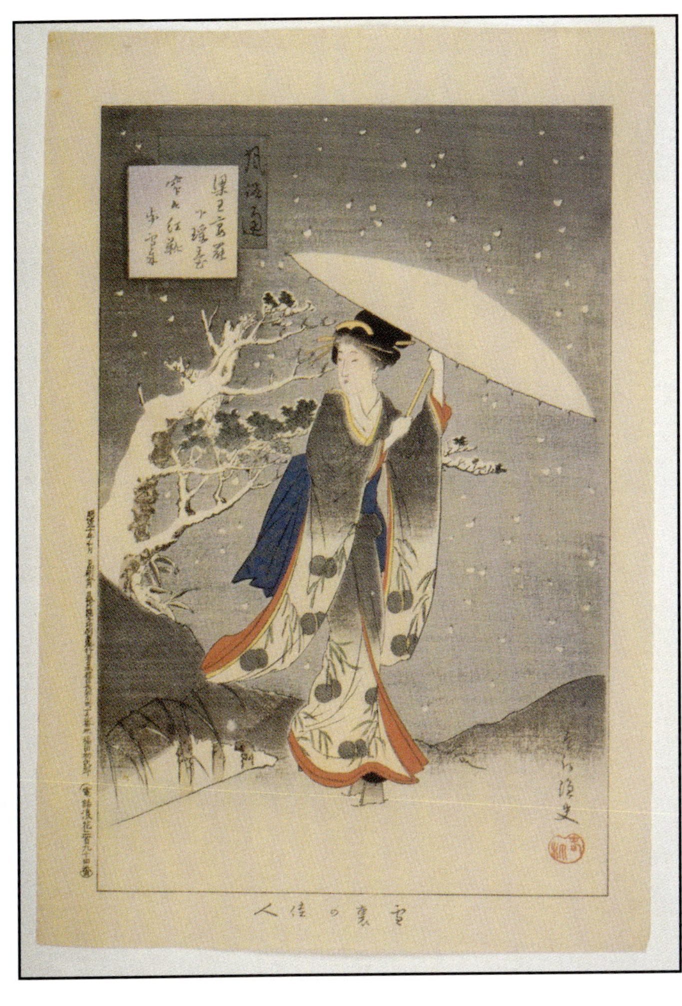

Shuntei, oban tate-e, "Bijin With Umbrella on a Snowy Night," dated Meiji 30 (1897), very good impression, color, and condition (not from an album), $375-500.

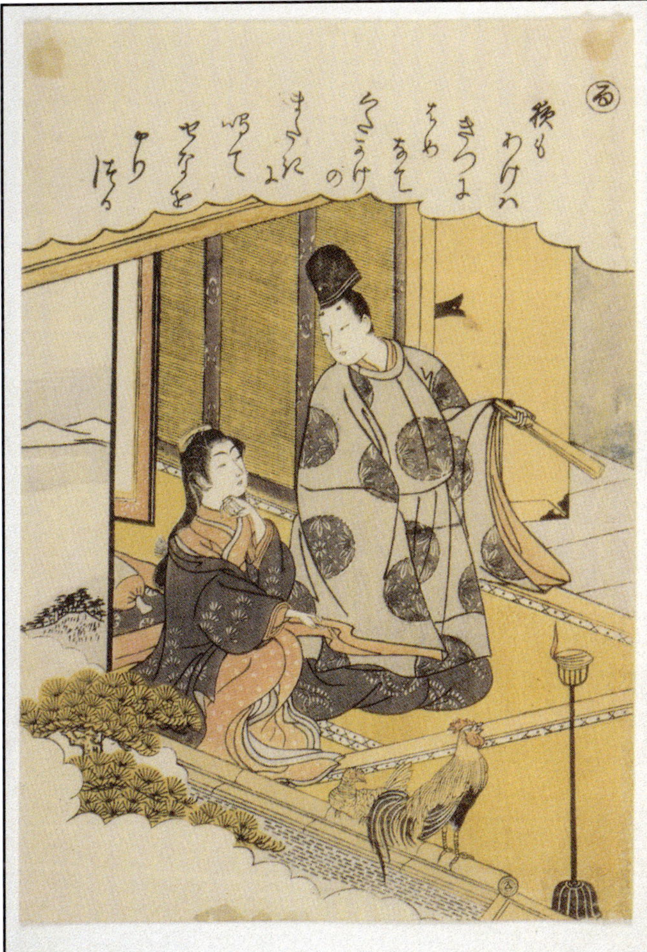

Shunsho, Katsukawa, chuban, "Isei Monogatari," a series of prints with letters of the old Japanese alphabet instead of number. This print has the 11th letter Ru, c. 1770, very good impression, color, and condition , a bit of residue from old mat on the upper corners of reverse, $1000-1500.

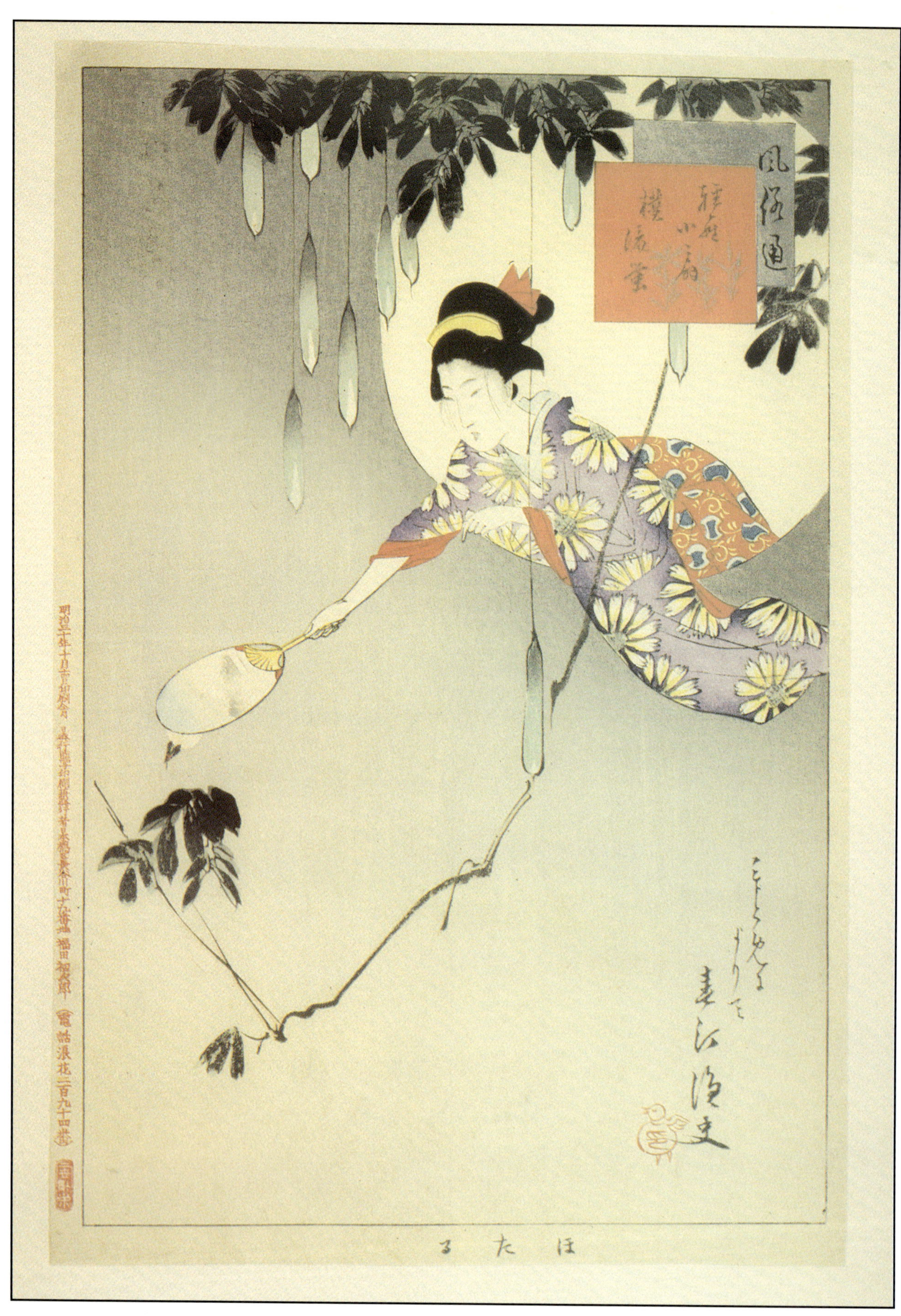

Shuntei, oban tate-e, dated Meiji 30 (1897), mica, fine impression, color, and condition, $375-500.

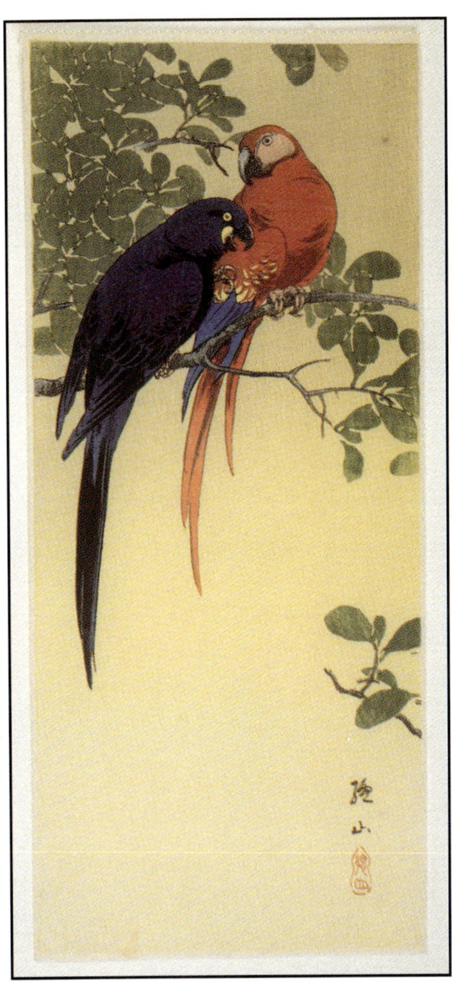

Sozan Ito, tanzaku, "Parrots," artist signed and sealed, published by Watanabe, c. 1927, fine impression, color, and condition, $775-975.

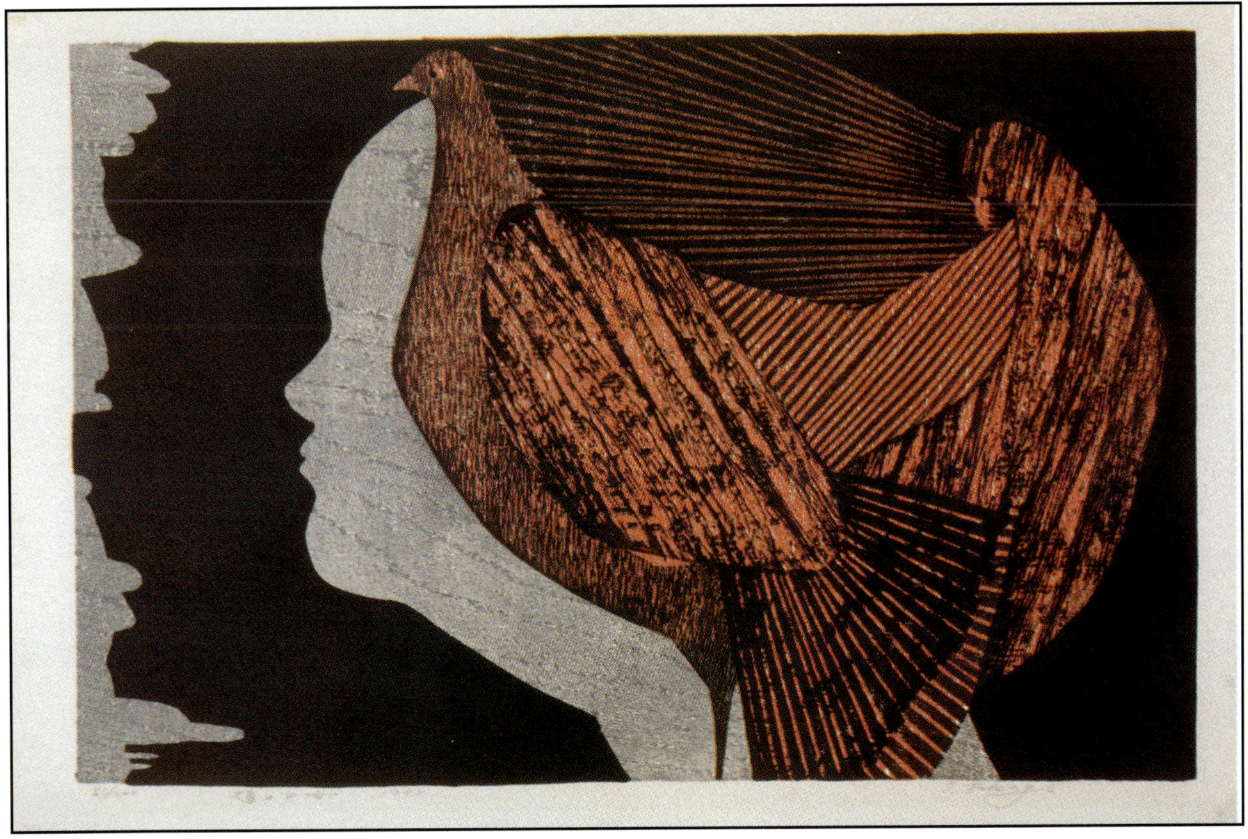

Takagi Shiro, 17 1/4" x 11 3/4", from an edition of 200, dated 1972, signed in pencil on bottom margin "S.Takagi," very good condition, $300-475.

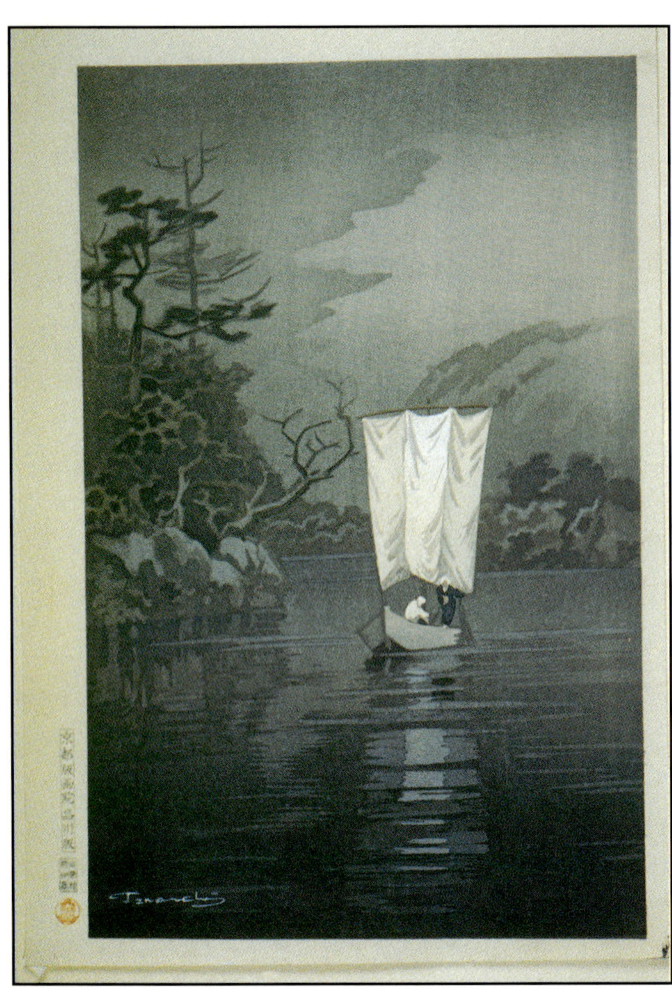

Terauchi Manjiro, oban tate-e, 15 3/4" x 11 3/4", "Sailboat", signed in white in lower left within image, published Kyoto Hanga-In, c. 1950, fine condition, color, and impression, $700-950.

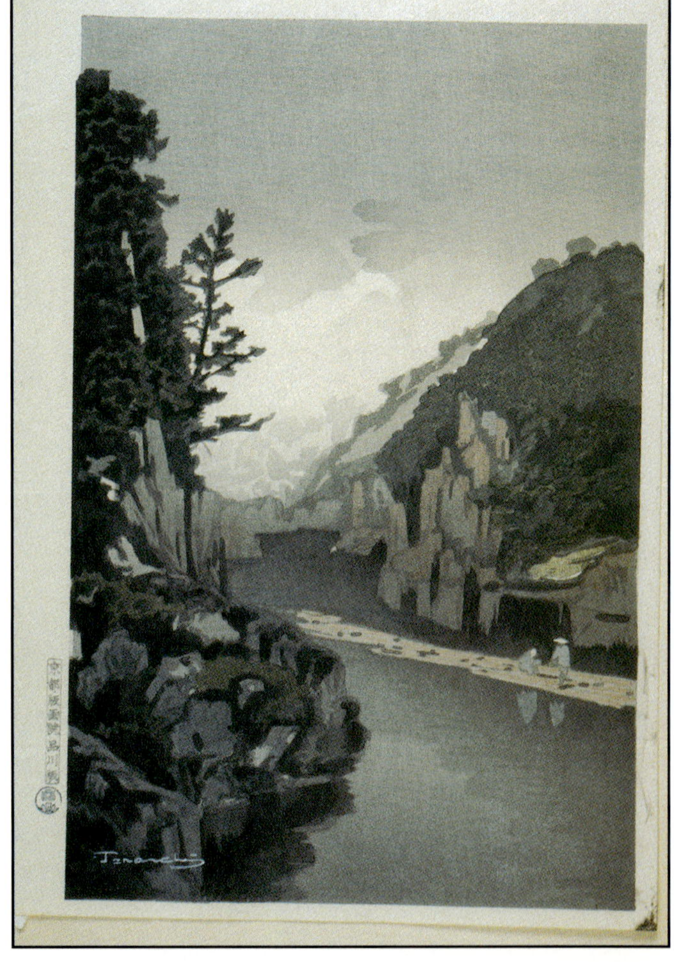

Terauchi Manjiro, oban tate-e, "Riverscape," published by Kyoto Hanga-In, c. 1950, fine impression, color, and condition, $700-950.

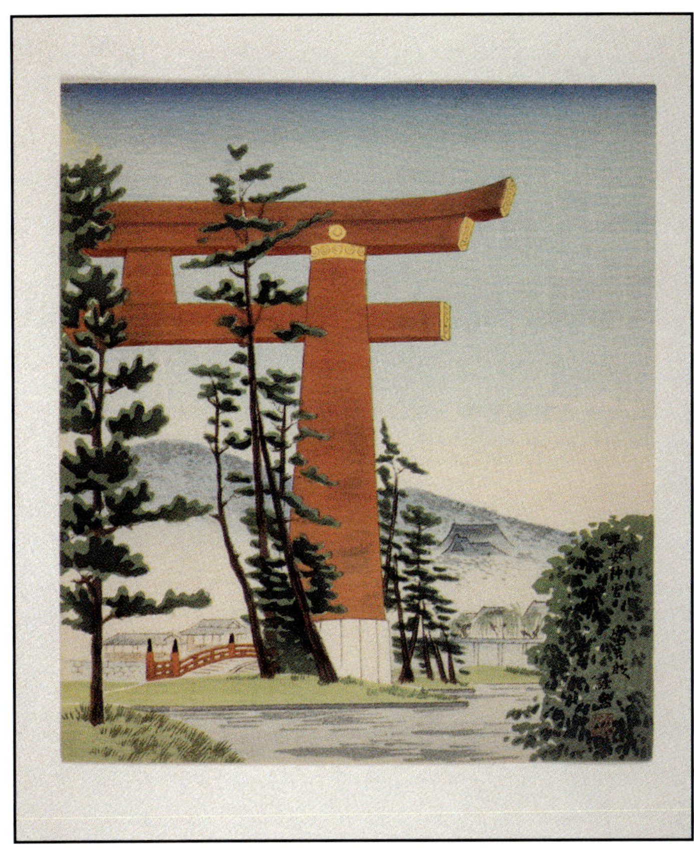

Tokuriki Tomikichiro, shishiban, "Torii Gate," published by Uchida, from a set of 15 Views of Japan, c. 1955, very good condition, color, and impression, $100-150.

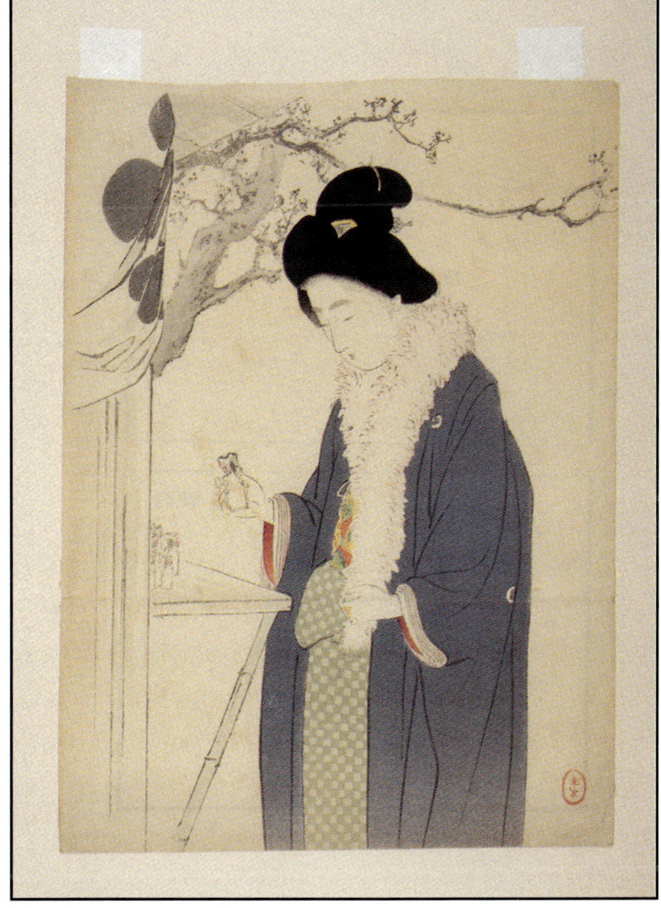

Toshikata Mizuno, kuchi-e (12" x 9"), c. 1903, fine impression and color, slightly soiled, crease, $300-475.

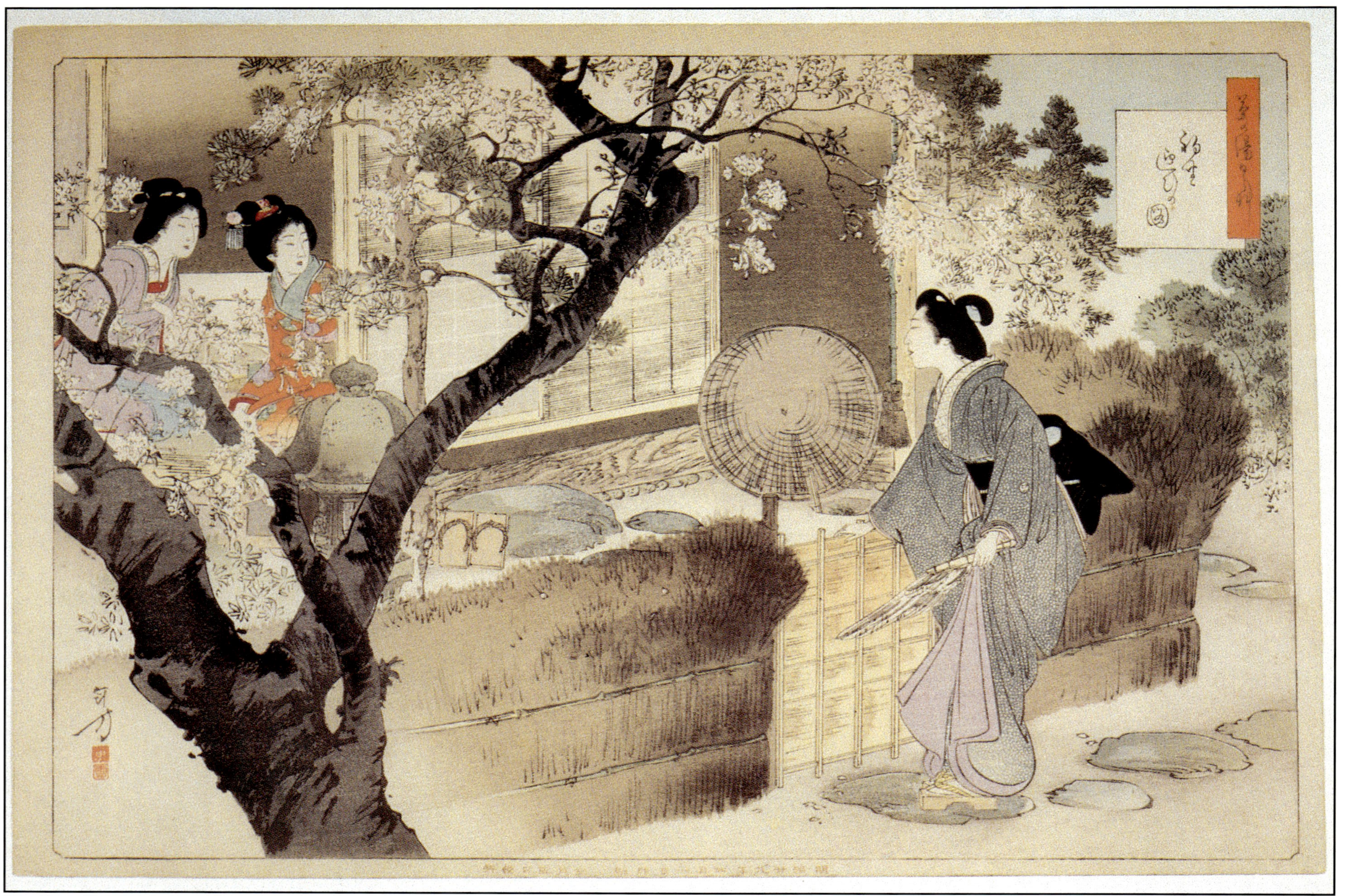

Toshikata Mizuno, oban yoko-e, c. 1902, fine impression, color, condition, backed, $475-675.

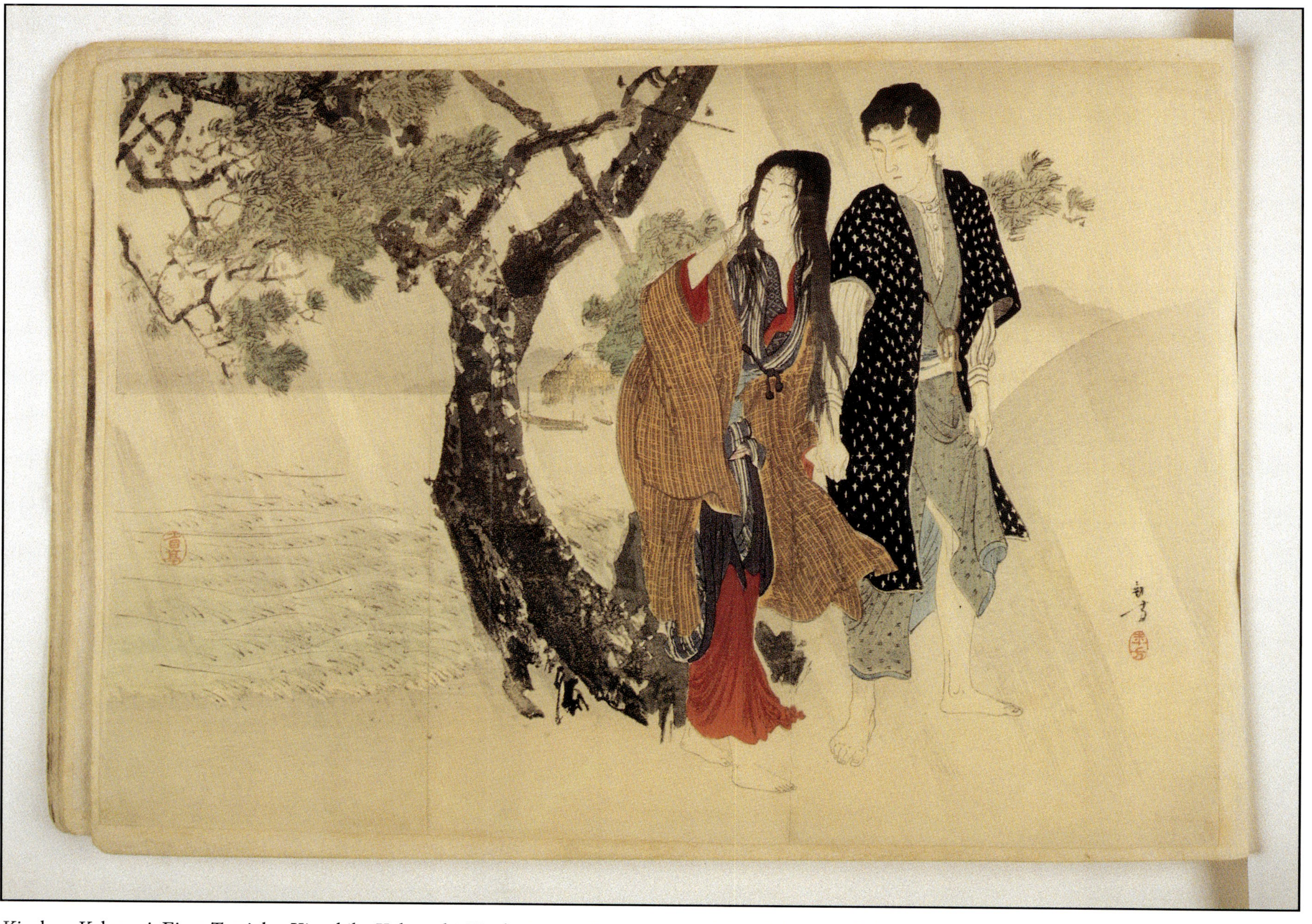

Kiyokata Kaburagi, Eisen Tomioka, Kiyochika Kobayashi, Hanko Kajita, Kason Suzuki, Keishu Takeuchi, Chikanobu Yoshu, Toshimine Tsutsui, Toshikata Mizuno, oban yoko-e, 11 1/2" x 8 1/2", (Toshikata Mizuno), 24 woodblock illustrations for Romantic Novels, late Meiji period c. 1900, fine impressions, very good color and condition, mica, gauffrage, $2500-4500.

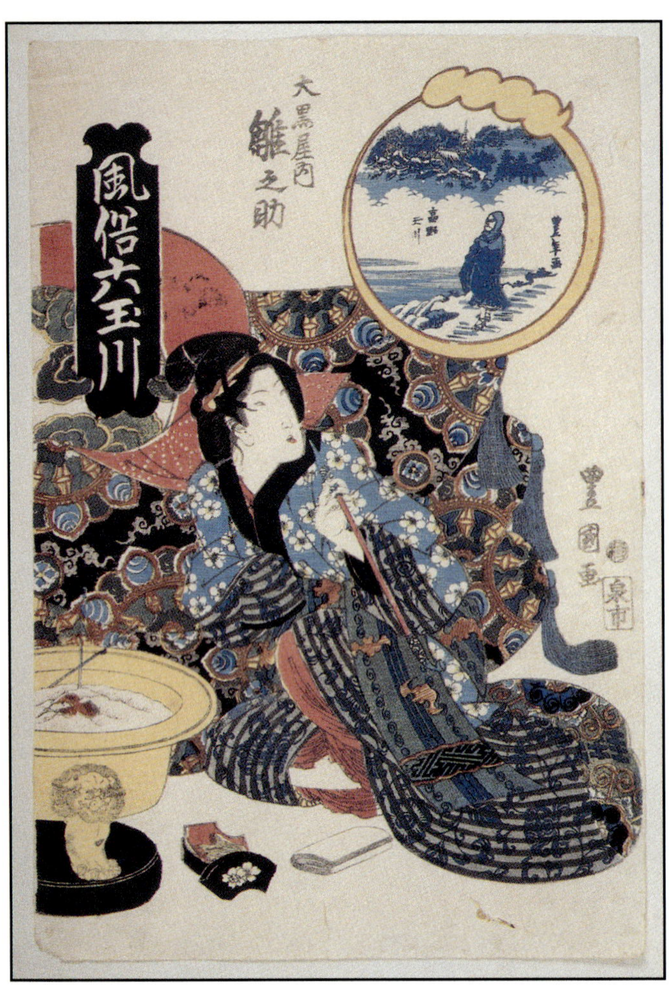

Toyokuni II, oban tate-e, azuri-e rebus, bijin holding her pipe, fine color, impression, and condition, $950-1500.

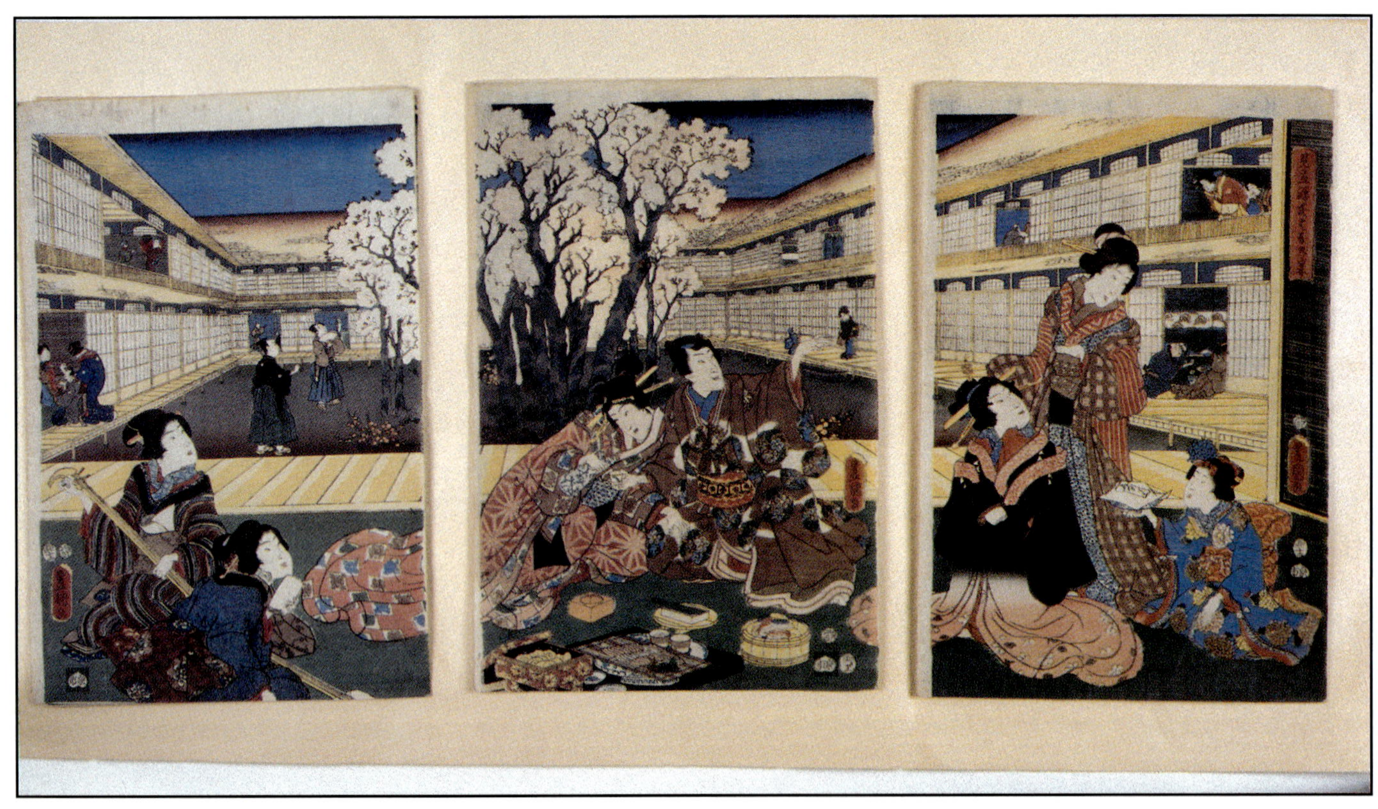

Toyokuni III, oban tate-e triptych, "Yoshiwara," 12th month year of the Hare, fine use of perspective and bokashi, fine impression, color, and condition, $2000-3000.

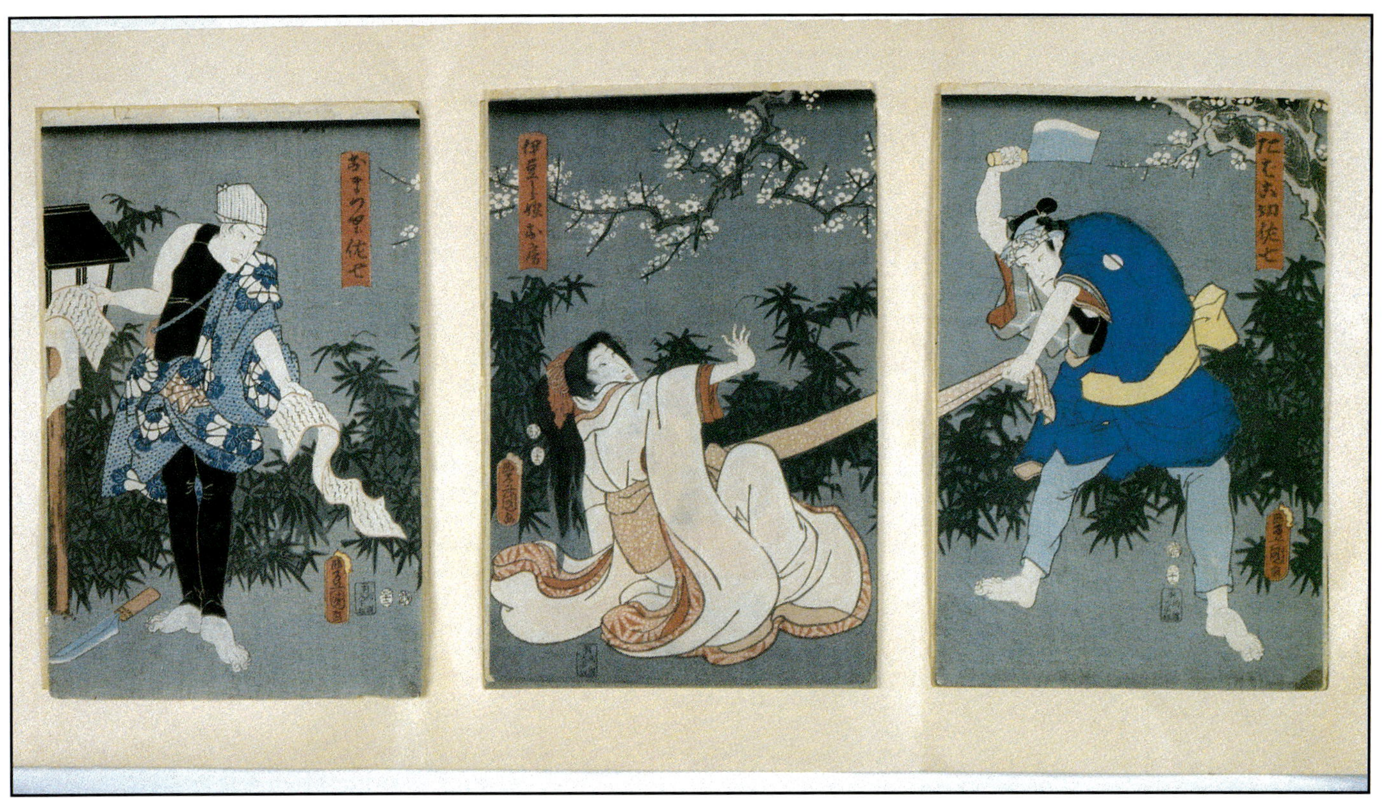

Toyokuni III, oban tate-e triptych, "Actors," dated twelth month year of the Snake 1857, fine imrpession, and color, gauffrage, bottom edges slightly rubbed, $1000-1500.

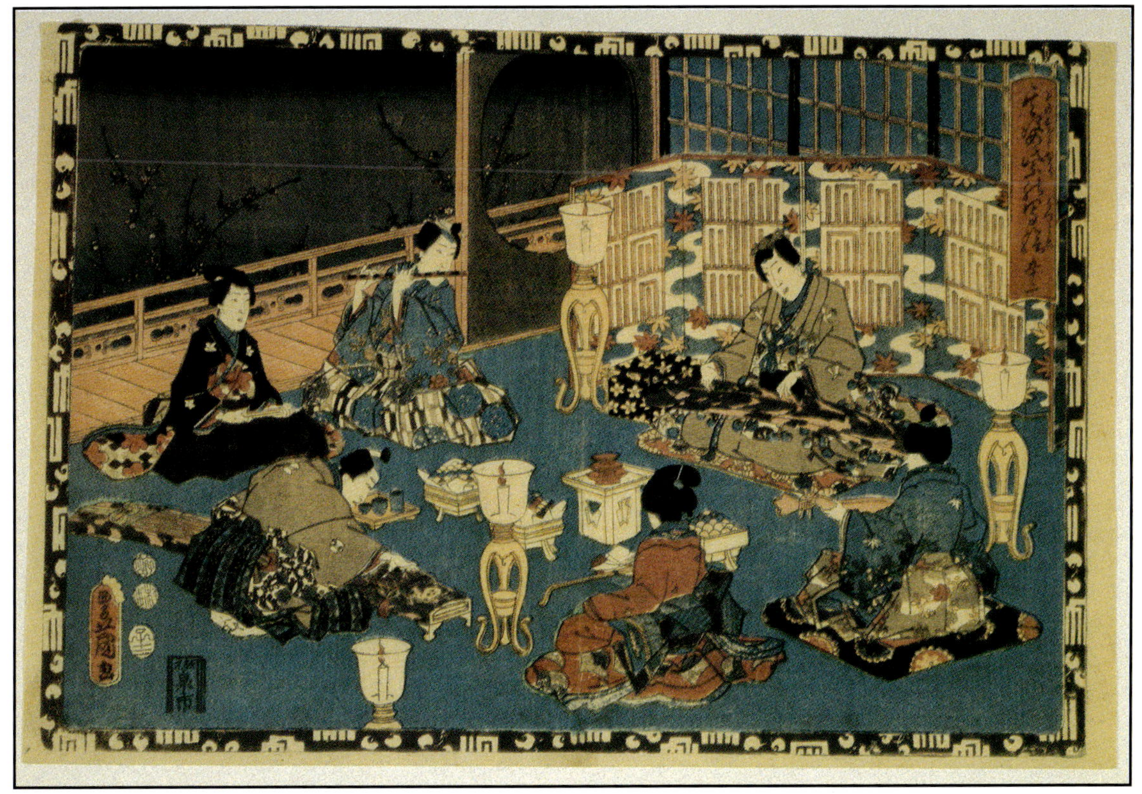

Toyokuni III, oban yoko-e, from the series Tale of Genji, c. 1852 year of the Rat 3, bokashi and perspective, fine impression, color, and condition, $500-750.

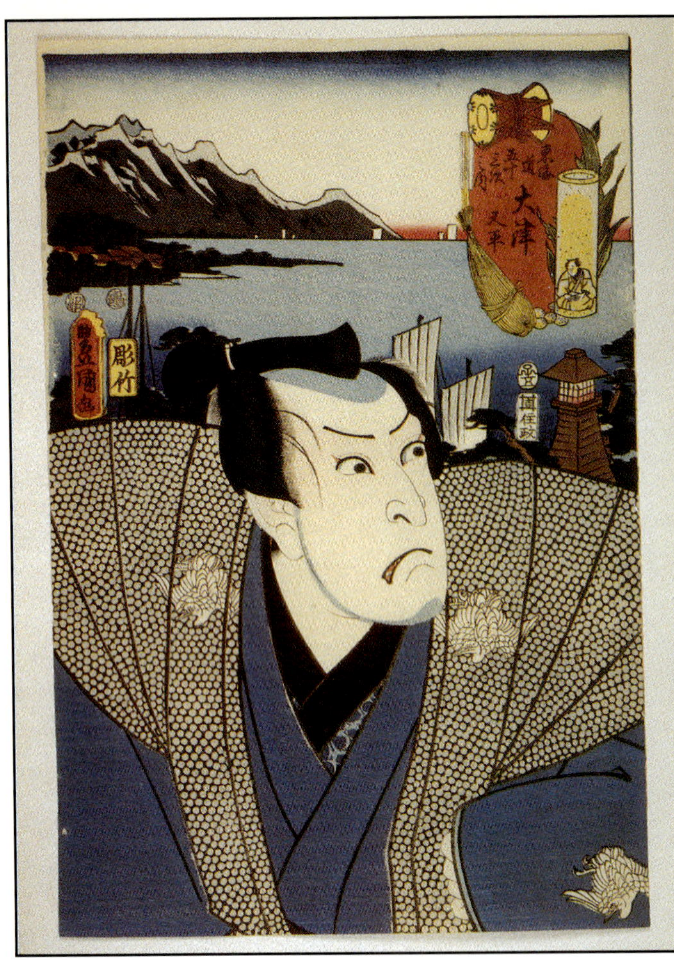

Toyokuni III, oban tate-e, "Nakamura Taemon III as Matahei 'Otsu'," from the series Fifty-three Stations Along the Tokaido, published by Sumiyoshiya Masagoro, 1852, very good impression, color, and condition, $500-700.

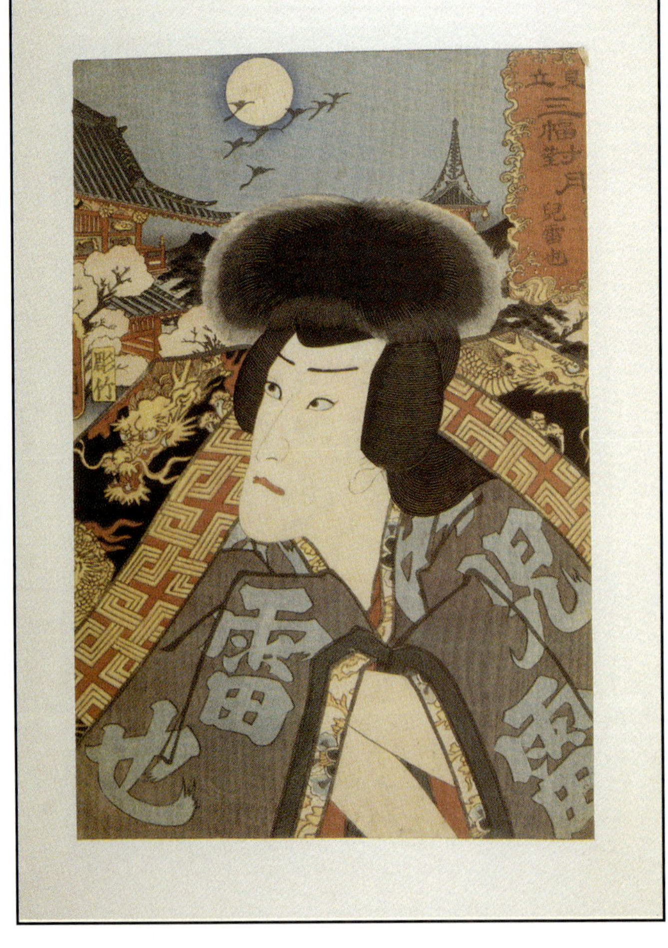

Toyokuni III, oban tate-e, from Minata River, c. 1845-60, fine impression, color, slightly trimmed into image, $275-375.

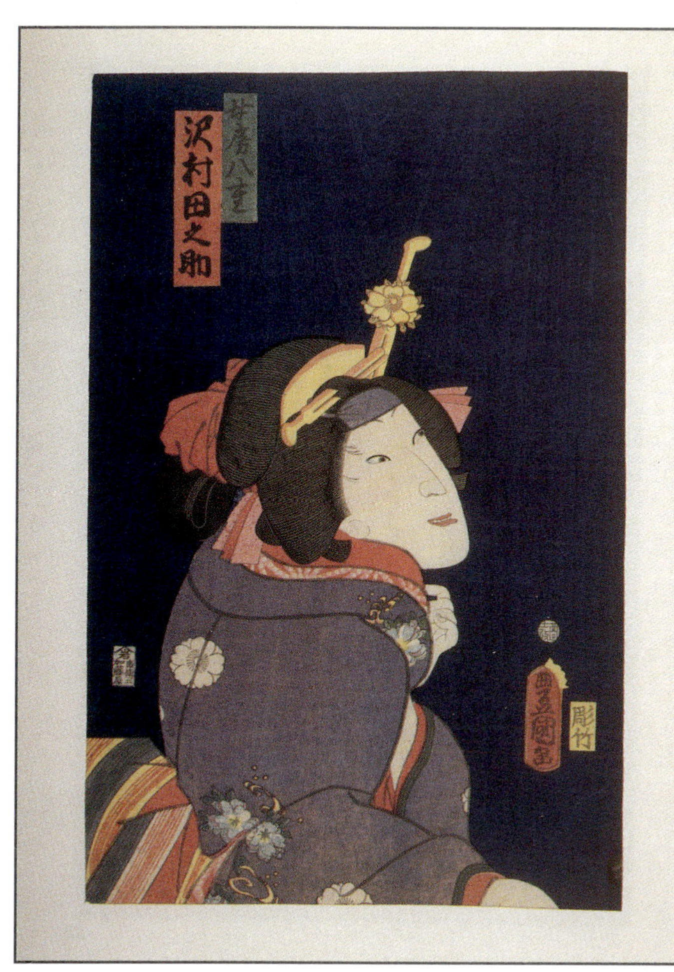

Toyokuni III, oban tate-e, "Horitake," fine impression, color, and condition, $300-475.

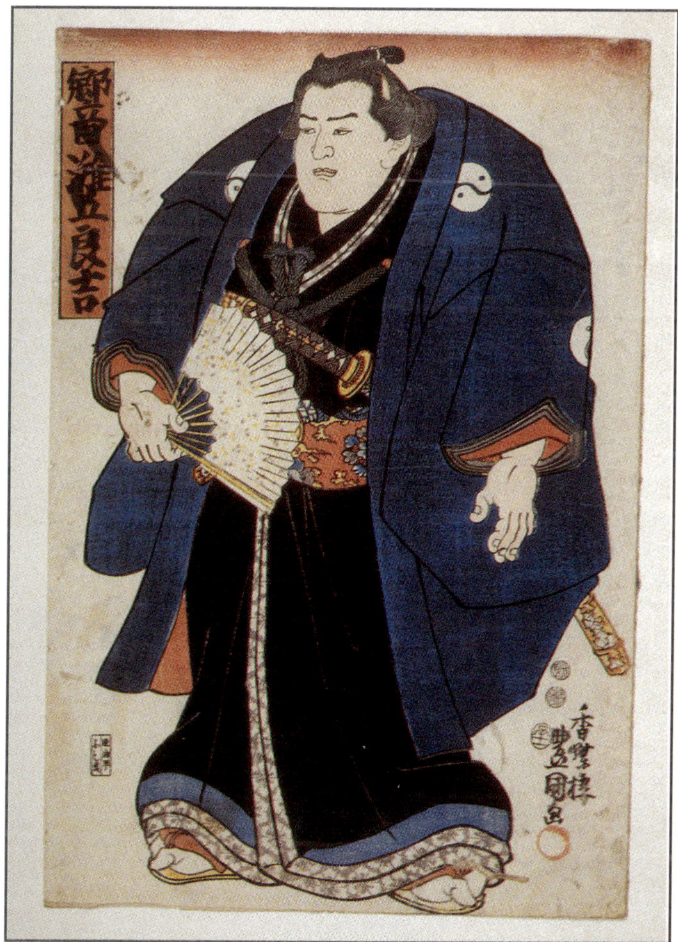

Toyokuni III, oban tate-e, "Sumo," sealed 1852, gauffrage, fine impression, color, condition, slight wormage, binding holes on left, $1000-1500.

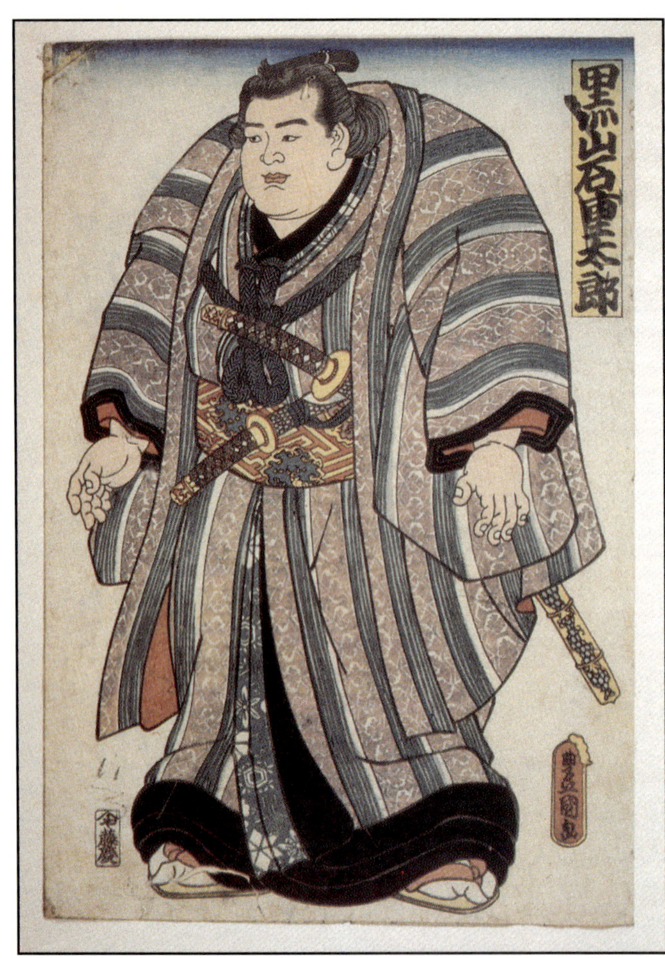

Toyokuni III, oban tate-e, "Sumo," gauffrage, fine impression, color, condition, slight wormage, $900-1200.

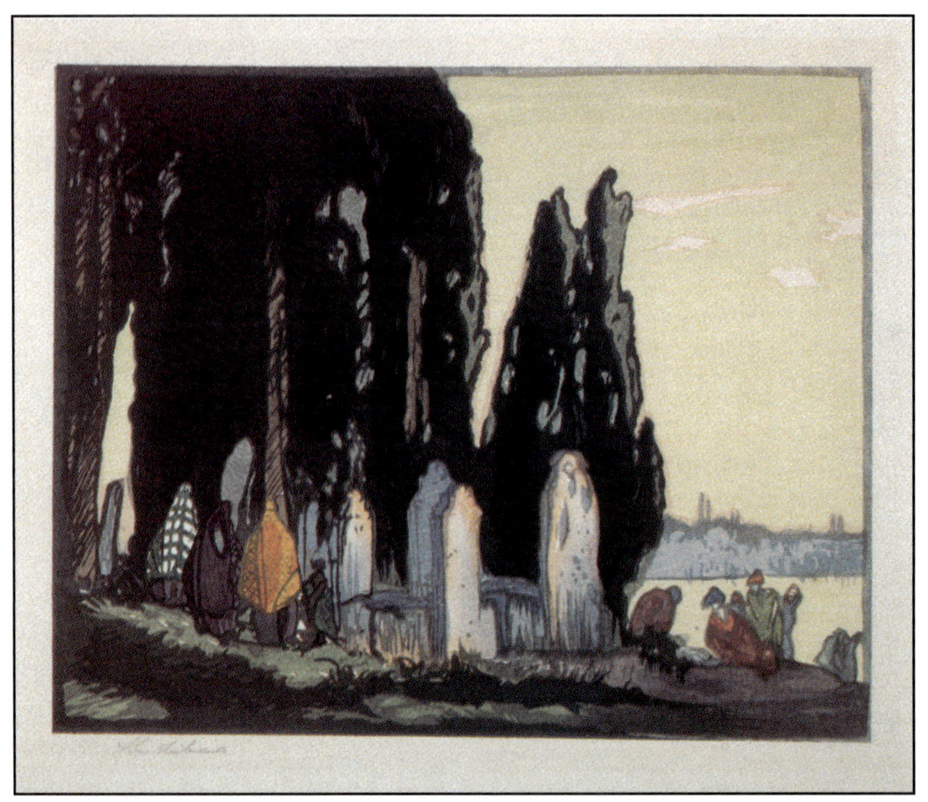

Urushibara Yoshijiro, from a series of 10 prints made in collaboration with Frank Brangwyn, signed Y. Urushibara in pencil, c. 1924, original folio, fine impression, color and condition, $1500-2000.

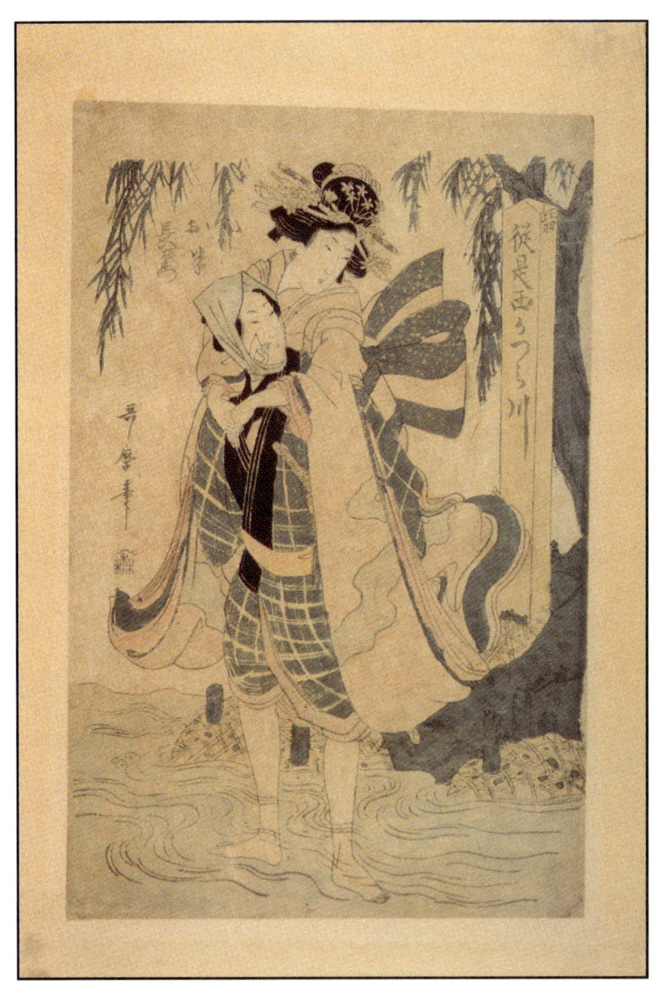

Utamaro II, oban tate-e, "Bijin Being Carried Through Water, "This print has an obvious carving mistake (one foot has the toes facing the wrong way), fair condition, color, and good impression, $1500-2200.

Sanzo Wada, 7" x 9 1/2", "A Dancing Girl Preparing Tea," signed "Wada Sanzo," signed and sealed Sanzo, 1950, fine condition, color, and impression, $550-775.

The following information accompanied this print:

A 20 impression woodblock print. Woodblock prints are Japan's special handicraft that express a pictorial sense impossible for any mechanical printing to attain. Their artistic value is recognized throughout the world.

Because the process of making a woodblock print depends entirely on the skill of the fingers, painstaking efforts by master craftsmen and amazingly precise technique are necessary.

After a painting has been selected, the engraver must have remarkable patience and exact technique in order to carve the design from different blocks of cherry wood, depending on the lines and the final color effect desired. In particular, where extra fine lines must be carved, the ability even to split a hair lengthwise into two is required.

The printer next used these block to secure one impression after another. One can only be amazed at the skill with which even the minutest detail is printed on Japanese paper without the trace of the slightest flaw. A great number of impressions are particularly necessary in order faithfully to express the perspective, lighting and cubic effect that modern painting possess.

This woodblock print is the work of the Kyoto Hanga-In (Kyoto Color Print Institute), Yanagino Bamba, Shijo Minami, Kyoto, which is carrying on the most progressive study of color prints in Japan.

Twenty impression were required to complete this color print. Painting by Sanzo Wada, member of the Japan Art Academy. Carving and printing by craftsmen of the Kyoto Hanga-In.

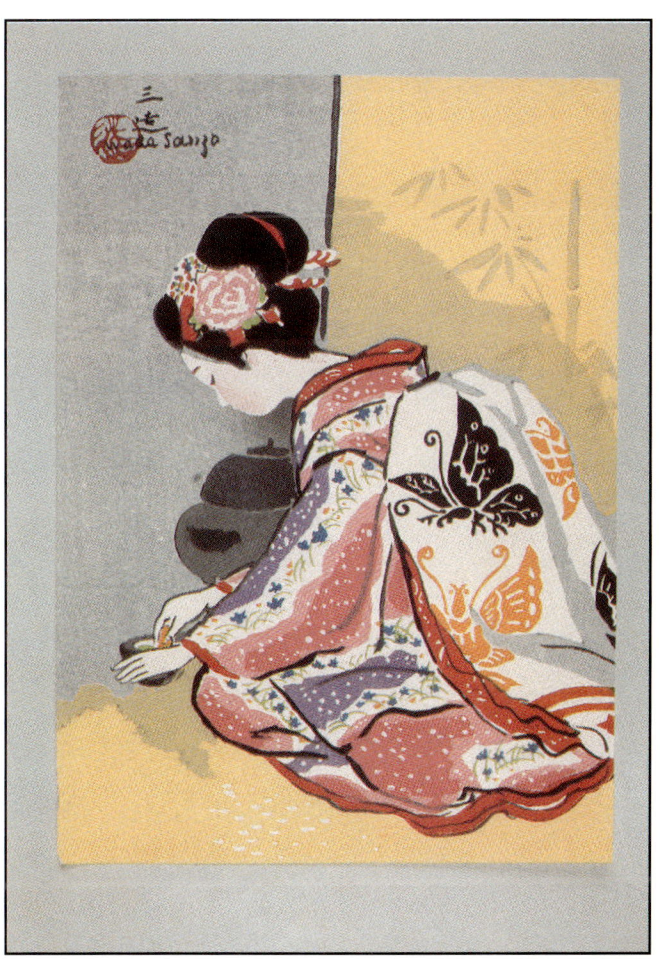

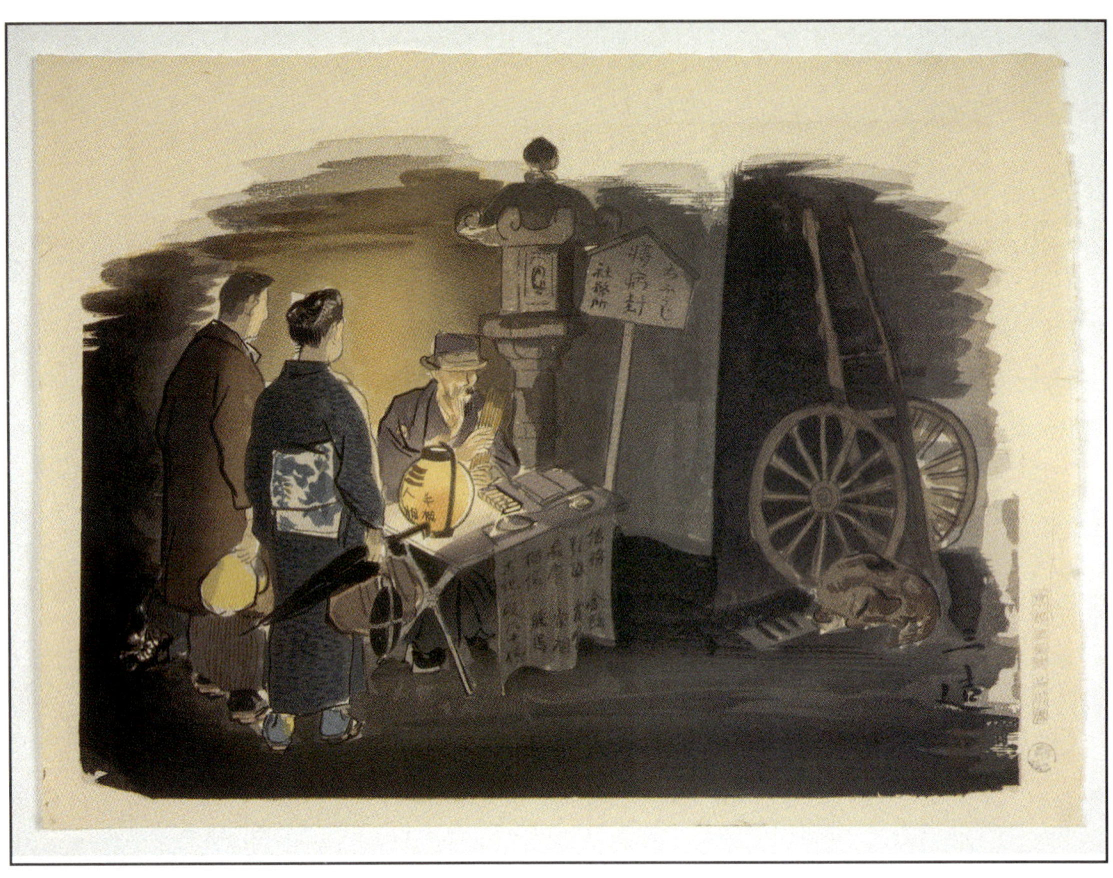

Wada Sanzo, oban yoko-e, 16" x 11 1/2", "The Fortune Teller," c. 1952, signed and sealed lower right within image, published by Kyoto Hanga-In, fine condition, color, and impression, $375-575.

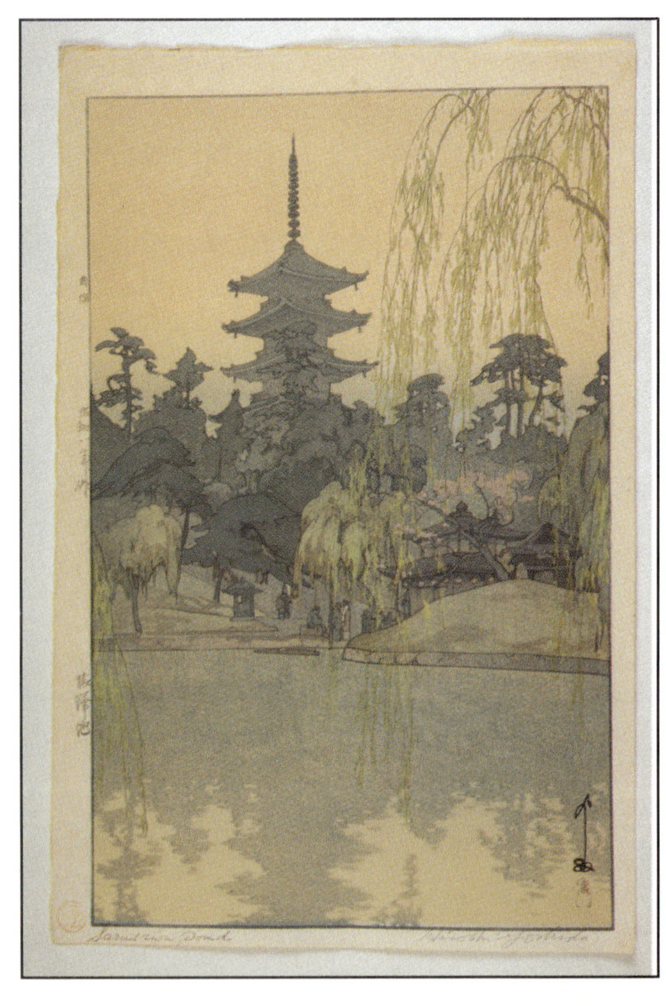

Yoshida Hiroshi, oban tate-e, "Sarusawa Pond (in Nara)," dated Showa 8 (1933), signed and sealed, with jizuri seal, very good impression, color, and condition, $1200-1800.

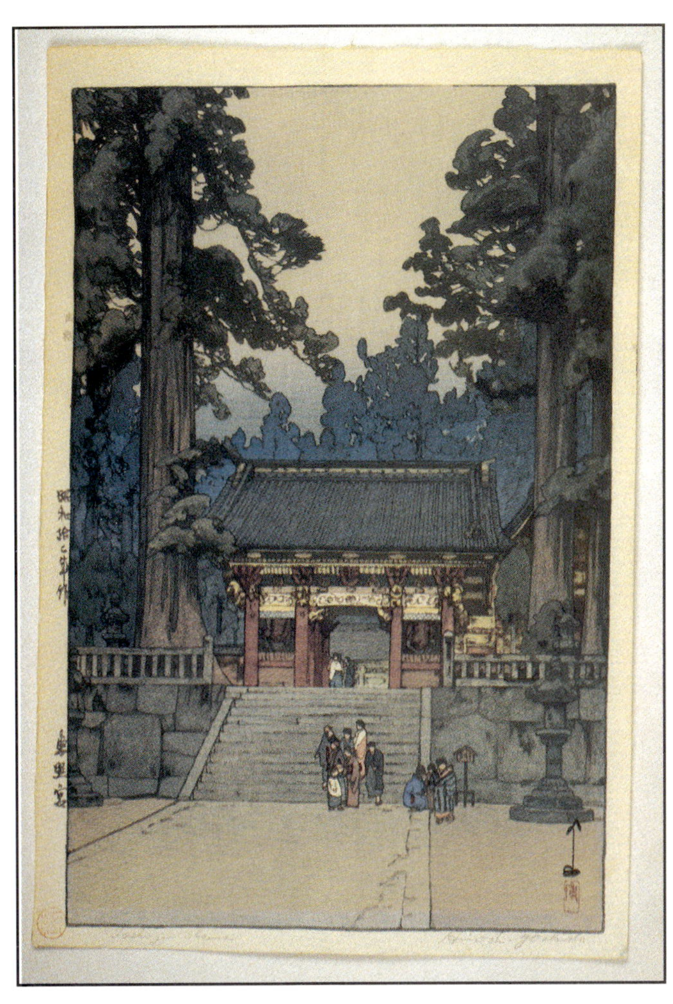

Yoshida Hiroshi, oban tate-e; "Toshogu Shrine," Showa 2 (1927), jizuri seal, signed in pencil "Hiroshi Yoshida," very good impression, color, and condition, $1000-1500. (When this print was new it retailed for $15.)

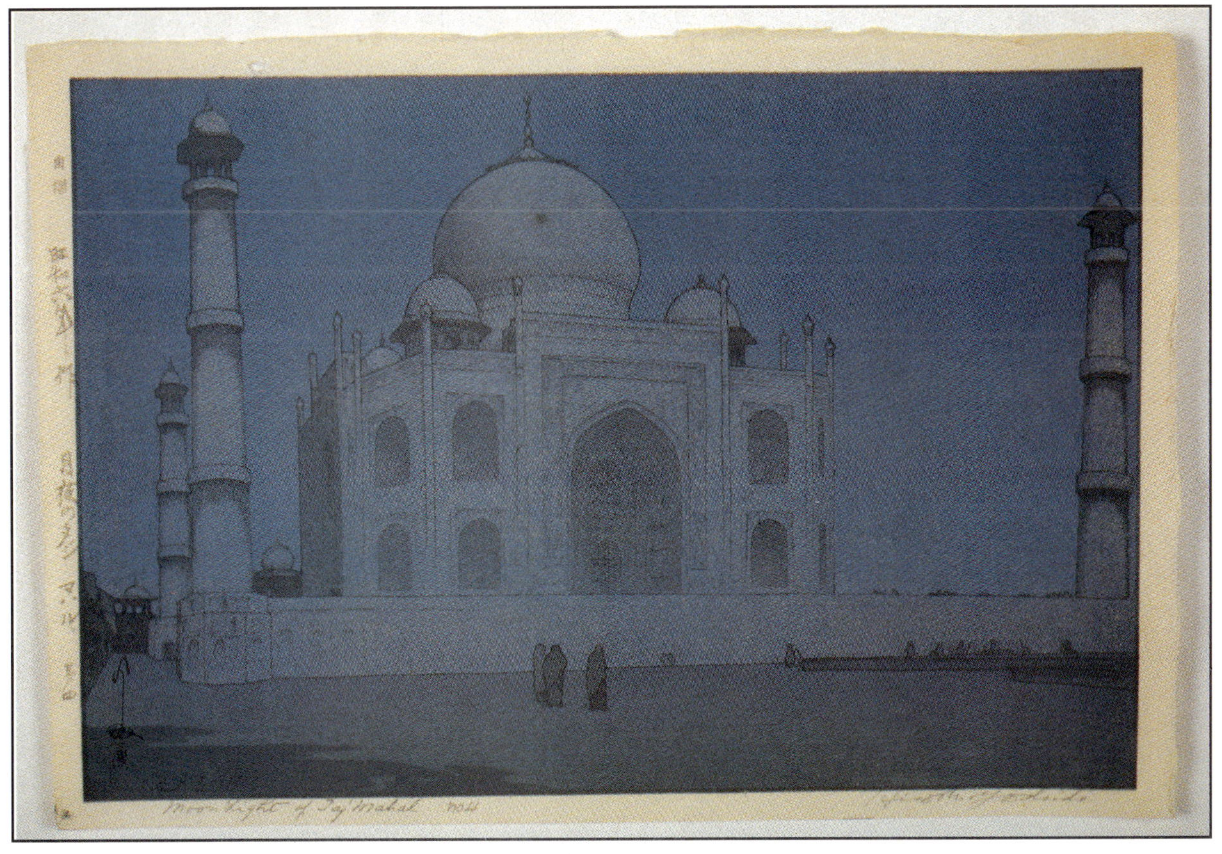

Yoshida Hiroshi, oban yoko-e, "Moon Light of Taj Mahal No 4," dated Showa 6 (1931), jizuri seal, fine condition, color, and impression, $1200-1800.

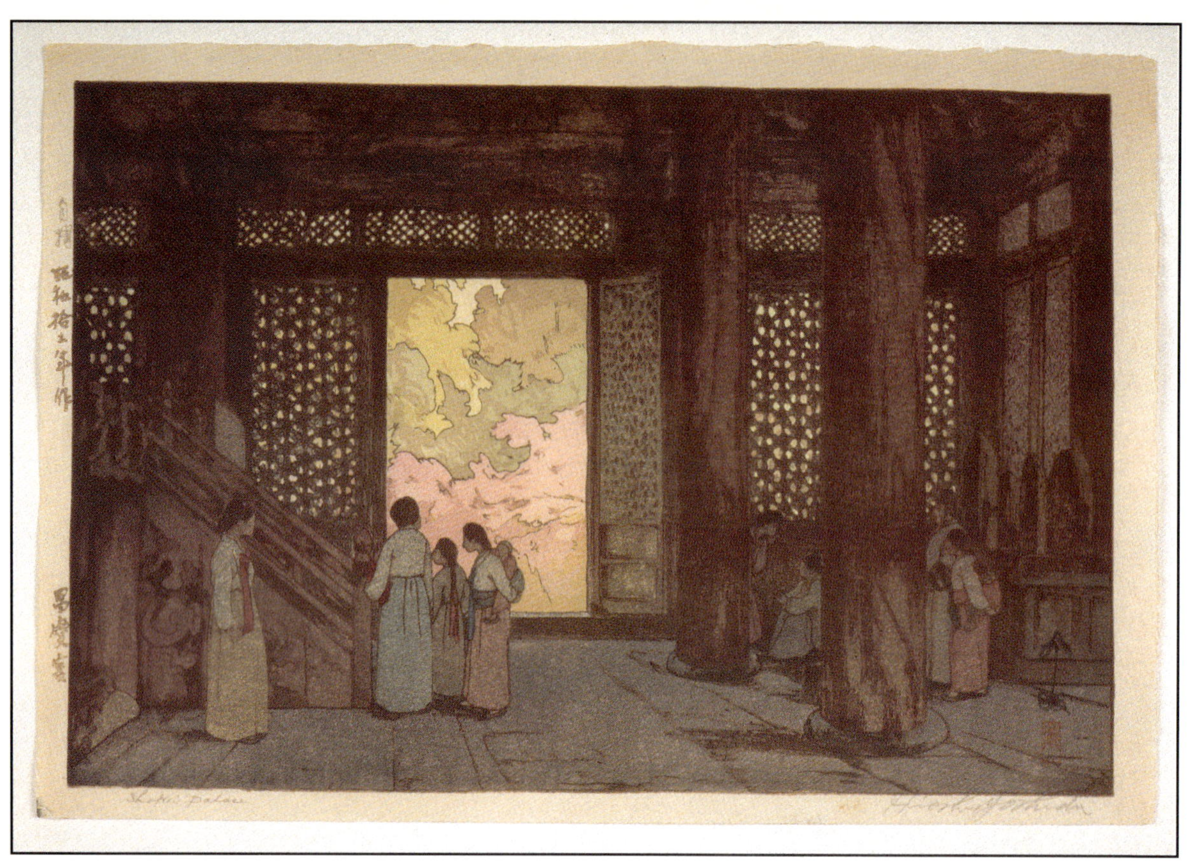

Yoshida Hiroshi, oban yoko-e, "Shokai Palace," dated Showa 12 (1937), jizuri seal, fine condition, color, and impression, $1200-1800.

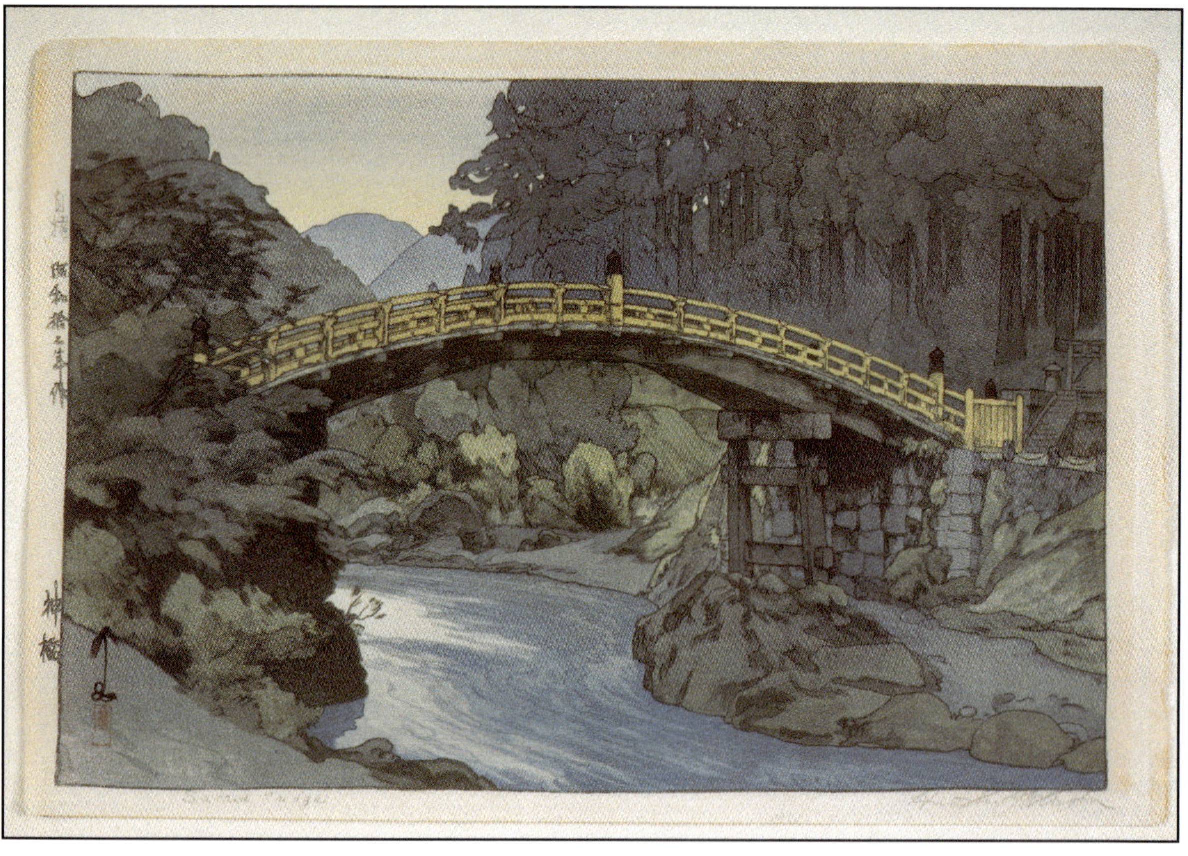

Yoshida Hiroshi, oban yoko-e, "Sacred Bridge," dated Showa 12 (1937), jizuri seal, fine condition, color, and impression, $1200-1800.

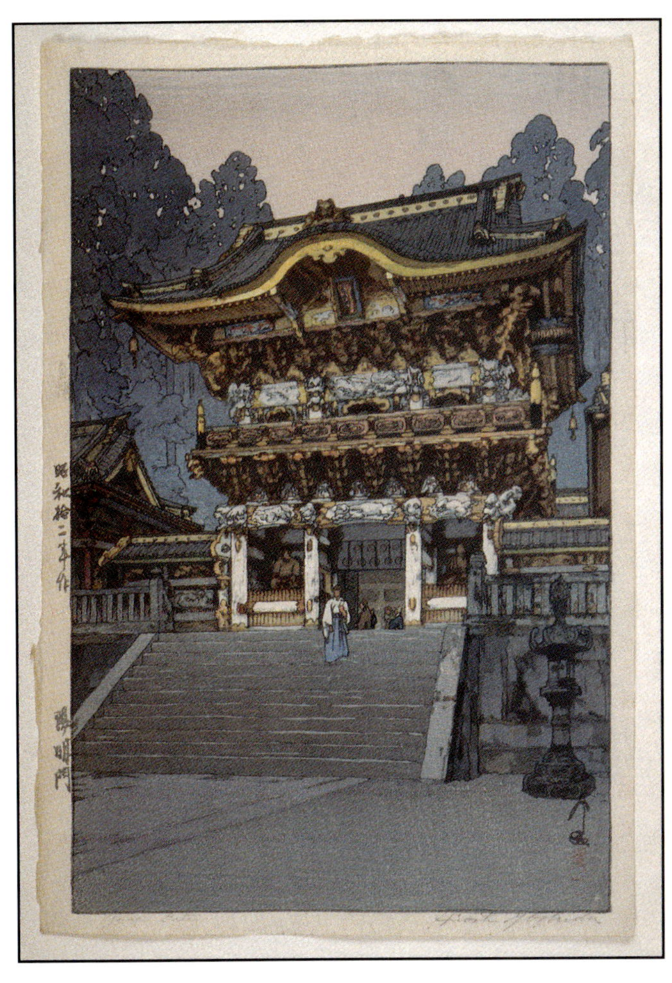

Yoshida Hiroshi, oban tate-e, "Yomei Gate," dated Showa 12 (1937), jizuri seal, fine condition, color, and impression, $1200-1800.

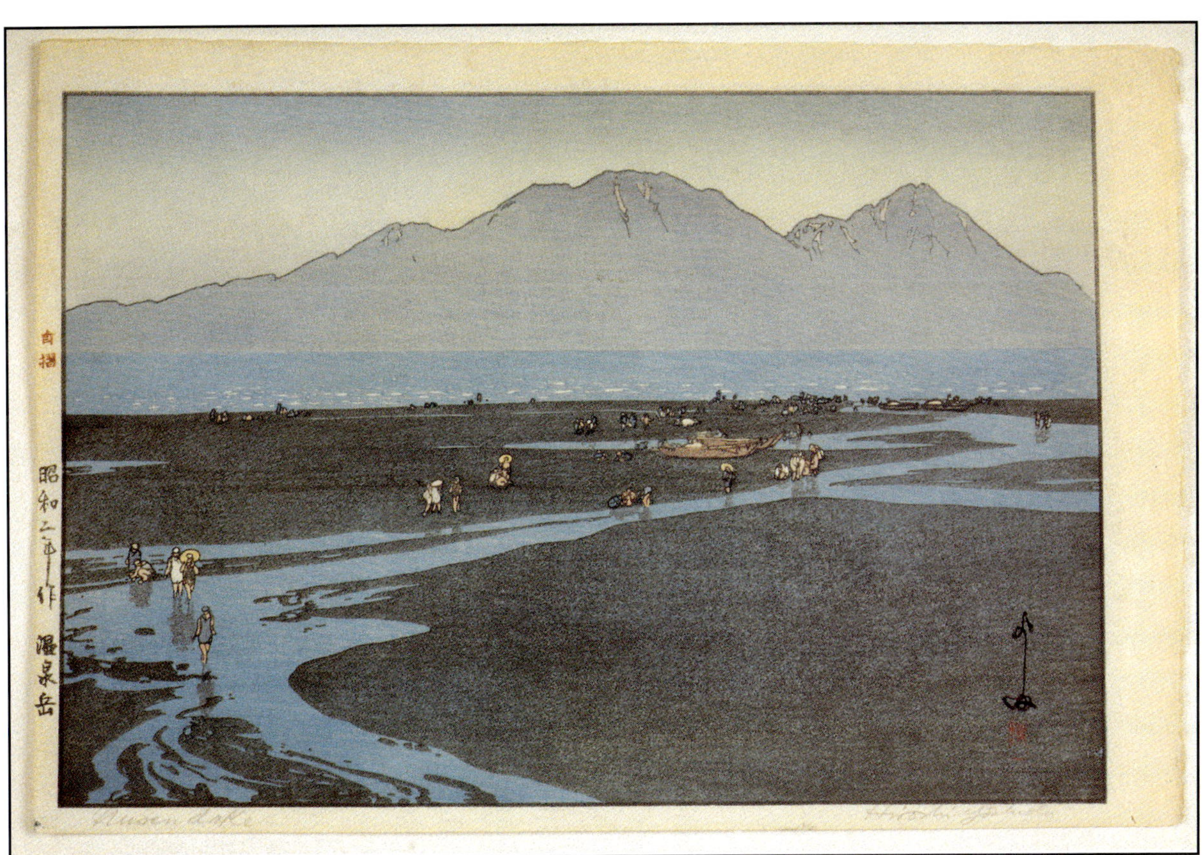

Yoshida Hiroshi, oban yoko-e, "Usendake," dated Showa 2 (1927), jizuri seal, fine condition, color, and impression, $1500-1800.

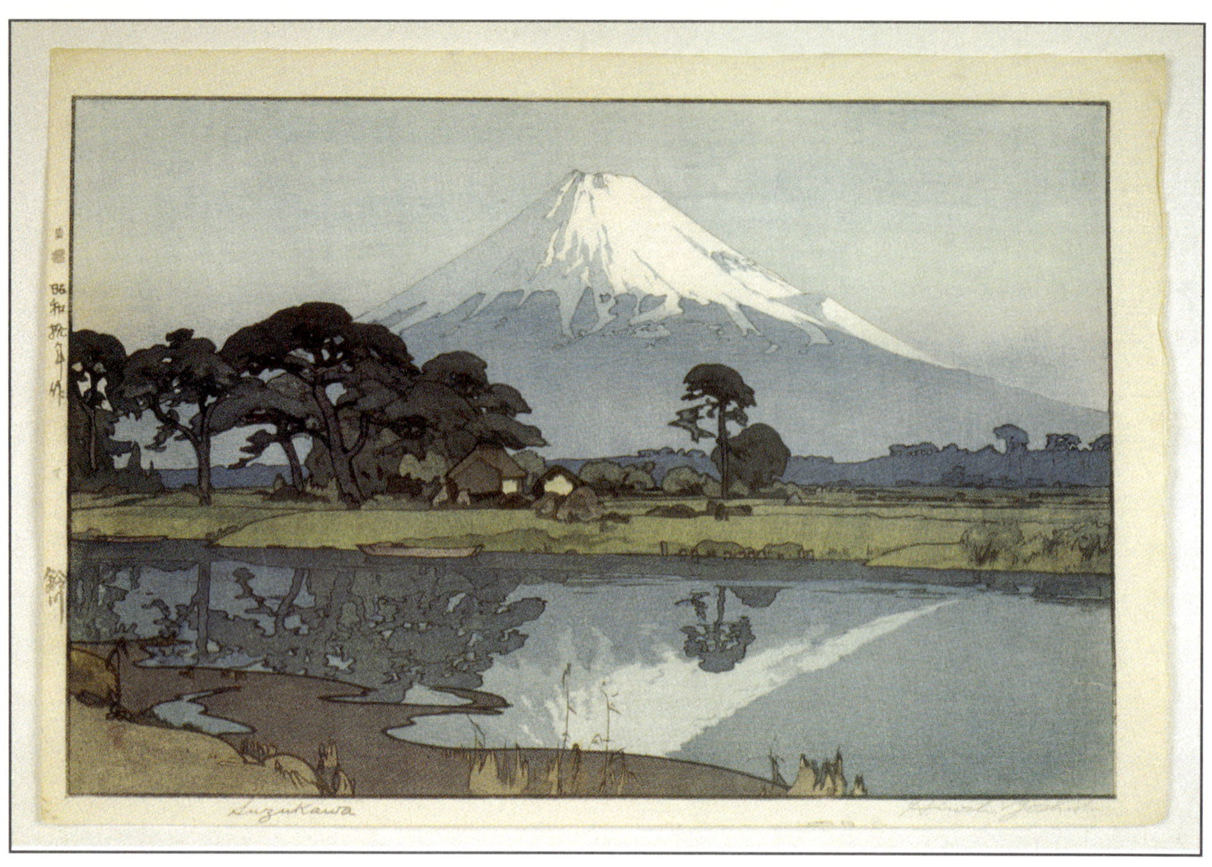

Yoshida Hiroshi, oban yoko-e, "Suzukawa," dated Showa 9 (1935), jizuri seal, fine condition, color, and impression, $1200-1800.

Yoshida Hiroshi, oban tate-e, "Temple Gate," dated Showa 8 (1933), very good impression, color, and condition (void of jizuri seal), $150-250.

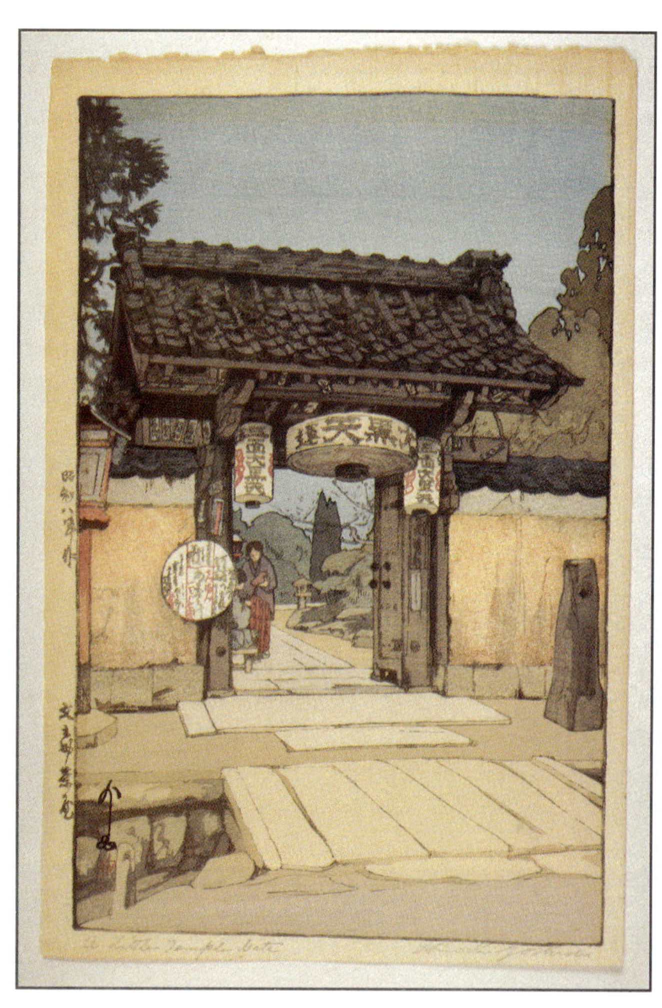

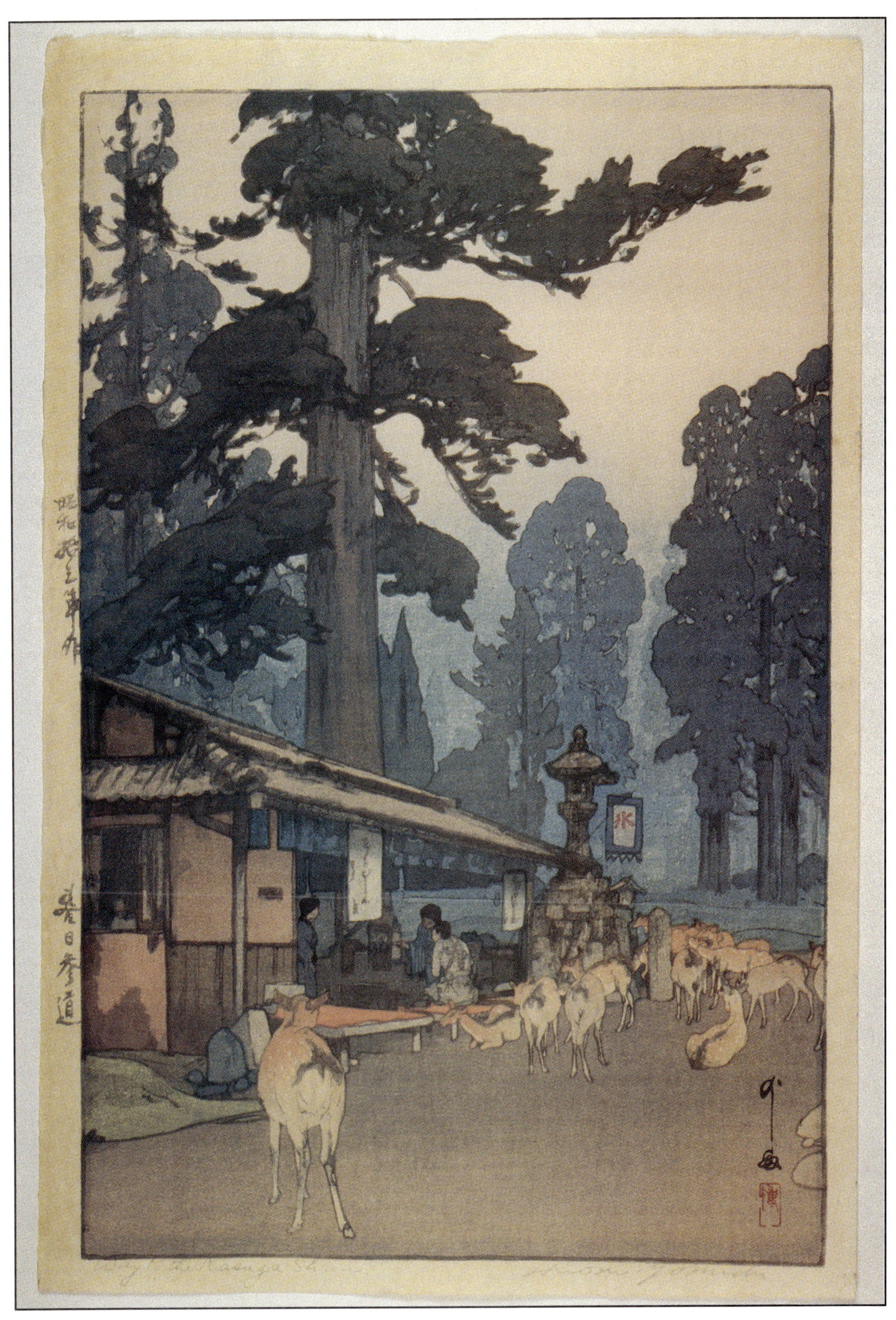

Yoshida Hiroshi, oban tate-e, "Way to the Kasuga Shrine," dated Showa 13 (1938), (void of jizuri seal), fine impression, color, and condition, $200-275.

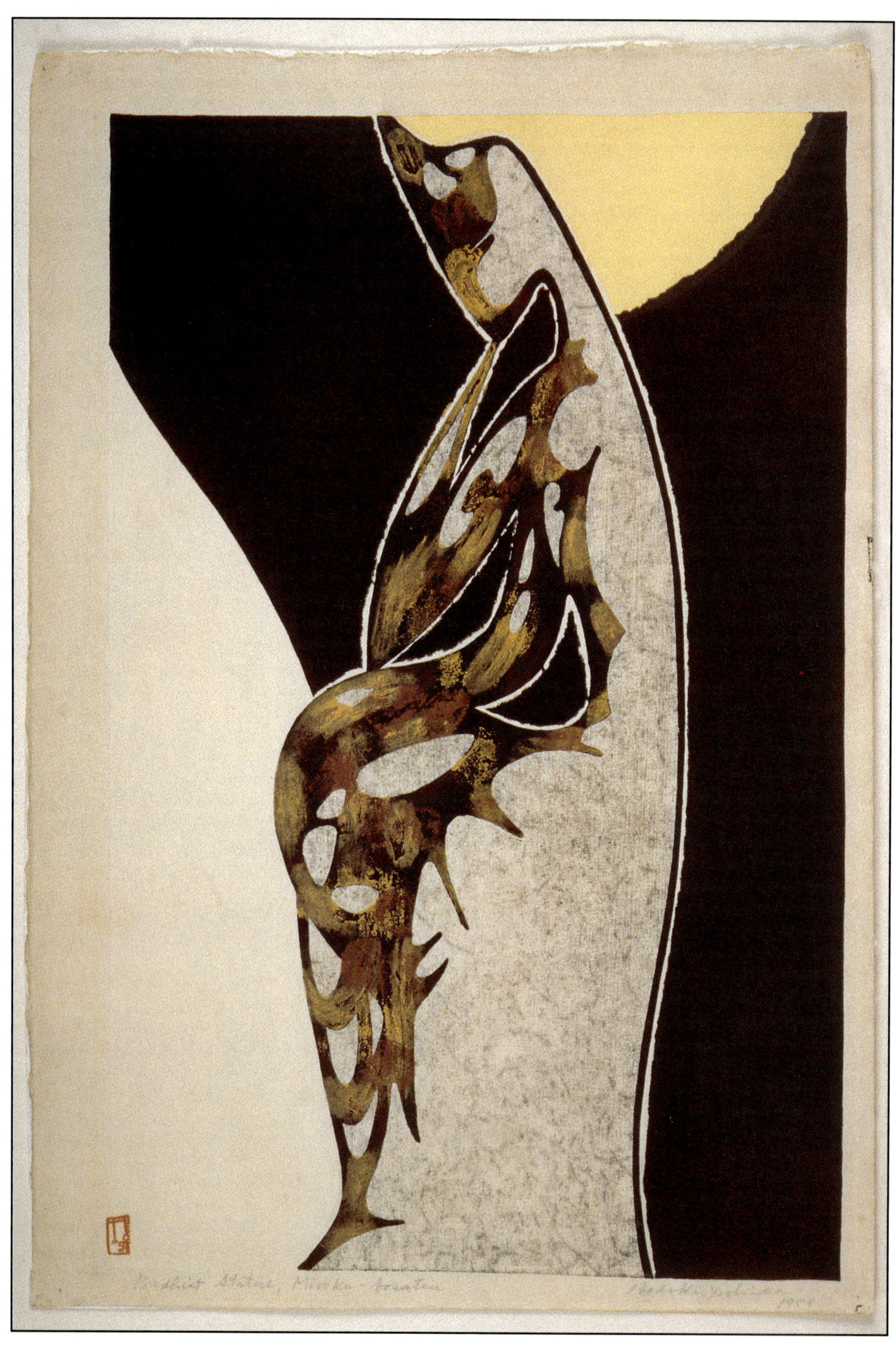

Yoshida Hodaka, oban tate-e, 16" x 11", penciled title "Budhist Statue, Miroka-Bosatsu," (spelled with only one d), sealed in the lower left within the image, mica, lower margin with "Hodaka Yoshida 1959," fine impression, color, and condition, $1800-2500.

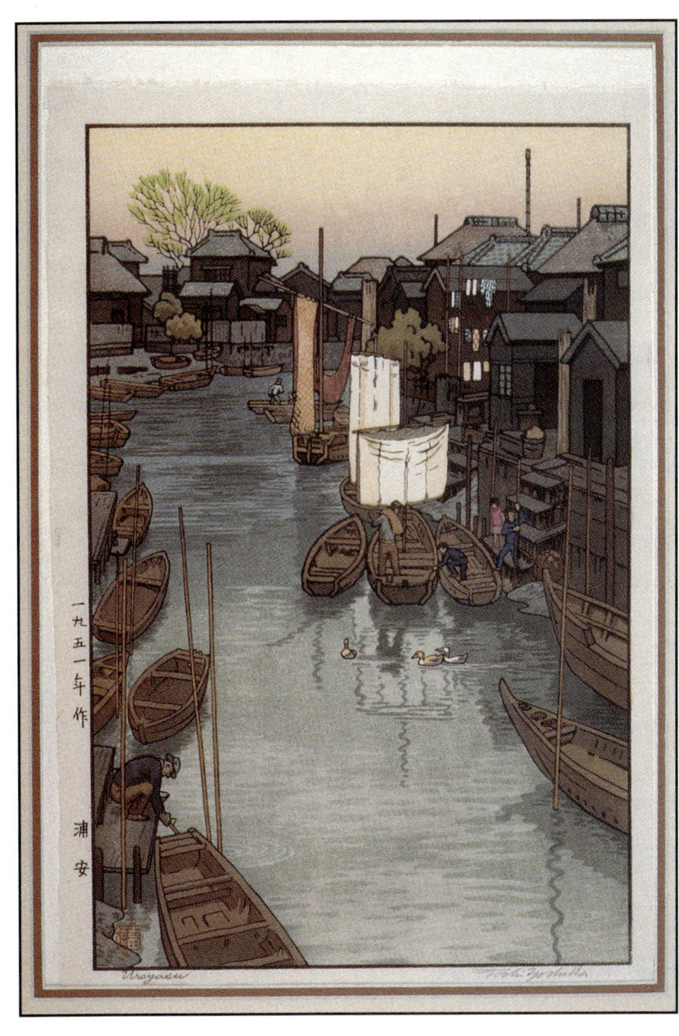

Yoshida Toshi, oban tate-e, "Urayasu," dated 1951, sealed, signed on lower margin, fine impression, condition, and color, $900-1500.

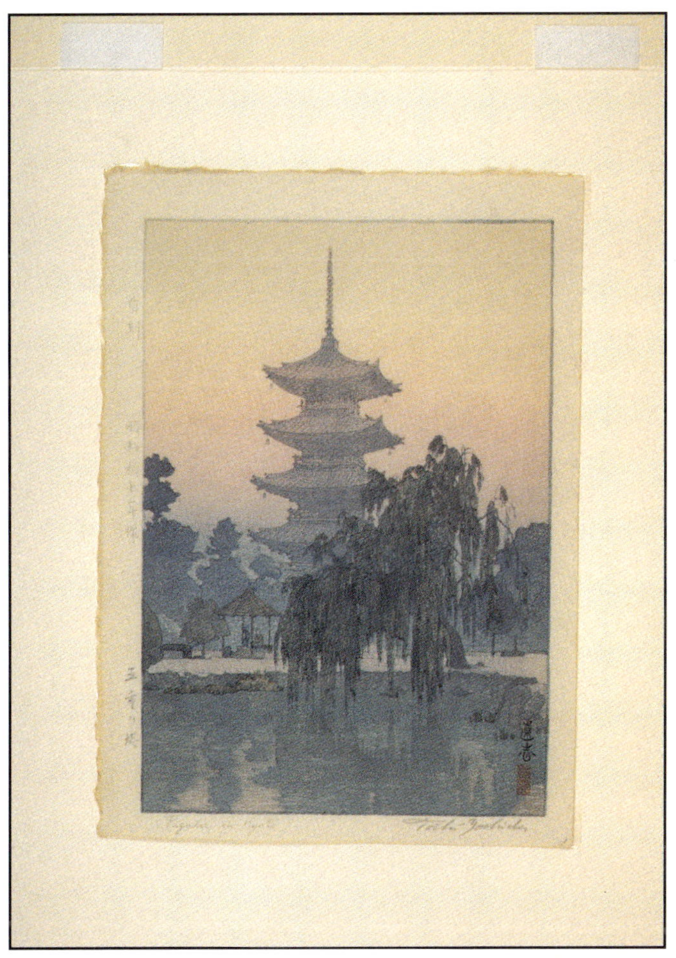

Yoshida Toshi, 10 1/2" x 7 3/4", "Pagoda In Kyoto," signed and sealed, dated 1942, fine impression, color, and condition, $750-950.

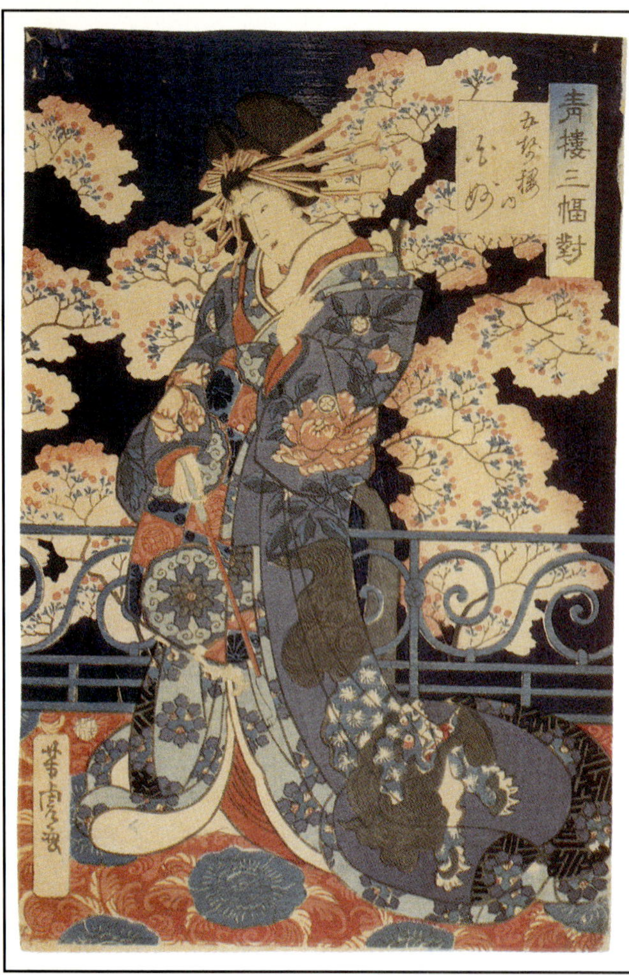

Yoshitora,Utagawa, oban tate-e, a geisha on a verandah in the Yoshiwara, her kimono with huge shishi design, c. 1859, signed "Yoshitora ga," very good impression, good color, and condition, $300-485.

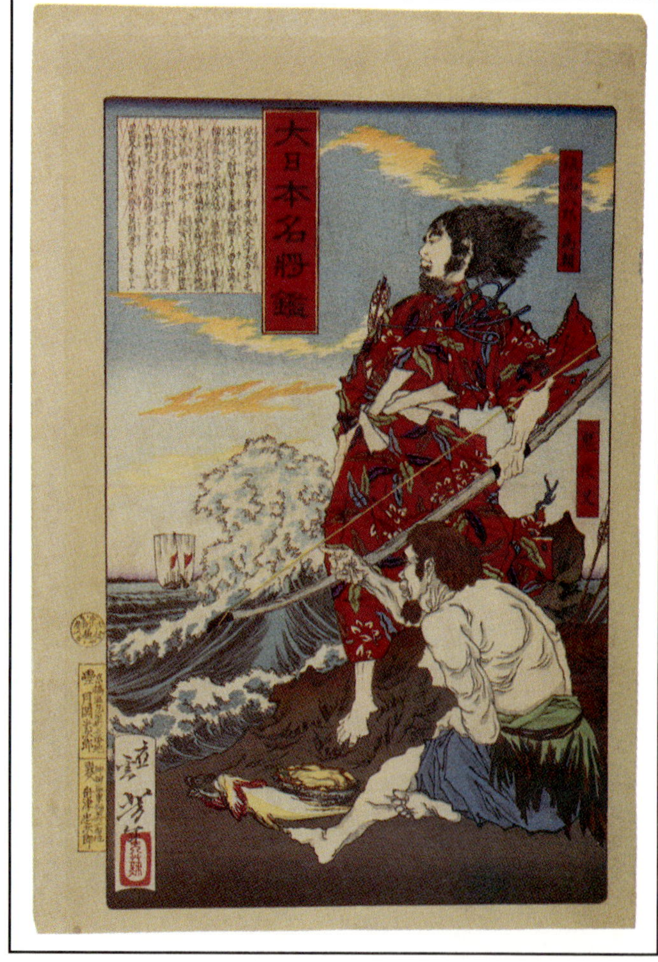

Yoshitoshi, oban tate-e, "Chinzei Hachiro Tametomo and Oniyasha," from the series A Mirror of Famous Japanese Generals, dated Meiji 12 (1879), signed "Oju Yoshitoshi," seal Taiso, $750-900.

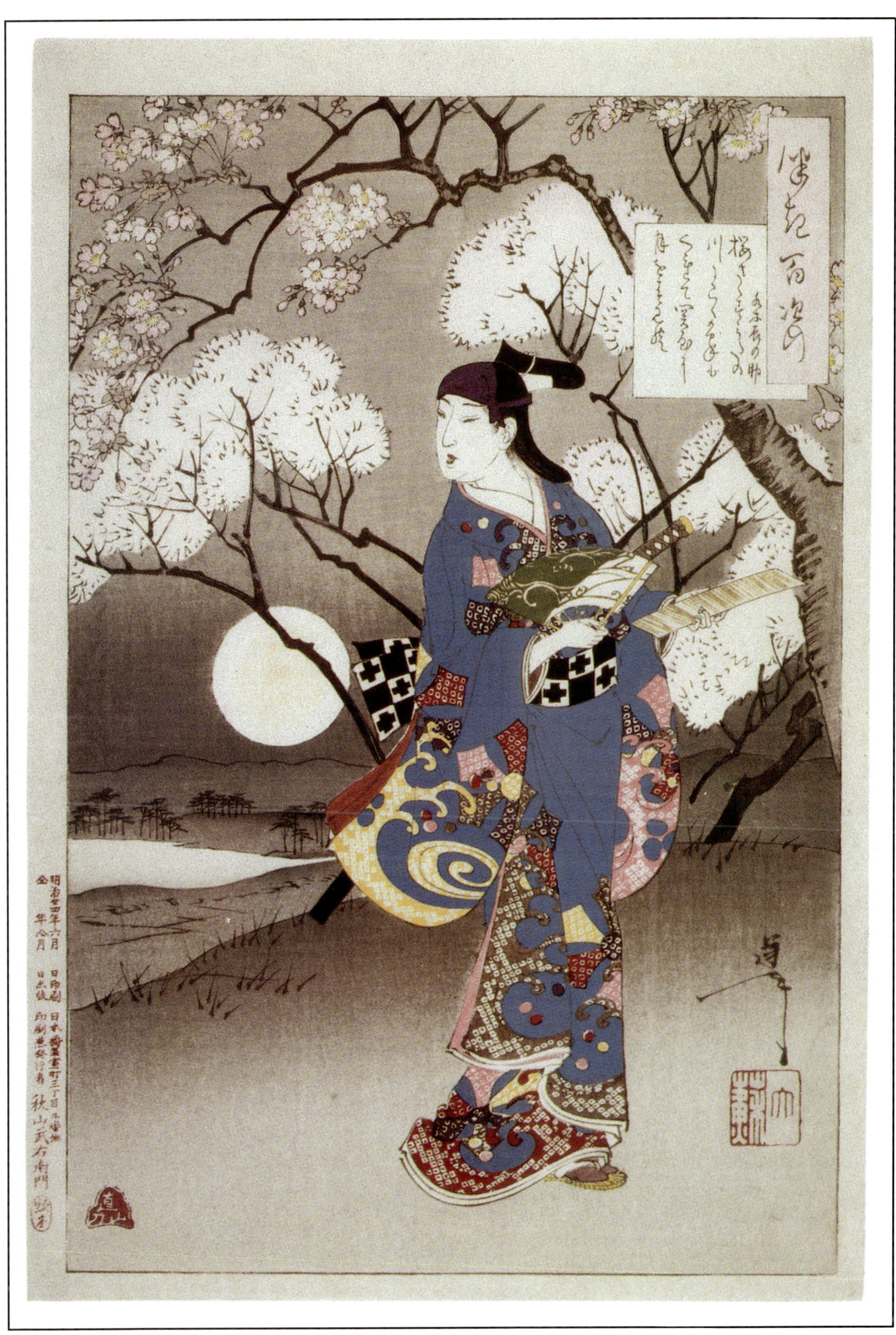

Yoshitoshi, oban tate-e, "A Poem by Mizuki Tatsunosuke," from the series: The 100 Aspects of the Moon , dated Meiji 24 (1891), 6th month (June), signed "Yoshitoshi," seal Taiso, published by Akiyama Buemon, carved by Chokuzan, fine impression, color, and condition, $800-1200.

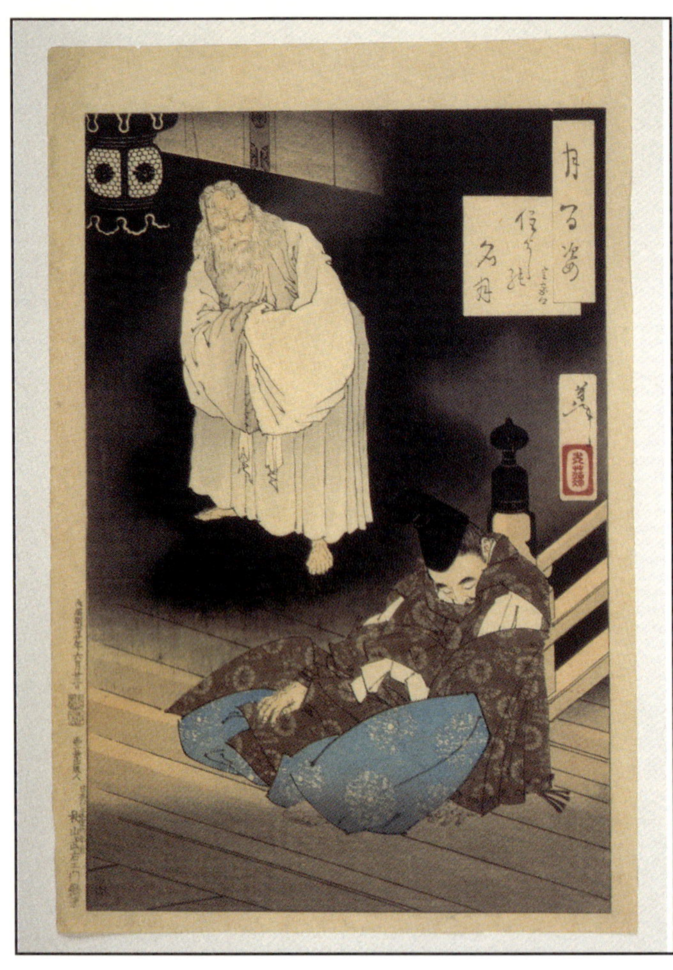

Yoshitoshi, oban tate-e, "The Moon of Sumiyoshi," from the series The 100 Aspects of the Moon, dated Meiji 20 (1887), 6th month 23rd day (June 23), signed "Yoshitoshi," seal Taiso, published by Akiyama Buemon, carver Yamamoto, fine impression, color, and condition, $800-1200.

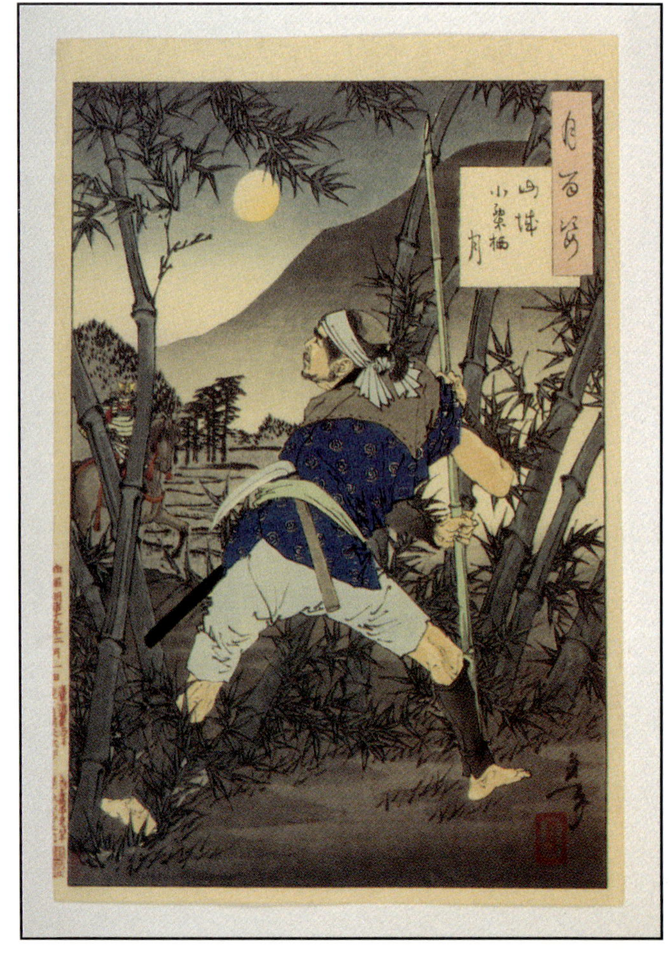

Yoshitoshi, oban tate-e, "Moon at Ogurusu: The Ambush of Akechi Mitsuhide by Moonlight," from the series The 100 Aspects of the Moon, signed "Yoshitoshi," seal Taiso, published by Akiyama, carver Enkatsu, dated Meiji 19 (1886), fine impression, color, and condition, $900-1200.

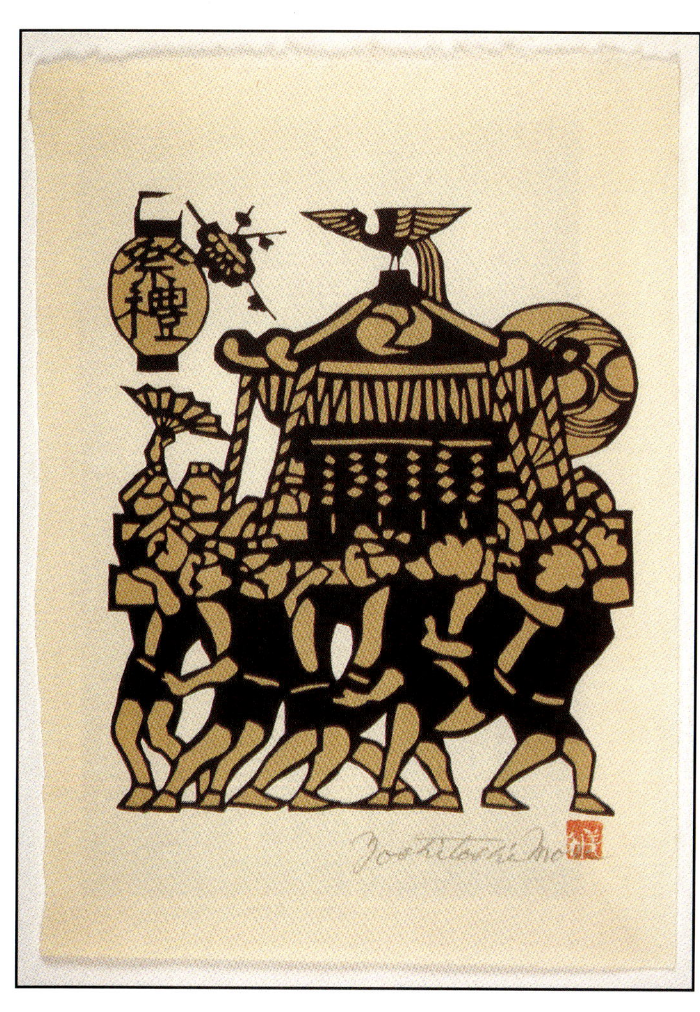

Yoshitoshi Mori, 12" x 16 1/2",stencil, "Festival," signed in pencil and sealed, unlimited edition, fine condition, $300-400.

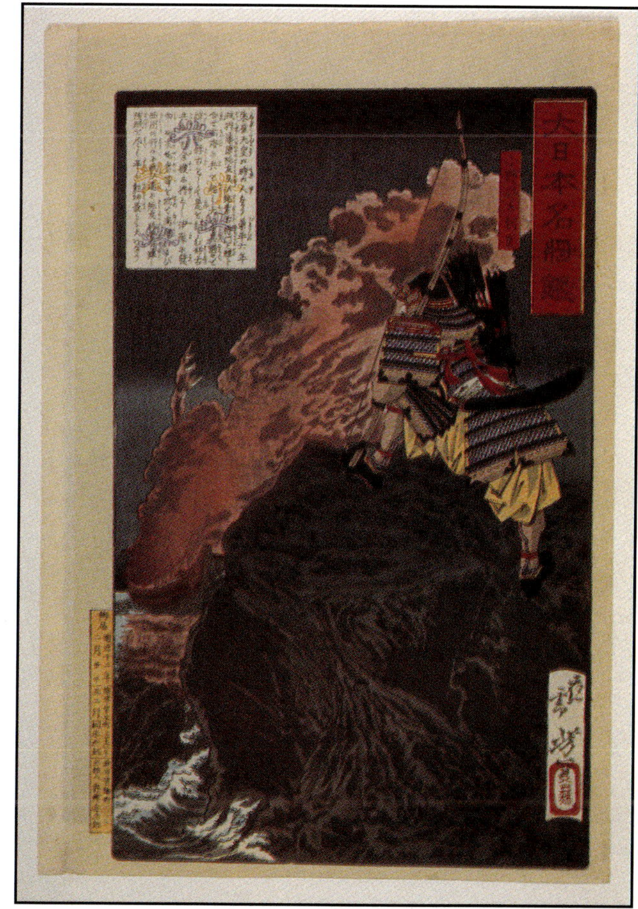

Yoshitoshi, oban tate-e, "Ono no Yoshifuru Ason," from the series A Mirror of Famous Japanese Generals, dated Meiji13 (1880), signed "Oju Yoshitoshi," published by Chujiro Funazu, sealed Taiso, very good color, condition, and impression, $575-875.

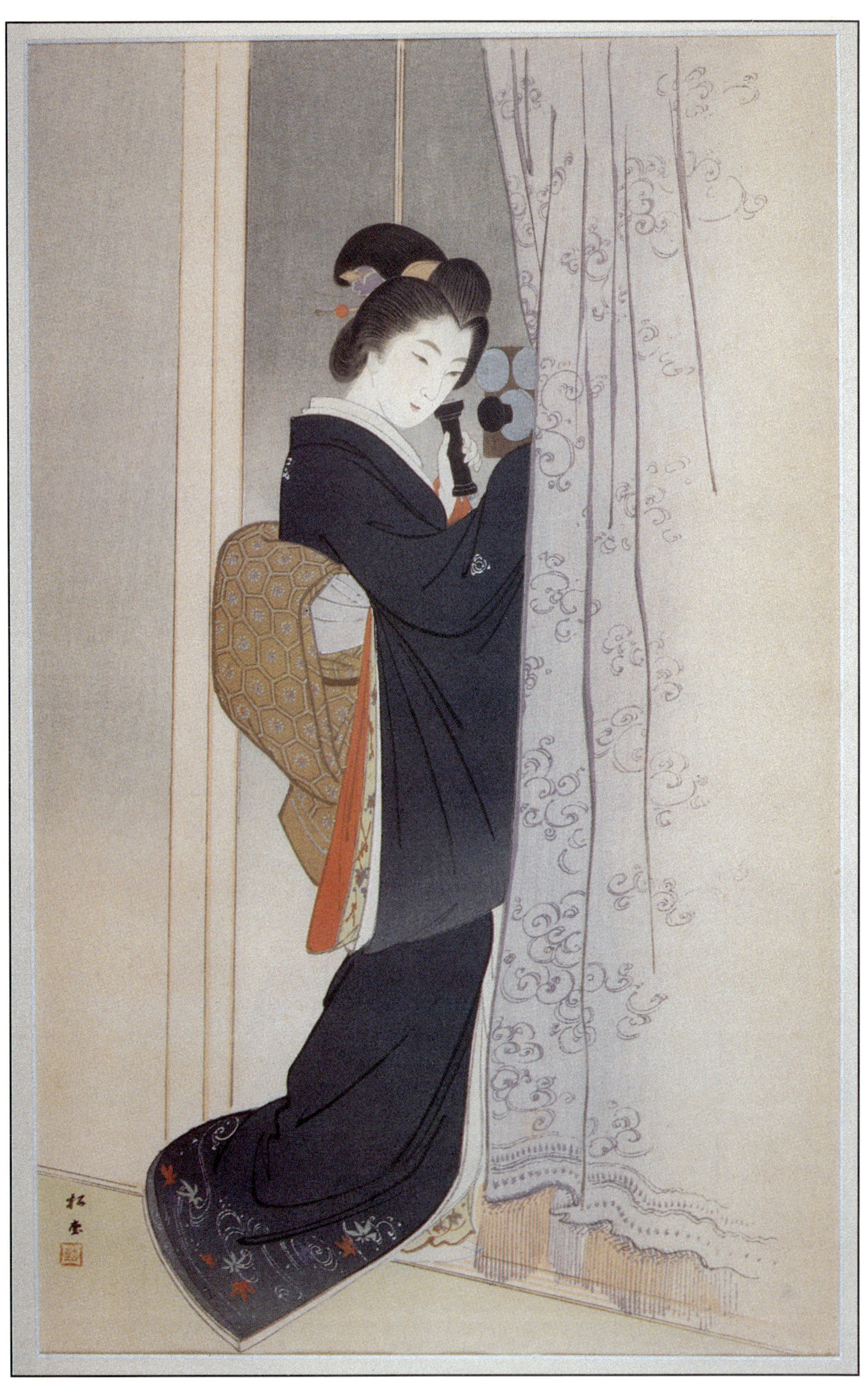

Yukawa Shodo, oban, "Bijin With Telephone," from the series One Hundred Beauties, Past and Present, signed and sealed "Shodo," dated 1903, mica, handpainted embellishment, fine impression, condition, and color, $1500-2000.

Appendix A

The Numerals

Characters		*Sino-Japanese*	*Pure Japanese*	*Reading for days of the month*	*Alternative readings for first month and first day*
1. 一	or 壹	ichi	hito(stu)	tsuitachi	
2. 二	or 貳	ni	futa(tsu)	futsu(ka)	
3. 三	or 参	san	mi(tsu)	mik(ka)	
4. 四	or 肆	shi	yo(tsu)	yok(ka)	shogatsu (first month) 正月
5. 五	or 伍	go	itsu(tsu)	itsu(ka)	
6. 六	or 陸	roku	mu(tsu)	mui(ka)	
7. 七	or 柒	shichi	nana(tsu)	nano(ka)	
8. 八	or 捌	hachi	ya(tsu)	yō (ka)	
9. 九	or 仇	ku	kokono(tsu)	kokono(ka)	tsuitachi (first day) 朔日
10. 十	or 拾	ju	to, tō	tō (ka)	
11. 十一		juichi		juichi(nichi)	
12. 十二		juni		juni(nichi)	shonichi (first day) 初日
15. 十五		jugo		jugo(nichi)	

Characters		*Sino-Japanese*	*Pure Japanese*	*Reading for days of the month*	*Alternative readings for first month and first day*
17. 十七		jushichi		jushichi(nichi)	ganjitsu (first day of the month) 元日
20. 二十	or 廿	niju		hatsu(ka)	
23. 二十三		nijusan			
29. 二十九		nijuku			
30. 三十	or 卅	sanju			
40. 四十		shiju			
50. 五十		goju			
60. 六十		rokuju			
77. 七十七		shichijushichi			
88. 八十八		hachijuhachi			
100. 百		hyaku			

Characters		*Sino-Japanese*	*Pure Japanese*	*Reading for days of the month*	*Alternative readings for first month and first day*
101. 百一		hyakuichi			
113. 百十三		hyakujusan			
500. 五百		gohyaku			
1,000. 千		sen			
2,000. 二千		nisen			
10,000. 万	or 萬	man			
100,000. 十万		juman			
1,000,000 百万		hyakuman			
10,000,000 千万	senman				
100,000,000 億兆	oku				

Appendix B

Japanese Year Dates and Chronology Arranged for Dating Prints

Year A.D	*Japanese Period (nengō)*	*Year of the Cycle*	*Zodiacal Name of the Year*	*Intercalary Month*	*Short Months*
1744	Yenkiō	1	Rat		1,3,5,6,8,9,12
1745		2	Ox		4,6,7,9,10,12
1746		3	Tiger	Jan./Feb.	3,5,7,9,10
1747		4	Hare		1,3,6,8,10,12
1748	Kwanyen	5	Dragon	Nov./Dec.	1,4,6,9,10,12
1749		6	Snake		2,3,5,8,11
1750		7	Horse		1,3,4,6,8,12
1751	Hōreki	8	Sheep	July/Aug.	2,4,5,6,8,11
1752		9	Monkey		2,4,5,7,8,11
1753		10	Cock		3,4,5,6,8,9,12
1754		11	Dog	March/April	2,5,6,8,9,12
1755		12	Wild Boar		3,5,7,9,10,12
1756		13	Rat	Dec./Jan.	3,5,8,10,11,12
1757		14	Ox		2,5,7,10,12
1758		15	Tiger		2,3,5,7,10,12
1759		16	Hare	Aug./Sept.	1,3,4,6,7,10
1760		17	Dragon		1,3,4,6,7,10
1761		18	Snake		2,4,5,7,8,10
1762		19	Horse	May/June	3,4,5,7,8,10
1763		20	Sheep		2,4,6,8,9,11
1764	Meiwa	21	Monkey		2,5,7,9,10,12
1765		22	Cock	Jan./Feb.	1,4,7,9,11,12

Year A.D	*Japanese Period (nengō)*	*Year of the Cycle*	*Zodiacal Name of the Year*	*Intercalary Month*	*Short Months*
1766		23	Dog		2,4,7,10,12
1777		24	Wild Boar	Oct./Nov.	1,3,5,7,9,12
1778		25	Rat		2,3,5,6,9
1769		26	Ox		1,3,4,6,7,9
1770		27	Tiger	July/Aug.	2,4,5,6,7,9
1771		28	Hare		1,3,5,7,8,10
1772	Anyei	29	Dragon	July/Aug.	1,4,6,8,9,11
1773		30	Snake		1,4,6,8,10,12
1774		31	Horse		1,4,6,8,10,12
1775		32	Sheep		2,4,6,9,12,12
1776		33	Monkey	Jan./Feb.	2,4,6,8,12
1777		34	Cock		2,3,5,6,8,12
1778		35	Dog	Aug./Sept.	3,4,6,7,8,12
1779		36	Wild Boar		2,4,6,7,9,12
1780		37	Rat		3,5,7,8,10,12
1781	Temmei	38	Ox	June/July	4,5,7,8,10,12
1782		39	Tiger		3,5,7,9,11
1783		40	Hare		1,3,6,8,10,12
1784		41	Dragon	Feb./March	1,3,5,8,10,12
1785		42	Snake		2,4,5,8,11
1786		43	Horse	Nov./Dec.	1,3,5,6,8,11
1787		44	Sheep		2,3,5,6,8,11
1788		45	Monkey		2,4,6,7,9,11
1789	Kwansei	46	Cock	July/Aug.	3,5,6,7,9,11
1790		47	Dog		2,5,7,8,10,12
1791		48	Wild Boar		2,5,7,9,11
1792		49	Rat	March/April	1,2,4,7,9,11
1793		50	Ox		1,3,5,7,10,12

Year A.D	*Japanese Period (nengō)*	*Year of the Cycle*	*Zodiacal Name of the Year*	*Intercalary Month*	*Short Months*
1794		51	Tiger	Dec./Jan.	2,4,5,7,11,12
1795		52	Hare		2,4,5,7,10
1796		53	Dragon		1,3,5,6,8,10
1797		54	Snake	Aug./Sept.	2,4,6,7,7,9
1798		55	Horse		1,4,6,7,9,10
1799		56	Sheep		1,5,6,8,10,11
1800		57	Monkey	May/June	2,4,6,8,10,12
1801		58	Cock		2,4,6,9,11
1802	Kiowa	59	Dog		1,3,4,6,10,12
1803		60	Wild Boar	Feb./March	1,3,4,6,9,12
1804	Bunkwa	1	Rat		2,4,5,7,9
1805		2	Ox	Sept./Oct.	1,3,5,6,7,8,12
1806		3	Tiger		3,5,6,7,9,12
1807		4	Hare		4,6,7,9,10
1808		5	Dragon	July/Aug.	1,4,6,7,9,10,12

Zodiac Year Cycle for Dating Woodblock Prints

Zodiac Year Sign		*Operative Years*					
RAT	ne	1804	1816	1828	1840	1852	1864
			(8)			(2)	
OX	ushi	1805	1817	1829	1841	1853	1865
		(8)			(1)		(5)
TIGER	tora	1806	1818	1830	1842	1854	1866
				(3)		(7)	
HARE	u	1807	1819	1831	1843	1855	1867
			(4)		(9)		
DRAGON	tatsu	1808	1829	1832	1844	1856	1868
				(11)			(4)
SNAKE	mi	1809	1821	1833	1845	1857	1869
						(5)	
HORSE	uma	1810	1822	1834	1846	1858	1870
			(1)		(5)		(10)
GOAT / RAM	hitsuji	1811	1823	1835	1847	1859	1871
		(2)		(7)			
MONKEY	saru	1812	1824	1836	1848	1860	1872
			(8)			(3)	
COCK	tori	1813	1825	1837	1849	1861	1873
		(11)			(4)		(6)
DOG	inu	1814	1826	1838	1850	1862	1874
				(4)		(8)	
BOAR	i	1815	1827	1839	1851	1863	1875
			(6)				

Japanese Chronology

1	2	3	4	5	6	7	8	9	10
一	二	三	四	五	六	七	八	九	十

NUMERALS

Rat	Ox	Tiger	Hare	Dragon	Snake	Horse	Goat	Ape	Cock	Dog	Boar
子	丑	寅	卯	辰	巳	午	未	申	酉	戌	亥

YEAR NAMES

Hōei	Shōtoku	Kōhō	Gembun	Kwampō	Enkō	Kwanen	Hōreki
宝永	正徳	享保	元文	寛保	延享	寛延	宝暦
1704	1711	1716	1736	1741	1744	1748	1751

Meiwa	Anei	Temmei	Kwansei	Kôwa	Bunkwa	Bunsei	Tempō
明和	安永	天明	寛政	享和	文化	文政	天保
1764	1772	1781	1789	1801	1804	1818	1830

Kōkwa	Kaei	Ansei	Man-en	Bunkyu	Genji	Kei-ō	Meiji
弘化	嘉永	安政	萬延	文久	元治	慶應	明治
1844	1848	1854	1860	1861	1864	1865	1868

NENGŌ

Appendix C

Common Character Index

Notes on character index

These characters are the ones most commonly used in Japanese artists names. Some characters may be read in more than one way. The character ichi is used in forming many names such as ip, ik, is, etc., the sounding depends on the character that follows. The character zan (san) is also pronounced yama in some cases.

NOTE: When you are researching an artist and cannot find a listing under one name, try looking under his school name. When using older books while researching you will find that the spelling has changed. The ones most commonly found are (Ye)/E., (Kwa)/Ka, (Gwa)/ga.

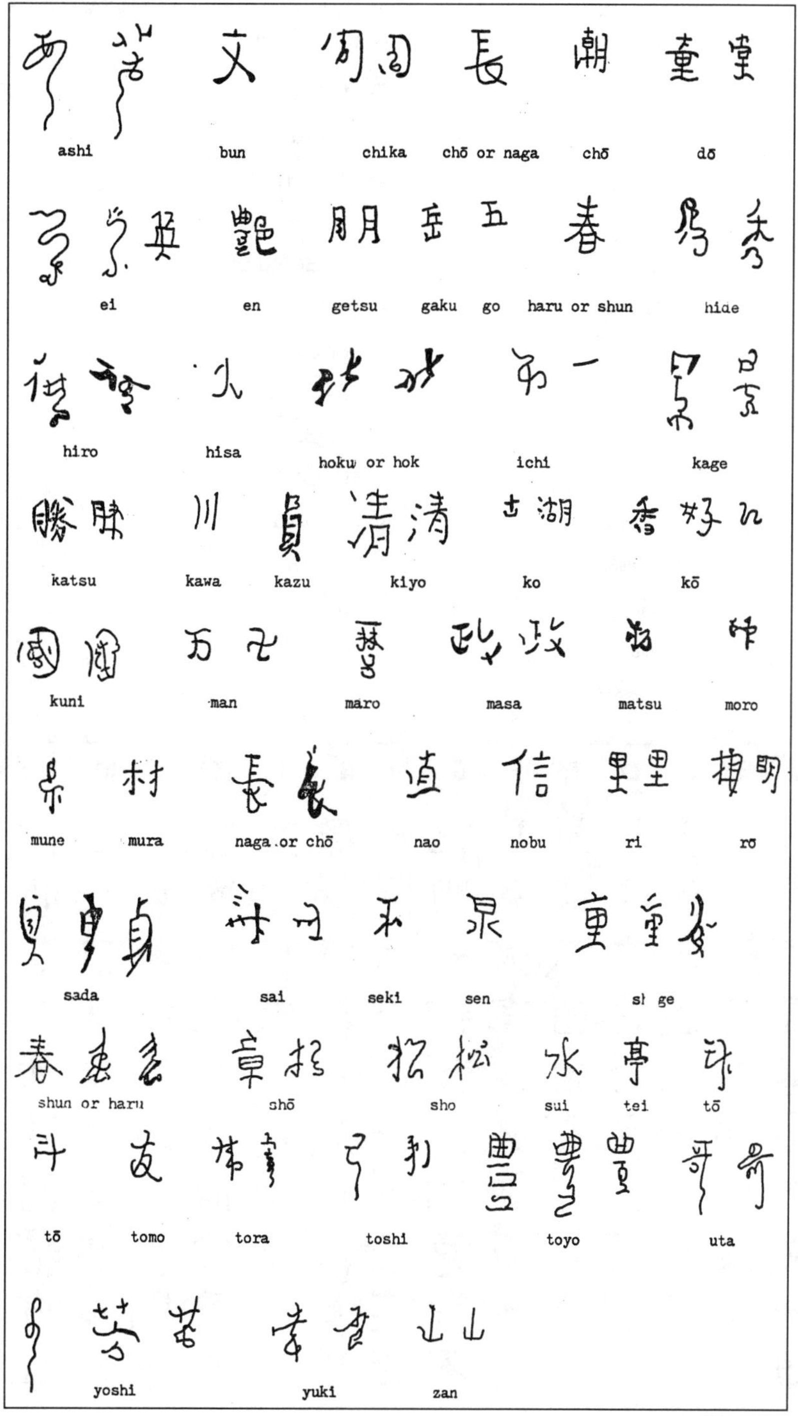

Appendix D

Characters Commonly Found in the Names of Ukiyo-e Artists

These characters are arranged in the alphabetical order of their transliterated readings. Japanese characters may often be read in two or more ways. In the following list, where the alternative reading is restricted to only one or two instances among the names of the artists, it is given in brackets after the common reading. Where alternative readings are fairly common, the character is given in alphabetical order two or three times. The table should be of use in turning the Japanese into the English transliteration, and may also be of use in turning the English back into the Japanese character. However, in this use it will obviously not be immediately apparent which of two or more characters with the same reading should be used and a choice will have to be made on other evidence in this instance. It is thought that the names of all known artists of this school are covered by the characters of the present table.

A. 1. An
2. Ashi
3. Aki
4. Ba
5. Be
6. Boku
7. Boku
8. Bun
9. Chi
10. Chika

B. 1. Chika
2. Chika
3. Cho
4. Cho
5. Cho
6. Cho
7. Cho
8. Cho
9. Do
10. Do

C. 1. Do
2. Da
3. Den
4. Fuji
5. Fu
6. Fusa
7. Fusa
8. Ga
9. Gaku
10. Gaku

D. 1. Gawa
2. Ge
3. Gen
4. Gen
5. Getsu or Ges
6. Gioku
7. Go
8. Go
9. Guchi
10. Gun

E. 1. Gwa
2. Gwa
3. Hachi
4. Haku
5. Haku
6. Hana
7. Han
8. Hara
9. Haru
10. Ha

F. 1. He
2. Hide
3. Hide
4. Hiko
6. Hisa
7. Hishi
8. Ho
9. Ho
10. Ho

G. 1. Hoku or Hok

	A	B	C	D	E	F	G	H	I	J	K	L	M	N	O
1	安	近	童	川	画	兵	北	治	監	蕙	錦	紅	麿	杭	森
2	芦	設	田	下	峨	英	細	壽	兼	溪	京	嵩	九	明	師
3	朋	鳥	傳	玄	八	秀	一	常	勝	軒	曉	與	政	峯	本
4	馬	朝	藤	源	碧	彥	衛	香	葛	氣	學	江	升	光	宗
5	邊	長	風	月	伯	廣	井	霞	景	喜	喬	好	雅	満	村
6	墨	調	房	玉	花	之	爲	狩	幾	龜	兆	湖	倍	宮	妙
7	卜	晁	宇	五	半	菱	衛	兼	河	枝	清	好	妍	門	南
8	文	蝶	雄	江	原	芳	意	景	川	木	公	花	眞	猛	年
9	地	藤	岳	口	春	抱	居	系	員	菊	香	國	磨	守	上
10	周	堂	嶺	郡	長	爲	石	上	主	吉	光	乇	松	益	野

2. Hoso

3. and 4. Ichi (Ik, Ip, It, Itsu or Kadzu) 5, 6, 7, 8, 9, all I

H. 1. Ji

2. Jui

3. Jo

4. Ka

5. Ka

6. Ka

7. Kado

8. Kage

9. Kage

10. Kami

I. 1. Kan

2. Kane

3. Katsu

4. Katsu

5. Katsu

6. Ki

7. Kawa

8. Kawa

9. Kazu

10. Kei

J. 1. Kei

2. Kei

3. Ken

4, 5, 6, 7, 8 all Ki

9. Kiku

10. Kichi

K. 1. Kin

2. Kio

3. Kio

4. Kio

5. Kio

6. Kita

7. Kiyo

8. Ko

9. and 10.Ko

L. 1., 2., 3., 4., 5., all Ko

6. Ko

7. Ko

8. Kwa

9. Kuni (Koku)

10. Man

M. 1. Maru

2. Maru

3. Masa

4. Masa

5. Masa

6. Masu

7. Masu

8. Ma

9. Maro

10. Matsu

N. 1. Matsu

2. Mei

3. Mine

4. Mitsu

5. Mura

6. Miya

7. Mon

8. Nen (Toshi)

9. No

10. No

O. 1. Mori

2. Moro

3. Moto

4. Mune

5. Mura

6. Myo

7. Nan

8. Nen (Toshi)

9. No

10. No

P. 1. Nabe

2. Naga

3. Naga

4. Naka

5. Nawo

6. Ni

7. Nichi

8. Nishi

9. Nobu

10. Nobu

Q. 1. Nobu

2. Nobu

3. Nori

4. Nori

5. O

6. O

7. O

8. Oku

9. Pitsu

10. Po

R. 1. Po

2. Raku

3. Ran

4. Ran

5. Rei

6. Ren

7. Ren

8. Ri

9. Rin

10. Ritsu (Riu)

S. 1. Riu

2. Riu

3. Ro

4. Riyo

	P	Q	R	S	T	U	V	W	X	Y	Z	Aa	Bb	Cc	Dd
1	鍋	濵	峰	栁	齋	泉	飾	嵩	田	且	留	洞	綱	尾	英
2	長	宣	樂	龍	鄉	仙	嶋	宗	太	種	富	樹	顧	翁	榮
3	水	完	蘭	棲	省	鮮	田	素	表	谷	乃	才	艶	谷	江
4	中	周	藍	旅	清	鴈	信	春	竹	貞	虎	到	豊	山	園
5	直	大	嶺	柳	而	四	焦	杦	瀧	亭	鳥	藤	雲	矢	豐
6	二	應	蓮	老	成	芝	洲	翠	濯	打	利	虎	歌	柳	遠
7	日	櫻	蓮	郎	雪	之	松	祐	爲	榮	俊	年	哥	安	燕
8	西	奥	理	六	石	玄	樵	鈴	民	權	年	若	上	保	容
9	信	筆	琳	貞	川	重	章	忠	丹	披	東	月	原	右	楊
10	延	鳳	立	載	扇	子	臺	廷	楳	時	等	經	渡	永	湯

5. Ro
6. Ro
7. Ro
8. Roku
9. Sada
10. Sai

T. 1. Sai
2. Sato
3. Sei
4. Sei
5. Sei
6. Sei
7. Sek (Sess) Set)
8. Seki
9. Sen
10. Sen

U. 1. Sen
2. Sen
3. Sen
4. Shu
5. Shi
6. Shi
7. Shi
8. Shiba
9. Shige
10. Shik(

V. 1. Shika
2. Shima
3. Shin
4. Shin
5. Shiu
6. Shiu
7. Sho
8. Sho
9. Sho
10. Sho

W. 1. So
2. So
3. So
4. Shun
5. Sugi
6. Sui
7. Suke
8. Suzu
9. Tada
10. Tada

X. 1. Ta
2. Ta
3. Taka
4. Take
5. Taki
6. Taku
7. Tame
8. Tami
9. Tan
10. Tan

Y. 1. Tan
2. Tane
3. Tani
4. Tei
5. Tei
6. Tei
7. Teru
8. Teru
9. To
10. Toki

Z. 1. Tome
2. Tomi
3. Tomo
4. Tora
5. Tori
6. Toshi
7. Toshi
8. Toshi
9. To or To
10. To

Aa. 1,2,3,4,5 all To
6. Tora
7. Toshi
8. Tsui
9. Tsuki
10. Tsune

Bb. 1. Tsuna
2. Tsura
3. Tsuya
4. Toyo
5. Um (Un)
6. Uta
7. Uta
8. Uye
9. Wara
10. Watana

Cc. 1. Wo
2. W›
3. Ya
4. Yama
5. Ya
6. Yama
7. Yasu
8. Yas

Dd. 1. Yei
2. Yei
3. Ye
4. Yama
5. Yen
6. Yen
7. Yen
8. Yo
9. Yo
10. Yu

	Ee	Ff	Gg	Hh	Ii
1	勇	芦	氣	辛	山
2	幽	義	雪	善	亢
3	芳	湯	之	三	藏

Appendix E

Signatures of Ukiyo-e Artists of the 18th and 19th Centuries

Ashiaki (fl.ca.1820's) Osaka school

Ashihiro (fl. ca. 1816-36) Osaka school. Pupil of Ashikuni

Ashihiro (Same as above)

Ashikyo (fl. ca. 1816-17) Osaka school

Ashikyo (fl. ca. 1816-1817) Osaka school

Ashikuni (ca. 1775-1818) Osaka school

Ashikuni (Same as above)

Ashimaru (fl. 1803-1830's) Osaka school

Ashinuki (fl. ca. 1817-31) Osaka school

Ashisato (fl. ca. 1800-16) Osaka school

Ashitomo (fl. ca. 1800-30) Osaka school, pupil of Ashikuni

Ashiyuki (fl. ca. 1814-33) Osaka school, pupil of Ashikuni

Baien (fl. ca. 1819) Osaka school

Baien (fl. ca. 1819-30) Osaka school

Baikei (fl. 1816) Osaka school

Bairi (1844-95) Kyoto painter, designed kacho-e

Bosia (1752-1826)

Buncho (fl. ca. 1765-92), (fl. ca. 1764-1801)

Bunkyo (1767-1830) pupil of Eishi

Bunro (fl. 1800-10) pupil of Buncho

Chikakuni (fl. ca. 1821-23) Osaka school, pupil of Ashikuni and Yoshikuni

Chikamaro, name used by Kyosai

Chikanobu (1838-1912) pupil of Kunichika, (fl. early 19th c.), pupil of Utamaro

Chikashige (fl. second half 19th c.) pupil of Kunichika

Chincho (1679-1754) pupil of Kiyonobu. Rare

Choki (fl. late 18th to early 19th c.) A great master

Ebikane (fl. ca. 1827-28) Osaka school

Eiju (fl. ca. 1830's-50's) Osaka school, (fl. ca. 1790's) pupil of Eishi

Eiri Chokyosai (fl. ca. 1790's-early 1800's), pupil of Eishi

Eiri Rekisentei (fl. ca. 1790's), (fl. early 19th c.), pupil of Eizan

Eisen (1790-1848) pupil of Eizan

Eishi (1756-1829) Master printmaker and painter

Eisho (fl. ca. 1790's) pupil of Eishi, (fl. early 19th c.), (fl. mid-19th c.)

Eisui (fl. ca. 1790-1823) pupil of Eishi)

Eizan (1787-1867) founder of the Kikugawa style, (fl. late 18th c.)

Enjaku (fl. ca. 1858-65) Osaka school

Enkyo (1749-1803)

Enshi (fl. ca. 1785-95) pupil of Shunsho

Fujikuni (fl. mid 1820's) Osaka school

Fujinobu (fl. ca. 1750's-60's) possible pupil of Shigenaga. Rare

Fusatane (fl. ca. 1849-70) pupil of Sadafusa

Gakutei (1786-1868) pupil of Shuei and Hokkei

Ginko (fl. 1874-97)

Gokyo (fl. ca. 1795), pupil of Eishi

Goshichi (ca. 1776-1831), pupil of Eizan

Goyo (1880-1912) master printmaker

Gyokuho (fl. 1810's), early name of Gyokuzan II

Gyokusen (fl. 1830's), Osaka school, rare

Gyokushu (fl. 1834), probably a pronunciation of Tamakuni

Hanzan (fl. 1850) Osaka school

Harunobu (ca. 1724-70), a great master. First to use full color

Harushige. Name used by Kokan on prints in the Harunobu style

Hatsukuni (fl. ca. 1820's) Osaka school

Hidekuni (fl. 1820's) Osaka school

Hidemaro (fl. ca. 1820's) Kyoto school, (fl. early 19th c.) pupil of Utamaro

Hikokuni (fl. ca. 1821-24) Osaka school, pupil of Ashikuni

Hirokuni, name used by Hirosada until 1847, early name used by Hironobu II

Hirokage (fl. ca. 1855-65) pupil of Hiroshige

Hironobu I (fl. ca. 1851-70) Osaka school, Hironobu II (fl. 1844-90)

Hirosada (fl. ca. 1820's-60's) Osaka school, pupil of Kunimasa

Hokkai (fl. ca. 1832)

Hokkei (fl. can 1818-20's) Osaka school, 1780-1850) pupil of Hokusai, (fl. 1830's)

Hokucho (fl. ca. 1820-30) Osaka school, pupil of Hokushu, (fl. ca. 1850's) Osaka

Hokuei (fl. ca. 1820's-37) Osaka school, pupil of Hokushu

Hokuga (fl. ca. 1821-26) Osaka school

Hokugan (fl. ca. 1820-32) Osaka school, pupil of Yoshikuni

Hokui (fl. ca. 1830-40) Osaka school, pupil of Hokusai

Hokuju (fl. ca. 1830-40) Osaka school, (fl. 1789-1818) pupil of Hokusai

Hokumei (fl. 1830's) Osaka school, pupil of Hokuei

Hokumyo (fl. ca. 1830-37) Osaka school, possibly early name used by S. Shinshi

Hokusei (fl. ca. 1826) Osaka school, pupil of Hokushu

Hokusei name used by Hokkai before 1832

Hokusho (fl. ca. 1822-32) Osaka school

Hokushu (fl. ca. 1808-32) Osaka school Pupil of Hokusai

Hokusui (fl. ca. 1860) Osaka school

Hokusui (fl. ca. 1854-57) Osaka school. Name used by Yoshitoyo I

Hokuto (fl. ca. 1835) Osaka school

Hiroshige (1797-1858) Edo artist. Pupil of Toyohiro. Master printmaker. Famous ofr his landscapes and kacho-e. The period of the signature style is below each one

Hiroshige II (1826-69), pupil and adopted son of Hiroshige. Used name from 1858-65

Hiroshige III (1843-94), pupil of Hiroshige. Used name from 1865 on

Hokusai (1760-1849), pupil of Shunsho. Considered one of the world's greatest draftsmen. Very prolific. Used many names which are listed below with their periods of use. Some of these names were also used by his pupils later on.

Shunro: 1779-94

Banri?: 1780-82

Zewasai: 1781-82

Gyobutsui: 1782

Gumbatei: 1785-94

Shishoku Ganko?: 1788-1810, used on shunga

Sori: 1795-98

Hyakurin Sori?:1795-97

Tawara-ya Sori II or IV: 1796?

Hokusai Sori: 1979-98

Hokusai: 1797-1819

Kako: 1798-1811

Fusenkyo Hokusai: 1799

Tatsumasa Shinsei: 1799-1810

Senkozan: 1803

Kintaisha: 1805-9

Gakyojin: 1800-8

Kyukyushin: 1805

Gakyo-rojin: 1805-06, 1834-49

Katsushika: ca. 1807-24

Taito: 1811-20

Kyorian Bainen: 1812

Raishin: 1812-15

Tengudo Nettetsu: 1814

Iitsu: 1820-34

Zen saki no Hokusai Iitsu: 1821-33

Fusenkyo Iitsu: 1822

Getshi-rojin: 1828

Manji: 1831-49

Tsuchimochi Nisaburo: 1834

Hyakusho Hachiemon: 1834-46

Miura-ya Hachiemon: 1834-46

Fujiwara Iitsu: 1847-49

Ikkei (fl. ca. 1870's) Edo artist, pupil of Hiroshige II

Kagematsu (fl. ca. 1830's-40's) Osaka school

Kagetoshi (fl. ca. 1830's) Osaka school, pupil of Sadakage

Katsunobu (fl. ca. 1716-35), two artists of this name at this time

Keisai (1764-1824) pupil of Shigemasa, name used by Eisen

Kishikuni (fl. ca. 1820's) Osaka school

Kiyochika (1847-1915) innovative artist, who used western techniques

Kiyoharu (fl. ca. 1820's-30's) Osaka school, (fl. ca. 1700-30), (fl. ca. 1704-20)

Kiyohiro (fl. ca. 1737-76) Torii school

Kiyokuni (fl. ca. 1827) Osaka school, (fl. ca. 1830's-40's) Torii school

Kiyomasu (fl. ca. 1696-1716), K. II (1706-63) possibly same as Kiyonobu II

Kiyomine (1787-1868) Torii school, pupil of Kiyonaga

Kiyomitsu (ca. 1735-85) K. II (1787-1868) K. III (1832-92) all Torii school

Kiyonaga (1752-1815) pupil of Kiyomitsu I. Last major Torii artist

Kiyonobu (1664-1729) founder of the Torii school. K. II (1706-63)

Kiyosada (fl. ca. 1848) Osaka school, (1844-1901) Torii school

Kiyoshiga (fl. 1720's-60's) Torii school, pupil of Kiyonobu I

Kiyotada (fl. 1720-50), K. II (fl. early 19th c.), K. III (1817-25) all Torii school

Kiyotomo (fl. 1720's-40's) Torii school, possible pupil of Kiyonobu I

Kiyotsune (fl. ca. 1757-79) Torii school, pupil of Kiyomitsu I

Kochoro (1848-1920) Utagawa school, became Kunisada III in 1889

Kokan (1747-1818), first to produce copperplate engraving

Konobu (fl. 1867-80's), son and pupil of Sadanobu I, became Sadonobu II

Koryusai (fl. ca. 1764-88) possibly a pupil of Shigenaga

Kosei (fl. 1860)

Koson, early name used by Shoson

Kuniaki (1835-88) Yokohama school, pupil of Kunisada

Kunichika (1835-1900) pupil of Toyohara Chikanobu and Kunisada

Kuniharu (1803-39) pupil of Toyokuni II, (fl. ca. 1840's-50's) Osaka school

Kunihiro (fl. ca. 1815-43) Osaka school, pupil of Toyokuni II

Kunihisa II (1832-91) Yokohama school, pupil of Kunisada, K. I (1800's-1810's)

Kunikage (fl. ca. 1831) Osaka school

Kunikazu (fl. ca. 1849-67) Osaka school, pupil of Kunisada

Kunikiyo (fl. mid 19th c.) Utagawa school, pupil of Toyokuni I

Kunimaru (1794-1829) Tuagawa school, pupil of Toyokuni I

Kunimasa (1773-1810) Utagawa school, pupil of Toyokuni I

Kunimatsu (fl. mid-late 19th c.) Utagawa school, pupil of Toyokuni II

Kunimune (fl. ca. 1818) Utagawa school, K. II (fl. ca. 1825-44) both pupils Toyokuni

Kunimitsu (fl. 1801-18) Utagawa school, pupil of Toyokuni I

Kunimori (fl. 1818-43) pupil of Toyokuni I, K. II (1848-60) pupil of Kunisada

Kuninaga (?-1829) Utagawa school, pupil of Toyokuni I

Kuninao (1793-1854) Utagawa school, pupil of Toyokuni I

Kunisada (1786-1865) prolific artist, became Toyokuni III in 1844*

Kunishige, name used by Shigeharu

Kuniteru (1808-76) Utagawa school, pupil of Kunisada and Toykuni, (fl. mid-19th c.) Utagawa school, pupil of Kunisada, (fl. early Meiji era), Utagawa school pupil of Kunisada and Kunishika, K. II (1829-74) pupil of Kunisada

Kunitomo (early 19th c.) pupil of Toyokuni II

Kunitora (fl. ca. 1810's-30's) Utagawa school, pupil of Toyokuni I

Kunitoshi (fl. 1847-99) Utagawa school, pupil of Kunisada and Kunitsugu

Kunitsuna (1805-68) Utagawa school, pupil of Toyokuni I

Kunitsuru (fl. ca. 1830's) Utagawa school, pupil of Toyokuni II

Kuniyasu (1794-1834) Utagawa school, pupil of Toyokuni I

Kuniyoshi (1798-1861) Utagawa school, pupil of Toyokuni, prolific artist with his own unusual style using western techniques

Kaigetsude Doshu (fl. 18th c.) Kaigetsudo is a school of painters and printmakers founded by Ando Kaigetsudo. The following pupils all used the name: Anchi, Dohan, Doshu, Doshin and Doshu. Old spelling Kwagetsudo.

Kyosai (Gyosai) (1831-89) Innovative painter and printmaker. Pupil of Kuniyoshi

Kunisada II (1823-80) pupil of Kunisada. Used this name from 1846-70

Kunisada III (1848-1920) pupil of Kunisada II, started to use this name in 1889, both Utagawa school

Magosaburo, early name used by Ishikawa Toyonobu

Mangetsudo (fl. ca. 1760), possibly name used by a publisher for pirating activities. Rare

Masakuni (fl. ca. 1823) Osaka school, pupil of Yoshikuni

Masanobu Kitao (1761-1816), pupil of Shigemasa

Masanobu Okumura (1686-1764), a major innovator in printmaking

Masayoshi (1764-1824) pupil of Shigemasa

Masuharu (fl. ca. 1850's) Osaka school, pupil of Kunimasu

Masunobu (fl. 1770's), (fl. ca. 1850's) Osaka school, pupil of Kunimasu

Minko (fl. ca. 1764-72)

Mitsunobu (fl. ca. 1730's-60's) Osaka school, pupil of Sukenobu

Moromasa (ca. 1712-72) Hishikawa school, pupil of Moroshige

Moronobu (ca. 1618-94) Pioneer of Ukiyo-e. Founder of the Hishikawa school

Munehiro (fl. ca. 1846-67) Osaka school, pupil of Hirosada

Nagahide (fl. ca. 1804-48) Osaka school

Nagakuni (fl. ca. 1814-20's) Osaka school, pupil of Nagahide

Nan yosai early name used by Hokuga

Naomasa (?) Yokohama school, possibly pupil of Kuninao

Niho (fl. ca. 1850's) Osaka school

Nobuharu (fl. ca. 1832) Osaka school

Nobuhiro (fl. ca. 1839) Osaka school, pupol of Sadanobu

Nobukatsu (fl. ca. 1824-41) Osaka school, pupil of Sadamasa and Shigenobu

Nobumasa (fl. ca. 1832-48) Osaka school

Nobumitsu (fl. ca. 1850's) Osaka school

Nobusada (fl. ca. 1823-32) Osaka school, pupil of Shigenobu

Osencho (fl. early 19th c.) pupil of Eisen?

Rankosai (fl. ca. 1805) Osaka school

Reizan (fl. ca. 1871) Osaka school

Riko (fl. ca. mid 1820's) Osaka school

Roko (fl. ca. 1790's-1800's) Osaka school, pupil of Shokosai or Ryukosai

Ryukoku (fl. ca. 1800's), follower of Utamaro

Ryukosai (1772-1816), a founder of the Osaka school. Rare

Ryunsai (fl. ca. 1788), follower of Kiyonaga

Sadafusa (fl. ca. 1825-50) Utagawa school, pupil of Kunichika

Sadaharu (fl. ca. 1830-44) Osaka school

Sadahide (1807-73) Utagawa school, pupil of Kunisada

Sadahiro I (fl. ca. 1825-75) Utagawa school, pupil of Kunisada, worked in Osaka

Sadahiro II (fl. ca. 1864-76) Osaka school pupil of Hirosada

Sadakage (fl. ca. 1820's-30's) Utagawa school, pupil of Kunisada, worked in Osaka

Sadamasa (fl. ca. 1830's-40's) Osaka school, pupil of Sadanobu

Sadamasa, same as above

Sadamasu I, name used by Kunimasu from 1834-48

Sadanobu I (1809-79) Osaka school, S. II (1848-86) Osaka school, son of I

Sadanobu (fl. ca. 1730's)

Sadashige, name used by Kuniteru II

Sadatora (fl. ca. 1817-30's) Utagawa school, pupil of Kunisada, worked in Osaka

Sadatsuga (fl. ca. 1835-39) Osaka school, pupil of Kunisada

Sadayoshi (fl. ca. 1760's), (fl. ca. 1837-60's) all Osaka school

Sadayuki (fl. ca. 1839-40's) Osaka school, pupil of Sadamasu

Seiko (fl. 1810's-20's) Osaka school

Sekiho (fl. early 19th c.) pupil of Sekien

Sekijo (fl. ca. 1800-7) pupil of Sekien

Senman (fl. ca. 1820's) Osaka school

Sharaku (fl. 1794-5) produced 159 prints in ten months, known for psychological insight

Shibakuni (fl. 1821-26) Osaka school, pupil of Yoshikuni

Shigefusa (fl. ca. 1740's-60's) follower of Sukenobu, (fl. ca. 1820's) Osaka school

Shigefusa II (fl. ca. 1850) Osaka school

Shigeharu (1803-53) Osaka school, pupil of Shigenobu

Shigehiro (fl. ca. 1865-78) Osaka school

Shigekatsu (fl. ca. mid 1820's) Osaka school

Shigemaro (fl. ca. 1816) Osaka school

Shigemasa (1739-1820) one of the great teachers of his time

Shigenara (ca. 1697-1756), great teacher and innovator

Shigenao (fl. 1824-41) Osaka school, became Nobukatsu in 1929

Shigenobu (fl. can 1716-36) Torii style, (fl. 1720-40) Masanobu style, (fl. ca 1724-1735) Nishikawa style, (fl. ca. 1764-79) Harunobu style, (1787-1832 pupil of Hokusai, S. II (fl. ca. 1820's) pupil of Shigenobu, name used by Hiroshige II

Shikan (fl. can 1778-1838) Osaka school, name used by Nakamura Utaemon III

Shikimaro (fl. ca. 1810) pupil of Tsukimaro

Shimamaru (fl. ca. 1830) Osaka school

Shiseki (1712-86) Nagasaki school

Shicho, name used by Choki

Shokosai (fl. ca. 1795-1809) one of the founders of the Osaka school

Shoraku (fl. ca. late 1810's) Osaka school

Shoson (1877-1945) pupil of Kason, known for his Kacho-e

Shozan (fl. 1875) Yolohama school?

Shujin (fl. ca. 1858-61) pupil of Hiroshige, known for his Kacho-e

Shucho (fl. ca. 1790's-early 1800's) pupil of Buncho

Shuncho (fl. ca. 1815-23) Osaka school, pupil of Shunkosai

Shuncho, early name of Hokusho

Shuncho Gajuken (fl. ca. mid-1820's) Osaka school

Shuncho Katsukawa (fl. ca. 1780-95) pupil of Shunsho

Shundo (fl. 1780-92) pupil of Shunsui and Shuncho

Shunei (fl. ca. 1810's-20's) Osaka school

Shunei (1762-1819) pupil of K. Shunsho, a leader of teh Katsukawa school

Shunjo (fl. ca. 1830's) Osaka school, (?-1787) pupil of Shuncho

Shunju (fl. 1828-29) Osaka school, pupil of Hokuei

Shunkei (fl. ca. 1840) Osaka school

Shunkin (fl. ca. 1816's) Osaka school

Shunko II, name used by Shusen (1762-1830) after 1812

Shunko, name used by Hokushu from 1810-18

Shunko (1743-1812) pupil of Shunsho, a leader of the Katsukawa school

Shunkyo (fl. ca. 1814) Osaka school

Shunkyo (fl. ca. 1800's) pupil of Shunsho and Shuntei

Shunman (1757-1820) pupil of Shigemasa

Shun'o, (?) Osaka school

Shunpo (fl. ca. 1820's) Osaka school

Shunsei (fl. ca. 1820's) Osaka school, pupil of Shunshi

Shunsen (1762-ca. 1830) Katsukawa school, pupil of Shun'ei

Shunsen (fl. ca. 1780-90's) Katsukawa school, pupil of Shunsho

Shunshi (fl. ca. mid-1820's-30's) Osaka school, pupil of G. Shunshi

Shunshi, G. (fl. ca. 1820's) Osaka school

Shunshi (fl. ca. 1826-28) Osaka school

Shunshin (fl. ca. 1820's) Osaka school, pupil of Hokushu

Shunsho (1726-93) founder of the Katsukawa school

Shunsho, name used by Hokusho, (fl. ca. 1830's-40's) Utagawa school

Shunshi (fl. ca. 1740's-60's) pupil of Chochun

Shuntei (1770-1820) Katsukawa school, pupil of Shun'ei, (fl. ca. mid 1810's-early 20's), Osaka school, (fl. ca. 1820's) Osaka school

Shuntoku (fl. ca. 1820's) Katsukawa school, pupil of Shun'ei

Shunyei, Old spelling of Shun'ei

Shunyo, name used by Hokei from 1813-18

Shun-Yosai, go of Hokkei

Shunzan (fl. ca. 1827-29) Katsukawa school of Shunsho

Sugakudo, a name of Shujin's

Sukenobu (1671-1751) important member of teh Kyoto school

Taito II (fl. ca. 1810-53) pupil of Hokusai (who was Taito I)

Tamakuni (fl. 1823) Osaka school, (fl. 1834) Osaka school

Terushige (fl. can 1715-25) Katsukawa school

Tokyo (fl. ca. 1860's) Osaka school

Tomikuni (fl. ca. 1821-22) Osaka school

Tominobu (fl. mid 18th c.) Miyagawa school

Tomiyuki (fl. can 1850's) Osaka school

Torin I (fl. late 18th c.) founder of the Tsutsumi school, T. II (fl. ca. 1789-1801) T. III (ca. 1743-1820)

Toshiei (fl. late 1800's) possibly a pupil of Yoshitoshi

Toshikuni, name used by Hokugan from 1816-32

Toshinobu (fl. ca. 1717-50) pupil of Masanobu, (fl. ca. 1857-86) pupil of Yoshitoshi

Toshiyoshi (fl. ca. 1890's) possibly a pupil of Yoshitoshi

Toyoharu (1735-1825) founder of the Utagawa school

Toyohide (fl. ca. 1839-41) Osaka school, (fl. ca. 1860's) Osaka school

Toyohisa (fl. ca. 1801-18) Utagawa school, pupil of Toyoharu, T. II (fl. ca. 1830's)

Toyokawa, name was used by Hikokuni in 1821

Toyokuni I (1769-1825) Utagawa school, pupil of Toyoharu

Toyokuni II (1777-1835) pupil of Toyokuni I, used name off and on from 1825

Toyokuni III (Kunisada) took this name in 1844, pupil of Toyokuni I, his name is always enclosed

Toyomasa (fl. ca. 1770-80) pupil of I. Toyonobu

Toyonobu, I (1711-85), (fl. 1770-80), (?-1886) Utagawa school, pupil of Kunihisa

Toyoshige II (fl. ca. late 1800's) Yokohama school

Tsukimaro (fl. ca. 1800's-20's) Kitagawa school, pupil of Utamaro

Umekuni (fl. ca. 1823-26) Osaka school, pupil of Yoshikuni

Umekuni, same as above

Unsen (fl. ca. 1870's)

Utakuni (1777-1827) Kamigata school, Osaka artist

Utamaro (1754-1806) one of the great masters, U. II (?-1831

Utatora (?) Yokohama school

Yasuji (1864-89) pupil of Kiyochika

Yoshiiku (1833-1904) Utagawa school, pupil of Kuniyoshi

Yoshiharu (1828-88) Utagawa school, pupil of Kuniyoshi

Yoshikazu (fl. 1850-70) Yokohama school, pupil of Kuniyoshi

Yoshikuni (1855-1903) Kyoto artist, pupil of Yoshiume

Yoshikuni (fl. ca. 1803-40) Osaka school, pupil of Ashikuni

Yoshimine (fl. ca. 1855-75) Osaka school, pupil of Yoshiume

Yoshimitsu (fl. ca. 1873-80) Osaka school, pupil of Toshitaki

Yoshinobu (fl. ca. 1730's-40's) follower of Kiyonobu, (fl. ca. early 1840's) Osaka school, (1848-54) pupil of Kuniyoshi

Yoshitaki (1841-99) Kamigata school, pupil of Yoshiume

Yoshitomi (fl. ca. 1850's-70's) Yokohama school, pupil of Kuniyoshi

Yoshitora (fl. ca. 1850-80) Utagawa school, pupil of Kuniyoshi

Yoshitoshi (1839-92) leading artist of the Meiji era. pupil of Kuniyoshi. The first two signatures were used after 1873

Yoshitoyo (fl. 1840-60) Osaka school, Y. II (fl. ca. 1890's-1900) Osaka school, son of Yoshimine, (1830-66) Kamigate-e school, pupil of Kuniyoshi

Yoshitsuga (fl. ca. 1830's) Osaka school, pupil of Sadayosh

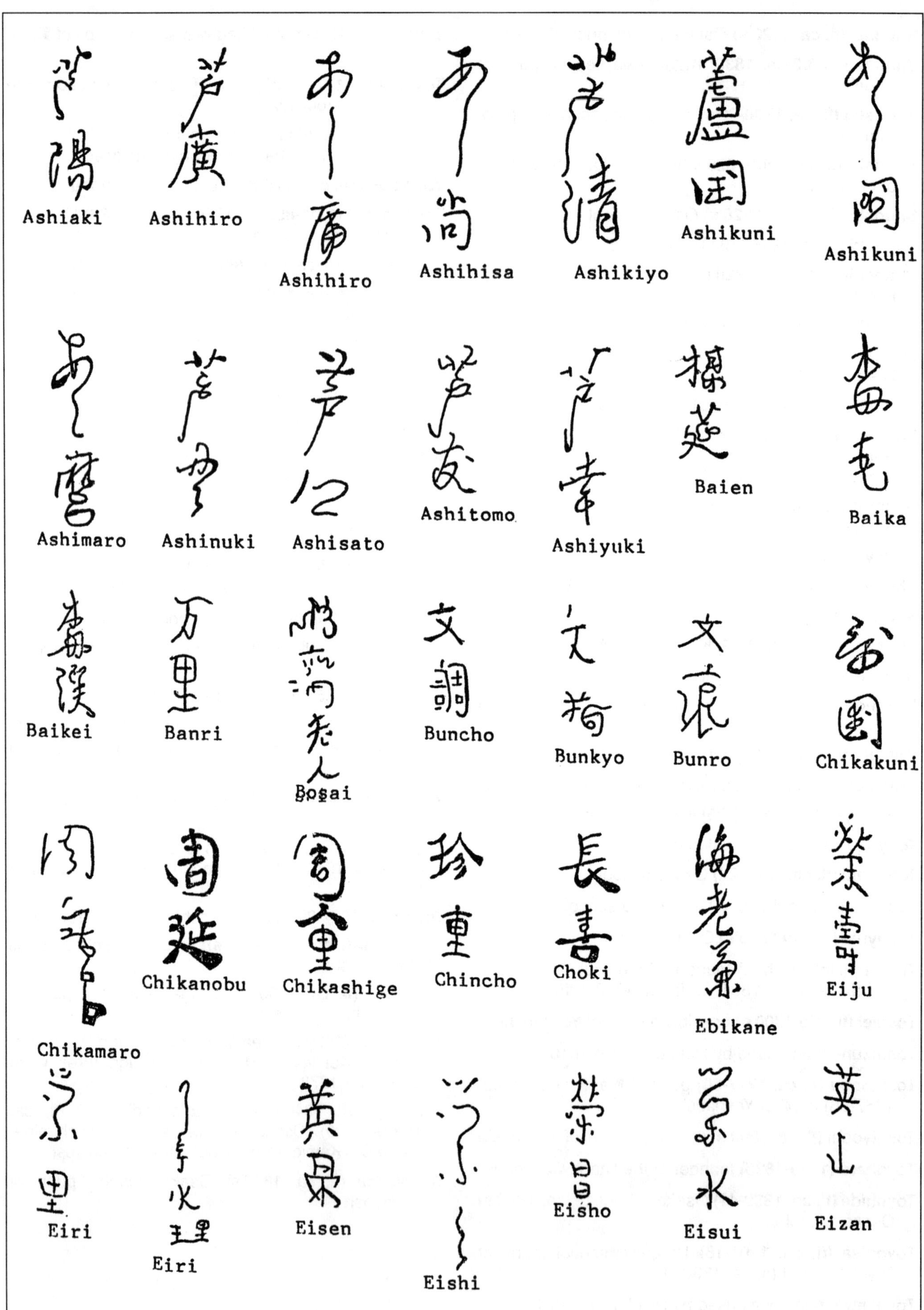
Ashiaki
Ashihiro
Ashihiro
Ashihisa
Ashikiyo
Ashikuni
Ashikuni
Ashimaro
Ashinuki
Ashisato
Ashitomo
Ashiyuki
Baien
Baika
Baikei
Banri
Bosai
Buncho
Bunkyo
Bunro
Chikakuni
Chikamaro
Chikanobu
Chikashige
Chincho
Choki
Ebikane
Eiju
Eiri
Eiri
Eisen
Eishi
Eisho
Eisui
Eizan

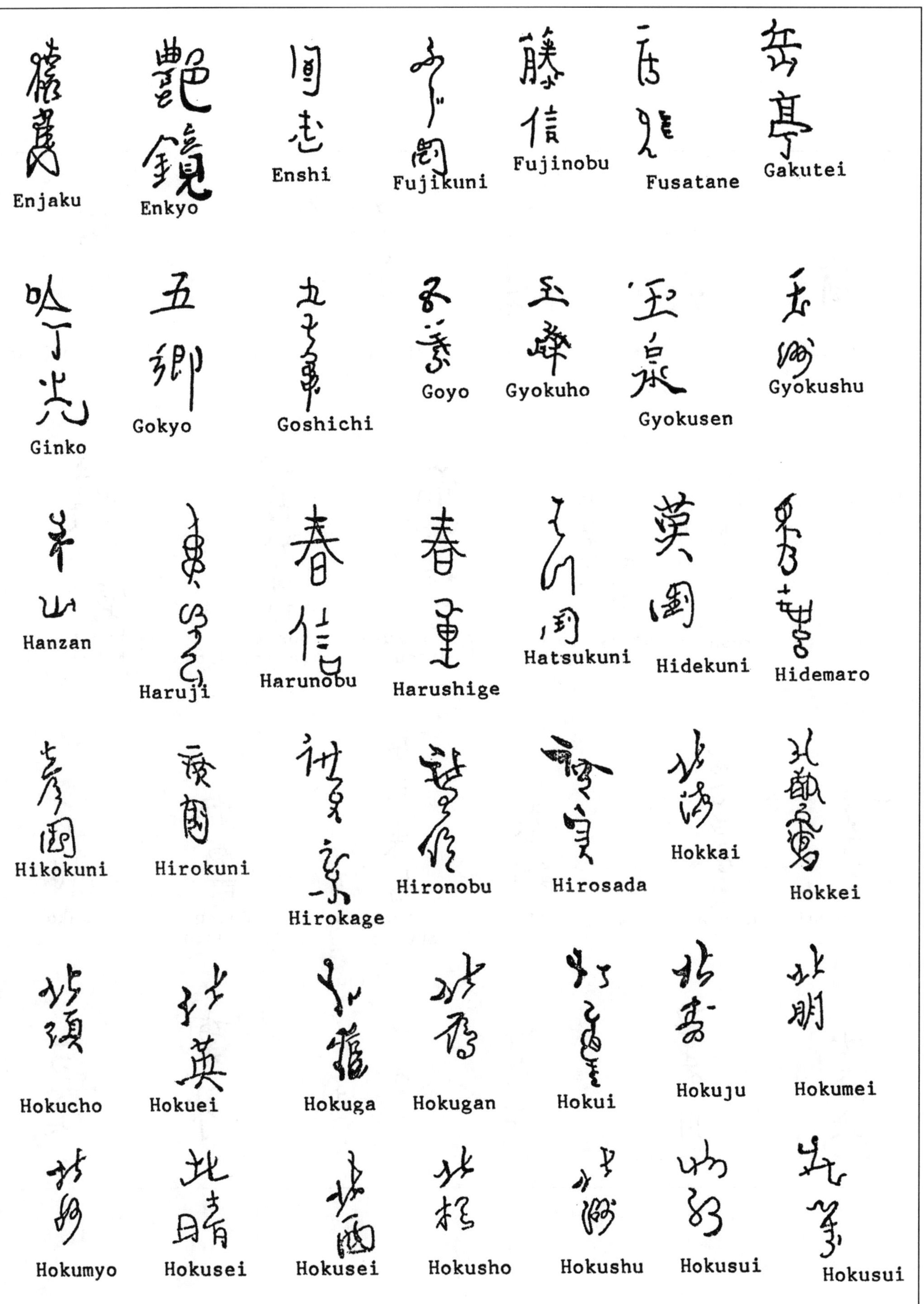
Enjaku
Enkyo
Enshi
Fujikuni
Fujinobu
Fusatane
Gakutei
Ginko
Gokyo
Goshichi
Goyo
Gyokuho
Gyokusen
Gyokushu
Hanzan
Haruji
Harunobu
Harushige
Hatsukuni
Hidekuni
Hidemaro
Hikokuni
Hirokuni
Hirokage
Hironobu
Hirosada
Hokkai
Hokkei
Hokucho
Hokuei
Hokuga
Hokugan
Hokui
Hokuju
Hokumei
Hokumyo
Hokusei
Hokusei
Hokusho
Hokushu
Hokusui
Hokusui

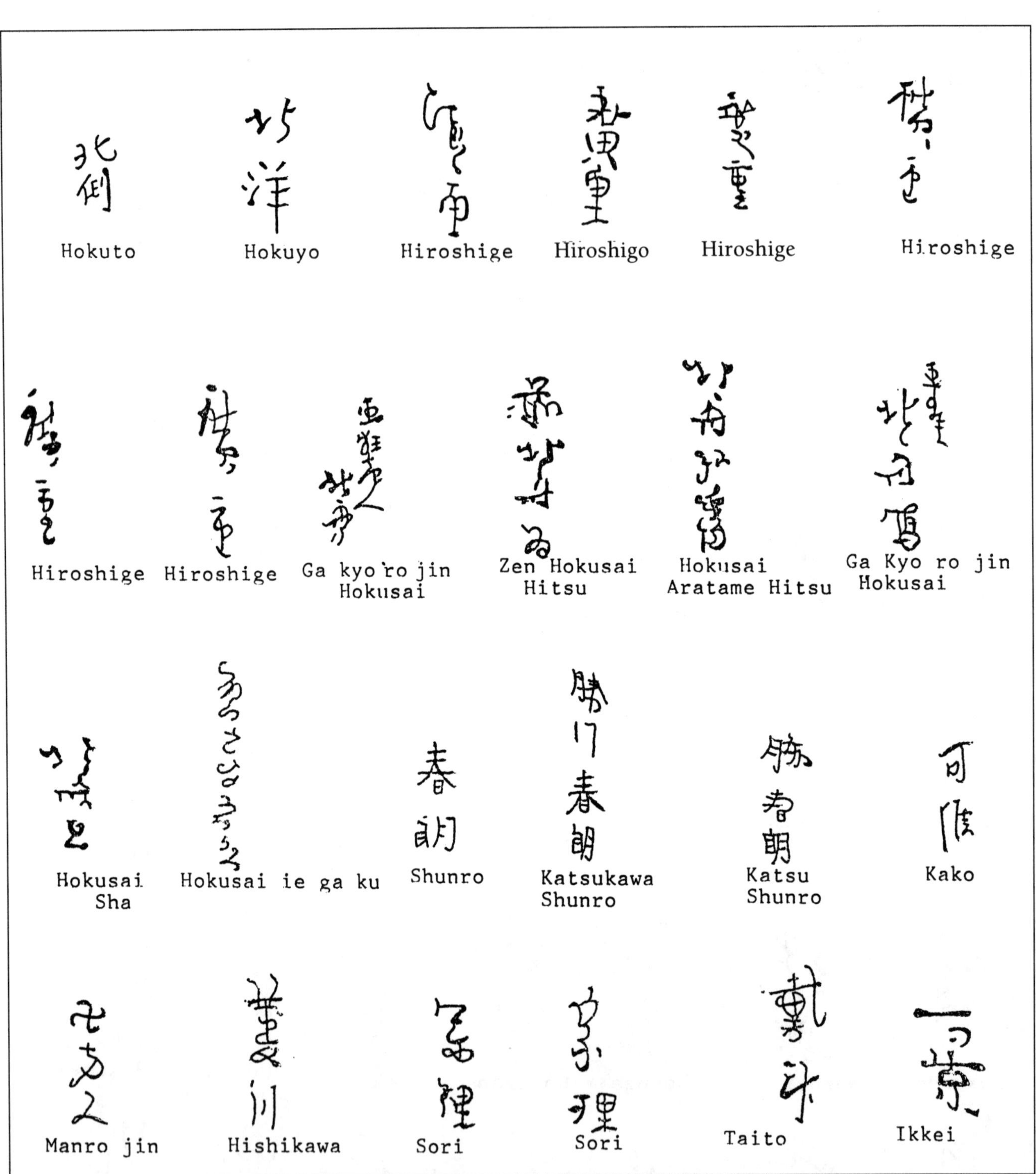

Hokuto
Hokuyo
Hiroshige
Hiroshigo
Hiroshige
Hiroshige
Hiroshige
Hiroshige
Ga kyo ro jin Hokusai
Zen Hokusai Hitsu
Hokusai Aratame Hitsu
Ga Kyo ro jin Hokusai
Hokusai Sha
Hokusai ie ga ku
Shunro
Katsukawa Shunro
Katsu Shunro
Kako
Manro jin
Hishikawa
Sori
Sori
Taito
Ikkei

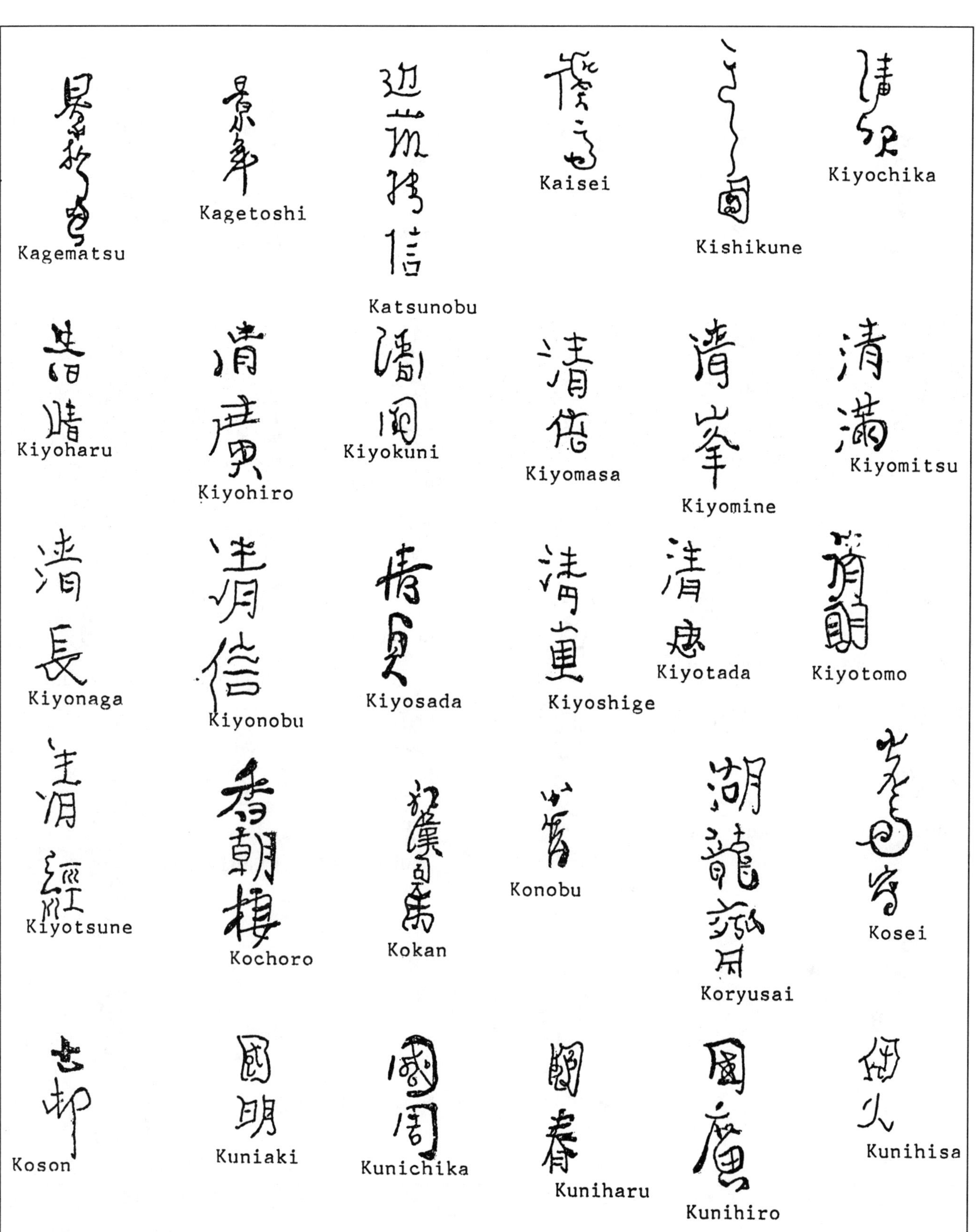
Kagematsu
Kagetoshi
Katsunobu
Kaisei
Kishikune
Kiyochika
Kiyoharu
Kiyohiro
Kiyokuni
Kiyomasa
Kiyomine
Kiyomitsu
Kiyonaga
Kiyonobu
Kiyosada
Kiyoshige
Kiyotada
Kiyotomo
Kiyotsune
Kochoro
Kokan
Konobu
Koryusai
Kosei
Koson
Kuniaki
Kunichika
Kuniharu
Kunihiro
Kunihisa

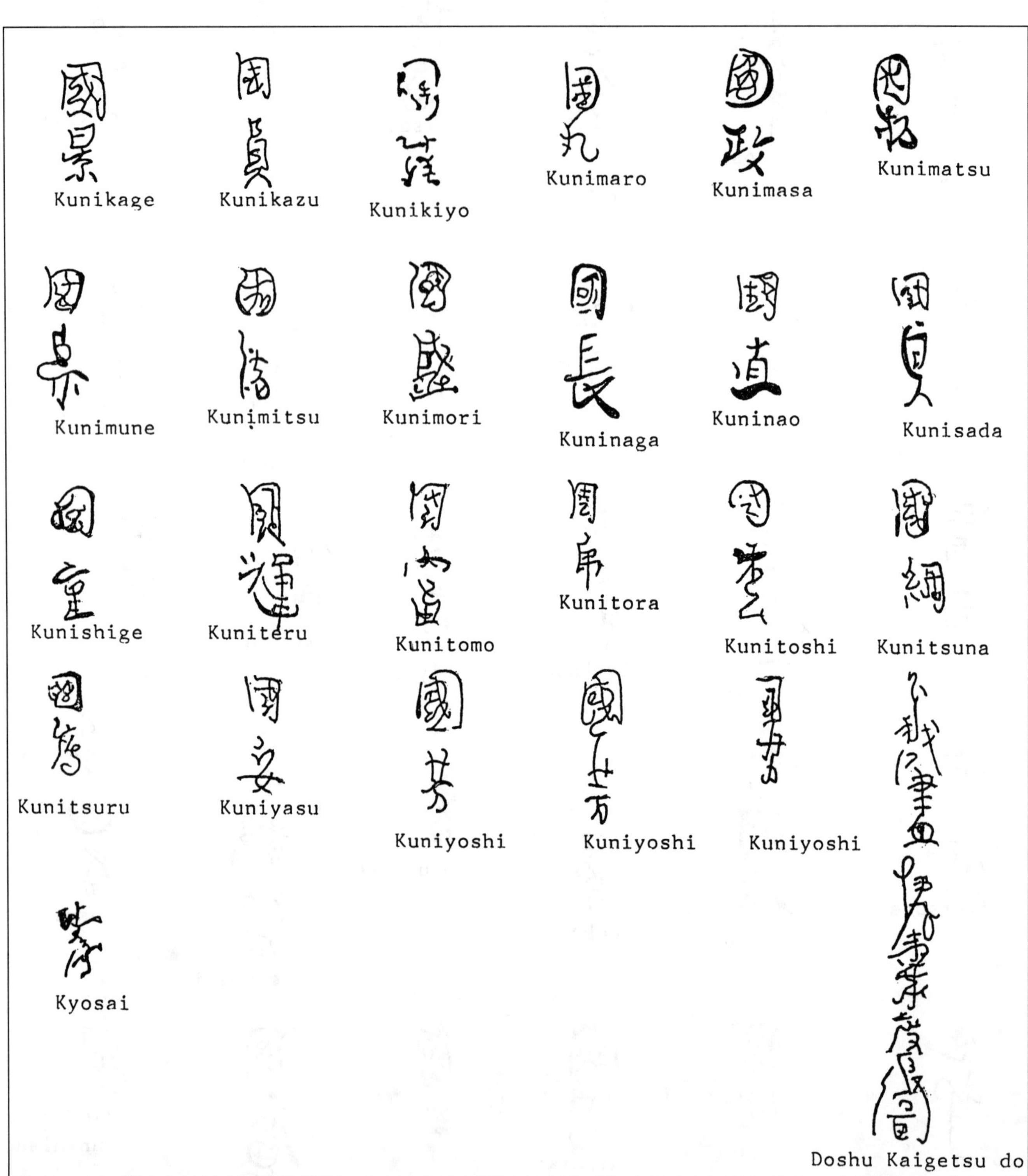
Kunikage
Kunikazu
Kunikiyo
Kunimaro
Kunimasa
Kunimatsu
Kunimune
Kunimitsu
Kunimori
Kuninaga
Kuninao
Kunisada
Kunishige
Kuniteru
Kunitomo
Kunitora
Kunitoshi
Kunitsuna
Kunitsuru
Kuniyasu
Kuniyoshi
Kuniyoshi
Kuniyoshi
Kyosai
Doshu Kaigetsu do

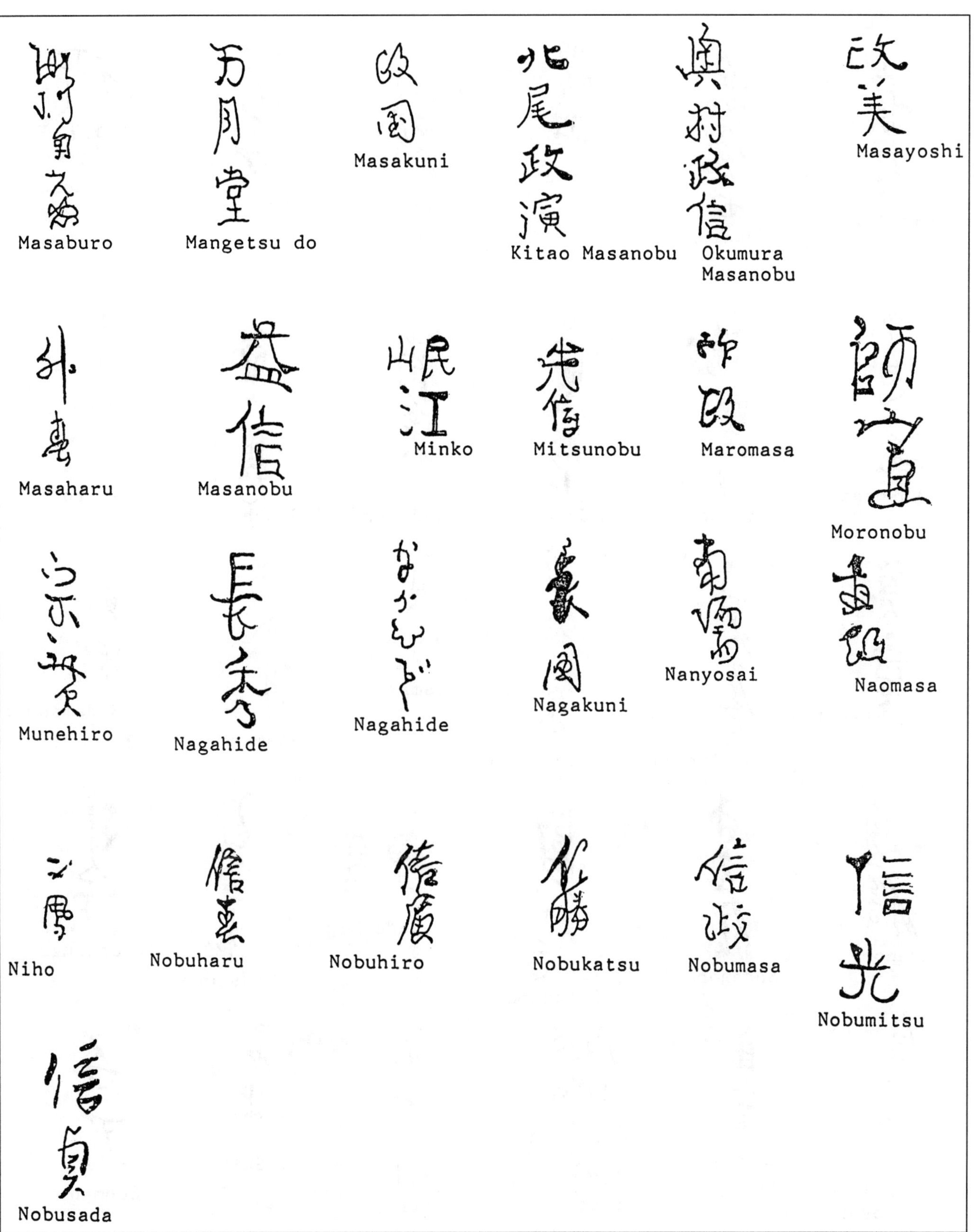
Masaburo
Mangetsu do
Masakuni
Kitao Masanobu
Okumura Masanobu
Masayoshi
Masaharu
Masanobu
Minko
Mitsunobu
Maromasa
Moronobu
Munehiro
Nagahide
Nagahide
Nagakuni
Nanyosai
Naomasa
Niho
Nobuharu
Nobuhiro
Nobukatsu
Nobumasa
Nobumitsu
Nobusada

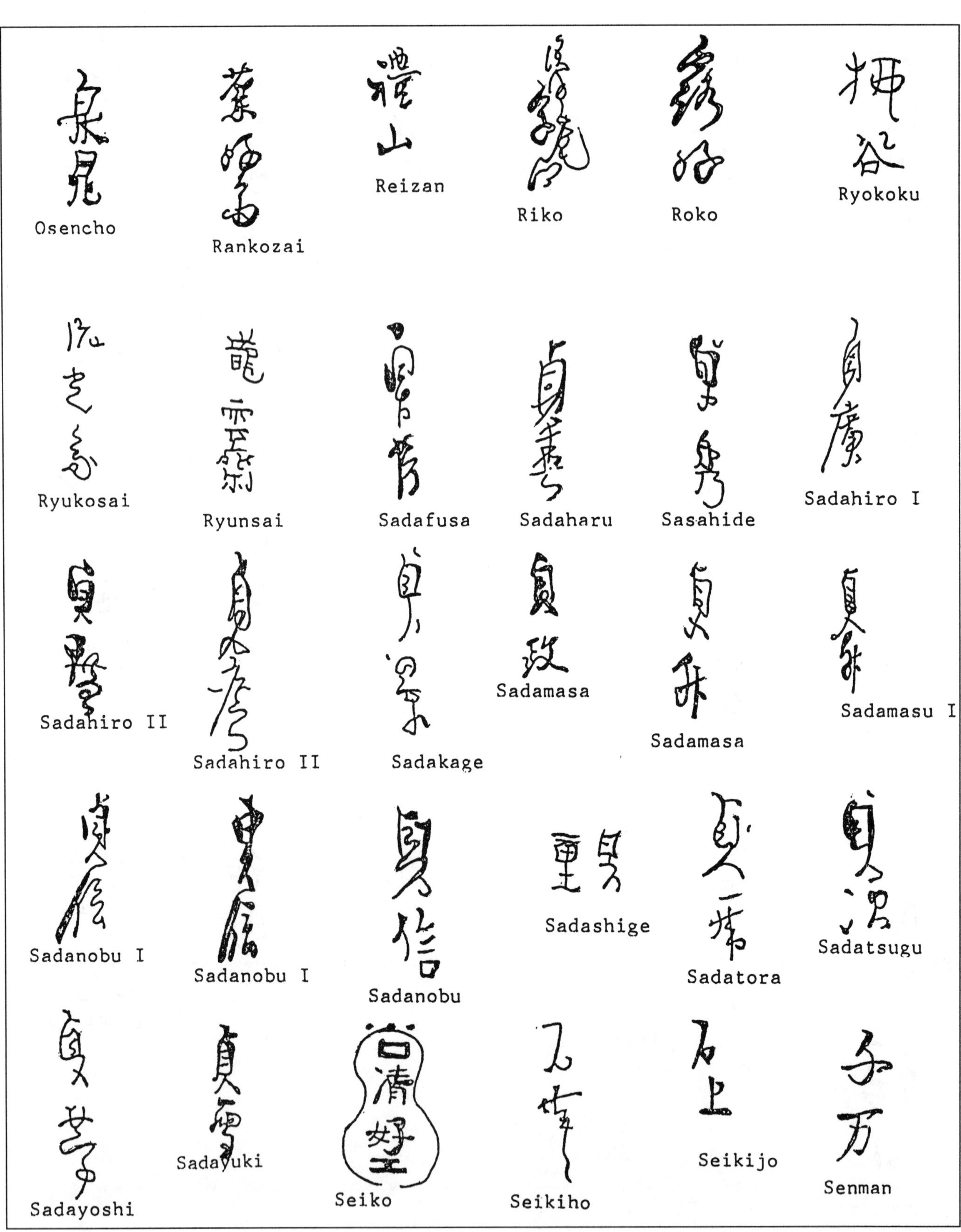
Osencho
Rankozai
Reizan
Riko
Roko
Ryokoku
Ryukosai
Ryunsai
Sadafusa
Sadaharu
Sasahide
Sadahiro I
Sadahiro II
Sadahiro II
Sadakage
Sadamasa
Sadamasa
Sadamasu I
Sadanobu I
Sadanobu I
Sadanobu
Sadashige
Sadatora
Sadatsugu
Sadayoshi
Sadayuki
Seiko
Seikiho
Seikijo
Senman

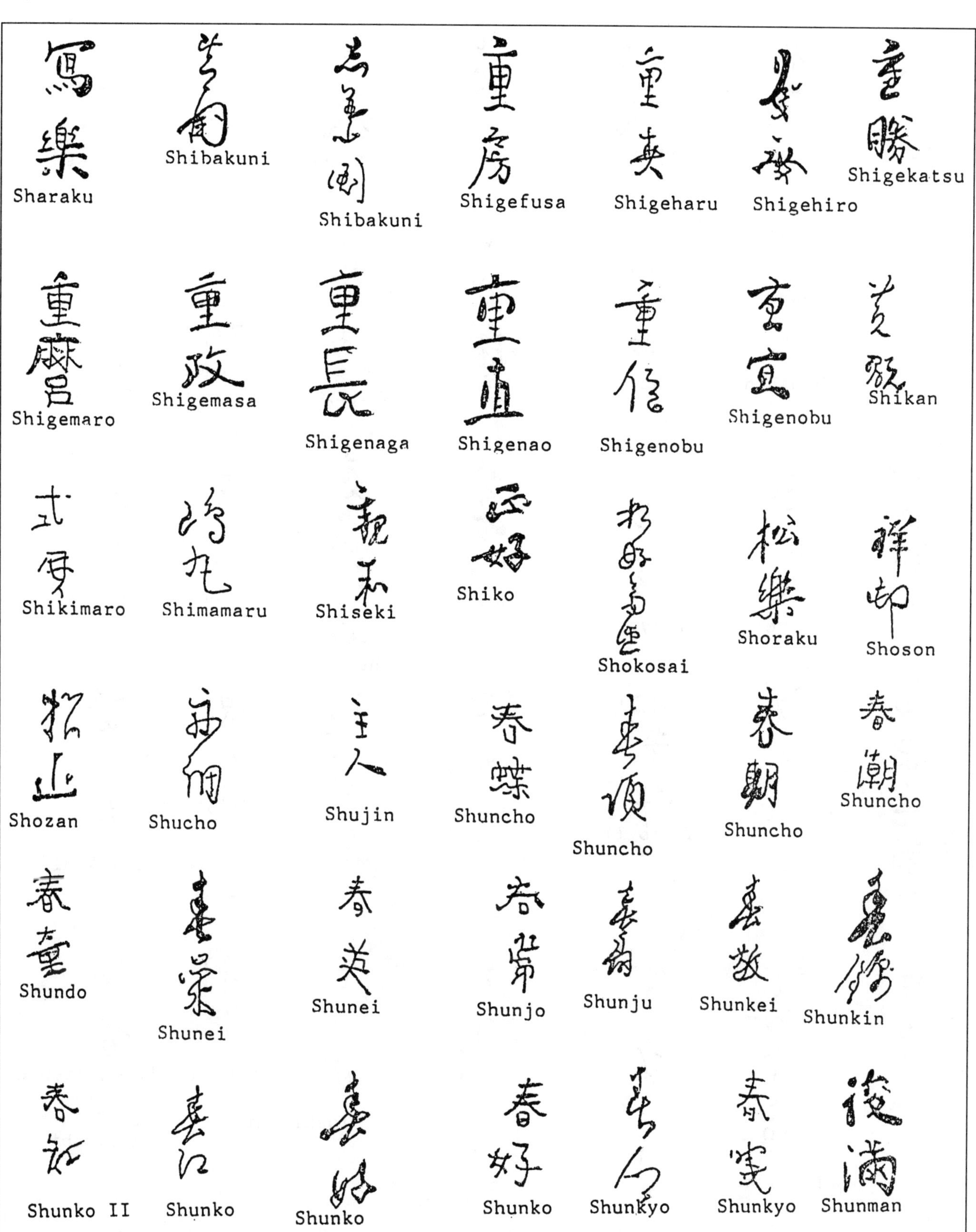
Sharaku
Shibakuni
Shibakuni
Shigefusa
Shigeharu
Shigehiro
Shigekatsu
Shigemaro
Shigemasa
Shigenaga
Shigenao
Shigenobu
Shigenobu
Shikan
Shikimaro
Shimamaru
Shiseki
Shiko
Shokosai
Shoraku
Shoson
Shozan
Shucho
Shujin
Shuncho
Shuncho
Shuncho
Shuncho
Shundo
Shunei
Shunei
Shunjo
Shunju
Shunkei
Shunkin
Shunko II
Shunko
Shunko
Shunko
Shunkyo
Shunkyo
Shunman

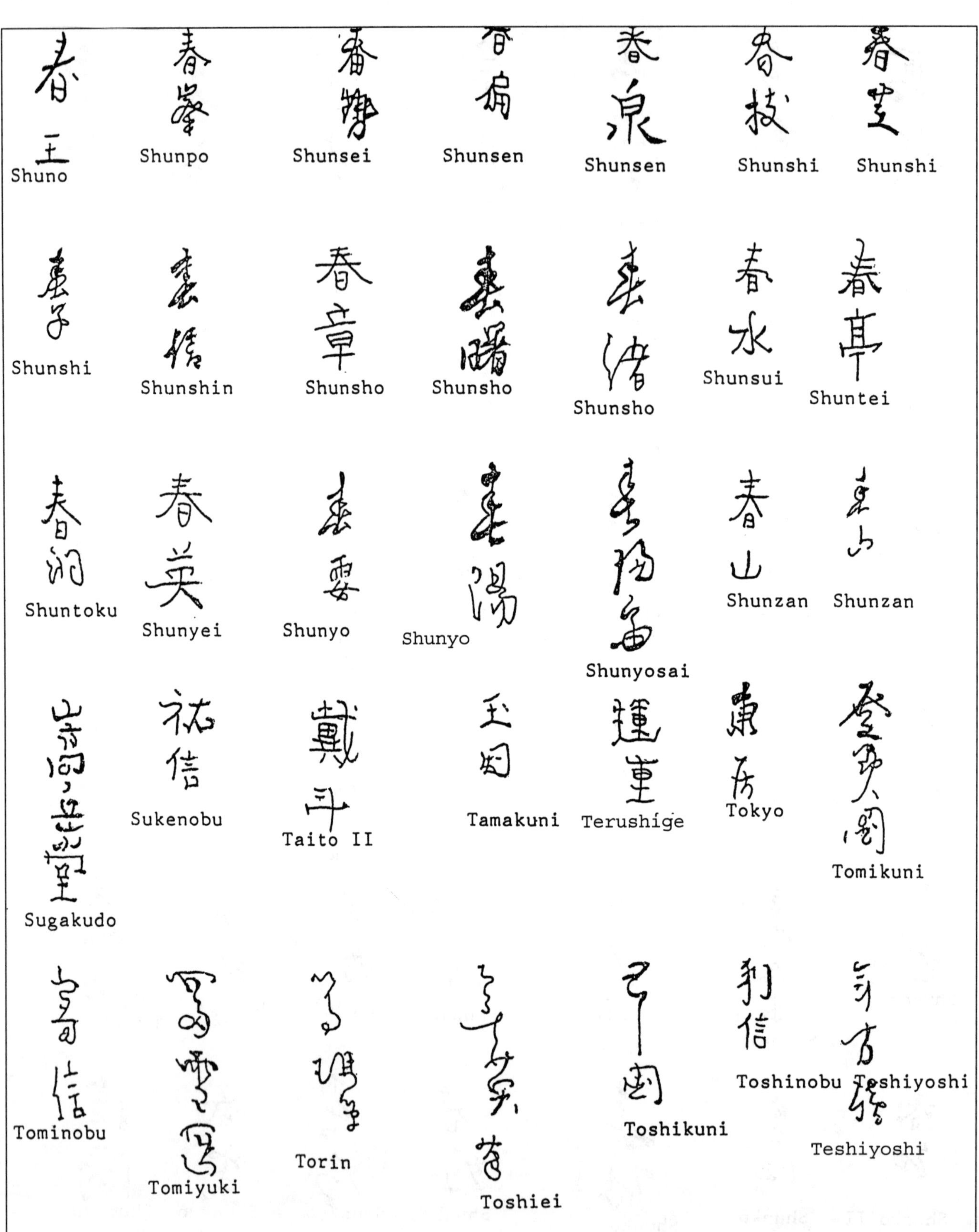

Shuno
Shunpo
Shunsei
Shunsen
Shunsen
Shunshi
Shunshi
Shunshi
Shunshin
Shunsho
Shunsho
Shunsho
Shunsui
Shuntei
Shuntoku
Shunyei
Shunyo
Shunyo
Shunyosai
Shunzan
Shunzan
Sugakudo
Sukenobu
Taito II
Tamakuni
Terushige
Tokyo
Tomikuni
Tominobu
Tomiyuki
Torin
Toshiei
Toshikuni
Toshinobu
Teshiyoshi
Teshiyoshi

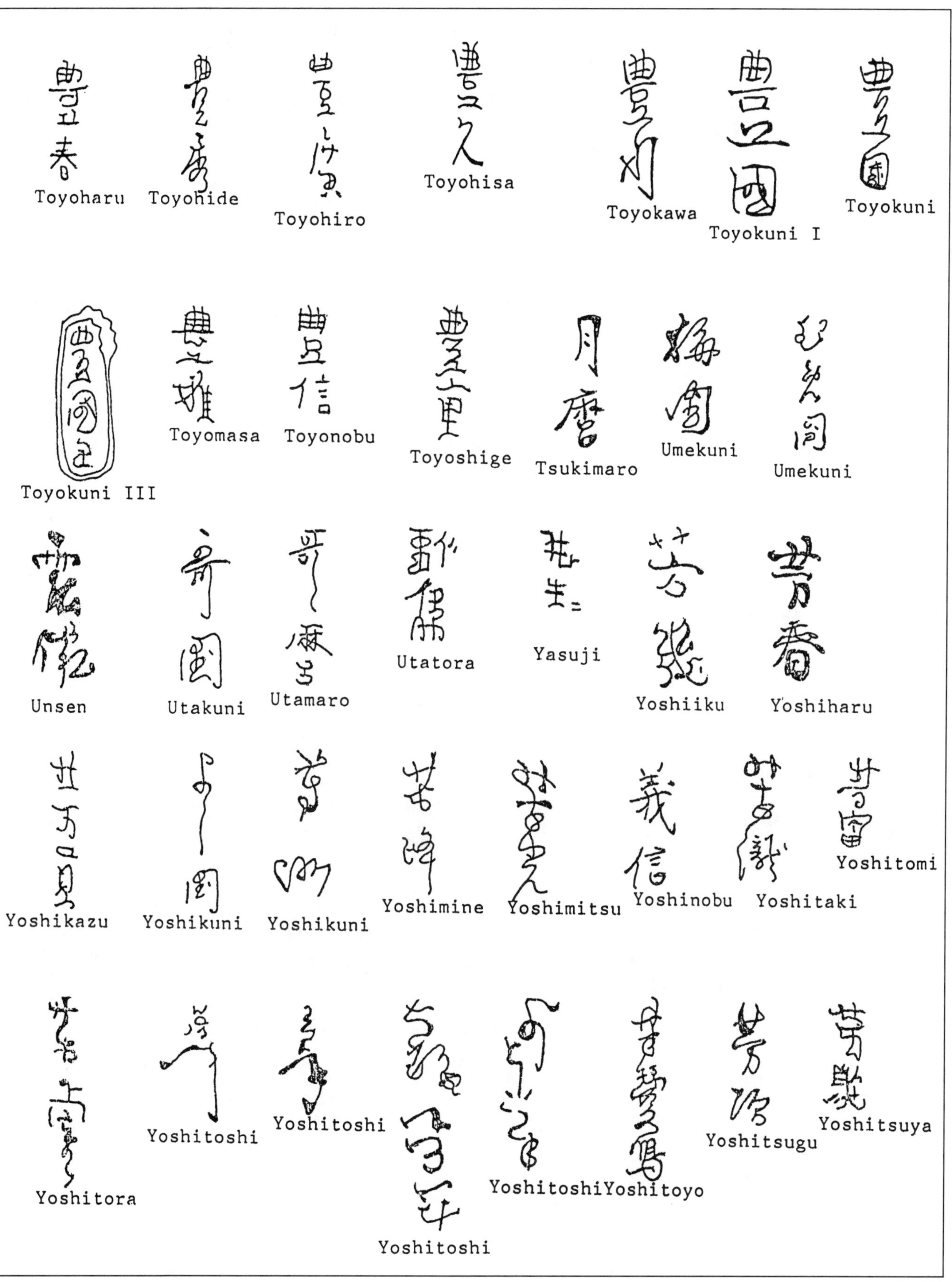
Toyoharu
Toyohide
Toyohiro
Toyohisa
Toyokawa
Toyokuni I
Toyokuni
Toyokuni III
Toyomasa
Toyonobu
Toyoshige
Tsukimaro
Umekuni
Umekuni
Unsen
Utakuni
Utamaro
Utatora
Yasuji
Yoshiiku
Yoshiharu
Yoshikazu
Yoshikuni
Yoshikuni
Yoshimine
Yoshimitsu
Yoshinobu
Yoshitaki
Yoshitomi
Yoshitora
Yoshitoshi
Yoshitoshi
Yoshitoshi
Yoshitoshi
Yoshitoyo
Yoshitsugu
Yoshitsuya

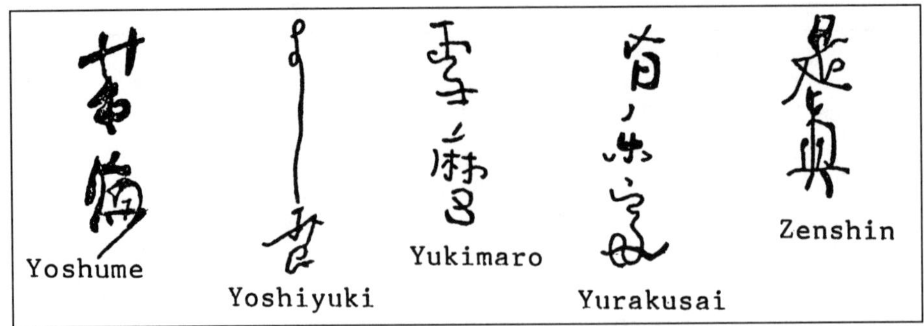
Yoshume
Yoshiyuki
Yukimaro
Yurakusai
Zenshin

Appendix F

Signatures and Seals of 20th Century Woodblock Artists and Publishers

Selected Signatures and Seals

The signature on a modern Japanese print may indicate the family name of the artist, a given name, some part of a name, or an art name. The seal may be any of these, a studio name, or the publisher. Signatures are ordinarily in kanji, which are Chinese characters used in Japanese writing. Signatures may also be in kana, the Japanese syllabary, or, in cases of Western-oriented artists, in Western script. Names may be read from top to bottom, from left to right, or from right to left. Signatures may be carved in the block or written in Western fashion in the bottom margin. Seals are traditionally stamped in red ink, but for prints they may be carved in the block. Artists frequently indulge in creative liberties with their signatures and seals. In the listing of signatures and seals, a question mark indicates that we have not deciphered the seal.

Various words preceding or following a name indicate the role of the person named:

e: picture. Indicates the artist.
ga: picture. Indicates the artist.
han: printing plate. Indicates the publisher.
hanken shoyu: copyright owner.
hanmoto: publisher
hitsu: brush. Indicates the artist.
hori: carved. This often precedes the name of an artisan carver.
in: seal. May indicate either artist or publisher.
ko: workshop. Indicates the publisher.
saku: made. May indicate either artist or publisher.
suri: printed. This often precedes the name of an artisan carver. It is also sometimes found after the name of the artist on so saku-hanga prints.
to knife. Indicates the carver. This is sometimes found after the name of the artist on so saku-hanga prints.

Akamatsu Rinsaku. Seal: Akamatsu Rinsaku.

Asahi Masahide. Seal: Asahi.

Asano Takeji. Signature: T. Asano.

Asano Takeji. Signature: Takeji to.

Asano Takeji. Signature: Takejo ga.

Asano Takeji. Signature: T.A.

Azechi Umetaro. Seal: U.

Azechi Umetaro. Signature: Azechi Umetaro.

Azechi Umetaro Seal: U (stylized).

Azechi Umetaro. Seal: Ume.

Bito. Signature: Bito (or Mito) ga. Seal: Sato Shotaro han.

Daigo. Signature: Possibly Daigo (or Taigo) ga. Seal: Daigo in.

Domoto Insho. Signature: Insho. Seal: Insho.

Ebata Yoichi. Signature: Yo. Eba

Eijiro. Seal: Eijiro.

Endo Eyozo. Signature: Kyozo. Seal: Kyozo ga.

Fujimori Shizuo. Seal: Shizu.

Fujimori Shizuo. Signauture: S. Fudimori. Seal: Shizu.

Fujimori Shizuo. Seal: Siz.

Fujimori Shizuo. Signature: S. Fudimore. Seal: Shizu.

Fujita Tsuguharu. Signature: Tsuguharu Foujita.

Fukazawa Sakuichi. Seal: Saku.

Furukawa Ryusei. Seal: Ryu.

Furukawa Ryusei. Signature: Ryusei.

Hashiguchi Goyo. ga. Seal: Hashiguchi Goyo.

Hashiguchi Goyo. Signature: Goyo ga. Seal: Goyo.

Hashiguchi Goyo. Signature: Goyo ga. Seal: Go (five) with a leaf.

Hashimoto Okiie. Seal: Hashi.

Hata Tsuneharu. Seal: Hata.

Hatsuyama Shigeru. Signature: Shigeru. Seal: Shigeru.

Hirakawa Seizo. Seal: H.S.

Hirano Hakuho. Signature: Hakuho ga. Seal: Haku.

Hirano Hakuho. Signature: Hakuho ga. Seal: Hirano.

Hiratsuka Un'ichi. Seal: Un.

Hiratsuka Un'ichi. Seal: UN.

Hiratsuka Un'ichi. Seal: Un'ichi in.

Hiratsuka Un'ichi. Signature: Hiratsuka Un'ichi.

Hir atsuka Un'ichi. Seal: Un Hiratsuka.

Hisaizumi Kyozo. Signature: Kyozo. Seal: Kyozo.

Hodo. Signature: Hodo. Seal: Takemura (publisher).

Hotei. Signature: Hotei. Seal: Hotei.

Ide Gakusui. Signature. Gakusui. Seal: Gakusui.

Inuzuka Taisui. Seal: Inuzuka.

Ishii Hakutei. Signature: Hakutei. Seal: Bonkotsu to.

Ishii Hakutei. Seal: Haku.

Ishii Tsuruzo. Signature: TU.

Ishii Tsuruzo. Signature: Tsuruzo ga.

Ishii Tsuruzo. Seal: T.

Ishikawa Toraji. Signature: Ishikawa. Seal: Tora.

Ishiwata Koitsu. Seal: Koitsu.

Isoda MataichiroSignature: Mataichirohitsu.

Ito Shinsui. Signature: Shinsui. Seal: Tatsumi.

Ito Shinshi. Signature: Shinsui ga. Seal: Shinsui.

Ito Shinsui. Signature: Shinsui (reading from right to left).

Ito Shinsui. Signature: Shinsui ga. Seal: Ito

Ito Sozan. Signature: Sogan. Seals: So and Zan.

ItoTakashi. Signature: Takashi. Seal: Takashi.

ItoYuhan.

Jo Signature: Jo e. Seal: Jo in.

Kaburagi Kiyokata. Signature: Kiyokata. Seal: Kiyokata.

Kajita Hanko. Signature: Hanko. Seal: Hanko.

Kajita Hanko. Signature: Hanko. Seal: Hanko.

Kako. Signature: Possibly Kako Seal: Kako

Kamei Tobei. Signature: To. Seal: Jikoku (self-carved).

Kamei Tobei. Seal: Kame.

Kano Koga. Signature: Koga. Seal: Koga saku.

Kasamatsu Shiro. Signature: Shiro. Seal: Shiro saku.

Kasamatsu Shiro. Seal: Kasamatsu.

Katsuhira Tokushi. Seal: Kasamatsu.

Katsuhira Tokushi. Seal: Toku.

Katsuki Sadao. Signature: Katu.

Kawai Gyokudo Signature: Gyokudo. Seal: Gyokudo

Kawakami Sumio. Seal: Sumio.

Kawakami Sumio. Seal: SK.

Kawakami Sumio. Seal: Sumi.

Kawakami Sumio. Seal: Sumi.

Kawakami Sumio. Seal: Sumi.

Sawakami Sumio. Seal: Sumio.

Kawakami Sumio. Signature: Sumi.

Kawanishi Hide. Signature: Hide. Seal: Hide.

Kawase Hasui. Signature: Hasui. Seal: Sui.

Kawase Hasui. Signature: Hasui. Seal: Kawase.

Kawase Hasui. Signature: Hasui. Seal: Sui.

Kikuchi Zenjiro. Signature: Zen.

Kishida Ryusei. Seal: Ryusei.

Kitano Tsunetomi. Signature: Tsunetomi hitsu.

Kiyohara Hitoshi. Seal: Hitoshi.

Kiyohara Hitoshi. Signature: Hitoshi. Seal: Hitoshi.

Kobayakawa Kiyoshi. Signature: Kiyoshi. Seal: Kobayakawa.

Kobayashi Kiyochika. Signature: Kiyochika. Seals: Kiyo and Chika.

Kobayashi Kiyochika. Seal: Kiyochika.

Koho. Signature: Koho.

Koizumi Kishio. Signature: Izumi.

Komura Settai. Seal: Settai.

Kosetsu. Signature: Kosetsu. Seal: Sato han.

Kosugi. Misei. Seal: Shikyo.Enka (one of his go,)

Kotozuka Eiichi. Upper seal: Koto. Lower seal: Uchida han (publisher).

Maeda Masao. Seal: Masa.

Maeda Masao. Seal: Masa.

Maeda Masao. Signature: Maeda Masao.

Maekawa Senpan. Signature: Sen.

Maekawa Senpan. Signature: Maekawa Senpan.

Maekawa Senpan. Signature: Pan.

Maekawa Senpan. Seal: Senpan.

Maki Haku. Seal: Maki Haku.

Matsubara Naoko. Seal: Matsubara Naoko.

Matsubayahi Keigetsu. Seal: Keigetsu.

Matsuoka Eikyu. Signature: Eikyu. Seal: Eikyu in.

Miki Suizan. Signature: Suizan.

Mizushima Nihofu. Signature: Nihofu. Seal: Nihofu.

Mori Yoshitoshi. Seal: Yoshitoshi.

Mori Yoshitoshi. Seal: Yoshi.

Morita Tsunetomo. Seal: M.

Munakata Shiko. Seal: Kegon.

Munakata Shiko. Seal: Hogan Munakata Shiko

Muto Kan'ichi. Seal: Kan.

Nagai Hyosai. Seal: Hyo.

Nakagawa Isaku. Seal: Nakagawa.

Nakagawa Yutaro. Signature: Yut.

Nakazawa Hiromitsu. Seal: Hiro.

Nakazawa Hiromitsu. Seal: Hiro.

Narazaki Eisho. Signature: Eisho.

Natori Shunsen. Signature: Shunsen ga. Seal: flower pattern.

Natori Shunsen. Signature: Shunsen. Seal: Natori.

Natori Shunsen. Signature: Shunsen. Seal: Shunsen.

Natori Shunsen. Signature: Shunsen ga. Seal: leaf pattern.

Natori Shunsen. Signature: Shunsen ga. Seals: Shun and Sen.

Natori Shunsen. Signature: Shunsen. Seal: Shunsen.

Natori Shunsen. Signature: Shunsen. Seal: Natori.

Natori Shunsen. Seal: Natori.

Natori Shunsen. Signature: Shunsen. Seal: ?

Natori Shunsen. Signature: Shunsen ga. Seal: Taishido.

Nishihara Hiroshi. Signature: Hiroshi. Seal: Hiroshi/child.

Nishimura Goun. Signature: Goun saku. Seal: Goun.

Noda Kyuho. Signature: Kyuho. Seal: Kyuho.

Nomura Toshihiko. Signature: Nomura Toshihiko.

Nomura Toshihiko. Seal: Toshihiko.

Nomura Yoshimitsu. Signature: Yoshimitsu. Seal: Sato Shohan.

Nomura Yoshimitsu. Signature: Yoshimitsu. Seal: Sankokai.

Oda Kazuma. Seal: Kazuma.

Oda Kazuma. Signature: Kazuma hitsu. Seal: Oda.

Ogata Gekko. Signature: Gekko. Seal: Gekko.

Ohara Hoson. Signature: Hoson. Seal: Hoson.

Ohara Koson. Signature: Koson. Seal: Koson.

Ohara Koson. Signature: Koson. Seal: Koson.

Ohara Koson. Signature: Koson. Seal: Koson.

Ohara Shoson. Signature: Shoson. Seal: Shoson.

Ohno Bakufu. Seal: Bakufu.

Ohno Bakufu. Signature B. Ohno.

Okamura Kichiemon. Seal: ?

Okuda Teruichiro. Signature: TERU

Okuyama Gihachiro. Seal: Gi.

Okuyama Gihachiro. Signature: Gihachiro. Seal: Okuyama.

Omura Koyo. Signature: Koyo. Upper seal: ? Lower seal: Shinagawa (a printer or proprietor at Kyoto Hanga-in).

Onchi Koshiro. Seal: K.

Onchi Koshiro. Signature: K. Onzi.

Onchi Koshiro. Signature: K. Onchi.

Onchi Koshiro. Signature: Ko.

Ryoji Chomei. Seal: Ryoji in.

Ryoko. Signature: Ryoko. Seal: Ryoko.

Saito Kiyoshi. Seal: Kiyoshi.

Seicho. Signature: Seicho. Seal: Seicho

Sasajima Kihei. Seal: Ki.

Seicho. Signature: Seicho. Seal: Seicho.

Seiko. Signature: Seiko.

Sekino Jun'ichiro. Seal. Jun.

Sekino Jun'ichiro. Seal: Sekino. Jun'ichiro.

Shimozawa Kihachiro. Seal: Hachi.

Shuho. Signature: Shuho. Seal: Possibly Jindo.

Suwa Kanenori. Seal: S.

Takahashi Hiroaki. Signature: Hiroaki. Seal: Shotei.

Takahashi Hiroaki. Signature: Hiroaki. Seal: Hiroaki saku.

Takahashi Hiroaki. Seal: Hiroaki.

Takahashi Hiroaki. Signature: Hiroaki saku. Seal: Hiroaki.

Takeda Shintaro. Signature: Shin.

Takehisa Yumeji. Seal: Takehisa Yumeji no in.

Takehisa Yumeji. Signature: Yumeji. Seal: Take.

Takehisa Yumeji. Seal: Take.

Takehisa Yumeji. Seal: Pattern.

Takeuchi SeihoSignature: Seiho. Seal: Seiho.

Takeuchi Seiho. Seal: Seiho.

Takeuchi Seiho. Signature: Seiho. Seal: Seiho.

Takeuchi Seiho. Signature: Seiho saku. Seal: Kachuan.

Tamamura Hokuto. Signature: Hokuto saku. Seal: Hokuto.

Tanaka Hisara. Seal: Hi.

Taniguchi Kokyo. Signature: Kokyo ga. Upper seal: Kokyo in. Lower seal: Sato Sho han.

Tobari Kogan. Signature: Kogan. Seal: Kogan.

Tobari Kogan. Seal: Kogan.

Toko. Signature: Toko. Seal: Sho.

Tokuriki Tomikichiro. Signature: Tomikichiro saku. Seal: Kiwame (former censor seal).

Torii Kotondo. Seal: Kotondo.

Torii Kotondo. Signature: Kotondo ga. Seal: Kotondo.

Torii Kotondo. Seal: Torii.

Torii Tadamasa. Signature: Tadamasa. Seal: Tadamasa.

Torii Tadamasa. Signature: Torii Tadamasa. Seal: Torii Rairyu.

Tsuchiya Koitsu. Seal: Shinsei (genuine) Koitsu.

Tsuchiya Koitsu. Signature: Koitsu. Seal: Shin (true).

Tsuchiya Koitsu. Seal: Shinsei (genuine).

Tsuchiya Rakuzan. Signature: Rakuzan Koshisei. Seal: ?

Tsuchiya Rakuzan. Upper seal: Ko in. Lower seal: Rakuzan.

Tsukioka Gyokusei. Signature: Gyokusei. Seal: Tsukioka.

Tsukioka Kogyo. Signature: Kogyo. Seal: Bokuun.

Tsuruta Goro. Signature: Goro.

Tsuruya Kokei. Seal: Tsuruya Kokei.

Tsuyahisa. Signature: Possibly Tsuyahisa.

Urushibara Mokuchu. Seal: Urushibara.

Urushibara Mokuchu. Seal: Mokuchu han.

Urushibara Mokuchu. Signature: Urushibara ga. Seal: Mokuchu.

Yamaguchi Gen. Seal: G.

Yamaguchi Ryoshu.

Yamaguchi Susumu. Seal: Yamaguchi.

Yamakawa Shuho. Signature: Shuho. Seal: leaf pattern.

Yamamoto Kanae. Seal: Kanae.

Yamamoto Kanae. Seal: Kanae.

Yamamoto Shoun. Signature: Koka. Seal: Shoun.

Yamamura Koka. Signature: Koka. Seal: Toyonari.

Yamamura Koka. Signature: Koka ga.

Yamamura Toyonari. Signature: Toyonari ga. Seal: Taisei.

Yamamura Toyonari. Signature: Toyonari e.

Yamamura Toyonari. Seal: Toyonari.

Yamaoka Beika. Signature: Beika. Seal: ?

Yasuda Hanpo. Signature: Hanpo. Seal: Hanpo no in.

Yorozu Tetsugoro. Seal: Tetsu.

Yoshida Fujio. Signature: Fujio. Upper seal: Fuji. Lower seal: O.

Yoshida Hiroshi. Signature: Yoshida. Seal: flower pattern.

Yoshida Hiroshi. Signature: Yoshida Seal: flower pattern.

Yoshida Hiroshi. Signature: Yoshida. Seal: Hiroshi.

Yoshida Masao. Signature: MAS.

Yoshida Toshi. Signature: Toshi. Seal: Yoshida Toshi.

Yoshida Toshi. Seal: Toshi.

Yoshida Toshi. Seal: Yoshida.

Yoshida Toshi. Signature: Toshi. Seal: Yoshida.

Yoshida Toshi. Signature: Toshi. Seal: Yoshida.

Yoshikawa Kanpo. Signature: Kanpo. Seal: Sato Sho han.

Yoshun. Seal: Possibly Yoshun.

Publishers

Doi Teiichi. Seal: Hanken shoyu (copyright owned by) Doi Teiichi.

Fusui Gabo. Seal:anken shoyu Fusui Gabo hakko.

Kato Junji. Seal: Hanmoto Kato Junji.

Nishinomiya Yosaku: Signature: Nishinomiya Yosaku.

Sato Shotaro. Seal: Sato Sho han.

Sato Shotaro. Seal: Sato han.

Sato Shotaro. Seal: Sato ko.

Sato Shotaro. Seal: Sato Sho han.

Sato Shotaro. Seal: Sato Sho han.

Shin Yamato-e Moku-hanga Kankokai. Seal: Shin Yamato-e Moku-hanga Kankokai.

Takamizawa. Seal: Adapted from the actor's seal of Uemura Kichizaburo.

Uchida. Seal: Hanmoto Uchida.

Uchida. Seal: Uchida han.

Uchida. Signature: Uchida Bijutsu Shoshi (art/book shop) han.

Unsodo. Seal: Gomei gaisha (mutually owned) Unsodo han.

Watanabe Shozaboro. Seal: Watanabe.

Watanabe Shozaburo. Seal: Watanabe ko.

Watanabe Shozaburo. Seal. Watanabe.

Watanabe Shozaburo. Hanmoto Watanabe Hanga Ten (shop).

Sample Seals of Carvers and Printers

Small twin seals of carver and printer are often seen together. Top character, right seal: hori (carver) followed by the carver's name. Top character, left seal: suri (printer) followed by the printer's name.

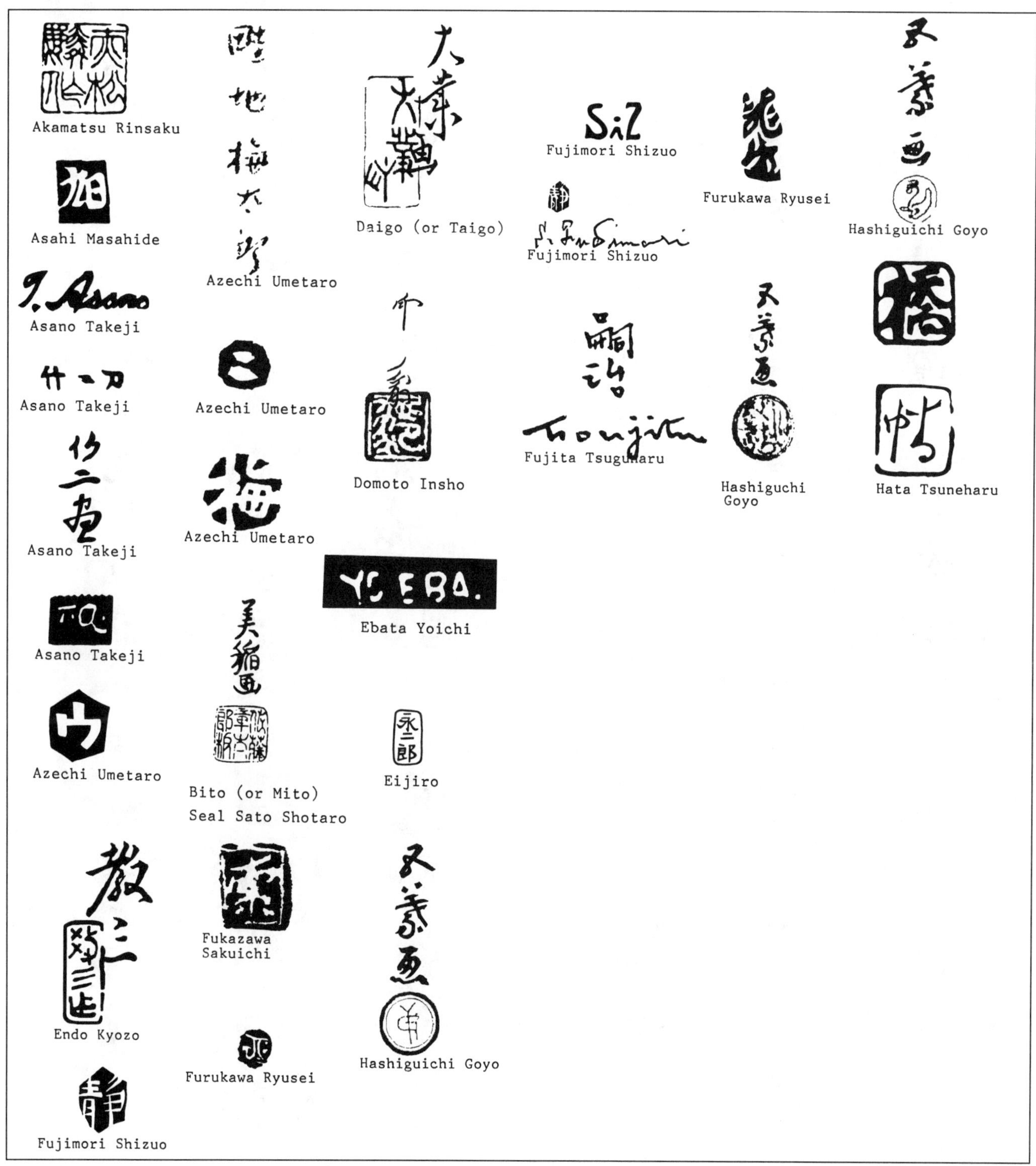

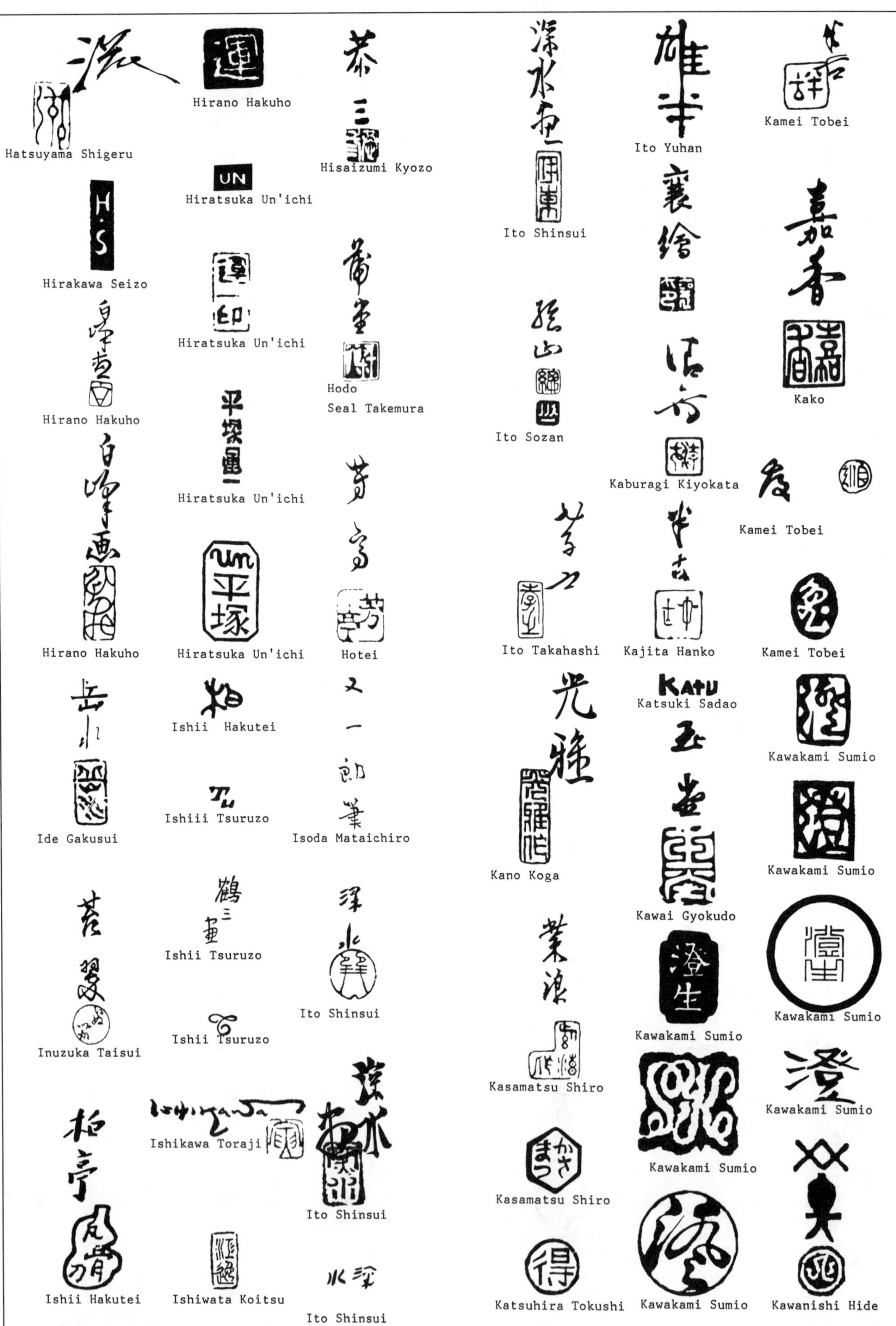
Hatsuyama Shigeru
Hirakawa Seizo
Hirano Hakuho
Hirano Hakuho
Ide Gakusui
Inuzuka Taisui
Ishii Hakutei
Hirano Hakuho
UN
Hiratsuka Un'ichi
Hiratsuka Un'ichi
Hiratsuka Un'ichi
Hiratsuka Un'ichi
Ishii Hakutei
Ishiii Tsuruzo
Ishii Tsuruzo
Ishii Tsuruzo
Ishikawa Toraji
Ishiwata Koitsu
Hisaizumi Kyozo
Hodo
Seal Takemura
Hotei
Isoda Mataichiro
Ito Shinsui
Ito Shinsui
Ito Shinsui
Ito Shinsui
Ito Sozan
Ito Takahashi
Kano Koga
Kasamatsu Shiro
Kasamatsu Shiro
Katsuhira Tokushi
Ito Yuhan
Kaburagi Kiyokata
Kajita Hanko
KATU
Katsuki Sadao
Kawai Gyokudo
Kawakami Sumio
Kawakami Sumio
Kawakami Sumio
Kamei Tobei
Kako
Kamei Tobei
Kamei Tobei
Kawakami Sumio
Kawakami Sumio
Kawakami Sumio
Kawakami Sumio
Kawanishi Hide

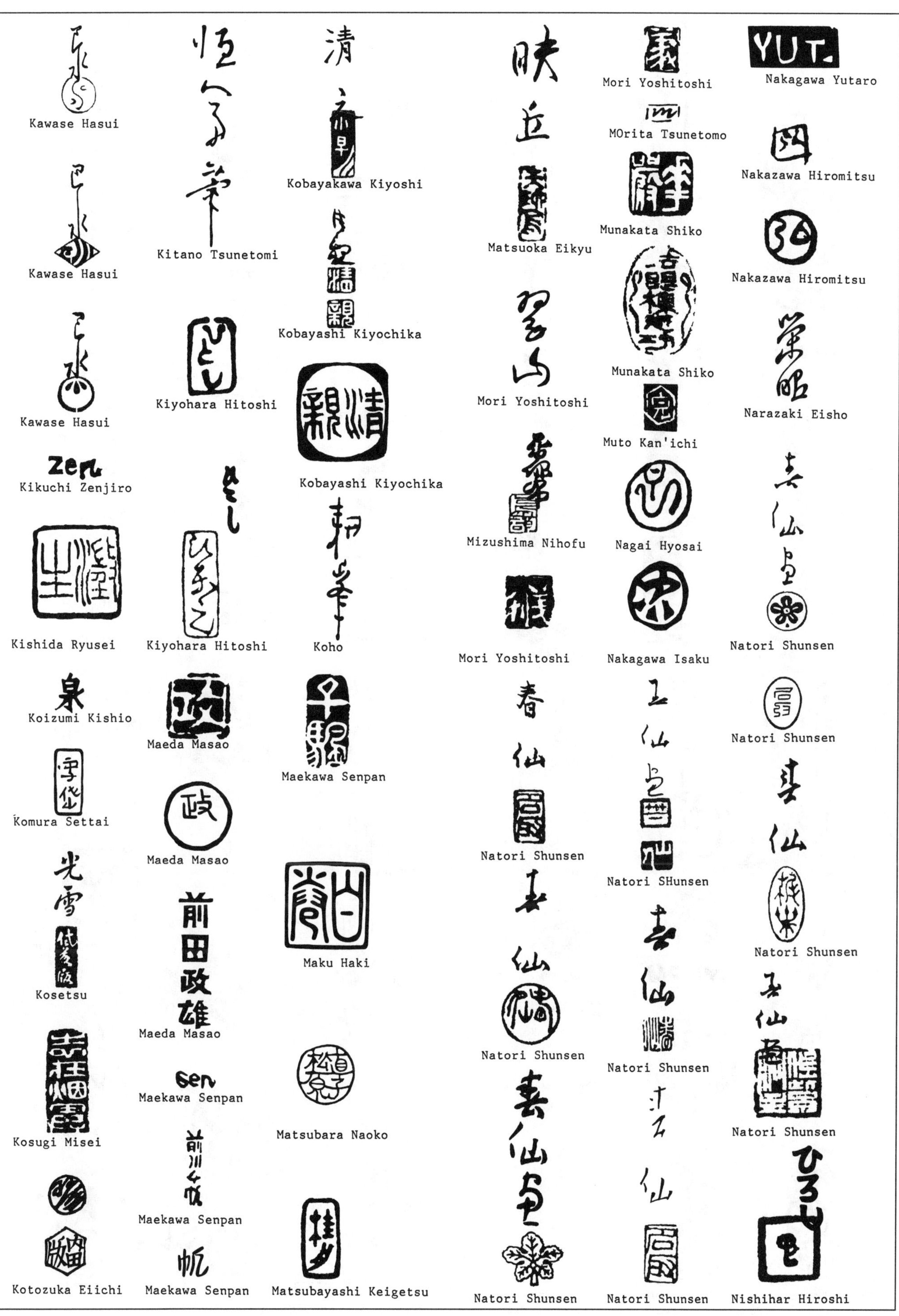
Kawase Hasui
Kawase Hasui
Kawase Hasui
zen
Kikuchi Zenjiro
Kishida Ryusei
Koizumi Kishio
Komura Settai
Kosetsu
Kosugi Misei
Kotozuka Eiichi
Kitano Tsunetomi
Kiyohara Hitoshi
Kiyohara Hitoshi
Maeda Masao
Maeda Masao
Maeda Masao
sen
Maekawa Senpan
Maekawa Senpan
Maekawa Senpan
Kobayakawa Kiyoshi
Kobayashi Kiyochika
Kobayashi Kiyochika
Koho
Maekawa Senpan
Maku Haki
Matsubara Naoko
Matsubayashi Keigetsu
Matsuoka Eikyu
Mori Yoshitoshi
Mizushima Nihofu
Mori Yoshitoshi
Natori Shunsen
Natori Shunsen
Natori Shunsen
Mori Yoshitoshi
MOrita Tsunetomo
Munakata Shiko
Munakata Shiko
Muto Kan'ichi
Nagai Hyosai
Nakagawa Isaku
Natori SHunsen
Natori Shunsen
Natori Shunsen
YUT.
Nakagawa Yutaro
Nakazawa Hiromitsu
Nakazawa Hiromitsu
Narazaki Eisho
Natori Shunsen
Natori Shunsen
Natori Shunsen
Natori Shunsen
Nishihar Hiroshi

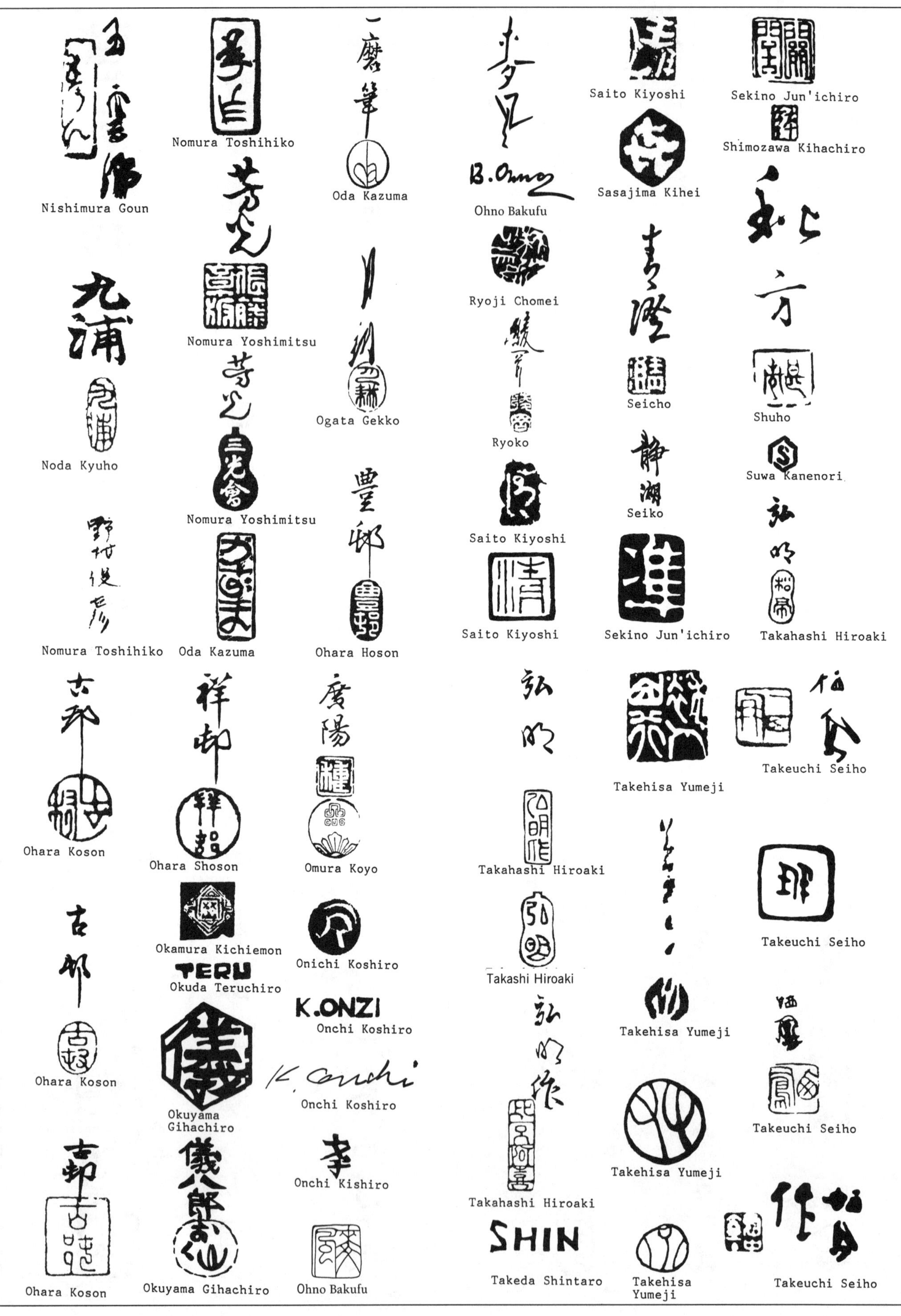
Nishimura Goun
Nomura Toshihiko
Oda Kazuma
B. Onno
Ohno Bakufu
Saito Kiyoshi
Sasajima Kihei
Sekino Jun'ichiro
Shimozawa Kihachiro
Nomura Yoshimitsu
Ryoji Chomei
Noda Kyuho
Ogata Gekko
Ryoko
Seicho
Shuho
Nomura Yoshimitsu
Saito Kiyoshi
Seiko
Suwa Kanenori
Nomura Toshihiko
Oda Kazuma
Ohara Hoson
Saito Kiyoshi
Sekino Jun'ichiro
Takahashi Hiroaki
Takeuchi Seiho
Takehisa Yumeji
Ohara Koson
Ohara Shoson
Omura Koyo
Takahashi Hiroaki
Okamura Kichiemon
Onichi Koshiro
Takeuchi Seiho
TERU
Okuda Teruchiro
Takashi Hiroaki
K.ONZI
Onchi Koshiro
Takehisa Yumeji
Ohara Koson
K. Onchi
Onchi Koshiro
Okuyama Gihachiro
Takeuchi Seiho
Onchi Kishiro
Takehisa Yumeji
Takahashi Hiroaki
SHIN
Ohara Koson
Okuyama Gihachiro
Ohno Bakufu
Takeda Shintaro
Takehisa Yumeji
Takeuchi Seiho

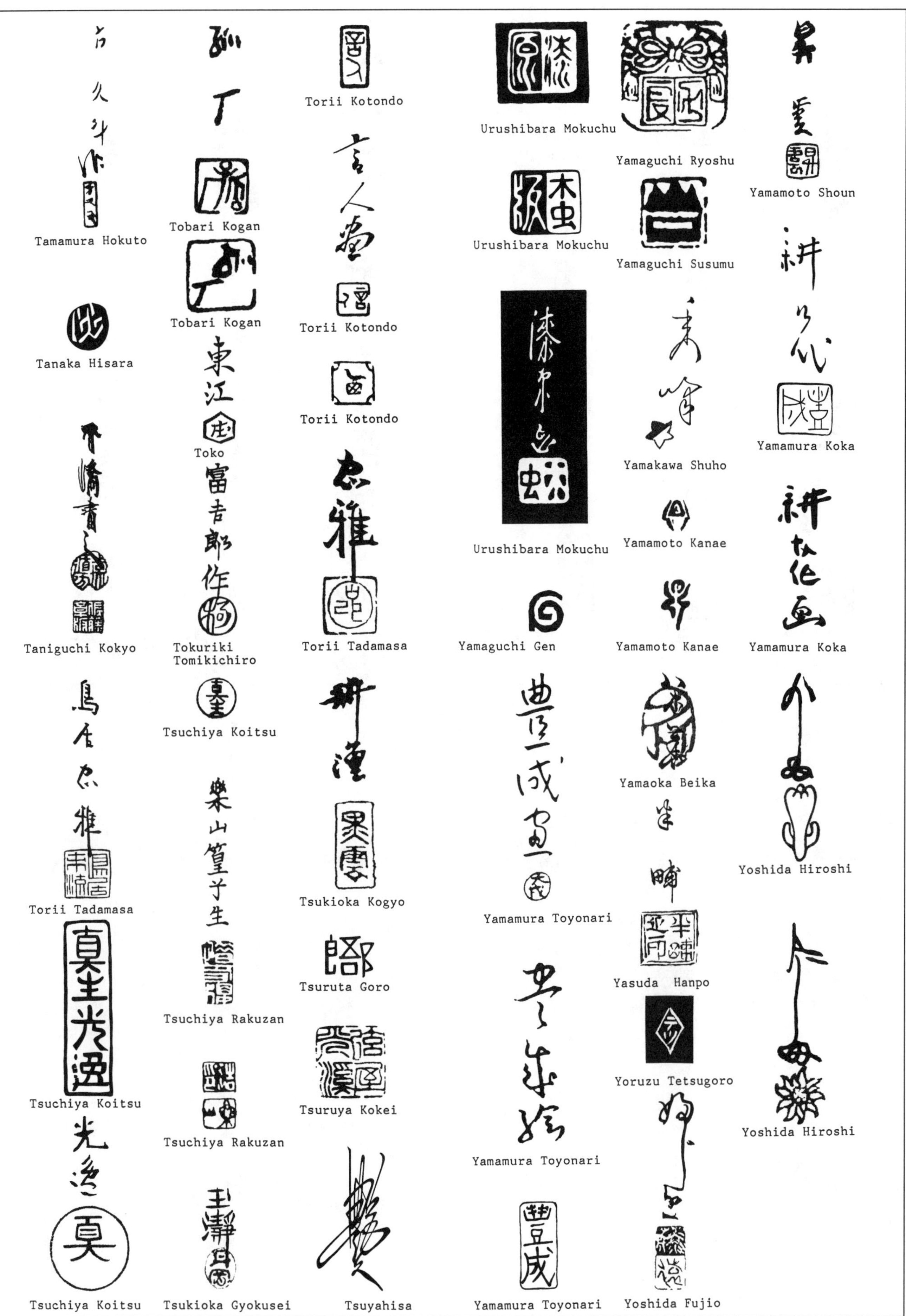

Tamamura Hokuto
Tanaka Hisara
Taniguchi Kokyo
Torii Tadamasa
Tsuchiya Koitsu
Tsuchiya Koitsu
Tobari Kogan
Tobari Kogan
Toko
Tokuriki Tomikichiro
Tsuchiya Koitsu
Tsuchiya Rakuzan
Tsuchiya Rakuzan
Tsukioka Gyokusei
Torii Kotondo
Torii Kotondo
Torii Kotondo
Torii Tadamasa
Tsukioka Kogyo
Tsuruta Goro
Tsuruya Kokei
Tsuyahisa
Urushibara Mokuchu
Urushibara Mokuchu
Urushibara Mokuchu
Yamaguchi Gen
Yamamura Toyonari
Yamamura Toyonari
Yamamura Toyonari
Yamaguchi Ryoshu
Yamaguchi Susumu
Yamakawa Shuho
Yamamoto Kanae
Yamamoto Kanae
Yamaoka Beika
Yasuda Hanpo
Yoruzu Tetsugoro
Yoshida Fujio
Yamamoto Shoun
Yamamura Koka
Yamamura Koka
Yoshida Hiroshi
Yoshida Hiroshi

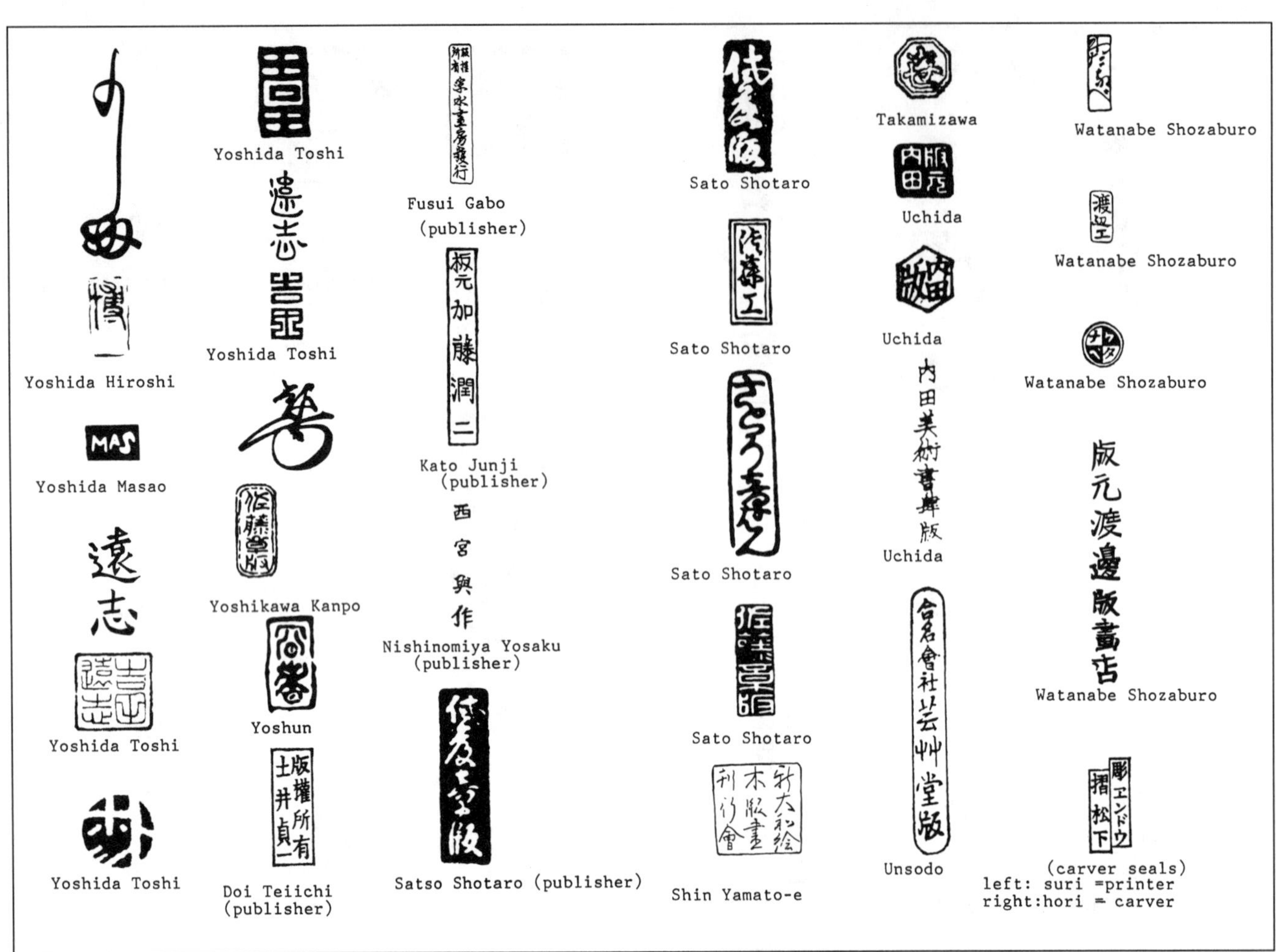
Yoshida Hiroshi
Yoshida Masao
Yoshida Toshi
Yoshida Toshi
Yoshida Toshi
Yoshida Toshi
Yoshikawa Kanpo
Yoshun
Doi Teiichi (publisher)
Fusui Gabo (publisher)
Kato Junji (publisher)
西宮與作
Nishinomiya Yosaku (publisher)
Satso Shotaro (publisher)
Sato Shotaro
Sato Shotaro
Sato Shotaro
Sato Shotaro
Shin Yamato-e
Takamizawa
Uchida
Uchida
内田美術書肆版
Uchida
Unsodo
Watanabe Shozaburo
Watanabe Shozaburo
Watanabe Shozaburo
版元渡邊版畫店
Watanabe Shozaburo
(carver seals)
left: suri =printer
right:hori = carver

Appendix G

Ukiyo-e Artists by School

The Osaka School

1. Ashihiro. Portraits of actors, 1820-1830.

2. Ashiyuki actor portraits and surimono, 1820-1830.

3. Ashikiyo. Portraits of actors, about 1825.

4. Ashimaro. Portraits of actors, about 1825.

5. Ashikuni. Prehaps the same as Shunshi and a little earlier than the others. Actors.

6. Hokuju, 1748-1815, real name Asai Shotei. Pupil of Hokusai. Also in Edo.

7. Hokutsui. Worked about 1810-1820.

8. Hokubi. Earlier signature "Shunko." Worked 1825-1849 approx. Actors, surimono and illustrations to editions of kabuki dramas.

9. Shunshosai hokucho. Actors. Pupil of Hokushu.

10. Sekkotei hokumiĺ. Actors and rare surimono.

11. Hokuga.

12. Hokui no fude. Mostly book illustrations, c. 1830-1850.

13. Seiyosai Shunshi. Actor portraits, 1820-1830. Perhaps the same as Ashikuni.

14. Shunyo. Perhaps pupil of Hokushu. Actors and dramatic scenes.

15. Shummansai Hokkaku. Said to have been an actor. Prints of actors 1835 onwards.

16. Enjaku. Perhaps an actor. Very fine dramatic prints, c. 1850. Rare.

17. Baika.

18. Kunihiro. Many actor portraits, c. 1820-1840.

19. Masunobu. Rare actor portraits, c. 1850.

20. Sadahiro. Actors and illustrations, about 1830.

21. Gochotei Sadamasu (= Kunimasu). Actors, c. 1830-1850.

22. Hirosada. Many portraits of actors, some of great merit, during the period 1835-1845.

23. Hironobu. Rare portraits.

24. Sadahiro

25. Sadakage. Actors, bijin-e (rare in this school) and surimono, c. 1840.

26. Sadanobu. Portraits, illustrations and landscapes (some good but derivative), c. 1835-1855.

27. Shigeharu. Actors and illustrations of some merit in certain instances; born 1802, died 1853.

28. Sadafusa. Portraits of actors, c. 1830.

29. Niho. Landscapes (very rare) and surimono of good quality, c. 1850.

30. Nobuhiro. Rare actor portraits.

31. Kunikazu. Actors and dramatic scenes from contemporary theatre, c. 1845.

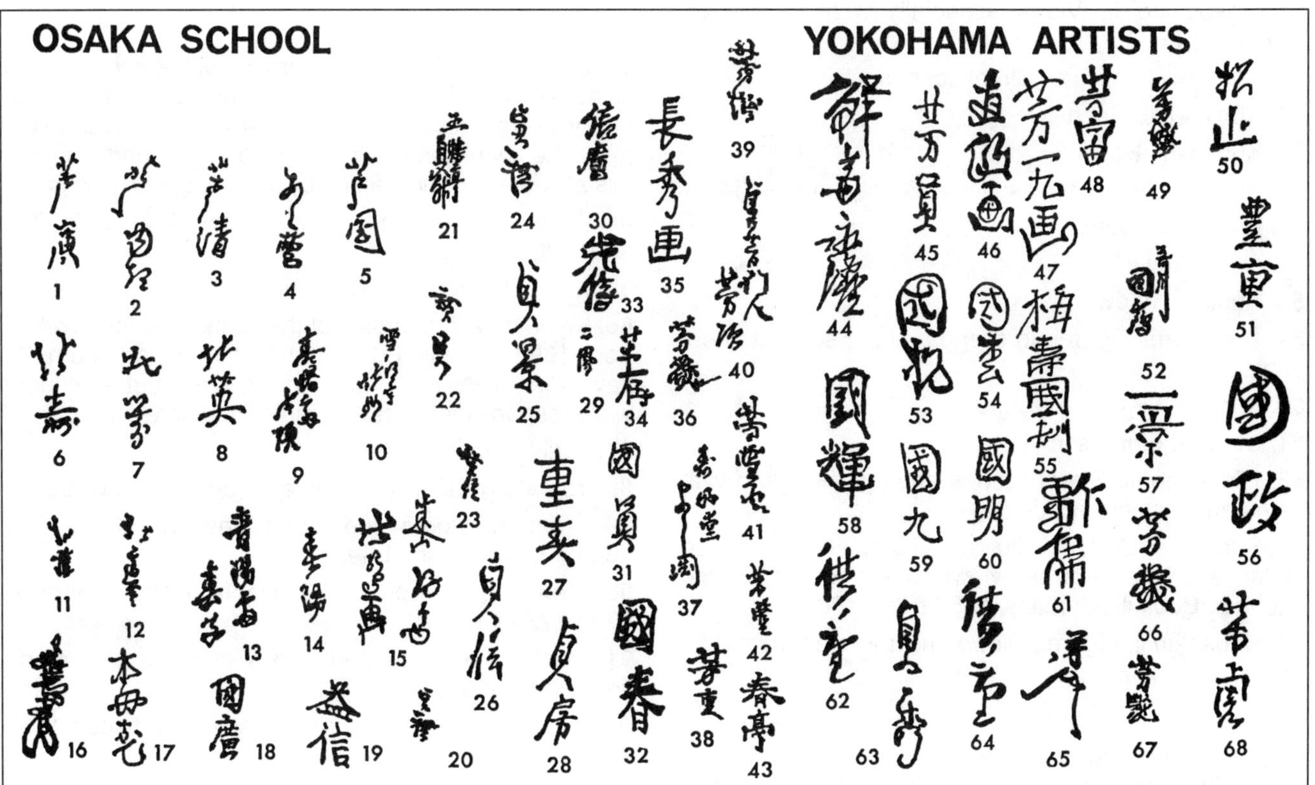

32. Kuniharu.

33. Mitsunobu. Rare portraits of actors,

c. 1850. Usually of sombre colour and striking pose.

34. Yoshiume. Pupil of Kuniyoshi. Actors, c. 1850-1860.

35. Nagahide. (So read by Kurth and also Hajek but there is some doubt) see 135.

36. Yoshichika. Actors, c. 1850.

37. Jukodo yoshikuni. Actors, c. 1850.

38. Yoshishige. Book illustrations, c. 1850.

39. Yoshitaki. Actors and landscapes, 1840-1899.

40. Sadayoshi's pupil Yoshitsugu.

41. Yoshiyuki. Actors and landscapes in the 1860's.

42. Yoshitoyo. Actor portraits, c. 1850.

43. Shuntei. Illustrations - a few of some merit, c. 1800-1810.

Artists of the Yokohama-e

Most of these artists of course produced other kinds of print as well and the very short note of themes given here refers only to their work in this genre.

44. Sensai eitaku. Figures.

45. Yoshikazu. Figures.

46. Naomasa ga. Figures.

47. Yoshiiku ga. Figures.

48. Yoshitomi. Figures.

49. Yoshimori. Figures.

50. Shotan. Views, figures and scenes in both the European and Chinese quarters. An interesting artist perhaps influenced by the Nagasaki-e and active about 1875.

51. Toyoshige II. Views especially with trains (Not Toyoshige I = Gosotei Toyokuni).

52. Utagawa kunitsuru. Street scenes, etc.

53. Kunimatsu. Scenes.

54. Kunitoshi. Scenes.

55. Baiju Kunitoshi. Views; perhaps not same as 54.

56. Kunimasa. Views.

57. Ikkei. Views.

58. Kuniteru. Views.

59. Kunimaru. Figures in scenes. Often several sheet prints.

60. Kuniaki. Figures in scenes.

61. Utatora. Figures in views.

62. Hiroshige iii. Street scenes and figures; often with trains and western buildings.

63. Sadahide. Certainly the best and most experienced of these artists. Figures, views, shipping, etc. Some interiors. Book illustrations, 1850's and 1860's.

64. Hiroshige ii. Figures, views and imported animals.

65. Yoshitoshi. Figures.

66. Toshichika. Figures.

67. Yoshitsuya. Figures.

68. Yoshitora. Figures and scenes in European countries and America.

Primitives.

Used here in a loose sense and mainly for those not so obviously in the Torii traditions.

69. Gwashi Hishikawa Moronobu (?-1694) Bijin-e, Interiors of Yoshiwara. Ichimai-e, very rare.

70. Hishikawa Moronobu (cursive style)

71. Morofusa, fl. 1685-1703. Several books and half a dozen single sheets.

72. Sukenobu (1671-1751). Many books which inspired several later artists. Sheet prints very rare. He influenced at least two generations.

73. Hanegawa chinchĺ hikko with seal "Chincho" (1679-1754). A samurai. Work rare.

74. Kumeido shinshi.

75. Ando Kaigetsudo, active 1710-1725. Courtesans. The wonderful prints of the Kwaigetsudo are the most sought after of all–as they are the rarest. Only thirty-nine are known to exist today.

76. Doshu Kaigetsudo.

77. Seal of Dohan Kaigetsudo.

78. Seal of Doshin Kaigetsudo.

79. Okumura Masanobu (1686-1764). Prolific artist, publisher and bookseller. Figures, interiors, courtesans, actors and shunga.

80. Ishikawa Ryusen, fl. 1680-1710's. Book illustrations and rare single sheets.

81. Toshinobu, fl. 1717 to about 1745. Fine urushi-e in hoso-ban format.

82. Toyonobu (1711-1785). One of the finest ukiyo-e artists especially of benizuri-e.

Tori School

83. Kiyonobu i (1664-1729). Founder of this school which is noted for actor prints of great power, delineated in highly calligraphic line. A poster artist, his prints are very rare. The kabuki handbills designed by him and others of this school are distinguished by a swirling heavy script.

84. Kiyoshige (worked a little before 1725 to a little after 1760). Rare.

85. Kiyotada (about 1718-1748).

86. Kiyomasu. Two artists of this name, the first worked from 1696 to early 1720's, whilst the secind seems to have died in 1763. Both did fine work but also both were responsible for rather more mediocre prints.

87. Torii Kiyonobu fude.

88. Yamato gwashi Torii Kiyotada" and seal Kiyotada.

89. Torii Kiyotomo fude and seal (fl. 1720-1745 approx.). Mostly urushi-e.

90. Terushige. Pupil of Kiyonobu, worked approx. 1725-1735.

91. Yoshinobu. Illustrated books of plays and made some rare benizuri-e, c. 1740's.

92. Toyomasa. Designed early nishiki-e between 1767 and 1773.

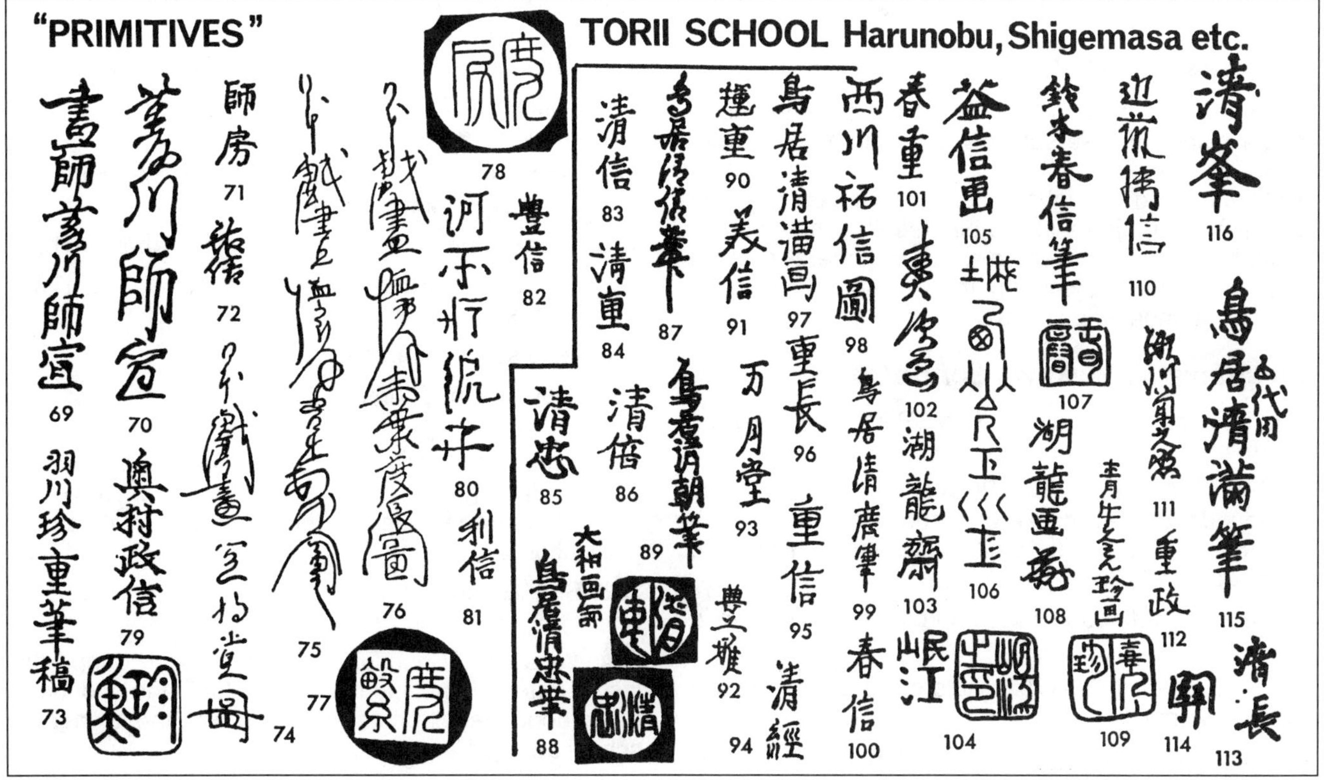

93. Mangetsudo. Pupil of Masanobu working 1740's.

94. Kiyotsune, active 1760's and 1770's. Mostly actors.

95. Shigenobu. An early name and signature of 82.

96. Shigenaga (1697-1756). Interiors, figures and fine bird prints.

97. Torii Kiyomitsu ga (1735-1785). Produced much work including some very fine hashirakake-e. Many bijin-e and some of the finest nudes in Japanese art.

98. Nishikawa Sukenobu zu (see No. 72).

99. Torii Kiyohiro fude (active 1750's and 1760's). Mostly actors in benizuri-e.

Kawamata School

100. Harunobu (1725-1771). One of the most important artists of the ukiyo-e style. Nearly all his prints were of courtesans or bijin-e. The best of his prints were probably produced for limited circles of art connoisseurs and other highly refined and literate Edo citizens. Almost all of his work has a persuasive charm and innocence.

101. Harushige. This used to be thought as earlier art name of Sha Kokan but is now believed to be that of a separate artist, see No. 186. Copied Harunobu's work.

102. Harutsugu (also read Haruji) fl. 1760's. Pupil of Harunobu; work rare.

103. Koriusai (fl. 1760-1784). A samurai and friend of Harunobu. Earlier signature Haruhiro. His subjects are similar to those of his friend with the addition of children–to which several of his prints are devoted–and a fine series of birds. He excelled in the form of the pillar-print. His colour range is darker than that of Harunobu and his work has a greater expanse of rust red. In the hosoban prints his figures are often clustered nearer together and make his designs seem more static than Harunobu's. The work of both, however, is very similar.

104. Minko (fl. about one decade from 1762). Work resembles Harunobu's. His Saigwa shokunin burui was produced with stencils and is very fine.

105. Kuninobu. Pupil of Masunobu. Produced urushi-e 1734.

106. Josei Sanjin. Kyosen ko. (fl. 1760's). His signature on prints has long puzzled scholars. He was the chairman of one of the chief literary clubs which commissioned prints from Harunobu and others. He may himself have designed some of the prints so signed but more likely he devised what others executed.

107. Sukuki Harunobu fude with seal. See No. 100.

108. Koriusai ga with a kakihanj (written seal). See No. 103.

109. Seigyo Gyochin ga with seal gyochin. (Also transliterated kyochin) (fl. 1740's?)

110. Kondo Katsunobu (fl. 1720) son of Kiyoharu who was noted for his Kompira-bon, he produced some rare but meritorious urushi-e.

111. Nishimura Magosaburo (Shigenobu). Earlier name of Ishikawa Shuha Toyonobu.

112. Shigemasa (1739-1820). Founder of Kitao School. Calligrapher and book illustrator. His scarce prints are unsigned.

113. Kiyonaga (Torii IV) (1752-1815). His work shows several influences besides Torii traditions. Very notable prints in the 1780's but the earlier work is but mediocre.

114. Seki sig. of Kiyonaga (no. 113).

115. The 5th Torii Kiyomitsu fude = Kiyomitsu II (1787-1869) sig. after 1815 of Kiyonaga's pupil, Kiyomine, see No. 116.

116. Kiyomine. Early name of Kiyomitsu II.

Hanabusa School

117. Hanabusa Itcho (1652-1724) an unorthodox Kano school painter whose subjects, often humerous, were drawn from plebeian life. His sketches were extensively published throughout the eighteenth century and reprinted many times in the nineteenth. They were a constant influence on ukiyo-e but in general show a wider and deeper sympathy than anything in ukiyo-e itself. He founded the Hanabusa school.

Miyagawa-Katsukawa Schools

118. Tominobu Miyagawa School. Prints very rare but of some grace and marked by boldness of design.

119. Shunsho (1726-1792). Pupil of Miyagawa Shunsui and founder of the Katsukawa school. Noted for theatrical prints and a prolific producer of them in the two decades from 1770.

120. Shunsen (fl. 1800-1820 approx.). Mostly bijin-e in landscape.

121. Shundo (fl. 1780-1792). Actors in dramatic roles in hosoban format.

122. Shunjo (died Aug. 1787). All his single sheet prints seem to date from the last two years of his life; previously he illustrated kibyoshi.

123. Shunko (1743-1812). Produced some outstanding prints and is credited with the invention of the large head portrait which, however, seems to have been earlier than his time.

124. Shuncho (fl. 1778-1795 approx.). Pupil of Shunsho; almost all his great prints are in the style of Kiyonaga whom he surpasses in the best of his work.

125. Shuntei (1770-1820). Some early actor prints but most commonly met with are prints of warriors, battles, etc. Some interesting landscapes in European manner.

126. Shunyei (1762-1819). Some actor prints of great merit. May have influenced Sharaku.

127. Shunzan (fl. 1782-1798). Actor prints but later influenced by Kiyonaga.

128. Shunkyo produced a few rare pirnts about 1810.

129. Katsukawa Shunsho with kakihan (1726-1792) see No. 119.

130. Vase seal of Shunsho

131. Vase seal of Shunko.

132. Shunto. Pupil of Shunyei. Produced a few rare but fine prints in the first years of the nineteenth century. Some mitate themes are known by him in whch young women play analogues of the main acts in theatrical productions.

133. Shunko (II) Shunsen's signature after 1812. See No. 120.

134. Yanagawa Shunsui. Worked in Kyoto during the last quarter of the eighteenth century and produced some good stencil prints. Relations with the Miyagawa school are problematical.

135. Choshu. This name is also read Nagahide.

Kitao School (Founder Shigemasa see No. 112).

136. Masayoshi (1764-1824). Pupil of Masanobu. His early work ws in pure ukiyo-e style but later he worked in other styles, some highly individualistic such as that of the rapid sketches called ryaku-ga-shiki.

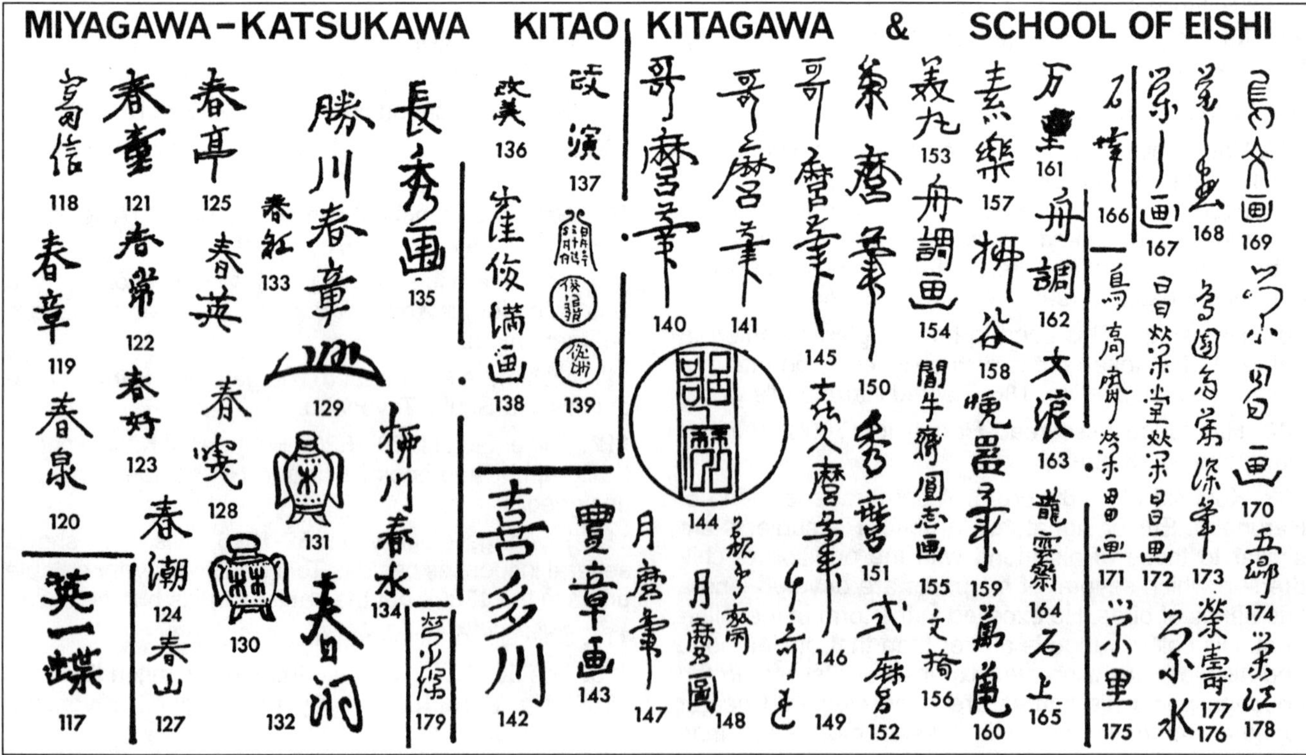

137. Masanobu (Kitao) (1761-1816). All his sheet prints–mostly bijin-e–were done in his early life. In middle age he became famous as the novelist Santo Kyoden.

138. Kubo Shunman ga (1757-1820). A very individualistic artist drawing his primary inspiration from Kiyonaga rather than from his master, Shigemasa. Most of his single sheet prints are bijin-e of women of noble presence and reposeful gesture. He is also one of the great masters of the surimono using, quite frequently, still-life" themes.

139. Seals of Shunman occurring on surimono.

Kitagawa School

140. Utamaro fude" signature of 1794

141. Kitagawa" (Utamaro) sig. on the Shell Book. Utamaro (1754-1808) is considered by some to be the greatest of all the ukiyo-e artists and, in so far as such a generalization can have any meaning, this may be true. He was undoubtedly limited in his themes, the work of his maturity being almost restricted to bijin-e. That he had great gifts in other directions is attested by the Shell Book ("Gifts of the Ebb Tide"), the Insect Book (Mushi Erabi) and the work on birds (Momoshidori awase) but these remain somewhat isolated in his output. His influence dominated ukiyo-e for the last twenty years of his life.

143. Toyoaki. Early name of Utamaro.

144. Seal Utamaro.

145. Utamaro (II) fude (fl. 1800-1810). With very few exceptions his work is not impressive.

146. Kikumaro (I) fude. Best of Utamaro's pupils. Signed thus, 1795-1805.

147. Tsukimaro fude. Signature of No. 146, from 1805 to 1820.

148. Kwanunsai tsukimaro fude. A late signature of **147.**

149. Senkwa.

150. Kikumaro II fude pupil of Kikumaro I, worked in the 1830's. Does not appear to be the same as Yukimaro, son of Kikumaro I.

151. Hidemaro. Pupil of Utamaro I. Active during Bunkwa (1804-1817).

152. Shikimaro. Contemporary of last.

153. Yoshimaro. Pupil of Kikumaro I. Active 1810's. About 1819 took the name of Kitao Shigemasa III. Sometimes signed Yoshimaro. Active until 1840.

154. Shucho ga. Active c. 1795-1800. Study of his rather rare prints gives him an increasing reputation. Bijin-e, fine surimono, kwa-cho and Eurpoean influenced uki-e.

155. Angyusai Yenshi (active 1787-1793). Rare bijin-e and actors (=? Angyusai Shudo).

156. Bunkyo (1767-1830). Is the novelist Sakuragawa Jihinari. Very rare prints.

157. Soraku. Pupil of Yeishi. Portrait busts of young women but his work in prints is rare. Was a noted kyoka poet.

158. Ryukoku (active c. 1808-1816?). Work in style of Utamaro.

159. Banki fude (=Banki II) Worked at same period and in similar style to 158.

160. Banki (I). Seems to have been influenced by Utamaro, Shunsho and Kiyonaga. His prints are rare but repesent a rather wide range of subjects. He designed at least one successful hashirakake-e of half length figures in the style of Utamaro.

161. Banri. Rare artist. Work shows influence both of Kiyonaga and early Utamaro.

162. Shuchí. Another signature of 154.

163. Bunro (active 1795-1800) pupil of Tamagawa Shucho.

164. Ryunsai. Some fine figure studies, somewhat in the manner of Kiyonaga but with a certain resemblance to early Utamaro. Dates unknown.

165. Sekijo (active c. 1798-1807). Pupil of Sekiyen.

166. Sekiho. Same master and same period of activity as last.

School of Eishi (the so-called "Hosoda School").

167. Eishi ga. An early signature.

168. Eishi ga. A later signature (1756-1829). A highly individual artist of very great talent. His restrained and rather low colouring and the unusually perfect placing of accessories combine to give an impressively aristocratic atmosphere to his work.

169. Chobun ga. In seal script. A signature of Chobunsai Eishi (No. 168).

170. Eisho ga. (active 1790's-1810). Pupil of 168 but influenced also by 142. Mostly designed pictures of courtesans.

171. Chokosai Eisho ga. Signature of 170.

172. Shoeido Eisho ga. Another signature of No. 170.

173. Choensai Eishin fude (active c. 1793-1805) variously stated to be the pupil of 168 and of eizan but the former is certainly correct.

174. Gokyo (active around 1795). Pupil of 168 whose style he followed with great exactitude. Prints by him are very rare but of high quality.

175. Eiri (active 1788-1805). Designed but few prints in manner of Eishi. He also illustrated some kibyoshi with a certain success.

176. Eisui (active 1795 to about 1801). Responsible for some rather individualistic designs in the style of his master, Eishi.

177. Eiju. Active about same time as last. Probably an amateur.

178. Eiko. Known only as a painter of ukiyo-e and not as print designer. Some of his work has been illustrated however in later block printed illustrated books.

179. Eitoku. A rare artist active about 1800. Designed very few prints.

Independent Artists.

180. Toshusai Sharaku (worked 1794 and 1795). One of the most highly valued artists of ukiyo-e school. Nothing is known for certain of his life although there is perhaps some slight evidence that he was a No actor of this name. He designed prints for Tsutaya but being unsuccessful at this time disappeared the following year. All his work concerns people of the kabuki theatre except for one portrait of a wrestler.

181. Ichijusai Kunimasa (1773-1810). Pupil of Toyokuni whose style he followed in some early prints but later did some impressive actor portraits much influenced by Sharaku yet with individual characteristics of his own. His work is perhaps even rarer than Sharaku's.

182. "Kabukido". Signature of Kabukido Enkyo (worked 1796). An amateur who designed a few actor portraits very much in the style of Sharaku. These are highly prized but very rare.

183. Buncho (active 1760's and 1770's). Work for all its high individuality shows the influence of Harunobu. Portraits of actors. Thought by some to be among the greatest artists of the school. His work is rare and not easily accessed. (See Plate 13).

184. Hanzan (active 1840's-1860's) An Ísaka artist most noted for his surimono which are in an exceptional, broad, sketchy style.

185. Sugakudo (Worked 1859-1860). A native of Osaka whose Kacho prints are sometimes of quite exceptional merit.

186. Kokan Shiba (1747-1818). Pupil of Harunobu. Much influenced by western art which he studied at Hagasaki. Worked also with oil painting, copper-plate engraving and lithography as well as a few ukiyo-e style woodcuts. Also used the name Harushige, see No. 101.

187. (Kono) Bairei (1844-1895). Studied Shijo school methods but produced some woodcuts of merit although of somewhat garish colour. Noted mostly for volumes of bird and flower studies produced in the 1880's and 1890's. Signed also Chokuho and Shijun.

188. Zesshin (1807-1891). Noted painter and lacquerer.

School of Hokusai.

189. Hokusai Tatsumasa (1760-1849) signature of about 1800. Perhaps the most prolific of all ukiyo-e artists and certainly the most experimental. His work is very uneven in quality. He used more than twenty other names, many for quite short periods in the different stages of his career. He did work in all the subjects known to ukiyo-e art and to some other schools as well. The best of his work is now rather hard to come by although late reprints of his books are not uncommon.

190. Katsu (Shika) Shunro. Name given to him by Shunsho whose pupil he was. Hokusai used the name at various times until 1796. This signature dates from 1786.

191. Hishikawa Sori. A signature used by Hokusai about 1797 and found in his hibyoshi and surimono of this period. He was, in fact, Sori IV. The first two of the name were painters only, the first (early eighteenth century) studied both Sumiyoshi and Korin schools. The third was the illustrator of Kyosen's "Segen Jui".

192. Gakyojin Hokusai. A signature adopted abou;1800.

193. Zen Hokusai Iitsu.

194. Hokusai. Name in seal script from the "Mangwa".

195. Hokusai. With phonetic reading in kana script.

196. "Gakyo" rojin manji Hokusai signature from1838.

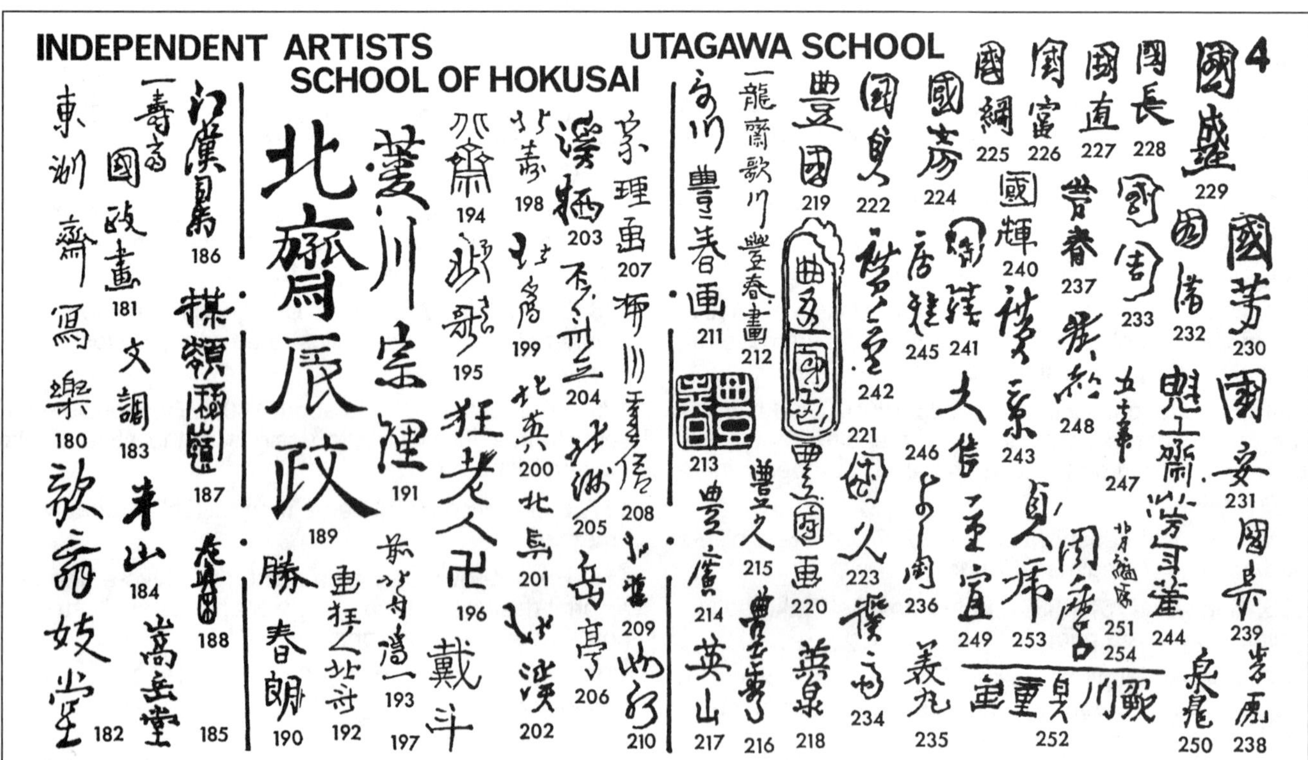

197. Taito (II) Hokusai himself was Taito I. This pupil was active from 1821 to about 1853. He was given the name in 1820 when Hokusai took the name Iitsu (no. 193). He was earlier known as Hokusen. Because he copied the master's prints without authority, he was known as "Dog Hokusai".

198. Hokuju (active c. 1802-1834). Book illustrations and some meritorious surimono.

199. Hokui (active c. 1830-1840).

200. Hokuei. An Osaka artist (see No. 8), pupil of Hokusai.

201. Hokuba (1770-1844). Pupil of Hokusai. Noted for book illustrations, some humorous single sheets and certain exquisitely detailed surimono.

202. Hokkei (worked 1810-1856). Perhaps the best of the master"s pupils. He was responsible for some very fine surimono, a few Ísaka school prints and several illustrated books.

203. Kiko Keisei. A pupil of the last. Perhaps an amateur: he produced a few rare surimono.

204. Shinsai (active 1803 to about 1815). Several books, some good surimono and some rare and interesting landscape prints. Hokusai gave him the name in 1800.

205. Hokushu. A pupil of Hokusai's active in the Osaka school about 1830-1840.

206. Gakutei (active 1800 to about 1840) pupil of Hokkei and of Hokusai. A good book illustrator, he also produced some rare and effective landscape sheets but is mostly remembered as one of the masters of the surimono. These last are rich and detailed and usually with all the refinements of printing reserved for this kind of work.

207. Sori ga. A signature of Hokusai's from 1798.

208. Yanagawa Shigenobu (1784-1832). Pupil of Hokusai and later son-in-law. Worked in Osaka and Edo. Known for a few interesting prints of No actors.

209. Hokuga. A pupil of Hokusai. His work is of poor quality but he is said to have been expert at mixing colours.

210. Hokusui. A member of this school who, about 1850, was responsible for some small landscape sheets which have a surprising charm and are drawn and printed with considerable care. He had a rather restrained colouring.

Utagawa School

211. Utagawa Toyoharu ga. An early signature (1735-1814). Founder of the school. His work is lacking in power and his early landscapes are little more than topographical essays. His uki-e and battle scenes were very important historical developments in ukiyo-e.

212. Ichirysai Utagawa Toyoharu ga. A later signature.

213. Seal of Toyoharu.

214. Toyohiro (1763-1828). Essayed almost all subjects but remains a petit maitre of charming atmosphere and gentleness - characteristics apparent in his surimono particularly.

215. Toyohisa (active 1808-1818?). Made a few actor prints.

216. Toyohide. An Osaka artist.

217. Yeizan (1787-1867). Founder of the Kikugawa school. Produced many prints, some in style of Utamaro. He also copied Toyokuni. Figure subjects.

218. Yeisen (1790-1848). Prolific designer of prints of women.

219. Toyokuni (I) (1769-1825). An influential artist who, although prolific, has claim to only a few really great works. The name was also used by Toyokuni II, Toyoshige and Toyokuni III (Kunisada).

220. Toyokuni II (Toyoshige) (1777-1835). Signs also Gosotei, Ichiyeisai adn Ichiryusai Toyokuni.

221. Toyokuni (III) (Kunisada) (1786-1865). Produced an enormous quantity of work usually of negligible quality but among it probably more fine prints than are usually accredited to him.

222. Kunisada, see 221.

223. Kunihisa. Three of this name; two women pupils of Toyokuni I and II and a man signing Ichiryusai, Ipposai, and Ichiunsai Toyokuni.

224. Kunihiko (Kokkisha).

225. Kunitsuna (Ichiransai and Ichirantei).

226. Kunitomo. Pupil of Toyokuni II.

227. Kuninao. Two artists of this name, the first a pupil of Toyokuni I (1793-1854).

228. Kuninaga. Ichiunasi (active 1801-1829).

229. Kunimori. Ipposai, Kochoro, pupil of Toyokuni II.

230. Kuniyoshi (1797-1861). Known for his musha-e (pictures of heroes) but was responsible for some fine landscape, shunga and pictures of cats.

231. Kuniyasu (1794-1834) Ipposai. Fellow student with 230 under Toyokuni I.

232. Kunimitsu (active 1802-1810s) Ichiosai.

233. Kunichika. Pupil of Toyokuni I: Ichiyosai, Ikkeisai and Keseisha.

234. Keisai (Eisen).

235. Yoshimaru (active 1807-1840). Pupil of Tsukimaro but did not escape Utagawa influence.

236. Yoshikuni. Pupil of Kuniyoshi, worked in Ísaka. Signed Jukodo, Shunkodo, Toyokawa.

237. Yoshiharu.

238. Yoshitora (active 1850-1880). Ichimosai, Kinchoro and Mosai. Some satirically humorous work of slight interest among much rubbish.

239. Kunimune. Student of Toyokuni I.

240. Kuniteru. Pupil of Toyokuni I. Used name Issai. A Kuniteru II, pupil of Kunisada.

241. Kunikiyo. Pupil of Toyokuni I.

242. Hiroshige I (1797-1858). Artist with enormous output. Noted for some of the finest atmospheric landscape prints especially those depicting snow and rain.

243. Hirokage (worked 1851-1866). Pupil of Hiroshige I.

244. Kwaisai Yoshitoshi (died 1892). His best work was worthy of a better place in history.

245. Fusatane (worked 1849-1859) Isshosai.

Artists of the Utagawa School

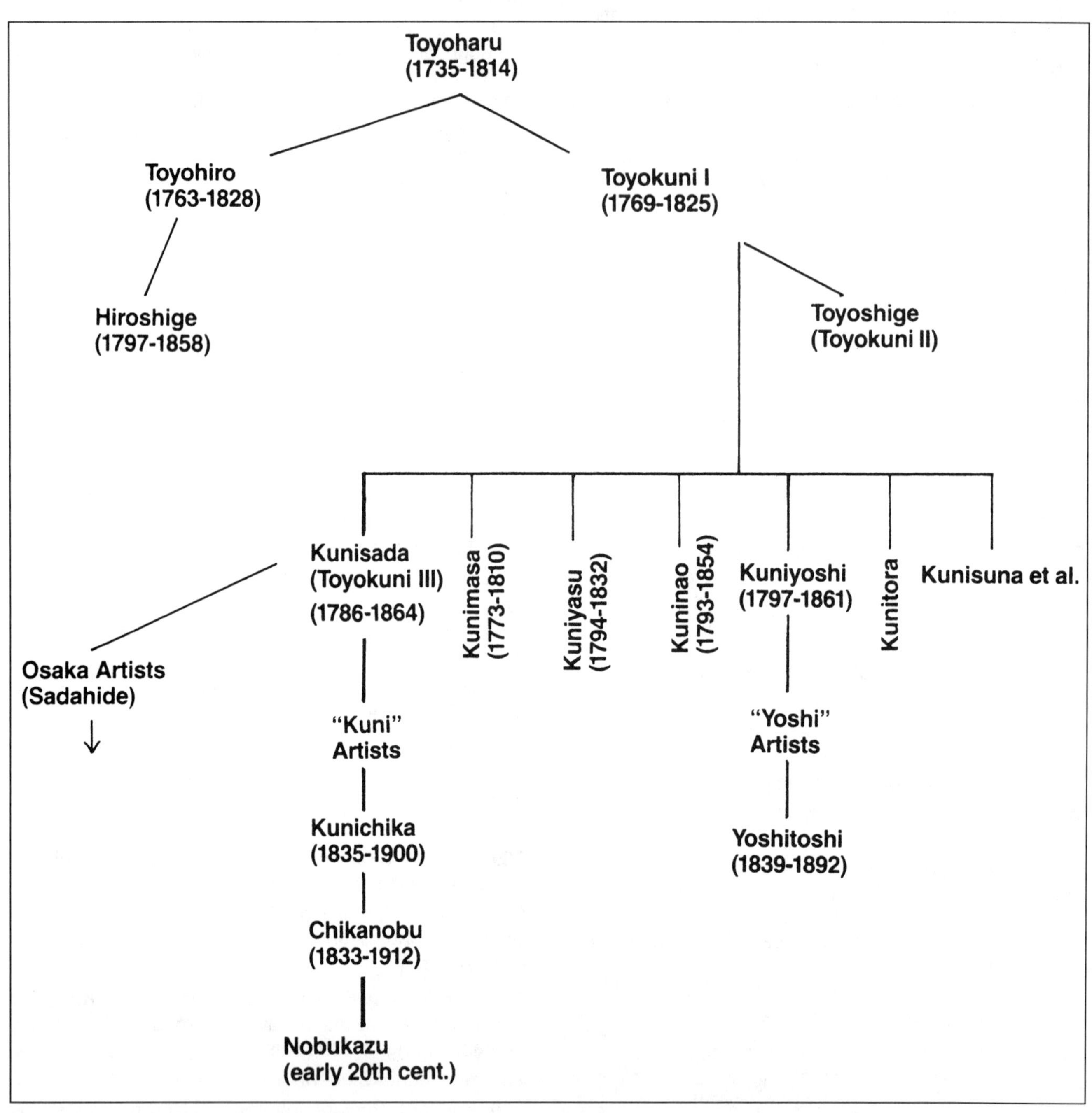

246. Hisanobu (worked 1800 to about 1820) of uncertain affinities.

247. Goshichi (worked around 1802). Pupil of Yeizan. His surimono are often excellent.

248. Kyosai (1831-1889). Pupil of Kuniyoshi. Had individual style. Often humerous.

249. Shigenobu (1826-1869) was Hiroshige II and the son-in-law of Hiroshige I.

250. Sencho. A pupil of Yeisen, No. 218.

251. Yoshitsuna. A pupil of Kuniyoshi, No. 230.

252. Utagawa Sadashige (1830-1874) was Kuniteru II and of some merit.

253. Sadatora (worked 1830s and 1840s). Pupil of Kunisada. Some interesting prints.

254. Chikamaro. A name used by Kyosai, No. 2.

Appendix H

Trademarks of Edo Publishers

1. Komatsuya Dembei
2. Urokogataya
3. Nakajimaya Risuke
4. Hiranoya Kichibei
5. Iseya Sanjiro
6. Iseya Kimbei
7. Kseya ?
8. Kiyomidzuya
9. Yedoya
10. Maruya Kuzayemon
11. Ezakiya Kichibei
12. Ibaya Sensaburo
13. Tsuruya Kihei
14. Yamaguchiya Kihei
15. Ibaya Kyubei
16. Kawaguchiya Chozo
17. Takenouchi Magahachi
18. ? Maruya Tetsujiro
19. Iseya Tokichi
20. Maruya Kohei
21. Mikawaya Rihei
22. Nishimuraya Genroku
23. Iwatoya Kisaburo
24. Matsumura Yahei
25. Yoshimaya Sonokichi
26. Tambaya
27. Maruya Jimpachi
28. Sugiwaraya ?
29. Tsuruya Ume?
30. Masuya Jimpachi
31. Eimiya Kichiyemon
32. Maruya Bunyemon
33. Murataya Jirobei
34. Nishimaya Shinroku

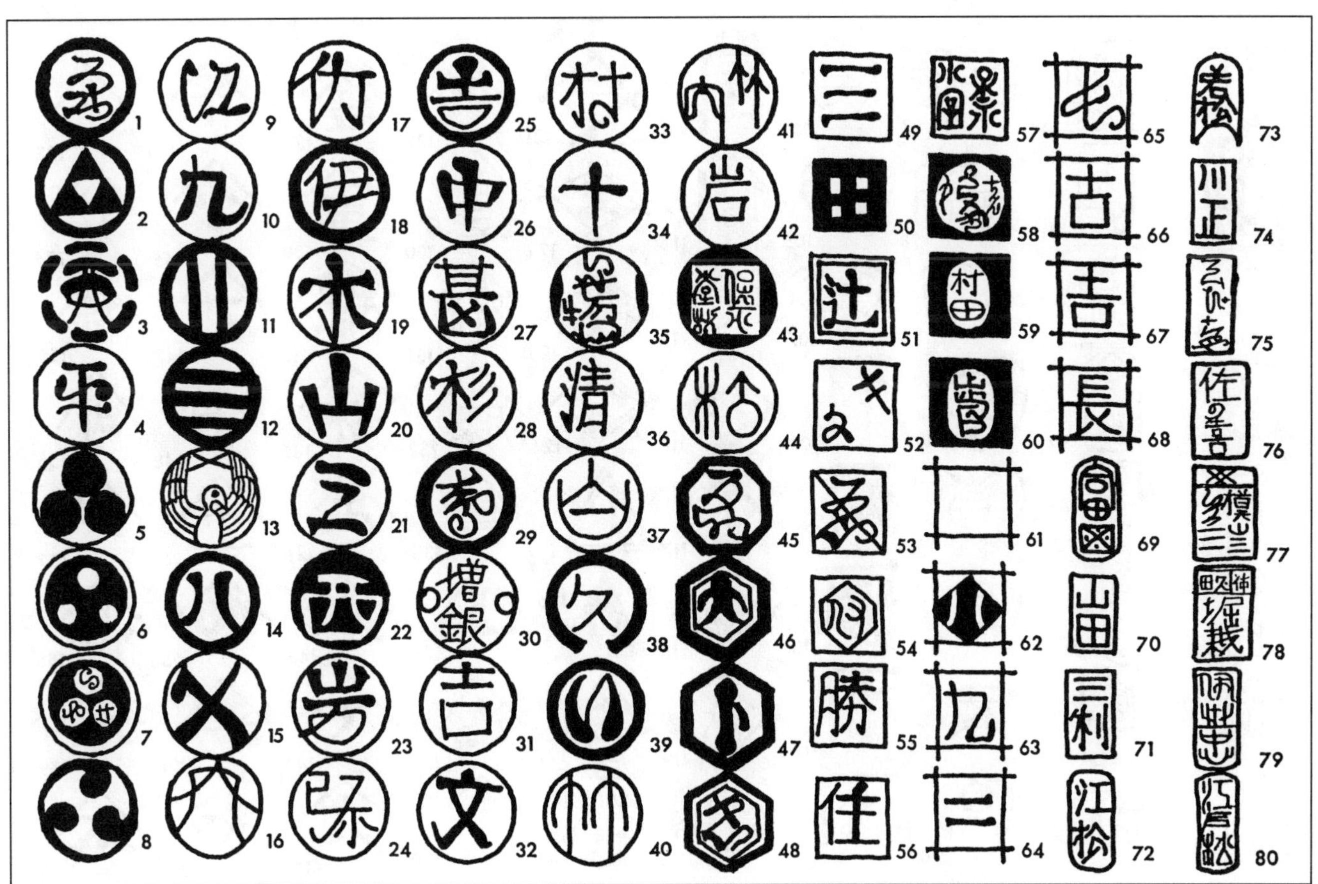

35. Iseya Soyemon
36. Maruya Seijiro
37. Ísakaya Shosuke
38. Ibaya Kyubei
39. Sawamuraya Rihei
40. Takenouchi Magohachi
41. Takenouchi Kikwakudo.
42. Iwatoya Yamagata.
43. Hoyeido
44. Wakamatsuya Gensuke
45. Yamatoya
46. Daikokuya Kinnosuke
47. Yenshuya Hikobei
48. Igaya Kanyemon
49. Shimidzuya
50. Kagiya Shojiro
51. Tsujiya Yasubei
52. Aritaya Kiyoyemon
53. Masuya ?
54. Izutsuya Kanyemon II
55. Nakamuraya Katsugoro
56. Sumimaruya Jinsuke
57. Hoyeido
58. Sakaiya
59. Murataya
60. Nakajimaya
61. Omiya Yohei
62. Kogaya Katsugoro
63. Sakaiya Kurobei
64. Kawaguchiya Chozo
65. Aridaya Seiyemon
66. Kogaya Kitsugoro
67. Sumiyoshiya Masagoro
68. Aritaya Kiyoyemon
69. Tomitaya ?
70. Yamadaya Sanshiro
71. Mikawaya Rihei II
72. Yedoya Matsugoro
73. Wakamatsuya Yoshiro
74. Kawaguchiya Shohei
75. Ebisuya ?
76. Sanoya Kihei
77. "Idzusan"
78. Horikoshi ?
79. Iseya Chusei

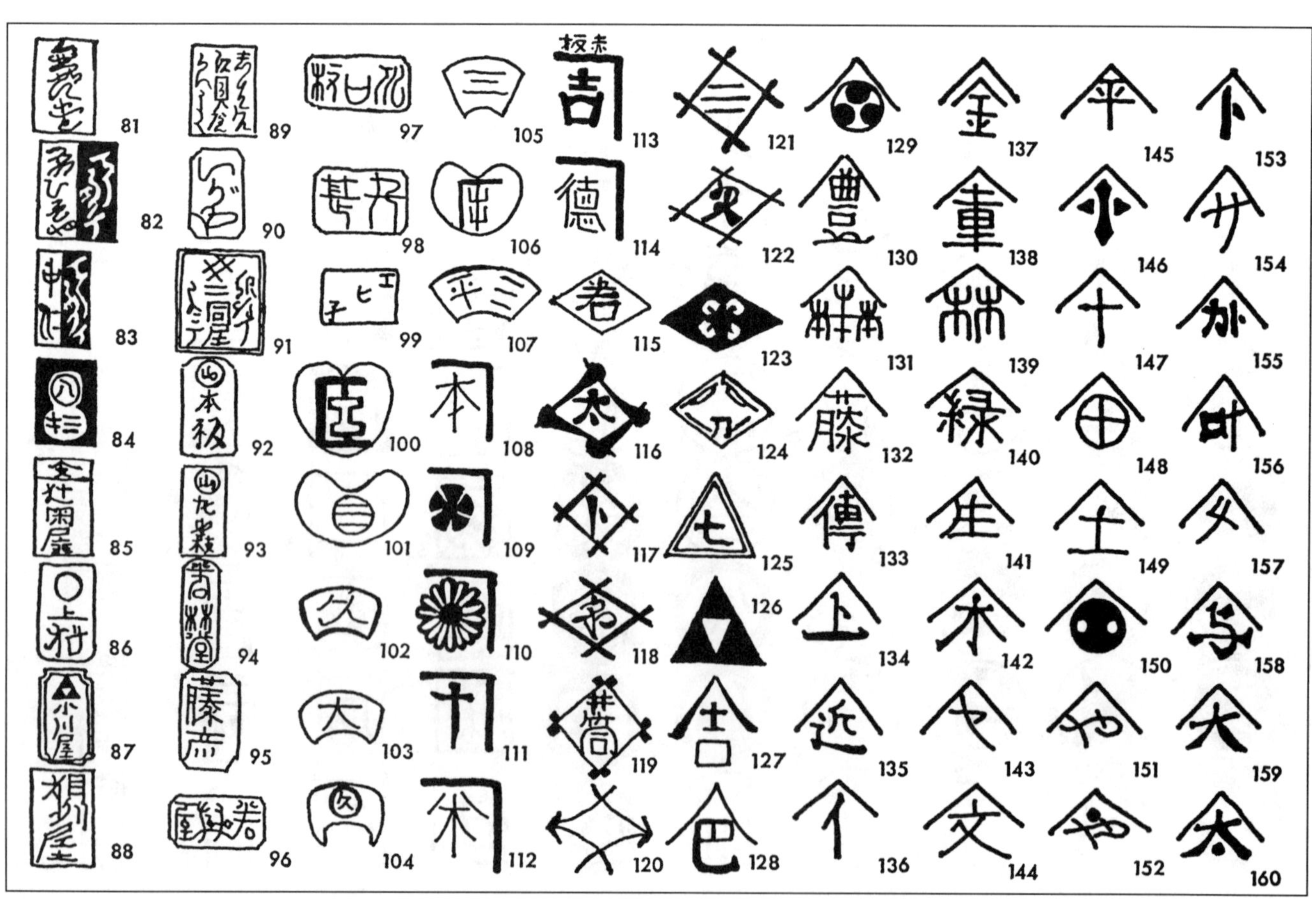

80. Edoya Matsugoro
81. Enkakudo
82. Ebisuya Shoshichi
83. Kinshodo
84. Mitaye Kihachi
85. Tsujiokaya Bunsuke
86. Uemuraya
87. Urokogataya
88. Sagamiya
89. Emiya
90. Igaya
91. Igaya
92. Yamamoto = Maruya Kohei
93. Maruya
94. Jakurindo = Yokasaya Yoichi
95. Fujiokaya Hikotaro
96. Wakasaya Yoichi
97. Isekane ? Kawaguchi
98. Maruya Jimpachi
99. Ebiya.
100. Hirabashiya Shogoro
101. Ibaya Sensaburo
102. Ibaya Kyubei = Kinseido
103. Omiya Kuhei
104. Ibaya Kyubei
105. "San"=? Sanmaido
106. Rinshodo
107. Sankindo
108. Daikokuya Heikichi
109. Azumaya Daisuke
110. Kikuya Ichibei
111. Kojimaya ?
112. Idzusan ?
113. Iseya Kanekichi
114. Hamadaya Tokubei
115. Wakasaya Yoichi
116. Ningyoya Takichi
117. Ebiya Rinnosuke
118. Izutsuya Chuzayemon
119. Izutsuya Sanyemon
120. Sagamiya
121. Yenami
122. Marukyudo
123. Uyedaya Kyujiro
124. Fujiwaraya Bunjiro
125. Ogawa Shichirobei and Yenomoto Kichibei

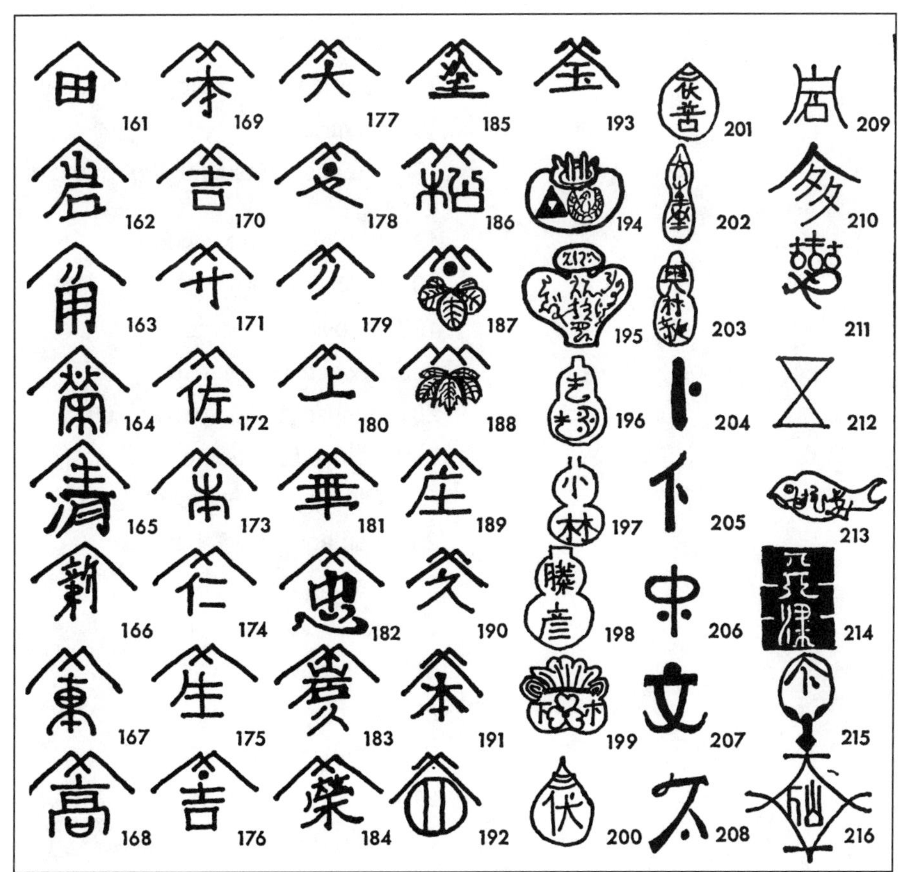

126. Urokogataya
127. Yamashiroya (Shokwakudo) and Izudtsuya
128. Iwaiya
129. Nishimuraya Yohachi
130. Toyojimaya Bunjiyemon
131. Mariya Jihei
132. Yamashiroya Tokei
133. Yamaden
134. Kawaguchiya Uhei
135. Soshuya Yohei
136. Sanoya Kihei
137. Yamazakiya Kimbei
138. Joshuya Juzo
139. Iseya Rihei
140. Echizenya Heisaburo
141. Yamadaya Shobei
142. Echigoya Chohachi
143. Fujiokaya Hikotaro
144. Tsujiokaya Bunsuke
145. Omiya Heihachi
146. Shin Iseya Kohei
147. Yamadaya Juhei
148. Daikokuya Kyubei
149. Muraya Kyushiro
150. Daikokuya Kinjiro
151. Fujiokaya Hikotaro
152. Fujiokaya Keijiro
153. Yenshuya Matabei
154. Ídaya Takichi
155. Tsuruya Kiyemon
156. Gusokya Kahei
157. Tajimaya Yehei
158. Hori Takichi
159. Joshuya Kinzo
160. Ningyoya Takichi
161. Yamaden ?
162. Katoya
163. Kadomaruya
164. Takahashiya
165. Kiyomidzuya
166. Shinsenyendo
167. Surugaya
168. Takasu Shoshichi
169. Iwatoya Gempachi and Izumiya Ichibei
170. Kagaya Kichibei
171. Matsumoto Sahei
172. Yamadaya Sasuke
173. Takatsuya Isuke
174. Kinshodo (NOT Kinshodo!)
175. Yebisuya Shoshichi = Kinshodo
176. Yorozuya Kichibei
177. Joshuya Kinzo
178. Fujiokaya Keijiro
179. ? Kuwagataya
180. Iseya Soyemon
181. ? Herindo
182. Chusuke ?
183. Iwamoto Kyubei
184. Takahashiya
185. Mikawaya
186. Matsumura Yahei
187. Tsutaya Kichizo
188. Tsutaya Jusaburo
189. Ebisuya Shoshichi
190. Yamamotoya Heikichi
191. Kawaguchiya Shozo
192. Yezakiya Tatsukura
193. Moritaya Hanjiro
194. Tsuruya and Urokogataya together
195. Izumiya
196. Reads “Mitsuoki” the gourd seal of Okumuraya (Masunobu)
197. Kobayashiya Matsugoro
198. Fujihiko
199. Kinoshita Jinyemon
200. Fushimiya Genroku
201. Fushimiya Genroku as 200
202. Shioya Shosaburo
203. Okumuraya Genroku
204. Yamaguchiya Tobei
205. Yamaguchiya Chusuke
206. Akamatsuya Shotaro
207. Shiuwaya Bunshichi
208. Nishikiya Takemura
209. Kadusaya Iwakichi
210. Ningyoya Takichi
211. Kiriya

212. Iseya Heibei

213. Ebisuya

214. Amamatsuya Hosuke

215. Yenshuya Matabei

216. "Senichi" see list

The following publisher"s seals are chosen only as examples. When the publisher"s name is printed in full the seal often follows it. A seal under the artist"s name on a print is most frequently that of the artist himself and not the publisher.

217. Reads "Tori shio cho Okumuraya Hammoto" i.e. the publisher Okumuraya in Tori Shio Street.

218. Sakaiya hammoto

219. Murata han

220. Mikawaya Ai (hei han)

221. Maruko

222. Uemura

223. Nakajimaya

224. Tsurushin-later used by Moriji

225. Hangiya Shichirobei

226. Surugaya

227. Ezakiya Tatsukura

228. Hoyeido

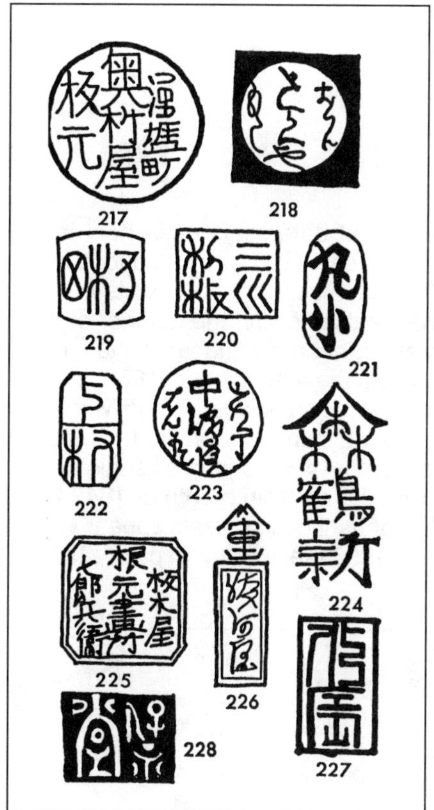

Appendix I

Date and Censor Seals

Censor seals and date seals often help to date the prints. The kiwame seal (1,2) was introduced in the ninth month of 1790 and occurs on most prints until 1842. In 1805 additional seals showing the number of the month of publication appear and continue until the fourth month of 1806 (3-8). From the fifth month of 1806 until 1811 the year is designated by its zodiacal symbol with a numeral for the month (9-14, numerals omitted to avoid confusion). Between 1811-14 various gyoji seals appear (not illustrated). From the seventh month of 1842 to the end of 1846 single nanushi censor seals appear (15-26) and from early 1847-1852 these occur in pairs (27-35). From the second month of 1852 to the eleventh month of 1853 an added date seal gives the year and month (35-43). From the last month of 1853 to the end of 1857 the aratame seal replaces the nanushi seals (44-47). In 1858 the date seal appears alone (48). From 1859-71 a single seal combining aratame, the zodiacal year symbol and a number denoting the month (mostly omitted from the table) occurs (49-62). Between 1872 and 1875 a simple year-month date seal is found (63-65). From 1876 formal censorship ceased but dates are often given by reference to the years of the Emperor's reign (66-68).

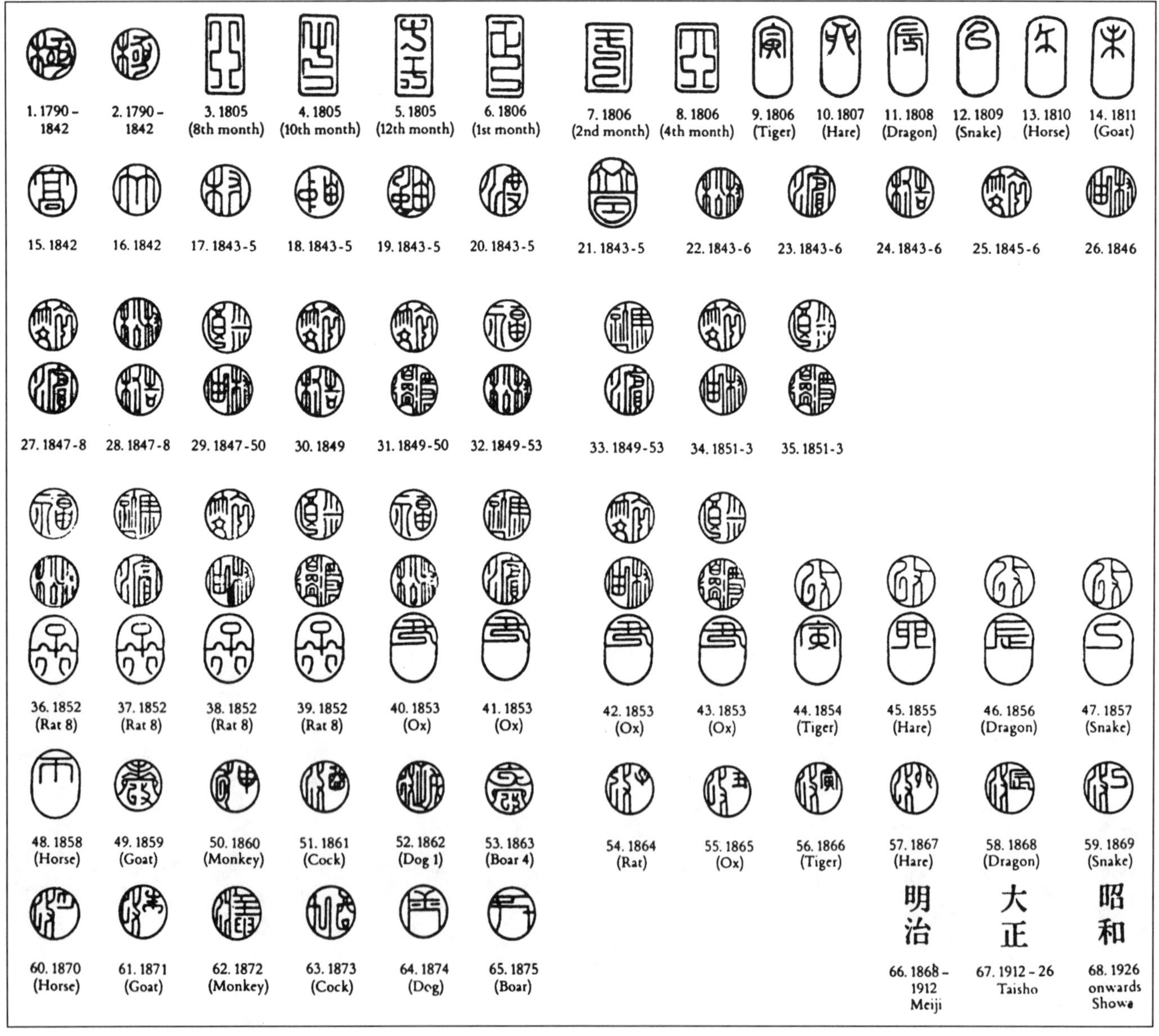

The dating of prints 1790 to 1874

Japanese prints are dated by determining the period in which certain censor seals are used. The appear either singly on in conjunction with other censor's seals and date seals.

There are four types of censor's seals. The kiwame (approval), aratame (examined), the Gyoji and Nanushi. The Gyoji and Nanushi and circular and contain one syllable of the censor's name.

The name Gyoji refers to members of the Wholesale Publishers Guild, to whom the artist's designs were submitted for approval. Late in the 1840's, the headmen of the city's wards were appointed to this duty. There are called the Nanushi censors.

Date seals are seals that contain a zodiacal symbol for the year and a numeral for the months. During the early 1800's a month seal was briefly used.

Censor seals are not found on private printings, pirated prints, shunga (erotic prints), or on prints before 1790. Due to the lack of research in the area of dating before 1840, inaccuracies are bound to occur as more material is being researched.

Examples of Seals 1790-1874

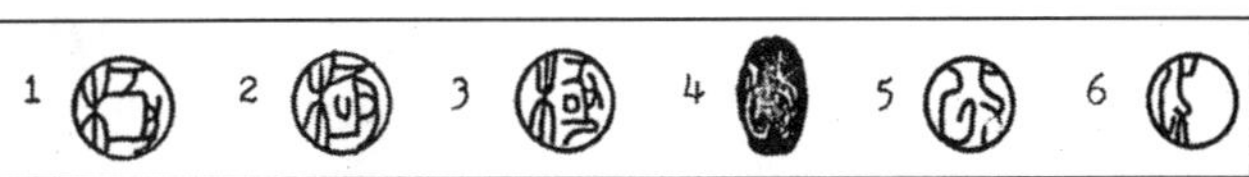

1. Kiwame (approval) seal, this seal and its variations were used from 1790-1845. This one is the earliest, found singly 1790-1804.
2. Used singly or with other from 1800-1845.
3. Same as above
4. Oval aratame (examined) used from 1848-1851
5. Round aratame (examined) used from Dec., 1853-1859.
6. Aratame incorporated with date seal 1859-1874.

Appendix J

Actor's Mon (Crests)

1. Agemaki Rinza but before 1756 was Azuma.

2. Anekawa Shinshiro (1609-1749) but jo-mon of the whole school.

3. Arashi jo-mon

4. Arashi Sangoro (1726-1729)

5. Arashi Wakano.

6. Arashiotohachi (1732-1768)

7. Bando jo-mon.

8. Bando Hikosaburo II.

9. Bando Mitsugoro I jo-mon.

10. Bando Mitsugoro kae-mon: jomon as 9.

11. Bando Hikosaburo III, 1759-1803/1806-1811.

12. Fujimura Hantayu jo-mon.

13. Hayakawa Shinkatsu, 1703-1711/1712-1738.

14. Ichikwa Danjuro II and the mon of the Naritaya and Kuraiya.

15. The jo-mon of the Osaka branch of the Naritaya. Sumizo Ichikawa occurs in late prints.

16. Ichikawa Danzo I, 1695-1740 (after 1731 he removed the characteroichi').

17. Ichikawa Sosaburo, 1731-1753.

18. Ichikawa Raizo I (kaemon) – his jo-mon was 14 - and Ichikawa Monnosuke II, 1756-1794.

19. Ichikawa Masugoro, 1727-1741.

20. Ichikawa. Jo-mon of the ke Omodokaya.

21. Ichikawa Danzo III, 1739-1772 intermittently.

22. Ichikawaomezo, 1776-1800/1804-1824.

23. Ichikawa Danjuro VI, 1782-1799.

24. Ichikawa Koamazo II, 1770-1801.

25. Ichikawa Yaozo II, 1751-1777. Kae-mon. For jo-mon he used No. 27.

26. Ichikawa Monnosuke, 1700-1727.

27. Ichikawa Yaozo I, 1747-1759.

28. Ichikawa Komazo.

29. Ichikawaomezo.

30. Ichikawa Monnosuke III?

31. Ichikawa Danzo who also used No. 16

32. Ichimura Uzayemon VIII.

33. Ichimura Uzayemon IX. 1731-1785.

34. Ichimura Uzayemon XII for whose successors it became the jo-mon. Also used by Kakitsu.

35. Iwai Sagenda (1700-1718).

36. Iwai Hanshiro II (1700-1710) and Hanshiro III (1722-1756).

37. and 38. Jo- and kae-mon of Iyai Hanshiro IV, 1753-1800 intermittently.

39. Kametani Kikusan jo-mon.

40. Kamimura Kichisaburo, 1700-1708.

41. Katsuyama Matsugoro, 1707-1723.

42. Kirinami Onoe (kae-mon).

43. Matsumoto Koshiro, 1700-1729.

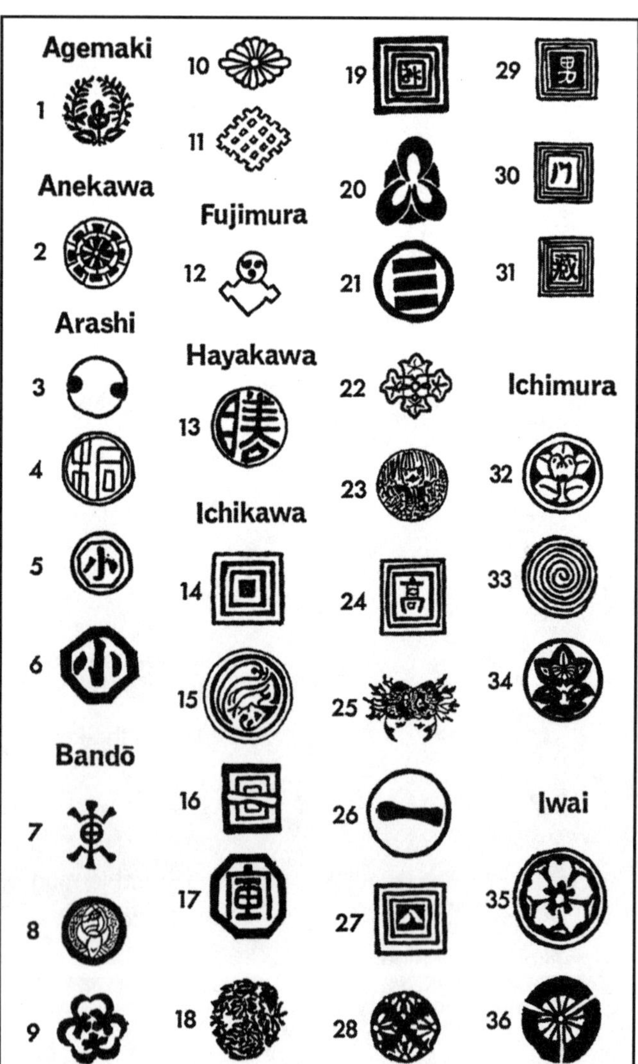

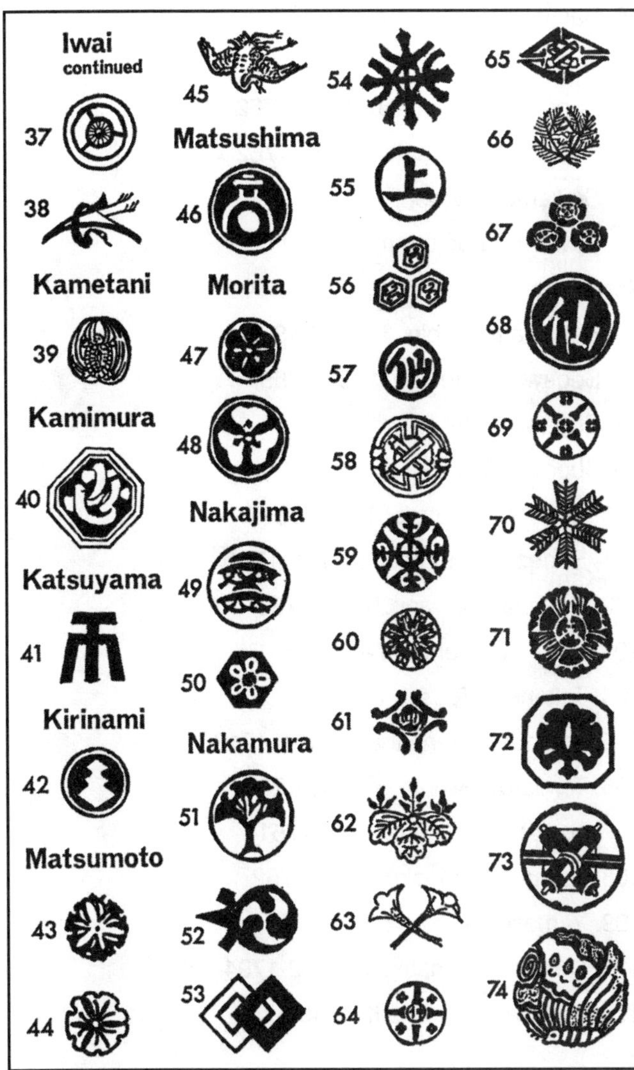

44. Matsumoto Koshiro II, 1719-1776. Took No. 45 as kae-mon.

45. Matsumoto Koshiro IV, 1754-1800 intermittently. Kae-mon. Took No. 44 as his jo-mon.

46. Matsushima Hyotaro, 1700-1725 intermittently.

47. Morita Kanya became the jo-mon used by most of the ke.

48. Morita Kanya VI, 1736-1770.

49. Nakajima Kanzayemon, 1700-1710. Jo-mon also of Miyoyemon I, 1714-1762, and Miyoyemon II, 1755-1782.

50. Makajima Sambozo and several others of the ke.

51. Nakamura Senza, 1716-1718.

52. Nakamura Takesburo, 1700-1720.

53. Nakamura Shichisaburo I, 1700-1713 and jo-mon of Shichisaburo II who used No. 56 for his kae-mon.

54. Nakamura Denjuro I, 1700-1713.

55. Nakamura Kichibei, 1716-1739.

56. Nakamura Shichisaburo I and II.

57. Nakamura Sukegoro, 1725-1763.

58. Nakamura Utayemon I, 1757-1770.

59. Nakamura Denkuro II, 1733-1755.

60. Nakamura Tomijuro I, 1731-1778 intermittently and Noshi I, 1770-1777.

61. Nakamura Kiyosaburo I, 1749-1758.

62. Nakamura Kumetaro I, 1748-1755.

63. Nakamura Nakazo I Kaemon. Acted intermittently with several changes of mon, 1745-1786. Used No. 54 as jo-mon.

64. Nakamura Nakazo II, 1778-1796.

65. Nakamura Matsue, 1761-1785. Usedo. 66 as the jo-mon.

66. Jo-mon of No. 65.

67. Nakamura Sukegoro II, 1761-1798. Kae-mon. Used 68 for jo-mon.

68. Nakamura Sukegoro I, 1725-1763.

69. Nakamura Nakazo. It is as No. 64 without theooni' character in the centre and was used as a jo-mon by several later actors of the school.

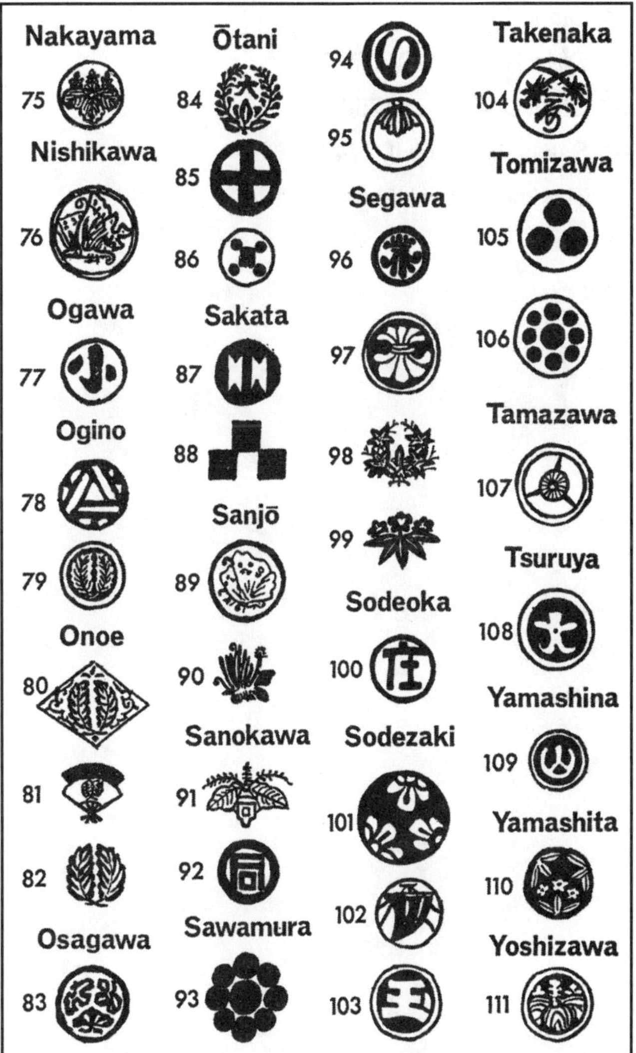

70. Used by anosaka Branch of the Nakamura (Tennojiya?).

71. Used by Baigyoku I and Fujusake I and found on someosaka prints.

72. Used as jo-mon in this school by the long line of actors with the name Kanzaburo.

73. Used by the later actors of the Nakamura, with the name Utayemon and by the family Shikan.

74. A common mon in the school in later times and found on a late print of the actor Shibajaku (III?). Note differences from other butterfly mon.

75. Nakayama

76. Nishikawa Konsuke, 1700-1702

77. Ogawa Zengoro, 17111-1732

78. Ogino Isaburo, 1724-1747

79. Ogino Isaburo, 1724-1747

80. Onoe Kikugoro I (Baiko), 1742-1773

81. Jomon of Onoe Kikugoro I

82. Onoe Matsusuke, 1756-1814

83. Osagawa Tsuneyo II, 1763-1808

84. Otani Hiroji I

85. Otani Hiroji I, 1701-1743

86. Otani Oniji, 1735-1756

87. Sakata Hangoro II, 1742-1782

88. The kaemon of Hangoro II

89. Sanjo Kantaro, 1714-1749

90. Sanjo Kantoro

91. Sanokawa Ichimatsu, 1741-1762

92. Sanokawa Ichimatsu, 1741-1762

93. Sawamura Kodenji, 1700-1702

94. Sawamura Sojuro II, 1749

95. Sawamura Sojuro III, 1759-1800

96. Segawa Kikunojo, 1730-1748

97. Segawa Kikunojo I, 1731-1755

98. Sugawa Yujiro

99. Sugawa Yujiro

100. Sodeoka Shotaro, 1716-1733

101. Sodezaki Niunosuke, 1702-1711

102. Sodezaki Miwano, 1725-1735

103. Sodezaki Iseno, 1726-1745

104. Takenaka Tosshi, 1743

105. Tomizawa Hansaburo, 1710-1718

106. Tomizawa Montaro, 1740-1749

107. Tomazawa Saijiro, 1733-1751

108. Tsuruya Namboku, 1732-1752

109. Yamashina

110. Yamashita Kinsaku II, 1752-1794

111. Yoshizawa Ayame II, 1745-1752

Appendix K

Names of Famous Courtesans Depicted in Woodblock Prints

1. Hitofude (also a locution used in letters written by women and meaning "just a line" or "a few lines")
2. Yayegiri
3. Tokayeri
4. Nanasato
5. Kokonoye
6. Kawanoto
7. Sanshu
8. Mitsuharu
9. Chidori
10. Chitose
11. Chiharu
12. Chibune
13. Yugiri
14. Yubaye
15. Kumegawa
16. Kodayu
17. Nakayama
18. Oi
19. Shirosumi
20. Shiroharu
21. Tamagawa
22. Tamanoye
23. Tamatoko
24. Tamasho
25. Tamagiku
26. Tamagoto
27. Tamahagi
28. Tamateru
29. Tamakadzura
30. Shiramono
31. Shirakawa
32. Shiro
33. Shirotaye
34. Shirotama
35. Shiroito
36. Shirabei
37. Shiragiku
38. Shiratsuya
39. Uriuno
40. Motosuye
41. Suyehiro (lit. a type of folding fan)
42. Takehime
43. Yegawa
44. Handayu
45. Taye
46. Yemon
47. Jigoku-dayu
48. Sayoginu
49. Koromode
50. Kinugasa
51. Yemon
52. Yoshino
53. Yoshikawa
54. Ariwara
55. Koshikibu
56. Sata

一	川	春11	太	川21	琴26	白32	白	半	夜	川53	妙58
筆1	戸6	千	夫16	玉	玉	白	露38	太	絹48	在	杣
八	三	船12	中	ノ	萩27	妙33	瓜39	夫44	衣	原54	川59
重	州7	夕	山17	江22	玉	白	木	江	手49	小	大
桐2	三	霧13	大	玉	照28	玉34	末40	妙45	衣	式	町60
十	春8	夕	井18	床23	玉	白	末	江	笠50	部55	吾
返3	千	栄14	代	玉	葛29	絲35	廣41	門46	衣	佐	妻61
七	鳥9	久	墨19	菖24	白	白	竹	地	紋51	多56	呉
里4	千	米	代	玉	物30	葉36	姫42	太	吉	佐	竹62
九	歳10	川15	春20	菊25	白	白	江	夫47	野52	香	小
重5	千	小	玉	玉	川31	菊37	川43	早	吉	保57	車63

57. Sakao
58. Taye
59. Somakawa
60. Omachi
61. Adzuma
62. Kuretake
63. Oguruma
64. Oyama
65. Hatsuse
66. Koya
67. Koya
68. Matsuyama
69. Matsumura
70. Matsukaze
71. Matsundo
72. Matsuhana
73. Matsumagi
74. Akashi
75. Nagato
76. Nagao
77. Nagohama
78. Choto
79. Nagaho
80. Tsumagoto
81. Makinoto
82. omaki
83. Toriwa
84. Hanasaki
85. Kwacho
86. Hanayanagi
87. Kwayu
88. Hanando
89. Hananoto
90. Hanagoromo
91. Hanamachi
92. Hananowatashi
93. Hanateru
94. Hanatsuma
95. Hanazome
96. Hanamurasaki
97. Hanaogi
98. Hanamado
99. Hanatsuya
100. Hanatsuru
101. Toragozen
102. Otobane
103. Shinateru
104. Shigeoka
105. Shigemoto
106. Shigeririye
107. Senju
108. Harushiba
109. Haruno
110. Yoshito
111. Mitsuma
112. Wakamatsu
113. Wakana
114. Wakana
115. Wakataye
116. Wakaura
117. Wakaume
118. Wakamurasaki
119. Wakaba
120. Minaduru
121. Somekawa
122. Somenosuke
123. Yamato
124. Suzunami
125. Ukishima
126. Ukifume (this is also the title of chapter 51*

of the Genji Monogatari).

127. Kuranosuke
128. Takagi
129. Takao
130. Takamura
131. Takamadodayu
132. Miyagawa

尾山64泊瀬65阿古66許也67松山68松
村69松風70松人71於花72政那木73明
石74長門75長尾76長濱77長登78長端79
妻琴80巻戸81大巻82鳥岩83花咲84花
鳥85花柳86花遊87花人88花ノ戸89花
衣90花町91花ノ渡92花照93花妻94花
染95花紫96花扇97花窓98花露99花鶴100
虎御101音羽102品照103重岡104重本105重
枝106泉壽107春芝108春野109美人110美妻111
若松112若菜113若那114若妙115若浦116若
梅117若紫118若葉119皆鶴120染川121染之
助122倭123涼波124浮島125浮舟126倉之助127

133. Miyagi

134. Makinoto

135. Morokoshi

136. Karagiku

137. Morokoshi (this name seems originally to have been taken by prostitutes from the Ryukyu Islands

138. Ogino

139. Asaju

140. Michinoku

141. Umegaye

142. Onoyama

143. Onodaki

144. Toriiwa

145. Tokidzu

146. Tokigi

147. Tokiyoshi

148. Komurasaki

149. Renzan

150. Sushore

151. Agemaki

152. Katsuyama

153. Utanosuke

154. Yosogi

155. Asadzuma

156. Miyakoji

157. Kumoi

158. Kumodori

159. Tomikawa

160. Kisegawa

161. Kicho

162. Morinosuke

163. Hanaogi

164. Sugawara

165. Suganosuke

166. Nioteru

167. Makinosuke

168. Terutaye

169. Daisei

170. Manshu

171. Mitsusode

172. Makino-o

173. Kasen

174. Utahime

175. Sugaoka

176. Katsumi

177. Kawasemi

178. Yeishi

179. Masuharu

180. Kotobiki

181. Koine

182. Tagasode

183. Shidzu-no-o

184. Misayama

185. Ohashi

186. Ainare

187. Nishikinokoji

188. Shinoura

189. Hamamurasaki

190. Oiso

191. Agemaki

192. Kasumino

193. Usugumo

194. Yenishi

195. Shigeteru

196. Kaoi

197. Kayede

198. Toyooka

199. Toyohara

200. Toyoteru

201. Segawa

202. Seyama

203. Takigawa

204. Takahashi

205. Tsuyazumi

206. Fujiwara

207. Kozakura

高城128 高雄129 高村130 高恋太夫131 宮
川132 宮本133 眞木の戸134 唐土135 唐菊136
唐師137 扇野138 淺ゞ[illegible]139 陸奥140 梅枝141
野山142 野瀧143 鳥岩144 常津145 常木146 常
芳147 小紫148 連山149 須捕150 揚巻151 勝山152
雅樂助153 粧木154 朝妻155 都路156 雲井157
雲鳥158 富川159 喜瀬川160 喜長161 盛之
助162 華扇163 菅原164 菅之助165 鳩照166 萬
紀之助167 照妙168 大勢169 滿州170 滿袖171
槙ノ尾172 歌川173 歌姫174 壽加岡175 壽
津美176 翡177 榮司178 增春179 彈琴180 小稲181
誰袖182 賤ノ尾183 操山184 大橋185 鴨緑186

錦小路187篠
浦188濵紫189大
磯190總角191霞
野192薄雲193緣194
繁照195顔居196
雛冠197豊岡198
豊原199豊照200
瀬川201瀬山202
瀧川203瀧橋204
艶壽美205藤
原206小櫻207

Locutions Used in Prints of Women

1. *Bijin* (a Beauty)
2. *Biyo* (a Beauty)
3. *Waka* (young)
4. *Yuri* (a prostitute quarter)
5. *Musume nana Komachi* (Girls as the Seven Komachi)
6. *Go (Shichi) kenjin.* Five (Seven) courtesans from as many houses.
7. *Seiro maikun* (Famous courtesans)
8. *Yoshiwara*
9. *Joro*
10. *Seirobijin* (Beauties of the Pleasure Quarters)
11. *Oiran* (a prostitute of the highest class).
12. *Oidan* (Literally, "a flower bed" - a euphemism for a brothel).
13. *Hanaguruma* (Literally, "a flower chariot" a cant name given to a serving maid in a brothel but in this sense it is read "kwasha").
14. *Ogi* (a prostitute, a substitution for the next . . .)
15. *Ogi* (a fan, see No. 14)
16. *Haru* (read thus it means "Spring" but read "Shun" it means "erotic")
17. *Ten (Den).* (A shop. Usually one dealing in dried goods is understood. It is found on prints depicting lovely shop assistants)
18. *Shoka* (a brothel)
19. *Kuruwa no naka or kuruwa no uchi.* (Literally "within the quarter". It is said of inmates of the Yoshiwara)
20. *Yugeijo* (courtesans)
21. *Joshi* (Lovers' Double Suicide)
22. *Yukun* (a courtesan)
23. *Yujo* (a courtesan)
24. *Keisei* (a courtesan)
25. *Ageya* (a brothel)

美人1美女2若3
狹邪4娘七小
町5五[七]軒人6
青樓名君7吉
原8女郎9青樓
美人10花魁11花
壇12花車13妓14[扇15]
春16店17娼家18郭
中[内19]遊藝女20
情死21遊君22遊
女23傾城24揚屋25

Appendix L

Genji Mon

The Genji Monogatari is a 10th century novel by Lady Murasaki Shikibu. The story has been the subject of many woodblock prints and each of it's 54 chapters may be associated with a series of related small geometric devices known as Genji Mon.

Recognition of these will indicate the chapter from which the print subject is taken, each chapter having its own special mon.

1.Kiritsubo
2.Hahkigi
3.Utsusemi
4.Yugao
5.Wakamuasaki
6.Suyetsumuhana
7.Momiji no Ga
8.Hana no Yen
9. Aoi
10. Sakaki
11. Hanchirusato
12. Suma
13. Akashi
14. Miozukushi
15. Yomgiu
16. Sekiya
17. Eawase
18. Matsukaze
19. Usugomo
20. Asago
21. Otome
22. Tamakazura
23. Hatsune
24. Kocho
25. Hotaru
26. Tokonatsu
27. Kagaribi
28. Nowake
29. Miyuki
30. Fujibakama
31. Makibashira
32. Umegaye
33. Fuji no Uraba
34. Wakana no Jo
35. Wakana no Ge
36. Kashiwagi
37. Yokobuye
38. Suzumushi
39. Yugiri
40. Minori
41. Maboroshi
42. Niou-Miya
43. Kobai
44. Takegawa
45. Hashihime
46. Shii-ga-moto
47. Agemaki
48. Sawarabi
49. Yadorigi
50. Azumaya
51. Ukifune
52. Kagero
53. Tenarai
54. Yume no Ukihashi

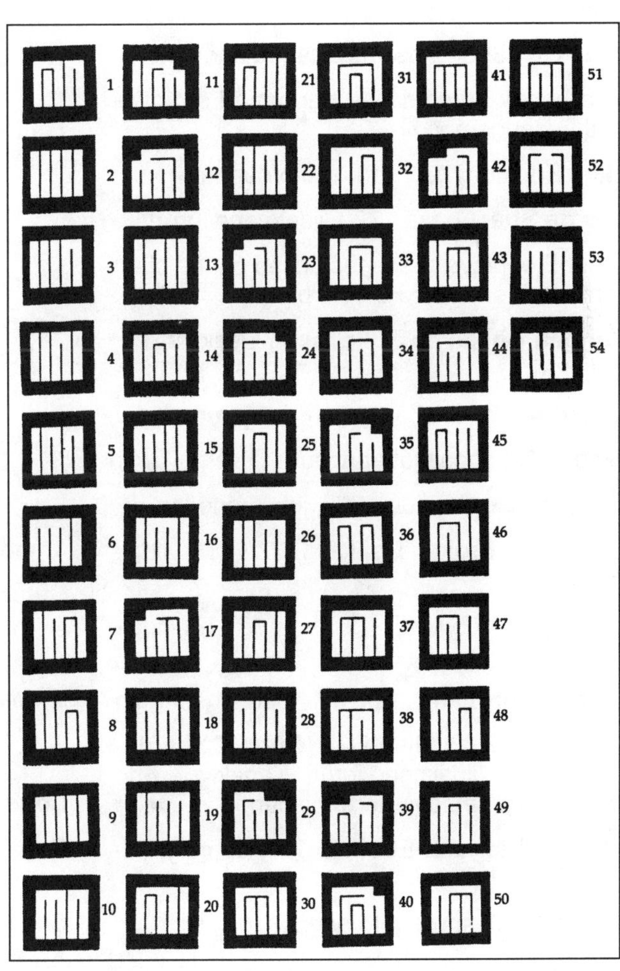

Appendix M

Kabuki Plays

The underlined parts of the list indicate abbreviated play titles and alternative titles are added in brackets.

Play titles were often changed and, as a result of modifying or combining of plots, many plays remained undeveloped. Many 18th century plays originate from the Kamigata area since their plots were adapted from Ningyo Joruri, the puppet theatre based on Osaka.

Banzui Chobei Shojin no Mamaita, Edo 1803, sewamono (see also Kiwame tsuki Banzui Chobei).

Benten Kozo, Edo, 1862, sewamono

Date Kurabe O-Kuni Kabuki (Kasane), a part of Meiboku Sendai Hagi, end of 1770's, sewamono.

Ehon Taikoki, Osaka 1800, jidaimono/joruri

Funa Benkei, Tokyo 1885, shosagoto and ghost play

Gion Sairei Shinkoki, Osaka 1757, jidaimono/joruri

Godairiki Koi no Fujime, Kyoto 1794, sewamono

Gonin Otoko, Osaka 1703

Go Taiheiki Shiraishi Banashi, Edo 1780, jidaimono/joruri

Hagoromo, Tokyo 1898, shosagoto/nagauta/tokiwazu

Harugoma, a hobby horse dance performed as interlude or within hengemono

Hashi Benkei, Edo ca. 1790, shosagoto/nagauta

Heike Nyogo ga Sha, Osaka 1720, jidaimono/joruri

Hencho Nijushiko, plays or scenes based on the classis ÔTwenty-four examples of filial piety'

Hikosan Gongen Chikai no Sukedachi, Osaka 1790, jidaimono/joruri

Hiragana Seisuiki, Kyoto 1739, jidaimono/joruri

Ibaraki, Tokyo 1883, shosagoto/nagauta

Ichinotani Futaba Gunki, Edo 1752, jidaimono/joruri

Igagoe Dochu Sugoroku, Osaka 1777/1783, jidaimono/joruri

Imoseyama Onna Teikin, Osaka 1771, jidaimono/joruri

Iro Moyo Chotto Karimame, Edo ca. 1820, shosagoto

Kagamiyama Kokyo no Nishiki-e (Onna Chushingura), Edo 1782, jidaimono/joruri Kagekiyo, Edo early 18th century, semeba (torture scene)

Kanadahon Chushingura, Edo mid 18th century, jidaimono/joruri

Kanjincho, Edo 1840, shosagoto/naguta

Katakiuchi Tengajaya Mura, Osaka 1781, jidaimono

Kiwame Tsuki Chobei, Tokyo 1881, sewamono

Koi Hikyaku Tamato Orai (Umegawa Chubei), Osaka ca. 1706, sewamono

Koi Nyobo Somewake Tazuna, Osaka 1751, jidaimono/joruri

Kokusenya Kassen, Kyoto 1716 (played in aragoto style in Edo), jidaimono/joruri

Meiboku Sendai Hagi, Osaka 1777, jidaimono/joruri

Michiyuki mono (lovers on the way to commit suicide), shosagoto

Modori Bashi (Rashomon), performed since the second half of 18th century, but the current version was established in Tokyo 1890

Modori Kago, Edo 1788, shosagoto/tokiwazu

Momiji Gari, Tokyo 1887, shosagoto/nagauta/tokiwazu/gidayu

Musume Dojoji, Edo 1753, shosagoto/nagauta

Narukami, Osaka 1742, jidaimono

Natsu Matsuri Naniwa Kagami, Osaka 1745, sewamono/joruri

Omi Genji Senjin Yakata, Osaka 1770, jidaimono/joruri

Oshi no Fusuma Koi no Mutsugoto (Oshidori), shosagoto/nagauta

Saikaku Gonin Onna, Osaka ca. 1700, shosagoto

Sanbaso, a dance often performed at the opening of a Kabuki program

Shakkyo, a lion dance

Shibaraku, usually performed on kaomise programmes, Edo 1697, jidaimono in aragoto style

Shin Usuyuki Monogatari, Osaka ca. 1745, jidaimono, joruri

Shishimai, a lion dance, performed independently or with hengemono, shosagoto

Soga cycle (a play named variously, most of them are with the Soga name) Edo 1676, jidaimono. Soga plays were inclined to be performed in the first month of the year

Sonezaki Shinju, ca. 1705, sewamono

Sugawara Denju Tenarai Kagami, Osaka 1746, Edo 1747, jidaimono/joruri

Sukeroku Yukari no Edo-Zakura (part of the Soga cycle), Edo 1713, sewamono

Sumidagawa Gonishi no Omokage, Osaka 1784, sewamono

Tsuchigumo, Tokyo 1881, shosagoto/nagauta. The subject of the play has ben popular since the early 19th century

Ukiyozuki Hiyoku no Inazuma (Nagoya Sanza), Edo 1824, sewamono

Yanone Goro, Edo 1719, jidaimono/aragoto style

Yasuna, Edo 1818, shosagoto

Yoikoshin, Osaka 1723, sewamono

Yoshitsune Senbon-Sakura, Ise/Edo 1748, jidaimono

Yotsuya Kaidan (Tokaido Yotsuya Kaidan), Edo 1825 (?), sewamono

Yukari no Murasaki Zukin, sewamono

Kabuki Roles and Scenes

Role-names written in Japanese can be read in various ways. Kabuki role-names may also sound the same as those of historical personalities although they are sometimes modified intentionally because of certain governmental restrictions. In addition, role-names are sometimes take from Western documentation in which the corresponding Japanese characters are not included and no indication of long vowels is provided.

Role-names sometimes include additional terms which specify the nature of the character. A number of such terms and their meanings are given within the following list:

baba old woman, grandmother

bokon ghost

bozu *(bonzu)* priest

geisha singing and/or dancing female professional entertainer

gozan formerly honorary title added to the name of the lady of a certain rank

hyakusho peasant

imoto younger sister

keisei courtesan

kitsune fox

musume young girl, daughter

ningyo doll

nyobo wife

odori dance

onna woman

otoko man

sarumawashi monkey trainer

sendo boatman

shinzo young courtesan, often escorting a courtesan of higher rank

shirabyoshi court style dancer

tsubone assistant of a court lady

uri dealer, street peddler

yakko namservant or maid

GLOSSARY

actor's crest: Mon (heraldic crest or family crest) were widely used by kabuki actors. The mon was used as a decorative pattern on their robes. In prints, the mon is often the only way of identifying the actor. Many generations of the same family used the same mon, thus one must identify the dating of a print in order to determine which generation, of a specific actor family, is depicted.

airo: Pigment(s).

aizuri-e: Prints which were produced only in shades of blue. They were popular during the 1830s-40s and again in the 20th century. The color blue may be traced back to *airo*, a pigment which tended to fade to buff when exposed to humidity and sunlight. It was discarded before the 18th century ended. It can be found in early Harunobu prints. The darker blues ("*ai*" / indigo) were used until c. 1810. In 1818, a new blue pigment was used sparingly. A darker version was added and used for backgrounds. These are thought to have been produced with powdered azurite which was finely ground. The finer the powder the lighter the hue. Darker tones were used extensively into the 1820s and printed so as to create *bokashi.* By c. 1829-31, a Prussian blue was introduced. This was a synthetic that was brought to Japan by the Dutch and originated in Germany. The new blue pigment , termed *berorin*, was stable and did not fade.

aquatint: A method of printmaking in which tonal areas, ranging from light to dark, rather than lines, are created on a metal plate. The print made from that plate resembles a drawing done with watercolor washes.

***aratame*:** Censorship seal, used from early 1854-1871. (See section on Dating Prints and Seals.)

art name: The name used by the artist to sign his/her work.

ato-zuri: Late impression of a print.

baren: A disk made of tightly twisted and coiled bamboo leaves, backed with several layers of lacquered paper and covered with a bamboo leaf. The *baren* is used for applying pressure when printing with woodblocks. A circular rubbing pad.

***beni*:** Pink/red pigment made from safflower.

***beni-e*:** A *sumizuri-e* hand colored in water base vegetable pigments including yellow, red, red/orange, blue and green.

benizuri-e: A print that is rose, green, sometimes yellow, blue or gray, all printed from blocks (sometimes with over-printing in order to produce three colors from two blocks).

bijin: A beautiful woman.

bijin-ga: A print of a beautiful woman (women).

bijutsu: Art, visual art, fine art.

blind printing: See gauffrauge.

bokashi: Gradation of color.

calendar: Dates employing *nengo* (era-names). (See *Appendix B*)

censor's seal: (See Appendix I)

crepe paper print: (The following is reprinted from *The Orientalia Journal.* Please note the original spelling for the term crepe.) The following excerpt was taken from *Japan: Its Architecture, Art and Art Manufactures,* C. Dresser, 1882:

"The crape paper, which is a most perfect imitation of real crape, is made by a very ingenious and most simple process. In the first place, that which may be called the matrix-paper is prepared by laying a moistened sheet of strong paper on a wooden board cut with fine grooves running either parallel or crossing one another at very small angles, and by beating it with hard brushes so as to force it into these grooves. It is then painted over with the frequently mentioned "*shibu,*" in consequence of which operation the paper becomes so elastic that when let go after having been stretched out it refolds by itself. For the production of crape, several sheets of thin moistened paper are laid alternately with sheets of the above mentioned matrix-paper, one upon the other. The package is then wound onto a round piece of wood, and pressed several times with a strong lever, as if it were to be stripped off from this piece of wood. By means of this operation the soft and moistened paper is forced into the folds of the matrix, and consequently folded in a similar manner. By repeating this manipulation ten or twelve times, each time unrolling it in order to change the position of the paper between the sheets of matrix-paper, and by winding it again onto the piece of wood, the paper becomes gradually folded in all directions, the intersecting points of all these folds producing the craped surface. Naturally, this process causes the paper to shrink considerably. This kind of craping is done with printed pictures, and also with colored papers."

daimyo: Feudal lord.

daisen: Printed slip pasted on the cover of a book and/or the cartouche giving the title.

danjuro: Actor's crests.

detcho: Single-leaf book binding.

diptych: Two prints forming one continuous picture.

doban: Copperplate printing.

do-bori: Engravers who carve non-intricate portions of a woodblock.

doro-e: Semi *ukiyo-e* landscape done in *uki-e* style.

dosa: A sizing agent applied to paper or silk.

drypoint: A method of printmaking in which the design is scratched directly into the metal plate with a sharply pointed tool. The most distinctive characteristic of a drypoint print made from that plate is the raised "burr" left on both sides of the cut line, similar in appearance to an image drawn with a felt-tip pen on dampened paper.

e-daisen: An illustrated slip title.

Edo: The old name of the city of Tokyo.

e-goyomi: A calendar print. (See *surimono*)

edori-bon: Early printed books with illustrations that were hand colored.

ehon: A picture book(s).

emaki (emakimono): A horizontal hand-scroll.

embossing: (See gauffrauge.)

etching: A method of printmaking in which the surface of a metal plate is scratched and then exposed to acid in order to deepen and widen the etched design. The print made from that plate can look like a sketch.

fude: Generally found below the artist's name. It means "painted by."

fude-bokashi: Gradation of a color produced by shading pigment on a woodblock with a brush.

fue: Flute.

Fuji san: Mt. Fuji.

fokei-ga: A landscape print.

fuki-bokashi: The technique of shading by partially wiping off pigment from the woodblock.

fukesi: A reproduction or facsimile print.

fukesi-hanga: A print made as a reproduction of a painting.

futon: Quilt coverlet.

ga: When used after a signature on a work of art (drawing, painting, picture, print), it signifies that the signature is that of the artist. (Drawn by.) Older reference books use the term gwa. The meaning is the same.

gafu: An album.

gako: Painter.

gauffrauge: To achieve gauffrauge, also termed blind printing or embossing, a woodblock would be cut to print the textured effect without charging the block with color. The block would be pressed into the dampened paper and rubbed hard enough to make an impression that would remain after the paper dried.

geimei: Professional name of public entertainers.

geisei: Personal, professional name of artists.

geisha: A woman entertainer accomplished in music, dance, and conversation.

Genji monogatari: *The Tale of Genji*, a novel of classical Japanese literature, written by Lady Murasaki, detailing the romantic adventures of Prince Genji in 54 chapters and is closely associated with woodblock prints.

giga: Drawn for fun.

Gion: The eastern ward of Kyoto.

go: Art name used by the artist to sign his/her work. There are many artists that used many *go*. e.g. Kunisada: Gototei Kunisada, Ichiyusai Kunisada, Kochoro Kunisada, Utagawa Kunisada, etc.

gofun: An opaque white pigment made from calcium carbonate.

gyosho: Informal calligraphy.

haiga: Sketches illustrating themes of *haiku* poetry.

haiku: A 17-syllable verse.

hakkake: Double or overprinting used to deepen a color (sometimes used for grading color).

han: A woodblock which has an engraved design.

hanga: Print(s).

hangi: A woodblock.

hanji-e: A print based upon a rebus.

hankoku: A reprint.

hanmoto: Publisher, or published by.

hanshi-bon: Medium-sized book (6 1/2" x 9"), 23 x 16 cm.

hanshita-e: The design for engraving.

haori: Half-jacket.

harimaze: Two or more prints on one sheet.

hayu: Actor.

hexaptych: Six prints (on separate sheets)forming one continuous picture.

hikitsuke: The drawstop of the *kento* register system.

hitsu: Drawn by.

hon: Book (also *bon*).

hori-shi: The engraver or carver.

hosho: Handmade paper.

hotoke-bon: Sacred books.

hyoshigi: Two pieces of wood tied with a string and

used as clappers to announce the beginning of a play or to accent a particular scene.

ichimai-e: A single-sheet print.

impression: A single printing, all the copies printed in one continuous operation (approx. 200 sheets).

ippai: The number of print impressions for a given printing (approx. 200).

iro-ita: The color block(s) used in a *nishiki-e* printing.

ishizuri-e: A rare printing technique that imitates Chinese stone rubbings. (stone print)

itame-mokuhan: Printing with the woodgrain visible.

jizuri: Self printed.

joboku: Term for "published" (used in colophons).

johan: Term for "published" (used in book colophons).

joruri-bon: Books containing the texts of dramas, usually illustrated.

kabuki: The popular theater of Japan.

kacho-e: Prints of flowers and birds.

kagi: The right-angle guide mark of the *kento* registration.

***kakemono*:** A hanging scroll.

kakihan: A hand seal.

***kamei*:** A family name.

kami: Paper.

kamigata prints: Prints of the Osaka School.

kanban: Theater poster.

Kano: A leading school of Japanese art.

kansu-bon: Book in scroll form.

kappazuri-e: Prints produced by stenciling. Either part, or the whole design or the colors, were applied by means of stencils within a block printed outline.

kara-zuri: Gauffrauge (blind printing) or embossed printing using an uninked block(s).

***katsura no tsuyazuri*:** The printing of black on black to give a shine to the surface.

***keisei*:** Courtesan.

***kento*:** Border marks of the printing blocks, ensuring perfect register during the printing with consecutive blocks (the *kento* is generally cut at a right angle).

kimekomi: Blind printing or gauffrauge of full figures.

kirara-e: Prints with mica background.

kira-zuri: Mica ground impression (mother-of-pearl dust).

kiwame: Meaning approved, this censor's seal was used on prints from c. 1790-1842. (See Appendix I)

kizuri-e: Prints with a yellow background.

kokyo: Stringed musical instrument played with a bow.

koma-e: A picture in a cartouche found within a print.

koto: A harp-like, 13-stringed musical instrument played in horizontal position.

koyaku: Child actor.

kozo: The plant fiber used in making print paper.

kubari-hon: Privately printed works.

kumadori: Theatrical makeup.

***kusa-zoshi*:** Picture novels.

kusazuribiki: Tearing off of armor, a scene frequently presented in Soga plays.

kusa-zuri-e: Prints rendered in yellow and grass green (*rokusho-e*).

kyogen-bon: Illustrated *kabuki* plays.

maiko: An apprentice geisha in Osaka or Kyoto.

mame-ban: A miniature print.

mame-hon: A miniature book.

mica: Fine grained, half-glossy pigments obtained from milled mother-of-pearl and other opaque materials.

mikado: Emperor or Empress.

moji-e: Picture composed of written words.

moku-hanga: Woodblock print.

mokume-zuri: Printing with the woodgrain pattern.

***mon*:** Crests which designate individual actors, actors' families, narrators' families, schools, theaters, specific roles, chapters of *Genji.*

monogatari: A novel, story, tale.

musha-e: Prints of famous warriors.

Nagasaki-e: Prints from Nagasaki depicting foreigners.

namban: Term for the first Europeans in Japan.

nigao-e: Actor's portrait.

nishiki-e: A full-color print (brocade picture).

Noh (No): Classical masked drama.

odori: Dance.

okubi-e: A bust portrait.

onnagata: A male actor who specializes in female roles.

Osaka: A school of printing that generally portrays theatrical subjects.

pentaptych: Five prints (on separate sheets) forming one continuous picture.

Perry: Commodore Matthew Perry (1794-1858), an

American navy officer, whose mission, in 1853-54, opened the ports of Shimoda and Hakodate to foreign vessels.

pigments: The colors used in *ukiyo-e*. Prior to 1860, the colors used were water based vegetable dyes. From 1860 imported aniline dyes were also used.

primitives: The earliest *ukiyo-e* prints.

proof: The test impression of a print (often rendered in *sumi* and from the key block).

rakan: The 500 Buddhist deities.

rokkasen: The six classical poets.

ronin: A knight without a lord, a samurai who lost his position.

saga-bon: A book printed by use of movable type.

sanbaso: A dance derived from *Noh* performed by one dancer (*sanbaso*) or three dancers (*okina*, *senzai*, *sanbaso*), most frequently as a starting ceremony. One of the few occasions on which *kabuki* actors may wear masks.

***sanbukutsui*:** Term used especially for triptychs showing representatives of the principal towns of Edo, Kyoto, and osaka at each other's sides.

sansui: A landscape.

sashi-e: A book illustration.

school: After the name of the artist, when known, the school is listed. There are two types of schools; regional style and the style of a known/famous artist.

seiro: "Green House" or brothel.

sekiban: A lithograph.

shakkyo: Lion dance performed with swinging peony branches.

shibai: Theater.

shibai-e: A theatrical print.

shin hanga: Creative print(s).

shincho: Newly printed.

shini-e: A commemorative picture.

shinkoku: A new edition.

shinpan: New publication.

shita-e: A preliminary design.

shogun: Military dictator.

shohan: First edition.

shomei: Genuine name.

***shomen-zuri*:** Polishing the surface of a print.

shomotsu-bon: The sewn binding for books.

shozuri: The earliest edition of a book.

shunga: Erotic paintings, prints, and illustrated books. *Shunga* were drawn by artists of great skill who simply portrayed everyday sexlife as simply as the *kabuki* prints advertised the pleasures of the theater. Not all erotic depictions contain total nudity. Suggestive and/or partial nudity was more expressive, beautiful clothing concealing and revealing was more stimulating. The complex folds of layers of kimono, multiple sleeve openings, exposure of the nape of the neck, a curling of the toe, etc., were all part of the symbolic language of *shunga.*

signatures: When a signature/same-name was used by more than one artist, one can determine the differences and make an identification by becoming familiar with the various schools, when the artists were working, and by checking date seals, censor seals, zodiac seals.

states: The term for describing the differences between existing variant editions of a print.

sumi: Black ink.

sumizuri-e: Black (ink) and white print(s) (printed from one block).

sumo: Japanese wrestling.

sumo-e: A wrestling print.

surimono: Literal meaning "something prints." *Surimono* were privately printed and designed The techniques were the same as those used for standard woodblock prints. *Surimono* with verses (calligraphy) required an additional carver who specialized in calligraphy. Blocks were also cut to print textured effects, color overlays, gold, silver and/or bronze (mica effects) and gauffrage (blind printing). There are three kinds of *surimono* that appear by the mid-1700s.

1. Sheets of *haiku* verse.

2. Announcements of musical performances.

3. Calendar prints.

Of the three, the calendar prints (also termed *egoyomi*) were commissioned for the New Year and were given as gifts to members of poetry clubs. Poetry clubs practiced writing verse as a way of discovering one's wisdom and talent. Poetry groups were called *gawa*. There were groups throughout Japan. Every group or club had their own *mon* which often appeared on the *surimono* as part of the design.

suri-shi: A printer.

tanto: A dagger.

tate-banko: A print(s) which is cut out and mounted on cardboard.

toba-e: Caricatures in styles derived from medieval scroll painting ascribed to *Toba Sojo*.

Tokai-do: Travelers' route from Edo to Kyoto with 53 rest stations along the way.

torii: Monumental porch to a *Shinto* shrine.

Tosa: The traditional school of Japanese art.

toshidama: A seal consisting of a jeweled ring used by members of the Utagawa artists' school. It is derived from a ring given to Toyokuni I by the Shogun.

triptych: Three prints (on separate sheets) forming one continuous picture.

tsuji banzuke: Theater program poster.

tsuya-dashi: Overprinting in black to give luster to certain areas of a print(s).

uchiwa-e: A fan print.

uki-e: Perspective picture (prints using Western style perspective).

ukiyo-e: Pictures of the floating world.

ukiyo-e school: The school of Japanese art based on the floating world.

urushi: Lacquer.

urushi-e: Lacquer pictures; woodblock prints in black to which colors, or a glossy black containing a lacquer binder, are added.

wakazashi: The shorter of the two swords of the samurai.

washi: Handmade paper.

yakusha: Actor.

yakusha-e: An actor print.

Yamato: Ancient name for Japan.

Yokohama-e: Prints which depicted life in Yokohama after Perry's opening of Japan in the 1850s. These prints were largely concerned with the Western influences that were entering Japan in the latter half of the nineteenth century. Themes found in Yokohama prints include ships and maps of Yokohama; people of the five treaty nations (United States, Britain, France, Russia and the Netherlands); leisure and entertainment; language prints; and enlightenment and internationalism as Meiji Japan looked at the world abroad.

Yoshiwara: Licensed pleasure quarters in Edo.

-za: Theater.

zensho: A complete collection.

zoho: A supplement work.

zu: Picture.

Bibliography and Sources

The author suggests that a good reference library, containing both general references and volumes on specific areas of interest, is essential for collectors and dealers. Suggested titles:

Andacht, Sandra. *The Orientalia Journal Annual of Articles.* Little Neck, New York: Sandra Andacht Publishing. 1982

Andacht, Sandra. *Collector's Value Guide To Oriental Decorative Arts,* Dubuque, IA, Antique Trader Books. 1998

Art Institute of Chicago. *Japan's Modern Prints-Sosaku Hanga.* Exhibition catalog 1960

Azechi, Umetaro. *Japanese Woodblock Prints: Their Technique and Appreciation,* Tokyo, 1963

Blakemore, Frances. *Who's Who in Modern Japanese Prints.* New York, Weatherhill, 1975

Gonse, Louis. *Catalogue de l'Exposition retrospective de l'art japonais.* Paris, 1883

Fenollosa, Ernest, F. *The Masters of Ukiyo-e,* New York, 1896

Hillier, J. *Japanese Colour Prints.* Phaidon Press, London, 1966

Illing, Richard. *Later Japanese Prints.* London, 1978

Keyes, Roger S. & Mizushima Keiko. *The Theatrical World of Osaka Prints.* Philadelphia, PA, 1973

Lane, Richard, *Images From The Floating World,* Tabard Press, New York, 1978

Michener, James. *The Floating World.* Random House, New York, 1954

Michener, James. *Japanese Prints from the Early Masters to Modern.* Tuttle, Rutland, VT, 1959

Michener, James. *The Modern Japanese Print: An Appreciation.* Tuttle, Rutland, VT, 1968

Narazaki, Muneshige. *The Japanese Print: Its Evolution and Essence.* Kodansha Intl, Tokyo, Japan, 1966

Statler, Oliver. *Modern Japanese Prints: An Art Reborn.* Tuttle, Rutland, VT, 1956

Stewart, Basil. *Japanese Color Prints.* Kegan Paul, Trench, Trubner & Co., London, 1920

Strange, Edward F. *Japanese Colour Prints,* Wymand & Sons, London, 1931

Yoshida, Hiroshi. *Japanese Woodblock Printing,* The Sanseido Co. Ltd., Tokyo & Osaka, 1939

Publications

Edited and published by Sandra Andacht, *The Orientalia Journal* is issued four times a year for collectors, dealers, and appraisers. Each issue contains special features and illustrations on such topics as woodblock prints, cloisonné, hardstones, pottery, porcelain, netsuke, rugs, paintings, and all other aspects of Orientalia. A question-and-answer column provides reader responses. The Orientalia Journal costs $21/yr.; $38/2 yrs.(in the US). Its foreign rate is $38 payable in US funds. A single copy and index of articles $7.50. Payment should be made direct to The Orientalia Journal, PO Box 94, Little Neck, New York 11363.

Museums

The Art Institute of Chicago
Michigan Ave. and Adams St.
Chicago, IL 60603

The Boston Museum of Fine Arts
465 Hunt Ave.
Boston, MA 02115

The Brooklyn Museum
188 Eastern Pkwy.
Brooklyn, NY 11238

The Cincinnati Art Museum
Eden Park
Cincinnati, OH 45202

The Cleveland Museum of Art
11150 East Blvd.
Cleveland OH 44106

The Denver Art Museum
100 W 14 Pkwy.
Denver. CO 80204

The M.H. De Young Memorial Museum
Golden Gate Park
San Francisco, CA 914118

The Freer Gallery of Art (The Sackler)
Washington, DC

Los Angeles County Museum Of Art
5905 Wilshire Blvd.
Los Angeles, CA 90036

The Metropolitan Museum of Art
5th Ave. at 82nd St.
New York, NY 10028

The Minneapolis Institute of Arts
2400 3rd Ave.
Minneapolis, MN 55404
William Rockhill Nelson Gallery of Art
Mary Atkins Museum of Fine Art
4525 Oak St.
Kansas City, MO 64111

The Portland Art Museum
Portland, OR

Royal Ontario Museum
100 Queen's Park
Toronto, Ontario Canada M5S 2C6

Seattle Art Museum
Volunteer Park
Seattle WA 98112

The Walters Art Gallery
222 State St.
Springfield, MA 01103

Yale University Art Gallery
New Haven, CT 06520

Organizations

Asia Society
725 Park Ave.,
New York, NY 10021

Society for Japanese Arts
Mr. Pankenstraat 12
5571 CP Bergeyk
The Netherlands

Japan House
33 E. 47 St.
New York, NY 10017

The Ukyio-e Society of America
Box 665, F.D.R. Station
New York, NY 1015

INDEX

A

actor's crests (mon): 262-264
aiban: 11
aniline dyes: 9
anyei (anei): 213, 216
aratame seal: 260, 261
art name: 11, 30, 32

B

backing: 12
baren: 10
beni-e: 7
benizuri-e: 7
bijin-ga: 6, 7, 27, 34, 73
"bird and flower prints": 6, 31
bokashi: 10
bunkwa: 214, 216

C

care and keping of prints: 12
censor's seal: 9, 260-261
Cezanne: 10
chonin: 5
chronology: 212-214, 216
chuban: 7, 11
condition: 12
courtesans: 6, 7, 265-268
creasing: 12
"creative prints": 9, 10, 67
cycle charts: 215

D

daimyo: 5, 9
dai-oban: 11

E

e: 237
ebankiri: 11
Edo: 5, 6, 8
Eishi, School of: 251

F

fading: 12
format and size: 11
foxing: 12
fude: 11

G

ga: 11, 237
geisha: 271
Genji Mon: 269
Genji monogatari: 269
go: 11
gyoji seal: 260, 261

H

han: 237
Hanabusa School: 250
hanashita-e: 10
hanken shoyu: 237
hanmoto: 237
harugoma: 270
Harunobu Suzuki: 7, 23
Hashikawa Moronobu: 7
hashira-e: 11
Hasui Kawase: 25-26, 27
Hideyoshi Toyotomi: 5, 87
Hiroshige: 27
hitsu: 237
Hokusai 30, 31, 32
Hokusai, School of: 252, 253
horeki: 212, 216
hori: 237
hosho: 7
hosoban: 7,11

I

impression: 12
in: 237
Ishikawa Toyonobu: 7

J

Jacoulet, Paul: 37, 38

K

kabuki: 6, 7
- origins of: 6
- play titles: 270, 271
- roles and scenes: 272

kacho-e: 6, 14, 15, 20, 34, 70, 74, 77, 82, 86
Kaigetsudo Ando: 7
kakemono-e: 11, 17, 18,
kaku-surimono: 11

kamban: ...11
Kamigata School: ... 86, 92
Kano School: ... 5, 6, 86, 250
kara-zuri: ... 7
Kawamata School: ... 249, 250
keisei: ... 271
kento: ... 10
kimekomi: ... 7
kiowa: ... 214, 216
Kitagawa School: ... 82, 96, 251
Kitao School: ... 250, 251
kiwame seal: ... 260, 261
koban: ...11
kwansei: ... 213, 214, 216
kwanyen (kwanen): ... 212, 216
Kyoto: ... 5, 6, 8
Kyoto Hanga-In: ... 60, 62

L

lithograph: ... 10

M

Meiji Period: ... 9
meiwa: ... 212, 213, 216
Miyagawa-Katsukawa School: ... 250
moku-hanga: ... 10, 12, 13, 20, 23, 34, ... 41, 43, 44, 47, 48, 49, 57, 67

N

naga-ban: ...11
Nagasaki School: ... 73
nanushi seal: ... 260, 261
nengo charts: ... 212-214, 216
"new prints": ...10, 11, 25
nigao-e: ... 8
Nihon Hanga Kyokai: ... 67
nishiki-e: ... 7
Noh (No): ... 47, 82
Numerical Table: ... 209-211

O

oban: ...11
odori: ... 271
ogata-chuban: ...11
o-hosoban: ...11
okubi-e: ...
O-Kuni: ... 6
onna kabuki: ... 6
Osaka School: ... 13, 14, 15, 16, 17, ... 18, 20, 23, 39, 43, 52, 57, 65, ... 66, 67, 70, 73, 74, 78, 86, 91, 96, 247, 248
Osaka: ... 5

P

Perry, Commodore Matthew C.: ... 8
"pictures of the floating world": ... 5
polychrome print: ... 7, 8, 31
print condition: ... 11, 12
publishers' seals: ... 259
publishers' trademarks: ... 255-259

R

restoration: ... 12
retouching: ... 12
rubbing: ... 12

S

Saito Kiyoshi: ... 67, 70
saku: ... 237
samurai: ... 5, 9
sanbaso: ... 270
serigraphy: ... 11
shakkyo: ... 270
shikishiban: ... 11
Shimabara: ... 6
shin hanga: ... 10, 13, 26
sho-tanzaku: ... 11
signatures on prints: ... 11, 221-236
soiling: ... 12
sosaku hanga: ... 9, 10, 41
stains: ... 12
sumi-e: ... 7
sumizuri-e: ... 7
surimono: ... 16, 20, 28,
suri: ... 237

T

Taikoki: ... 87
Takashi Shotei: ... 10, 73
tan-e: ... 7
tate-e: ... 11
temmei: 213, 216
to: ... 237
Tokaido: ... 8
Tokugawa government: ... 5, 8, 9, 87
  ban on Christianity: ... 5
  decline of: ... 8
  isolationist policy of: ... 6, 8, 9
  social hierarchy of: ... 5, 6

Tokugawa Ieyasu: 5, 6
Tokyo earthquake of 1923: 26, 37
toning: 12
Torii Kiyomitsu: 7
Torii Kiyonobu: 7
Torii School: 7, 43, 44, 248, 249
Tosa School: 5, 6
Treaty of Kanagawa: 8
trimming: 12

U

ukiyo: 5
ukiyo-e: 5, 6, 7-8, 9, 30, 31
- history of: 7-9
- popularity of: 6, 7, 8, 30
- subjects of:... 6, 7
- use of color in : 7

urushi-e: 7
Utagawa School: .... 25, 47, 52, 53, 65, 66, ... 78, 80, 81, 91, 92, 253, 254
Utamaro: 8, 86, 87, 88

V

Van Gogh: 10

W

wakasashu kabuki: 6
Watanabe Shozaburo: 10, 25, 241, 246
wear: 12

Y

yakusha-e: 6, 7
Yamamoto Kanae: 10, 90
yaro kabuki:.. 6
yenkio (enko): 212, 216
yoko-e: 11
Yokohama: 8, 9
Yokohama School: 50, 52, 81, 92, 248
Yoshiwara: 6, 7

Z

zodiac year cycle (for dating woodblock prints): 215
zu: 11

Index to Illustrations

Surname	First name or initial	Pages
Amano	Kunihiro	97
Aoyama	M	12
Asada	Benji	13
Asano	Takeji	13, 14, 97
Azechi	Umetaro	14, 15
Bartlett	Charles	16
Capelari	Fritz	98
Chikanobu		16, 17, 98, 99
Eisen		18, 100
Eisen	Tomioka	19, 101
Eizan		100, 101
Fujita	Fumio	102
Fusatane		20
Gesso	Yoshimoto	20, 21
Goyo		21, 22
Hagiwara	Hideo	23, 102
Hamaguchi	Yozo	23
Hanzan		103
Harunobu		24
Hasui	Kawase	25, 26, 103-116
Henmi	Takashi	27
Hiratsuka	Un'ichi	28
Hiroaki	Takashi	117-120
Hiroshige		28, 29, 30, 121-125
Hiroshige II		30, 126
Hiroshige III		31
Hokusai		32, 33
Hyde	Helen	33
Ikeda	Masuo	34, 35
Ikeda	Terukata	127
Inagaki	Nenjiro	35
Ishii	Hakutei	36
Ito	Nisaburo	35
Ito	Takashi	36
Iwami	Reika	36, 37
Jacoulet	Paul	37, 38, 127, 130, 131
Kampo	Yoshikawa	131
Karhu	Clifton	39
Kasamatsu	Shiro	40, 41, 132-137
Katsuhira	Tokushi	41, 40
Kawano	Kaoru	42
Keith	Elizabeth	42
Keishu	Takeuchi	42
Kitaoka	Fumio	43
Kiyochika		47, 141
Kiyokata	Kaburagi	43-46, 140-142
Kiyonaga		47
Kiyosada		142
Kogyo		143
Koichi	Okada	144
Koitsu	Ishiwata	48, 144
Koitsu	Tsuchiya	48, 145-151, 152
Koson	Ohara	49, 50, 152, 154
Kotondo	Torii	50, 51, 153, 154
Kotozuka	Eichi	154, 155-156
Koyo	Omura	157
Kuniaki		157
Kunichika		51, 158-160
Kunimatsu		52
Kunisada		53, 161-162, 163
Kunisada II		54, 163
Kuniyoshi		55, 56, 164-165, 166
Lum	Bertha	56, 166, 167
Mabuchi	Toru	57, 58
Maekawa	Senpan	167
Masanobu	Okumura	58
Migata	Toshihide	168
Mizufune		59
Morikuni		59
Munakata	Shiko	59
Nagai	Iku	60
Nagasaki		60, 61

Surname	First name or initial	Pages
Nakayama	Tadashi	61
Nishijima	Katsuyuki	61
Nishimura	Hodo	168
Nishiomiya		62
Nobukazu		169
Noda	Tetsuya	62
Nouet	Noel	169
Ogata	Gekko	62, 63, 170-171
Ohashi	Gekko	63
Ohno	Bakufu	64, 65
Okada	Koichi	63, 174
Okuyama	Gihachiro	174, 175
Onchi	Koshiro	65
Osaka	School	65
Ota	Gako	176
Rakuzan		66
Sadahide		176, 177
Sadanobu III		66, 67
Saito	Kiyoshi	68, 69, 70, 71, 177, 178, 179
Sakamoto		179
Seiler	Willy	71
Sekino	Jun'ichiro	72, 73
Shibuya	Eichi	73
Shigenaga		74
Shima	Tamami	74
Shinsui	Ito	75, 76, 77, 180
Shodo	Kawarazaki	77
Shoun		182, 183
Shuho	Yamakawa	180
Shunsen	Natori	77
Shunsho	Katsukawa	183
Shuntei		183, 184
Simon	T. F.	78
Sozan	Ito	185
Tadakiyo		79
Takagi	Shiro	185
Tanaka	Ryohei	79
Terauchi	Manjiro	186
Tokuriki	Tomikichiro	187
Toshikata	Mizuno	80, 187, 188, 189
Toshimine	Tsutsui	80
Toyoharu		81
Toyohide		81
Toyokuni		82
Toyokuni II		82, 190
Toyokuni III		82, 83, 84, 85, 190, 191-193, 194
Toyonari		86
Toyonobu		85
Ueno	Tadamasa	86
Urushibara	Yoshijiro	194
Utamaro		87, 88
Utamaro II		195
Watanabe	Sadao	89, 90
Yoshida	Hiroshi	91, 196, 197-201
Yoshida	Hodaka	91, 202
Yoshida	Toshi	92, 203
Yoshitora	Utagawa	93, 204
Yoshitoshi		94, 95, 204, 205-206, 207
Yoshitoshi	Mori	207
Yoshitsuya		94
Yoshitsuya II		95
Yukawa	Shodo	96, 208

About the Author

Sandra Andacht is a faculty member of the Appraisal Studies Programs at George Washington University (DC), CW Post College, and the Brookville Campus of Long Island University. Her specialty is Far Eastern Oriental decorative works of art and fine art, which includes: pottery, porcelain, ivory and ivory substances, lacquer, wood, furniture, textiles, cloisonné, screens, glass, snuff bottles, netsuke, sagemono/inro, tea ceremony objects, swords and sword furnishings, woodblock prints, paintings, hardstones (jadeite, nephrite and all the hardstones and related stones on the Mohs scale), water droppers and other writer's accoutrements, etc. She is also a member of the New England Appraisers Association and eppraisals.com (found at www.eppraisals.com).

Ms. Andacht is the Editor and Publisher of the *Orientalia Journal*, now in its 21st year. Her column, "East Meets West" is a regular feature in *Antique Trader Weekly*. She has written hundreds of articles in her discipline, as well as nine books including *The Collector's Value Guide to Oriental Decorative Arts* and *Oriental Antiques and Art*. Her articles have been published in *Antique Trader Weekly, Orientalia Journal, the Ukiyo-e Society Newsletter, Interior Design Magazine, Andon (Society for Japanese Art), Arts of Asia,* etc.

A popular speaker, Ms Andacht has lectured to the Ukiyo-e Society, the Art Forum at the University of Arkansas, in Jonesboro, the Greater New York Bead Society, Yeshiva University, New York University, George Washington University, CW Post College, and the Glass Society of Toledo among others.

Ms. Andacht appraises for US Customs, various corporations, individuals and insurance companies, as well as other appraisers (generalists and specialists in Asian Art). She is the appraiser and consultant in Asian Art for the Oklahoma City Art Museum, the Museum at the University of Illinois, and the Nassau County Museum of Art. She also acts as consultant and appraiser for many well-known collectors. Sandra Andacht has performed curatorial duties in her specialty for three major museum exhibitions.

The last exhibition, *Louis Comfort Tiffany and Stanford White and Their Circle*, ran from September 1998 to January 1999 at the Nassau County Museum of Art in Roslyn Harbor, New York.

Sandra Andacht is a member ADCA (Antiques Dealers and Collector Association), and has been a dealer in Orientalia Decorative and Fine Arts for 25 years.

Sandra Andacht can be reached via email at: Orientalia@aol.co

WOODBLOCK ARTIST'S SIGNATURES

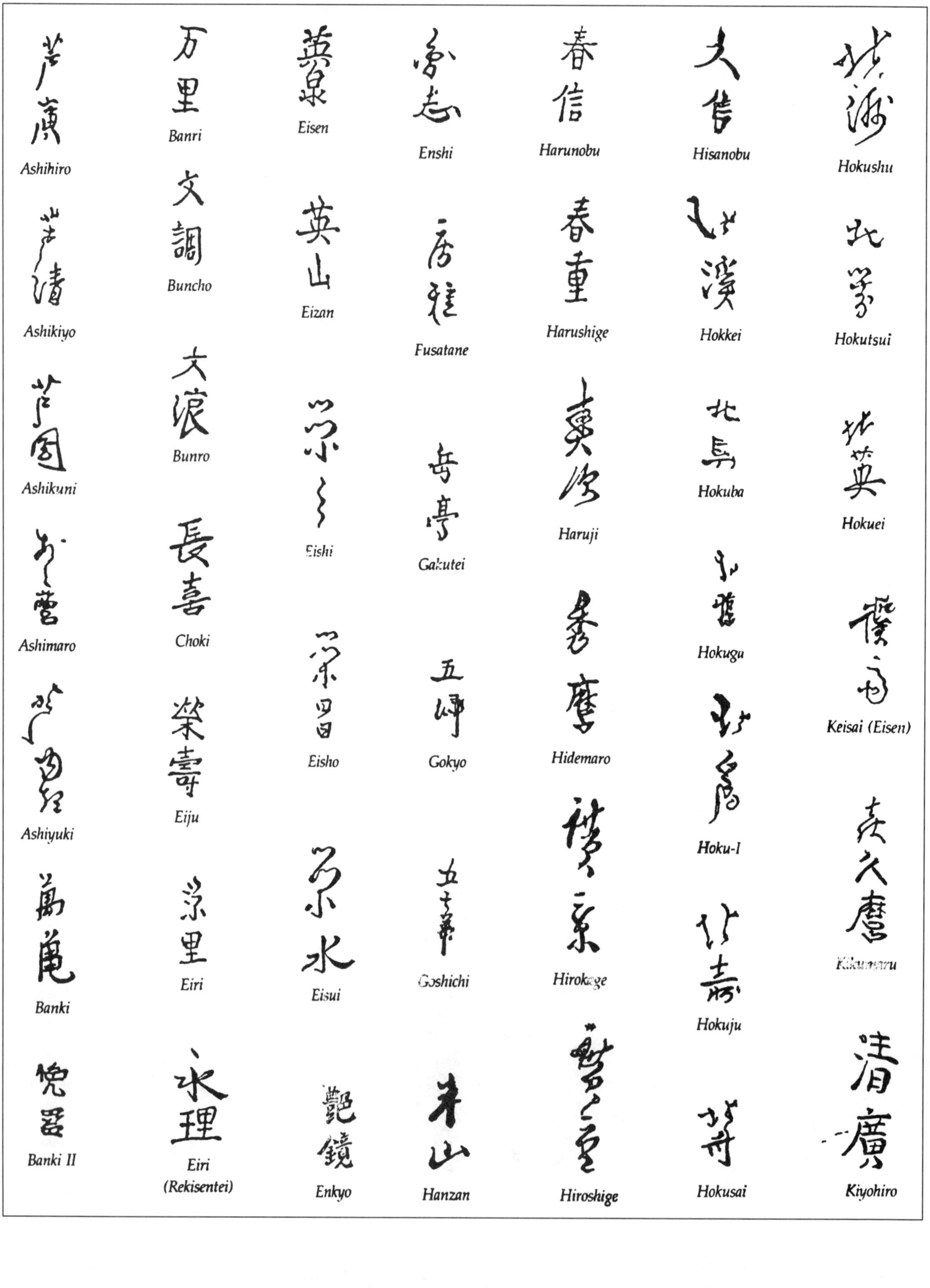

Ashihiro

Ashikiyo

Ashikuni

Ashimaro

Ashiyuki

Banki

Banki II

Banri

Buncho

Bunro

Choki

Eiju

Eiri

Eiri (Rekisentei)

Eisen

Eizan

Eishi

Eisho

Eisui

Enkyo

Enshi

Fusatane

Gakutei

Gokyo

Goshichi

Hanzan

Harunobu

Harushige

Haruji

Hidemaro

Hirokage

Hiroshige

Hisanobu

Hokkei

Hokuba

Hokugu

Hoku-I

Hokuju

Hokusai

Hokushu

Hokutsui

Hokuei

Keisai (Eisen)

Kikumaru

Kiyohiro

WOODBLOCK ARTIST'S SIGNATURES

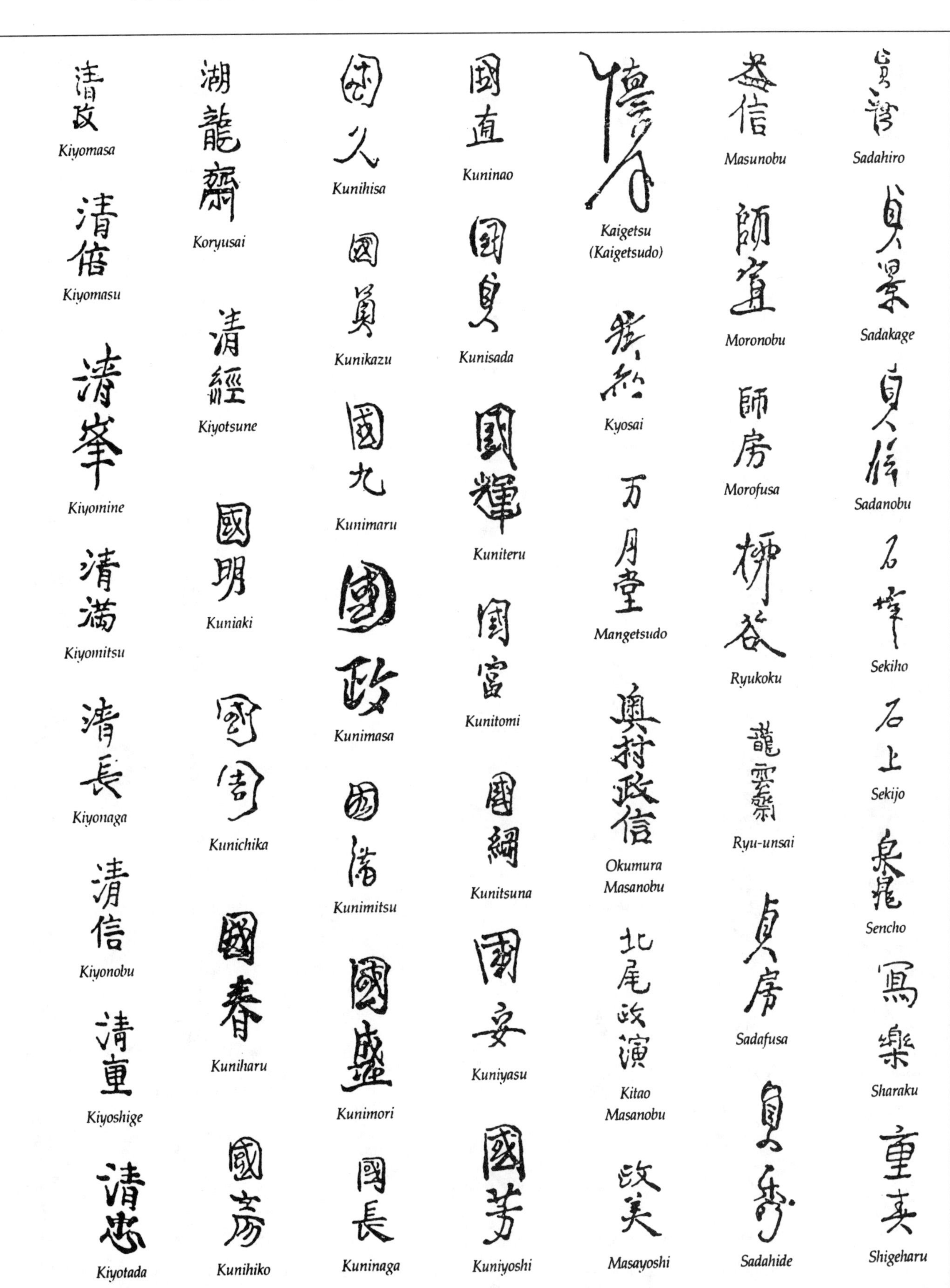

WOODBLOCK ARTIST'S SIGNATURES

Shigemasa

Shigenaga

Shigenobu

Shigenobu (Yanagawa)

Shigenobu (Hiroshige II)

Shikimaro

Shiko

Shinsai

Shucho

Shuncho

Shundo

Shunjo

Shunko

Shunkyo

Shunman

Shunro (later Hokusai)

Shunsen (Katsukawa)

Shunsen (Kashosai)

Shunsho

Shuntei

Shunei

Shunzan

Sori (Hokusai)

Sugakudo

Sukenobu

Taito (Hokusai)

Terushige

Tominobu

Toshinobu

Toyoharu

Toyohide

Toyohiro

Toyohisa

Toyokuni (also used by Toyokuni II (Toyoshige) and Toyokuni III (Kunisada))

Toyomaru

Toyomasa

Toyonobu

Toyoshige

Tsukimaro

Utamaro

Yoshichika

Yoshiharu

Yoshikazu

Yoshikuni

Yoshimaru

Yoshinobu

Yoshitora

Yoshitoshi

WOODBLOCK ARTIST'S SIGNATURES

- Ashihiro
- Ashikiyo
- Ashikuni
- Ashimaro
- Ashiyuki
- Banki
- Banki II

- Banri
- Buncho
- Bunro
- Choki
- Eiju
- Eiri
- Eiri (Rekisentei)

- Eisen
- Eizan
- Eishi
- Eisho
- Eisui
- Enkyo

- Enshi
- Fusatane
- Gakutei
- Gokyo
- Goshichi
- Hanzan

- Harunobu
- Harushige
- Haruji
- Hidemaro
- Hirokage
- Hiroshige

- Hisanobu
- Hokkei
- Hokuba
- Hokuga
- Hoku-I
- Hokuju
- Hokusai

- Hokushu
- Hokutsui
- Hokuei
- Keisai (Eisen)
- Kikumaru
- Kiyohiro

WOODBLOCK ARTIST'S SIGNATURES

Kiyomasa
Kiyomasu
Kiyomine
Kiyomitsu
Kiyonaga
Kiyonobu
Kiyoshige
Kiyotada

Koryusai
Kiyotsune
Kuniaki
Kunichika
Kuniharu
Kunihiko

Kunihisa
Kunikazu
Kunimaru
Kunimasa
Kunimitsu
Kunimori
Kuninaga

Kuninao
Kunisada
Kuniteru
Kunitomi
Kunitsuna
Kuniyasu
Kuniyoshi

Kaigetsu (Kaigetsudo)
Kyosai
Mangetsudo
Okumura Masanobu
Kitao Masanobu
Masayoshi

Masunobu
Moronobu
Morofusa
Ryukoku
Ryu-unsai
Sadafusa
Sadahide

Sadahiro
Sadakage
Sadanobu
Sekiho
Sekijo
Sencho
Sharaku
Shigeharu

WOODBLOCK ARTIST'S SIGNATURES

Shigemasa

Shigenaga

Shigenobu

Shigenobu (Yanagawa)

Shigenobu (Hiroshige II)

Shikimaro

Shiko

Shinsai

Shucho

Shuncho

Shundo

Shunjo

Shunko

Shunkyo

Shunman

Shunro (later Hokusai)

Shunsen (Katsukawa)

Shunsen (Kashosai)

Shunsho

Shuntei

Shunei

Shunzan

Sori (Hokusai)

Sugakudo

Sukenobu

Taito (Hokusai)

Terushige

Tominobu

Toshinobu

Toyoharu

Toyohide

Toyohiro

Toyohisa

Toyokuni (also used by Toyokuni II (Toyoshige) and Toyokuni III (Kunisada))

Toyomaru

Toyomasa

Toyonobu

Toyoshige

Tsukimaro

Utamaro

Yoshichika

Yoshiharu

Yoshikazu

Yoshikuni

Yoshimaru

Yoshinobu

Yoshitora

Yoshitoshi